SIGNIFICANCE TEST	=	SIZE OF EFFECT	×	SIZE OF STUDY
t	=	d	×	$\dfrac{\sqrt{df}}{2}$
F	=	$\dfrac{r^2}{1 - r^2}$	×	df
F	=	$\dfrac{eta^2}{1 - eta^2}$	×	$\dfrac{df \text{ error}}{df \text{ means}}$
F	=	$\dfrac{S^2 \text{ means}}{S^2}$	×	n
t^*	=	$\dfrac{r}{\sqrt{1 - r^2}}$	×	$\sqrt{df}$
t^*	=	$\dfrac{\bar{D}}{S_\mathrm{D}}$	×	$\sqrt{n}$
t^*	=	d	×	$\sqrt{df}$

* Correlated observations.

ESSENTIALS OF BEHAVIORAL RESEARCH
Methods and Data Analysis

McGraw-Hill Series in Psychology

Consulting Editor

Norman Garmezy

Adams: *Human Memory*
Berlyne: *Conflict, Arousal, and Curiosity*
Bernstein and Nietzel: *Introduction to Clinical Psychology*
Blum: *Psychoanalytic Theories of Personality*
Bock: *Multivariate Statistical Methods in Behavioral Research*
Brown: *The Motivation of Behavior*
Campbell, Dunnette, Lawler, and Weick: *Managerial Behavior, Performance, and Effectiveness*
Crites: *Vocational Psychology*
D'Amato: *Experimental Psychology: Methodology, Psychophysics, and Learning*
Dollard and Miller: *Personality and Psychotherapy*
Ferguson: *Statistical Analysis in Psychology and Education*
Fodor, Bever, and Garrett: *The Psychology of Language: An Introduction to Psycholinguistics and Generative Grammar*
Forgus and Melamed: *Perception: A Cognitive-Stage Approach*
Franks: *Behavior Therapy: Appraisal and Status*
Gilmer and Deci: *Industrial and Organizational Psychology*
Guilford: *Psychometric Methods*
Guilford: *The Nature of Human Intelligence*
Guilford and Fruchter: *Fundamental Statistics in Psychology and Education*
Guion: *Personnel Testing*
Hetherington and Parke: *Child Psychology: A Contemporary Viewpoint*
Hirsh: *The Measurement of Hearing*
Hjelle and Ziegler: *Personality Theories: Basic Assumptions, Research, and Applications*
Horowitz: *Elements of Statistics for Psychology and Education*
Hulse, Egeth, and Deese: *The Psychology of Learning*
Hurlock: *Adolescent Development*
Hurlock: *Child Development*
Hurlock: *Developmental Psychology: A Life-Span Approach*
Klein: *Motivation: Biosocial Approaches*
Krech, Crutchfield, and Ballachey: *Individual in Society*
Lakin: *Interpersonal Encounter: Theory and Practice in Sensitivity Training*
Lawler: *Pay and Organizational Effectiveness: A Psychological View*
Lazarus, A.: *Behavior Therapy and Beyond*
Lazarus, R.: *Patterns of Adjustment*
Lewin: *A Dynamic Theory of Personality*
Maher: *Principles of Psychopathology*

Marascuilo: *Statistical Methods for Behavioral Science Research*
Marx and Hillix: *Systems and Theories in Psychology*
Morgan: *Physiological Psychology*
Novick and Jackson: *Statistical Methods for Educational and Psychological Research*
Nunnally: *Introduction to Statistics for Psychology and Education*
Nunnally: *Psychometric Theory*
Overall and Klett: *Applied Multivariate Analysis*
Porter, Lawler, and Hackman: *Behavior in Organizations*
Robinson and Robinson: *The Mentally Retarded Child*
Rosenthal and Rosnow: *Essentials of Behavioral Research: Methods and Data Analysis*
Ross: *Psychological Disorders of Children: A Behavioral Approach to Theory, Research, and Therapy*
Shaw: *Group Dynamics: The Psychology of Small Group Behavior*
Shaw and Costanzo: *Theories of Social Psychology*
Shaw and Wright: *Scales for the Measurement of Attitudes*
Sidowski: *Experimental Methods and Instrumentation in Psychology*
Siegel: *Nonparametric Statistics for the Behavioral Sciences*
Steers and Porter: *Motivation and Work Behavior*
Vinacke: *The Psychology of Thinking*
Winer: *Statistical Principles in Experimental Design*

ESSENTIALS OF BEHAVIORAL RESEARCH
Methods and Data Analysis

Robert Rosenthal

Harvard University

Ralph L. Rosnow

Temple University

McGraw-Hill Book Company

New York   St. Louis   San Francisco   Auckland   Bogotá   Hamburg
Johannesburg   London   Madrid   Mexico   Montreal   New Delhi
Panama   Paris   São Paulo   Singapore   Sydney   Tokyo   Toronto

ESSENTIALS OF BEHAVIORAL RESEARCH
Methods and Data Analysis

1 2 3 4 5 6 7 8 9 0 H A L H A L 8 9 8 7 6 5 4 3

ISBN 0-07-053871-9

This book was set in Times Roman by Bi-Comp, Incorporated.
The editors were David V. Serbun and Barry Benjamin;
the production supervisor was Leroy A. Young.
The drawings were done by Danmark & Michaels, Inc.
The cover was designed by Merrill Haber.
Halliday Lithograph Corporation was printer and binder.

Library of Congress Cataloging in Publication Data

Rosenthal, Robert, date
    Essentials of behavioral research.

    (McGraw-Hill series in psychology)
    Bibliography: p.
    Includes index.
    1. Psychology—Research—Methodology. I. Rosnow,
Ralph L. II. Title. III. Series.
BF76.5.R629   1984   300'.72   83-5430
ISBN 0-07-053871-9

To our students
past, present, and future

CONTENTS

Preface   xv

Part 1   The Character of Scientific Investigation

1   Behavioral Science and Natural Science   3
What Is Behavioral Science? / The Scientific
Method / Serendipity / Deliberate Observation and
Replicability / Reactive Observation / Constructing
Hypotheses

2   The Contexts of Discovery and Justification   14
Good Hypotheses / Phantoms and False Conceptions /
Origins of Research Ideas / Falsifiability /
Significance Testing / Levels of Inquiry

3   Research Variables and Causality   26
The Assumption of Lawful Causality / Understanding
Behavior / Difficulties for Clear Inference / Metatheories
of Understanding / Independent Variables / Dependent
Variables / Operational and Theoretical Definitions

Part 2 Levels of Empirical Inquiry

4 Descriptive Research   41

A Paradigm Case / Higher-Order Relationships /
The Enumerative Survey / Secondary Records /
Meta-Analysis / Functions of Descriptive Research

5 Relational Research   51

A Paradigm Case / The Analytic Survey / Participant
Observation / Synchronic and Diachronic Research /
Historical Comparisons / Functions of Relational Research

6 Experimental Research   62

A Paradigm Case / Simulation / Role-Play Experiments /
Naturalistic Experimentation / Functions of Experimental
Research

Part 3 The Principles of Measurement and Control

7 Validity, Reliability, and Precision   75

The Concept of Error / Statistical Conclusion
Validity / Internal Validity / Construct Validity /
External Validity / Reliability in Test Construction /
Test Validity / Criteria of Precision

8 The Logic of Research Design   87

The Concept of Control / Experimental and Control
Groups / Pre- and True Experimental Designs /
The Solomon Design / Comparison of Experimental
Designs / Cross-Lag Design / Controlling for Age and
Cohort / Improvement on One-Shot Analysis

9 Subject-Experimenter Artifacts and
Their Control   102

Defining Systematic Error / Types of Role Motivations /
Controls for Demand Characteristics / Noninteractional
Experimenter Effects / Interactional Experimenter Effects /
Expectancy Bias / Representative Research Design /
Expectancy Control Design

Part 4 Techniques of Data Collection and Measurement

10 Field, Laboratory, and Archival Observations   117
Range of Procedures / Ethnographic Field Work /
Observers as Judges / Content Analysis /
Disguised Measures

11 Self-Report Data: Interviews and Questionnaires   128
Nature of Each / Structured and Unstructured Items /
Developing an Interview Schedule / Developing a
Questionnaire / Response Sets

12 Methods of Rating Behavior   140
Nature of Rating Scales / Errors and Their Control /
The Semantic Differential / The Q-Sort / The Likert
Scale / The Thurstone Scale

Part 5 Implementation of the Research

13 The Selection of Participants   155
The Paradox of Sampling / Requirements of Survey
Sampling / Simple Random Sampling / Other
Probability Samples / Nonresponse Bias /
Stimulating Participation / Selection of Judges
and Observers / Nonrandomized Selection

14 Ethics and Values in Human Research   170
Costs and Utilities / The Milgram and Humphreys
Studies / Deception in Research / Ethical
Guidelines / Debriefing / Scientific and Societal
Imperatives

15 Practices and Limitations of Research   180
Tensions of Corroboration / Replications and Their Relative
Utility / Limitations of Strong Inference / Assessing
Limitations Logically / Gathering Evidence / Statistical
Analysis of Data

Part 6   Fundamentals of Data Analysis

16   Describing Data   195
Displays / Measures of Location / Measures of
Spread / The Normal Distribution

17   Correlations   204
Pearson r / Interpretations of Correlations / Binomial
Effect-Size Display / Spearman Rank Correlation /
Point Biserial Correlation / Phi Coefficient /
Curvilinear (Quadratic) Correlation

18   Comparing Two Means: The t Test   225
t and d / Maximizing t / Interpreting t / Computing t /
t Tests for Nonindependent Samples / Assumptions
Underlying the Use of t Tests

Part 7   Fundamentals of Analysis of Variance

**19   Comparing Several Means: The Analysis
of Variance**   243
The F Test / An Illustration / The Table of Variance /
Distributions of F / After the F / Protecting against
"Too Many t Tests"

20   Factorial Design of Experiments   256
An Economy of Design / Effects and the Structure of
Analysis of Variance / Individual Differences as
Error / The Table of Variance / Testing the Grand
Mean / Computational Procedures: Equal and Unequal
Sample Sizes / Higher-Order Factorial Designs

21   Interaction Effects   277
Separation of Interaction from Main Effects / Defining
Interaction / Displaying the Residuals / More Complex
Two-Way Designs / Three-Way Designs / Further Notes
on Interpretation / Simplifying Complex Tables of Residuals

Part 8   Intermediate Topics in Data Analysis

22   Repeated-Measures Designs   305
Use of Repeated Measures / Computations / Fixed and
Random Effects / Latin Squares / Other Counterbalancing

Designs / Three or More Factors / Two Within-Subjects
Factors / Three Within-Subjects Factors / Fixed or
Random Factors / Did Repeated Measures Help? / A Note
on Assumptions

23 Contrasts: An Introduction   344

Background / Definitions and an Example / Additional
Examples / Unequal n per Condition / Orthogonal
Contrasts / Nonorthogonal Contrasts

24 Considerations of Power   355

Power Analysis / Effect Size / Power Tables / Indices
of Effect Size

Part 9   Additional Topics in Data Analysis

25 Comparing and Combining Independent
Research Results   369

Background / Comparing Two Studies / Combining Two
Studies / Comparing Three or More Studies / Combining
Three or More Studies / The File Drawer Problem

26 Chi-Square and the Analysis of Tables   383

Table Analysis and Chi-Square / Larger Tables of
Counts / An Illustration / The Analysis of Variance of
Qualitative Data / Testing Specific Hypotheses by
Subdividing Larger Tables / Complete Partitioning of Larger
Tables / Standardizing Row and Column Totals

27 Multivariate Procedures   414

Background / Relationships Within Sets of Variables:
Redescriptors / Relationships among Sets of Variables

Appendixes

A Writing the Research Report   431

Communicating Ideas / Form / Content /
Typing the Paper

B Statistical Tables   447

Table of Standard Normal Deviates (Z) / Summary Table
of t / Extended Table of t / Table of F / Table of
χ^2 / Significance Levels of r / Table of Fisher's z

Transformation of r / Table of r Equivalents of Fisher's z / Table of Random Digits

Glossary of Terms   468
References   484
Indexes   501
   Name Index
   Subject Index

PREFACE

This book evolved out of our lectures at Harvard University and Temple University, and many of the chapters, particularly in the last half, were originally handouts that were used in our methods courses. Thus much of the material has been undergoing the process of development and refinement for years on a wide range of undergraduate and graduate students primarily in psychology, sociology, education, and communication. These students had at least one course in statistics as a prerequisite, and we assume that our readers will also have had one course in quantitative methods. Nevertheless, we do review elementary topics (Chapters 16–19) as a brushup for those who may have forgotten some of their basic statistics, and we also review concepts and assumptions of research methods in the first few chapters in order to establish a common ground of understanding for the later discussions. Even in these reviews, however, we try to include some conceptually less common material to make them of interest also to more experienced students and researchers. For example, in talking about descriptive procedures we include a discussion of stem-and-leaf displays, trimmed statistics, etc., which will be of interest to researchers trained before the advent of robust procedures.

What if highly motivated students with no prior work in statistics wanted to go through this book on their own? They could do it, but it might be useful for them to read a more introductory text before (or while) consulting ours. A good selection for them would be the latest edition of *Introductory Statistics for the Behavioral Sciences* by Joan Welkowitz, Robert B. Ewen, and Jacob Cohen. For advanced graduate students and more experienced researchers we have written a supplementary volume on data analysis, which gives far more detail on the very central and flexible procedures of contrasts. It has been our experience that the chapters in the present volume are well suited for advanced undergraduate students and for beginning graduate students; in more advanced courses, we recommend using the supplementary volume along with the present one.

This volume opens with the substantive nature of behavioral research, and the point of view is decidedly pluralistic in keeping with our recent thinking (Rosnow, 1981). Some of this discussion began as an expanded version of our earlier primer of methods, and we thank John Wiley & Sons Publishers for permission to incorporate passages from that book. However, there are a number of topics in the first half which were not previously covered, for example, synchronic and diachronic research, cohort analysis, references to philosophers of science, and the limitations of research.

The later chapters on data analysis also have several themes or points of view which serve to integrate this material. One of these is the general relationship between tests of significance and size of effect under investigation, i.e.,

$$\begin{matrix} \text{Significance} \\ \text{test} \end{matrix} = \begin{matrix} \text{size of} \\ \text{effect} \end{matrix} \times \begin{matrix} \text{size of} \\ \text{study} \end{matrix}$$

Another is the strategy of employing focused rather than diffuse tests of hypotheses. A third is that a test of significance without an effect size estimate is an incomplete story under almost all conditions. Finally, to accompany our emphasis on effect size estimation, we show how the practical importance of even "small effects" is much greater than most behavioral researchers had been aware (see discussion of BESD in Chapter 17). The behavioral sciences have not been doing quite so badly after all!

Our approach to the teaching of data analysis is intuitive, concrete, and arithmetic rather than rigorously mathematical. There are two reasons for this. First, we ourselves are not rigorously mathematical in our approach to data analysis. Second, experience in teaching young researchers from the sophomore to the postdoctoral level convinces us that we can be more effective in our preferred mode. We pay a price for this. When we have a mathematically sophisticated student he or she will miss out on something valuable, and we encourage such a student to take course work in a department of mathematical statistics. We would still advise such a student to read this book, however—our approach will prove complementary, not contradictory.

The statistical examples we employ are in most cases hypothetical, constructed specifically to illustrate the logical bases of the computational procedures. The numbers were chosen to be clear and instructive; therefore, they are neater than real-life numbers tend to be. There are also fewer of them in any single example than we would find in an actual data set. Students who have looked at the primary literature of the behavioral sciences will know that most real-life examples involve more observations than are found in our statistical examples, and all our readers should keep that in mind.

We are indebted to many colleagues who read and criticized drafts of the manuscript incorporated in this book. Among them are Pierce Barker, Bella DePaulo, Susan Fiske, George Gitter, Judy Hall, Chick Judd, Dave Kenny, Mark Pavelchak, Gordon Russell, and Ed Tufte, who read all chapters in either or both the research methods and data analysis sections. Robin DiMatteo, Howie Friedman, David Goldstein, Dan Isenberg, and Charles Thomas read selected chapters, and we thank them for their suggestions. The first author also thanks William G. Cochran, Jacob Cohen, Paul W. Holland, Frederick Mosteller, and Donald B. Rubin, who were influential in developing his philosophy of research, and the National Science Foundation for its support of much of the research leading to the methodological developments described in this book and in the supplementary volume. The second author is grateful for the support that has been forthcoming from Temple University in the form of the Thaddeus Bolton Professorship. Both authors express their appreciation to Blair Boudreau for her superb typing. We also thank the following authors, journals, and publishers for generously granting permission to adapt tables, figures, excerpts, and illustrations: Freed Bales, Earl Baughman, Arnold Buss, Jacob Cohen, Donald Campbell, W. Grant Dahlstrom, Jack Friedman, John Haviland, Louise Kidder, Joseph Lev, Irwin Mahler, Conrad Smith, Academic Press, the *Alberta Journal of Educational Research,* the American Educational Research Association, the American Psychological Association, the American Sociological Association, the American Statistical Association, Elsevier Scientific Publishing Company, Houghton Mifflin, the *Journal of Communication,* the Journal Press, McGraw-Hill, *Psychological Reports,* the Rand Corporation, *Social Behavior and Personality,* the University of Chicago Press, and John Wiley & Sons Publishers. Finally, we thank Mary Lu Rosenthal and Mimi Rosnow for their helpful suggestions and particularly for their tireless support.

A wise researcher, Edward Tolman, once said that in the end the only sure criterion is to have fun. This is our fourth book together, and throughout the course of our long collaboration we have indeed had fun.

Robert Rosenthal
Ralph L. Rosnow

ESSENTIALS OF BEHAVIORAL RESEARCH
Methods and Data Analysis

PART
ONE

THE CHARACTER OF
SCIENTIFIC INVESTIGATION

Chapter **1.** **Behavioral Science and Natural Science**

Chapter **2.** **The Contexts of Discovery and Justification**

Chapter **3.** **Research Variables and Causality**

BEHAVIORAL SCIENCE AND NATURAL SCIENCE

WHAT IS BEHAVIORAL SCIENCE?

There are many fields of inquiry in the study of the nature of motivation and behavior—psychology, anthropology, sociology, communications, and educational research are some of these. Because these various disciplines share many common features, it has become convenient to group them together under a single heading, that of the behavioral sciences. One fundamental assumption they share is that it is possible to gather facts that reveal the principles or laws of behavior by using empirical methods. An *empirical method* is any effective manner or mode of procedure using objective experience, systematic observation, or experiment to map out the nature of reality.

That assumption, however, must be qualified, since there are aspects of human reality that are important and theoretically meaningful yet are beyond the reach of particular empirical methods. It is important that we recognize these boundaries so that we do not credit empirical methods with properties they do not have. Further, many of the "facts" of behavioral science, in particular, are conditioned by chance events and historical circumstances that are constantly changing, and thus introduce variability and uncertainty into the principles of behavior. As a consequence, there are few relatively permanent or invariant laws in behavioral science, in the sense that there are in physics, such as Newton's laws of motion or Einstein's $E = mc^2$.

The principles of behavior are based on *assumed probabilities*. That means the scientist assumes, based on empirical evidence, that a particular scientific prediction or conclusion is probably correct. Sometimes the odds that a prediction or conclusion is likely to be true are explicitly stated by the scientist, perhaps in the way that the weather forecaster will predict a "90 percent chance of rain" or give odds of "50–50 for the chance of snow." For instance, an opinion pollster who makes inferences from survey samples will also state the probability that opinions in the population at large are similar to those in the sample of responses. The researcher might say that "in 95 cases out of 100 the results based on the entire sample differ by no more than 2 percentage points in either direction from what would have been obtained by interviewing everyone in the population." More often, these assumed probabilities are not explicitly given, but are implicit—as when an experimental psychologist asserts that "frustration leads to aggression" or that "similarity leads to attraction." The implication of the experimenter's assertion is that there is ample empirical evidence for belief that, under specifiable conditions, the principle is probably correct.

Apart from the common assumption that empirical methods can reveal the principles or laws of behavior, each of the behavioral sciences also has a body of theories, concepts, data, and empirical methods that make it possible, on the whole, to distinguish one field of inquiry from another. Each also has its own area of application, although those areas are often overlapping. It is possible to distinguish at least four levels of human activity: (a) the individual personality, (b) interactions among individuals, (c) the group or social system, and (d) the cultural system (Applebaum, 1970). Level (a) has historically been the province of personality psychologists; level (b), that of social psychologists; level (c), of sociologists; and level (d), the subject matter of anthropologists. But personality and social psychologists have also begun to make empirical inquiries at levels (c) and (d) in order to establish how psychological facts are governed by cultural circumstances; and sociologists and anthropologists have begun to look at how complex interactions of societal and cultural events have influenced the evolution of the individual personality at level (a).

When (as in these instances) a behavioral scientist draws heavily on the theoretical orientations and methods of more than one field (as is the case in this book), that is called *interdisciplinary research*. If there are enough scientists who find a similar combination of theories, concepts, data, and methods useful, the labeling problem is solved by inventing a new discipline. Examples of new disciplines in the behavioral sciences are sociolinguistics, behavioral medicine, psychochemistry, behavioral genetics, and psychological anthropology. Most of those boundary-melting disciplines are of recent origin. Behavioral scientists hope that the new fields will show the same vigor and potential for breakthrough found in the combination of formerly differentiated disciplines in other sciences.

A prime example at the present time is that of psychological economics (Katona, 1975, 1979). The traditional science of economics most commonly proceeds on the premise that everyone behaves the same way, as if human beings were complex machines or robots without individual needs, wishes, and expectations. For example, the principle that "consumer expenditures are a function of income" is usually understood to mean that human beings will automatically spend the same proportion of their incomes and, therefore, there is no need to analyze the motives or attitudes or behavior of the people involved. The hybrid science of psychological economics proceeds on a different premise, to argue that human behavior is not at all like that of a machine that runs with clockwork precision, but that there are individual differences to be considered. This new field cuts across the time-honored boundaries of economics and psychology in order to consider economic processes as a function also of individual needs and behavior: the needs and behavior of consumers, of business people and government policy makers, and of the motives and attitudes of all those who spend, save, invest, set prices, and engage in other economic activities.

Another common feature of the behavioral sciences is, of course, their concern with the nature of motivation and behavior—human and nonhuman. Besides psychologists, anthropologists, sociologists, communication specialists, and educational researchers, there are other behavioral researchers (who call themselves ethologists) specializing in the comparative study of animal and human behavior, especially in relation to habitats. Konrad Lorenz (1966, 1977, 1979), the Nobel laureate, is an ethologist who has studied territoriality and aggression among lower organisms; he speculates that representations of these behaviors are present at the human level. Some animal behaviorists have emphasized the differences rather than the similarities between human and nonhuman aggression, and they point out that territorial behavior and aggression are not universal in lower animals. Among those behavioral scientists is sociobiologist Edward O. Wilson, who has sought to explain human aggression by referring to Darwin's idea that there is a constant struggle for species survival in which the most successful evolutionary modifications are those that survive. Wilson (1971) argues that some degree of human aggression is the result of a continuous developmental adaptation that was genetically programmed by means of natural selection to contribute to fitness in the narrow reproductive sense.

One final point: behavioral science is not synonymous with *behaviorism*. According to so-called methodological behaviorism, only the observable relationships between stimuli and responses are permissible as data and there is no need to speculate about what goes on beyond these visible relations. Many researchers, however, reject this narrow view of what is acceptable in behavioral science, and they argue that one cannot fully understand human behavior without also knowing the cognitive basis underlying it. Thus "behavioral science," as we use the term in this book, also includes cognitive and social scientists who are empirically interested in the nature of motivation and behavior.

THE SCIENTIFIC METHOD

To find empirical answers to the kinds of questions posed by behavioral scientists, a methodical system of procedures and techniques has evolved, and it is called the "scientific method." Philosophers of science, such as the American philosopher Charles Sanders Peirce, whose ideas flourished early in this century, have long pondered the nature of that method and have tried to reconstruct the logic of scientific practice. Peirce argued that the method of science is actually one of four ways to advance toward the truth (Reilly, 1970).

The poorest of these he called the *method of tenacity*. This means that a person stubbornly clings to a familiar idea just because this familiarity brings peace of mind. There is, in fact, experimental evidence to show that hearing some statement over and over can foster belief in it (Hasher, Goldstein, & Toppino, 1977). The notion seems to be that familiarity leads to "cognitive closure," which may explain why people find it satisfying to believe certain unfounded assertions, such as rumors, simply because they have been heard on a number of different occasions (cf. Allport & Lepkin, 1945).

A second approach, Peirce called the *method of authority*. This means that some ideas are held to be true merely because they have been approved by an institution or by a person whose expertise we respect or who is in a position of relative power. Of course, the perception of who is an "authority" is in the eye of the beholder; someone who sounds or looks "powerful" or seems like an "expert" to one person may not to another. Peirce thought that the method of authority made up for some of the shortcomings of the method of tenacity, but he realized that neither method encouraged careful thinking.

A third approach, which Peirce called the *a priori method,* means that one reasons from cause to effect, or from a general idea to a particular instance, independently of any scientific observation. Peirce thought this approach to be more reliable than the preceding two, since it calls for intelligent reasoning. However, it is still not much of an improvement, he argued, since it makes inquiry a matter of taste or fashion. If there is a disagreement about what is "true," there is no way that we can say which view is the correct one using the a priori method, he further argued.

It is only the fourth approach which allows us to *find out* what is "true." This, of course, is the *scientific method,* Peirce noted. It is the most satisfactory approach because it lets nature answer the questions that the scientist asks.

However, the term "scientific method" is itself surrounded by controversy, and is a misnomer to boot, since there are *many* recognized and legitimate methods of science. Each of these methods has its own set of formal and informal rules by which to assess its adequacy as a scientific technique. The rules have evolved as a result of good scientific practice. That is to say, because a substantial segment of the scientific community feels that such practices "work" or "produce" or "pay off," they have come to be regarded as good scientific practices (Campbell, 1974, 1979).

In sum, there are three distinct problems with Peirce's idealization of the scientific method. First, in spite of his own authority as an eminent philosopher, not everyone would agree with Peirce's contention that the method of science is the only proper way to advance to the truth. Painters, novelists, and theologians are also concerned with truth, but they do not use the scientific method to answer questions or to settle a dispute. Their method of intelligent reasoning is similar to the a priori method. As a consequence, they themselves are not scientists (nor ordinarily would they wish to be considered as such), although they may have much of intuitive significance to suggest to the behavioral scientist.

Second, scientists do not subscribe to one method, but to many different methods that cannot be easily defined in logical terms. Paul Feyerabend (1975), a modern philosopher, has said that success in science occurs only because scientists break every methodological rule and adopt the motto "anything goes" (Broad, 1979). Another philosopher of science, when he was asked to define the scientific method, answered that "the scientist has no other method than doing his damndest" (Kaplan, 1964, p. 27).

Thirdly, there is also disagreement among modern theorists as to what Peirce and classical philosophers of science meant by the terms "truth" or an "advance toward the truth." In ancient times it was held that truth consisted of an adequate conception of, or correspondence with, reality. But theorists now argue that ascriptions of truth always depend on societal norms and expectations which are constantly changing. Therefore, what one generation of scientists calls "truth" may be superseded by the theoretical formulations and empirical discoveries of following generations (Margolis, 1973). We return to this important point in a later chapter when we discuss the notion of "error" in behavioral science.

SERENDIPITY

Granted that the scientific method is constantly evolving, we can expect that new and innovative research methods will continue to be developed as theoretical and technological advances expand our scientific horizons. The field and laboratory methods of the behavioral scientist may be somewhat different from those of the natural scientist. However, the habits of good scientific practice are identical in both cases. The scientific method requires that the scientist observe with a keen, attentive, inquisitive, and open mind (Oppenheimer, 1955), for sometimes discoveries are made by accident. This faculty for making discoveries in the course of investigations designed for another purpose is called *serendipity,* a term derived from "Serendip," which was once the name for Sri Lanka. Horace Walpole, the eighteenth-century English novelist and essayist, claimed that the three princes of Serendip were constantly making discoveries by good luck, hence, "serendipity" (Medawar, 1979). Luck plays a part in scientific research when the researcher hits upon a right idea based on some felicitous discovery (Cannon, 1945; Merton, 1968).

To give an example, a British scientist at Cambridge University was observing the scintillation (the variations in strength) of radio signals from distant objects in the universe during specific periods. One of the professor's research students noticed during a period that was not being officially monitored, near midnight when the normal interplanetary pattern is generally absent, that there were also scintillations occurring. After months of careful exploration it was finally concluded that the phenomenon observed by serendipity was caused by a pulsating signal of extraterrestrial origin. The new data prompted a whole new direction of investigation. It is now theorized that these pulsating radio sources (called "pulsars") may be rapidly spinning neutron stars which resulted from the collapse of stars in supernova explosions. This theoretical breakthrough might never have been made at this time had the research student not kept a watchful eye out for the unanticipated discovery.

Murray Sidman (1960) has mentioned a similar example in behavioral science, in the behind-the-scenes story of a series of experiments that came to be known as the "ulcer project." It started with experiments that were being done by Joseph V. Brady in his laboratory at Walter Reed Army Hospital. Brady was running monkeys in some long-term conditioning experiments using electric shocks, food-reinforcements, and brain-stimulation. There was an unusually high mortality rate among the monkeys, which the researchers might have continued to treat simply as an unavoidable problem were it not for an accidental discovery. R. W. Porter, a pathologist, was also working at Walter Reed, and when he heard about the large number of deaths, he asked Brady for permission to do a post-mortem on the next few monkeys that became available. During the next few months, Porter would occasionally appear in Brady's office holding a piece of freshly excised monkey gut. Somewhere in the tissue there would be a clear round hole, which, Porter would explain to Brady, was a perforated ulcer.

One day, however, Porter remarked that of several hundred monkeys that he had examined before coming to Walter Reed, not one had shown any sign of a normally occurring ulcer. This remark was enough to cause Brady to change the course of his research. Could the ulcers have had something to do with the role the monkeys were obliged to play in the stress situation? Brady began doing experiments in which monkeys were subjected to electric-shock avoidance training and were paired with other monkeys who received the same shocks but without the opportunity to avoid them. When the monkeys were finally sacrificed, there were the lethal stomach ulcers in the monkeys that had been called upon to make "executive" decisions in the stress situations, while the "subordinate" monkeys showed no unusual pathology (Brady, 1958; Brady, Porter, Conrad, & Mason, 1958).

DELIBERATE OBSERVATION AND REPLICABILITY

Philosophers of science puzzle over the nature of the scientific method, but there is one fundamental characteristic on which all agree. It is that science is a process of deliberate observation as contrasted with the casual and largely passive observations of everyday life (Kaplan, 1964). Even many philosophers who reject the claim that science is a strictly logical process in which scientists advance inexorably toward the truth, concede nonetheless that good scientific practice is a process of controlled and disciplined observation.

The usual reason given to explain the restraint or direction the scientist exercises over his or her observations is that they can be repeated and authenticated by other scientists. In the case of physics or chemistry, where the long-established fact can usually be directly observed by each new generation of scientists, it is possible to repeat and authenticate a general fact as a law. But, as noted earlier, in the behavioral sciences it is not always possible to repeat and authenticate every observed fact at will. That is because the principles of behavior are influenced to some degree by events that do not occur with the same degree of predictable regularity with which many events in natural science occur. To be sure, the ability to repeat or duplicate an experiment (termed *replicability*) does have an important place in behavioral science, in that it is one means of determining the boundaries of an area of application.

Replicability is almost universally accepted as the most important criterion of genuine scientific knowledge, but it is not *always* possible to repeat and authenticate every laboratory event at will even in natural science. Michael Polanyi (1966) has introduced the concept of *tacit knowledge* to refer to our awareness of things that we cannot easily communicate verbally—the basis of hunches and intuitions—which we usually learn from direct experience and training. I know how to ride a bicycle, but I know from experience more about the skill involved than I can tell. When a novice takes a spill, he or she may conclude that no one can ride a bicycle if the skill has not been demonstrated.

This analogy also helps to point out the difficulties that can be encountered when replication is attempted without benefit of tacit knowledge acquired through experience. An interesting example occurred in the early 1970s, when British scientists were trying to replicate a certain sort of laser. This device was invented in the late 1960s, but details were not made public for several years. The laser turned out to be very difficult to replicate without having already done some work at the source of the original one. It was like learning to ride a bicycle, since it called for tacit knowledge acquired through direct experience (Collins, 1978).

The scientist who fails to replicate a device or an experiment, whether in behavioral or natural science, may conclude that the claimed phenomenon is not replicable—which, of course, is one possibility. It is also possible that the scientist did not carry out the study "properly" because he or she did not have the benefit of tacit knowledge. Tacit knowledge pertaining to rat handling, for example, is different in experimental psychology and pharmaceutical science. Experiments in these different fields, which also usually require different things to be measured or held constant, call for tacit knowledge which can only be acquired through experience or training (Collins, 1978).

REACTIVE OBSERVATION

However, replicability is not the major reason why the behavioral scientist practices deliberate observation. The reason is to try to ensure that what he or she observes can be explained impartially, that is to say, independent of the observer's own theoretical bias or some other prejudice. There are rules of logic that can help us to avoid some biases, although there is one form of bias against which it may be difficult to insulate unless special precautions are taken. That form of bias can produce *artifacts*, defined as threats to validity or as confounded aspects of the scientist's observations, a subject to which we devote an entire chapter. One example of this type of bias is the observer's expectancy. This expectancy can lead the observer, consciously or unconsciously, to behave in ways that are excessively conducive to the confirmation of the hypotheses.

It would be impossible to eliminate every form of bias in science. Indeed some artifacts seem to go hand in hand with deliberate observation. The terms *reactive* and *nonreactive* are used to distinguish observations that do (reactive) from those that do not (nonreactive) affect the behavior being observed (Webb et al., 1966, 1981). For example, in an experiment on therapy for weight control, the initial weigh-in might be a reactive stimulus to weight reduction, even without the therapeutic intervention (Campbell & Stanley, 1966).

The distinction between reactive and nonreactive observation also applies in natural science. The beam of light necessary to the observation of a subatomic particle must affect the particle's position and momentum (Kaplan, 1964). Hence, the more precisely that two related observable quantities are directly measured in quantum physics, the greater is the probability that the measurement process will produce uncertainties in the quantities. That is what Werner Heisenberg called the "principle of uncertainty" (Heisenberg, 1974; Lanz, 1976). In behavioral science we find that predicting human behavior may also be limited by reactive observations that impose uncertainties on the behavior observed.

Although it is difficult to avoid or reduce biases that seem to go hand in hand with reactive observations, there are logical rules that show how artifacts can be isolated and assessed by using control groups. These groups provide a standard of comparison by which to assess the magnitude and direction of the possible bias. For example, a number of strategies have been developed to assess the effects of the experimenter's expectancies, since it has been found that sometimes the experimenter's expectation for the experimental outcome can quite unwittingly become a more accurate prediction simply for its having been made. The idea—called the *self-fulfilling prophecy*—is that someone who predicts an event may behave in ways that are likely to increase the probability that the event will occur. One way to control for this artifact involves the use of an *expectancy control design* in which a given experiment is repeated by several experimenters, some of whom expect to find a certain effect and some of whom do not. If both groups of experimenters obtain the same size of effect, we can be fairly sure that the effect is "real" and not the consequence of the bias introduced by the theoretical orientation or expectancies of the experimenters. However, if the experimenters who expect to find that effect do so, and those who don't expect to find that effect do not, we may conclude that the effect was probably due to the expectations of the experimenters as much as to any "real effect" (Rosenthal, 1966, 1976).

CONSTRUCTING HYPOTHESES

Good scientific practice is more, of course, than an exercise in deliberate observation and the use of adequate control groups to expose and assess bias. Whether a program of research will "pay off" by casting new light on some difficult problem or perplexing aspect of behavior will also depend on the quality of the scientist's research ideas, or *hypotheses*. The scientist views facts not as isolated or separate entities or events, but as meaningfully connected. The scientist's hypotheses are the starting points for approaching this sort of connectedness, by making a theoretical guess as to the significance or meaning of a given fact (Cohen, 1959).

In any research project we begin by selecting and narrowing the question originally asked, to make it manageable for study within our available resources. The importance of extensive preparation cannot be stressed too strongly. The literature should be carefully reviewed, and the task at hand should be thought about at length. In this way it is possible to select the most simple and basic elements that will constitute the crux of the hypotheses. A classic principle illustrative of this intellectual ruminative and winnowing process is known as *Occam's razor,* after William of Occam, the fourteenth-century Franciscan philosopher. The principle of Occam's razor, also called the *principle of parsimony,* teaches that hypotheses introduced to explain relationships should be as parsimonious as possible. We "cut away" what is superfluous. Occam's razor is a qualified demand for prudence so that we do not overcomplicate the search for truth.

There are several kinds of hypotheses in behavioral science (Kaplan, 1964). A *working hypothesis* is a proposition, or set of propositions, that serves to guide and organize an empirical investigation. For example, social psychologist Leon Festinger (1957), in trying to account for the fact that some earthquake victims in India spread rumors about future catastrophes instead of seeking gratification in fantasy, was inspired to develop two basic hypotheses that became the starting point for an elaborate program of experimental research.

Festinger wondered why those rumors arose and were so widely accepted, since the belief that terrible disasters are coming seems frightening. He theorized that there should be "cognitive dissonance" arising from the experience of having survived a devastating earthquake in which other people had perished. The rumors, he reasoned, gave the survivors something to be frightened about—and this was reassuring for them in a way! That is, since the rumors provided them with information that fit with the way they already felt, the rumors were anxiety-justifying and dissonance-reducing instead of anxiety-provoking, he theorized. On the basis of this interpretation, he then developed two working hypotheses to explain why individuals strive for psychological consistency (or consonance) when they are experiencing, or expect to experience, cognitive dissonance (i.e., inconsistent knowledge, opinions, or beliefs about the environment). One hypothesis was that this dissonance, being psychologically uncomfortable, will motivate the person to reduce the dissonance and achieve consonance. The second hypothesis was that when this dissonance is present, besides trying to reduce it, the person will try to avoid situations and information that might increase the dissonance.

Scientists also speak of *plausible rival hypotheses,* which simply means that, instead of becoming attached to a single hypothesis, we consider reasonable alternatives which rival the working hypothesis as an explanation for the occurrence of some specified phenomenon (Campbell & Stanley, 1966). This idea was first put forward by a geologist, T. C. Chamberlin, before the turn of the century. Chamberlin argued that the moment we offer an explanation for a phenomenon we begin to feel "parental affection" for the idea. The more we think about it, the more this affection grows—and soon we find ourselves pressing the hypothesis to fit the facts and pressing the facts to make them fit the hypothesis. "To avoid this grave danger," Chamberlin (1897) suggested, "the method of multiple working hypotheses is urged. It differs from the simple working hypothesis in that it distributes the effort and divides the affections."

Others, including Feyerabend (1975), also believe that it is always a good idea to entertain strongly competing rival hypotheses. They argue that it is best to consider all possibilities with an open mind, since a specific working hypothesis may screen out important observations that are vital to our understanding of a phenomenon. By way of an example, suppose that a male and a female student decide to conduct, as a team, an experiment on verbal learning. Their particular interest is in the effect of stress, in the form of loud noise, on the learning of prose material. In order to divide the work fairly, the experimenters flip a coin to determine which of them will run the subjects of the stress condition and which of them will run the subjects of the no-stress condition. Suppose they find that better learning occurred in the stress condition. Can we ascribe the effect to the experimental stress? Probably not, because we have a plausible rival hypothesis to the working hypothesis of "result is due to stress." In this example, the plausible rival hypothesis is "result is due to sex of experimenter." That plausible rival hypothesis could have been fairly well ruled out in this experiment by having each of the two experimenters contact half the subjects of the stress condition and half the subjects of the no-stress condition. Such a plan would avoid the confounding (or intermixing) of the effects of stress and the effects of the experimenter's sex. The concept of plausible rival hypotheses is so important that an entire book has recently been devoted to giving practice in thinking them up (Huck & Sandler, 1979).

Sometimes we say of a hypothesis that it is *heuristic*, which means that it serves to stimulate interest as a means of furthering investigation. We often say this when it is a model or representation of reality developed informally, for example, on the basis of an analogy, since it serves as a starting point for inquiry. To give an example, social psychologists have recently developed the theory that gossip can be better understood if it is thought of as a commodity, like any commodity that is traded, bought, or sold in the marketplace (Rosnow, 1977; Rosnow & Fine, 1976). This theory hypothesizes, for example, that consumers of gossip, like consumers of any commodity, will have their own "brand loyalties" in the form of specifically "patronized" columnists, tabloids, and magazines. Another hypothesis derived from this theory asserts that the "consumption" of gossip is like the consumption of goods and services in societies where needs have been conditioned by competitive pressures. That is, when news is scarce, the gossipmonger should be able to exact a higher "price" for his or her tales. Still another hypothesis states that when the "market" for news expands, the amount of gossip in circulation should also expand. On the other hand, it is hypothesized that a community deprived of hard news, living on gossip, should become increasingly skeptical and suspicious of all news sources and extremely unbelieving of anything. Heuristic hypotheses, then, are meant to stimulate investigation by pointing out interesting possibilities based on a model of reality, and in this way to elicit further empirical research.

The development of clear, testable hypotheses is usually the first step in a program of empirical research, although in a later chapter we shall see how both observation and hypothesis are methods of corroboration which vie in competition with one another. Some hypotheses are not merely starting points but the end points of an investigation. Before approaching this more complicated idea, there are other basic assumptions of empirical research to consider, particularly with regard to the nature of the discovery and justification of the principles of behavior.

THE CONTEXTS OF DISCOVERY AND JUSTIFICATION

GOOD HYPOTHESES

Imagine we were considering a young woman with a new Ph.D. for a faculty position as an assistant professor. The search committee would interview her, observe her manner, her answers to their questions, and the questions she herself raised. In this way each member of the committee would begin to form an impression of her. As the interview progressed, additional observations would cause them either to crystallize their original impressions or to change them. If they began by examining her résumé—reading about her teaching experience, education, publications, and research interests—that background information could lead them to speculate further on her abilities and limitations. Suppose at some point in the interview that something unexpected happened, a fire alarm, a spilled cup of coffee, an embarrassing slip of the tongue. Her behavior could suddenly reveal a whole new positive side to her personality. On the other hand, the committee members might detect a subtle inconsistency in something she said and begin to form a different impression of her in order to reconcile the discrepant bit of information with their highly positive initial impression of her.

The structure of scientific discovery proceeds along similar lines. Just as tentative impressions about the applicant's aptitudes would emerge and gradually attain more definite form for each perceptive interviewer with each bit of significant new data, so will hypotheses emerge and crystallize for the perceptive scientist as new bits of evidence enter the picture. Not all impressions or hypotheses will be correct, although logic and the scientific method can provide the means of ascertaining their probable correctness.

There appear to be three relatively distinct stages in the development of scientific hypotheses (Kordig, 1978). In the first stage, *initial thinking,* the scientist "hits upon" an idea. The idea may be quite vague and difficult to articulate—like the first impression each committee member got in interviewing the applicant. In the second stage, *plausibility,* the scientist thinks about whether the idea is worthy of further consideration—in the same way that each committee member would think whether there were plausible reasons to support the first impressions as valid ones. In the third stage, *acceptability,* the scientist accepts the plausibility of the idea and molds it into a hypothesis that can be empirically tested. In the same way, a criterion for assessing the search committee's good judgment in deciding to hire the applicant would be her subsequent performance as a teacher and as a scholar.

The development of scientific hypotheses is thus usually seen as a natural deductive process, stimulated initially by cues that trigger the scientist's fertile imagination. But it also requires the ability to "guess" good ideas that will prove plausible and acceptable as hypotheses for empirical confirmation. One characteristic of "good ideas" that distinguishes them from "bad ideas" is that the former have a *high antecedent probability.* "Antecedent" means prior or going before, and to have a high antecedent probability thus means that the research idea is believed, even before being empirically tested, to be sound and likely to prove relevant to the problem under investigation. Apart from common sense and experience, however, there is no certain way of telling in advance if a research idea is likely to be supported. It is not always easy to take no for an answer when we are testing some pet hypothesis, and some scientists have spent weary and scientifically profitless years pursuing some pet idea that later proved to be groundless (Medawar, 1979). On the other hand, many good ideas were given up on too soon, and a "discovery" had to wait for years to be discovered by someone else.

In addition to being willing to take no for an answer if the evidence points that way, we must also try not to fall victim to what Abraham Kaplan (1964) has called the *principle of the drunkard's search.* It seems that a drunkard lost his house key, and he began searching for it under a street lamp although he had dropped the key some distance away. When asked why he didn't look where he had dropped it, he replied, "It's lighter here!" Kaplan makes the point that, like the drunkard's search, much effort in behavioral science is lost or vitiated when the researcher looks in a convenient place but not in the most likely one. It is important, therefore, that the thing sought—whether it be a key or some vital scientific evidence—have a high antecedent probability of being in the place where we are looking for it.

PHANTOMS AND FALSE CONCEPTIONS

A second characteristic of the "good hypothesis" is that it is not so narrow that it prevents a scientific breakthrough from occurring. The hypothesis should be parsimonious (Occam's razor), but it should not blind us by making us ignore any vital evidence just because that evidence does not fall within a very narrow range of acceptable facts. Serendipity has to be exploited—the lucky find must be noticed, explored, and interpreted for it to contribute to the body of scientific knowledge (Kaplan, 1964).

Scientists, being human and fallible, sometimes act on the strong presumption that any evidence or hypothesis that contradicts an established view has to be disregarded, even if it cannot be accounted for. They hope or rationalize that the exception will eventually turn out to be false or irrelevant (Polanyi, 1962). As long ago as the seventeenth century, the philosopher Francis Bacon realized that presumptions such as this one could affect the creativity of human thought and limit the chance for a scientific breakthrough. He called these preconceived ideas "phantoms and false conceptions." Facts and theories previously learned, common sense and hearsay, methodological biases, professional norms—those and other phantoms are so deeply rooted as to cloud our minds and make it very difficult for innovative ideas to penetrate (cf. Barber, 1961; Hurvich, 1969; Mahoney, 1976).

To illustrate: Michael Polanyi (1963) tells a story about his own experience when he first published his theory of the adsorption (adhesion) of gases on solids, in 1914. Within a few years of its publication he had gotten convincing experimental evidence to support the theory, but the then-current conception of atomic forces made his work unacceptable. Asked to state his position publicly, Polanyi was chastised by Albert Einstein for showing a "total disregard" for what was then "known" about the structure of matter. Polanyi, of course, was later credited with having been correct.

It seems that some of the best-known scientists have suffered in this way because of phantoms and false conceptions that clouded the minds of their distinguished colleagues. Lavoisier, the great French chemist, said in 1785: "I do not expect my ideas to be adopted all at once. The human mind gets creased into a way of seeing things. Those who have envisaged nature according to a certain point of view during much of their career rise only with difficulty to new ideas." Often it is only the passage of time, he noted, which can confirm or destroy innovative ideas (Hurvich, 1969). The point is that it is important to approach science with an open mind tempered by good judgment.

ORIGINS OF RESEARCH IDEAS

What are the circumstances that inspire scientific creativity? Although there are no hard-and-fast rules on this subject, it does seem that scientific creativity can be cultivated by approaching all things with a logical, inquisitive, and open frame of mind. The variety of situations that can stimulate research ideas might be compared to the energy that excites a neuron in the human nervous system. The energy used to excite the neuron is nonspecific. That is to say that the same ion flow occurs whether you hit your finger with a hammer, burn it on the stove, or have it bitten by a dog. As long as the excitation is intense, the result will be the same—ignition. In science it also makes little difference as to what circumstances provide the initial inspiration to light the fuse of creativity. As long as the situation is sufficiently stimulating to excite thought in the scientist, there will be "ignition."

William McGuire (1973) has discussed the kinds of situations that have been the basis of good research ideas in behavioral science. These include the use of intensive case studies, paradoxical incidents, metaphors, rules of thumb, accounting for conflicting results, and straightening out complex relationships.

For example, some scientists have been inspired to develop hypotheses based on *intensive case studies* of small groups and societies. They may either observe the group at a distance or actually become part of the group as a "participant observer." One behavioral scientist studied information exchange among the reindeer owners of Lapland. On the basis of this intensive case study, he developed and verified hypotheses about the psychology of gossiping in which he saw it as an exchange of one thing (information) in return for another (other information, esteem, etc.) (Paine, 1970). Another researcher made an intensive case study of gossiping in a Polynesian community. On the basis of his observations he also confirmed that gossip is not merely "idle talk," but talk that can help people to achieve goals under certain circumstances (Firth, 1956).

Other researchers have been inspired by *paradoxical incidents* to formulate research hypotheses. In Chapter 1 we mentioned how Festinger (1957) was inspired to develop two basic hypotheses after he had accounted for the paradox that earthquake victims gossiped about future catastrophes instead of seeking gratification in fantasy. Another well-known example in social psychology concerns the research of Bibb Latané and John Darley (1970) on the "diffusion of responsibility" hypothesis. The incident that stimulated their curiosity was a lurid murder in a respectable Queens neighborhood in New York City. The victim, Kitty Genovese, was coming home from work at three o'clock in the morning when she was set upon by a man who stabbed her repeatedly. Thirty-eight of her neighbors came to their windows to see what was the matter when they heard her cries of terror. However, not one of them went to her aid, even though the stalker took over a half hour to murder her. She died before anyone even bothered to telephone the police. When Latané and Darley started their research on bystander responses to emergencies, they had heard of dozens of such incidents. They also had heard many different explanations to account for this frightening passivity on the part of bystanders. None of the explanations seemed satisfactory to them. They instead theorized that, paradoxically, the key to understanding these failures of intervention can be found in the fact that *so many* people fail to intervene! There are several ways in which a crowd of onlookers can make each individual member of that crowd less likely to act, and one way, they theorized, may be because each bystander is picking up cues which produce a diffusion of responsibility. That is, social responsibility is dissipated when many people are present during an emergency, inasmuch as each member of the crowd believes that some other members will take control of the situation. Latané and Darley subsequently confirmed this hypothesis on the basis of many laboratory and field experiments where critical elements of the situation were manipulated to test their predictions.

A third source of research ideas is made up of *metaphors*. These are words or phrases applied to a concept or phenomenon that they do not literally denote. The expressions "Her life was an uphill climb" and "He was between a rock and a hard place" are examples of metaphors. That is, the expression suggests comparisons with another situation. Whether used in everyday speech or in science, the metaphor can sometimes supply us with greater linguistic flexibility simply by depicting one thing in terms of another (Billow, 1977). In Chapter 1, for example, we referred to how gossip has been metaphorically described as a "commodity" in the marketplace. Another example concerns how a biological metaphor was used by McGuire (1964) to develop hypotheses on the ways to "inoculate" people against the effects of propaganda. In essence, exposing them to fragments of the full set of arguments they may encounter at a future date, particularly in a *safe* setting where counterarguments can be rehearsed, will serve to inoculate them against a full-scale assault on their beliefs. McGuire's idea was that cultural truisms (such as "cigarette smoking is bad for your health" or any other statement which, in a particular culture, would be taken as obvious or self-evident) are especially vulnerable to counterarguments and propaganda because the truisms exist in a kind of "germ-free" environment where their validity is never challenged. He compared that to the biological situation in which a person brought up in a germ-free environment will be highly vulnerable to diseases because the person's body, never having been exposed to weakened doses of viruses, has not built up an immunity to disease. Using various forms of prior defenses to test this theory, McGuire was able to establish procedures for inoculating people against propaganda that was counter to their beliefs.

The *rule of thumb* is a fourth source of research ideas. It refers to a general principle or rule based on practical experience rather than on scientific knowledge. In this case one starts with the practitioner's rule based on experience and, seeing that it works, then tries to duplicate the experience and explain it scientifically. Irving Janis and his students took this approach in studying the time-honored method used by salesmen for softening up their clients by discussing business over a good lunch. To duplicate and try to explain this experience, the investigators fed hungry Yale undergraduates soda pop and peanuts at the same time that the students read propaganda messages. The researchers then compared the effects with those in an unfed control group. The results of this and similar research led to the finding that there was a "momentary mood of compliance" operating in the fed group. That mood is apparently what made them more susceptible to the propaganda than the comparison group which read the propaganda but got nothing to eat (Dabbs & Janis, 1965; Janis, Kaye, & Kirschner, 1965).

A fifth approach involves trying to *account for conflicting results*. Robert Zajonc (1965) neatly integrated a body of conflicting results to develop a theoretical synthesis to explain the psychological effects upon one's work of the presence of other people. The studies he integrated were done on such diverse populations as cockroaches, ants, rats, college undergraduates, and Army reservists. Some results showed that performance improved when passive observers were present. Other results showed it becoming poorer in the presence of others. To account for those conflicting results, Zajonc based his explanation on the familiar finding in psychology that a high drive level will cause people to give the dominant response to a stimulus, that is, the response which is fixed by or resulting from habit. When the task is familiar and well learned, the dominant response should be the correct one. When the task is new or not well learned, the dominant response could just as well be incorrect as correct. Zajonc further reasoned that the presence of others must serve to increase the subject's drive level, and the increase in drive is what leads to dominant responses. He hypothesized, therefore, that the presence of others should inhibit the learning of new responses and it should facilitate the performance of well-learned ones. From Zajonc's "social facilitation hypothesis" it follows that a student should study new material alone, preferably in an isolated place. Once the material is well learned, the student should take the exam with as many other students as possible, preferably on a stage before a large audience!

A sixth way of developing research ideas involves reducing complex relationships to a simpler, more parsimonious theoretical structure. That approach of *straightening out complex relationships* was used by Uriel Foa and Edna Foa (1974) to develop a formulation, which they call "resource theory," to explain how complex forms of interpersonal behavior can be understood simply as patterns of social exchange. There are six classes of social resources, they postulate: information, status, love, services, goods, and money. In any given situation the pattern of exchange will be predicted from the general characteristics of each resource according to specifications of the theory. For example, the more that the value of a given resource is influenced by the particular persons involved in exchanging it and by their relationship, the narrower is the range of resources with which it can be exchanged. Thus few resources can be exchanged for love, but several can be obtained for money. It follows, according to this theory, that money should be an appropriate means of exchange in many situations, while love should be suitable only in some situations. Specific predictions are made for particular situations following the general principles of resource exchange.

These six approaches are some of the ways in which creative hypotheses are stimulated. There are other situations as well that can lead to the development of research ideas in behavioral science (McGuire, 1973, 1976). Peter Caws has compared the structure of scientific discovery to the kind of inference that one makes in a game of chess. It requires an ability to keep a lot of information in mind at once, to be sensitive to feedback from experience, to assess strategies for further moves, and to perceive the relevance of one fact to another or to a theory.

FALSIFIABILITY

By a *theory* is meant something "bigger" than a hypothesis, since theories are really interrelated clusters of hypotheses. We are theorizing all the time, of course, even when we make the most trivial statement. If we say "This is a big house," certainly what we say is based on an observable property—size or "bigness"—but it transcends experience because the word "house" is a unifying term for an abstraction which goes far beyond observation. By calling something a "house" we attribute to it the theoretical properties of houses in general (Popper, 1961).

In behavioral science there are a number of distinctive theories which researchers have developed to comprehend the logic of human experiences. The term *discovery* is used by philosophers of science to refer to the origin, creation, and invention of theories. The term *justification* refers to the evaluation, defense, truth, and confirmation of the theories. Once having "discovered" a good theory, the logical next step in science would be to put the working hypotheses to some direct test in order to validate the theory as true.

The way this is supposed to work is based on what Karl Popper called *falsifiability*, an idea which became popular in the 1930s. It holds that a theory is "scientific" only if it is stated in such a way that it can, if incorrect, be falsified by empirical tests. Thus if one theory, T', were more falsifiable than another theory, T, and if T' had survived more severe testing than had T, we would conclude that T' was a better theory than T.

Popper's idea is widely accepted by scientists, but it is not universally accepted by everyone. Some have sought to challenge it based on another argument which states that theories instead form a complex system in which one part cannot be made to function except when its most remote parts are called into play (Duhem, 1954). Thus there can be no such thing as a completely decisive falsifying test, for whenever a refutation occurs, this merely tells us that the whole system needs to be adjusted, not that it needs to be discarded.

Festinger's cognitive dissonance theory is a good example to show that a theory is not usually discarded just because one or two hypotheses derived from it were falsified. Instead the whole theory is modified, and in the end may look very different from the way it originally looked. In the case of dissonance theory, there have been a great many experiments over the past twenty years to test specific hypotheses, and the results of some experiments have tended to disconfirm one or two core assumptions. Nevertheless, cognitive dissonance has survived, although its area of application is now more restricted. As a consequence, some of the studies originally discussed by Festinger no longer even apply. For instance, it is now theorized that being responsible for one's actions is essential for dissonance reduction to occur. However, earthquake survivors would not *feel responsible* for surviving, since the earthquake was a surprise to them and a natural occurrence beyond their control. Thus this central study, which Festinger originally used as a point of departure in developing his theory, no longer even pertains to his theory (Greenwald & Ronis, 1978).

There is another way of looking at theories, to be sure. We can also appraise them on the basis of whether their content and test records are adequate. By *content* is meant the theory's potential scientific interest and intellectual value, and by *test record* our reasons for believing it to be true (Koertge, 1979). To assess a theory's test record, most researchers ask only whether the specific hypotheses of the theory can be justified on the basis of significance testing, which concerns the statistical evaluation of conclusions. Significance testing is very closely tied to falsifiability, however, as we shall see.

SIGNIFICANCE TESTING

There is an old story in science about the danger of being overzealous in our philosophical analysis of what we do and how we do it. A grasshopper confronted a centipede with the question: "With all those legs moving at once, how can you keep from tripping?" The more the centipede philosophized about it, the more he came up with reasons for why he *could not* be doing what he had been doing all his life!—and he began to trip. The point is that many scientists, like centipedes, would prefer not to question the mechanics behind their methods, but instead to proceed on the basis of tried and true habits. Significance testing is one of these habits in behavioral science.

Significance testing refers specifically to the use of statistical probability when a decision is made about a hypothesis. It is not the only means available to the behavioral scientist for reaching a decision, but it has traditionally carried most of the weight of scientific inference in psychology, social psychology, and other behavioral sciences in which the experiment is a preferred method of scientific practice. Some behavioral scientists argue that it carries too much of the burden of scientific inference and that it is credited with properties it does not have (Bakan, 1967).

In later chapters we review the mechanics of significance testing in detail, but it is important here to understand the logic of this procedure. When the behavioral scientist uses significance testing to make a decision about a hypothesis, there are two distinct types of error that may occur. One of these, called *type I error*, consists of claiming a relationship that does not exist. The other, called *type II error*, consists of failing to claim a relationship that does exist. The probability of a type I error is called *alpha*, and the probability of a type II error is called *beta*. When behavioral scientists do significance testing they are asking the question: "What is the probability of a type I error?" That does not mean they are indifferent to the probability of committing a type II error, but the fact is that they do usually attach a greater psychological importance to type I errors.

To understand why this is so, we must introduce another concept that is pertinent to the criterion of falsifiability, that of the null hypothesis. The null hypothesis is characteristic of a great deal of experimentation as conducted in the behavioral sciences, and it is central to the statistical definition of the two types of decision error (Fisher, 1935). *Null hypotheses* entertain the possibility that there is no relationship or that nothing happens when we manipulate a variable. They are reference points against which working hypotheses are judged (cf. Strong, 1980). Thus if the working hypothesis states that "jogging makes you feel better" or that "similarity leads to attraction," the null hypothesis will state that "jogging does *not* make you feel better" or that "similarity does *not* lead to attraction."

Type I errors consist of mistakenly rejecting null hypotheses, and type II errors consist of mistakenly failing to reject null hypotheses. The probability of the type I error (alpha) is also called the *significance level*. When we do significance testing we are trying to state precisely the significance level to be more sure that we have not accepted a falsehood. In theory, then, the behavioral scientist attaches a greater loss to accepting a falsehood (type I error) than to failing to acknowledge a truth (type II error). This habit of being conservative in one's judgment is usually explained—some would say, rationalized—as "the healthy skepticism characteristic of the scientific temper" (cf. Axinn, 1966; Kaplan, 1964).

Another aid to reaching a decision about a hypothesis, which is also discussed in detail in the later chapters, is the *effect size* of the phenomenon under study. Effect size is defined as the degree to which the relationship studied differs from zero. Related to this concept is another called the *power of a statistical test*; it refers to the probability that the test will lead to the rejection of the null hypothesis given that the null hypothesis is indeed false. Put another way, power means the likelihood that the test will result in the conclusion that the relationship is not zero (Cohen, 1977). Procedures such as significance testing and estimating the size of the effect can be used at all levels of inquiry in behavioral science, wherever we must reach a decision about a hypothesis based on some empirical observations.

LEVELS OF INQUIRY

The experiment is the preferred method in many areas, but it is not the only approach the behavioral scientist uses when subjecting hypotheses to empirical testing. It is possible to distinguish two major empirical approaches, the descriptive and the relational, and a special case of the second type which would be the experimental approach. Once the research problem has been identified and the hypotheses have been clearly stated, it is important to select the level and method of inquiry that are most appropriate to the situation. These methods are not mutually exclusive, however, and many studies encompass aspects of more than one approach.

One approach, *descriptive inquiry,* tends to have as its goal a careful mapping out of what happens behaviorally. The researcher who is interested in the study of children's failure in school may spend a great deal of time observing the classroom behavior of children who are doing poorly. He or she can then describe as carefully as possible what it was that was observed. Careful observation of failing pupils might lead to some revision of our concepts of classroom failure, to suggestions as to factors that may have contributed to the development of failure, and even perhaps to ideas for the remediation of failure.

The careful observation of behavior is a necessary first step in the development of a program of research in science, but it is rarely regarded as sufficient. Sooner or later someone will want to know *why* something happens behaviorally or *how* what happens behaviorally is related to other events. If our interest is in children's failure, we are not likely to be satisfied for very long with even the most careful description of that behavior. Sooner or later we will want to know the antecedents of failure and the outcomes of various procedures designed to reduce classroom failure. Even if we were not motivated directly by the practical implications of knowing the causes and cures of failure, we would believe our understanding of it to be considerably improved if we knew the conditions increasing and decreasing its likelihood. To learn about the increase or decrease of failure behavior, or any other behavior, observations must focus on at least two elements at the same time. Two sets of observations must be made that can be related to one another.

This second approach, *relational inquiry,* has as its goal the description of how what happens behaviorally changes along with changes in some other set of observations. Continuing with the classroom example, let us suppose that the researcher noted that many of the scholastically failing students were rarely looked at or addressed by their teachers and seldom exposed to new academically relevant information. At this stage the researcher might have only an impression about the relation between the pupils' learning failures and teachers' teaching behavior. Such impressions of relationships are a frequent, and a frequently valuable, byproduct of descriptive observation. But if they are to be taken seriously as a relational principle, they cannot be left at the impressionistic level for very long. Our observer, or perhaps another observer who wanted to find out whether the first observer's impressions were accurate, might arrange to make a series of coordinated observations on a sample of pupils in classrooms that adequately represented the population of pupils about whom some conclusion was to be drawn. For each pupil it could be noted (a) whether the student was learning anything or the degree to which the student had been learning and (b) the degree to which the teacher had been exposing the student to material to be learned. From such coordinate observations, it should be possible to make a quantitative statement of the probable relationship between the amount of pupils' exposure to material to be learned and the amount of such material they did in fact learn.

To carry the illustration one step further, suppose that pupils exposed to less information were also those who tended to learn less. On discovering this relationship there might be a temptation to conclude that children learn less because they are taught less. Such a hypothesis, while plausible, would not be warranted by the relationship reported. In this case it might be that teachers teach less to those they know to be less able to learn. Differences in teaching behavior, then, may be as much a result of pupils' learning as a determinant of that learning. If we wanted to pursue our rival hypothesis, we could arrange to make further observations that would allow us to infer whether differences in information presented to pupils, apart from any individual differences among them, affected the pupils' learning. Such questions are best answered by manipulating the variables that one believes to be responsible for the effect.

This third possibility, *experimental inquiry,* has as its goal the description of what happens behaviorally when something of interest to the experimenter is introduced into the situation. It permits answers to the question: "What leads to what?" Nonexperimental relational observations can only rarely provide such information and then only under very special conditions. The increase in power in going from nonexperimental to experimental observations is the increase in power in going from statements of "X is related to Y" to statements of "X is responsible for Y." In our example, teacher teaching is X and pupil learning is Y. Our experiment is designed to reveal the effects of teaching on pupil learning. We might, therefore, select a sample of youngsters and, by tossing a coin or by means of some other random method, divide them into two equivalent groups. One of these groups would have more information given them by their teachers. The other group would be given less information. We could then assess which group of children's learning was superior. If the two groups differed, we would be in a position to ascribe the difference to the different treatments we had applied—more, compared to less, information.

There might still be a question of what it was about the better procedure that led to the improvement. In the case of increased teacher teaching, for example, we might wonder whether it was the information, the increased attention from the teacher while presenting the additional material, any accompanying increases in eye contact, smiles, warmth, or other possible correlates of increased teaching behavior. Each of these more-refined working hypotheses about the effective agents or active ingredients could be investigated in further studies involving descriptive and relational observations. In fact, the amount of new material teachers present to their pupils is sometimes predictable not so much by the children's actual learning ability, but by the teachers' beliefs or expectations for the pupils' learning ability (Beez, 1968; Rosenthal, 1973b). It has been experimentally found that teachers' expectations about pupils' performance can come to serve as "self-fulfilling prophecies" (Rosenthal, 1973c; Rosenthal & Jacobson, 1968; Rosenthal & Rubin, 1978).

In Chapters 4 to 6 we consider in detail further examples to illustrate the possibilities of descriptive, relational, and experimental inquiry. As a handy summary of what we have said so far, Table 2.1 gives examples of hypotheses that have been supported using those three approaches. We see that descriptive research tells "how things are." Relational research tells "how things are in relation to other things." Experimental research tells "how things are and how they got to be that way."

Table 2.1 Examples of descriptive, relational, and experimental conclusions in three areas of investigation

Research area	Descriptive	Relational	Experimental
Primate behavior	Baboon groups vary in size from 9 to 185 (DeVore & Hall, 1965)	Baboon groups found at higher elevations tend to have fewer members (DeVore & Hall, 1965)	Monkeys separated from their mothers prefer cloth-covered mother-surrogates to wire-mesh-type surrogates (Harlow, 1959)
Behavioral study of obedience	A majority of research subjects were willing to administer an allegedly dangerous level of electric shock to another person when requested to do so by a person in authority (Milgram, 1963)	Research subjects who are more willing to administer electric shocks to other persons report themselves as somewhat more tense during their research participation than do subjects who are less willing to apply electric shocks to others (Milgram, 1965)	Research subjects are less obedient to orders to administer electric shocks to other persons when they are in close rather than remote contact with these persons (Milgram, 1965)
Speech behavior	When people are being interviewed for civil service positions, the length of their utterances tends to be short in duration with only a few lasting as long as a full minute (Matarazzo, Wiens, & Saslow, 1965)	In interviewing both normal subjects as well as mental patients, it was found that average speech durations were longest with normals and shortest with the most disturbed patients (Matarazzo, Wiens, & Saslow, 1965)	In interviewing applicants for civil service positions, the length of the applicants' utterances could be approximately doubled simply by the interviewer's approximately doubling the length of his utterances (Matarazzo, Wiens, & Saslow, 1965)

THREE

RESEARCH VARIABLES AND CAUSALITY

THE ASSUMPTION OF LAWFUL CAUSALITY

It is a convenience to be able to refer somewhat abstractly to the things we observe or measure or plan to investigate in descriptive, relational, and experimental research. In psychology, education, communication, and other behavioral sciences these things are called *variables*. The term derives from the fact that they are "liable to variation or change" and because in some cases they can be varied or changed by the researcher who studies them experimentally.

The notion of a variable is qualified by means of a distinction that is drawn between the dependent variable and the independent variable. The *dependent variable* refers to the response in which the researcher is interested, and is usually symbolized by Y. The dependent variable is, therefore, referred to as the "response variable," as it is the result of or the response to some identifiable "cause." The *independent variable*, usually symbolized by X, refers to the factors on which the dependent variable depends. Changes in the independent variable, X, are conceptualized as having "led to" changes in the dependent variable, Y. In the statement "jogging makes you feel better," the independent variable would be jogging status (i.e., jogging or not jogging) and the dependent variable would be feeling status (i.e., feeling better or not feeling better).

In saying that "X is responsible for Y," or when using terms such as "cause" and "led to," the behavioral scientist means that there is evidence of a *determinative relationship*—that X serves to determine Y. In turn, this means that behavior is subject to lawful causality, an assumption with which not everyone agrees. Adolf Grünbaum (1952) has discussed the particular objections or arguments that have been offered against this assumption, and he has tried to show why they are without foundation.

One argument states that human behavior is not amenable to causal description because each person is unique and we cannot, therefore, generalize from one individual to another. Grünbaum answers that *all* particulars in the world are unique, whether they are human beings or whether they are physical objects or events like trees or light flashes. Every tick of the watch is unique, since no two ticks can be simultaneous with a given third event—and indeed every individual is also unique by virtue of a distinctive combination of characteristics not precisely duplicated in any other individual. But the fact that things are unique does not rule out the possibility that there are lawful relationships that might hold.

A second argument against causality in human behavior is that, even if there is a causal order, it is too complex ever to be discovered. According to this view, human behavior involves so complex a profusion of variables that it is impossible to unravel them. Of course, similar arguments were raised against the physics of motion before the time of Galileo. Critics said that it was hopeless to attempt to reduce the vast complexity of terrestrial and celestial motion to a few simple laws. The development of Newtonian physics is tangible evidence of the refutation of this objection, and there is no reason to expect that the same will not be true of behavioral science.

Other objections have also been advanced (see Grünbaum, 1952), and it is certainly true that many people believe that behavior—human behavior, at least—is not subject to lawful causality. In behavioral science we proceed on the opposite assumption, although we recognize full well that it is not always easy to distinguish cause from effect (Cohen, 1959). Is feminism the cause or the effect of the greater economic opportunity open to women? Is poverty the cause or the effect of a higher birthrate? That is, does the greater number of mouths to feed in a family reduce the individual shares of the family income, or do the poor perhaps seek a hedge against their old age by having many children some of whom will likely care for them?

UNDERSTANDING BEHAVIOR

When there is doubt about the dependence of a variable (as is usually the case in relational research), the logical temporal sequence can be a possible basis for decision. Suppose we find a relationship between biological gender and height, and we want to say which is the independent variable and which is the dependent variable. Logic would lead us to conclude that biological gender is more likely to determine height than that height is to determine biological gender, because a person's gender is established at birth. Similarly, in examining the relationship between birth order and volunteering to participate in psychological experiments, we logically think of birth order as the independent variable because it is not reasonable to think that volunteering could be a determinant of one's order of birth. Biological gender and birth order, in these examples, are likely to be called "independent variables," because they are established so early in the history of the individual.

The issue of *social causality*—what variables of social reality are causes, *X*, and what are effects, *Y*—is further complicated by the fact that most things in life can operate both as causes and effects. For example, rumors may "cause" riots, but riots may also "cause" rumors to surface—rumors can operate both as independent variables and as dependent variables. Indeed rumors can also "cause" other rumors. A rumor can trigger needs which, in turn, instigate additional rumors to provide relief. The rumor contributes to the situation, and the situation then contributes additional rumors as a result (Rosnow, 1980).

The issue of social causality is also complicated by the fact that there are different kinds of causal explanations. To explain an event as having been caused by someone's intervention is very different from an explanation that it was caused by the "temper of the times" (or *Zeitgeist*). Yet, social causation does not always involve individual purposes—for example, that the overcrowding in cities leads to certain social diseases does not imply intentionality (Cohen, 1959).

To illustrate the different kinds of determinative relationships that are possible, one needs only to be reminded of Aristotle's distinction among four different uses of cause for purposes of explanation. First, there is the *material cause,* Aristotle noted, which refers to the material out of which something is made or comes about. Second, there is the *formal cause,* the implicit form or meaning of the thing. Third, there is the *efficient cause,* which is the propelling factor that produces the thing or sets it into motion or changes it. Fourth, there is the *final cause* (or the *teleologic factor*), which refers to the end reason for which a thing tends naturally to strive. For example, when an architect builds a skyscraper, the material cause is the concrete, bricks, steel, etc.; the formal cause is the idea in the architect's mind; the efficient cause is the actual work done by the architect, the laborers, and their tools; and the final or teleologic cause is the purpose in view, which for the architect may be to gain public recognition, and for the populace is to have a place to work (Wheelwright, 1951). (Since the mid-eighteenth century, the convention has been to refer to what Aristotle called the material, the formal, and the final as "explanations" and to refer only to the efficient as a type of "causation.")

Perhaps wisely, perhaps overcautiously, behavioral scientists have sidestepped the issues involved in defining causality, because the notion of causality is complex and confusing (cf. Lana, 1969). If pressed to say what they mean, most would probably prefer to talk about "understanding" rather than "causality" and to use the terms "independent variables" and "dependent variables" to mean "antecedent events" and "consequent events," respectively. However, we need only push a bit to see that understanding is a quite subjective matter. I understand a certain phenomenon, and if you don't see it my way, why then you simply don't understand it. But perhaps I can show you I understand it by making predictions about what will happen in the future, predictions based on my understanding of what are the antecedent (or prior) events and the consequent (or following) events. If we disagree in our understandings, then perhaps you will also want to make some predictions based on your understanding. If your rival hypothesis logically implies predictions that are better borne out by the observations we make than are my predictions based on my working hypothesis, then I am willing to concede your *greater* understanding of the causal factors of the phenomenon in question.

Of course, we can also try to "understand" behavior without thinking about what caused it. Ordinarily when we speak of dependent variables we mean that they are dependent relative to one or more independent variables. But in doing descriptive research we are not interested at all in what is likely to lead to what. Similarly, in relational research, we may want only to know how much two variables are related, with no implication of one serving as determinant, cause, or antecedent of the other. If we want only to understand the relationship, for example, between two measures of racial prejudice or authoritarianism or intelligence, we refer to them as variables, but we would not try to distinguish independent from dependent variables.

DIFFICULTIES FOR CLEAR INFERENCE

David Hume, the eighteenth-century Scottish philosopher, saw that when people say that "X causes Y," they really mean that X and Y constantly go together, not that there is some necessary connection between them. In fact, he argued, people usually have no other notion than that X and Y are united in this way. Because it is possible for all objects to become causes or effects of each other, what is needed are general rules by which we may know when they really do serve as causes or effects, he reasoned. The rules that Hume developed were condensed by John Stuart Mill, a century later, to three essentials that provide the basic logic required to judge causes and effects.

The first requirement, Mill argued, is to show that Y did not occur until after X. The second is to show that X and Y are related. The third (and the most difficult requirement) is to show that other explanations of the relationship between X and Y can be ruled out. Hume believed that wanting to know what leads to what suggests the need for what he called the "experimental method of reasoning," and Mill developed logical "methods" related to his three requirements which became the basis of experimental design. In a later chapter we turn to these methods of Mill's which have led to the belief that perhaps the only way to be sure that X leads to Y is to vary X and observe the consequences.

However, sometimes it is not possible to vary X, for ethical or technical reasons, in which case we may have to settle for the best evidence available, even if it is inconclusive. Suppose that we had discovered an outbreak of strange psychological symptoms all over the country. We might begin our efforts to understand the problem by interviewing some or all of the afflicted with the aim of discovering some common factor among those afflicted. Our interviews, let us say, suggest that all the people with the strange psychological symptoms had recently visited a physician and that they all had prescribed for them a new drug whose side effects were not yet fully established. Now we suspect that the drug may, for some persons at least, be the determinant of the strange psychological symptoms. Shall we take a sample of people visiting physicians and arrange to give half of them the suspected drug? That would allow us to compare the two groups to see whether those given the drug were more likely to develop the strange psychological symptoms. But the ethical cost of such experimental research would be too high, for we would not be willing to expose people to a drug we had good reason to believe to be harmful.

As a practical alternative, we might want to compare those persons who were given the new drug by their physicians with those persons whose physicians did not prescribe the new drug. If only those given the drug developed the new symptoms, the drug would be more seriously implicated. But its determining role would still not be fully established. It might have been, for example, that those people given the new drug differed in a number of ways from those who were not given the drug by their physicians. Not the new drug, then, but a correlate of being given the new drug could be the determining variable.

Other relational analyses are possible that might help us to judge whether the new drug is a determinant of the new symptoms. Among those patients given the drug some will very likely have been given large dosages while others will have been given small dosages. If it turns out that persons on larger dosages suffer more severely from the new symptoms, the drug will be more strongly implicated. However, we cannot be certain about the causal role of the drug. It might be the case that those who are judged to be more ill by the physicians are given larger dosages, so that it is the illness for which the drug is prescribed that is the effective agent rather than the drug.

How have we satisfied Mill's three essentials for judging causes and effects? Not very well in this case. The first rule was to show that the drug preceded the symptoms in time. Unless our medical records went back far enough, we would be unable to show that Y did not occur until after X. The second requirement was to show that taking the drug was related to the mysterious symptoms. Even if we could show that taking the drug was correlated with the mysterious symptoms, it might be argued that in order to be susceptible to the drug, a person had to be already in a given state of distress. It was not the drug, or *not only* the drug, that was related to the symptoms, according to this argument. If we have not done very well in trying to satisfy rules 1 and 2, it is even more difficult to satisfy the third requirement. If the subjects who were in a state of distress were the only ones given the drug, then it is possible to explain the cause-effect relationship by saying that the subjects were "self-selected" into the treatment group. What we need is a comparison group of other subjects who were in a similar state of distress but were not given the drug.

Despite the difficulty of clear inference in this case, many scientists would probably be willing to be convinced by strong evidence even if inconclusive. Thus, if persons taking the drug were more likely to show the symptoms, if those taking more of the drug show more of the symptoms, and if those taking it over a longer period of time show more of the symptoms, a prudent scientist would be cautious about deciding that the drug *was not* a determinant of the symptoms. Even if an investigator was not willing to conclude that the drug was surely at the root of the symptoms, at least not on the basis of the type of evidence outlined, he or she might well decide that it would be wisest to act as though it were. In this case the scientist would be more concerned about making the type II error of underestimating the drug's harmful effects than about making the type I error of exaggerating the possible harmful effects.

METATHEORIES OF UNDERSTANDING

In focusing on one independent variable to the relative exclusion of others, the behavioral scientist will be guided by a theoretical preconception of what is and is not worth studying. For someone interested in why people don't help others in an emergency, the "number of witnesses to a crisis" would certainly be a variable worth studying. Other variables might be eliminated from empirical consideration if they were thought to be theoretically irrelevant. However, some variables tend to be overemphasized merely from force of habit, or because they are so simple to assess (e.g., birth order), or because it is fashionable for everyone in the field to focus on those particular variables. This kind of "tunnel vision" may lead to an artificially constricted theoretical view, and it would be far better to throw a wider net, to look at as many relevant variables as possible over the course of the research. The more kinds of relevant variables that are examined, the more generality and applicability the research findings can have, and the more precisely the relationship between X and Y can be stated.

One type of theoretical preconception that can greatly influence the thinking and perceptions of behavioral scientists is the *metatheory*, or conceptual scheme, with which they approach the study of human behavior. The metatheory that seems to influence the thinking of many experimentalists is a *mechanistic model*, which compares social causation to a complex machine and assumes human nature to be a matter of social engineering (Rosnow, 1981). To affect a machine, it is necessary to exert some influence on it—to push it, lift it, or let other forces act on it. Our intuitive idea is that such a machine is operating as if "frozen" in space (as opposed to something organic that evolves or develops), and that motion is connected with the acts of pushing, lifting, or pulling. The mechanistic model approaches human behavior as if it had reached a state of rest or balance, and that further "motion" was always first connected with some outside stimulation. As a consequence, the model tends to overemphasize relatively immediate states of behavior, without regard for the history or the teleologic causes of the behavior.

An alternative metatheory is that of an active (as opposed to reactive) and developing organism, known as the *organismic model* (cf. Overton, 1976). In this case the focus is usually on an organized whole and on the progressive changes in behavior patterns. The changes can be looked at, for instance, from the perspective of the history of the behavior or from the perspective of the development of one human being from birth to death. The research methods required to study the development of human behavior are also different from those used to study only the current state of behavior.

What independent variables might be favored by someone who envisioned behavior in terms of a mechanistic as opposed to an organismic model? While not all mechanists are experimentalists, many are and they tend to favor independent variables that can be experimentally manipulated. That does not mean that all mechanists are insensitive to the notion of social change or to the notion of an active rather than a reactive organism. We will find that certain variables can be defined from both points of view, but that the empirical emphasis is usually that of a reactive organism. The reactive organism is easier to study experimentally, which tends to compromise the organismic model in actual practice.

Suppose we were interested in the relatively short-term and long-term effects of biological variables on eating behavior. Short-term variables would be those having a momentary or transitory effect on eating behavior, while the effects of long-term variables would be to emphasize stability or change over time. An example of a short-term variable would be biological drives in a heightened state of arousal. By comparing food-deprived animals with others who already were quite satiated on food, the independent biological variable of the organism's hunger drive could be studied for its effect on any given dependent variable relevant to eating behavior. Alternatively, we might develop a hypothesis which argued that aspects of eating behavior evolved as a biological adaptation. While that notion allows for change over time, it does not emphasize "activity" but instead "reactivity." It is a kind of "quasi-organismic" hypothesis, in other words.

Such a theory was suggested recently by Michael Stock and his coworkers in Britain and Canada (Rothwell & Stock, 1979). They hypothesized that the biological mechanism preventing obesity evolved as an adaptation to allow animals to burn off excess food energy as heat instead of storing it as fat. In this case the long-term variable would be the processes of evolution and biological adaptation, but in order to study these "organismic" processes empirically it would be necessary to isolate biological variables in the here and now for examination. Stock has done precisely this, and he and his coworker Nancy Rothwell have begun experimenting on small deposits of fat cells called "brown fat" (because they are literally brown). Thus they have defined the biological independent variable causing obesity from the perspective of both a mechanistic and a quasi-organismic model of eating.

INDEPENDENT VARIABLES

Biological variables constitute one class of independent variables. The *social environment* constitutes a second class which would include the physical setting of the research, the evolution of social systems, and a wide range of other possibilities. For example, if one were to read while eating, the reading matter might be construed as a distracting environmental variable that turned the eater's attention away from food and led him to eat much more than usual. An organismic approach with emphasis on the social environment might focus on how the evolution of social systems could explain the development of civilized eating habits, customs, and food preferences. Anthropologist Michael J. Harner (1970) developed a scale for measuring population pressures in agricultural societies, which he used to test the theory that growth of population pressure was a major determinant of human social evolution through the process of competition for increasingly scarce subsistence resources.

Hereditary factors constitute a third class of independent variables, that is to say, factors associated with the individual's genetic endowment. For example, there was the case of a child born with a cortico-adrenal insufficiency who showed an enormous and continual craving for salt (Wilkins & Richter, 1940). His malfunctioning adrenals were not discovered until his death. When his perplexed parents brought him to the hospital to find a cure for his unusual salt-craving drive, the unsuspecting dietician kept the child on a normal hospital diet and he died within a few days. His great appetite for salt was what had been instrumental in keeping him alive, unbeknownst to his parents or the dietician in charge. Looked at from either a mechanistic or an organismic perspective, it would be the child's malfunctioning adrenals that constitute the independent variable, although this might be further conceptualized in terms of the cause or origin of this malfunctioning.

Previous training and experience is a fourth class of independent variables. For example, experiments by Paul Rozin (1967, 1979) have demonstrated that rats maintained on a diet that is deficient in thiamine will prefer one that is supplemented by this vitamin over one that is not. He has also shown that the behavior is learned, not innate. The rat eats the more favorable diet because of its more favorable consequences, not because the rat necessarily "knows" what is good for him. Given a choice of several diets, only one of which contains the nutrient he lacks, the hungry rat will consume one of the diets for several days until its effects are felt. If it is not a healthy diet, the rat will experiment with another, and so on until he learns which diet has the most favorable consequences.

Maturity constitutes a fifth class of independent variables. We might, for example, find an age correlation with eating behavior. Of course, age is related to other classes of independent variables, and it may be difficult to distinguish whether the eating behavior was influenced only by the organism's maturity or by some related variable or variables.

We can also think of these classes of independent variables in terms of their point of origin. There are *internal variables* that can "push" a human being in a particular direction or toward a specific goal or object (cf. Buss, 1978). The person's need for social approval, biological drives, hereditary predispositions—all of these might be worth exploring. The person might also be "pulled" by *external variables:* aspects of the social environment, group pressures, and societal norms. Good scientific practice requires that we explore both kinds of variables, that we consider how the person could be "pulled" and "pushed" at the same time.

DEPENDENT VARIABLES

The same considerations in selecting the independent variable will weigh in the selection of the dependent variable. Choosing one variable over another is often a matter of convention and convenience, but the choice is always better dictated on theoretical grounds for its relevance to the scientific problem under investigation. Further, just as tapping several kinds of independent variables can increase the generality and applicability of the research findings, so can the measurement of more than one dependent variable increase the scope of the findings by describing the area of application more specifically.

Animal behaviorists usually distinguish among three kinds of dependent measures: (a) the direction of behavioral change, (b) the quantity or persistence of change, and (c) the ease with which changes are effected. For example, in a learning experiment that consisted of teaching a thirsty rat to run through a complicated maze toward a thimbleful of water, the dependent variable could be the *direction* the rat chose on each trial (whether the animal turned right or left; i.e., toward or away from water). The dependent variable could also be how long the rat *persisted* in the correct response when the water was no longer available at the end of his run and all that greeted him each time was an empty thimble. A third dependent variable would be the *ease* with which the rat reacquired the correct response when the thimble of water was again made available to him.

We find variables similar to these three in human research. Suppose we were interested in the effects on a person's beliefs of two types of propaganda, emotional and rational. We could begin by observing how much the person's beliefs changed when he or she was exposed to each type of propaganda (disregarding the direction of change). That would tell us something about the relative strength of the two types in a concrete situation. We could then measure the direction of the person's beliefs to determine if there were any changes in the predicted direction or any "boomerang effects," that is, changes in the opposite direction of that advocated by a communicator. If we found changes, we could subsequently track them over a period of time to see how long they persisted.

Another way of viewing dependent variables has been suggested by Uriel G. Foa (1968), who puts them into three categories corresponding to three types of behavioral change. One type refers to the *diffusion* (or irradiation) of changes in a response onto other responses that are close in time to the primary one. For example, a series of studies dealt with the beliefs of some high school students about Pablo Picasso, the famous artist, when the students were in a generally favorable or unfavorable mood. Four sets of arguments were prepared. Two were pro-and-con positions on the genius of Picasso. Two others were pro-and-con positions on the question, "Should we have a longer school week?" The latter pro argument was intended to put them in an unfavorable mood (a longer school week), and the shorter-week argument was to put them in a favorable mood. The experimental design consisted of exposing groups of students to both Picasso arguments in conjunction with one or the other of the school-week arguments, varying the sequence and timing of the presentations, and measuring the resulting shifts of opinion. It was found that the argument against a longer school week put students in a frame of mind that was highly receptive to whichever Picasso argument accompanied it more closely in time. On the other hand, the argument in favor of a longer school week caused students to be more receptive to the Picasso argument that was presented farther away in time (Corrozi & Rosnow, 1968; Rosnow, 1968).

A second type of change concerns the *degrees of relationships* among people. Suppose we wanted to study the effects of different communication patterns on problem-solving behavior in groups. We could try experimenting with different patterns in order to observe the way in which each affected the behavior of the group, for example, the effects on morale that altered the cohesiveness of the group. Three such patterns that have been studied are shown in Figure 3.1: the "circle" (where a member may communicate with the person to his left and right), the "chain" (where communications must travel up and down a chain of command), and the "wheel" (where one central member may communicate with all the other members). Research has shown that the wheel typically provides the fastest speed of solution and greatest accuracy, and that the circle is usually the slowest and least accurate. More to the point, however, morale is found to be best in a circle and poorest in a wheel—which tells us about the degrees of emotional relationships that are characteristic of these patterns (Bavelas, 1950; Collins & Raven, 1969; Leavitt, 1951).

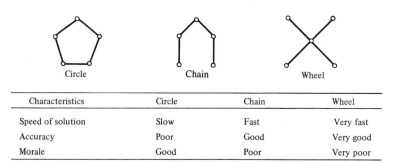

Characteristics	Circle	Chain	Wheel
Speed of solution	Slow	Fast	Very fast
Accuracy	Poor	Good	Very good
Morale	Good	Poor	Very poor

Figure 3-1 Three patterns in a chain of communication and the characteristic findings associated with each.

Going from one pattern to another should thus reveal changes in the degrees of relationships among the members.

A third type of change is that having to do with the *structure of hierarchies*. The word "hierarchy" means a system in which one thing is ranked above another. In group psychotherapy the so-called marathon group involves a continuous meeting lasting as long as three or four uninterrupted days. It provides an intensive experience in group processes, so that person A may increase his liking for person C and decrease his liking for person B. The hierarchical structure ABC thus changes to ACB. Another example has to do with changes in the structure of people's needs. Abraham H. Maslow (1962) hypothesized the existence of a "motive hierarchy" in which hunger, thirst, and similar physiologically-based drives were at the bottom and where the drive ranked highest was that of self-actualization (characterized by a superior perception of reality, increased self-acceptance, increased spontaneity, autonomy, and so on). For someone to achieve this highest state, Maslow assumed that all the person's other needs must first be satisfied since the structure of the need hierarchy never changed. However, it might be interesting to study whether Maslow's hierarchy is truly stable or whether the structure is influenced by cultural factors and personal experiences.

OPERATIONAL AND THEORETICAL DEFINITIONS

Whatever the variables under investigation are, it is important that we try to describe them in clear and precise terms. That tells others exactly what is being studied and allows them to try to integrate their own relevant findings within the body of research and to challenge or build on it. A good place to begin is with the dictionary definition and the derivation (or etymology) of the word. The *Oxford English Dictionary* (called the *OED*) is a multivolume etymological dictionary that has proven to be a valuable source of clues about the nature of particular variables in behavioral science. For example, a sociologist who was interested in the variable of gossip used the *OED* to learn how "gossip" developed from a positive term applied to both sexes into a derogatory term applied to women (Rysman, 1977).

It is possible to distinguish between two types of definitions in science, the operational and the theoretical (cf. Easley & Tatsuoka, 1968). The *operational definition* is one that assigns meaning to a variable in terms of the operations necessary to measure it in any concrete situation. The *theoretical definition* is one that assigns meaning in more abstract terms, since it is sometimes true that there is no procedure for measuring a variable directly.

In behavioral science, the operational definition of intelligence can be stated as "intelligence is equivalent to a person's score on a given IQ test." It is also possible to operationally define a variable in terms of the experimental methods involved in its determination. For example, John Dollard and his coworkers studied whether the existence of frustration always leads to some form of aggression, called the "frustration-aggression hypothesis" (Dollard, Doob, Miller, Mowrer, & Sears, 1939). They defined "frustration" on the basis of certain experimental operations as "a condition which exists when a goal response suffers interference."

The notion of an operational definition was first put forward by the physicist P. W. Bridgman (1937), who also realized that not every variable can be operationally defined in *directly* measurable terms. It is perfectly acceptable to speak of some variables even if there is no procedure for measuring them. For instance, we can speak meaningfully of the weight of an object while it is falling, even though the only instruments for measuring its weight would require that its motion be stopped (Easley, 1971).

Because it is also overly restrictive in behavioral science to insist that all variables be operationally defined in directly measurable terms, we find that many variables are defined in more abstract terms and measured indirectly, based on theoretical assumptions about their nature. For example, it is impossible to measure an attitude directly, since an attitude is an abstract concept referring to things that exist inside a person's mind. It is possible, nonetheless, to give a clear theoretical definition of an attitude as an individual's feelings, beliefs, and tendencies to behave as he or she does toward a certain social

		Physical aggression	Verbal aggression
Active aggression	Direct aggression	Punching someone	Insulting someone
	Indirect aggression	Playing a practical joke on someone	Maliciously gossiping about someone
Passive aggression	Direct aggression	Blocking someone's passage	Refusing to talk to someone
	Indirect aggression	Refusing to do some necessary task	Refusing to give one's consent

Figure 3-2 A typology of aggression to show all possible classes of aggressive behaviors in humans. (*A. H. Buss, "Aggression Pays," in J. L. Singer [ed.], The Control of Aggression and Violence, Academic Press, New York, 1971. Adapted by permission of the author and Academic Press.*)

object. On the basis of this definition, instruments have been developed for measuring attitudes indirectly, by asking questions about how a person feels, what the person believes, and how the person intends to behave.

Looking in the dictionary can be a good starting place, but it can also be limiting if what we want is a clear and precise operational or theoretical definition of an independent or a dependent variable. That is because the nature of some variables is difficult to capture precisely in a single sentence. Consider the definition of "aggression," which various world bodies, including the United Nations, have struggled over for years. Behavioral scientists also struggle with its meaning. A social psychological definition of aggression is "behavior whose intent is the physical or psychological injury of another" (Goldstein, 1975). But how can we enter someone's mind and find out what the person's "intent" was? Some animal behaviorists define aggression as "any offensive or threatening action or procedure" (Baenninger, 1974). That definition avoids the problem of trying to peer into the aggressor's mind, but the notion of what is offensive or threatening is also a matter of conjecture. Another way to describe a variable is in terms of its *typology*, which means a systematic classification of types. The typology of aggression shown in Figure 3.2 thus shows all possible types of aggressive behaviors, and it avoids the problem of trying to reduce this complex behavior to a single sentence. Models such as this one can be developed intuitively, or they can be developed empirically by using quantitative methods.

TWO

LEVELS OF EMPIRICAL INQUIRY

Chapter **4.** **Descriptive Research**

Chapter **5.** **Relational Research**

Chapter **6.** **Experimental Research**

FOUR

DESCRIPTIVE RESEARCH

A PARADIGM CASE

In Chapter 2 we defined descriptive research and gave brief examples drawn from the areas of primate behavior, the behavioral study of obedience, and speech behavior (see Table 2.1). We now look at more detailed cases for the purpose of introducing some alternative approaches to mapping out what happens behaviorally. In these examples, and in those discussed in subsequent chapters, we shall see that the three levels of inquiry—descriptive, relational, and experimental—are not mutually exclusive. Some studies may have characteristics of more than one type, although it is usually possible to classify a study as being *primarily* in one category on the basis of its principal objective.

We begin with a paradigm case in the field of human personality, an area that deals with the individuality and characteristics of normal and abnormal behavior. We call this a *paradigm case* because it represents a model as well as an exemplary case of descriptive research in behavioral science. This particular study also shows how descriptive methods are sometimes used in applied research to tell "how things are."

The Office of Strategic Services (OSS) was a World War II government agency in the United States charged with tasks as varied as intelligence gathering, sabotage behind enemy lines, mobilization of guerilla groups to resist the Nazi occupation, and preparation and dissemination of propaganda (OSS Assessment Staff, 1948). Thousands of men, drawn from both military and civilian life, were recruited to carry out the often hazardous missions of the OSS. Initially it was not known what type of men to select for each of the various missions, and a group of psychologists and psychiatrists was assembled to aid in the assessment of the special agents of the OSS. The chief contribution of these researchers was to set up a series of situations that would permit more useful and relevant descriptions of the personalities of the candidates.

The original intent of the assessment group had been more ambitious. It had been hoped that it would be possible to lower appreciably the error rate in the selection of men and women for the OSS and to increase the likelihood of assignment of agents to those missions they could best perform. Unfortunately, from the point of view of this intent, several factors made impossible the development of a screening and placement system that could be fairly and properly evaluated. Chief among those factors were the assessment staff's not knowing what particular mission would finally be assigned to a recruit and, perhaps most important, several weaknesses in the final appraisal of how good a job an agent had actually done.

From December 1943 to August 1945, more than 5000 recruits were studied by the assessment staff at one or another station. The primary station, S, was located about an hour's ride from Washington, D.C., in a rustic setting of rolling meadows and stately trees. To this station recruits were sent for a $3\frac{1}{2}$-day period, during which they were given identical clothes to wear and carried a pseudonym so that colonels and privates and college professors would be indistinguishable to the assessment staff. Besides a false name, each recruit had to invent a cover story giving himself a new occupation, new residence, new place of birth, and a new educational background. Candidates were warned that the assessment staff would try to trick them into breaking cover and giving away their true identity.

Virtually everything that a recruit did from the moment he arrived at Station S was grist for the assessment mill: how he got off the truck that brought his group of recruits, the manner in which he asked questions of the staff member who explained the Station S procedures to the candidates, what he said at the first dinner, and what he chose to do after dinner when he was free to read, or talk, or withdraw. That first evening, candidates filled out a great many paper-and-pencil tests of personality and ability and also answered questions concerning personal background information.

The next few days were filled with many situational tests in which the staff would have the opportunity to see each man's level of initiative, leadership, functioning intelligence, social relationships, and physical ability. For example, in one situation a group of four to seven men had to move a log and a rock across an 8-foot-wide brook. The situation was rigged so that either a bridge or an overhead cable system could be constructed to solve the problem, but the achievement of a solution was not the main purpose of the exercise. Instead it was to give the staff an opportunity to see which man played what role in the team effort required to achieve a solution.

One of the most trying, and possibly most revealing, situations was another task in which the candidate was to direct the efforts of two helpers in building a 5-foot cube out of a giant Tinker Toy set. Ostensibly the task was to assess the candidate's leadership ability. In actuality, it was a test of stress tolerance.

"Kippy" and "Buster," the two helpers, were really two members of the assessment staff. Kippy was a passive sort who did nothing unless ordered to, except occasionally to get in the way. Buster offered useless suggestions, griped repeatedly, and excelled in finding and harping on the candidate's weaknesses. Kippy and Buster together were sufficiently obstructive that, in the history of the OSS assessment program, no recruit was ever able to complete the task in the allotted 10 minutes.

Some of the candidates saw immediately that the two helpers were confederates; that insight sometimes, but not always, helped the candidates to contain their temper and persist in trying to get the job done. Other candidates wondered why the OSS could not afford better farmhands around the estate and admitted that the obstreperousness and insolence of the helpers tempted them more than once to lay an uncharitable hand upon one or the other of them. On more than one occasion such a laying on of hands did occur. Some candidates learned enough about themselves from this experience that they asked to be excused from the program, deciding that they could not deal with stress of this kind.

During the candidates' half-week assessment period, they underwent many situational tests of the kind described. Table 4.1 lists some of those tests, each one providing an opportunity for the staff to observe and describe the behavior of the candidate. It seems unlikely that, either before or since, have so many people been observed and described so carefully by so many experts in human behavior.

HIGHER-ORDER RELATIONSHIPS

We have viewed the OSS project as a paradigm case of applied descriptive research, but it must be noted again that description was not the only goal of the assessment staff. They also had a hope of relational observations in which the assessments made of the candidates could later be correlated with how good a job the men did in the field. Such correlations define the adequacy of the selection procedures, and when the correlations are high they tell that the *predictor variable* (the assessment in this case) did its job of predicting the outcome or *criterion variable,* the actual job performance.

The OSS project is, in this respect, typical of the intensive case study, in that it had the capacity to stimulate research ideas that could be followed up in relational and experimental investigations. The later investigations would be designed to tease out (a) *how* what happened behaviorally is related to other events and (b) *why* something happened behaviorally. Unfortunately, this type of relational outcome research had not been planned from the beginning, so there was no satisfactory evaluation of just how good a job had been done by the agents in the field. Even if such criterion information had been available, there is reason to suspect that the OSS assessment program could hardly have been very effective since the staff had only the vaguest, and probably some-

Table 4.1 Some situational tests employed by the OSS assessment staff

Situation	Props and materials	Objective
Personal belongings	A man's personal effects including clothing, news clippings, timetables, ticket receipt	Assess the type of person who left these personal belongings
The brook	Log, rock, boards, rope, pulley, barrel	Transport log and rock across 8-foot brook
The wall	2 walls, 10 feet high, 8 feet apart, heavy log, old board, short 2 × 4s	Transport heavy log up first wall over to second wall, down second wall
Construction task	Giant Tinker Toy	Direct two uncooperative assistants in building a 5-foot cube
Intelligence interview	Escaped prisoner	Interrogate prisoner for strategic information
Captured spy	Secret files	Explain why he was found at night going through secret files in building
Discuss the captured-spy stress interview	Sympathetic staff member cordially trying to break cover	Poststress attempt to break cover
Captured document analysis	Four captured documents	Abstract the core of reliable intelligence contained
Mined road	Long logs, stones, rope, 2 × 4s	Lead a group across a mined road
Room search	Friendly agent's room	Search room and report its contents by radio despite arrival of German guard
Blown bridge	Bridge abutments, pilings, and debris	Lead a group across a river using only the remains of the blown bridge

times erroneous, ideas about the nature of the jobs for which the candidates were being selected. It would be unreasonable indeed to think that one could select people for the performance of unspecified functions.

We sometimes suspect a higher-order relationship even when the data are employed in a generally descriptive manner, as in this case. For example, Gordon W. Allport and his colleagues (Allport, Bruner, & Jandorf, 1953) collaborated on a descriptive research project that involved an analysis of over 200 autobiographies on the subject of "My life in Germany before and after January 30, 1933." Of this collection of case studies, 90 were subjected to a searching psychological analysis. Most of the autobiographers were male, Jewish or Protestant, aged 30 to 60, middle or upper class, and from Germany or Austria. A striking finding was that despite the increasing likelihood of potential persecution during this period before World War II, the evidence was minimized or denied by the 90 respondents, as if the truth had been too hard for them to accept. Although there were severe stresses reported, including physical assaults, no one guessed the concentration-camp horrors that were to come. The physical assaults were perceived as isolated incidents and tended to be dismissed as such. Another finding characteristic of the 90 respondents was that, despite the stresses to which they had been exposed, there were no radical transformations in their personalities. A person might change, to be sure, but he or she was still clearly identifiable in personality as the same individual.

All the respondents in the sample of 90 had experienced severe frustration, and the frustration-aggression hypothesis had just been formulated. It will be recalled from our discussion in Chapter 3 that it was hypothesized by Dollard et al. (1939) that aggression and its derivatives should always be the reaction to frustration. This was not the final statement on the relationship between frustration and aggression, and the case studies of these 90 lives by Allport et al. was one of several studies which uncovered the fact that there were other reactions to frustration besides aggression and its offshoots. There were also responses of defeat, resignation, fantasy, conformity, and perhaps above all, of planning and problem-solving. The revised frustration-aggression hypothesis took all this into account. While it allowed for other responses to frustration, it was at the same time more difficult to verify or disprove than the 1939 formulation.

A similar type of descriptive study, one that took over where the Allport et al. study left off, was conducted by David P. Boder (1949). Following Germany's surrender in World War II, General Dwight D. Eisenhower sent out a call to the American press that can best be summarized by the phrase, "Come and see for yourself." The dead of Auschwitz, Bergen-Belsen, Buchenwald, Dachau, and Treblinka outnumbered their survivors, but there *were* survivors, and Boder, who spoke Russian, German, Spanish, Yiddish, and English, set out to collect first-person narratives of what had happened and how the survivors had responded. The wire recorder (predecessor of the tape recorder) had just been developed and made available commercially, so Boder was able to collect a narrative from each of the concentration-camp victims he interviewed. The statement he posed first to each respondent was: "We know very little in America about the things that happened to you people who were in concentration camps. If you want to help us out . . . tell us . . . your name, how old you are, and where you were and what happened." Altogether, 70 people, selected for representativeness of the survivors, were interviewed for a total of 120 hours.

In a sense, the case-study narratives collected by Boder were temporal continuations of those collected by Allport et al. The narratives collected by the latter went only up to the beginning of the war, while the bulk of Boder's narratives were concerned only with the World War II years. The earlier investigators could hardly have imagined that the next several years would bring such a deluge of horrors and atrocities: confiscation of personal belongings; loading of human beings onto cattle cars without food, water, or ventilation, so that most victims died before the destination was reached; the sorting into groups of those strong enough to be able to do forced labor versus those too sick or weak or young to work, who were taken to the "showers," which emitted not water but poison gas; the loading of bodies onto the crematorium piles when it was not certain that the gas had done its work. To help him better understand the reactions of concentration-camp victims to these horrors, Boder developed a system of classification of the stresses in the inmates' life situation. From this came the "Traumatic Index," an indicator that permitted the classification of the common trauma reported by many of the survivors.

In sum, the personal documents studied by Allport et al., and those later studied by Boder, were used in a descriptive manner, but there is also an implied relationship in these studies. Looking only at the samples examined, the data would be called "descriptive." But if we emphasize that both studies were interested in learning more about behavior under conditions of a catastrophe of human origin, we might also regard the combination of findings as relational. By implication, at least, the scientific question could be viewed as, "What is the effect of people's being exposed to catastrophic situations compared to their not being exposed to such situations?"

THE ENUMERATIVE SURVEY

Descriptive research is not restricted only to narrative descriptions of behavior, such as the behavior of the OSS recruits during World War II or that of the victims of Nazi persecution in the 1930s and 1940s. It can also involve an *enumerative* type of survey, the purpose of which is to count (enumerate) a representative sample (when it cannot count everyone) and then to make inferences about the frequencies of occurrence in the population as a whole.

A *sample* can be defined as a small part of anything, while a *population* refers to the total number of parts from which the sample was taken. The enumerative survey is one important way of sampling a population in its normal surroundings. This type of research is not meant to explain a causal relationship, or even to show relationships between one variable and another, but only to tell us how many members of a population have a specified attribute or how often certain events occur (Oppenheim, 1966). However, even though it is primarily descriptive, there may be relational aspects that are implicit in the findings.

Research done by R. E. Peterson (1968a, 1968b) on the scope of organized student protest in the 1960s is illustrative of the enumerative survey. During the 1960s, student activism was rampant on many college campuses in America, and sociologists and psychologists postulated various reasons to explain the unrest. Although the activists outwardly appeared to be rejecting or rebelling against parental values and ideologies, experience suggested that they were in fact closer to their parents' ideals than the nonactivist students were (Flachs, 1967; Keniston, 1967).

Peterson's research approached the problem from the descriptive rather than from the causal perspective (although there were also relational aspects to it) and simply enumerated the clear-cut, consistent, and growing trends. His data were obtained from questionnaires that he sent out in 1965 and again in 1968 to college deans at more than 800 of all regionally accredited four-year, degree-granting institutions in the United States.

Peterson defined organized student protest as "planned, public expressions of disapproval." He coded the results of his survey in summary categories based on whether the deans reported that they had experienced organized protests in connection with instruction and curriculum issues, faculty concerns, freedom of expression, student-administration problems, or extracurricular activities. He also divided the responding institutions into four geographical areas, in order to identify regional differences with regard to particular social issues; he then examined the type of educational institution in which protest was most frequent, i.e., whether it was the public liberal arts college, public university, independent liberal arts college, and so forth. Thus we see that, although Peterson's research was *primarily* descriptive, there were relational aspects; for example, relating protest events to type of school or region of country is a relational rather than a simply descriptive form of research.

Peterson's enumerative survey helped to establish an institutional and national profile of the types of schools that had experienced organized student protests for the academic years 1964–65 and 1967–68. It established that some issues were consistently more salient than others throughout the United States, but that in certain regions of the country, such as the south, the unrest was not as active as in other regions. It also revealed an increasing tendency, during the period of 1964 to 1968, for organized dissent about United States policies in Vietnam, but a decrease in civil rights protests during the same period. This suggested that, although the mood of dissension may not have changed very much, the outward display of behavior focused on entirely different issues as time passed.

Particularly interesting was the observation that only a small minority of college students actually participated in organized dissent, in spite of the fact that many Americans during this period had the impression of overwhelming student dissent. One explanation for this difference between the reality of the situation and people's impressions was that the student activists were unusually talented at making themselves and their causes highly visible (Keniston, 1969). Organized student protests were also likely to occur in the largest universities, the ones where student populations were most mixed and the faculty had many celebrities. These "high protest campuses" were simply superactive places in which everyone was more intense, more active, and more involved, and they were the types of educational institutions most likely to be publicized by the mass media (Hodgkinson, 1970).

SECONDARY RECORDS

Records of observations or measures made by others amount to a kind of "second-hand" naturalistic observation, since the researcher has no control over the original data-collection procedures (Scott & Wertheimer, 1962). Examples of such secondary records include the federal census and the kinds of raw data depositories available at the Human Relations Area Files at Yale University and elsewhere, the University of Chicago's National Opinion Research Center (NORC), and the University of Michigan's Survey Research Center. To illustrate: the Roper Center of the University of Connecticut offers survey data collected by NORC going back to the early 1950s. The data come from personal interviews administered to national samples using a standardized questionnaire with the same questions appearing in every survey or according to a rotation pattern. All the data are in the public domain and are readily accessible to researchers for duplication, analysis, and publication without clearance from NORC. A wide range of variables is tapped, including demographic, sociopsychological, political, socioeconomic, and other aspects of behavior.

There are many others kinds of public data that are available for analysis, from the simple birth, wedding, and death entries in town-hall ledgers to various census records. Data such as these can be used for making profiles for use in either descriptive or relational research in the same way that Peterson's data were the bases of institutional and national profiles. For instance, there are extensive records and documents in research libraries which are available to investigators wishing to do research based on census information. In the United States there are census records available on variables such as population growth, race, industrialization, urbanization, migration, and fertility. Using those records it is possible to generate descriptive historical profiles of regional and metropolitan areas going back over a century. Then, switching again to a relational mode of research, one can look for trends and growth patterns of old urban centers and the multiplication of new ones as a consequence of industrialization drawing more and more of the rural population toward the city. One can also see how, over the past one hundred years, the United States has grown more native-born and more female, and then (doing further relational research) correlate the records with others to highlight the relationships between one variable and another (Warner & Fleisch, 1977).

Another use of secondary records is in what is called *documentary research,* an area of inquiry in which many historians and some sociologists specialize. For example, a researcher might be interested in tracing the historical origins of some occurrence or type of behavior pattern. Those who do research in this area must take into consideration several problems, such as how to establish the authenticity of documents, whether the relevant documents are available, problems of sampling, how to establish whether the documents are telling the truth, and so on. Documentary research is not a clear-cut and well-recognized category, like survey research or experimental research, although for a specialized discussion of problems of documentary research the reader will find recent work by Jennifer Platt (1981 *a*, 1981 *b*) to contain helpful guidelines.

META-ANALYSIS

The reanalysis of someone else's analysis of data is known as secondary analysis, and a particular type of secondary analysis is called *meta-analysis,* which means the analysis of analyses. It is usually applied to a collection of independent replication results for the purpose of describing the findings, and in a later chapter we discuss in detail the methodology of meta-analysis.

To give an example, however, Rosenthal (1978) used this type of secondary-analytic approach to answer the following questions: (a) How often do recording or observer errors occur in psychological experimentation? and (b) Are the errors that do occur likely to be biased in favor of the observer's hypothesis? He began by searching the literature for research reports that gave an estimate of the frequency of recording errors and/or the degree to which those errors were biased in the observer's favor. Although he found only 21 studies that satisfied either criterion, the data from the studies were based on over 300 observers making about 140,000 observations.

Since almost all of the studies were designed, at least in part, to permit the quantitative assessment of error rates, they cannot be regarded as truly representative of behavioral research in general, nor can we have any way of knowing whether the studies give overestimates or underestimates of rates of error-making in the population of psychological experiments as a whole. Given those qualifications, Rosenthal found (a) that about 1 percent of all observations were wrong and (b) that of the observational errors that were made, about two-thirds supported the observer's hypothesis. The latter finding reflects the operation of a bias, since only half should do so by chance if the observers were unbiased.

FUNCTIONS OF DESCRIPTIVE RESEARCH

Briefly in Chapter 2, and again in this chapter, we have touched on the wide range of possibilities for descriptive-level research. We have seen that such research, whether it deals with a basic question (as in the meta-analytic study above) or an applied problem (as in the OSS study), is always directed toward the same objective—to tell "how things are." That defines the scope of all descriptive research, but we have also seen how the research findings may carry implications of a more complex relationship (as in the case studies bearing on the frustration-aggression hypothesis). In particular, however, we find that descriptive research can serve three important functions in any program of investigation in behavioral science.

One function is to provide groundwork by which to take a complex behavioral or organizational structure with which we are unfamiliar and get a sense of it. When thrown into a strange, ambiguous situation, the first thing we do is to try to orient ourselves by making use of reference points, and in this way the nature of the situation is gradually revealed to us. The psychologists and psychiatrists who aided in the assessment of the special agents of the OSS had no idea of what particular missions would be assigned to the recruits, but on the basis of descriptive research they were gradually able to perceive ways of dealing with this ambiguous problem.

A second function is to establish the boundaries of the research problem, once the nature of the situation is revealed. Descriptive research serves not only as a guide in adjusting to new surroundings, but it also helps us to clarify the shape and structure of phenomena. By methodically establishing frequencies of occurrence of events or of limiting demographic conditions, we can begin to specify the boundaries of the problem under investigation.

A third function is to raise, by implication, ideas that can be tested in relational or experimental studies. To be sure, the descriptive and the relational can also serve as a kind of "counterpoint" to one another in the same study. Peterson's research was basically descriptive, but it also showed how protest events were related to other variables.

RELATIONAL RESEARCH

A PARADIGM CASE

Relational research, like descriptive research, can involve gathering data in the natural environment or in a simulated environment, using electronic equipment or a simple diary with which to record behavior, making observations from afar or as a participant observer. The objective of relational research is always the description of how what happens is related to other events, although these descriptions may themselves be explanatory—the "how" may imply a "why" and not just a "what" (Kaplan, 1964). That is to say, we may suddenly see *why* something happened once we have described what happened and the events surrounding it.

In this chapter we discuss detailed examples of relational research to illustrate this wide area of application. Chapter 4 began with a paradigm case of applied descriptive research from the field of human personality, the OSS study carried out during World War II. The OSS assessment staff had been in a position to make a great many detailed observations relevant to many of the motives of the candidates. However, there was not a planned, systematic attempt to relate the scores or ratings on any one of these motives to the scores or ratings on some subsequently measured variable that, on the basis of theory, should show a strong correlation with the predictor variable. In the field of personality there are, however, many studies that could serve well to illustrate relational research. There are hundreds of studies showing how one personality attribute is related to some other personality attribute. For our illustration, we shall discuss the development of a personality construct known as "social desirability" (or the motive to be approved by others).

By a *construct* we mean an abstract variable that is constructed from ideas or images in order to serve as an explanatory term. Constructs—such as the motive to be approved by others—are variables that cannot be directly observed, but are defined on the basis of observations. The "government" is another example of a construct, since we do not observe the government in action, but only the members of government (the president of the United States, the members of Congress, and so on). Constructs are also sometimes called "auxiliary symbols" or "intervening variables" or "abstracta" (Kaplan, 1964; Reichenbach, 1938). In behavioral science, constructs are developed by a process in which a means for their measurement is devised and (in a procedure known as *construct validation*) then related to subjects' performance in a variety of other spheres as the construct would predict. (We return to the subject of construct validity in Chapter 7.)

Even when we narrow the range of personality research to such enterprises, there is still much from which to choose. For example, there are the investigations of David McClelland (1961) on the "achievement motive" and Stanley Schachter (1959) on the "affiliation motive." The paradigm case we have chosen is from research done at the very end of the 1950s by Douglas Crowne and David Marlowe, both then at Ohio State University. Crowne and Marlowe set out to develop an instrument that would measure the need for social approval independent of the subjects' level of psychopathology.

The researchers began by considering hundreds of personality-test items that were answered in a true-false format. To be included, an item had to be one that would reflect socially approved behavior but yet be almost certain to be untrue. In short, the items had to reflect behavior too good to be true. In addition, answers to the items could not have any implications of psychological abnormality or psychopathology. By having a group of psychology graduate students and faculty judge the social desirability of each item, and by having another group of psychology graduate students and faculty judge the degree of psychopathology implied by each item, it was possible to develop a set of items that would reflect behavior too virtuous to be probable and yet carrying no implication of personal maladjustment. The final form of the test, called the Marlowe-Crowne Social Desirability Scale, included thirty-three items (Crowne & Marlowe, 1964). In about half the items a "true" answer reflects the socially desirable or higher-need-for-approval response, and in about half the items a "false" answer reflects the socially desirable response. An example of the former type item might be: "I have never intensely disliked anyone." An example of the latter might be: "I sometimes feel resentful when I don't get my way."

The items, combined to form a personality scale, showed a high degree of relationship with those measures with which the scale was expected to show high correlations. First, it correlated well with itself. That is to say, an impressive relationship was obtained between the two testings of a group of subjects who were tested one month apart. Thus, the test seemed to be measuring what it measured in a consistent manner. In addition, though the test did show some moderate correlations with measures of psychopathology, there were fewer of these and they were smaller in size than was the case for an earlier developed scale of social desirability. These were promising beginnings for the Marlowe-Crowne scale, but it remained to be shown that the concept of need for approval (and the scale developed to measure it) had a utility beyond predicting responses to other paper-and-pencil measures. Hence, as part of their program of further validating their new scale and the construct that underlaid the scale, Crowne, Marlowe, and their students undertook an ingenious series of studies relating scores on their scale to subjects' behavior in a number of non-paper-and-pencil test situations.

In the first of these studies, subjects began by completing various tests, including the Marlowe-Crowne scale, and then were asked to get down to the serious business of the experiment itself. That "serious business" required subjects to (a) pack a dozen spools of thread into a small box, (b) unpack the box, (c) repack the box, (d) re-unpack the box, and so on, for 25 minutes while the experimenter appeared to be timing the performances and making notes about them. After these dull 25 minutes had elapsed, subjects were asked to rate how interesting the task had been, how instructive, how important to science, and how much the subject wanted to participate in similar experiments in the future. The results of this study showed quite clearly that those subjects who scored above the mean on need for approval said that they found the task more interesting, more instructive, more important to science, and that they were more eager to participate again in similar studies than those subjects who had scored below the mean. Apparently, then, just as we would predict, subjects higher in the need for social approval said nicer things to their high-status experimenter about the task and the experiment that he had set for them.

Next, the investigators conducted a series of studies employing the method of verbal conditioning. In one variant of this method, the subject is asked to say all the words he or she can think of to the listening experimenter. In the positive reinforcement condition, every time the subject utters a plural noun the experimenter approves by saying "Mm-hmm" and nodding his head affirmatively. In the negative reinforcement condition, every time the subject utters a plural noun, the experimenter disapproves by saying "Uh-uh." In these methods the magnitude of verbal conditioning is often defined by the increase in production of plural nouns from the pre-reinforcement level to some subsequent time block after the subject has received the reinforcements (e.g., head nods). Magnitude of verbal conditioning is often thought to be a good index of a simple type of susceptibility to social influence. Subjects who are more susceptible to the experimenter's reinforcements are thought to be also more susceptible to other forms of elementary social influence.

In the first of their verbal conditioning studies, the investigators found that subjects higher in the need for social approval responded with far more plural nouns when positively reinforced for them than did subjects lower in the need for approval. Similarly, subjects higher in need for approval responded with fewer plural nouns when punished for them than did subjects lower in the need for social approval. In this particular experiment, pains were taken to screen out those subjects who saw the connection between their utterances and the experimenter's reinforcement. In this way the relationship obtained was between subjects' need for approval as measured by the Marlowe-Crowne scale and subjects' responsivity to the approval of their experimenter but only when they were not explicitly aware of the role of the experimenter's reinforcement.

In the second of their verbal conditioning studies, the investigators wanted to use a task for subjects that would be more lifelike and more engaging than producing random words. For this purpose, subjects were asked to describe their own personality, and every positive self-reference was reinforced by the experimenter's saying "Mm-hmm" in a flat monotone. A positive self-reference was defined as any statement reflecting favorably upon the subject, and, despite this seemingly vague definition, two judges working independently showed a very high degree of consistency in identifying positive self-references. Results of the study showed that subjects above the mean in need for social approval made significantly more positive self-references than did subjects scoring lower in the need for approval. It now appeared that, regardless of whether the subjects' responses were as trivial as the production of random words or as meaningful as talking about themselves, these responses could be increased much more by subtle social reinforcement if the subjects were higher in their measured need for social approval.

In their third verbal conditioning study the investigators employed a vicarious (or substitute) reinforcement method. In this procedure subjects are not reinforced for a given type of response, but they are in a position to observe someone else receive reinforcement. The actual subjects of the study observed a pseudosubject, a confederate of the experimenter, make up a series of sentences using one of six pronouns and a verb given him by the experimenter. Whenever the pseudosubject began his sentence with the pronouns "I" or "We" the experimenter said the word "good." Before and after the observation period, subjects themselves made up sentences using one of the same six pronouns. Results of the study showed that subjects higher in need for approval showed a significantly greater increase in their use of "I" and "We" from their preobservational to their postobservational sentence construction sessions than did subjects lower in the need for social approval. Thus, once again it was shown that subjects can be successfully predicted to be more responsive to the approving behavior of an experimenter when they have scored higher on a test of the need for approval.

Still another set of studies was undertaken to extend the validity of the Marlowe-Crowne scale and of the construct of need for approval. This time the procedure employed was a derivative of a conformity method developed by social psychologist Solomon Asch (1952). In this situation a group of subjects must make judgments on some issue or other. Judgments are announced by each subject, and the purpose of the technique is to permit an assessment of the effects of earlier subjects' judgments on the judgments of subsequent judges. In order to control the earlier-made judgments, accomplices are employed to play the role of subjects, and they usually are all instructed to make the same judgment, one that is quite clearly in error. Conformity is defined as the real subject's going along with the majority in his or her own judgment rather than giving the objectively correct response.

In Marlowe and Crowne's variation of this method, the subjects listened to a tape recording of knocks on a table and then reported their judgment of the number of knocks they had heard. Each subject was led to believe that she was the fourth subject and was hearing the responses of three prior subjects to each series of knocks that were to be judged. The earlier three subjects were, of course, accomplices, and they all agreed with one another by consistently giving an incorrect response on twelve of the eighteen trials. For each real subject, then, it was possible to count the number of times out of twelve that she yielded to the wrong but unanimous majority. Results showed that subjects scoring higher in the need for social approval did indeed conform more to the majority judgment than did subjects scoring lower in the need for approval.

In the Asch-type situation employed, the wrong but unanimous majority had not been physically present in the room with the subjects, and the investigators wanted to know whether they would obtain the same results using "live" accomplices. This time the task was a discrimination problem in which subjects had to judge which of two clusters of dots was larger. Once again, accomplices were employed to give responses that were clearly wrong but that were unanimous. As before, the results showed that subjects scoring above the mean on the need-for-approval measure yielded more often to the unanimous but erring majority than did the subjects scoring below the mean.

We have now seen a substantial number of studies that support the validity of the Marlowe-Crowne scale and document the utility of their construct of the need for social approval. There are studies, to be sure, that do not support the investigators' major findings, but there are also additional findings that do. Our purpose here is not to be exhaustive, but to document an unusually elegant series of studies that serves well to illustrate the nature of relational research.

THE ANALYTIC SURVEY

In Chapter 4 we discussed Peterson's use of an enumerative survey to study the scope of organized student protest in the 1960s. It is possible to distinguish between two types of surveys; Peterson's is illustrative of the primarily descriptive type. The purpose of that kind of survey is to count, and therefore it is essentially fact-finding and actuarial (which means that it is primarily used to describe or uncover certain facts). The second type is the *analytic* survey, which is primarily designed to explore the relationships among variables (Oppenheim, 1966). This type is usually less oriented toward representativeness and more toward finding associations and explanations that can tell us "what goes with what." The analytic survey is also an example of naturalistic observation, since questionnaires and interviews are used to study what is happening in its natural state.

The construction of these questionnaires and interview schedules usually involves many weeks of planning prior to the actual carrying out of the survey. During those weeks, pilot work will be done to test all significant aspects of the project, especially those connected with problems of questionnaire design. This piloting may involve doing lengthy, unstructured interviews with subjects, in order to get a "feel" for the research problem. Once the pilot work is completed, the questionnaire or the interview schedule is pretested on a sample chosen for its similarity to the final sample. Only when the researchers are satisfied that they have developed a sound measuring instrument, and that they have smoothed out any anticipated rough spots in the data-collection procedures, is the survey ready to be undertaken.

The analytic survey has been called the "poor man's experiment" (Oppenheim, 1966), since both the analytic survey and the true experiment use "controls" to help in the analysis of relationships. However, the experiment contains at least one manipulated independent variable, which is not true of the survey. Suppose we decided to do an analytic survey of children's bedtime behavior (snacking behavior, time to doze off, etc.); we might try to control some variables by excluding them, by holding them constant, or by random sampling. We know that children usually go to bed later in the summer and on school holidays, and we might control these variables by collecting the data during one short period in the school term. We also know that children with older brothers or sisters usually go to bed later, and we might control this variable by random sampling. We would make sure that children with older brothers or sisters were randomly distributed throughout the sample. (In later chapters, we discuss the procedure of random sampling, the logic of control-group designs in experimental research, and other ways of controlling for extraneous variables and artifacts.)

PARTICIPANT OBSERVATION

A quite different use of relational research, also involving naturalistic observation, is called *participant observation* (Becker & Geer, 1960). In this case a group or a community is studied from within by a researcher who makes careful observations of the behavior as it proceeds. Participant observation is usually more appropriate than the analytic survey for studying people in their normal surroundings when the research involves an examination of complex social relationships or intricate patterns of interaction that cannot be precisely quantified or anticipated (Warwick & Lininger, 1975).

There are many examples of the use of participant observation in sociology and cultural anthropology, including the work of Bronislaw Malinowski, Raymond Firth, Margaret Mead, Ruth Benedict, and other leading social scientists.

These researchers spent many months, sometimes years, methodically recording their impressions and reflections based on field work in a particular culture. In all societies, human beings relate to one another by role and by affect (or emotion), and the research diaries of Malinowski, Firth, Mead, Benedict, and other investigators help us to flesh out the bare bones of human personality.

A classic example is the research done by Ruth Benedict (1934), who took two personality constructs discussed by Friedrich Wilhelm Nietzsche, the nineteenth-century philosopher, to differentiate between two types of cultures that she had studied through participant observation. Nietzsche had argued that human personality has an essential core consisting of both rationality and irrationality, which he represented by the constructs "Apollonian" (for Apollo, the ancient Greek god of light, healing, and poetry) and "Dionysian" (for Dionysus, the god of fertility and wine), respectively. We are dominated by these opposing forces, Nietzsche argued, although he also believed that the Victorian era in which he lived was too much under the domination of an Apollonian temperament, and that the Victorians needed to be liberated from this controlled, extreme rationality. While Nietzsche himself did not attempt to divide human beings on this basis, his constructs were later used by Benedict in this way. As a result of her observations of American Indians living in Arizona and New Mexico, she developed the theory that the Pueblos were Apollonian types in their cultural characteristics and that the surrounding tribes were Dionysian in their general way of life. (We return to the method of participant observation in Chapter 10, where we discuss specific data-collection procedures.)

Labels such as these do a certain amount of disservice to the uniqueness of each culture. However, they do make it possible to reduce a complex array of cultural characteristics to stereotypes which can serve as independent variables in hypotheses to be empirically tested (Klineberg, 1940). For many types of behavior the cultural context in which role expectations are played out is an important variable, although it is also true that no society is *completely* different from any other. To some extent, all have borrowed over the years from each other's customs and traditions, and are therefore complex admixtures of unique and general characteristics (Linton, 1936). Participant observation, in which behavior is studied naturalistically within its usual surroundings, helps us to identify the cultural context of social facts. The scientist who enters a community to record the natural behavior of the group has access to a body of information firsthand, and he or she can sense the frustrations and exhilarations of the community in a way that perhaps cannot be felt from an analytic questionnaire (Goode & Hatt, 1952).

SYNCHRONIC AND DIACHRONIC RESEARCH

In our discussions of descriptive research (Chapters 2 and 4), we saw that much investigation at this level is concerned with taking a single cross-sectional slice of time, so that the observations or measures have reference to a particular variable only as it exists in the here and now. This kind of temporal approach is also known as *synchronic research*, since the variable is observed as it exists at one brief period in time, not using information about its development. The OSS assessment study (Chapter 4) would be illustrative of a paradigm case of synchronic (as well as descriptive) research.

In contrast to the synchronic research approach, there is the diachronic research approach. In *diachronic research*, a phenomenon or a variable is observed in such a way as to uncover changes that occur during successive periods of time. Diachronic research is inherently relational, since it examines descriptions at varying points in time. The descriptions are the dependent variables, and time is the independent variable. That kind of temporal orientation makes it possible to study stability and social changes in behavior (cf. Barber & Inkeles, 1971; Rosnow, 1981). Unlike synchronic research (which forecloses on the temporal dimension), diachronic research lets us look for long-term trends and growth patterns on the basis of which it may then be possible to plan further relational research. Diachronic research also allows us the freedom to search for persistent or continual or regularly recurrent patterns of behavior (since change cannot be understood except in reference to stability), which in turn may give us a hint about future trends and growth patterns.

A study done by Stanley Coren and Clare Porac (1977) illustrates what we mean by diachronic research. In this study, Coren and Porac did an analysis of more than 5000 years of art works in order to gather evidence as to whether right-handedness is a recent trait or an age-old human characteristic. Previously it had been hypothesized that the development of right-handedness in humans was a physiological predisposition that was possibly heritable in nature. A rival hypothesis asserted that social or environmental pressures (or both) led to the high incidence of right-handedness in humans, which was seen as an adaptive response that resulted from the suppression of left-handedness. Coren and Porac submitted these alternative hypotheses to an empirical test by simply counting instances of unimanual tool or weapon usage in works of art from various cultures and times over fifty centuries.

They examined more than 12,000 photographs and reproductions of drawings, paintings, and sculpture, dated at approximately 15,000 B.C. to A.D. 1950, drawn from European, Asian, African, and American sources. Each plate or reproduction was carefully coded for figures displaying a clear hand preference, and from these a final sample of 1180 scorable instances was obtained. Of those, an average of 92.6 percent depicted the use of the right hand, and the geographical and historical distribution of right-handedness tended to be uniformly very high. Since there were no clear differences emerging among the various cultural subgroupings or in different historical epochs, these results would seem to support a physiological interpretation of handedness rather than one that proposes cultural and social determinants of handedness. It is not possible to ensure that the 12,000 photographs and reproductions are truly representative of the actual (as opposed to idealized) state, or the diffuse population of art works as a whole. Nevertheless, it does seem safe to conclude that, as far as *this historical record* takes us, human beings have always been depicted as predominantly right-handed.

HISTORICAL COMPARISONS

A particularly interesting form of diachronic research is that which uses secondary records to pinpoint types of behavior or events in time. The purpose of this form is usually to show how the *Zeitgeist* acts as a mediatory link to the social, political, and economic conditions of society within a larger conceptual frame than is considered in more "microlevel" (or smaller-scale) research.

For example, William J. McGuire (1976) painstakingly gathered basic demographic information on over 37,000 famous people of all times and places. He then used this historical data archive to search for cycles and trends as a function of historical periods. In one analysis, which was done of the past 2500 years, he looked at eight broad areas of endeavor (government, religion, arts and literature, humanities, and so on) in which the famous people of each era attained fame. He found striking variations that showed how achievements in these various fields of human culture waxed and waned alternately, in unison, or in sequence.

Working along similar lines, Dean Keith Simonton (1975a, 1975b, 1976a) has also done several diachronic studies in which he has investigated possible causal links among interdisciplinary relationships, sociocultural contexts, and ideological diversity in individual creativity over many generations of European history. By cross-tabulating secondary records, he has shown how it is possible to study the effects of improbable circumstances, such as war or political fragmentation, which cannot be investigated in the laboratory or using other data sources.

When studying social and historical processes in the ways pioneered by McGuire, Simonton, and other social psychologists, quantitative historians, and sociologists, it is often helpful to use a heuristic model of social change which serves as a blueprint to point out interesting possibilities. There are a number of such models among which to choose. One possibility is that of a linear (resembling a straight line) pattern of social and historical processes, analogous to the idea of unilinear evolution. Behavioral scientists have developed such models with reference to many kinds of nonhuman and human developmental processes, from the evolution of courtship behavior in spiders (Platnick, 1971) and of altruism in other lower-order animals (Wilson, 1975) all the way up the phylogenetic scale to the development of agriculture as a function of population pressures.

Michael J. Harner (1970) was inspired by this model to propose a scarcity theory to predict how rising population pressure in societies has affected the degree of dependence on agriculture for subsistence. He also theorized that, in much the same way, the resulting competition for scarce subsistence resources when population density increased is what led to ever larger and more complex social units (to ensure success in holding on to these scarce resources). The source of Harner's data to test these hypotheses was the *Ethnographic Atlas* (Murdock et al., 1962–67), a compendium of cross-cultural information on subsistence as well as codified data on kinship, social stratification, and political complexity in over a thousand cultures. Examining the pertinent correlations, Harner's findings were, in fact, consistent with his hypotheses. Thus his theoretical model was successful in predicting a variety of social evolutionary trends as a function of population pressure.

Another heuristic model for historical comparisons is the cyclical conception of social and historical processes (Rosnow, 1978; Sorokin, 1927). *Cycle* implies regular repetition over a fixed time or period, and a popular statistical approach to the study of these processes is known as *time-series analysis* (see Gottman, 1981, for an introduction to this approach). According to the cyclic model as applied to historical comparisons, there are some relationships that tend to recur in periodic cycles and rhythms. Pitirim A. Sorokin (1927) mentions, for example, the fluctuation of the periods of business increase and depression, the fluctuations in the composition of governments and in political opinions, the growth and decline of cultures and states, and the beginning and fall of dynasties. At the level of the individual, he notes that in each twenty-four hours, the maximum death and suicide cases happen about 6 A.M. to 7 A.M. and 7 P.M. to 8 P.M., while the minimum occur about 12 midnight to 2 A.M. Edward R. Dewey (1970), who made a career of cycle study, reported a remarkable number and variety of periodic rhythms in physical, biological, economic, and sociological phenomena.

There are other possible patterns to consider besides the unilinear pattern based on an idealization of the evolutionary tree of life and the cyclic pattern based on the conception of recurrence in cycles. The "dialectical pattern" is another that has begun to attract considerable attention in sociology and in developmental and social psychology (Laslett, 1980). This model envisions historical change as the progressive balancing of opposing forces. There are also more complex patterns (Rosnow, 1981). Each of these can provide a theoretical point of embarkation for the development of specific relational-type hypotheses.

FUNCTIONS OF RELATIONAL RESEARCH

Thus far in our discussion we have seen that behavioral science is not merely adding facts. All science requires that we view facts not as isolated or separate, but as related or connected in some systematic and logical way (Cohen, 1959). To make sense of the chaos of bewilderingly unconnected social facts, we therefore do relational research which tells us "how things are in relation to other things."

There are three major functions that such research can serve. One of these, of course, is to uncover the relations among different variables. From our discussion in Chapter 3 of John Stuart Mill's three essentials for judging causes and effects, we know that a fundamental requirement is to show that X and Y are actually related to one another. Relational research lets us see which variables are correlated (and how much), and which are not.

A second function, and a distinct advantage of relational research, is that it allows us to make comparisons where time is the independent variable. In this way, we search for long-term patterns which may then suggest future trends and growth patterns. This diachronic approach gives us a unique vantage point from which to develop models to suggest how social, political, and economic conditions can influence behavior over a long period of time.

A third function is that, as in Crowne and Marlowe's research, we can begin to establish the validity of our intervening variables (or constructs). In behavioral science, especially, there are countless examples of these abstract terms that are validated only by relating subjects' performance in a variety of situations as the construct would predict.

EXPERIMENTAL RESEARCH

A PARADIGM CASE

To experiment literally means "to test" or "to try," although in many areas of behavioral science the term is simply defined as "controlled manipulation of independent variables." We shall use *experimental research* to denote that case in which the primary interest of the investigator involves introducing some new feature into the environment for some of the research participants and then comparing their reactions with those of subjects who have not been exposed to the new feature. (To be sure, the subject can also serve as his or her own control, if we compare the subject's usual reactions with those when the new feature was then introduced.) In both the OSS assessment program (Chapter 4) and the Crowne and Marlowe research program on need for social approval (Chapter 5), there were many instances in which investigators introduced some new feature, some experimental manipulation, into the situation. We did not regard those manipulations as exemplifying experimental research because the *primary interest* was not in the comparison between the behavior of participants exposed to the new feature and the behavior of subjects not exposed to the new feature.

There are a dozen or so types of experiments (Kaplan, 1964): methodological, pilot, heuristic, boundary, to name a few. In this chapter we discuss the kinds of approaches or general circumstances in which many of these types have been used in the study of behavior. Once again we begin with a paradigm case from the field of personality, the important program of research of Harry and Margaret Harlow and their collaborators dealing with affection in primates.

There are few personality theories that do not consider early-life experiences to be of special importance in the development of personality. Among the early-life experiences often given special attention are those involving mother-child relationships. A generally posed proposition might be this one: Loving mother-child relationships are more likely to lead to healthy adult personality than hostile, rejecting mother-child relationships. To investigate this proposition experimentally, we would be required to assign half our sample of young children to loving mothers and half to rejecting mothers and follow up the development of each child's adult personality. Such an experimental plan is an ethical absurdity in our culture's value matrix although there are no special problems of experimental logic involved. Does this mean that we can never do experimental work on important questions of human development and human personality? One approach to the problem has capitalized on the biological continuities between nonhuman organisms and human beings. Primates especially have been shown to share attributes with humans sufficiently to make them valuable, if far from exact or even very accurate, models of humankind. We cannot, for the sake of furthering our knowledge of personality development, separate a human baby from its mother, but the important lessons we might learn from such separation make it seem justifiable to separate a nonhuman primate from its mother.

In their extensive research program at the University of Wisconsin, the Harlows and their collaborators have employed a great array of the research methods and approaches of both the psychologist and the biologist. Much of their research on the affectional system of monkeys has been of the descriptive type (e.g., young monkeys become attached to other young monkeys) and of the relational type (e.g., male monkeys become more forceful with age; female monkeys become more passive). Our interest here, however, will focus on their experimental research, although we shall be able to describe only a fraction of it.

As part of that research program, infant monkeys were separated from their mothers just a few hours after birth and were raised by bottle with great success. The Harlows had been advised by Dr. Gertrude van Wagenen to have available for their infant monkeys some soft, pliant surfaces, and folded gauze diapers were consequently made available to all the baby monkeys. The babies became very much attached to these diapers, so much so that they could only be removed for laundering with great difficulty. These observations led to an experiment designed so that it would show more systematically the shorter- and longer-term effects of access to a soft material. The research was planned also to shed light on the question of the relative importance to the development of the infant's attachment to its mother of being fed by her as opposed to being in close and cuddly contact with her (Harlow, 1959, 1966).

Two pseudomothers were built: one a bare, welded-wire cylindrical form with a crude wooden head and face attached, the other a similar apparatus but covered with terry cloth. Eight newborn monkeys were given equal access to the wire-and-cloth mother figures, but four of the monkeys were fed at the breast of the wire mother, and four were fed at the breast of the cloth mother. Results showed that when the measures were of the amount of milk consumed or the amount of weight gained, the two mothers made no difference. The monkeys fed by the two mothers drank about the same amount of milk and gained about the same amount of weight. However, regardless of which mother had fed them, baby monkeys spent much more time climbing up on the cloth mother and clinging to her than they did on the wire mother. This finding was important for a number of reasons; not only for demonstrating the importance of contact comfort but also for showing that a simple earlier formulation of love for mother was really much too simple. That earlier formulation held that mothers became prized because they were associated with the reduction of hunger and thirst. The Harlow results show quite clearly that being the source of food is not nearly as good a predictor of a baby's subsequent preference as is being a soft and cuddly mother. When the monkeys were about 100 days old, they spent an average of about 15 hours a day on the cloth mother but only about 1.5 hours on the wire mother, regardless of whether it had been the cloth or the wire mother that had fed the baby monkey.

Later experiments showed that when the infant monkey was placed into a fear-arousing situation, it was the cloth monkey that was sought out for comfort and reassurance. A frightened monkey, confronted by a mechanical bear that advanced while beating a drum, would flee to the cloth mother, secure a dose of reassurance, then gradually explore the frightening objects and begin to turn them into toys. When the cloth mother was not in the room, the infant monkeys hurled themselves onto the floor, clutched their heads and bodies, and screamed in distress. The bare-wire mother provided the infant with no greater security or reassurance than did no mother at all.

A collaborator in the Harlow group, Robert A. Butler, had discovered that monkeys enclosed in a dimly lit box would spend hour after hour pressing a lever that would open a window in the box and give them a chance to see something outside. Monkeys barely able to walk will press the lever for a brief peek at the world outside. One of the variables that determines how hard the monkey will work to look out the window is what there is to be seen. When the monkey infants we have been discussing were tested in the "Butler box" it turned out that monkeys worked as hard to see their cloth mothers as to see another real monkey. On the other hand, they worked no harder to see the wire mother than to see nothing at all outside the box. Not only in this experiment, but to a surprising degree in general, a wire mother is not much better than no mother at all, but a cloth mother comes close to being as good as the real thing. (The Harlows have, however, found other views prevalent among monkey fathers.)

A number of female monkeys became mothers themselves although they had not had any monkey mothers of their own and no physical contact with age-mates during the first year of their life (Harlow & Harlow, 1965). Compared to normal monkey mothers, these unmothered mothers were usually brutal to their firstborn offspring, hitting them, kicking them, and crushing them. Those motherless mothers who were not brutal were indifferent. The most cheerful result of this experiment was that those motherless monkeys who went on to become mothers for a second time, treated their second babies in a normal or even an overprotective manner.

A very important series of studies required that infant monkeys be raised in social isolation (Harlow & Harlow, 1970). When the isolation is total the young monkey is exposed to no other living organism; all its physical needs are met in automated fashion. A major independent variable is length of isolation since birth: zero, three, six, or twelve months. All the monkeys raised in isolation were physically healthy, but when placed into a new environment they appeared to crouch in terror. Those monkeys that had been isolated only three months recovered from their neurotic fear within a month or so. Those monkeys that had been isolated for six months never did quite recover. Their play behavior, even after six months, was minimal and usually isolated. Their social activity, when it did occur, was directed only to monkeys that had also been raised in isolation. Those monkeys that had been isolated for twelve months showed the most severe retardation of play and of the development of aggression. Apathetic and terrified, these monkeys were defenseless against the attacks of the healthy control-group monkeys.

Longer-term effects of early social isolation have also been discovered. Several years later, the six-month-isolated monkeys showed a dramatic change in orientation to other monkeys. Whereas earlier they had been attacked by other monkeys and had not bothered to defend themselves, they had by now developed into pathological aggressors, attacking other monkeys large and small, acts virtually never occurring among normal monkeys of their age. Another long-term effect of early social isolation can be seen in the inadequacy of the sexual behavior of these monkeys. Even females who were only partially isolated in infancy avoid contact with breeding males, do not groom themselves, engage in threats, in aggression, in clutching themselves, biting themselves, and often failing to support the male should mounting occur. Normal females rarely engage in any of these behaviors. Male monkeys who have been isolated show even more serious sexual inadequacy than do the isolated females. When contrasted with normal males, they groom less, threaten more, are more aggressive, initiate little sexual contact, engage in unusual sexual behavior, and almost never achieve intromission.

In the extensive research program of the Harlow group, there were many other experiments. Some monkeys were raised without mothers but with access to age-mates, while other monkeys were raised by their mothers but without access to age-mates (Harlow & Harlow, 1966). The overall results, while complicated, suggested that both normal mothering and normal age-mate contact are important to normal social development but that to some extent each can substitute for some deficits in the other. Both types of experience are better than either alone, but either alone appears to be very much better than neither.

SIMULATION

The program of experimentation conducted by Harlow and his coworkers emphasizes the power of the experimental method to permit us to make inferences of a causal nature. The research also illustrates some of the many kinds of experiments that are possible in behavioral science (Kaplan, 1964). The entire program is illustrative of the use of *heuristic experiments*, which are designed to generate ideas, provide leads for further inquiry, and open up new lines of investigation. There were also *methodological experiments*, which serve to develop or to improve some particular technique of inquiry, as in the development of the "Butler box" for studying whether monkeys will work as hard to see their cloth "mothers" as they will to see another live monkey. There were *exploratory experiments*, which invited serendipity, as in the early stages of Harry Harlow's research, when he first began experimenting with the cloth surrogate mothers. There were *fact-finding experiments* aimed at determining some magnitude or property of the dependent variable, and *boundary experiments* which were designed to fix the range of application (or boundaries) of relationships.

We now turn to another kind of experiment, a *simulation experiment,* also illustrated by Harlow's program of research. These are experiments on a model, to learn what will happen under conditions that are designed to mimic the natural environment in a definite way (Kaplan, 1964). We simulate when more realistic experiments are morally impossible (e.g., Harlow's use of primates instead of humans to study the development of personality) or when simulation can serve a training function (e.g., driver simulation or astronaut simulation). We also use simulation in order to "telescope" time and thus predict future events from present ones (e.g., internation simulations to predict future world outcomes from present "nation" characteristics). Finally, we simulate when the real situation is too complex or when more realistic experiments would be too costly. The fundamental task of simulation is that of scaling down the natural environment to a laboratory size that still contains the *key* elements which are thought to account for the dynamics of the real-world phenomenon under investigation.

An example of a simulation experiment is the recent work of Joseph V. Brady and his associates at the Johns Hopkins University School of Medicine, where a programmed environment has been constructed for the experimental analysis of individual and social behavior over extended time periods (Brady, Bigelow, Emurian, & Williams, 1974; Brady & Emurian, 1979). This environmental design consists of a complex of rooms for individual living quarters, a larger social-living unit, and a workshop, in which volunteers reside over a continuous period while they are monitored by electromechanical control devices interfaced with a computer. Various activities are programmed, such as 10 minutes of light calisthenics, access to reading and art materials, social recreation, etc., and the emotional interactions and reactions within this programmed environment are coded and quantified for statistical analysis of trends and cycles. In this way, Brady and his collaborators have been able to explore the continuous effects of living in a self-contained programmed environment. They hope to extrapolate from this simulation to the daily environment of astronauts, submarine crews, and others who are confined to a self-contained environment.

Two important criteria for assessing the effectiveness of a laboratory simulation such as this one (or indeed *any* laboratory experiment) are its *experimental realism,* which refers to its psychological impact on the participants, and its *mundane realism,* or the extent to which the laboratory events are likely to occur in a naturalistic setting (Aronson & Carlsmith, 1968). Brady's methodological experiments suggest that these criteria have been adequately met by his design of a programmed environment. Sometimes, however, the natural environment is scaled down so much that neither criterion is satisfied. Early experiments into the psychology of rumor, which attempted to simulate rumormongering using an artificial environment, reveal some of the difficulties encountered in trying to satisfy these two criteria when the experimental simulation is scaled down too much.

As a means of isolating the kinds of message distortions that can occur in rumormongering, an experimental simulation was used that consisted of projecting a slide depicting a semidramatic scene of a large number of related details (Allport & Postman, 1947). Six or seven participants who were unfamiliar with the picture waited in an adjoining room. The first participant entered and took a position from which he or she could not see the picture. The experimenter or another participant described the picture, giving about twenty details in the account. A second participant then entered the room and stood beside the first, who told the second participant everything that could be recalled about the picture. This "hearsay account" was next communicated to a third participant, and so on. Once the subjects had completed this "rumor chain," their reports were analyzed and contrasted with the picture on the slide. As a consequence of observations made in a number of such experiments, it was concluded that the subtle interpenetration of cognitive and emotional processes in rumormongering which leads to the obliteration of some details (called "leveling") and the pointing up of other details ("sharpening") is due to the cognitive effort to assimilate information by twisting new materials to build a better overall structure. It was also concluded that particular details were most susceptible to leveling and others to sharpening.

One problem with this kind of simulation is that there is very little emotional or psychological involvement required of the participants. In "real life" there is usually some ego-involvement and concern when passing on or listening to a nice juicy rumor. (Perhaps the only ego-involvement in this case would be that elicited in the participants as a consequence of their interaction with the experimenter and their desire to project a favorable image.) There is a question, then, as to the simulation's experimental realism.

Another problem is that in normal conversation a person hears a rumor and, if the message is not understood, usually asks for clarification. In real life we tend to use our critical faculties to work out the meaning of a rumor, but in these early simulation experiments the subjects were always passive receivers. Thus there is also a question as to the simulation's mundane realism.

In fact, later field and laboratory research findings revealed that, as the early experiments showed, it is true that intellectual pressures and the natural porosity of human memory can cause a message to become simplified and ordered in the retelling, due to the processes of leveling and sharpening. But the later studies also found that rumors can become more diffuse and complex. There seem to be situational and individual differences in leveling and sharpening that were not evident in the early findings. It appears that rumor distortions can take a variety of specific forms besides those resulting only from leveling and sharpening (Rosnow, 1980).

ROLE-PLAY EXPERIMENTS

In our earlier discussions we alluded to research studies in which some form of deception was used to prevent the subjects from guessing the researcher's hypotheses or true intent. A leading example was alluded to in Table 2.1 (see page 25), the behavioral studies of obedience done by Stanley Milgram (1963, 1965). Milgram subjected volunteers to an elaborate deception to make them believe that they were giving painful electric shocks to a hapless (confederate) victim. Each volunteer was seated in front of a "shock generator," on which there were switches indicating increases in voltage from 15 to 450 volts, and was told to administer shocks to a "learner" every time the learner made a mistake in a simple memory test. The first mistake was punished by a 15-volt shock, the second by a 30-volt shock, and so on up the scale.

In a later chapter, we return to this study for a detailed discussion of ethical considerations and debriefing procedures in human research. However, many researchers object to the use of deception, and there have been efforts to develop realistic alternatives to laboratory deceptions in particular. One such alternative is called *role play*, since it consists of having subjects act out a given scenario—which means that they enact the role of a research subject in a simulated drama devised by the experimenter. To be sure, there have also been questions raised about the mundane realism of role play as well as questions about whether it is "exactly comparable" to more direct experimental manipulations (Miller, 1972).

A methodological experiment addressed to the latter question was done by Martin S. Greenberg (1967), who attempted to replicate earlier experimental findings on anxiety and affiliation. In a well-known series of experiments by Stanley Schachter (1959), subjects had been allowed to wait with others or to wait alone before participating in a research project. For some subjects (the "high-anxiety group") the anticipated project was described as involving painful electric shocks, while for others (the "low-anxiety group") it was represented as involving no physical discomfort. Significantly more of the high-anxiety subjects chose to wait with others in a similar plight. (This finding inspired the remark that "misery prefers miserable company.") Another of Schachter's findings was that anxious firstborns and only children showed this desire to affiliate with others more than did laterborns. In Greenberg's role-play experiment, the participants were told to *act as if the situation were real*. They were then subjected to a scenario that was closely modeled after Schachter's original experiments. Although some of the primary results of Greenberg's role-play experiment were not statistically significant, the direction of his major findings was consistent with Schachter's earlier experimental findings.

The qualified success of this methodological experiment would seem to support the idea that role-play experiments can play a useful part when the scenario is realistic. Other methodological experiments on role play have been done in recent years (e.g., Darroch & Steiner, 1970; Horowitz & Rothschild, 1970; Wicker & Bushweiler, 1970; Willis & Willis, 1970), although opinions remain divided on the usefulness of role play as a substitute for more traditional experimental methods (cf. Hendrick, 1977; Miller, 1972). Nonetheless, there is evidence that role play may be a reasonable alternative to laboratory deception when appropriate steps are taken to make this approach realistic by increasing the participants' emotional involvement. This is sometimes known as *emotional role play*.

To illustrate: an imaginative application of emotional role play was done in research by Irving Janis and Leon Mann (1965; Mann, 1967; Mann & Janis, 1968) which was designed to study how self-improvised emotional arguments can produce a "saying is believing" effect. The volunteer subjects in this role-play experiment were young women, all between the ages of 18 and 23, none of whom knew that the objective of the research involved modifying their smoking habits and attitudes toward smoking. Each subject averaged about a pack of cigarettes a day. Randomly assigned to either an experimental or a control group, the participants were told at the beginning of the study that the research was intended to examine two important problems about the human side of medical practice: how patients react to bad news, and how they feel when a physician tells them to quit an enjoyable habit such as smoking.

In the experimental group, each participant was instructed to imagine that the experimenter was a physician who had been treating her for a persistent cough and that on this third visit he was going to give her the results of x-rays and other diagnostic tests previously carried out. The experimenter then outlined five different scenes, and he instructed the participant to "act out" each scene as realistically as possible. The first scene took place in the doctor's office while the patient awaited the diagnosis. She was asked to imagine and express aloud her thoughts, her concern, her feelings about whether to give up cigarettes. The second scene was the imagined confrontation with the physician. She was told that according to the results of his diagnostic tests, there was a small malignant mass in her right lung. She was also told that there was only a moderate chance for surgical success for treating this condition. She was then encouraged to ask questions. In the next scene she was instructed to express her feelings about her misfortune. The physician could be overheard in the background phoning for a hospital bed. In the fourth scene, the physician described details of imminent hospitalization. He told the subject that chest surgery typically requires a long convalescent period, at least six weeks. He then raised questions about the woman's smoking history and asked whether she was aware of the relationship between smoking and cancer. He stressed the urgent need for her to stop smoking immediately and encouraged her to talk freely about the problems she thought she might encounter in trying to break the smoking habit. Subjects assigned to the control group were exposed to similar information about lung cancer from a tape recording of one of the experimental sessions, but they were not given an opportunity to engage in emotional role play.

As Janis and Mann had hypothesized, the immediate impact of the emotional role-play condition in producing attitude change was consistently greater than it was in the control condition. There was greater fear of personal harm from smoking, a stronger belief that smoking causes lung cancer, and a greater willingness and intent to quit smoking in the experimental group. To determine the relatively long-term effects of this role-play manipulation, the researchers conducted follow-up interviews at different points over an 18-month interval. The purpose of these postexperimental inquiries was disguised, however, by representing them as local public-opinion surveys. None of the participants showed any signs that she suspected the real purpose of the interviews. The main findings were exactly as before. On the average, women who had participated in the emotional role-play sessions reported that they had reduced their daily cigarette consumption by more than twice the amount of those who participated in the control condition, and this advantage of "saying is believing" persisted *even after a year and a half!*

NATURALISTIC EXPERIMENTATION

So far we have looked at examples of experiments that used various kinds of simulation methods, including the heuristic experiments of Harlow, the environmental simulations of Brady, and the role-play experiments of Janis and Mann. Many experimenters believe that the ideal context for behavioral science is the natural environment, and in recent years there has been a movement toward the greater use of field experiments in behavioral science. These researchers believe that field experiments can also be an effective way of circumventing the problems that may accompany the use of reactive measurements in the laboratory.

A famous example of this naturalistic approach was a study of the comparative effects of rational and emotional political propaganda. The study was carried out by George W. Hartmann in Allentown, Pennsylvania, during a statewide election campaign in 1935. Hartmann, whose own name had been entered on the ballot as a Socialist party candidate, wrote two political leaflets, one designed to appeal to the voters' reason and the other to their emotions. He then had the leaflets distributed in different wards matched on the basis of their size, population density, assessed property valuation, previous voting habits, and socioeconomic status. By comparing the election results in the wards that got the rational appeal versus those that got the emotional appeal, he deduced that the emotional propaganda must have had the stronger impact. That is to say, the voting returns showed that the emotional message was associated with greater increases in voting for the Socialist party relative to both the control regions and to the increases in voting for Democratic and Republican candidates.

A more recent example of field experimentation is a cross-national research study on helping behavior that was conducted by Roy E. Feldman (1968). For many kinds of behavior, the cultural context in which the behavior is enacted can be an important variable. Feldman repeated several standard experiments in Athens, Paris, and Boston, using both foreigners and natives of the region as confederates. In one study he had the confederates ask directions from passersby. In another they asked strangers to mail a letter for them, explaining that they were waiting for someone and couldn't leave the spot right then. In a third study, confederates overpaid merchants or taxi drivers and then observed whether the people were honest and returned the money. By cross-tabulating the results of the reactions of more than 3000 subjects, Feldman was able to show that when a difference in helping behavior occurred, Parisians and Bostonians treated compatriots better than they did foreigners, whereas Athenians were more helpful to foreigners than to compatriots.

What is termed *social experimentation* is also illustrative of the naturalistic approach (Riecken, 1975). It involves the application of experimental methods to the analysis of social problems and to the development, testing, and assessment of workable intervention procedures to reduce the problems. For example, it may be possible to use quasi-experimental research to evaluate the effects of low-cost public housing or of age-graded penal institutions. A design is called *quasi-experimental* if it resembles an experimental design but there are factors operating that would make a true experiment impossible (Campbell & Stanley, 1966). If one were doing an "experiment" to evaluate the effects of low-cost public housing, it might be difficult or impossible (for administrative and ethical reasons) to have *full* control over the assignment of subjects to experimental and control conditions. This makes a true experiment impossible. However, a kind of experimental design could be used to permit comparisons of the effectiveness of the particular intervention procedures used.

The technical capacity to carry out social experiments is not well developed in the United States, although in other countries it has been used quite effectively to develop social programs and social policy. A lingering problem with social experimentation is that there is no guarantee that similar conditions will prevail in the future as obtained in the past. This means that, unless it is possible to develop and apply forecasting techniques, there is a degree of risk in attempting to generalize from past experimental (or quasi-experimental) conditions to future social conditions (Horowitz, 1979).

FUNCTIONS OF EXPERIMENTAL RESEARCH

In Harlow's experiments on personality development, in Janis and Mann's role-play experiment, and in other studies discussed in this chapter, we have seen how experimental research has the capability to reveal (to some extent) "how things get to be the way they are." We have also seen that some experiments are done not in the context of verification and hypothesis testing, but in the context of discovery (cf. Henshel, 1980 a).

The typical one-shot experiment is another example of a synchronic method, but there are two functions of experimental research that are different from the functions of some other synchronic methods. One of these functions, of course, is to test for possible causal patterns in which changes in one variable lead relatively quickly to changes in another. Experimental research allows us actively to observe behavior by introducing conditions relevant to what we expect to observe. By making use of experimental and control groups (discussed in Chapter 8), we can also establish that variable X actually precedes variable Y in time.

The second function, which is related to the first, is to provide empirical reference points (called *pointer readings*) to help pin down or pinpoint a theoretical relationship at a moment in time. Imagine, by way of an analogy, that we have a mechanical system in space that contains a number of bodies moving with respect to each other. Each body exerts an influence on the others, and our task is to discover the exact nature of this system. We cannot, on the basis of a single experimental observation, reveal the distant past and look far into the future. However, we can begin to generate pointer readings to show the state of the system at several moments. When faced with complex patterns of behavior and of changing social events, the experimenter proceeds by observation, hypothesis, prediction, and test. The results of experimental tests help the behavioral scientist to pin down parts of the entire picture in terms of causal relationships, even though no single experiment has the capacity to reveal the complete picture. Thus it is desirable to examine more than one specimen of the independent variable under investigation and to investigate the effects on more than one dependent variable, if possible over time and in different environments, with different types of participants chosen for reasons related to the hypotheses.

PART
THREE

THE PRINCIPLES OF
MEASUREMENT AND CONTROL

Chapter **7.** **Validity, Reliability, and Precision**

Chapter **8.** **The Logic of Research Design**

Chapter **9.** **Subject-Experimenter Artifacts and Their Control**

VALIDITY, RELIABILITY, AND PRECISION

THE CONCEPT OF ERROR

The dictionary definition of "error" is that it is a deviation from the correctness or truth of something. Behavioral scientists, as indeed all researchers, aspire to a high degree of correctness and truth in their work. They try to ensure that their research findings are relatively free of error. In aspiring to this ideal, however, they proceed on an assumption which is actually something of a fiction, called "the fiction of the true measure" (Kaplan, 1964). According to this ideal, there is some pure or absolute state of affairs in human reality which is the sole proper objective of genuine knowledge. What we measure or infer in science is regarded, then, as an approximation to this pure or absolute state.

However, human reality is not that simple. There are many aspects which are not at all "pure" or "absolute," but are instead intellectual abstractions that gradually attain some form or shape as ideas and then change. These ideas are informally negotiated by members of a society almost in the way that the terms of a transaction are formally negotiated in a business deal. The difference is that what is negotiated in preliminaries to a business deal usually exists in some concrete form, but what is "negotiated" by members of a society exists only as an idea. The "true measure" or "true inference" is, then, an intellectual abstraction which also represents an idealized state that does not really exist.

There is, to be sure, another way in which to proceed, pointed out by Abraham Kaplan (1964). It helps us to avoid the problem of the fiction of the true measure. What we *can* say, as empiricists, is that as we reduce error, we find (or hope to find) that our observations increasingly converge on a particular value, which we call the "real value." It is this value that we regard as the magnitude of the dependent variable, provided that we do not take the idiom too literally. In other words, our observations are corrected and any errors are reduced by a process of successive approximation, in which the obtained values increasingly converge on some real value.

In this chapter we discuss three criteria by which to judge how well our observations are able to achieve this objective. We cannot, of course, guarantee that our findings are error-free, since all human endeavors involve some degree of error, and the scientific endeavor is no exception. One criterion, termed *validity,* essentially means the degree to which we observe what we purport to observe. The second criterion, *reliability*, is the degree to which our observations are consistent or stable. The third criterion, *precision*, refers to the sharpness or exactness of our observations. These three criteria are related (both statistically and logically), and we shall see how a potential threat to any one criterion can seriously jeopardize another in very specific ways.

We start by considering how the criterion of validity is approached in research design, since in the next two chapters we return to these ideas to discuss the logic of research design and some ways of controlling error. One category of error is *insufficient validity,* which occurs when a research result is unable to accomplish what it sets out to do.* To say that a research design (or a test measurement) is valid means that it is a relatively accurate approximation to the real value. The most recent theoretical work on this topic, by Thomas D. Cook and Donald T. Campbell (1979), distinguishes among four types of validity: statistical conclusion validity, internal validity, construct validity, and external validity. Each bears a relationship to a different question in the unfolding of the research process. We begin by defining these four types of validity with reference to those specific research questions.

STATISTICAL CONCLUSION VALIDITY

In Chapter 3 we discussed some essentials of causal inference that were condensed by John Stuart Mill from the rules of logic developed by David Hume in the eighteenth century. One requirement is to show that X is at least a potential contributory condition of Y. The expression for this relationship is to say that the two variables *covary*, which means that variations in one are related to variations in the other. *Statistical conclusion validity* involves the specific question as to whether the presumed independent variable, X, and the pre-

---

* Validity is also the major consideration in the choice of a particular instrument or test measurement, a point to which we return later in this chapter.

sumed dependent variable, Y, are indeed related. If they are *not* related—that is, if they do *not* covary—the one cannot have been a cause of the other.

To know whether X and Y covary involves addressing three further questions, however. First, is the study sufficiently sensitive to permit reasonable statements about covariation? Second, given that it is sensitive enough, what is the evidence that X and Y covary? Third, given this evidence, how strongly do X and Y covary? In order to answer each of these questions we must take into consideration the power of the statistical test, a procedure (alluded to in Chapter 2) that we discuss in detail in later chapters. We must also consider the reliability of the experimental manipulation of the independent variable. If, for example, different experimenters are responsible for manipulating the independent variable, then we must be sure that the manipulation does not differ very much from one person to another. If the same experimenter is responsible for manipulating the independent variable, then we must be sure that there are no differences from occasion to occasion. We could do pilot-testing to see whether there were any differences and then make changes in the procedures to make them more rigorously standardized.

INTERNAL VALIDITY

Once we have seen that two variables covary, we may then want to ask whether they are causally related. *Internal validity* refers to the degree of validity of statements made about whether X causes Y. In Chapter 1 we discussed an example concerning plausible rival hypotheses. A male and a female student decided to conduct, as a team, an experiment into the effects of stress on verbal learning. Because they had divided the work fairly (but confoundedly), it was impossible to rule out whether the result was caused by what they thought was the independent variable (experimental stress) or whether the result was caused by the effects of the experimenter's sex. The male experimenter had given one treatment, and the female experimenter had given the other. This experimental design had low internal validity because it was impossible to determine whether the relationship between X and Y was causal; that is, Y might have been due not to stress but to the sex of the experimenter. This problem could have been avoided by having each experimenter contact half the subjects of the experimental condition and half the subjects of the control condition. That would have avoided the confounding of stress with the experimenter's sex.

There are other plausible threats to internal validity which can sometimes be anticipated and avoided, or at least controlled for. One type is simply designated as "history." This is an event or incident that takes place between the premeasurement and the postmeasurement and, in turn, contaminates the results. A second threat to internal validity is called "maturation." Results can be contaminated by the participant's having grown older or wiser or stronger or more experienced between the pretest and the posttest. Internal validity can also be jeopardized by a third type of error called "instrumentation." This is said to have occurred when the result might be due to changes in the measuring instrument, for example, if the instrument has deteriorated over time. A fourth challenge to internal validity is called "selection." This means that different kinds of people have been selected to take part in one experimental group than have been selected for another. This is typically a problem in quasi-experimental research, where it is impossible to have full control over the assignment of subjects.

CONSTRUCT VALIDITY

Suppose, however, that we have relatively high statistical conclusion validity and internal validity. We can say with some confidence (a) that there is a relationship between two variables, and (b) that it is a plausibly causal relationship. The next question to ask is, given the plausibly causal relationship between X and Y, what are the cause and effect constructs (the intervening variables) involved in the relationship? This leads us to the third type of validity, which is concerned with the psychological qualities contributing to the relationship between X and Y—known as *construct validity* (Caws, 1965; Cronbach & Meehl, 1955). It will be recalled that in Chapter 5 we discussed Crowne and Marlowe's validation of the construct of social desirability or need for approval, and in other chapters we have alluded to constructs such as "cognitive dissonance" and "diffusion of responsibility." Each had to be validated by logical analysis and empirical research, in which a means for theoretically defining the construct was related to subjects' performance in different situations.

Some researchers have attempted to formalize this process on a statistical basis. They argue that assessing construct validity ideally depends on two processes (and two further types of validity): (a) the testing for a "convergence" across different measures or manipulations of the same behavior, and (b) the testing for a "divergence" between measures or manipulations of related but conceptually distinct behaviors.

To illustrate, suppose we were developing a new test of sensitivity to nonverbal cues. Suppose the test assessed people's ability to read other people's emotions from still photographs. We would want that test to correlate fairly highly with other tests of sensitivity to nonverbal cues, for example, tests that used films of real people as stimulus materials. If it did so, we would have achieved *convergent validity*. However, we would not want our new test to correlate very highly with ordinary intelligence as measured by some standard IQ test. If it did correlate highly, it could be argued that what we had developed was simply one more test of general intelligence. That result would argue for poor *discriminant validity*. We want our measures to correlate highly with the measures that our theory says they should correlate highly with (convergent validity), but we want them to correlate much less with the measures our theory says they should not correlate so highly with (discriminant validity).

We can now see how these ideas would be applied in an actual situation to assess the validity of a particular construct, the social attitude. Although researchers have debated, and indeed continue to debate, the nature of social attitudes, one view that is widely accepted is that an attitude is composed of three components: the cognitive, the affective, and the behavioral. The "cognitive component" refers to a person's beliefs, ideas, and the way he or she sees things. The "affective component" refers to the way a person evaluates things, how he or she feels about them. The "behavioral component" refers to whether the person is inclined to act upon his or her beliefs. The most compelling evidence for this multidimensional construct derives from a study in which the researcher constructed a number of different scales to measure "attitude toward the use of contraceptives" (Kothandapani, 1971). To tap the cognitive component he included positive and negative statements, such as: "Birth control *will help* me postpone childbirth as long as I want" and "I believe that birth control *causes* many birth defects." For the affective component he included statements such as: "I am *happy* to learn about the benefits of birth control" and "The very thought of birth control *disgusts* me." For the behavioral component he used statements such as: "I would volunteer to *speak* about the merits of birth control" and "I would *walk* a mile to get my birth control supplies." He then administered all the scales to a randomly selected sample of nearly 500 black, low-income, married women who were residents of a public housing project in North Carolina. He also asked each woman about her use of birth control devices. The results of this study yielded strong evidence of discriminant validity among the dimensions as well as convergent validity, thus indicating (a) that the scales were indeed measuring three different dimensions, and (b) that these three dimensions, or components, were part of the same general construct.

EXTERNAL VALIDITY

Among the major threats to construct validity are certain types of experimenter- and subject-artifacts, for example, the well-known experimenter-expectancy and good-subject effects, which we discuss in Chapter 9. Let us assume, however, that we have been successful in establishing the validity of our construct. Having gotten to this point in the deductive process, we might now ask: "How generalizable is the causal relationship between X and Y across persons, settings, and times?" *External validity* refers to the generalizability of a relationship beyond the circumstances under which it is observed by the scientist (Cook & Campbell, 1979).

A summary term which is used to refer to the fact that a relationship that is obtained between two variables in a laboratory situation is free of confounding (has internal validity) *and* is a relationship that would occur outside the laboratory under nonreactive conditions (external validity), is that of *inferential validity* (Rosnow & Aiken, 1973). That is, given a high degree of internal and external validity, we may legitimately draw inferences (make valid generalizations) from our observations in a precisely controlled laboratory situation.

To illustrate a possible threat to external validity, there is extensive research which suggests that subjects who volunteer to serve as research participants are more sensitive and accommodating to certain coercive task-orienting cues than are nonvolunteer or captive participants (Rosenthal & Rosnow, 1975). This has obvious and serious consequences for psychological research that uses primarily volunteers. One such study was done by Irwin A. Horowitz (1969), who was interested in the role dynamics of volunteers and nonvolunteers when they were exposed to persuasive communications designed to influence their opinions on a controversial issue. In his review of the literature, Horowitz was struck by the fact that volunteer subjects had been used in many experiments in communication, particularly in those on the effects of so-called fear appeals—messages that are intended to arouse emotional tensions. Horowitz observed that the usual finding in these studies was that the volunteer subjects were more apt to be persuaded by the fear appeal the more threatening it was. He wondered, however, if the results might be lacking in external validity. In real life we are exposed to all sorts of fear appeals whether we choose to be subjected to them or not, so perhaps we learn to ignore some in real life.

Horowitz randomly assigned volunteers and nonvolunteers to two groups, in one of which there was a high level of fear aroused and in the other, a low level of fear. The high-fear group read pamphlets on the abuse and effects of drugs and watched two films that depicted the hazards of LSD and other hallucinogens and the dangerous effects of amphetamines and barbiturates. The low-fear group did not see the films, but instead read pamphlets on the hazards of drug abuse that omitted the vivid verbal descriptions of death and disability to which the high-fear group was exposed. The subjects were then given a questionnaire asking them to respond on scales corresponding to statements contained in the pamphlets. To provide a check on the effectiveness of the manipulation of anxiety (called a *manipulation check*), the subjects were also given another scale that asked them to tell the extent, if any, to which they had been concerned and upset. The results of this manipulation check confirmed that the high-fear manipulation had been more distressing than the low-fear manipulation. As to the main finding, it was indeed true that the volunteer subjects had been more persuaded by the high- than by the low-fear manipulation, but the nonvolunteer subjects were more persuaded by the low- than by the high-fear manipulation! The point, of course, is that we have to consider the interdependence of such variables as the subjects' volunteer status and the independent variable of interest, if our conclusions are to have external (and inferential) validity.

Thus we see how external validity may be jeopardized "across persons" and "across settings" when generalizations that are purported to apply to the population as a whole are, in fact, based *only* on the behavior of volunteers. Previously we discussed the difference between synchronic and diachronic research, and there is also a danger inherent in the idea of trying to generalize "across times" on the basis of observations made *only* at a particular moment in time. These are important limitations to keep in mind when we ponder the external validity of our conclusions.

RELIABILITY IN TEST CONSTRUCTION

One type of error is insufficient validity, and a second type is *insufficient reliability*. This second type occurs when an observation is repeated and it fails to yield sufficiently similar results even though the situation is unchanged. The less error there is, the more reliable the observation, so that a measurement that is free of error is a correct measure. We noted that one threat to statistical conclusion validity was the unreliability of measures, and we now discuss several methods of evaluating reliability in test (or scale) construction in order to show how reliability is tied together with validity.

There are three simple but useful methods of evaluating reliability in test construction. In each, reliability is expressed mathematically using a correlation coefficient, such as r, which means the degree to which variables are linearly related to each other. One of these is called the *test-retest method,* in which the correlation coefficient is calculated on data obtained from the same test but from results gotten at different times. The test is administered twice to the same group of people, and the objective is to determine how consistently they respond after we correct for any general effect on responding of the time interval employed or for the effect of testing a second time.

Of course, when we repeatedly measure someone we do not expect to get exactly the same value each time. If we repeatedly measured a child's height, there would be small differences in the values with each measure. The child will slouch a bit more or stand a little differently on the measuring spot or the measurer may have a slightly different angle of viewing the markings (Stanley, 1971). What we take as the "real value" will be the average figure. The more highly correlated the group members' scores are on the two occasions, the more reliable the measuring instrument.

A second approach is called the *equivalent-forms method*. This method calculates the correlation coefficient on data from comparable forms of the same test. For example, we might have two forms of a test of intelligence or of an attitude scale. The two forms would use different but comparable items. Both forms are administered to the same group of people, with the aim of determining whether the two forms actually measure the same thing. If the values closely converge, this means that there is high equivalent-forms reliability. The advantage in having comparable forms of an IQ test or an attitude scale derives from the fact that familiarity with a test (or scale) can often enhance performance. That is because the items are likely to be remembered the second time around. Thus, reliability assessment would be contaminated otherwise by subjects' having taken the same test twice (an *error of testing*).

A third approach to evaluating reliability in test construction is called the *method of internal consistency,* in which components of the test are correlated with one another. A common example of this method is the *split-half method*. The instrument is split in two, and both parts are administered to the same group of people. The responses to the two parts are then correlated. The objective in this instance is to determine the degree to which the instrument is internally consistent. Internal consistency reliability can also be evaluated in more elegant ways by employing statistical procedures besides *r* (Rosenthal, 1982).

TEST VALIDITY

When we speak of *test validity* (e.g., in the sense of achievement tests) we mean something a little different from the four kinds of validity discussed earlier. The definition of validity is the same (that something actually does what it purports or claims to do), and the procedures for assessing validity are logically similar, in that some good criterion is needed against which the test's accuracy can be checked. However, the particular criteria are different in that they specifically pertain to the past, present, or future. If we were developing a test of college aptitude we might employ as our (future) criterion the successful completion of the first year of college or maybe grade-point average after each year of college. If we were developing a test to measure anxiety, we might use as our (past or present) criterion the pooled judgments of a group of highly trained clinicians who have rated each person to whom we have administered the test. In the validation of our observations we try to select the most sensible and meaningful criterion in the past, present, or future.

One important type of test validity is called *predictive validity*. Can the test "predict" the future? Tests of college aptitude are normally assessed for predictive validity, since the criteria of graduation and grade-point average are events that will occur in the future. The aptitude-test scores are saved until the future-criterion data become available and are then correlated with them. The resulting correlation coefficient serves as a statement of predictive validity.

When the criterion is in the present, we speak of *concurrent validity*. Clinical diagnostic tests are normally assessed for concurrent validity, since the criterion of the patients' true diagnostic status is in the present with respect to the tests we are trying to validate. Shorter forms of longer tests are often evaluated with respect to their concurrent validity using the longer test as the criterion. It could reasonably be argued in such cases that it is not validity but reliability that is being assessed. Indeed, while reliability and validity are conceptually distinguishable, it is sometimes difficult to separate them in practice.

When the criterion is in the past, we speak of *postdictive validity*. Clinical tests in forensic psychiatry and psychology are normally assessed for postdictive validity since the criterion of criminal or psychopathological behavior is in the past with respect to the observations being validated. Thus, a court may want a determination of whether the accused was capable of a given unlawful act, whether the accused knew at the time that it was "right" or "wrong," and whether the accused was capable of controlling his or her actions. To assist the psychiatrist or psychologist in making this retrospective assessment, a psychological test of some sort may be administered. On the basis of the accused's responses, it may be decided to enter a plea of insanity, since it appears that he or she was unable to distinguish right from wrong at the time of committing the unlawful act.

In the predictive, concurrent, or postdictive validation of our instruments we try to select the most sensible and meaningful criterion that is also a reliable criterion. Grade-point average tends to be a fairly reliable criterion, while clinicians' judgments about complex behavior may be a less-reliable criterion. In a later chapter we discuss how the reliability of pooled judgments can be increased by adding more judges. Thus we can increase the reliability of pooled clinical judgments by adding more clinicians to the group whose pooled judgments will serve as our criterion (Rosenthal, 1973a, 1982).

Sometimes we must be concerned about the validity of the criterion. Suppose that we want to develop a short test of anxiety that will predict the scores on a longer test of anxiety. The longer test serves as our criterion, and the new short test may be relatively quite valid with respect to the longer test. But the longer test may be of dubious validity with respect to some other criterion, for example, clinicians' judgments. Sometimes, then, criteria must be evaluated with respect to other criteria, and there are no firm rules (beyond the consensus of the researchers in an area of inquiry) as to what shall constitute an ultimate criterion.

Predictive, concurrent, and postdictive validities can often be expressed by a single correlation between the test (or observations) being assessed for validity and the data based on a single criterion. There is another type of test validity, *content validity,* in which a more subjective evaluation is called for. The criterion for the assessment of content validity is an exhaustive listing of all the material that the observations to be validated were designed to sample. The common use of content validation is in the assessment of tests of achievement, or content mastery. In the same way that a student's final exam should include questions from all of the assigned chapters, not just the final chapter, if the instructor wishes to claim that the test has content validity, so must any achievement or mastery test adequately sample all relevant material. A test is thus regarded as more content-valid the more it covers the facts, ideas, and concepts that define the material of the area, course, or unit of study. While the other forms of test validity can be expressed by a correlation coefficient, content validity is usually expressed as a global, nonquantitative judgment or in terms of the adequacy of sampling of the contents to be covered.

More sophisticated views of the validation of tests, or of observations generally, require that we be sensitive not only to the correlation between our measures and some appropriate criterion but also to the correlation between our measures and some inappropriate criterion. Suppose we developed a measure of adjustment and found that it correlates positively and substantially with our criterion of the pooled judgment of expert clinicians. That would be an attractive outcome of a concurrent validation effort. Suppose further, however, that we administer a test of intelligence to all of our subjects and find that the correlation between our adjustment scores and intelligence is also positive and substantial. Would our new test be a reasonably valid test of adjustment, of intelligence, of both, or of neither? That question is difficult to answer, but we could not claim on the basis of these results to understand our new test very well. It was not intended, after all, to be a measure of intelligence. In short, our test has good concurrent validity but poor discriminant validity. It does not correlate differentially with criteria for different types of observation.

CRITERIA OF PRECISION

To say that someone is "very sensitive" implies that the person possesses a high degree of susceptibility to stimulation. A person who is very sensitive to noise, for example, is someone who has a low threshold of response to the slightest sound. To say that a scientific instrument is sensitive also implies a high degree of susceptibility to stimulation. That means the instrument is capable of detecting the slightest changes. Many instruments in behavioral science only approach this ideal. Others are capable of making relatively fine discriminations of changes in behavior. The term for this sharpness or exactness of some instruments is *precision* (and a third type of error, therefore, is *insufficient precision*).

When we talk of a precise *instrument* or of precise *instrumentation,* we are using terms with rather general meaning in science (Hackmann, 1979). One category of instrumentation consists of representations of what is observed to take place in the real world. That would include the kinds of simulation methods that were previously discussed, which were designed to mimic naturally-occurring events. However, it is quite possible in some instances to create a laboratory procedure and then mimic *it* in a natural situation (Henshel, 1980*a*, 1980*b*). An illustration would be the recent development of biofeedback investigation, in which subjects learn to control some of the supposedly involuntary processes of the body (such as heart rate or blood pressure) by monitoring these functions as they change under certain circumstances. In this case, a potentially beneficial effect was observed in the laboratory using precise methods, and an effort was then made to make the external world match the laboratory (rather than to make the laboratory match the external world, as is usually done). Subjects took their newly acquired lab skills into their day-to-day activities.

A second category of instrumentation consists of the tools of data collection with which discoveries are made. For many years the research data of behavioral science were dominated by self-reports, since interviews and questionnaires were used extensively in descriptive, relational, and experimental studies to measure many dependent variables. These instruments are useful for many purposes, but only when they are carefully constructed to probe into the behavior under investigation. If you ask me my opinion of something controversial, I may respond superficially in ways that mask a host of complex feelings. Unless the instrument is sufficiently sensitive to probe into the ulterior motives behind my responses, it will not be possible to get precise answers about my true feelings. However, a good case can be made for self-report measures under some circumstances where they are equal or superior to other means of assessment (Mischel, 1968).

The extent to which a research design or a test measurement is precise implies that it is also a relatively sensitive instrument. The scale in the pediatrician's office that measures a baby's weight is a more sensitive measuring instrument than the average bathroom scale. It is more precise for the doctor to report that the baby weighs "10 pounds and 5.8 ounces" than to say only that the baby "tips the scales at 10 pounds." Of course, there is such a thing as *pointless precision,* when the measure is more exact than can be taken advantage of in the situation. Loose approximation can be misleading, but the anxiety to be overly precise may reflect a lack of assurance of the scientific worth of one's endeavors (Kaplan, 1964). The researcher's efforts might be more profitably directed toward other aspects of the project or design which could be improved upon.

Scientists also use the term *false precision* when something relatively vague is reported as if the measuring instrument were sensitive to very slight differences (Kaplan, 1964). Suppose we asked 100 people to respond to the statement: "Cigarette smoking is bad for your health,"

_____1. I agree strongly with the statement.
_____2. I agree moderately with the statement.
_____3. I neither agree nor disagree with the statement.
_____4. I disagree moderately with the statement.
_____5. I disagree strongly with the statement.

We see that the responses are numbered from 1 to 5. We could add up all the individual replies and then divide by 100 to get the average response of these 100 persons. Suppose that the average response was strongly in favor of the statement, and we reported that it was 1.5 or 1.55 or 1.555 or 1.5555. If we reported 1.5555 that would appear to be a more precise figure than if we said 1.5. However, the three extra decimal places add nothing but false precision intended to put a better scientific face on the data. Given the relatively low discriminating power of many instruments in behavioral science (as compared with those in natural science), we find that one or two decimal places will suffice for most purposes when rating scales are employed.

The precision of a statistical procedure is also determined by its discriminating power. Let us say that we wanted to study the relationship between intelligence and persuasibility. We begin by giving IQ tests to a group of subjects. We expose them to some controlled amount of propaganda and then measure their opinions using a rating scale. A simple procedure for establishing whether there was a relationship between IQ and persuasibility would be to divide the group equally into "high IQ" and "low IQ" subjects by splitting the group at the median IQ (called a *median split*). If the mean opinion-change score were the same in the "high IQ" as in the "low IQ" subgroup, this would tell us that intelligence is unrelated to persuasibility. Or would it? The answer is that we cannot say with certainty, since it is also possible that the median split masks a curvilinear relationship. If we had equally divided the group into three or four subgroups on the basis of their IQ scores, we would have more than two reference points. With two points it is only possible to draw a straight line, but with three or four or more points we can detect a curvilinear relationship (if there is one). Suppose that people with average IQs tend to be more persuaded by propaganda than those either lower or higher in IQ. The median-split technique would be considered to have relatively poor discriminating power under these circumstances, since it was insensitive to the actual curvilinear relationship. (A similar problem frequently arises with correlational data. Investigators often assume linearity, do not construct a scatterplot of the data points, and report a correlation coefficient based upon an assumption of linearity.)

Precision, reliability, and validity are important considerations in all aspects of research. However, the most important of these three criteria is validity, for without adequate validity we have nothing. In the following two chapters, we consider in more detail how specific threats to validity are theoretically approached in the design of experimental and nonexperimental studies.

EIGHT

THE LOGIC OF RESEARCH DESIGN

THE CONCEPT OF CONTROL

The word "control" was derived from "counter-roll," a master list that was used to check and correct other lists. In modern usage, there are four distinct meanings of *control* in behavioral science (Boring, 1969).

One of these pertains to the *constancy of conditions,* that is, the importance of maintaining those conditions that affect the variables of the research at the levels or values at which we want them, or at which we believe them to be. We might at some time want to study the effect of temperature variation on human behavior under controlled conditions, but it would not be good scientific practice to allow the temperature in our laboratory to vary capriciously from very chilly to very hot under uncontrolled conditions. If that occurs, we would not be able to claim the constancy of conditions that allows statements of relationships to be made with precision. In this case we control the ambient temperature by holding it constant (constancy of conditions), in order to eliminate the possibility that it may introduce error into our findings.

A second usage is that of *control series,* which refers to the calibration of various elements of the research, including in some cases the apparatus used or even the subjects' mental set. For example, in psychophysical research, the subjects may be asked to judge whether their skin is being touched by one or two fine compass points. If the subjects know that two points will always be applied, they may never report the sensation of being stimulated by only one point. Yet we know that when two points are sufficiently close to one another they are invariably perceived as only one point. In this situation a control series might consist of applying only one point on a certain percentage of the trials. Thus if the subjects do not know when they are receiving one or two points, their responses are less apt to be influenced by the power of suggestion or by their expectation of what they are receiving.

A third usage refers to the ability to manipulate or shape behavior based on a particular schedule of reinforcement. For example, B. F. Skinner (1980) has discussed a remarkable case, in which two brothers, the Colliers, were found dead in a house completely filled with rubbish, as an example of "control by a worsening schedule." The Collier brothers, Skinner explains, had been inveterate collectors of string, newspapers, and boxes. The collection, however, slowly became "aversive" as it grew, since the addition of one more piece of string or one more newspaper or box could hardly have been as rewarding to the brothers as when they began their collection. Throwing things out would have been a form of escape, but the collection was not made noticeably more aversive by any one addition. Furthermore, it would have required a monumental effort to clean up the house, and the Colliers would have had to call in outsiders who no doubt would have ridiculed them. Thus their compulsive behavior was shaped, or "controlled," by saving or collecting in which reinforcement must have been very rare. Skinner (1972) and others have also used the term *behavioral control* in connection with the shaping of animal or human behavior, by which is usually meant the manipulation of the environmental conditions to which the organism is exposed in order to bring about a definite behavioral outcome.

It is the fourth meaning of "control" that is most closely and specifically linked to the principles of experimental design. In this case the term generally refers to the use of a condition against which we compare the effects of the treatment (or experimental) condition. For example, the story is told of how the ancient Egyptians discovered citron to be an antidote for poison (Jones, 1964). It seems that a magistrate had sentenced some convicted criminals to be executed by being exposed to poisonous snakes. It was reported back to him, however, that none of the criminals had died despite the care in carrying out the sentence. Inquiring into the matter, he learned that the criminals, just before they were bitten by the snakes, had been given some citron to eat by an old woman who took pity on them. The magistrate hypothesized that it must have been the citron that had saved them, and he had the criminals divided into pairs in order to test his hypothesis. Citron was fed to one of each pair and not to the other. When the criminals were again exposed to the poisonous snakes, the ones who had eaten the citron suffered no harm while the untreated "controls" died instantly. The story illustrates the early use of *control groups*.

EXPERIMENTAL AND CONTROL GROUPS

This sense of the term also embodies certain ideas subsequently developed by John Stuart Mill. We have mentioned Mill's name in previous chapters. By setting down a logical method consisting of a set of principles, he essentially laid the foundation for the later use of various statistical procedures in experimental design (which we discuss in later chapters). One of Mill's principles is called the *method of agreement*. It simply states: "If X, then Y." This statement means that whenever X is present, Y follows. When this occurs, X and Y are said to covary. It also means that X is a *sufficient condition* of Y. "Sufficient" tells us that X is adequate for the occurrence of Y.

Another of Mill's principles, called the *method of difference,* states: "If not-X, then not-Y." In other words, when X isn't present, Y does not occur. This means that X is a *necessary condition* of Y. "Necessary" tells us that X is requisite or essential for the occurrence of Y.

We can also put these two principles together: "If X, then Y" and "If not-X, then not-Y." When we combine them in this way, the combinatory principle is called the *joint method of agreement and difference* (or the "joint method"). The joint method tells us that X is both necessary and sufficient for the occurrence of Y.

Let us suppose that X represents a new and highly touted tranquilizer which can be obtained without prescription, while Y represents a decrease in measured tension. Say that we have a group of subjects who complain of tension, that they take a certain dosage of tranquilizer X and then show a reduction in tension. What we have described so far is a standard *experimental group* in which X occurred and then Y occurred. But could we conclude from this single observation that it was the tranquilizer which led to the reduction in tension? Not yet, since we have established only that X is a sufficient condition of Y. What we seem to require is a *control group* against which to compare the reaction in the experimental group. For our control let us suppose we have a group of comparable subjects who were not given any pills, and that they did not show any tension reduction. In other words, when X did not occur then Y also did not occur. We can diagram this two-group design as follows, and we quickly see that it corresponds to Mill's joint method:

Experimental group	*Control group*
If X, then Y	If not-X, then not-Y

Could we now conclude that taking the drug is what led to tension reduction? Yes—but with the stipulation that "taking the drug" means something quite different from getting a certain chemical into the blood system. "Taking the drug" means among other things: (a) having someone give the subject a pill; (b) having someone give the subject the attention that goes with pill giving; (c) having the subject believe that relevant medication has been administered; and (d) having the ingredients of the drug find their way to the blood system of the subject.

Usually when testing a new drug the researcher is interested only in the subject's physical reaction to active ingredients. The researcher does not care to learn that subjects will get to feel better if they believe they are being helped, because this fact is already established. But if the researcher knows this, then how is he or she to separate the effects of the drug's ingredients from the effects of pill giving, subject expectations of help, and other psychological variables that may also be sufficient conditions of *Y*? The answer is by the choice of a different (or an additional) control group.

This time we will employ not a group given nothing, but instead a group given something that differs only in terms of the ingredients whose effects we would like to establish. The need for this type of control is so well established in drug research that virtually all trained investigators routinely use *placebo-control groups* (a placebo being a substance without any pharmacological effect but given as a "drug" to a control group). The general finding is, incidentally, that placebos are often effective and sometimes even as effective as the far more expensive drug for which they serve as the relevant control. Thus, we see that it is not always immediately apparent how one should select his or her control group or groups. Only experience in a given research area is likely to teach the investigator what shall constitute adequate controls.

PRE- AND TRUE EXPERIMENTAL DESIGNS

In our tranquilizer research we first used a no-pill control group and then a placebo control (probably a sugar pill). Assuming that there is often a choice of control groups, how can the researcher decide on the most appropriate control groups? That question is not a simple one, but two major factors to be considered are: (a) the specific question of greatest interest to the researcher, and (b) what is known generally about the research area. Even a very experienced scientist may go astray in choosing control groups when he or she makes a major shift of research areas. By constantly asking ourselves how the validity of the findings might be increased by some improvement in the design we begin to get an intuitive idea of what additional groups are required.

Recent theoretical attempts have been made by Donald T. Campbell and Julian C. Stanley (1966) and by Thomas D. Cook and Campbell (1979) to systematize the choice of control groups. In the preceding chapter we discussed some of the theoretical work by Cook and Campbell on the identification of possible threats to internal validity, and we mentioned four specific threats: (a) history, (b) maturation, (c) instrumentation, and (d) selection. Table 8.1 shows how these four threats to internal validity are theoretically related to three types of research designs.

The first two designs are labeled "preexperimental" because of the fact there is such a total absence of control that they are of minimal value in establishing causality. The first of these, called a "one-shot case study," would consist of observing or measuring some behavior once an event has occurred. For example, following the introduction of a new educational treatment designed to improve students' concentration, the students might be interviewed to ascertain their psychological reactions. They might also be tested on a standard achievement test. However, in designs of this type there is no allowance made for a comparison with the reactions of other students who were not subjected to the new treatment.

The second example of a preexperimental design is called "one-group pre-post." It makes a slight improvement on the first design in that the students would be measured both before and after exposure to the treatment. However, there is still no allowance made for a comparison with the reactions of other students who were not exposed to the treatment.

The table also indicates how four sources of internal invalidity discussed in the preceding chapter are pertinent to each design. The first type of error, history, becomes a plausible rival explanation of change in both these designs since specific contaminating events occurring before the postmeasurement cannot be controlled and assessed by either design 1 or design 2. Suppose that a sudden snow storm resulted in an unexpected cancellation of classes. Designs 1 and 2 do not allow us to isolate the effects on motivation of a school closing and

Table 8.1 Sources of invalidity for two preexperimental designs and the Solomon experimental design

	Sources of invalidity			
	History	Maturation	Instrumentation	Selection
1. Preexperimental: one-shot case study X O	−	−	not relevant	−
2. Preexperimental: one-group pre-post O X O	−	−	−	+
3. True experimental: four-group design I R O X O II R X O III R O O IV R O	+	+	+	+

Note: An X symbolizes the exposure of a group to an experimental variable or event, the effects of which are measured by O (which represents an observation or measurement). An R symbolizes random assignment to separate treatment groups. A minus (−) indicates a definite weakness, a plus (+) that the source of invalidity is controlled.

Source: D. T. Campbell and J. C. Stanley, *Experimental and Quasi-Experimental Designs for Research,* Rand McNally, Chicago, 1966 (republished by Houghton Mifflin). Copyright 1963, American Educational Research Association, Washington, D.C. Adapted by permission of the first author, Houghton Mifflin Co., and the American Educational Research Association.

to assess this possible factor apart from the effects of the new educational treatment that was explicitly designed to improve concentration.

The second type of error is maturation, which might refer to the students' concentration improving as a result of getting older. If they indeed become better at the task, we could not tell whether the gains were due to their having grown older or to the fact that they were subjected to a particular educational treatment.

The third type of error, instrumentation, is relevant only to design 2. This type of error could be accounted for as a change in the calibration of the measuring instrument, or due to changes in the observers or scorers, rather than changes due to the impact of the treatment. For example, observers might over time become better judges of student concentration, and erroneously infer improvement.

The fourth type, selection, refers to the particular characteristics of the participants themselves. In design 1 there is no way of knowing beforehand anything about the state of the participants, since they are observed or measured only once (after the treatment has been administered). The addition of a preobservation in design 2 results in an improvement over design 1, inasmuch as it allows us to ascertain the prior state of the participants.

THE SOLOMON DESIGN

We turn now to design 3, which is a rather complicated model also known as the "Solomon design" (after the scientist who developed it, Richard L. Solomon). While it is not a common design, it is an elegant example of the fundamental logic of experimental design. To understand the nature of this four-group design, it is best to begin with a study that actually used it. Because the Solomon design becomes even more complicated when there are multiple independent variables for consideration (Solomon, 1949), the study we have chosen is one done by Solomon and Michael Lessac (1968; Lessac & Solomon, 1969) in which there was only one type of identifiable difference between the experimental and the control groups.

Previous research had led to the development of what is called the "critical period hypothesis." This hypothesis states that there are optimum periods in the life of an infant animal during which it learns how to make adaptive responses to its environment. Withholding various kinds of stimulation early in the organism's development should, it was theorized, impede the learning of sensory and motor associations important to adult behavior. Solomon and Lessac questioned this assumption because it ignores two rival possibilities: first, that the early deprivation destroys an already formed behavioral organization, not one that has yet to form, and second, that the early deprivation creates unusual patterns of responding that simply interfere with the later behaviors. To rule out these alternatives, it is necessary (a) to pretest the organism's behavior before it is subjected to a state of isolation, and (b) at the same time to control for the effects of this required pretesting. By pretesting the organism, we can then establish whether any effects of the isolation were merely a passive arrest of learning processes or an active impediment to existing perceptual-motor patterns.

Unfortunately, the pretesting might, theoretically at least, serve to enrich the experience of the supposedly deprived subjects. It is necessary, therefore, to devise a means of determining the possible confounding effect of the pretest on reactions to the treatment. That is why the four-group design was developed, and Table 8.2 shows another way of looking at it. The design calls for subjects to be assigned to one of four groups on a purely chance (or random) basis. Group I is pretested on whatever dependent variables are theoretically relevant, then subjected to a state of isolation, and finally retested on the dependent variables. Group II is not pretested, but undergoes the same isolation treatment and is given the same posttests as in group I. Group III is pretested and posttested, but is treated normally instead of being subjected to a period of isolation. Group IV only gets the posttests.

In carrying out this experiment, beagle pups were the subjects studied (Lessac & Solomon, 1969). Those assigned at random to groups III and IV were reared normally in the same way they would have been reared in a kennel, and those assigned at random to groups I and II were raised in isolation in 18 × 24 × 30-inch aluminum cages through which light entered by a 2½-inch space between the bottom tray and the door. All the pups were fed and medicated at the same times, and the dependent variables (the measures of which included testing each pup's response to pain, how it responded to its physical environment, and various tests of learning) were observed for all groups after one year had passed.

What can this four-group design tell us? First, by averaging the pretest performances of groups I and III we can estimate what the initial performances would have been in groups II and IV if they, too, had been pretested. We assume these pretest scores will be very similar or identical because the subjects were assigned at random; random assignment tends to maximize the probability that the groups are comparable by giving each subject an equal

Table 8.2 The Solomon four-group research design

Procedure	Treatment conditions	
	Isolation	No isolation
Pretesting	I	III
No pretesting	II	IV

Note: The design shown in this table corresponds exactly to design 3 in Table 8.1.

chance of being assigned to any particular group. Second, we can now examine the posttest performance in group II without having contaminated it by the pretesting procedures. A comparison of the estimated mean pretest score in group II with its actual mean posttest score would enable us to decide whether the isolation produced a deterioration in performance, an improvement, or whether it had no effect at all; and this effect can be compared to the effect obtained in group IV. Third, by comparing the differences in posttest scores between groups I and III with those found between groups II and IV—that is, (I–III)–(II–IV)—we can calculate the effects of the pretesting on the response to the treatment. This is called the "interaction of pretesting and the treatment." A positive difference score would suggest that the pretesting had an enriching effect, i.e., it weakened the effect of isolation. A negative score would suggest the opposite. In the study by Lessac and Solomon, use of this four-group design enabled them to conclude that behavioral development may not merely be retarded by isolation but, in fact, distorted.

COMPARISON OF EXPERIMENTAL DESIGNS

Table 8.3 compares the Solomon design with two simpler designs in terms of the four sources of internal invalidity and two of external invalidity. We see that design 4, called a "pre-post control group design," is composed only of groups I and III of the Solomon design. Design 5, called a "posttest-only control group design," consists only of groups II and IV of the Solomon design. We also see that, except for the two sources of external invalidity, there is no loss in the relative validities of the two-group designs as compared to the Solomon design. The differences occur only in the case of the threats to external validity. Design 4 is seriously deficient when it comes to the interaction of pretesting and the treatment manipulation, but design 5 is not flawed in this respect since the subjects are only measured after the manipulation of X. To be sure, design 5 would not have been a good choice in the Solomon and Lessac study, because they raised specific questions that could only be answered by estimating the state of the pups' behaviors before the isolation treatment began. Design 5 would be recommended in situations where it was not necessary to get a precise estimate of the interaction of pretesting and X.

We also see that questions can be raised about the possible threat to external validity resulting from the interaction of selection and X. None of these three experimental designs can control, for example, for the kind of interaction with the subject's volunteer status that was found by Horowitz in his research on persuasion (discussed in Chapter 7). This is not an exhaustive list of the sources of internal and external invalidity, and for further discussion the reader should refer to Campbell and Stanley (1966) and to Cook and Campbell (1979). These are some of the types of errors that can jeopardize validity, and which can be isolated for quantitative analysis (as in the Solomon design) or avoided by using other research designs.

Table 8.3 Sources of invalidity for three true experimental designs

	Sources of internal invalidity				Sources of external invalidity	
	History	Matu-ration	Instru-mentation	Selection	Interaction of pretesting and X	Interaction of selection and X
3. Solomon four-group design	+	+	+	+	+	?
I R O X O						
II R X O						
III R O O						
IV R O						
4. Pre-post control group design	+	+	+	+	−	?
I R O X O						
III R O O						
5. Posttest-only control group design	+	+	+	+	+	?
II R X O						
IV R O						

Note: A question mark (?) indicates a possible source of concern.

Source: D. T. Campbell and J. C. Stanley, *Experimental and Quasi-Experimental Designs for Research,* Rand McNally, Chicago, 1966 (Republished by Houghton Mifflin). Copyright 1963, American Educational Research Association, Washington, D.C. Adapted by permission of the first author, Houghton Mifflin Co., and the American Educational Research Association.

CROSS-LAG DESIGN

We have seen how random assignment and adequate control groups can provide a sound basis of comparison in drawing conclusions about the relative magnitude of some effect. Suppose I tell you that I went fishing last weekend and caught "a very big fish." You might ask me, "compared to what?" My assertion that the fish was "very big" is predicated on a basis of comparison with other fish that I have caught or been told about, as well as with my knowledge about what size fish of that type can be characterized as "small" or "big" or "very big." Those experiences are "controls" that provide a basis of comparison in estimating just how large my own fish was. Whatever conclusions we want to draw, we always predicate them on some comparison or "control group" in order to arrive at valid ones

So far we have only looked at the kinds of control groups that might be used in experimental research. However, we are also interested in tracking some variables over a long period of time in order to establish trends and cycles. For example, in Chapter 5 we alluded to the historical comparisons made by McGuire (1976), in which he searched for cycles and trends in achievements in various fields of human culture over more than 2000 years of recorded history. To serve as a basis of comparison, he decided to analyze the biographical directories published in different countries. In this way one sample of famous people drawn from one culture served as control for another sample of famous people drawn from another culture. The extent to which McGuire was led to conclusions about the distribution of famous people "across time" was, then, predicated on two universal biographical dictionaries.

There are other ways of approaching diachronic research in which the stability or reliability of probable causal relationships can be compared over long periods of time. One possibility is to use a *cross-lag research design*, so called because one variable lags behind the other. To understand how that design works, we begin with a relatively simple example using relational data to test a causal hypothesis.

Suppose we were interested in the relationship between television violence and aggression, and we had access to data on the TV-viewing habits of a representative sample of children. If we also had peer ratings of their aggressiveness (arrived at by posing the question, "Who started fights over nothing?"), we could describe a positive (correlation) relationship by saying the children who watched more violent TV were also the more aggressive. If the relationship were negative, that would tell us the children who watched more violent TV were less aggressive. Neither finding, by itself, could reveal whether TV viewing and aggressiveness were linked in a causal fashion. There are at least three rival hypotheses to consider: (a) aggression is the independent variable and the preference for violent TV is the dependent variable; (b) aggression is the dependent variable and the preference for TV violence is the independent variable; or (c) both are dependent variables and some other variable is their common cause.

One way to begin to unravel the puzzle of causality is to look at the relationships between the two variables over time, as indexed by cross-lag correlations. By examining these cross-correlations it may be possible partially to rule out one or more of the rival hypotheses and narrow the field a little. A great deal could be said about the procedure (e.g., Kenny, 1979), but it will suffice here simply to diagram the obvious possibilities in this example.

Figure 8.1 represents these correlational possibilities by the symbol r followed by a subscript to designate the two variables correlated.* In this case,

---

* The correlation coefficient, r, can take on values from -1.0 through zero to $+1.0$. A correlation near zero means that the two variables in question are relatively unrelated. A positive correlation means that the greater the value or score on one variable, the *greater* the value or score on the other variable. A negative correlation means that the greater the value or score on one variable, the *lower* it is on the other variable. From the point of view of estimating a value or score on one variable from our knowledge of it on the other variable, it makes no difference whether the correlation is very close to $+1.0$ or -1.0; both correlations would predict equally well.

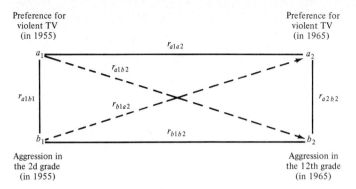

Preference for
violent TV
(in 1955)

Preference for
violent TV
(in 1965)

Aggression in
the 2d grade
(in 1955)

Aggression in
the 12th grade
(in 1965)

Figure 8-1 Hypothetical cross-lag research design for two variables: (a) preference for violent TV and (b) aggression. The dashed lines show the direction of the two cross-lag correlations, r_{a1b2} and r_{b1a2}.

variable a is TV-watching behavior and variable b is aggressive behavior, and our task is to decide whether one variable causes the other to occur.

There are several factors for us to consider. One criterion of causality discussed earlier is that the two variables, a and b, must actually covary. That should be made evident from examining the correlations between a and b within some period, say the period of 1955 and the period of 1965. If r_{a1b1} is satisfactorily high, this tells us that a and b covary in 1955; if r_{a2b2} is satisfactorily high, then we know that a and b also covary in 1965.

We also want to know whether the measures of the two variables are stable (reliable) measures. That can be seen by examining the correlations r_{a1a2} and r_{b1b2}. If they are both satisfactorily high, we can conclude that the measurements are relatively stable.

The key question, however, is whether there is evidence of a causal relationship. The cross-lag correlations give us a clue as to whether there is or is not a causal relationship between a and b. One cross-lag correlation, r_{a1b2}, involves the relationship between preferences for watching violent TV in 1955 and aggression in 1965. The other correlation, r_{b1a2}, refers to the relationship between aggression in 1955 and preferences for watching violent TV in 1965. A minimal or weak correlation between $b1$ and $a2$, especially in relation to a larger correlation between $a1$ and $b2$, would weaken the probability that aggressiveness is the independent variable and the preference for violent TV is the dependent variable. A much stronger correlation between $b1$ and $a2$ than between $a1$ and $b2$ would suggest that b may be causally implicated in the relationship between a and b. Similarly, a minimal or weak correlation between $a1$ and $b2$, especially in relation to a larger correlation between $b1$ and $a2$, would weaken the probability that aggressiveness is the dependent variable and the preference for TV violence is the independent variable. A much stronger correlation between $a1$ and $b2$ than between $b1$ and $a2$ would suggest that a may be causally implicated in the relationship between a and b.

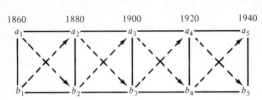

Figure 8-2 Hypothetical cross-lag design for two variables, a and b, at 20-year intervals over the period from 1860 to 1940. Cross-lagged correlations are shown (in dashed lines) only between adjacent time periods; in practice they would be computed from each period to all subsequent periods.

In fact, a field study along these very lines was done by Eron, Huesmann, Lefkowitz, and Walder (1972), who looked at the relationship between the preference for TV violence and subsequent behavior on the part of children ten years later. Their findings, which have now been replicated in other countries (Eron & Huesmann, 1980), indicated a substantially more positive correlation between preference for TV violence and subsequent aggression than between aggression and subsequent preference for TV violence.

The application of this type of design over many cross-lag periods allows us to assess the stability or reliability of a causal relationship over eras. That approach is diagrammed in Figure 8.2, which shows two variables, a and b, that have been repeatedly measured at twenty-year intervals. To do that kind of analysis would require that we have access to a good source of historical records on the variables in question. Obviously the analysis could not be applied to TV watching, since television has not been around that long. The solid lines in the figure show some of the possible correlations that could be calculated for analyzing stability of measures and whether the variables covary. The dashed lines show some of the possible cross-lag correlations to test the causal hypothesis that a leads to b or the rival hypothesis that b leads to a.

CONTROLLING FOR AGE AND COHORT

There are, of course, other ways of approaching diachronic relationships, depending on the particular hypotheses under investigation. Suppose we were interested in drawing conclusions about the possible changes that are related to becoming older. One popular approach is to do synchronic research using a *cross-sectional design*, which takes a slice of time and compares subjects of different ages on some variable. A better approach would be to do diachronic research in addition to the synchronic, for example, using a *longitudinal design* in which a collection of individuals was studied over a long period of time.

There is a particular deficiency in the cross-sectional design, which can be illustrated by a well-known example from developmental psychology. For many years it was taught that the age-curve for intelligence increased to a maximum at 30 years of age and then declined. This curve, however, was based on cross-sectional data, that is, on the results of IQ tests which had been given at the same time to younger and older persons whose scores were then plotted as a function of their calendar ages. It was later discovered, in an analysis of the extensive testing records of military draftees during World Wars I and II, that the average IQ of young adults tested in the early 1940s coincided with the eighty-second percentile of young adults tested twenty-four years earlier. That the World War I recruits, when they were the same age as the World War II recruits, scored so much lower in IQ, may have been due to differences in the life experiences (education, child rearing, cultural advantages, etc.) of the two generations. If, in the 1940s, however, both generations had been tested at the same time, it would surely have *looked as if* the older generation had lost some intelligence points over the intervening period of twenty-four years (when actually the older generation would not have performed as well on the tests even when they were the same age as the younger generation). The term for a generation (i.e., a collection of people born in the same period) is a *cohort* (Ryder, 1965), and the problem, then, is that the cross-sectional design fails to take into account the cohort as a confounding temporal variable (Schaie, 1965; Wohlwill, 1970).

By implication, it would seem that using a longitudinal design might have prevented the confounding of age and cohort effects by comparing the differences between the age categories within one particular cohort. The use of a *cohort table*, such as that in Table 8.4, allows us to see whether there are any discrepancies and contradictions as a result of the type of research design. This cohort table was adapted from a more complete table developed by sociologists Jacques A. Hagenaars and Niki P. Cobben (1978), based on data showing estimated percentages of women in the Netherlands with no religious affiliation according to age and period. The table also shows seven different cohorts or "generations" of respondents.

Table 8.4 Estimated percentages of women in the Netherlands with no religious affiliation according to age and period

	Period 1 (1909)	Period 2 (1929)	Period 3 (1949)	Period 4 (1969)
Age 20–30	Cohort 4 4.8%	Cohort 5 13.9%	Cohort 6 17.4%	Cohort 7 23.9%
Age 40–50	Cohort 3 3.1%	Cohort 4 11.9%	Cohort 5 17.2%	Cohort 6 22.0%
Age 60–70	Cohort 2 1.9%	Cohort 3 6.7%	Cohort 4 11.9%	Cohort 5 19.4%
Age 80–	Cohort 1 1.2%	Cohort 2 3.8%	Cohort 3 6.6%	Cohort 4 12.2%

Note: An example of a cross-sectional design is shown by the vertical analysis (Period 4), and an example of a longitudinal design is shown by the diagonal analysis (Cohort 4).

Source: J. A. Hagenaars and N. P. Cobben, "Age, Cohort and Period: A General Model for the Analysis of Social Change," *Netherlands Journal of Sociology*, 1978, *14*, 59–91. Reprinted by permission of Elsevier Scientific Publishing Co.

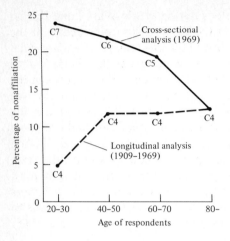

Figure 8-3 Percentages of nonaffiliation to church of women in the Netherlands, as shown by a cross-sectional design in 1969 and a longitudinal design from 1909 to 1969. (*After Hagenaars and Cobben, 1978.*) Cohorts are symbolized as C7 (Cohort 7), C6 (Cohort 6), and so on.

The analysis of one particular column would be comparable to the one-shot case study design discussed earlier in this chapter, for instance, a survey that is carried out once. An example of this is shown with reference to Period 4, and Figure 8.3 shows the shape of the age curve in 1969. These data seem to support the hypothesis that with the passing of years, and the approach of the end of life, religious observance increases (percentage of nonaffiliation decreases). The analysis of one particular cohort would be equivalent to a longitudinal survey which is carried out periodically to follow the life course of that cohort. An example of this is shown with reference to Cohort 4 (on the diagonal of Table 8.4), and Figure 8.3 shows the shape of the age curve from 1909 to 1969. We now see that the conclusion based on the cross-sectional survey cannot be correct.

IMPROVEMENT ON ONE-SHOT ANALYSIS

When we have an adequate cohort table, such as Hagenaars and Cobben's, other analyses are also possible. Thus, we could improve on the one-shot analysis by plotting all of the cross-sectional curves, as shown in Figure 8.4a. We now see that the exact percentages of affiliation, and the slopes of the age curves, are quite different for different periods. We could also plot the data according to cohort of women, as shown in Figure 8.4b, which helps us to avoid the mistake of assuming that the results of an analysis of one particular moment are generalizable to other periods (known as the *fallacy of period centrism*). There are, to be sure, other possibilities, and in a later chapter we discuss these alternative sampling designs.

We have discussed how, depending on the problem under investigation, a longitudinal design may be preferable to a cross-sectional design, but we have also seen that other designs (Figure 8.4b, for example) can provide even further improvements. There are also quasi-experimental designs for use in field stud-

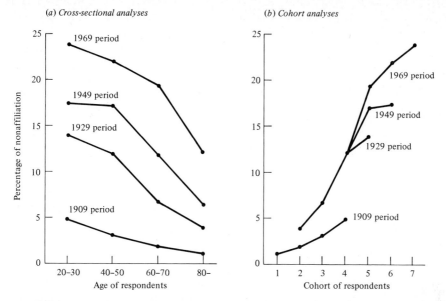

Figure 8-4 Percentages of nonaffiliation to church of women in the Netherlands, according to (a) age of women and (b) cohort of women. (*After Hagenaars and Cobben, 1978.*)

ies in education and other areas (Cook & Campbell, 1979), cohort designs for problems in student development and counseling (Whiteley, Burkhart, Harway-Herman, & Whiteley, 1975), and experimental designs for making clinical observations (Mahoney, 1978). We have looked at some types of threats to internal and external validity and examples to illustrate the logic of a variety of different designs, but we have not tried to be exhaustive in this coverage. Particularly in some of its more statistical aspects, the design of relational and experimental investigations is a very specialized and highly developed field, and in later chapters we shall have recourse to return to the topic of research design.

SUBJECT-EXPERIMENTER ARTIFACTS AND THEIR CONTROL

DEFINING SYSTEMATIC ERROR

In defining artifacts as threats to validity, we have also alluded to the idea that some artifacts can pose a direct threat to construct validity. Subject and experimenter artifacts are an example. They are a type of systematic error, however, and like most systematic errors they can often be assessed, reduced, and possibly even avoided altogether once we have discovered their underlying causes or processes.

Systematic errors can be contrasted with *random errors*, which are defined as the effects of uncontrolled variables that cannot be specifically identified but are "self-canceling." For instance, when we repeatedly take a measurement of something, the measurements do not, as a rule, yield identical results. The results may be very close, but there are almost always some random fluctuations in the data, which cannot be completely eliminated. However, the average of these errors would probably equal zero. In contrast, *systematic errors* are those that are also attributable to uncontrolled variables, which often *can* be specifically identified, but that are not "self-canceling," that is, the average error does not equal zero.

This difference between random and systematic errors has important implications in the design of experiments. When subjects are randomly assigned to conditions, we can usually assume that any differences among the subjects that appear as random errors should be self-canceling. Some subjects may be more intelligent than other subjects, or taller or more sociable etc., but we assume that random assignment will achieve comparability by equating the average unit within each treatment group (Cook & Campbell, 1979). This is not true in the case of subject and experimenter artifacts, however, because the equivalence achieved by random assignment does not automatically mitigate the effects of systematic errors.

To understand why this is so, and how we can effectively deal with the problem, it is important to understand the nature of the social interaction between the experimenter and the subject. The experimenter is studying an active and aware human being who might not be participating were he or she not interested and probably somewhat involved in the research, since even in subject pools and in surveys, people can say no. Indeed, there is considerable evidence to suggest that, within our western society, the role of the research subject is well understood by the majority of normal adults who find their way into behavioral scientists' subject pools. In this chapter we begin by discussing what is known about the nature of this interaction from the subject's side of the experimenter-subject equation.

However, experimenters can also have an effect on the results of research, and we turn next to the experimenter's side of the equation. The systematic errors generated by the experimenter are usually unintentional, and it is useful to think of them as falling into two classes. One type occurs without affecting the actual response of the human or animal subject; it is in the mind, the eye, or the hand of the experimenter. This type of error is *noninteractional,* and we will discuss the various kinds of noninteractional experimenter effects. The second type is *interactional,* in that it operates by affecting the actual response of the participant. There are also several kinds of interactional experimenter effects, but one kind in particular—the experimenter expectancy effect—is of greatest interest to us, and we discuss how it can be assessed or reduced using special control groups and other strategies.

By *control* we again mean the use of a comparison group to isolate something or the use of a procedure to serve as a check on validity. However, we often mean something more general when dealing with systematic errors, namely, ways of exercising restraint or direction or of holding certain events in check in order to avoid artifacts. We also use the term *experimenter* more generally in this chapter, to mean any researcher who tests or tries some observational method, using human or animal subjects, in order to gather scientific data about behavior. To the extent that we hope for dependable knowledge in behavioral science, we must have dependable knowledge about the experimenter-subject interaction. We can no more hope to acquire accurate information for our discipline without an understanding of the data-collection situation than astronomers and biologists could hope to acquire accurate information for their disciplines without understanding the effects of their telescopes and microscopes.

TYPES OF ROLE MOTIVATIONS

One way of thinking about the subject-artifact problem is in terms of what sociologists and social psychologists know as *role theory*. That theory derives from the dramaturgical analogy, and it assumes that a large part of human behavior is guided by the wishes, expectations, and behavior of others. For the human research subject, it is recognized that he or she, no less than other socialized human beings, is sensitive to the wishes, expectations, and behavior of the other participants and the experimenter.

In an experiment, the object is usually to observe behavior in a precisely controlled situation where the experimenter can manipulate the independent variable or interfere with some normally occurring relationship while holding other variables constant. To be able to draw valid inferences from the research findings that are generalizable to a comparable situation outside of the laboratory setting requires that the experimental conditions closely resemble the naturalistic processes under investigation. Insofar as the research subject is playing a different role than he or she would play in the corresponding naturalistic situation, it may be difficult, even impossible, to draw conclusions that can be generalized beyond the laboratory setting (thus jeopardizing the study's inferential validity).

There are several such roles which the subject might play. One is that of the *good subject,* whose creed could be a paraphrase of the old song about Lola: "Whatever experimenters want, experimenters get." The good subject is excessively sensitive and accommodating to the experimenter's implicit wishes and expectations for the experimental outcome. Of course, not everyone is willing to play the good subject, although many volunteer subjects seem quite willing to do whatever the experimenter asks of them.

Martin T. Orne (1962) has done extensive research into this type of role enactment, and he has introduced the expression "demand characteristics of the experimental situation" to denote the mixture of various hints and cues that govern the subject's perception of his or her role and of the experimenter's hypothesis. At one point in his research on hypnosis, Orne tried to devise a set of dull, meaningless tasks which he hoped the control subjects would either refuse to do or would try for a short time and abandon. One task was to add hundreds of thousands of two-digit numbers until the experimenter told them to stop. Five and a half hours after the subjects began, the experimenter gave up! The subjects never did quit. Even when they were told to tear each individual sheet from a stack of arithmetic work sheets into no less than thirty-two pieces and then go on to the next and do the same thing, the subjects kept on working. Orne's (1962) explanation for this unusual behavior was that the volunteers were reacting to demand characteristics and to the fact that they were research subjects. Feeling that they had a stake in the outcome of the experiment, they attributed meaning to an utterly meaningless task. It was as if they reasoned that no matter how trivial the task seemed to them, the experimenter must surely have an important scientific purpose to justify their working so hard on the addition problems.

A second type of role motivation, discussed by Milton J. Rosenberg (1969) and Irwin Silverman (1977), is similar to the social desirability set studied by Crowne and Marlowe (discussed in Chapter 5). Rosenberg has coined the term *evaluation apprehension* to characterize this attitude, and he has argued that many research situations are highly conducive to a fear of being judged or evaluated. The average research participants, it is argued, are apprehensive (or fearful) that the experimenter plans to evaluate them psychologically and will evaluate their performance unfavorably. Because most people would like to "look good" in front of other people, the subjects put their best foot forward. In fact, several experiments have shown that when there is a conflict between complying with demand characteristics and projecting a good appearance, most subjects prefer to look good rather than to cooperate with the experimenter (Rosnow, Goodstadt, Suls, & Gitter, 1973; Sigall, Aronson, & Van Hoose, 1970; Page, 1971).

A third type of role motivation is that of the *negativistic subject,* who approaches the experimental situation with an uncooperative attitude. This type is just the opposite of the good subject and may even be hostile at times. Instead of going along with demand characteristics, the negativistic subject does everything possible to disconfirm the experimenter's hypothesis. This type is also different from the subject who is simply disinterested in the experiment, although it is not easy to distinguish one from the other unless we take pains to learn from subjects whether they did not comply with demand characteristics because they wanted to "mess up" the experiment (the negativistic subject) or because they did not care about the outcome (the uninterested subject).

It is easy to see how subject artifacts resulting from a particular role enactment might be a threat to construct validity. That type of validity is what experimenters are concerned with when they worry about *confounding*; this is a general term (to be discussed later) which in this case means that what one experimenter interprets as a causal relationship between X and Y may be seen by another researcher as the relationship between some role variable and Y (Cook & Campbell, 1979). In interpreting the research data, it is important to consider the interdependence of the intentionally imposed research conditions and whatever systematic errors might inadvertently have resulted from the type of role enacted by the subjects.

CONTROLS FOR DEMAND CHARACTERISTICS

Various types of controls have been developed which proceed on the assumption that how the subject responds to demand characteristics is mediated by a three-step process (Rosnow & Davis, 1977). First, there is the subject's *sensi-*

tivity and receptivity to demand characteristics. The scientific atmosphere of the research setting, how experienced the subject is in the ways of behavioral science, the subject's perspicacity and intelligence—these variables tend to affect the subject's facility at recognizing and interpreting demand characteristics. Second, there is the subject's *motivation to respond to the demand characteristics of the situation.* To play a role requires some knowledge of what is expected, but also the *desire* to play it. Third, there is the subject's *capability to respond to demand characteristics.* There may be restraints which would make it difficult or even impossible for the subject to respond to demand characteristics. Coping with subject artifacts seems to depend on which of these three processes we want to control.

One possibility is to minimize the presence of demand characteristics, for example, by the use of field experiments and quasi experiments that use nonreactive measures. Because the subject is unaware that he or she is "participating" in a scientific experiment, receptivity to demand characteristics is nil.

Another possibility is to "short-circuit" the motivational process, for example, by telling the subject that the purpose of the experiment cannot be revealed and that it is important he or she *not* try to figure it out. This creates a role demand in direct conflict with the demand characteristics of the situation. If the subject is acquiescent (and not suspicious) and capable of response, then compliance with this new "demand" essentially creates motivation not to comply with the demand characteristics of the experiment.

Still another possibility is to use a posttest-only control group design rather than a pre-post control group design. The use of a pre-post design has been shown to "sensitize" volunteer subjects so that they respond more to the treatment than if they had not been pretested (Rosnow & Suls, 1970). Elimination of the pretest, and the use instead of unobtrusive measures, should reduce the probability of demand characteristics being communicated and received. In some instances, of course, it may be essential to use a pre-post design. In that case it would be wise to use the Solomon design, since it controls for the pretest-by-treatment interaction.

Other methods have been tested (Adair, 1973; Barber, 1976; Rosenthal & Rosnow, 1969; Rosnow & Davis, 1977; Silverman, 1977), and the reader is referred to those sources for discussions of other ways to control for subject artifacts. Orne (1969) has also used what are called *quasi-control subjects* (in addition to the usual controls) to help pinpoint the demand characteristics. The idea is to have the quasi-control subjects step out of their traditional roles and serve as "coinvestigators" rather than objects for the experimenter to manipulate. These subjects should be drawn from the same population as the other subjects, but the quasi-control subjects are then instructed to reflect clinically upon the context in which the experiment is being conducted. They also speculate on ways in which it might influence their behavior if they were in the experimental group.

There are three further possibilities when we use quasi-control subjects. One possibility is to have the experimental subjects function as their own quasi-controls. This involves eliciting from the subjects, by judicious and exhaustive inquiry in a postexperimental interview or in an interview conducted after a pilot study, their perceptions and beliefs about the experimental situation without making them unduly suspicious or inadvertently cueing them about what to say. A second possibility, called "preinquiry," uses quasi-control subjects who are told to imagine they are research subjects. Although these subjects never actually take part in the experiment, they are given the same information about the experiment that is provided the research subjects. A third possibility is to use "blind controls" who are unaware of their status, and compare their reactions with the quasi-control subjects who were told to imagine they were research subjects.

Few studies use elaborate experimental designs to tease out subject artifacts. Another procedure that is sometimes possible would be to observe the dependent variable more than once in different contexts (Rosnow & Aiken, 1973). In a study on hypnosis, the hypnotized subjects and a control group of subjects who simulated being hypnotized were given the suggestion that, for the next two days, every time they heard the word "experiment" mentioned, they would respond by touching their forehead (Orne, Sheehan, & Evans, 1968). First the researchers tested the suggestion in the original experimental setting. They then tested it when the situation was changed. They had a secretary in the waiting room confirm the time of the subject's appointment "to come for the next part of the *experiment*." Later she asked the subject if she could pay him "now for today's *experiment* and for the next part of the study tomorrow." On the following day she met the subject with the question: "Are you here for Dr. Sheehan's *experiment*?" In this way it was possible to repeatedly observe the critical response both outside and inside the laboratory setting. We know the subjects were aware of being observed, but it is assumed that they did not connect the fact of being observed by the secretary with the demand characteristics of the experimental situation. In fact, no simulating subjects responded to the secretary's suggestion in the waiting room on both days, but five out of seventeen hypnotized subjects did so. The results of this experiment thus support the hypothesis that posthypnotic behavior is not limited to the experimental setting.

NONINTERACTIONAL EXPERIMENTER EFFECTS

Where some researchers have focused on the subject's perceptions and reactions to demand characteristics, other researchers have been concerned with the types of systematic errors due to experimenter effects. One type of noninteractional effect is termed an *observer effect,* so-called because the experimenter must make provision for the careful observation and recording of the events under study. It is not always easy to be sure that one has, in fact, made an accurate observation. That lesson was first taught to us by astronomers near the end of the eighteenth century. The royal astronomer at the Greenwich

Observatory in England, a man named Maskelyne, discovered that his assistant, Kinnebrook, was consistently "too slow" in his observations of the movements of stars across the sky. Maskelyne cautioned Kinnebrook about his "errors," but the errors continued for months. Kinnebrook was fired. Twenty years later, an astronomer at Königsberg, a man named Bessel, arrived at the conclusion that Kinnebrook's "error" was probably not willful, that is, different people perceive at different speeds. Bessel studied the observations of stellar transits made by a number of senior astronomers. Differences in observation, he discovered, were the rule, not the exception (Boring, 1950). That early observation of the effects of the scientist on the observations of science made Bessel perhaps the first student of the "psychology of scientists."

A second noninteractional effect is called an *interpreter effect*. The interpretation of the data is part of the research process. A glance at any of the technical journals in behavioral science will suggest strongly that while researchers only rarely debate the observations made by one another, they often debate the interpretation of those observations. It is as difficult to state the rules for accurate interpretation of data as it is for accurate observation, but the variety of interpretations offered in explanation of the same data imply that many researchers must turn out to be wrong. The history of science generally, and the history of behavioral science more specifically, suggests that more researchers are wrong longer than they need to be because they hold their theories in too tight a grip. The common practice of "theory monogamy" has its advantages, however. It does keep researchers motivated to make more crucial observations. In any case, interpreter effects seem less serious than observer effects, because the former are public while the latter are private. Given a set of reported observations, the interpretations become generally available to the scientific community. We are free to agree or disagree with any specific interpretation. Not so in the case of the actual observations. Often those are made by a single investigator, so that we are not free to agree or disagree. We can only hope that no observer errors occurred, and we can (and should) repeat the observations where that is possible by replication.

A third noninteractional effect is called an *intentional effect*. It happens sometimes in undergraduate laboratory science courses when students "collect" and report data too beautiful to be true. (That probably happens most often when students learning science are told what results they must get to do well in the course, instead of being taught the logic of scientific inquiry and the value of being quite open-eyed and open-minded.) Unfortunately, the history of science tells us that not only undergraduates have been dishonest in science (Weinstein, 1979). Such instances do, however, seem to be rare. Nevertheless, intentional effects must be regarded as part of the inventory of the effects of investigators themselves. Recently there was the case of the late Cyril Burt. In three separate reports of more than twenty, more than thirty, and more than fifty pairs of twins, Burt reported a correlation coefficient between IQ scores of those twins, who had been raised apart, of exactly .771 for all three studies!

Such consistency of correlation would bespeak a statistical miracle if it were true (Kamin, 1974).

Intentional effects, interpreter effects, and observer effects all operate without the experimenter's influencing the subject's actual response. A powerful, necessary, though insufficient tool for the control of these effects is our awareness of them. That some of these effects are fully public events ensures that in time they may be discovered by the addition of new observations (through the process of replication) or by new theoretical insights that may focus our attention on the inconsistencies in previous data. This is also true in the case of those effects of the experimenter himself or herself (to be described next), in which the subject's behavior is directly affected.

INTERACTIONAL EXPERIMENTER EFFECTS

There are *biosocial effects* of the experimenter. The sex, age, and race of the investigator have all been found to affect the results of research. What we do not know, and what we need to learn, is whether subjects respond differently simply to the presence of experimenters varying in those biosocial attributes. It is also possible that experimenters varying in those attributes behave differently toward their subjects and, therefore, obtain different responses from them because they have, in effect, altered the experimental situation for their subjects. So far the evidence suggests that male and female experimenters conduct the "same" experiment quite differently, so that the different results they obtain may well be due to the fact that they have unintentionally conducted different experiments. Male experimenters were found in two experiments to be more friendly to their subjects (Rosenthal, 1977). Biosocial attributes of the subject can also affect the experimenter's behavior, which in turn affects the subject's responses. In one study, the interactions between experimenters and their subjects were recorded on sound films. The study found that only 12 percent of the experimenters ever smiled at their male subjects, while 70 percent of the experimenters smiled at their female subjects. Smiling by the experimenters, it was found, affected the results of the experiment (Rosenthal, 1967). The moral is clear. Before claiming a gender difference in the results of behavioral research, we must first be sure that males and females were treated identically by the experimenter. If they were not, then gender differences may be due not to constitutional or socialization factors, but simply to the fact that males and females did not in effect participate in the same experiment; that is, they were treated differently.

Psychosocial effects are a second type of interactional effect. The personality of the experimenter has also been found to affect the results of research. Experimenters who differ in anxiety, need for approval, hostility, authoritarianism, status, and warmth tend to obtain different responses from their subjects. Experimenters higher in status, for instance, tend to obtain more conforming responses from their subjects, and experimenters who are warmer in their interaction with their subjects tend to obtain more pleasant responses from their subjects. Warmer examiners administering standardized tests of intelligence are likely to obtain better intellectual performance than are cooler examiners or examiners who are more threatening or more unfamiliar to their examinees.

Situational effects constitute a third type of interactional experimenter effect. Experimenters who are more experienced at performing a given experiment obtain different responses from their subjects than do their less-experienced colleagues. Experimenters who are acquainted with their subjects obtain different responses than do their colleagues who have never met their subjects. The things that happen to experimenters during the course of their experiments, including the responses they obtain from their first few subjects, can all influence their behavior, and changes in their behavior can lead to changes in their subjects' responses. When the first few subjects of their experiments tend to respond as they are expected to respond, the behavior of the experimenters changes in such a way as to influence their subsequent subjects to respond too often in the direction of their hypothesis.

EXPECTANCY BIAS

Some expectation of how the research will turn out is virtually a constant in science, and another type of interactional effect is that which is due to the researcher's expectancy. Behavioral scientists, like other scientists generally, conduct research specifically to test hypotheses or expectations about the nature of reality. In the behavioral sciences, the experimenter's hypothesis may unintentionally influence his or her behavior toward the subjects in such a way as to increase the likelihood that they will confirm the investigator's hypothesis or expectation; this is known as an *experimenter expectancy effect* (Rosenthal, 1966). We are speaking, then, of the investigator's hypothesis as a self-fulfilling prophecy. The experimenter prophesies an event (the working hypothesis), and the expectation of the event then changes the behavior of the prophet (the experimenter) in such a way as to make the prophesied event more likely. The history of science documents the occurrence of this phenomenon with the case of "Clever Hans" as a prime example.

Hans was the horse of Mr. von Osten, a German mathematics instructor, at the turn of this century. By tapping his hoof, Hans was able to "verbalize" difficult mathematical calculations, and he spelled, read, and solved problems of musical harmony as well. A distinguished panel of scientists and experts on animals ruled that no fraud was involved. There seemed to be no cues given to Hans to tell him when to start or when to stop the tapping of his hoof. But, of course, there were cues, although it remained for Oskar Pfungst, a promising psychologist of that period, to demonstrate the fact. Pfungst, in a series of brilliant experiments, showed that Hans could answer questions only when the questioner or experimenter himself knew the answer and was within the horse's view. Pfungst learned that an unconscious forward movement of the experimenter's head was all the signal that Hans needed to start tapping. A tiny upward movement of the questioner's head or a raising of his eyebrows was the unconscious signal to Hans to stop his tapping. The questioners had expected Hans to give correct answers, and their expectancies were reflected in their unwitting signals to Hans that the time had come for him to stop his tapping. Thus the questioner's expectation became the reason for the horse's amazing abilities.

Recent experiments have shown that an investigator's expectation can also come to serve as a self-fulfilling prophecy. In one study, a dozen experimenters were each given five rats that were to be taught to run a maze. Half the experimenters were told their rats had been specifically bred for maze-bright-ness; the remaining experimenters were told their rats had been bred for maze-dullness. There were, of course, no actual differences between the rats as-signed to each of the two groups. At the end of the experiment the results were clear. Rats that had been run by experimenters expecting brighter behavior showed significantly superior learning compared to rats run by experimenters expecting dull behavior (Rosenthal & Fode, 1963). The experiment was re-peated, this time using a series of learning trials, each conducted in Skinner boxes. Half the experimenters were led to believe their rats were "Skinner box bright" and half were led to believe their rats were "Skinner box dull." Once again there were not really any differences in the two groups of rats, at least not until the end of the experiment. Then, the allegedly brighter animals really were brighter, and the alleged dullards really were duller (Rosenthal & Lawson, 1964).

REPRESENTATIVE RESEARCH DESIGN

Replicating the research with different experimenters is one way of controlling for experimenter artifacts. Replication is science's empirical system of checks and balances to expose and reduce errors of observation. Where it would appear that the error effect is mediated by demand characteristics, the controls discussed earlier in this chapter can be employed. However, let us say we wanted to test the hypothesis that men and women respond differently to an experimental treatment when the experimenter is a man as opposed to a woman. A typical design might consist of randomly assigning subjects of both sexes to a male or female experimenter whose experimental role was carefully programmed. The problem with this design is that it is only representative in the context of the selection of subjects. It is not representative as regards the stimulus, the experimenter. Since the design did not sample from among popu-lations of experimenters and situations, we would be hard pressed to say whether there is or is not a general relationship of the type hypothesized. It is possible that using other male or female experimenters would have produced quite different results, since our use of only one person of each sex as a stimulus does not preclude the possibility that some of the other characteristics of this person may have stimulus value that is unknown and uncontrolled (Maher, 1978).

There are, in other words, two principal limitations of this "single-stimulus design" (Maher, 1978). First, it is possible that obtained differences between those subjects who were exposed to the male experimenter and those who were exposed to the female experimenter may be due to the effects of uncontrolled stimulus variables. We cannot tell, based only on the information furnished by these data, whether the obtained differences are due to the validity of the tested hypothesis or to the effects of the uncontrolled variables. Second, a lack of difference between those subjects who were exposed to the male experimenter and those exposed to the female experimenter may also be due to the presence of an uncontrolled stimulus variable operating either to counteract the effect of the intended independent variable or to increase that effect artificially to a "ceiling value" (a top limit) in the different groups. Again, we have no way of distinguishing between this explanation and the possibility that the lack of difference is due to the invalidity of the tested hypothesis. To deal with these two possibilities, Egon Brunswik (1947) introduced the notion of a *representative research design*, which simply involves sampling from both subjects and stimuli. If the stimulus is a person, then no satisfactory alternatives exist to adequate sampling of stimulus persons.

EXPECTANCY CONTROL DESIGN

The logic of research design also allows us to control for an expectancy effect, using what is called an *expectancy control design* (Rosenthal, 1966). In this four-group design, the expectancy variable is permitted to operate separately from the independent variable in which the researcher is ordinarily most interested. An example is given in Table 9.1, which shows the results of a discrimination-learning experiment done by J. R. Burnham (1966).

Table 9.1 Expectancy control design used by Burnham (1966) to study discrimination learning in rats as a function of brain lesions and experimenter expectancy

(a) Brain state	(b) Expectancy		Totals
	Lesioned	Unlesioned	
Lesioned	46.5	49.0	95.5
Unlesioned	48.2	58.3	106.5
Totals	94.7	107.3	

The design of Burnham's research consisted of having twenty-three experimenters each run one rat in a T-maze discrimination problem. About half the rats had been lesioned by removal of portions of the brain. The remaining rats had received only sham surgery, which involved cutting through the skull but no damage to brain tissue. The purpose of the study was explained to the experimenters as an attempt to learn the effects of lesions on discrimination learning. Expectancies were manipulated by labeling each rat as lesioned or unlesioned. Some of the really lesioned rats were labeled accurately as lesioned but some were falsely labeled as unlesioned. Similarly, some of the really unlesioned rats were labeled accurately as unlesioned but others were falsely labeled as lesioned.

By comparing the margin totals and the differences between these totals, we get an idea of the relative effectiveness of the two manipulations: (a) manipulation of the brain state of the animals, and (b) manipulation of the experimenters' expectancies concerning the brain state of the animals. The higher the scores, the better the rats' performances are. We see that rats that had been lesioned did not perform as well as those that had not been lesioned, and we also see that rats that were believed to be lesioned did not perform as well as those that were believed to be unlesioned. What makes this experiment of special interest is that the effects of experimenter expectancy were similar to those of actual removal of brain tissue.

Table 9.2 Strategies for the reduction of experimenter expectancy effects

1. Increasing the number of experimenters
   decreases learning of influence techniques
   helps to maintain "blindness"
   minimizes effects of early data returns
   increases generality of results
   randomizes expectancies
   permits the method of collaborative disagreement
   permits statistical correction of expectancy effects

2. Observing the behavior of experimenters
   sometimes reduces expectancy effects
   permits correction for unprogrammed behavior
   facilitates greater standardization of experimenter behavior

3. Analyzing experiments for order effects
   permits inference about changes in experimenter behavior

4. Developing training procedures
   permits prediction of expectancy effects

5. Maintaining "blind contact"
   minimizes expectancy effects

6. Minimizing experimenter-subject contact
   minimizes expectancy effects

7. Employing expectancy control groups
   permits assessment of expectancy effects

If an experimenter interested in the effects of brain lesions on discrimination learning had employed only the two most commonly used conditions, the researcher could have been seriously misled by the results. Had he or she employed experimenters who believed the rats to be lesioned to run the lesioned rats and compared their results to those obtained by experimenters running unlesioned rats and believing them to be unlesioned, the experimenter would have greatly overestimated the effects on discrimination learning of brain lesions.

For investigators interested in assessing for their area of research the likelihood and magnitude of expectancy effects, there appears to be no substitute for the employment of expectancy control groups. For the investigator interested only in the reduction of expectancy effects, other strategies—such as "blind experimenters," minimized experimenter-subject contact, and even automated experimentation (Kleinmuntz & McLean, 1968; McGuigan, 1963; Miller, Bregman, & Norman, 1965; Rosenthal; 1966)—have been proposed. Table 9.2 summarizes seven strategies for the reduction of experimenter expectancy effects, and for each strategy some consequences of its employment are listed. These techniques proceed on the premise that the mediation of the experimenter expectancy effect depends to some important degree on various processes of nonverbal communication that can be controlled or circumvented (Rosenthal, 1979; Rosenthal, Hall, DiMatteo, Rogers, & Archer, 1979).

FOUR

TECHNIQUES OF DATA COLLECTION AND MEASUREMENT

Chapter **10.**   **Field, Laboratory, and Archival Observations**

Chapter **11.**   **Self-Report Data: Interviews and Questionnaires**

Chapter **12.**   **Methods of Rating Behavior**

FIELD, LABORATORY, AND ARCHIVAL OBSERVATIONS

RANGE OF PROCEDURES

When the variables under investigation cannot be manipulated in the laboratory, the method of study known as *field observation* is often used. Several major types of sampling for observational studies of social behavior have been used by researchers (Altmann, 1974). Some have involved watching and making field notes based on impromptu or extemporaneous sampling, where the observers simply recorded as much as they could. Others involved recording all occurrences of some specified behavior only during a given sample period, using tally sheets and field notes. Still others consisted of supplementing with interviews and participant observation what was observed extemporaneously, in order to reveal specific relationships and preferences. There are other approaches as well, and which approach is preferable in a given situation will depend upon the questions about behavior that the researcher is attempting to answer.

To illustrate one approach: Louise H. Kidder (1972) did a field observation study in which tape recordings, interviews, and participant observation in a hypnosis workshop were used to investigate the role interaction between the hypnotist and the person becoming hypnotized. Kidder was curious to learn how the skeptical subject, who says "How do I know if I was hypnotized?" or "I still don't consider it an experience any different from others," ends up being convinced of the reality of the power of hypnosis and the ability of hypnotists to implement and control it. She did her field observations over a three-day period while attending a workshop given for practicing psychologists who were there to learn the procedures of how to hypnotize someone. Using a tape recorder and written notes, Kidder made verbatim accounts of the interactions between hypnotists and their subjects (see examples in Table 10.1). By the end of the workshop, the skeptical subjects had become convinced that hypnosis was a real phenomenon and had also lowered their criteria for what could pass as "hypnosis."

Methods of field observation are also used by anthropologists, animal behaviorists, and comparative psychologists to investigate animal behavior in the wild. In one study, done in East Africa, the researchers patiently watched and recorded the course of actions taken by a troop of baboons when it encountered a cheetah drinking in the river (Baenninger, Estes, & Baldwin, 1975). Although other researchers had stated that adult male baboons actively defend their troops against predators (DeVore & Washburn, 1963), there were few accepted records of this behavior at the time of the study. The observations made in this study dispelled any doubts as to the reality of baboon defensive behavior. As the researchers watched, two male members of the baboon troop continued to harass the cheetah until they had successfully chased him far away from the main body of the troop.

The advantage of this approach, using a single case study, was that it looked at behavior in its usual uncontrolled natural environment. At the other extreme of observational methods are those used by operant behaviorists, who have extended the laboratory analysis of animal behavior to human situations. We noted an example of this method of study in Chapter 6, when we discussed the work of Joseph Brady using a structured environment for the experimental analysis of human behavior. This type of work, in most cases, is characterized by a degree of experimental control and objective measurement that would be impossible in a field setting or indeed in the usual laboratory experiment. This is achieved by placing human subjects within a totally programmed environment (cf. Brady & Emurian, 1979; Findley, 1966).

Between these field and laboratory extremes, there are a variety of methods of observation and data-collection procedures. The particular measurements or instruments may, in part, depend on whether our questions have to do with *events*, which are relatively instantaneous, or with *states*, which have more appreciable durations (Altmann, 1974). We can, for instance, record the course of actions of baboons chasing a cheetah (an event), or the organizational structure of a troop of baboons (a state). We can record that participants at a hypnosis workshop behaved in ways that suggest trying to be a good subject (an event), or that one participant seemed to be feeling skeptical and unsure about the power of hypnosis (a state). In this, and in following chapters, we discuss some of the major data-collection procedures that are possible in research on human behavior. Whether field or laboratory research is undertaken, the data collection must be done purposefully and systematically, in order to enhance control and precision of the observations.

Table 10.1 How skeptics became convinced of the power of hypnosis

Examples	Interpretations
Subject: The question in my mind is, how do you know if you were in a trance or not? I mean, I know I did some things, but I think they were all under conscious voluntary control.	
Hypnotist 1: This is the one question that all patients will ask . . . And they'll say, "You see, it doesn't work." I think you can tell if someone is in a trance by looking at them. . . . the facial expressions. I could walk around the room and tell who wasn't and who was, by how they responded. I thought you were, but maybe you didn't think you were.	Shows the ambiguity and the fine line between what one person calls "hypnosis" and what another calls "playing the game."
Hypnotist 2: You were actually the one that I thought went into trance the quickest. . . . The question is not were you in trance, but why did you feel compelled to do those things. And why did you follow the suggestions?	
Subject: My conscious perception was that I was kind of going along with the thing all the way. I was kind of playing the game the way it's supposed to be. I was trying to achieve something which somehow felt different from just playing the game, and as far as I was consciously aware, I didn't succeed.	
Hypnotist: Dr. Z tried to help those of you who weren't able to do the arm lift. He said, "For those for whom this was difficult, the arm can get very heavy" (so persons could let their arms go down instead of up). . . . He pointed out the successes instead of failures and gave other possibilities for achieving success.	Shows how the responsibility for "successes" and "failures" is placed on the subject rather than on the hypnotist.
Subject: You make it sound as if it's the patient's fault instead of yours if he doesn't go into trance.	
Hypnotist: Well, let me say this. Earlier hypnosis was done in an authoritarian fashion—now it is much more permissive and we conceive of hypnosis as the achievement of the subject, in which the hypnotist helps.	
Subject 1: I'm surprised, most of us don't think it's so different from other things.	Shows how the subject gives up his original idea that hypnosis is a dramatically different state of being and accepts even mildly different experiences as evidence that he was hypnotized.
Subject 2: Yes, I guess my expectations have changed. Now if I experience anything like it I'm satisfied. And I'm not sure about what the different depths means. But now if I'm under I still notice if another person comes over, but I say "I don't care."	

Source: L. H. Kidder, "On Becoming Hypnotized: How Skeptics Become Convinced: A Case of Attitude Change?" *Journal of Abnormal Psychology,* 1972, *80,* 317–322. Reprinted by permission of the author and the American Psychological Association.

ETHNOGRAPHIC FIELD WORK

When field observation is used in the study of a society's culture, the method is known as *ethnography* (since it deals with the description of a particular tribal or ethnic group). A natural unit of this type of field observation is commonly referred to as an *activity*. An activity is any intentional act or behavior or incident that is aimed at affecting the status of events. Ethnographic observation is usually addressed to such questions as: "What is happening?" and "What are the people doing?" The answers to these questions tell us the objective of the act, behavior, or incident: "They are gossiping" or "They are taking a siesta" or "They are preparing a meal."

An example of ethnography is a study done by John Beard Haviland (1977), in which he observed the various uses of gossip in Zinacantan, a small village in Mexico. Over a period of ten years, he and his family set up housekeeping from time to time in the village. Each time, he observed and tape-recorded the behavior and conversations of the villagers. Table 10.2 gives examples of those conversations, based on fragments transcribed from tape recordings or field notes. Haviland's own interpretation is also given. Based on his wide sampling of conversations such as these, Haviland was able to develop insights into Mexican village culture and to theorize on how gossip is part of a pattern of behaviors that encourages mutual spying among households at the same time that it isolates households from one another.

When making ethnographic observations, there are general questions that are useful to keep in mind (Goodenough, 1980). First, what is the *purpose* of the activity? That is, what are the goals and their justifications? In Haviland's study, several objectives of gossiping were identified, which led him to conclude that, despite fences erected between households, the people were constantly scrutinizing one another's dealings.

Second, what *procedures* are used? What are the operations performed, the media or raw materials used, the skills and instruments involved, if any? Haviland observed that the medium of gossip was word of mouth, and he carefully noted the linguistic and psychological skills required in effective gossipmongering.

Third, what are the *time and space requirements?* How much time is needed for each operation, what areas or facilities are required, and are there any obstacles in the way of the activity? Haviland noted when and where gossiping occurred, as well as what natural obstacles to the transmission of information existed.

Fourth, what are the *personnel requirements?* How many people participate, and what are their specializations if any? Haviland noted the elaborate conversational devices by which certain people in positions of authority protected themselves against charges of slander.

Fifth, what is the nature of the *social organization?* What are the categories of personnel, their rights, duties, privileges, and powers, the structure of management, and the types of sanctions used? Haviland observed how Zinacanteco

Table 10.2 Translated fragments of Zinacanteco gossip and their interpretation

Examples	Interpretations
"Didn't I hear that old José was up to some mischief?" "Perhaps, but that never became public knowledge. It was a secret affair." "The magistrate settled the whole business in private." "Yes, when a dispute is settled at the townhall, then a newspaper report goes out to every part of town . . . Ha ha ha." "Yes, then we all hear about it on the radio . . . Ha ha ha." "But when the thing is hushed up, then there's nothing on the radio. There are no newspapers. Then we don't hear about it. Ha ha ha."	Shows how some villagers even gossip about gossip.
"Is it true that old Maria divorced Manuel?" "Yes. She complained that she awoke every morning with a wet skirt. Old Manuel used to piss himself every night, just like a child." "When he was drunk, you mean?" "No, even when he was sober. 'How it stinks!' she said." "Ha ha ha. She spoke right out at the townhall."	Shows how some gossip trades on a separation, but also on a connection, between the public and the private domain.
"This is what I told him: All right, I'll see how deeply I must go into debt to take this office. But I don't want you to start complaining about it later. If I hear that you have been ridiculing me, saying things like: 'Boy, he is just pretending to be a man; he is just pretending to have money to do ritual service. He stole my office, he took it from me . . .' If you say such things, please excuse me, but I'll drag you to jail. I'll come looking for you myself. I don't want you to tell stories about me, because you have freely given me your ritual office. If there is no dispute, then I too will behave the same way. I won't gossip about you. I won't ridicule you. I won't say, for example, 'Hah, I am replacing him; he has no shame, acting like a man, asking for religious office when he has no money.' I won't talk like that. 'He wanted to serve Our Lord, but he ran away. I had to take over for him.' I won't say things like that, if we agree to keep silent about it . . ."	Shows a common theme in gossip about shady dealings and how the villagers take pains to ensure that the matter is kept quiet.

Source: J. B. Haviland, "Gossip as Competition in Zinacantan," *Journal of Communication,* 1977, *27,* 186–191. Reprinted by permission of the author and the *Journal of Communication.*

gossip was a form of behavior by which villagers managed their social faces and at the same time protected their privacy.

Sixth, what are the *occasions for performance?* When is the activity mandatory, permitted, and prohibited, and what is the relation of the initiator's role to the roles of others? Haviland noted the occasions that were most and least conducive to gossiping, and the particular role interactions of the gossipmongers within those circumstances.

In the early development of anthropology, researchers had yet to formulate a tradition of how to obtain the most objective results through ethnographic observation. This has recently led to discussions concerning the validity of seminal studies (by Margaret Mead and others) whose objectivity is now in doubt. Modern anthropologists such as Haviland frequently work in teams and also use various checks and balances to control for observer bias. They will try to establish rapport with a wide range of individuals (men and women, young and old, etc.) by framing their specific questions during interviews in a context of the indigenous folklore of the culture. They will also compare one another's observations, to ensure that the study has arrived at a sophisticated awareness of the entire culture.

OBSERVERS AS JUDGES

It often helps to use *category scales,* in the form of checklists or tally sheets, to focus our observations on specific behaviors. In developing such scales to be used in field studies, the researcher begins by defining each of the categories of behavior that is relevant as specifically as possible (based on experience in pilot studies). The next step is to decide where and when the observations will be made, and by whom. The final step before going into the field involves the selection and training of judges in the use of the scales to record the particular variables under investigation.

Such scales have also been used in a variety of other, including laboratory, settings to classify what is observed into theoretically meaningful categories. For example, Robert F. Bales (1950*a*, 1950*b*) developed a set of scales to be used by judges to categorize the behaviors of persons engaged in a small-group interaction in the lab. The particular categories chosen by Bales (which have been successfully used in the field as well) are given in Figure 10.1; also shown are the relations among them according to his theoretical model for group interaction. Through a one-way screen, trained observers record every event that occurs among several people who are brought together to have a discussion of some complex human relations problem. The observers are trained to record whether a person asks a question or answers one, gives help or withholds it, agrees or disagrees with someone, and so on. Using this approach, Bales has succeeded in identifying standard sequences when a small group of persons engages in problem-solving for a period of time. He has found, for

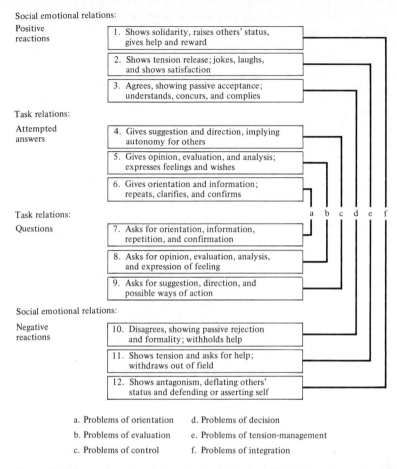

Social emotional relations:
Positive reactions

1. Shows solidarity, raises others' status, gives help and reward
2. Shows tension release; jokes, laughs, and shows satisfaction
3. Agrees, showing passive acceptance; understands, concurs, and complies

Task relations:
Attempted answers

4. Gives suggestion and direction, implying autonomy for others
5. Gives opinion, evaluation, and analysis; expresses feelings and wishes
6. Gives orientation and information; repeats, clarifies, and confirms

Task relations:
Questions

a b c d e f

7. Asks for orientation, information, repetition, and confirmation
8. Asks for opinion, evaluation, analysis, and expression of feeling
9. Asks for suggestion, direction, and possible ways of action

Social emotional relations:
Negative reactions

10. Disagrees, showing passive rejection and formality; withholds help
11. Shows tension and asks for help; withdraws out of field
12. Shows antagonism, deflating others' status and defending or asserting self

a. Problems of orientation d. Problems of decision
b. Problems of evaluation e. Problems of tension-management
c. Problems of control f. Problems of integration

Figure 10-1 Categories of socioemotional (directed at friendship and emotional needs) and task-related (directed at achieving concrete problem-solving) interactions in small groups. (*R. F. Bales, "A Set of Categories for Analysis of Small Group Interaction," American Sociological Review, 1950, 15, 257–263. Reprinted by permission of the author and the American Sociological Association.*)

instance, that there are between fifteen and twenty codable interactions a minute, about half of which are problem-solving. The remaining interactions usually consist of positive and negative reactions and questions. Giving information tends to be the most frequent behavior in the first third of a 40-minute meeting. Opinions tend to be given most often during the middle portion of a meeting, and offering suggestions is most frequent in the last third.

Other researchers have used category scales for coding active behavior as well as records of behavior. For example, David Kipnis (1976) has developed simple categories for classifying the major tactics of power that people use to influence one another, which he discovered after extensive field and laboratory research in ongoing and simulated work situations (Goodstadt & Kipnis, 1970; Grey & Kipnis, 1976; Kipnis & Cosentino, 1969). One category consists of "strong tactics," such as actively criticizing someone's point of view as foolish or childish, or getting angry at someone and demanding that the person give in. A second category includes "weak tactics," such as giving in on one issue so that the person will agree on another, or being especially sweet or helpful before bringing up some subject of disagreement. A third category, that of "rational tactics," includes stating one's point of view and letting the other person decide, or holding mutual talks without arguments. Kipnis has begun to apply these categories to an analysis of plays and literature in order to study beliefs about power based on how protagonists attempt to influence other characters. Tally sheets are used by judges to code what happens, and to identify common elements which can then be related to other literary variables in order to show how protagonists influence behavior in other characters.

CONTENT ANALYSIS

Category scales are also used in the technique known as *content analysis*. This is a multipurpose research method, based on exact counts of frequency, that permits quantification of archival or other subjective data making use of public records. Content analysis can be employed, for instance, to examine the substance of news messages or some other communications, using a set of categories that have been logically derived to describe and analyze various aspects of messages. The researcher interested in using content analysis will find extensive discussions of this method in Bernard Berelson's classic book *Content Analysis in Communication Research* (1952), in a more recent review by Ole R. Holsti in the revised *Handbook of Social Psychology* (Lindzey & Aronson, 1968–1969), and in Klaus Krippendorff's *Content Analysis* and Karl Rosengren's *Advances in Content Analysis* (both published by Sage, 1980, 1981).

A recent investigation using content analysis was that by Jack Levin and Allan J. Kimmel (1977), who employed this method to study gossip columns and "media small talk." They asked three questions: (a) What kinds of well-known people were the subject of gossip? (b) In what social contexts did this gossiping take place? (c) To what extent did gossip columns emphasize norms and values of American society? To answer these questions, they developed an elaborate coding sheet on the basis of pilot testing. They then chose a sample of gossip columns from the 1950s to the 1970s and had three judges analyze each column using the coding categories.

Each category was carefully defined, to avoid the possibility of coding errors resulting from ambiguity. For example, one category had to do with the "normative focus of the gossip." A large number of alternative possibilities were listed, and the judges were instructed to code each alternative that was discussed in a particular gossip column. They were also given specific examples to help them in deciding how to code; for instance: "If they say a target person didn't hit someone in a bar, code under *fighting and altercation* anyway, because that norm is being discussed."

With regard to the particular questions that guided the study, it was found, first of all, that for all time periods, the well-known subjects of gossiping were usually white males, of whom about two-thirds were in show business. Only a very small percentage of names were those of politicians, although this percentage increased over the years. Secondly, it was found that one-half of all the gossip directly pertained to some aspect of the occupational role of the subjects as opposed to their private lives. But the period of the mid-1970s seemed to be an especially "gossipy time," judging from the finding that small talk about the private affairs of others was so prevalent in the media. Romance and relationships, their establishment and dissolution, were also perennial favorites of the gossip columnists, although the representation of romantic tales declined from the early to the later periods. Thirdly, the findings suggested that media small talk does have a strong normative bias. Almost one-half of all gossip was centrally concerned with the prescription or proscription of some behavior or attitude.

When choosing this method of data collection, there are three points to remember (Berelson, 1954). First, it is extremely important that the analyses be consistent among judges, that is, different coders should produce the same results. If two judges are to code the normative status of gossip and they cannot agree on what constitutes "fighting and altercation," then the resulting analysis cannot be very useful. If each category and unit of analysis is carefully defined, and if the judges are adequately trained, the intercoder reliability should be satisfactorily high.

Second, it is important that the specific categories and units be relevant to the questions or hypotheses of the study. In choosing categories, it is a good idea to ask "What is the communication about?" and "How is it said?" This helps to focus our attention on the substance (the *what*) and the form (the *how*) of the subject matter. It is also well to consider several different units of analysis before settling on any one unit. For example, we might consider coding words and word compounds (or phrases), or perhaps themes (or assertions).

Third, it is important to decide on a good sampling procedure. Because content analysis is so time-consuming and expensive, we must be sure that the materials to be analyzed are representative enough to justify the effort.

DISGUISED MEASURES

In Chapter 9 we discussed a potential problem with all empirical research, which is that in the process of watching or recording an event or a state of behavior the observer may affect its course. One way that researchers deal with this problem is by concealment or deception, but that raises important ethical questions (which we discuss in a later chapter). Nonetheless, there are various *disguised measures* that researchers have used either to study behavior indirectly or to study it unobtrusively.

When we say that behavior is studied *indirectly,* we mean that the subject is aware of being observed but not of the consequences of his or her responses. A familiar example of an "indirect disguised measure" would be the Rorschach test, which is also an example of what is called a *projective test.* To "project" means to ascribe to another person one's own feelings, thoughts, or attitudes. Projection tests such as the Rorschach operate on the principle that subjects will project some unconscious aspect of their life experience and emotions onto ambiguous stimuli in the spontaneous responses that come to mind. The Rorschach consists of ten ambiguous ink blots reproduced on ten different pieces of cardboard which are presented individually to the subject in a standard sequence. The subject is instructed to look at each card as long as he or she wants and then to tell the examiner what the blot seems to represent. The examiner keeps a record of everything the subject says and also notes any peculiarities of expression or of bodily movement by the subject.

There are other types of projective tests which are also examples of indirect disguised measures. For example, there are *word association tests,* in which the subject is read a list of words and responds with the first thing that comes to mind. There are also *sentence completion tests,* where the subject responds to an incomplete sentence with whatever comes to mind ("Being with someone makes me _____ ").

When we say that behavior is studied *unobtrusively,* we mean that the measures are hidden in such a way that they do not intrude on people's awareness of being measured. For example, Lawrence S. Wrightsman (1969) counted bumper stickers and tax stickers as unobtrusive measures of attitudes and behaviors in his field observational study of "law and order" during the 1968 American presidential campaign. The major candidates that year were Nixon and Agnew on the Republican ticket and Humphrey and Muskie on the Democratic side, but there was also a third-party independent candidate, Governor George Wallace of Alabama, who campaigned using the slogan, "Law and Order." Wrightsman wondered whether supporters of Wallace were, in fact, more law-abiding than were supporters of the major-party candidates. To answer this question he decided to do a survey of motor vehicles.

Wrightsman chose to study motor vehicles because an excellent unobtrusive measure of obeying one law could be readily found in Davidson County, Tennessee. The law that drew his attention mandated that all motor vehicles carry a new tax sticker. Wrightsman and his students made a five-day survey of parking lots and simply noted for each car whether it had the county tax sticker and also whether it had a bumper sticker supporting Nixon, Humphrey, or Wallace. For a control group he used those cars without a presidential bumper sticker that were parked adjacent to the above cars. On the basis of this survey, he found that Wallace supporters obeyed the new tax-sticker law proportionately less than did supporters of either Nixon or Humphrey, or even in comparison with the control cars. He also correlated the age of the car (as an unobtrusive measure of socioeconomic status) and presence of a tax sticker, and he found almost identical rates of old Wallace cars with the tax sticker on them as new Wallace cars with the tax sticker. On the basis of this finding, he ruled out the possibility that fewer Wallace supporters displayed a tax sticker because they were poorer and less able to pay the $15 tax.

In an entertaining and important reference book entitled *Nonreactive Measures in the Social Sciences,* Eugene Webb and his coauthors (1981) have provided a veritable encyclopedia of unobtrusive disguised measures. They mention, for example, how it was possible to measure the relative popularity of children's-museum exhibits with glass fronts. This was done unobtrusively simply by dusting the glass fronts of certain exhibits each evening for noseprints. Those with more noseprints on the glass were more, or at least more closely, observed. Distance of the noseprints from the floor even provided a crude index of the ages of the viewers. Besides noseprint counting, we might keep track of the wear and tear of tiles on the floor in front of each exhibit. Other examples of unobtrusive measures would include the study of language behavior by analyzing the content of messages that people composed on floor-sample typewriters in department stores, or estimating the degree of fear induced by a ghost story by observing the shrinking diameter of a circle of seated children. Some unobtrusive measures of anxiety in airports might be gotten from records of sales at airport bars, sales of trip-insurance policies, and, of course, records of decreased sales of air travel tickets.

Whatever observational procedures we decide to use, it would be well to keep in mind the relative imprecision of behavioral science measuring instruments. In physics the galvanometer reading may reflect, almost purely, the single measure of voltage, but in behavioral science our instruments are often incapable of differentiating among any of several motives all of which might be operating at the same time. The solution to this problem is to strive for *multiple confirmation,* by using two or more independent measures of the same behavior and then comparing the results. If no single measure is very precise, it may be possible to reduce error by confronting a working hypothesis by a series of measures and then "triangulating" on the results of all of them. Once the hypothesis has been supported by two or more independent measures, it becomes more convincing, especially if it stands up to a series of imperfect measures each with their own, often unique, sources of error (Webb, Campbell, Schwartz, Sechrest, & Grove, 1981).

ELEVEN

SELF-REPORT DATA: INTERVIEWS AND QUESTIONNAIRES

NATURE OF EACH

Where we feel that persons have the language and experience to describe their own behavior, interviews and questionnaires are useful instruments for gathering data in a natural setting (Kahn & Cannell, 1965; Ruehlmann, 1977). Each has its own distinct advantages, although there is also a close resemblance between the two. The essential difference, of course, is that the interviewer asks the questions directly of the subject, while in a questionnaire the subject reads the questions.

Among the advantages of the typical interview is that it provides an opportunity to establish rapport with the respondent and to stimulate the trust and cooperation needed to probe sensitive areas. The interview provides more opportunity to help the respondent in his or her interpretation of the questions and also allows a greater flexibility in determining the wording and sequence of questions. At the same time, the typical interview allows greater control over the situation, by letting us determine on the spot the amount of probing (Gorden, 1969). The obvious danger is that this also leaves more room for experimenter bias.

A study done by Perry London (1970) and his coworkers in the 1960s illustrates how the interview can be used in the context of discovery to reveal relationships which might be further explored in a followup investigation. London was specifically interested in finding out if there were character traits associated with the extremely heroic acts of Christians who risked their lives trying to save Jews in Nazi-occupied Europe during World War II. His strategy was to seek out both the rescuers and those who had been rescued and to do tape-recorded interviews with each person. The interview schedules were constructed using general questions that allowed them to be used across several different samples in the United States and in Israel, to be coded for quantitative analysis, and to tap a number of biographical and psychological variables. The interview began in each case by asking the subject to describe, in his or her own words, the relevant incidents. The interviewer then inquired about the background events that had led up to those incidents, and he parenthetically asked about personal details, attitudes, and seemingly incidental variables needed to fill in the information the researchers were seeking about character traits. The interviewer worked with a checklist of content areas and questions, all of which had to be covered before the interview was completed, but the sequence of questions was left to the interviewer. Thus, from the respondent's point of view, much of the personal information he or she communicated was spontaneous and the interview process was friendly and informal. From the interviewer's point of view, he was able to probe sensitive areas obliquely and tactfully, yet without being secretive or deceptive and without sacrificing any questions. The results of this exploratory study suggested three hypotheses about character traits which seemed to be related to heroic behavior: a spirit of adventurousness, a strong sense of identification with a parental model of moral conduct, and a feeling of being a socially marginal individual.

The questionnaire also has its advantages. It is more convenient to use because it can be administered to large numbers of people, as in mail surveys. For this reason, the questionnaire is also more economical than the interview— the mail survey eliminates the cost of travel and travel time. The questionnaire can also allow for a type of "anonymity" not provided by the interview: instead of having the respondent confronted by the researcher in a personal interview, a self-addressed stamped envelope can be provided which is to be sent directly to some research center that has no connection with anyone the respondent knows personally (Gorden, 1969).

For example, in a study done by Conrad Smith (1980) to investigate individual factors in viewers' choices of a favorite local television news program in Salt Lake City, a mail survey was undertaken of a subsample of subjects who had previously been interviewed. The questionnaire that was mailed to these subjects asked them to describe their TV-viewing habits and preferences and also asked them to give certain biographical details which had also been asked for in the interview. In this way, it was possible to examine the consistency of each subject's answers over time. By comparing the interview responses with the questionnaire responses, results showed that the respondents answered the questions consistently over time.

Like Smith, many researchers prefer to combine the use of the interview and the questionnaire. Depending on the topic under study, it may be possible to introduce questionnaire items during the course of an interview when the questions will be better grasped by rereading them several times. Or it may be helpful to use some interviewing to supplement a questionnaire when the nature of the questions is sensitive and some personal contact is needed to elicit a full, frank response (Gorden, 1969).

A disadvantage of interviews and questionnaires is that they may encounter resistance simply from the fact that they are used so frequently by research workers. The proliferation of field research, in general, also appears to be causing people to be more selective in cooperating with researchers, particularly with those who exploit their participants merely as a means to an end. One social scientist (Lotz, 1968) has told how forty anthropologists visited a single Indian settlement in the Northwest Territories of Canada in one summer and how, on another occasion, an American psychologist nearly ended up in the river after researching the same Indians! It is important not only to keep in mind the negative attitude of some people toward surveys, but to be sensitive to the fact that each person has an individual sense of the loss of privacy and the invasion of his or her personal life. We return to this point in Chapter 14 when we discuss in detail the ethical imperatives of human behavioral research.

STRUCTURED AND UNSTRUCTURED ITEMS

Something very basic to consider when developing the interview or questionnaire is whether the items should be structured or unstructured. *Unstructured items* (also called "open-ended") are those that offer the respondents an opportunity to expand on their answers, to express feelings, motives, or behavior quite spontaneously (Campbell, 1950). "Tell me, in your own words, how you felt the day you graduated from high school"—this would be an example of an unstructured item. *Structured items* are those with clear-cut response options. An item such as the following, which was included in a questionnaire given to junior high school teachers (Baughman & Dahlstrom, 1968), would be a structured one:

> Several things help children to make good grades, of course. Some students seem to make good grades easily, but others have to work hard in order to make their grades. We are interested in knowing how much each child *tries* to do well, even though his grades may or may not be the best.
> (1) Tries very, very hard
> (2) Tries somewhat more than the average student
> (3) Tries about like the average student
> (4) Tries somewhat less than the average student
> (5) Doesn't try at all

The interviewer who uses unstructured items can rely on a tape recorder to capture verbatim the entire reply, which frees the interviewer to attend to the direction of specific questions and to visual details and impressions which can be filled in later. If a tape recorder is used in the interview, permission should be asked of the subject and the confidentiality of the interview should be

CHILD'S NAME _____ INTERVIEWER _____

DATE _____

We are interested in spending time with your four-year-old child, _____ .
We believe there are many things that children can learn when they are young. There are some
things you may be able to tell us about _____that will help us to know him (her) better.
I will be asking you about what _____ is like and some of the things he (she) may or
may not like to do.

1. Could you tell me what X is usually like?

    a. Happy_____   d. Silly _____
    b. Serious _____   e. Other _____
    c. Sad _____

2. Would you describe him (her) as:

    a. Shy _____   h. Needs encouragement _____
    b. Active _____   i. Always in a hurry _____
    c. Careful _____   j. Plays well alone _____
    d. Fearful _____   k. Would rather play by himself _____
    e. Tries things _____   l. Would rather play with others _____
    f. Shows off _____   m. Does he have to do things just right (just so)?_____
    g. Laughs a lot _____ n. Asks a lot of questions _____

3. Do you have any special concerns about X?

    a. _____

    b. _____

4. Has X had a chance to spend time doing some of these things?

    _____ a. Marking with crayon _____
    _____ b. Marking with a pencil_____
    _____ c. Cutting with scissors _____
    _____ d. Pasting _____
    _____ e. Collecting things _____
    _____ f. Working puzzles _____
    _____ g. Building with blocks or sticks _____
    _____ h. Looking at magazines or catalogs_____

5. Does anyone read story books to him (her)?_____

    (If yes) Does he (she) seem to listen? _____
    (If no) Does he (she) listen to someone tell stories?_____
    Does he (she) seem to enjoy the stories?_____
    What kind does he (she) seem to like most? _____
    Does he (she) ever tell a story that he (she) has heard?_____

    Does he (she) ever make up a story to tell?_____

    Does he (she) ever try to tell a story that he (she) has seen on television? _____

6. Does X get to play with children other than his (her) brothers and sisters? _____

7. Where does he (she) see other children? _____

8. Does he (she) get to spend much time with his (her) daddy? _____

9. Does he (she) like to:

    _____ a. Throw a ball   _____ f. Jump
    _____ b. Run   _____ g. Play games
    _____ c. Climb   _____ h. Make believe (play house, play grown-up)
    _____ d. Dance   _____ i. Other things (list)_____
    _____ e. Sing   _____

10. Does X try to help around the house or farm? _____

Figure 11-1 Example of an interview schedule. (*E. E. Baughman and W. G. Dahlstrom,* Negro and
White Children: A Psychological Study in the Rural South, *Academic Press, New York, 1968.*
Reprinted by permission of the authors and Academic Press.)

stressed. The drawbacks attendant on tape recorders include the fact that they can break, make noise, interrupt the interview, and make people unnecessarily apprehensive.

The researcher who uses an unstructured interview must also be sensitive to the subtleties of what is said in order to keep asking the right questions and keep the interview on the topic. The researcher must be careful not to let personal bias or prejudice interfere in the interviewer-respondent dialogue, or in the earlier stages of work when questions that will constitute the format of the interview are being drawn up.

For large-scale studies, in which many interviewers are required, the unstructured interview is not recommended since interviewer biases can influence the results (Pareek & Rao, 1980). It is preferable to use at least a relatively structured interview, consisting of specifically worded questions presented according to a prescribed schedule. Figure 11.1 shows what such an interview schedule might look like. This particular schedule was used by E. Earl Baughman and W. Grant Dahlstrom (1968) in a sociopsychological study in depth of children in the rural south. We see that some items are more structured than others, which is typical of many interview schedules. The more structured items are 2, 4, and 9, and the most unstructured item is 3.

DEVELOPING AN INTERVIEW SCHEDULE

There are several important objectives to keep in mind when developing the interview schedule (Gorden, 1969). The most basic is to be able to *locate the potential interviewees*. This can usually be accomplished during the initial stage of development, when the types of questions to be asked are being tested in a preselected sample. If difficulties are encountered at this point, the researcher is forewarned about what to expect and modifications can be made. A researcher who wanted to interview the "opinion leaders" in a community would have no way of knowing whether someone selected at random to be interviewed was of the type needed. It might take a long series of interviews with many randomly selected individuals to lead the researcher to the type of person that he or she wanted to locate.

A second objective is to *define categories appropriate for the answers*. Given the basic hypotheses of the study, it should be possible to examine each question or item and ask how the answers will be relevant to these hypotheses. The format of the interview may require pruning to cut superfluous or undesired items. We also do not want the interview to be too long, and 90 minutes seems to be the outermost limit before boredom sets in (Pareek & Rao, 1980).

A third objective is to *determine certain ranges of response for some items in quantitative terms*. If we want to know someone's salary, it is well to present ranges of income levels rather than require an exact amount in the answer. Different studies will require different ranges, and these can be worked out in a pilot study.

A fourth objective is to *establish the best sequence of questions*. Specific questions seem to be less affected by what preceded them than are general questions, although when specific questions have a close substantive relationship to one another there is a general strain toward consistency in attitudes (Bradburn, 1982). When sensitive topics are to be discussed, it is usually better to ask these questions at the end of the interview or to raise them parenthetically (as was done in London's study), but only after rapport has been established. Questions about a person's age, education, and income may seem like an invasion of privacy, and when asked at the beginning of an interview they can interfere with the establishment of trust. Smith asked such questions at the end of his interview, and he prefaced them by informing the subject that the information was needed in order to find out how accurately the sample represented U.S. Census estimates of the area population. He added: "Some of the questions may seem like an invasion of your privacy, so if you'd rather not answer any of the questions, just tell me it's none of my business."

A fifth objective is to *establish the best phraseology* of items. Current survey practice relies almost exclusively on *standardized questions,* so-called because they are worded in the same way for all respondents. Use of such questions is based on the assumption that the wording in which the questions are posed can be readily understood in roughly equivalent ways by all respondents. Certain verbal expressions can inhibit rapport and break down the flow of communication, while others (depending on the circumstances) can facilitate the flow of communication. During the piloting stage, it can be discovered what jargon and expressions are inhibitors and facilitators of communication in these particular circumstances. Especially important is the phraseology of the opening question, since variations in wording can affect how respondents interpret questions (Bradburn, 1982). The opening question should be clearly connected with the explanation of the interview, so that the respondent knows immediately that the interviewer is pursuing the stated purpose.

DEVELOPING A QUESTIONNAIRE

Questionnaires are among the most widely used instruments for data collection (Fear, 1978; Kahn & Cannell, 1965). As in the development of an interview schedule, the earliest stages in the development of a questionnaire will usually be exploratory, including talks with key informants to give a "feel" for the problem (Oppenheim, 1966). Pilot work is also usually required in devising the actual wording of questions, which can take several forms to help elicit specific responses. They can be yes-no, either-or, acceptable-unacceptable items. Fill-in-the-blank is another form, useful when more specific responses are sought. Of course, these structured forms are effective only if the material to be covered can be simplified to this extent.

Piloting will allow us to determine whether the items are worded properly and whether response terms like "approve" and "disapprove," "like" and "dislike" are being used as synonyms or whether there are possible differences in implication. It is possible, for example, for people to like something without approving of it or to approve of something without liking it (Bradburn, 1982). We must also be sure that the way in which the items are worded and presented does not lead the respondent into giving a particular answer. A poor question will produce a very narrow range of responses or will be misunderstood by the respondents. The question may be so vague or ambiguous that the respondents cannot answer it precisely or correctly. It may be a leading question that produces a biased answer. It may be worded in such a way as to produce a meaningless answer (Oppenheim, 1966). These flaws can often be identified by piloting the questionnaire, and they usually can be corrected simply by rewording the items.

The choice of whether to use structured or unstructured questions, or both, can also be explored in pilot work. The chief advantage of the unstructured or open questionnaire is the flexibility it gives to the respondent to let his or her thoughts roam freely and spontaneously, in the same way that an unstructured interview gives flexibility. However, while these free-response questionnaires are relatively easy to construct, many people will find them difficult to answer if they seem too wide-ranging and time-consuming (Oppenheim, 1966). Structured or closed questionnaires are, of course, easier and quicker to answer (and also easier to code). However, they leave no room for spontaneity and expressiveness, and the respondent may feel that the closed questions are forcing him or her to choose between given alternatives none of which are exactly the best ones (Oppenheim, 1966).

One way of dealing with this problem is to use a combination of both types of questions and to order them in a "funnel sequence." That means the questions begin at the most general level and narrow down to the most specific. Some researchers prefer to use open-ended items at the start of a research project, and structured items at the end when ideas are more focused. As with all instruments, it is important that whatever form and structure are chosen, the questionnaire be piloted before it is actually used to gather information. Only in this way can we make sure that it elicits the kinds of information we are seeking.

Where we are interested in gathering information with regard to specific preferences or habits, a highly structured questionnaire will be most useful. It focuses the respondent's attention on specific questions and alternatives. We want to be sure, however, that we have a sufficient number of items so as to ensure reliability. In the following chapter we discuss some examples of attitude questionnaires which use rating scales according to a standardized format. Since the reliability of such a questionnaire is defined in terms of the number and average reliability of its items, we might also reduce one threat to reliability by making our questionnaire longer and selecting items for their high interrelationships. On the other hand, very long questionnaires can tend to discourage the subjects from answering. A way around this problem is to vary the format in order to keep the subjects interested.

An example of a highly structured questionnaire with a varied format is shown in Figure 11.2. A high degree of structure was recommended in this particular case because the responses were later computerized and scaled. This questionnaire was used by Smith (1980) in his one-year-followup survey to check on the reliability of certain answers to questions used in his interview research. The questionnaire was mailed to 10 percent of the respondents who had participated in his interview study of TV news preferences among viewers in Salt Lake City. There was also a covering letter and a self-addressed stamped envelope accompanying each questionnaire. A questionnaire such as this would be piloted on samples that were similar to the one that would be used in the investigation. In this way, the ideal length, as well as the specific items to be included, can be determined empirically. Smith's questionnaire would take about 20–30 minutes to complete.

RESPONSE SETS

In Chapter 5 we discussed in detail the relational research of Crowne and Marlowe (1964) on the approval motive. Other researchers have studied the influence of a social-desirability set on the responses to standardized personality questionnaires, that is, questionnaires distinguished by the fact that there are standards for administering, scoring, and interpreting them. When the researcher finds a correlation between scores on a social-desirability scale and responses on a questionnaire, it is usually interpreted to mean that there was a tendency on the part of subjects to present themselves on the questionnaire in a more favorable light. In one early study it was found that psychiatric patients who scored high on a measure of social desirability tended to produce sentence completions that were also high in socially desirable content (Rozynko, 1950). In fact, it has long been observed that scores on a personality questionnaire are influenced by factors other than the manifest content of the items. Simply because a person responds "no" to the statement, "Once in a while I think of things too bad to talk about," does not necessarily mean that the person's thoughts are indeed pure. The term for this type of artifact is a *response set* (Cronbach, 1946, 1950).

There are several ways of dealing with response sets. One method, noted above, is the use of a scale that measures social desirability. Several such scales have been developed, including one meant to be used in survey research (Schuessler, Hittle, & Cardascia, 1978) and another to be used in a clinical setting (Larsen, Martin, Ettinger, & Nelson, 1976). By far the most popular scale is the Marlowe-Crowne, although (perhaps like all measuring instruments) it suffers from certain deficiencies. One researcher found that children who scored high on the Marlowe-Crowne seemed more interested in refraining from presenting themselves in an unfavorable light than, as is usually assumed, in wanting to project only a favorable image (Crandall, 1966). For this reason, we must be cautious about assuming that the scale is measuring only the "need

TV News Followup Questionnaire

Instructions: The questions below are similar to those you answered in 1979. Answer each question by marking an "X" in the appropriate box, or by writing a number which expresses your response to the question or statement.

The first set of questions is designed to measure your news viewing habits now compared to those you expressed in 1979. Mark an "X" in the box which describes how often, on the average, you watch each of the weekday local newscasts at six and at ten.

1. At *6 pm weekdays,* how often do you watch local news on *Channel 2* (KUTV)?

☐ Nearly every day ☐ 2 or 3 times a week ☐ About once a week ☐ 1 or 2 times a month ☐ Occasionally (less than once a month) ☐ Never

2. At *6 pm weekdays,* how often do you watch local news on *Channel 4* (KTVX)?

☐ Nearly every day ☐ 2 or 3 times a week ☐ About once a week ☐ 1 or 2 times a month ☐ Occasionally (less than once a month) ☐ Never

3. At *6 pm weekdays,* how often do you watch local news on *Channel 5* (KSL–TV)?

☐ Nearly every day ☐ 2 or 3 times a week ☐ About once a week ☐ 1 or 2 times a month ☐ Occasionally (less than once a month) ☐ Never

4. At *10 pm weekdays,* how often do you watch local news on *Channel 2* (KUTV)?

☐ Nearly every day ☐ 2 or 3 times a week ☐ About once a week ☐ 1 or 2 times a month ☐ Occasionally (less than once a month) ☐ Never

5. At *10 pm weekdays,* how often do you watch local news on *Channel 4* (KTVX)?

☐ Nearly every day ☐ 2 or 3 times a week ☐ About once a week ☐ 1 or 2 times a month ☐ Occasionally (less than once a month) ☐ Never

6. At *10 pm weekdays,* how often do you watch local news on *Channel 5* (KSL–TV)?

☐ Nearly every day ☐ 2 or 3 times a week ☐ About once a week ☐ 1 or 2 times a month ☐ Occasionally (less than once a month) ☐ Never

7. If you got conflicting or different reports of the same news story from radio, television, the magazines and the newspapers, which of the four versions would you be most inclined to believe — the one on radio or television or magazines or newspapers?

☐ Television ☐ Newspapers ☐ Radio ☐ Magazines ☐ Don't know or Not Applicable

The next set of questions is to find out how your current opinions about local TV news compare to those you expressed in 1979. Following each statement, write a number between 0 and 8 indicating the degree to which your opinion is *similar to* or *different from* the opinion expressed.

I'm the Same   0 1 2 3 4 5 6 7 8   I'm Very Different

EXAMPLE: "The local TV news helps keep me informed." . . . . _____

You would write "0" if you completely agree with this statement, because your opinion is the same. A "1" or a "2" would indicate that you mostly agree, but not completely. A "6" or "7" would indicate that you mostly *disagree,* and an "8" would mean that you completely disagree; that your opinion is very different from the one expressed.

If you have no opinion about a statement, leave the space *blank.*

Remember: the more you agree, the *smaller* the number.

8. "The news stories are pretty much the same on all three local newscasts." . . . . _____

9. "It would bother me a great deal if I had to go several weeks without seeing any local TV news." _____

10. "I watch the local TV news to help me keep up with state and local government." . . . . _____

11. "I watch the local TV news because I don't have time to read a newspaper." . . . . _____

12. "I watch the local TV news to know I'm not missing something important." . . . . _____

13. "I watch the local TV news because I feel reassured after the news is over." . . . . _____

14. "I watch the local TV news to pass the time until something better comes on TV." . . . . . . _____

15. "I watch the local TV news so I can find out what is going on and follow it up in more detail by reading the newspaper." . . . . _____

16. "I watch the local weekday TV news on the channel(s) I do because I like the newscasters on that (those) channel(s)." . . . . _____

17. "I watch the local weekday TV news on the channel(s) I do because I'm in the habit of watching that (those) channel(s)." . . . . _____

18. "I watch the local weekday TV news on the channel(s) I do because that (those) channel(s) does (do) a better job of summarizing national and international news at 10pm." . . . . _____

19. "I watch the local weekday TV news on the channel(s) I do because I like the program(s) before the news on that (those) channel(s)." . . . . _____

20. "I watch the local weekday TV news on the channel(s) I do because I like the program(s) after the news on that (those) channel(s)." . . . . _____

21. "I watch the local weekday TV news on the channel(s) I do because that (those) channel(s) has (have) the best weather news." . . . . _____

22. "I watch the local weekday TV news on the channel(s) I do because the newscasters on that (those) channel(s) seem to like each other." . . . . _____

23. "I watch the local weekday TV news on the channel(s) I do because that (those) channel(s) make(s) the news interesting to watch." . . . . _____

24. "I watch the local weekday TV news on the channel(s) I do because the newscasters on that (those) channel(s) are like my personal friends." . . . . _____

25. "I watch the weekday local TV news on the channel(s) I do because that (those) channel(s) does (do) the best job of showing pictures of the news." . . . . _____

26. "I watch the local weekday TV news on the channel(s)
I do because that (those) channel(s) does (do) a better
job of showing names and weather statistics."

27. "I watch the local weekday TV news on the channel(s)
I do because that (those) channel(s) has (have) the
best quality news."

28. "I watch the local weekday TV news on the channel(s)
I do because the newscasters on that (those) channel(s)
are good-looking people."

29. "I watch the local weekday TV news on the channel(s)
I do because the newscasters on that (those) channel(s)
speak well."

30. "I watch the local weekday TV news on the channel(s)
I do because the newscasters on that (those) channel(s)
make the news easy to understand."

The next set of questions is to find out your current opinion about how much *alike* or *different* some of the local newscasters are from each other. "0" would mean that the two newscasters are identical in terms of the qualities you consider important in a newscaster, and a "1" or a "2" would indicate that there *is* a difference in your opinion, but not a very large one. "8" would mean that, in your opinion, the two newscasters are as different as they could be.

If you are not familiar with a newscaster in the pair, leave the space *blank*.

The Same 0 1 2 3 4 5 6 7 8 Very Different

Remember: The bigger the difference (in your opinion), the *bigger* the number.

31. Patrick Greenlaw and Terry Wood . . . . _____
32. Patrick Greenlaw and Dick Nourse . . . . _____
33. Patrick Greenlaw and Shelley Thomas . . . . _____
34. Patrick Greenlaw and Bruce Lindsay . . . . _____
35. Terry Wood and Dick Nourse . . . . _____

36. Terry Wood and Shelley Thomas . . . . _____
37. Terry Wood and Bruce Lindsay . . . . _____
38. Dick Nourse and Shelley Thomas . . . . _____
39. Dick Nourse and Bruce Lindsay . . . . _____
40. Shelley Thomas and Bruce Lindsay . . . . _____

The next few questions are designed to find out how much you now enjoy watching some of the local TV news personalities. For these questions, *the scale is reversed.* The more you enjoy the newscaster, the *larger* the number. "0" would mean that you do not enjoy a particular newscaster at all, while "8" would mean that you enjoy that person very much. Because of the frequency with which channel 4 newscasters change, none are listed here.

Don't Enjoy   0 1 2 3 4 5 6 7 8   Enjoy Very
At All   Much

If you are not familiar with a particular newscaster, leave the space *blank*.

Remember: the more you enjoy the newscaster, the *larger* the number.

41. Patrick Greenlaw . . . . _____
42. Terry Wood . . . . _____
43. Mark Eubank . . . . _____
44. Bill Marcroft . . . . _____
45. Dick Nourse . . . . _____

46. Shelley Thomas . . . . _____
47. Bruce Lindsay . . . . _____
48. Bob Welti . . . . _____
49. Paul James . . . . _____

The next few questions are to find out a little bit more about you in order to compare the sample selected for the TV news survey with census figures and the results of other surveys. For each question, write in the appropriate number or mark an "X" in the appropriate box.

If you feel that any of the questions invade your privacy, leave them blank.

50. On an average day (year-around basis) about how much time do *you personally* spend watching TV (including news and entertainment programs)?

hours _____   minutes _____

51. Your sex:

Female ☐   Male ☐

52. How old were you on your last birthday?

☐	☐	☐	☐	☐	☐	☐	☐
18–24	25–34	35–44	45–54	55–64	65–74	75–84	85–95

53. What is your religious preference?

☐	☐	☐	☐	☐	☐
Catholic	Jewish	LDS	Protestant	none	other

Thank you for taking the time to fill out the questionnaire. Without the cooperation of people like you, public opinion polls would not be possible. Don't forget to mail the completed form!

Figure 11-2 Example of a highly structured mail questionnaire with a varied format. (*C. Smith, "Selecting a Source of Local Television News in the Salt Lake City SMSA: A Multivariate Analysis of Cognitive and Affective Factors for 384 Randomly-Selected News Viewers," doctoral dissertation, Temple University School of Communication, November 1980. Reprinted by permission of the author.*)

for social approval" and not the need to avoid disapproval. A further consideration is that there may be situational variables which interact with or moderate the effects of this response set. It has been found, for instance, that responding anonymously to a questionnaire sometimes tends to reduce the social-desirability response set (Thomas et al., 1979).

In personality research, researchers have developed "keys" for scoring standardized questionnaires and "lie scales" which are used to detect "faking" by the respondent (Ruch, 1942). One way to develop a "fake key" is to compare the responses of subjects who were instructed to fake with those of subjects who were instructed not to fake. We would compare the differences in responding and then construct a scoring key using this information as a guideline.

Another procedure recommended as a means of coping with social desirability is the use of forced-choice items, where the respondent is "forced" to accept some statements that are clearly unfavorable or to reject some statements that are clearly favorable. This method, which we discuss in more detail in the following chapter, is believed to reduce the social-desirability set by suppressing certain defensive tendencies on the part of the respondent.

Still another way of suppressing certain response tendencies, which is particularly relevant in the context of this and the following chapter, is to vary the direction of the statements in a personality or attitude questionnaire. This simple procedure is thought to suppress a particular response set known as *yea-saying*. It refers to the fact that some people like to answer "yes" to almost every statement or question, even to those items with which they may not agree. A famous example came to light in the 1950s, with regard to a personality questionnaire called the "F Scale" (for Fascism Scale), which was developed to study the nature of the authoritarian personality. This research was begun during the 1920s in Germany, when a group of investigators at the University of Frankfurt conducted interviews with hundreds of German citizens. The results of the interviews convinced the investigators that anti-Semitic prejudices were rife in Germany and that the explosion of fascism was imminent. When Hitler came to power, the researchers left Germany and immigrated to the United States. The investigation continued, with the emphasis now directed upon the dissection of the fascist mentality. Working at the University of California at Berkeley, the researchers developed this personality questionnaire (the F Scale) which included thirty-eight statements such as the following:

> One should avoid doing things in public which appear wrong to others, even though one knows that these things are really all right.
> No insult to our honor should ever go unpunished.
> It is essential for learning or effective work that our teachers or bosses outline in detail what is to be done and exactly how to go about it.

Such statements were thought to go together to form a syndrome of behavior that renders the person receptive to antidemocratic propaganda (Adorno,

Frenkel-Brunswik, Levinson, & Sanford, 1950). This authoritarian personality was also seen as having a strong need to align himself or herself with authority figures and protective ingroups, a strong sense of nationalism, rigid moralism, definiteness, and a strong tendency to perceive things in absolutes, that is, as all good or all bad. Other psychological tests, including the Rorschach, were brought in to flesh out the authoritarian personality.

Although this is regarded as one of the most influential studies done in social psychology, it turned out that there were serious problems with the research. One problem concerned the "unidirectional wording" of the items making up the F Scale. They had been written in a way that only by disagreeing with a statement could you obtain a completely nonauthoritarian score. But some amiable, obliging souls, who were not the least bit authoritarian, liked to say "yes" to every statement. In other words, the F Scale probably measured two distinct but not readily distinguishable character traits, authoritarianism and the agreeing response set (Couch & Keniston, 1960). To remedy this problem, what was necessary was simply to vary the direction of the statements. Both positive and negative statements would have to be interspersed, preferably in a random sequence. Thus, to obtain a completely nonauthoritarian score would require that the subject agree with some statements and disagree with others.

Response sets can also pose a problem in interview research. Studies have shown that responding is apt to be in a socially desirable direction when the subject and the interviewer are of the same race and social class (Dohrenwend, 1969; Dohrenwend, Colombotos, & Dohrenwend, 1968). The interaction then seems to take on the character of a polite social exchange, in which the subject only says what is socially desirable rather than revealing what is accurate but not desirable. The way to avoid this problem seems to be to use interviewers who have a friendly but professional demeanor rather than those who are overly solicitous (Weiss, 1970).

TWELVE

METHODS OF RATING BEHAVIOR

NATURE OF RATING SCALES

In Chapter 10 we discussed certain types of category scales, which require an observer to use a checkoff sheet with which to classify behaviors. The observer who works with category scales is a classifier and not an evaluator, in that no assessment is made as to whether one behavior is more appropriate, more effective, etc., than another. The observer reads, listens to, or watches something and then classifies it as accurately as possible. However, of all the different methods of measuring or recording aspects of behavior, the most popular are *rating scales*. The observer who works with rating scales is an evaluator who does not merely classify or count frequencies, but gives a numerical value to certain judgments or assessments.

In this chapter we describe some of the major types of rating scales used in behavioral science. Rating scales can be used in many ways and in many different situations. For instance, they might be used in field observational research to evaluate the quality of some experience or activity. They might be used in a questionnaire or as part of a structured interview to provide an assessment of the subject's self-perceptions. Whatever objectives they may be designed to accomplish, they usually take one or a combination of three basic forms: numerical, forced-choice, and graphic.

The *numerical scale* represents one basic form. It is distinguished by the fact that the raters work with a sequence of defined numbers. The numbers may be quite explicit, as in the following example which was taken from a behavior rating scale for adolescents (Baughman & Dahlstrom, 1968):

How popular is each of your classmates?
(1) Extremely popular
(2) Above average
(3) About average
(4) Below average
(5) Quite unpopular

Other numerical scales carry no numbers, although they are implicit, for example:

Do you feel that a large-scale civil defense program would tend to incite an enemy to prematurely attack this country, or do you feel that such a program would lessen the chances of an enemy attack?
(Check one)
____It would considerably increase the chance of an enemy attack
____It would somewhat increase the chance of an enemy attack
____It would neither increase nor decrease the chance of an enemy attack
____It would somewhat decrease the chance of an enemy attack
____It would considerably decrease the chance of an enemy attack

In both examples above, the questions and alternative responses are written in simple, straightforward language. It is very important that statements such as these not be ambiguous or complexly worded, for that asks the respondent to provide a unidimensional response to a multidimensional question— quite impossible! In the second example, note that the middle alternative ("neither increase nor decrease") represents something like indifference. In general, the practice in survey research has been to omit middle categories, to try to push respondents to one or the other side (Bradburn, 1982).

These numerical scales are also among the easiest to construct and to use, and the simplest in terms of data analysis (Guilford, 1954). However, it is believed that they are more vulnerable to many biases and errors than other forms that have been specifically developed to overcome some of those problems. An item asking "How popular is each of your classmates?" and giving five alternative possibilities ranging from "quite unpopular" to "extremely popular" may be vulnerable to a particular type of response set known as the *halo effect*. This type of error refers to the fact either that a judge who forms a favorable impression of someone with regard to some central trait will then tend to paint a rosier picture of the person on other characteristics, or that, having knowledge of some previous outstanding performance (positive or negative) or trait, this knowledge influences one's current rating of the ratee for the better or the worse. That is, because we tend to judge a person in terms of a general mental attitude toward him or her, this "halo" will influence our opinions about specific qualities of the individual. For example, a student who was athletic or good-looking might be judged as more popular than was really the case. The halo effect is most prevalent when the trait or characteristic that is being rated is not easily observable, is not clearly defined, involves reactions with other people, and is of some moral importance (Symonds, 1925).

A second basic form, which was specifically developed to overcome the halo effect, is the *forced-choice scale,* briefly mentioned in the preceding chapter. (Readers interested in other plausible sources of the halo effect and other methods used to reduce halo will find a detailed discussion in Cooper, 1981.) An example of a forced-choice scale would be one that presented two equally favorable statements about someone, and asked the rater to choose only one of the statements to describe that person: "X is energetic" and "X is intelligent." The rater is "forced" to say whether person X has more of one trait than another of this pair. The theory behind this procedure is that if the judge is dominated by a desire to make the person "look good" and to avoid making him or her "look bad," the judge would simply pile up favorable ratings using a numerical scale. In using the forced-choice procedure it is thought that the judge is likely to mark the irrelevant traits as often as the relevant ones, since there is no inkling as to which favorable and unfavorable traits receive weight toward the score.

There are a number of variations on the forced-choice rating scale. One form that has been found to be most popular with raters and that also gives the highest validity consists of four items or statements, all favorable to the person being rated, and the rater must select the two that are more descriptive (Guilford, 1954). The forced-choice method also has liabilities, however. It is time-consuming, and it is sometimes resisted by subjects who object to being "forced" to make a choice between equally favorable or equally unfavorable alternatives (Cronbach, 1960).

A third basic form is the *graphic scale,* usually a straight line resembling a thermometer and presented either horizontally or vertically:

Extremely unpopular	About average	Extremely popular

One type of graphic scale is divided into segments, as in the following 7-point graphic scale:

Unpopular ＿＿ : ＿＿ : ＿＿ : ＿＿ : ＿＿ : ＿＿ : ＿＿ Popular

In choosing *anchor words,* such as "extremely unpopular" and "extremely popular," we try to select terms or short statements that are simple, unidimensional, and unambiguous. The anchor words should be clearly relevant to the behavior or variables being rated and consistent with other cues. Figure 12.1 shows a "mood questionnaire" that was based on the graphic type of rating scale, in which the same anchor words are relevant for all eight variables. It is also important that anchor words be as precise as possible and that they stay

Indicate the way you feel *now* by placing a check mark in the appropriate place.

	Not at all		A little		Quite a bit		Extremely
	1	2	3	4	5	6	7
Jittery	_____	_____	_____	_____	_____	_____	_____
Depressed	_____	_____	_____	_____	_____	_____	_____
Troubled	_____	_____	_____	_____	_____	_____	_____
Shaky	_____	_____	_____	_____	_____	_____	_____
Unhappy	_____	_____	_____	_____	_____	_____	_____
Excitable	_____	_____	_____	_____	_____	_____	_____
Downhearted	_____	_____	_____	_____	_____	_____	_____
Anxious	_____	_____	_____	_____	_____	_____	_____
	1	2	3	4	5	6	7
	Not at all		A little		Quite a bit		Extremely

Figure 12-1 A "mood questionnaire" that was based on the graphic type of rating scale. (*Rosnow, 1968.*)

clear of expressions with ethical or moral connotations, in order to avoid a social-desirability response set.

ERRORS AND THEIR CONTROL

The use of rating scales proceeds on the assumption that the person doing the rating is capable of some degree of precision and objectivity. However, our discussion of artifacts (in Chapter 9) and of response sets such as "yea-saying" (Chapter 11) and the halo effect should make us alert to the many sources of personal bias that the human observer brings to the rating situation. J. P. Guilford (1954) has noted other errors which also need to be controlled.

There is the *error of leniency,* named from the fact that observers will tend to rate someone who is very familiar, or someone with whom they are ego-involved, more positively than they should. (Some people who are aware of this failing will "lean over backwards" and rate the person more negatively than they should, thus making the opposite type of error.) When we anticipate the leniency error, a way to help counteract it is to arrange the scale differently. We might give only one unfavorable cue word ("poor") and have most of the range given to degrees of favorable responses ("fairly good," "good," etc.):

Poor	Fairly good	Good	Very good	Excellent

However, we treat or analyze the verbal labels numerically such that "good" is only a 3 on a 5-point scale.

Another type is called the *error of central tendency.* It occurs when the observer hesitates to give extreme ratings and instead tends to rate in the direction of the mean of the total group. This can also be counteracted in the way that the positive range was expanded in the sample shown above. Thus, in a numerical or a graphic scale, it is usually a good idea to allow for one or two more points than are absolutely essential. If it is essential, for instance, that we have at least five alternative responses, then it would be better to use a 7-point than a 5-point rating scale, since people are reluctant to use the extremes.

Still another type is called a *logical error in rating*. It refers to the fact that judges are likely to give similar ratings for variables or traits that seem logically related in the minds of the judges but may not be related in any given target person. This "logical error" is similar to the halo effect, in that both increase the intercorrelation of the variables or traits being rated. The difference is that the halo effect results from the observer's favorable attitude about one personality as a whole, whereas the logical error results from the observer's perception as to the relatedness of certain variables or traits irrespective of individuals.

There are other possibilities as well (see Cooper, 1981; Guilford, 1954). The most effective method for improving ratings in light of all these potential errors is to use multiple observers who have been very carefully trained, and then to pool their ratings by using the mean ratings within categories. Observers who have been lectured on rating errors will be more sensitive to the different kinds of biases and should also be mindful about how they respond. Training that includes practice sessions followed by discussions of each possible error will teach the observers what to watch for and how to be more precise and objective in their evaluations.

THE SEMANTIC DIFFERENTIAL

Among the major rating scales in actual use, the *semantic differential* is one popular type. It was developed by Charles E. Osgood and his coworkers, based on the graphic type of scale, to measure the subjective (or connotative) meaning of any given stimulus (Osgood, Suci, & Tannenbaum, 1957). It is also used in marketing research and in the measurement of attitudes with regard to particular social stimuli (Brinton, 1961; Oskamp, 1977; Triandis, 1964).

The semantic differential typically consists of a set of 7-point scales which are anchored at each end by pairs of adjectives, such as bad-good, tense-relaxed, stingy-generous, and so on. The particular adjectives are chosen on the basis of the underlying dimensions of meaning that are of interest to the researcher. The three usually of interest are the *evaluative dimension* (bad-good, unpleasant-pleasant, negative-positive, ugly-beautiful, cruel-kind, unfair-fair), the *potency dimension* (weak-strong, light-heavy, small-large, soft-hard), and the *activity dimension* (slow-fast, passive-active, calm-excitable). It was these three dimensions that Osgood and his collaborators repeatedly found to be the fundamental ones. Most researchers simply employ the pairs of adjectives used in the studies of Osgood and his coworkers, although a more rigorous approach would require them to choose the particular adjectives on the basis of those which best represent statistically determined dimensions that underlie the domain of interest to them. The behavior or concept to be evaluated is given at the top of the page, and the subject judges it against each successive scale by putting a check mark in the appropriate position. Numbers are then assigned to the ratings, e.g., +3 extremely good, +2 quite good, +1 slightly good, 0 equally good and bad or neither, −1 slightly bad, −2 quite bad, and −3 extremely bad.

This basic procedure has been put to a wide range of uses (cf. Snider & Osgood, 1969). One of Richard Nixon's first moves in putting together a team for the 1968 presidential campaign was the appointment of advertising researchers who traveled all through the country asking people to evaluate the presidential candidates on the semantic differential scale. Joe McGinniss (1969), in his book *The Selling of the President,* tells how the researchers had plotted the "Ideal Presidential Curve," which was the line connecting the points that represented the average rating in each category as applied to the ideal, and had then compared this profile with the plotted curves for Nixon, Hubert Humphrey, and George Wallace. The gaps between the Nixon profile and the "ideal line" represented the personality traits that Nixon should try to improve. It was considered especially important that he close the "personality gap" between himself and Humphrey.

The semantic differential is also used to establish group profiles to show how stereotypes (the "pictures in our heads") appear. Figure 12.2 shows two such profiles that were gotten by connecting the points that represented the

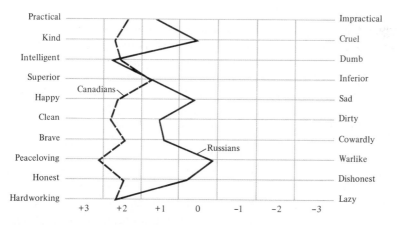

Figure 12-2 Profiles for Canadians (dashed line) and Russians (solid line) in a sample of 132 Canadian ninth-graders. (*J. G. Snider, "Profiles of Some Stereotypes Held by Ninth-Grade Pupils,"* Alberta Journal of Educational Research, *1962, 8, 147–156. Adapted by permission of the author and the journal editor.*)

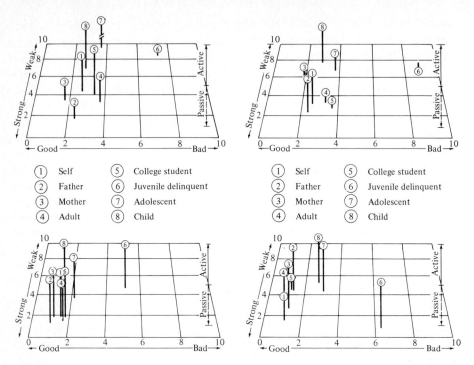

Figure 12-3 Actual (top) and ideal (bottom) locations of eight role concepts on three semantic dimensions for males (left) and females (right). The three dimensions are the evaluative (bad-good), the potency (weak-strong), and the activity (passive-active). (*C. J. Friedman and J. W. Gladden, "Objective Measurement of Social Role Concept via the Semantic Differential,"* Psychological Reports, *1964, 14, 239–247. Reprinted by permission of the authors and the journal editor.*)

average ratings of 132 Canadian boys and girls during the early 1960s (Snider, 1962). It is not surprising that the children rated their own Canadian culture more favorably than they did the Russian culture, since there is usually a tendency to hold a more favorable stereotype of our own culture.

Other pictorial representations are also possible, for example, that in Figure 12.3 which shows a three-dimensional representation of eight role concepts (self, father, mother, adult, college student, juvenile delinquent, adolescent, and child) that were rated by male and female college students. The instructions to the raters were first to evaluate the concepts "as you *actually* think they are, in terms of the meanings they have for you" (the two diagrams at the top of Figure 12.3) and then to rate each concept "on the basis of how it should *ideally* be, the way it is supposed to be as opposed to how it actually is" (the two figures at the bottom). The subjects were also told that this was not a test and, therefore, there were no "right" or "wrong" answers (Friedman & Gladden, 1964). The pictorial representations reveal differences in spatial relationships but also similarities. We see, for instance, the general clustering on the left side with the lone role number 6 ("juvenile delinquent") on the right; the roles "self" and "college student," which were perceived as somewhat weaker in actuality by men than by women; the role of "father," which was perceived to be stronger, ideally, by men than by women. The researchers theorized that these differences were due to the influence of learned expectancies regarding role attitudes—an interesting though speculative interpretation for further investigation.

THE Q-SORT

The scales discussed so far are designed to study groups *or* individuals. Another major rating scale is the *Q-sort,* which was developed by William Stephenson (1953) specifically to study a single or a few individuals at a time. (The scale takes its name from a type of statistical design.) The procedure has been shown to be particularly useful in personality assessment; for example, to arrive at a comprehensive picture of a person's attitudes, strengths, and weaknesses.

The Q-sort calls for the preparation of a set of stimuli (phrases, pictures, or statements) covering some aspect of behavior or personality. The stimuli usually differ from one study to the next, depending on the particular aspect of behavior under investigation. Each stimulus appears on a separate card, and the subject's job is to sort through the cards and place them into one of a number of different piles to resemble a "bell-shaped" curve. The sorting procedure might be seen as a variation on the forced-choice rating scale, since all the cards have to be used and only so many cards are allowed to be placed in each pile. The number of piles, and the number of cards that are allowed in each pile, is determined according to a formula discussed by Stephenson (1953). For instance, if there were eighty cards, then they would be sorted into eleven piles:

Pile number	11	10	9	8	7	6	5	4	3	2	1
Number of cards	2	4	6	9	12	14	12	9	6	4	2

If there were ninety-eight cards, they would be sorted into thirteen piles:

Pile number	13	12	11	10	9	8	7	6	5	4	3	2	1
Number of cards	2	4	6	8	10	12	14	12	10	8	6	4	2

As an example, Stephenson (1980) had children sort through forty-eight pictures of different faces. They were told to decide which *two* photos they liked *most* and to put them in the extreme favorable pile, and then to decide which *two* they liked *least* and to put them in the extreme unfavorable pile. They then decided which *four* photos they liked *next most* and put them in the corresponding pile, and which *four* they liked *next least,* and so on. In this case there were nine piles which were scored from -4 to $+4$:

Pile number	9	8	7	6	5	4	3	2	1
Number of photos	2	4	5	8	10	8	5	4	2
Score	-4	-3	-2	-1	0	$+1$	$+2$	$+3$	$+4$

To analyze the results, we might compute the median position of a particular subset of pictures. We might also compute a correlation showing how similar one rater is to another in their evaluations. When the Q-sort is used in assessing personality dynamics, statements are prepared covering dozens of aspects of behavior. The statements are then judged as fitting or not fitting the individual. A correlation is computed on the scores of each statement to see how closely the descriptions of the two raters correspond (Cronbach, 1960). The Q-sort has some advantage over the usual rating form, since the sorter can shift cards back and forth, and the fixed distribution eliminates some rater differences in sorting style, such as yea-saying. However, the use of this technique also requires a word of caution, since spurious results due to an overestimation of the correlation coefficient can result when stimuli are already inherently correlated. For discussions of this problem, the interested reader should refer to Sundland's article (1962) and Stephenson's reply (1963).

THE LIKERT SCALE

Rating procedures are also employed in the development of standardized attitude questionnaires, such as those used to describe people's evaluations in terms of a unidimensional scale. One popular approach is based on a method known as *summated ratings*, which was developed by Rensis Likert (1932) to produce what has been dubbed a "Likert scale." It is essentially a type of numerical rating scale, in that numbers are associated with five response alternatives ("strongly agree," "agree," "undecided," "disagree," "strongly disagree") to statements that are easily classifiable as favorable or unfavorable.

The first step in constructing a Likert scale is to gather a large number of statements on the issue in question. These are given to a sample of subjects from the target population, who indicate their evaluations by means of the 5-point rating scale. A technique called *item analysis* is then used to sort through the data in order to select the best statements for the final scale. It consists of calculating the extent to which the responses to individual statements are correlated with the total score (the sum of all the items), and statements that correlate well are then chosen for the final scale. The reasoning is that statements that have low correlations with the total score will not be good at discriminating between those respondents with positive attitudes and those with negative attitudes.

A questionnaire that was developed along these lines is shown in Figure 12.4 (Mahler, 1953). This is a 20-item Likert scale with a very high split-half

Please indicate your reaction to the following statements, using these alternatives:

> Strongly Agree = SA   Disagree = D
>
> Agree = A   Strongly Disagree = SD
>
> Undecided = U

*1 The quality of medical care under the system of private practice is superior to that under a system of compulsory health insurance.

SA A U D SD

2 A compulsory health program will produce a healthier and more productive population.

*3 Under a compulsory health program there would be less incentive for young people to become doctors.

4 A compulsory health program is necessary because it brings the greatest good to the greatest number of people.

*5 Treatment under a compulsory health program would be mechanical and superficial.

6 A compulsory health program would be a realization of one of the true aims of a democracy.

*7 Compulsory medical care would upset the traditional relationship between the family doctor and the patient.

*8 I feel that I would get better care from a doctor whom I am paying than from a doctor who is being paid by the government.

9 Despite many practical objections, I feel that compulsory health insurance is a real need of the American people.

10 A compulsory health program could be administered quite efficiently if the doctors would cooperate.

11 There is no reason why the traditional relationship between doctors and patient cannot be continued under a compulsory health program.

*12 If a compulsory health program were enacted, politicians would have control over doctors.

*13 The present system of private medical practice is the one best adapted to the liberal philosophy of democracy.

14 There is no reason why doctors should not be able to work just as well under a compulsory health program as they do now.

15 More and better care will be obtained under a compulsory health program.

*16 The atmosphere of a compulsory health program would destroy the initiative and the ambition of young doctors.

*17 Politicians are trying to force a compulsory health program upon the people without giving them the true facts.

*18 Administrative costs under a compulsory health program would be exorbitant.

*19 Red tape and bureaucratic problems would make a compulsory health program grossly inefficient.

*20 Any system of compulsory health insurance would invade the privacy of the individual.

Figure 12-4 Example of a Likert scale that was developed to measure attitudes toward socialized medicine. (*I. Mahler, "Attitudes Toward Socialized Medicine," Journal of Social Psychology, 1953, 38, 273–282. Reprinted by permission of the author and The Journal Press.*) Asterisk indicates negative items whose weights must be reversed for purposes of scoring. The same response alternatives are used with all items.

reliability. As regards validity, the scale has been found to predict known groups (106 Stanford University students with positive and negative attitudes about socialized medicine, as established by interviews). In scoring the scale, response alternatives for the pro-socialized-medicine statements are weighted from 4 ("strongly agree") to 0 ("strongly disagree"). For the anti-socialized-medicine statements (marked by an asterisk), the weighting is reversed. A person's score is the sum of the weighted responses, with a high score indicating a positive attitude toward socialized medicine.

THE THURSTONE SCALE

Another approach to attitude scaling is based on the *method of equal-appearing intervals*, developed by L. L. Thurstone (1929). The name derives from the assumption that the judges, who are asked to sort statements in different piles, can keep the intervals between piles psychologically equal. It is one of several methods devised by Thurstone, although this particular one is often called the "Thurstone scale."

The procedure again begins with a large number of statements, but this time each statement is typed on a separate slip of paper or index card. Judges (not the subjects to be tested later) then sort the statements into eleven piles, num-

The following statements express opinions about divorce. Please indicate your agreement or disagreement with each of the statements by marking them as follows:

(✓) Mark with a check if you agree with the statement.

(✗) Mark with a cross if you disagree with the statement.

Scale Value		
3.7	1	Divorce is justifiable only after all efforts to mend the union have failed.
6.6	2	Present divorce conditions are not as discreditable as they appear.
8.5	3	If marriage is to be based on mutual affection, divorce must be easy to obtain.
1.6	4	Divorce lowers the standards of morality.
.5	5	Divorce is disgraceful.
8.4	6	Divorce is desirable for adjusting errors in marriage.
4.8	7	Divorce is a necessary evil.
9.8	8	Divorce should be granted for the asking.
6.2	9	A divorce is justifiable or not, depending on the wants of the persons involved.
10.1	10	A person should have the right to marry and divorce as often as he or she chooses.
.5	11	Divorce is never justifiable.
8.8	12	Easy divorce leads to a more intelligent understanding of marriage.
3.3	13	Divorce should be discouraged in order to stabilize society.
5.8	14	The evils of divorce should not prevent us from seeing its benefits.
9.4	15	The marriage contract should be as easily broken as made.
.8	16	The best solution of the divorce problem is never to grant divorce.
1.2	17	Lenient divorce is equivalent to polygamy.
7.1	18	Divorce should be permitted so long as the rights of all parties are insured.
4.2	19	Divorce should be discouraged but not forbidden.
.8	20	Divorce is legalized adultery.
3.8	21	Long and careful investigation should precede the granting of every divorce.
8.1	22	Permanence in marriage is unnecessary for social stability.

Figure 12-5 Example of a Thurstone equal-appearing-interval scale that was developed to measure attitudes toward divorce. (*After Shaw & Wright, 1967; L. L. Thurstone,* The Measurement of Social Attitudes, *University of Chicago Press, Chicago, Ill., (C) 1931. Reprinted by permission of the University of Chicago Press.*) In actual practice the scale values would not be shown on the questionnaire that was administered to subjects.

bered from 1 ("most unfavorable statements") to 11 ("most favorable statements"). Unlike the Q-sort, the judges in this case are allowed to place as many statements as they wish in any pile. A scale value is calculated for each statement, which is simply the median of the responses of all judges to that particular item. In selecting statements for the final Thurstone scale, we choose those (a) that are most consistently rated by the judges and (b) that are spread relatively evenly along the entire attitude range.

A Thurstone scale that was constructed in this way is shown in Figure 12.5. This is a 22-item questionnaire with high test-retest reliability (Thurstone, 1931). Although this early scale of attitudes toward divorce contains items relevant to the issue today, with the passage of time the original scale positions might be expected to change. Thus the scale values shown in Figure 12.5 were more recently obtained from a sample of twenty-six graduate students in social psychology courses at the University of Florida (Shaw & Wright, 1967). In scoring this scale, the person's total score would be the median of the scale values of items checked to indicate agreement—with a high score indicating a favorable attitude toward divorce.

The researcher who uses a one-dimensional attitude scale to predict behavior must be mindful of the fact that there is not always a reliable positive correlation between people's beliefs and their subsequent behavior in a given situation. In Chapter 10 we discussed Wrightsman's (1969) "law and order" study in which he observed that the law-and-order automobile drivers were also the least likely to obey the new tax-sticker law. That does not mean, however, that we should expect a negative correlation between people's attitudes and their public behavior. A public identity is not only determined by what a person would like to do, but also by what the person thinks is required and by the expected consequences of the behavior (Triandis, 1971). Many researchers feel that it is necessary to use a multidimensional attitude scale as opposed to the unidimensional scales given as illustrations of the Likert and Thurstone techniques. Thus they argue that if we want to know what a person thinks, we had best measure the cognitive component. If we want to know how a person feels about something, then it would be preferable to measure the affective, or evaluative, component. However, if we want to know how the person will behave, we should measure the conative, or action potential, component, since behaviors can best be predicted from recently expressed intentions (Fishbein & Ajzen, 1975; Kothandapani, 1971). Some prefer to use the semantic differential, since it is a multidimensional rating scale, while other researchers choose the more traditional Likert or Thurstone scales but then give careful attention to several variables when analyzing the results.

FIVE

IMPLEMENTATION OF THE RESEARCH

Chapter **13.** **The Selection of Participants**

Chapter **14.** **Ethics and Values in Human Research**

Chapter **15.** **Practices and Limitations of Research**

THIRTEEN

THE SELECTION OF PARTICIPANTS

THE PARADOX OF SAMPLING

If we want to know whether a word has been used properly, we look in the dictionary. However, the dictionary is based on how words are in fact used. This situation is known as the "paradox of usage" (Kaplan, 1964); it means that the usage of words is validated by a method that is based on how the words are actually used!

There is a comparable situation in behavioral research, known as the "paradox of sampling" (Kaplan, 1964). It refers to the fact that the appropriateness of a sample is also validated by the method used to arrive at it. For instance, in market research or opinion polling, the researchers determine the characteristics of a population based on a survey sample. This sample, were it *not* representative of its population, would be of little use to the researchers. To know for sure that the sample is representative would, however, require a thorough knowledge of the population. In that case, the researchers would have no need of a sample!

Instead we use what is called a *sampling plan* to validate the appropriateness of the sample. A sampling plan is essentially a design, a scheme of action, or any such procedure that specifies how the participants are to be selected. To maximize the chances that a sample is representative of its population, a sampling plan would specify that there will be no preferential selection of participants who are different from the rest of the population in any way related to the variables or problems under investigation. Sampling plans similar to those used in market research and opinion polling also find applications in other areas, for instance, the selection of items to be included in a test or the selection of participants for an experiment. In this chapter we discuss several kinds of sampling plans that are possible in descriptive, relational, and experimental research.

REQUIREMENTS OF SURVEY SAMPLING

In deciding on a specific plan to use when doing a survey, there are practical considerations to weigh, such as the kinds of resources that are available. There are also two important statistical requirements of sampling plans.

One of these is that the sample values be *unbiased*. This means that they do not differ from the corresponding values in the population being studied. We say that a sampling plan is "acceptably free from bias" if it is a *probability sample*. In probability sampling every element in the population has a known probability of being selected. This probability is determined through some process of random selection, and the most basic selection process is known as *simple random sampling*.*

There are several modifications of simple random sampling, including stratified random sampling and cluster sampling, which are also types of probability sampling. In the following pages we discuss the nature of each of these types, although there are others as well which are used in field research (see Kish, 1965).

In addition to being free from bias, another statistical requirement of a sampling plan is *stability* in its samples. This means that all samples produced by the same sampling plan will yield essentially the same results (Kaplan, 1964). Instability usually results when the sample size is too small, even if the sample has been chosen without bias. Previously we discussed the nature of precision in measurement and in research design (see Chapter 7). A sample would be too small if its results also were not precise enough in terms of the research aims, and it would be too large if the results were more precise than was warranted by their likely uses ("pointless precision"). In general, it can be said that, for any given degree of precision, the more essentially alike (*homogeneous*) the members of the population, the fewer of them need to be sampled. The more unlike (*heterogeneous*) they are, the more sample cases that will be needed (Kish, 1965).

SIMPLE RANDOM SAMPLING

This simplest type of probability sampling is distinguished by the fact that we select the sample elements from a table of random digits, such as that shown in Appendix B. Let us say that we want to select ten men and ten women individually at random from a population totaling ninety-six men and ninety-nine women. To show how to develop this simple random sample we refer to Table 13.1, which reprints a portion of the more complete table of random digits in the appendix.

---

* As we shall see, however, this does not mean that generalization of the results of behavioral research is achieved because investigators *always* draw random samples; in fact, most research (particularly experimental) is done using nonrandom samples.

Table 13.1 Random digits

00000	10097	32533	76520	13586	34673	54876
00001	37542	04805	64894	74296	24805	24037
00002	08422	68953	19645	09303	23209	02560
00003	99019	02529	09376	70715	38311	31165
00004	12807	99970	80157	36147	64032	36653
00005	66065	74717	34072	76850	36697	36170
00006	31060	10805	45571	82406	35303	42614
00007	85269	77602	02051	65692	68665	74818
00008	63573	32135	05325	47048	90553	57548
00009	73796	45753	03529	64778	35808	34282

Note: The left-hand column is for reference only, while all the other columns and numbers are random digits.

We begin by numbering the men in the population consecutively from 01 to 96 and the women in the population consecutively from 01 to 99. We are now ready to use the random digit table. In any use of such a table, we only use the random digits and not the reference numbers in the left-hand column (numbered from 00000 to 00009), which are there to help us identify particular lines. We do the random sampling by putting our finger blindly on some starting position. Suppose we put our finger on the first 5-digit number on line 00004— that would be 12807. We will read across the line two digits at a time, then across the next line, and so on, until we have chosen individually at random the ten male subjects. We do the same thing, beginning at another blindly chosen point, until we have chosen the ten female subjects. Thus, beginning with the number 12807, we would select persons numbered 12, 80, 79, etc.

There are two variations of this procedure, either of which is acceptable from the point of view of random selection. In one variation, known as "sampling with replacement," the selected names are placed in the selection pool again and may be reselected on subsequent draws. Tossing a coin would also be sampling with replacement, in this case from a population consisting of two elements, heads and tails (Kish, 1965). In the second variation, known as "sampling without replacement," a previously selected name cannot be reselected and must be disregarded on any later draw. We usually prefer to do sampling without replacement because we do not want to test the same person twice. In the case of a duplication, then, we go on to the next 2-digit number in the row.

OTHER PROBABILITY SAMPLES

A popular modification of simple random sampling is known as *stratified random sampling*. The name refers to the fact that it is used when the population is divisible into subpopulations called "strata" (or layers). Within each stratum a separate sample is selected, and the stratum means are then statistically weighted to form a combined estimate for the entire population. For instance, in a survey of political opinions, it might be useful to stratify the population according to party affiliation, sex, socioeconomic status, and other meaningful categories theoretically related to voting behavior. This ensures that one has enough men, women, Democrats, Republicans, etc., to draw inferences about each respective subgroup.

Cluster sampling is another type of random sampling procedure, and it is often combined with stratification. It consists of taking "clusters" (bunches or groups) of elements as sampling units when individual selection of elements is too expensive. This procedure is also very useful when we do not have a complete list of the population available in order to do simple random sampling. Instead we divide the population into subclasses and then sample in a way so as to ensure that each subclass is represented in proportion to its population.

An illustration of this procedure is also known as *area probability sampling,* since the clusters are geographical areas. In area probability sampling the plan consists of selecting geographical areas and then randomly subsampling for dwelling units within the selected geographical areas. Except for a minor group of transients, people can thus be identified with a place of residence, and that residence with a particular area. This procedure is also cheaper than simple random sampling when doing a door-to-door survey, for example.

The study done by Conrad Smith (see Chapter 11), in which he interviewed and then sent questionnaires to TV viewers in Salt Lake City to find out about their preferences in news telecasts, used an area probability sample. Smith (1980) developed his sampling plan using tract and block estimates that he obtained from census data found in the library. Area probability sampling is used by professional pollsters, since it is economical and can be used repeatedly. To reuse this sampling plan, we merely vary the random selection of dwelling units within the sample areas (Warwick & Lininger, 1975). (For other variations, see Babbie, 1975; Cornell & McLoone, 1963; Furno, 1966; Kish, 1965; and Parten, 1950.)

Since both stratified random sampling and cluster sampling satisfy the criterion that every element in the population has a known probability of being selected, we said that they are types of probability sampling. Suppose that we needed an area probability sample of 300 out of 6000 estimated dwellings in a city. Since a good list of all the dwellings in the entire city does not exist, and would be too costly to prepare, we can instead obtain a sample of dwellings by selecting a sample of blocks using a city map. We might begin by dividing the entire area of the city's map into blocks and then selecting one of every twenty blocks into the sample. If we define the sample as the dwellings located within the boundaries of the sample blocks, then the probability of selection for any dwelling is the selection of its block. This has been set at one-twentieth to correspond to the desired sampling rate of 300/6000 (Kish, 1965).

NONRESPONSE BIAS

Not everyone who is contacted by an opinion pollster, or for that matter by any type of researcher, will automatically agree to participate as a research subject. Indeed it is almost impossible to obtain answers from every person in a large sample, no matter what sampling plan or data-collection procedures are used. For this reason, certain statistical procedures have been developed for estimating *bias due to nonresponse*. In addition, error due to nonresponse can usually be minimized by following up nonrespondents in order to stimulate responses (Filion, 1975–76).

Both the estimation and the minimization of nonresponse bias are illustrated in Table 13.2, which presents summary data reported by William Cochran (1963). Three waves of questionnaires were mailed out to fruit growers, and the number of respondents and nonrespondents to each wave was recorded. One of the questions dealt with the number of fruit trees owned, and data were available for the entire population of growers for just this question. Thus, it was possible to calculate the degree of bias attributable to nonresponse present after the first, second, and third waves of questionnaires. Rows 1 to 3 provide the basic data in the form of (1) the number of respondents to each wave of questionnaires and the number of nonrespondents, (2) the percentage of the total population represented by each wave of respondents (and nonrespondents), and (3) the mean number of trees owned by respondents in each wave and by nonrespondents. Examination of row 3 reveals the nature of the bias due to

Table 13.2 Example of bias due to nonresponse in survey research

	Response to three mailings				
Basic data	First wave	Second wave	Third wave	Nonre- spondents	Total population
(1) Number of respondents	300	543	434	1839	3116
(2) Percent of population	10%	17%	14%	59%	100%
(3) Mean trees per respondent	456	382	340	290	329
Cumulative data					
(4) Mean trees per respondent (Y_1)	456	408	385		
(5) Mean trees per nonrespondent (Y_2)	315	300	290		
(6) Difference ($Y_1 - Y_2$)	141	108	95		
(7) Percent of nonrespondents (P)	90%	73%	59%		
(8) Bias = (P) $\times$ ($Y_1 - Y_2$)	127	79	56		

Source: W. G. Cochran, *Sampling Techniques,* 2d ed., Wiley, New York, 1963; table reprinted from R. Rosenthal and R. L. Rosnow, *The Volunteer Subject,* Wiley-Interscience, New York, 1975, by permission of the publisher.

nonresponse, which was that the earlier responders owned more trees on the average than did the later responders.

The remaining five rows of data are based on the cumulative number of respondents available after the first, second, and third waves. For each wave, five items of information are provided: (4) the mean number of trees owned by the respondents up to that point in the survey, (5) the mean number of trees owned by those who had not yet responded up to that point, (6) the difference between these two values, (7) the percentage of the population that had not yet responded, and (8) the magnitude of the bias up to that point in the survey. Examination of this last row shows that with each successive wave of respondents there was an appreciable decrease in the magnitude of the bias, which appears to be a fairly typical result of studies of this kind. That is, increasing the effort to recruit the nonrespondents decreases the bias in the sample estimates.

Unfortunately, in most circumstances of behavioral research we can compute the proportion of our population who fail to participate (P) and the statistic of interest for those who volunteer their data (Y_1), but we cannot compute the statistic of interest for those who do not respond (Y_2). Therefore, we are often in a position to suspect bias but are unable to give an estimate of its magnitude.

STIMULATING PARTICIPATION

The followup or reminder using a telephone call, a registered letter, or a special delivery letter has been found to be an especially effective technique in stimulating responses to mailed questionnaires (Linsky, 1975). There are other ways of increasing participation besides following up the nonrespondents. Another technique that has proven effective in mail surveys is to contact the potential respondents before they receive the questionnaire in order to encourage their later participation. A third possibility is to send out the questionnaire using a "high-powered mailing," such as special delivery or airmail, and using hand-stamped rather than postage-permit return envelopes. Still another alternative is to enclose some small reward; but *promising* a reward (rather than enclosing one) is usually less effective than no reward. (For further details, see Heberlein & Baumgartner, 1978; Linsky, 1975.)

In experimental research using nonrandom samples, experimenters are often concerned with the problem of *volunteer bias,* which is analogous to the problem of nonresponse bias (Rosenthal & Rosnow, 1975). In the next chapter we discuss the ethical responsibilities of researchers, which include the responsibility for protecting the rights of the subject. The subject has a right to choose whether or not to participate in the experiment, and it is possible that many persons who decide to participate or not to participate as subjects do so for reasons that are related to the nature of the investigation. For instance, brighter individuals might be more likely to volunteer for an experiment in learning, while gregarious individuals might choose a social-psychological experiment on small-group interaction. The extent to which these subjects were different from those persons who chose not to volunteer could have serious effects on estimates of such population values as means, medians, proportions, variances, skewness, and so on, which we discuss later.

In recent years, a great deal has been learned about the situational determinants of volunteering to be a research subject. One of the consequences of this methodological research is that we also have a number of steps which may be useful in reducing the magnitude of volunteer bias by stimulating more "nonvolunteers" to enter the sampling pool. Of course, we do not want to exert undue pressures on the nonvolunteers to participate, since that would infringe on their right to privacy and free choice. The following recommendations may serve not only to reduce volunteer bias, but also to make us more thoughtful in the planning of experimental research (Rosnow & Rosenthal, 1976, p. 103):

1. Make the appeal for volunteers as interesting as possible, keeping in mind the nature of the target population.
2. Make the appeal as nonthreatening as possible, so that potential recruits will not be put off by unwarranted fears of unfavorable evaluation.
3. State the theoretical and practical importance of the research for which volunteering is requested.
4. State in what way the target population is particularly relevant to the research being conducted and the responsibility of individuals to participate in research that has the potential for benefiting others.
5. When possible, potential volunteers should be offered not only pay for participation but small courtesy gifts simply for taking time to consider whether they will want to participate.
6. Have the request for volunteers made by a person of status as high as possible, preferably by a woman of high status.
7. Whenever possible, avoid research tasks that are psychologically or biologically stressful.
8. Communicate the fact that volunteering is not an unusual behavior, but is usually the norm.
9. After a target population has been defined, an effort should be made to have someone known to that population make the appeal for volunteers. The request for volunteers may be more successful if a personalized appeal is made.
10. In situations where volunteering is regarded by the target population as normative, conditions of public commitment to volunteer may be more successful (e.g., raising your hand to participate); where nonvolunteering is regarded as normative, conditions of private commitment may be more successful (e.g., signing your name on a piece of paper that only the experimenter will see).

Another way of improving generalizability has been developed by medical researchers working in the psychopharmacology of antianxiety and antidepressant drugs. These researchers have found that it is not always possible to generalize from studies of indigent patients in hospital clinics to patients seen by nonpsychiatrist physicians in private practice. As a consequence, the researchers have turned to the use of *symptomatic volunteers* as research subjects (Overall, Goldstein, & Brauzer, 1971). These would be subjects, drawn from among volunteers for clinical drug studies, who share demographic and sociocultural characteristics of patients seen in private practice. Similarly, in behavioral research, once we have defined the nature of the population it may be possible to use "symptomatic volunteers" who most closely resemble those persons to whom we wish our generalizations to apply.

In a good deal of behavioral research, however, interest is centered less on such statistics as means and proportions and more on such statistics as differences between means and differences between proportions. The experimental investigator is ordinarily interested in relating such differences to the operation of the independent variable. The fact that volunteers may differ from nonvolunteers in their scores on the dependent variable may be of less interest to the behavioral experimenter. The experimenter would rather know whether the magnitude of the difference between the experimental and control group means would be affected if volunteers were used. In Chapter 15 we shall return to the problem of volunteer bias to discuss how we might predict whether volunteer status interacts with the experimental variables. There are also some instances in which the researcher would rather have a select sample than an average sample, such as in the selection of judges or clinical observers, which is discussed in the next section.

SELECTION OF JUDGES AND OBSERVERS

Whether we make ethnographic observations and rate or categorize activities as they proceed, or whether we make film records and then use judges to rate or categorize what they see, an important question to consider is: "Who should the judges or observers be?" Usually there is no special interest in individual differences among observers or judges when we consider issues of interobserver or interjudge reliability. We simply decide on the type of judges or observers we want (college students, clinical psychologists, linguists, mothers, etc.) and then regard each observer or judge within that sample as to some degree equivalent to, or interchangeable with, any other observer or judge within the sample.

In the case of judges, if we wanted an average sample we might be content to select college or high school students. If we wanted judgments of nonverbal cues to psychoses we might choose experts for our judges: clinical psychologists or psychiatrists. If we wanted judgments of nonverbal cues to discomfort in infants we might select pediatricians, developmental psychologists, or mothers. Similarly, if we wanted judgments of nonverbal cues of persuasiveness, we might invite trial lawyers, fundamentalist clergymen, or salespersons.

In any of these particular cases we would be perfectly content with a nonrandom selection of judges. Indeed, if we wanted to obtain the highest possible level of general accuracy of judgments of nonverbal cues, we might want to select our judges on the basis of prior research that has identified specific characteristics of people who are most sensitive to nonverbal cues. A recent review of research suggests that to optimize overall sensitivity to non-verbal cues we should probably select judges who are female, of college age, cognitively complex, and psychiatrically unimpaired (Rosenthal, Hall, DiMatteo, Rogers, & Archer, 1979).

An important consideration that goes along with the question of "Who should judge?" is that of the number of judges needed for effective reliability. The major factor determining the answer to the latter question is the average reliability coefficient $(\bar{r})$ between any pair of judges chosen at random from a prescribed population. If the reliability coefficient were very low, we would require more judges than if the reliability coefficient were very high.

Let us say that we had two judges rate a sample of teachers based on the videotaped behavior of the teachers. The correlation coefficient reflecting the reliability of the two judges' ratings would be computed to give us our best (and only) estimate of the correlation likely to be obtained between any two judges drawn from the same population of judges. That correlation coefficient is clearly useful; it is not, however, a very good estimate of the reliability of our variable, which is not the rating of warmth made by a single judge but rather the mean of two judges' ratings. Suppose that the correlation between our two judges' ratings of warmth is .50. The reliability of the mean of the two judges' ratings, termed the *effective reliability,* would then be .67 not .50. Intuition suggests that we should gain in reliability in adding the ratings of a second judge, because the second judge's random errors should tend to cancel the first judge's random errors. Intuition further suggests that adding more judges, all of whom agree with one another to about the same degree, defined by a mean interjudge correlation coefficient of .50 (for this example), should increase the effective reliability.

Our intuition would be supported by an old and well-known result reported by Charles Spearman and William Brown in 1910 (Walker & Lev, 1953). With notation altered to suit our present purpose, the well-known Spearman-Brown result is:

$$R = \frac{n\bar{r}}{1 + (n - 1)\bar{r}}$$

where R = effective reliability; n = number of judges; and $\bar{r}$ = mean reliability among all n judges. To illustrate the computation of R, given more than two judges, consider the following example.

Five persons are each rated on their degree of warmth by each of three judges yielding the following set of scores:

Persons	Judges		
	A	B	C
1	5	6	7
2	3	6	4
3	3	4	6
4	2	2	3
5	1	4	4

For the set of five persons we can compute the correlation between each pair of judges, AB, AC, and BC. For the ratings shown these correlations are:

$$r_{AB} = .645$$
$$r_{AC} = .800$$
$$r_{BC} = .582$$
$$\Sigma = 2.027$$

and the mean of these three rs $(\bar{r})$ is .676. To obtain R, the effective reliability, or the reliability of the sum or mean rating of all the judges, we simply apply the Spearman-Brown formula with $\bar{r} = .676$ and $n = 3$:

$$R = \frac{3\,(.676)}{1 + (2)(.676)} = .862$$

As an aid to investigators using this and related methods, Table 13.3 has been prepared based on the Spearman-Brown formula (Rosenthal, 1982). The table gives the effective reliability, R, for each of several values of n, the number of judges making the observations, and $\bar{r}$, the mean reliability among the judges. It is intended to help us to obtain approximate answers to questions such as the following:

1. Given an obtained or estimated mean reliability, $\bar{r}$, and a sample of n judges, what is the approximate effective reliability, R, of the mean of the judges' ratings? The value of R is read from the table at the intersection of the appropriate row (n) and column ($\bar{r}$). Suppose an investigator wants to work with a variable believed to show a mean reliability of .50 and can afford only four judges. The investigator believes he should go ahead with his study only if the effective reliability will reach or exceed .75. Shall he go ahead? The answer is yes, because the table shows R to be .80 for an n of 4 and an $\bar{r}$ of .50.
2. Given the value of the obtained or desired effective reliability, R, and the number, n, of judges available, what will be the approximate value of the required mean reliability, $\bar{r}$? The table is entered in the row corresponding to the n of judges available, and is read across until the value of R closest to the one desired is reached; the value of $\bar{r}$ is then read as the corresponding

Table 13.3 Effective reliability of the mean of judges' ratings

Number of judges (n)	Mean reliability (r̄)																		
	.05	.10	.15	.20	.25	.30	.35	.40	.45	.50	.55	.60	.65	.70	.75	.80	.85	.90	.95
1	05	10	15	20	25	30	35	40	45	50	55	60	65	70	75	80	85	90	95
2	10	18	26	33	40	46	52	57	62	67	71	75	79	82	86	89	92	95	97
3	14	25	35	43	50	56	62	67	71	75	79	82	85	88	90	92	94	96	98
4	17	31	41	50	57	63	68	73	77	80	83	86	88	90	92	94	96	97	*
5	21	36	47	56	62	68	73	77	80	83	86	88	90	92	94	95	97	98	*
6	24	40	51	60	67	72	76	80	83	86	88	90	92	93	95	96	97	98	*
7	27	44	55	64	70	75	79	82	85	88	90	91	93	94	95	97	98	98	*
8	30	47	59	67	73	77	81	84	87	89	91	92	94	95	96	97	98	*	*
9	32	50	61	69	75	79	83	86	88	90	92	93	94	95	96	97	98	*	*
10	34	53	64	71	77	81	84	87	89	91	92	94	95	96	97	98	98	*	*
12	39	57	68	75	80	84	87	89	91	92	94	95	96	97	97	98	*	*	**
14	42	61	71	78	82	86	88	90	92	93	94	95	96	97	98	98	*	*	**
16	46	64	74	80	84	87	90	91	93	94	95	96	97	97	98	98	*	*	**
18	49	67	76	82	86	89	91	92	94	95	96	96	97	98	98	*	*	*	**
20	51	69	78	83	87	90	92	93	94	95	96	97	97	98	98	*	*	*	**
24	56	73	81	86	89	91	93	94	95	96	97	97	98	98	*	*	*	**	**
28	60	76	83	88	90	92	94	95	96	97	97	98	98	98	*	*	*	**	**
32	63	78	85	89	91	93	95	96	96	97	98	98	98	*	*	*	*	**	**
36	65	80	86	90	92	94	95	96	97	97	98	98	*	*	*	*	**	**	**
40	68	82	88	91	93	94	96	96	97	98	98	98	*	*	*	*	**	**	**
50	72	85	90	93	94	96	96	97	98	98	98	*	*	*	*	**	**	**	**
60	76	87	91	94	95	96	97	98	98	98	*	*	*	*	*	**	**	**	**
80	81	90	93	95	96	97	98	98	98	*	*	*	*	*	**	**	**	**	**
100	84	92	95	96	97	98	98	*	*	*	*	*	*	**	**	**	**	**	**

Note: Decimal points omitted.
* Approximately .99.
** Approximately 1.00.

Note also: Use of this table proceeds on the assumption that a comparable group of judges would show comparable "mean" reliability among themselves and with the actual group of judges available to us. That assumption is virtually the same as the assumption that all pairs of judges show essentially the same degree of reliability.

column heading. Suppose an investigator who will settle for an effective reliability no less than .90 has a sample of twenty judges available. In the investigator's selection of variables to be judged by these observers, what should be their minimally acceptable reliability? The answer from Table 13.3 is .30.

3. Given an obtained or estimated mean reliability, $\bar{r}$, and the obtained or desired effective reliability, R, what is the approximate number (n) of judges required? The table is entered in the column corresponding to the mean reliability, $\bar{r}$, and is read down until the value of R closest to the one desired is reached; the value of n is then read as the corresponding row title. For example, we know our choice of variables to have a mean reliability of .40 and want to achieve an effective reliability of .85 or higher. How many judges must we allow for in our preparation of a research budget? The answer is nine judges.

It will sometimes happen that when we examine the intercorrelations among our judges we will find that one judge is very much out of line with all the others. Perhaps this judge tends to obtain negative correlations with other judges or at least to show clearly lower reliabilities with other judges than is typical for the correlation matrix. If this "unreliable" judge were dropped from the data, the resulting estimates of reliability would be biased, however, since they would be made to appear *too* reliable. If a judge must be dropped, the resulting bias can be reduced by an equitable trimming of judges. Thus, if the lowest agreeing judge is dropped, the highest agreeing judge is also dropped. If the two lowest agreeing judges are dropped, the two highest agreeing judges should also be dropped, and so on. Experience suggests that when large samples of judges are employed, the effects of trimming judges are small (as is the need for trimming). When the sample of judges is small, we may feel a stronger need to drop a judge, but doing so without equitable trimming is more likely to leave a residual biased estimate of reliability. A safe procedure is to do all analyses with and without trimming and to report *all* the differences in results.

NONRANDOMIZED SELECTION

There are other instances as well where nonrandomized selection is the norm, and we have alluded to some of these in earlier chapters. For example, the cohort design (discussed in Chapter 8) is sometimes considered to be a type of quasi-experimental design using nonrandomized selection. Of course, the cohort method can also be used with survey data which are based on random sampling; an example would be the personal interview data collected by the National Opinion Research Center (NORC), as referred to in an earlier chapter. Since respondent age is reported to the year, one can use the NORC data to study age trends by reexamining a particular age group (persons aged 21 to 29 in 1963) several years later (persons aged 30 to 38 in 1972).

Quasi means "resembling," and previously we said that quasi experiments resemble true experiments in that both types have treatments and dependent measures. However, in quasi experiments the participants are not randomly assigned to the different treatment groups. (They are also not randomly selected, but then neither are the subjects of most true experiments.) Instead the subjects already belong to existing groups, although in some cases we may be able to decide when some groups will be measured.

In our discussion of the cohort table, we also noted some of its advantages over the simple cross-sectional and simple longitudinal designs for studying behavior on the basis of age, cohort, and period. The precise meaning of these three concepts varies considerably from one study to another. In the literature on counseling and student development, for instance, "age" is often taken to mean the subject's year in school rather than chronological age (Whiteley et al., 1975); and in research on social change, "period" is often defined as some environmental effect or cultural change which is the result of lengthy historical processes such as industrialization or urbanization (Hagenaars & Cobben, 1978). Each design, to be sure, has its own inherent limitations when we are interested in controlling for age, cohort, and period no matter how they are defined.

Table 13.4 summarizes the various approaches that have been suggested (Schaie, 1965; Wohlwill, 1970), based on the model of a cohort table. In this case, "age" is defined as the subject's year in an elementary school consisting of grades 1–6. In the *simple cross-sectional design*, students in different grades are observed at the same time. The major deficiency of this sampling design is that it confounds the year of the subject and the cohort. In the *simple longitudinal design,* students of the same cohort are observed over several periods. The deficiency in this case is that the design does not control for the effect of history (or period). In the *cohort-sequential design,* several cohorts are studied, with the initial measurements taken in successive years. The design takes into account cohort and "age" but does not take time of measurement (period) fully into account. In the *time-sequential design*, students of different ages are observed at several different times. This design considers "age" and time of measurement but does not take cohort fully into account. In the *cross-sequential design,* several different cohorts that are observed over several periods are initially measured in the same period. This design takes into account the time of measurement and the cohort but does not take "age" fully into account.

It is clear that these designs are a distinct improvement over the simple cross-sectional design when studying maturational processes. But each leaves something to be desired nonetheless. In a given study the researcher might select a particular design depending on which of three variables (age, cohort, and period) he or she was willing to sacrifice and have confounded (Whiteley et al., 1975). A further improvement, of course, would be to employ representative samples (the NORC type, noted previously) or even census data and then to trace the effects of all three variables using a complete cohort table as in Chapter 8 (Table 8.4). Carrying out such an analysis is not simple, but it does

Table 13.4 Five sampling designs according to "age" (grades 1–6), period (history or time of measurement), and cohort (C1–C11)

Simple cross-sectional design (1980)

Age	Period					
	1975	1972	1977	1978	1979	1980
G1	C6	C7	C8	C9	C10	C11
G2	C5	C6	C7	C8	C9	C10
G3	C4	C5	C6	C7	C8	C9
G4	C3	C4	C5	C6	C7	C8
G5	C2	C3	C4	C5	C6	C7
G6	C1	C2	C3	C4	C5	C6

Simple longitudinal design

Age	Period					
	1975	1976	1977	1978	1979	1980
G1	C6					
G2		C6				
G3			C6			
G4				C6		
G5					C6	
G6						C6

Cohort-sequential design

Age	Period					
	1975	1976	1977	1978	1979	1980
G1						
G2						
G3	C4	C5	C6			
G4		C4	C5	C6		
G5			C4	C5	C6	
G6				C4	C5	C6

Time-sequential design

Age	Period					
	1975	1976	1977	1978	1979	1980
G1				C9	C10	C11
G2				C8	C9	C10
G3				C7	C8	C9
G4				C6	C7	C8
G5				C5	C6	C7
G6				C4	C5	C6

Cross-sequential design

Age	Period					
	1975	1976	1977	1978	1979	1980
G1	C6					
G2	C5	C6				
G3	C4	C5	C6			
G4		C4	C5	C6		
G5			C4	C5		
G6				C4		

Note: Each sampling design is accentuated by dotted lines. Only the first subtable is completely labeled to show all possible cohorts; in addition it shows the simple cross-sectional design for the 1980 period (set off by dotted lines).

give a more complete picture by letting us examine all possibilities on the basis of representative data (e.g., Hagenaars & Cobben, 1978).

One final instance in which nonrandomized selection is typical is in what is often referred to as "small-N research" or "N-of-one" or "single-case research." Conditioning experiments of the Skinnerian type employing programmed environments, inbred animal subjects, and continuous assessment of performance over time would be an example of the single-case approach using nonrandomized selection. The rationale behind this approach, in which the subjects serve as their own controls, is that the study of ongoing behavior in a highly controlled environment gives the experimenter an important tactical advantage. The behavior can be continuously monitored as treatment effects are replicated within the same subjects over time. Changes in the pattern of performance are taken as the basis for drawing inferences about treatment effects (Kazdin & Tuma, 1982). The researchers start by establishing a "baseline" for each subject—usually rats, mice, rabbits, etc.—from which to measure the effects of the treatments. Once such a baseline has been established, it is assumed that the researcher can generalize to any other subjects because their baselines are comparable. If there is any variability in the baselines of different subjects, the procedure then is to search for previously overlooked or ignored sources of differences in order to *impose* comparability on the data (see Sidman, 1960, for discussion). This approach has found widespread acceptance in many areas of animal behavioral research, where the vast majority of studies use partially or fully inbred strains and it can be assumed that genetic differences are minimized or eliminated by the breeding schedule.

Just as the choice of an appropriate sampling plan—whether it is a probability sampling plan or some nonrandomized plan—is a basic consideration, so too is the original decision to do the research using one set of procedures as opposed to another. Throughout the planning and execution of the research, the conscientious investigator will weigh the costs and benefits of alternative methods from the point of view of some particular value system. The discussion so far has emphasized the scientific values to be considered when making such a decision; we now turn to ethical imperatives which must be weighed in making this decision.

FOURTEEN

ETHICS AND VALUES IN HUMAN RESEARCH

COSTS AND UTILITIES

The term "value" refers to the standards or principles by which we judge the worth of something. By *ethics* we mean the system of moral values by which we judge behavior, including scientists' behavior. For a long time it was argued that science was neutral with regard to moral values. Some theorists drew a distinction between the natural and the behavioral sciences, arguing that the subject matter in the behavioral sciences makes it difficult to maintain scientific detachment. The subject matter of the natural sciences, they said, might be more easily viewed with ethical neutrality in that it does not have concerns about human beings at its core. However, along with the development of atomic physics and other scientific triumphs, there has been a growing unrest about the moral implications of some of the most basic research in natural science. The result is that no longer do we think of science, whether it be natural or behavioral, as an endless frontier unbounded by moral constraints of any sort (Holton & Morison, 1979).

Especially in behavioral science, this awareness of the moral implications of scientific investigation has led to dilemmas associated with the conduct of research with human participants (Reynolds, 1975; Suls & Rosnow, 1981). We begin with a discussion of the dilemma involved in attempting to balance the potential benefits from research against the risks to the human participants. The decision process by which researchers usually weigh the "cost" and the "utility" of doing research is illustrated in Figure 14.1. The "cost of doing" includes possible harm to subjects, time, expenditures of money, effort, etc., while the "utility of doing" includes benefits to subjects, to other people at

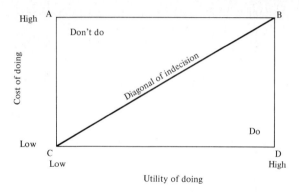

Figure 14-1 A decision-plane model of the costs and utilities of doing and not doing research. Studies falling at point A *are not* carried out, while studies at point D *are* carried out. Studies falling along the diagonal of indecision, B–C, are too hard to decide about.

other times and places, to the investigator, etc. "Better studies"—in the sense of internal and external validity—are more useful than "worse studies," and studies addressing important topics are more useful than studies addressing trivial topics.

The model is insufficient, however—the insufficiency stems from its failure to delineate the costs (and utilities) of *not* conducting a particular study. The failure to conduct a study that could be conducted is as much an act to be evaluated on ethical grounds as is the conducting of a study. The oncologist who could find a cancer preventive but feels the work to be dull and a distraction from his or her real interest is making a decision that is to be evaluated on ethical grounds as surely as the decision of a researcher to investigate tumors with a procedure that carries a certain risk. The behavioral researcher whose study might reduce violence or prejudice, but who refuses to do the study because it involves deception or harm risk, has not solved the ethical problem but only traded one problem for another.

THE MILGRAM AND HUMPHREYS STUDIES

There are two studies in particular, one experimental and the other nonexperimental, which have borne the brunt of the misgivings by behavioral researchers (Holden, 1979). The experimental research, which we have alluded to in earlier chapters, was that done by social psychologist Stanley Milgram, and the nonexperimental research was done by sociologist Laud Humphreys.

Milgram, beginning in the late 1960s, experimented on how far people would go in subjecting another person to pain at the order of an authority figure. He told volunteers they would be giving varying degrees of painful electric shocks to another person each time the person made a mistake in a learning task. He also varied the physical proximity between the teacher and the learner, to see whether the teacher would be less ruthless in administering the electric shocks the closer he or she was to the learner. The results were shocking to most people, since it was found that a great many subjects unhesitatingly obeyed the experimenter's command as they continued to increase the level of shocks administered to the learner. Even when there was feedback from the victim, who pretended to cry out in pain, many subjects were obedient to the authority of the experimenter's order to "please continue" or "you have no choice, you must go on" (Milgram, 1974).

In fact, the "learner" was a confederate of Milgram's, and there were no electric shocks actually transmitted. The participants were not told this at the outset, but they were extensively debriefed once the experiment was over. In spite of such precautions and the obvious social significance of the research, Milgram's studies were the target of criticism and debate with regard to the morality of what he had done.

Some people argued that it was wrong to deceive the participants, in spite of the fact that there was no physical harm done to the "learner." Others noted that Milgram himself had noticed nervous signs of sweating, trembling, stuttering, etc., in the participants, and those signs of psychological discomfort should have resulted in the immediate termination of the study. Milgram answered that there might have been discomfort, but there was certainly no lasting harm to the participants. The evidence of this fact was what they told him during the debriefing session and much later in a postexperimental interview. The study was further criticized on the grounds that Milgram had instilled in his subjects a distrust of authority, and this was also unethical, it was argued. Milgram responded to this criticism by saying that he considered it perfectly ethical if, indeed, the subjects' experience had taught them to be skeptical of this kind of authority.

The nonexperimental research that has borne the brunt of similar misgivings was that done by sociologist Laud Humphreys in 1969. He was working on his doctorate at Harvard University at the time and conducted a study designed to reveal how society treated homosexuals (Humphreys, 1975). He set himself up as a "watchqueen" in a public lavatory in St. Louis to warn homosexuals who were engaged in fellatio about intruders, but he also recorded the license numbers of the cars driven by the homosexuals. He then represented himself as a market researcher in order to obtain the names and addresses of the owners from the Department of Motor Vehicles. Once having identified the homosexuals by name, he then joined a public health survey team, changed his hairstyle, and interviewed them as a public health researcher (Holden, 1979).

Despite all this, Humphreys was scrupulous in protecting the confidentiality of his subjects. Nevertheless, it is true that he lied to them and to the Department of Motor Vehicles, and that he invaded the privacy of his subjects without their informed consent. This research, as indeed all research, raises an important value question which constantly confronts behavioral scientists: Does whatever scientific or social utility that is attributed to the research outweigh whatever costs may be incurred by the subjects as well as by society and science? However, there is a further question to consider: What of the social and scientific cost of *not doing* the research insofar as it involves deception, an invasion of privacy, or harm risk?

DECEPTION IN RESEARCH

Imagine an experiment similar to Milgram's in which the experimenter instead greeted his subjects by saying: "Hello, today we are going to investigate the effects of physical distance from the victim on willingness to inflict pain on him. You will be in the 'close condition.' In addition, you will be asked to fill out a test of fascist tendencies because we believe there is a positive relationship between scores on our fascism test and obedience to an authority who requests that we hurt others. Any questions?"

A completely honest statement to a research subject of what he or she is doing in the experiment might involve a prebriefing of the kind given. Such a prebriefing is manifestly absurd if we are serious in our efforts to learn about human behavior. If subjects had full information about our experimental plans, procedures, and hypotheses, we might very well develop a science of behavior based on what subjects thought the world was like or what subjects thought experimenters thought the world was like. Subjects' knowledge of or suspicions about the purpose of the research, coupled with their tendency to want to be "good subjects" or to "look good" in the eyes of the experimenter, could seriously jeopardize the validity of the research findings.

Indeed, the problem of subjects' knowledge of the true intent of the research is sufficiently threatening to the validity of research that behavioral scientists have almost routinely used one form or another of deception of subjects. There are few researchers who advocate the use of deception in and of itself. At the same time, there are few researchers who feel that we can do entirely without deception. No one seriously advocates giving up the study of racial prejudice and discrimination. Yet, if all measures of racial prejudice had to be labeled as such, it is questionable that it would be worth the effort to continue the research.

To adopt a rigid moralistic stance requires that a deception be labeled a deception and that by our dominant value system, which decries lying (at least in a formal sense), it be banished or ruled out. In fact, most people, including behavioral scientists, are willing to weigh and measure their sins, judging some to be larger than others. In the case of "lying" to subjects, most experimenters would probably agree on the proposition that refraining from telling a subject that an experiment in the learning of verbal materials is designed to show whether earlier, later, or more-midmost material is better remembered is not a particularly serious breach of ethical standards. The reason we do not view that particular deception with alarm seems due in part to its involving a sin of omission rather than commission. A truth is left unspoken, but a lie is not told. Suppose, however, that the same experiment were presented as a study of the effects of meaningfulness of verbal materials on their retention or recall. That would constitute a direct lie, designed to mislead the subject's attention from the temporal order of the materials to some other factor in which we really are not interested. Somehow, that change does not seem to make the deception so much more heinous even though now our sin is of commission and we have not withheld information from, but actively lied to, our subject.

It does not seem, then, that the style of deception is its measure, but instead its probable effect on the subject. Very few people would care whether subjects focused on meaningfulness of verbal material rather than temporal order, since there seems to be no consequence, positive or negative, of this deception. It seems that it is not deception as such so much as *harmful deception* that we would like to minimize. The degree of harmfulness is something on which we can agree fairly well. Most people would agree that it is not very harmful to subjects to be told that a test they are taking anonymously as part of the research is one of personal reactions (which it is) rather than a test of need for social approval (which it may also be). On the other hand, most people would probably agree that it could be harmful to college-age subjects to be falsely told that a test shows them to be homosexual even if they are later told they had been lied to. Most people would probably also agree that it may well be harmful to army recruits to be led to believe that they are in a stricken airplane about to crash, or that they have inadvertently killed some army buddies and that, to be able to report this, they have to repair a broken telephone ("the effects of stress on the performance of technical duties").

ETHICAL GUIDELINES

Some of the potentially most harmful deceptions, perhaps, ought never to be employed, but they are quite rare in any case. For the great bulk of deceptions where there may be a range of potentially negative consequences, the investigator, professional colleagues, and to some extent, ultimately, the general community, must decide whether a deception with a given degree of potentially negative effects is worth the potential increase in knowledge. A particular technique that may be useful, at least with regard to some research, is to use "mock subjects" who are selected from the same population as the actual subjects but are made fully aware of every aspect of the study (Atwell, 1981). If the mock group overwhelmingly agreed to being subjects in that study, then we may assume that the actual subjects (who are not aware of every aspect) would probably also agree. The procedure is not able to reveal every potential complication, to be sure, but it may be useful nonetheless for calculating the possible consequences of some research in behavioral science.

Through regulations promulgated by the United States government, it is also now required that every institution receiving federal support set up review boards for deciding on the ethical merits of any research involving human or animal subjects done under the institution's auspices. Professional organizations (such as the American Psychological Association) have also developed ethical guidelines for researchers. There are five simple guidelines that can provide us with a checklist of standards to judge our own research projects even before they are judged by our colleagues on the review boards.

First, it is important to realize the personal responsibility we have to ensure the ethical acceptability of the research, no matter whether we are directing the data collection ourselves or whether a graduate student or an undergraduate student of ours is doing the data collection. We cannot dismiss the personal responsibility by shifting the authority to the student.

Second, we must be as honest and open with the participants as we can. If we cannot be completely honest and open with them, and if we cannot find some alternative procedures that will allow us to be so, then we should ask ourselves whether the study is really worth doing. If the answer is a definite yes, then we must realize that we have an obligation to debrief them at some point once the study is completed, unless that procedure would introduce stress or anxiety.

Third, we must respect the individual's right to refuse to participate in our research or to drop out of the research at any time. Each person has a different sense of the loss of privacy or the invasion of his or her life, and these are not easy to erase or to overcome by debriefing (Bok, 1978; Kelman, 1968). Therefore, we must not pressure any person to go against his or her will.

Fourth, whenever possible we should practice *informed consent*. We first inform the subject of the nature of the research and only then request the subject's consent to participate, without exerting any psychological pressures on the person. If we think the procedures may put the subject in risk or danger of some serious and lasting harm, then we ought to abandon the procedures, even if the subject gives his or her informed consent to participate.

Fifth, we must protect the confidentiality of the participants. Indeed, whenever possible, the responses of the subjects should be treated anonymously. This means that if we have given them an "anonymous questionnaire" to complete, we must under no circumstances lie to them by surreptitiously coding the questionnaire in order to identify each respondent later by name.

In some cases, we incur even greater personal responsibility because the participants are unable to take responsibility for their own behavior. In research with children, for example, the privacy and sensitivity of parents must be considered in addition to the possible effects of the questioning on the child. Debriefing the child when the study is over is seldom desirable or possible. Therefore, it is imperative that extra precautions be taken in advance of the study to rule out even the slightest possibility of a harmful effect on the child. The informed-consent issue is also more complicated in research with children, since legally only parents or other guardians can consent on behalf of children (Smith, 1969).

In cases where the subject lies to us about medical or psychopathological conditions, there may be little we can do to protect either the subject or ourselves, except possibly to insure against anticipated liability. Recently there was the case of a young nursing student who died from cardiac arrest while participating in a sleep experiment at the National Institutes of Health (NIH). In volunteering for the study she had concealed that she suffered from anorexia nervosa and self-induced vomiting. Vomiting causes loss of hydrochloric acid, and that depletes intracellular potassium, which in turn can produce cardiac arrest. As part of this experiment, the subject was given lithium, which also depletes cells of potassium. When she was found dead at the sleep lab she had been taking lithium for nine days, and there were lines of evidence to indicate that she was vomiting prior to her death. Although of normal weight, she had been trying to lose weight in the preceding two months in preparation for her sister's wedding, and at the sleep lab there was dried vomitus in her handbag. The subject had been given a physical examination when she was accepted into the experiment, but her condition was not detected at the time. Even though it was later discovered that she had been an NIH patient for cardiac arrest, that information was never communicated to the researchers conducting the sleep experiment (Kolata, 1980). There would seem to be little the researchers could have done to further protect the subject in this case, although this incident points out the necessity for gathering complete information on the participants whenever there is even the slightest possibility of a medical complication resulting from the experimental treatment.

DEBRIEFING

Our research is not completed once the data are in. A careful debriefing interview of all the participants is desirable as the final step in the data-collection process, particularly so in experimental research. This may not be possible in some instances, such as when the debriefing might produce stress or might be ineffective given the nature of the participants (e.g., children, the aged, prisoners, the mentally ill or retarded). In most cases, however, debriefing is absolutely essential.

We mentioned the criticisms of Milgram's research on obedience to authority, in which he duped participants into believing that they were administering painful electric shocks to another person. Experimental procedures such as Milgram's are inherently disquieting, and it was of the utmost importance that all of his subjects be assured that their "victim" had not received electric shocks at all. Let us see how the debriefing was actually handled in this research (Milgram, 1977).

To be sure that each participant knew exactly what the reality of the situation was, Milgram administered a careful postexperimental treatment to all subjects, then sent them a followup report and questionnaires; a year later he conducted a psychiatric interview with a subsample of his group of subjects. During the postexperimental debriefing session, each subject had a friendly reconciliation with the "victim" and an extended discussion with the experimenter about the purpose of the study and why it was thought necessary to deceive the subject. Those subjects who had obeyed the experimenter when he told them to keep administering the electric shocks were assured that their behavior was normal and that the feelings of conflict or tension they had experienced were shared by other participants. The subjects were told they would receive a comprehensive written report at the conclusion of the research. The report they received detailed the experimental procedures and findings, and the subject's own part in the research was treated with dignity. They also received a questionnaire that asked them once again to express their thoughts and feelings about their behavior. One year after the experiment was completed, there was an additional followup study of forty of the experimental subjects, who were intensively interviewed by a psychiatrist to identify any possible injurious effects resulting from the experiment.

The followup treatments administered by Milgram were unusually extensive, and the typical experiment will not require debriefing covering so wide an area or span of time. However, there are several fundamental considerations that will enter into any debriefing. Social psychologists Eliot Aronson and J. Merrill Carlsmith (1968) have suggested six important points to consider.

First, the most essential requirement is that the researcher communicate her or his own sincerity as a scientist. If the research involved any sort of deception, then it is important to tell the subject why it was necessary to resort to it and how the use of deception was carefully considered by the researcher. Science is the search for truth, and sometimes it may be necessary to resort to deception in order to uncover the truth. Responsible researchers will not view this matter lightly, and their sincere concern should be apparent.

Second, in spite of the researcher's sincere wish to treat the subject responsibly, it is nevertheless possible that the subject will leave the experiment feeling gullible, as if he or she has been "had." The researcher must assure the subject that being "taken in" does not reflect in any way on the subject's intelligence or character. Rather it simply reflects on the effectiveness of the study's design, which the researcher has no doubt gone to some pains to achieve.

Third, the debriefing session should proceed gradually. Researchers should have as their chief aim a gentle unfolding of the details of any deceptions used. Together, in a dialogue led by the researcher, the subject and the experimenter should examine the entire research process. If done patiently, the dialogue may go far in assuaging any negative feelings the subject could be harboring. Instead of thinking of themselves as "victims" of the researcher, the subjects begin to think of themselves as "coinvestigators" in the search for truth.

Fourth, the researcher should reiterate assurances of anonymity. The subjects' responses will be treated confidentially. The data will be coded and statistically analyzed without reference to any respondent's name.

Fifth, for reasons known only to themselves, some subjects may give false assurances as to the effect of the study on how they feel. The researcher has a responsibility to alleviate the subjects' discomfort and restore a sense of well-being as much as possible. In turn, this may necessitate the questioning of remarks or reactions in detail, if they appear to mask hidden feelings of apprehension or residual anxiety on the part of the participant.

Sixth, there are no reliable shortcuts to debriefing the subject as soon after the research as possible. Promising to mail the subject a report of the research in lieu of a personal debriefing may be expedient, but it is a weak substitute. However, if it is possible that a personal interview may alert other subjects who have not yet participated in the research as to the nature of the study, then it may be reasonable to delay the debriefing, but only for as short a time as is practicable.

SCIENTIFIC AND SOCIETAL IMPERATIVES

In this chapter we have discussed the major questions concerning ethics and values which constantly confront behavioral scientists. Each researcher must weigh his or her responsibilities to science and to society very carefully. However, values enter into science not only in the ethics of the profession, but also in the selection of problems for scientific investigation (Reynolds, 1975). Even when research is not directly funded by some agency of society, it is at least countenanced and indirectly supported because our society places a high value on science and gives the scientist a relatively free hand to study whatever he or she wants to study. There are, to be sure, limits on how far the scientist can go in the quest for knowledge, and we discussed these limits earlier in this chapter. The point, however, is that our society provides the circumstances and a psychological environment that are conducive to good scientific practices. The question, then, is, what does the scientist owe society in return for that privilege?

Some would argue that the behavioral scientist owes society the assurance that the research will lead to the betterment of humankind. This position is widely heralded particularly during periods of social stress, when the clarion call is sounded for researchers to get out of their ivory towers and to formulate hypotheses that will be relevant to social problems. However, no scientist can guarantee the outcome of his or her work. Even the best motives can produce results that do not further the state of well-being for which we strive.

The very nature of behavioral science is that it also challenges or questions societies' values and often elicits emotional responses. When we describe certain behaviors as being normative (that is, usual), the implication to the layperson is that we are saying that such behaviors are to be expected and therefore desirable. When we study prejudice or mental illness, we are touching on highly charged social problems. Even when we study topics that may appear to us to be neutral (marriage and the family, the genetics of intelligence, learning behavior, etc.), we must realize that to others they may be supercharged with values and conflicts. The point is that our science must be conducted with a sense of responsibility and an awareness that research is not done in isolation from the surrounding society.

As a consequence, it has been suggested that behavioral researchers should openly acknowledge that their work forces them to tread on "thin ice," morally speaking (Atwell, 1981). In studying human behavior we are constantly in jeopardy of violating someone's basic right—if only the right of privacy—and it is prudent that we study and discuss the moral dimensions of our research. It is a good idea as well to ask ourselves what justifies the role we play in society, for if the role cannot be justified then perhaps it ought to be replaced by one that can be. In the end, the behavioral scientist's responsibilities are twofold. On the one hand, the researcher must protect the integrity of his or her work, in order to ensure that the work measures up to the standards of good scientific practice. On the other hand, the researcher must also respect the dignity of those he or she studies and the values that allow the pursuit of scientific knowledge in a free society.

FIFTEEN

PRACTICES AND LIMITATIONS OF RESEARCH

TENSIONS OF CORROBORATION

This book began by noting a fundamental presupposition of the behavioral sciences, the assumption that empirical methods can be used to gather social facts. The bulk of the discussion gives ample testimony to the scope and variety of empirical methods that are actually used in behavioral science. However, we qualified the assumption by noting that there are aspects of reality which go beyond the methods available to study them. This applies as well in natural science as it does in behavioral science.

Consider Newton's first law of motion, which states: A body not acted on by any force will continue in a state of rest or uniform motion in a straight line forever. Suppose we took the position that the only acceptable evidence for the certainty of this law would be that based on some method of direct observation. Were we to proceed on this assumption, we would never be willing to accept the first law of motion. That is because no one has ever seen "a body not acted on by any force" (for example, friction and gravity), much less corroborated its "motion in a straight line forever." Nevertheless, the first law of motion remains an indispensable part of physics and one of the most accurate descriptions of nature (Cohen, 1959).

There are no exact laws of behavior that are in any way comparable to Newton's law of motion. It is true, nonetheless, that what "laws" and "social facts" exist in behavioral science derive from the persuasive force of many bits of evidence, only some of which are based on direct observations. The reason why we draw on a combination of critical evidence has been explained by Stephen C. Pepper (1946).

There are essentially two types of corroboration, he notes, the "method of observation" and the "method of hypothesis." In the former, the critical evidence derives from the number of observations, and even more from the number of scientists whose observations concur. In the latter, the critical evidence derives instead from logical descriptions based on the relevant facts. The first method usually takes precedence over the second, since if I can get a number of corroborating observations it seems foolish to spend time over the logic of a hypothesis. The method of observation does not have unquestionable priority over the method of hypothesis, however, as the example of Newton's first law clearly shows. Since there is relative uncertainty associated with both methods, the solution is one of proportion.

Let us say I am interested in whether there are differences in influenceability between men and women. I may do a research study in which male and female subjects read a persuasive communication and then answer a questionnaire to reveal the extent to which they had been influenced by what they read. Suppose I analyze the data and discover that the female subjects were more influenced by what they read than were the male subjects. How can I now corroborate my belief that women are more easily persuaded than men? Using the method of observation, I can repeat the study and can ask my colleagues whether they have observed a similar relationship. If I agree with myself, and if we all agree, then we may feel justified in believing that women are more easily persuaded than men.

On the other hand, I may use the method of hypothesis. I may examine the nature of the facts about influenceability and about sex differences and then try to interpret the research to fit my hypothesis. Were I, for instance, to examine the nature of the facts very carefully, as Alice H. Eagly (1978) has done, I might conclude that the research finding does not reflect an "immutable law" but instead reflects the kind of social relationship that is also affected by historical and cultural variables. Thus, I accept the research evidence, particularly if it is based on very considerable agreement among many observers, but I interpret it to fit my hypothesis.

Whichever "method" I use, my belief is based on a cumulative corroboration of evidence and a sense of proportion. Ideally, I search for some plausible combination of social facts which can be further corroborated by observation and hypothesis. I realize, in this particular case, that facts about the role of the female sex, as indeed most social facts, are circumscribed by historical and cultural events which are in constant flux, and I must be careful, therefore, not to accept as "law" something which merely seems to hold true of present or past behavior (Cohen, 1959; Gergen, 1973). Eagly went further in testing her historical interpretation of sex differences, by sorting the research findings into periods; she found that studies reporting greater influenceability among females were indeed more prevalent prior to 1970 than during the period of the women's movement in the 1970s.

REPLICATIONS AND THEIR RELATIVE UTILITY

Eagly would not have been able to test her hypothesis had there not been a number of replications available for her to examine with reference to particular historical periods. The crucial role of replication is well-established in science generally, even apart from its particular role in connection with Eagly's investigation. The undetected equipment failure, the rare and possibly random human errors of procedure, observation, recording, computation, or report are well enough known to make scientists wary of the unreplicated experiment. When we add to the possibility of the random "fluke," common to all sciences, the fact of individual differences and the possibility of systematic experimenter effects in at least the behavioral sciences, the importance of replication looms larger still to the behavioral scientist.

In an earlier chapter we briefly discussed what is meant by replication, and we now discuss it in more detail. Clearly the *same* experiment can never be repeated by a different worker. Indeed the *same* experiment can never be repeated by even the same experimenter (Brogden, 1951). At the very least, the subjects and the experimenters themselves are different, and the experimental situation is influenced (as Eagly pointed out) by the historical period. But to avoid the not very helpful conclusion that there can be no replication in the behavioral sciences, we can speak of "relative replications." We can rank-order experiments on how close they are to each other in terms of subjects, experimenters, tasks, and situations. We can usually agree that *this* experiment, more than *that* experiment, is like a given paradigm experiment. When we speak of replication in this chapter, therefore, we refer to a *relatively* exact repetition of an experiment.

Replications may be crucial, as when we try to resolve the tensions of corroboration, but some replications are more crucial than others. Three of the variables affecting the value, or utility, of any particular replication are:

a. *when* the replication is conducted
b. *how* the replication is conducted
c. *by whom* the replication is conducted

The first variable—*when* the replication is conducted—is important because replicated studies conducted early in the history of a particular research question are usually more useful than replications conducted later in the history of a particular research question. The first replication doubles our information about the research issue; the fifth replication adds 20 percent to our information level; and the fiftieth replication adds only 2 percent to our information level. Once the number of replications grows to be substantial, our need for further replication is likely to be due not to a real need for further replication but to a real need for the more adequate evaluation and summary of the replications already available. That was the situation in the case of Eagly's investigation.

How the replication is conducted is another important variable to keep in mind. It has already been noted that replications are possible only in a relative sense. Still, there is a distribution of possible replications in which the variance is generated by the degree of similarity to the original study that characterizes each possible replication. If we choose our replications to be as similar as possible to the study being replicated, we may be more true to the original idea of replication but we also pay a price—that price is external validity. If we conduct a series of replications as exactly like the original as we can, and if their results are consistent with the results of the original study, we have succeeded in "replicating" but not in extending the generality of the underlying relationship investigated in the original study. The more imprecise the replications, the greater the benefit to the external validity of the tested relationship if the results support the relationship. If the results do not support the original finding, however, we cannot tell whether that lack of support stems from the instability of the original result or from the imprecision of the replications.

The third variable—*by whom* the replicated experiment is conducted—is important because of the problem of *correlated replicators*. So far in our discussion we have assumed that the replications are independent of one another. But what does "independence" mean? The usual minimum requirement for independence is that the subjects of the replications be different persons. But what about the independence of the replicators? Are a series of ten replications conducted by a single investigator as independent of one another as a series of ten replications each of which is conducted by a different investigator?

To begin with, an investigator who has devoted his or her life to the study of vision, or of psychological factors in somatic disorders, is less likely to carry out a study of verbal conditioning than is the investigator whose interests have always been in the area of verbal learning or interpersonal influence processes. To the extent that experimenters with different research interests are different kinds of people, and as such are likely to obtain different data from their subjects, we are forced to the conclusion that within any area of behavioral research the experimenters come precorrelated by virtue of their common interests and any associated characteristics. Immediately, then, there is a limit placed on the degree of independence we may expect from workers or replications in a common vineyard. But for different areas of research interest the degree of correlation or of similarity among its workers may be quite different. Certainly we all know of workers in a common area who obtain data quite opposite from that obtained by colleagues. The actual degree of correlation, then, may not be very high. It may, in fact, even be negative, as with investigators holding an area of interest in common but holding opposite expectancies about the results of any given experiment.

A common situation in which research is conducted nowadays is within the context of a team of researchers. Sometimes these teams consist entirely of colleagues; often they comprise one or more faculty members and one or more students at various stages of progress toward the Ph.D. Experimenters within a single research group may reasonably be assumed to be even more highly intercorrelated than any group of workers in the same area of interest who are not within the same research group. And perhaps students in a research group are more likely to be more correlated with their major professor than would be true of another faculty member of the research group. There are two reasons for this likelihood. The first is a *selection* factor. Students may select to work in a given area with a given investigator because of their perceived and/or actual similarity of interest and associated characteristics. Colleagues are less likely to select a university, area of interest, and specific project because of a faculty member at that university. The second reason why students may be more correlated with their professor than another professor might be is a *training* factor. Students may have had a large proportion of their research experience under the direction of a single professor. Other professors, though collaborating with their colleagues, have most often been trained in research elsewhere by other persons. While there may be exceptions, even frequent ones, it seems reasonable, on the whole, to assume that student researchers are more correlated with their adviser than another professor might be.

The correlation of replicators which we have been discussing refers directly to a correlation of *attributes* and indirectly to a correlation of *data* these investigators will obtain from their subjects. The issue of correlated experimenters or observers is by no means a new one. Over eighty years ago, Karl Pearson spoke of "the high correlation of judgments . . . [suggesting] . . . an influence of the immediate atmosphere, which may work upon two observers for a time in the same manner" (1902, p. 261). Pearson believed the problem of correlated observers to be as critical for the physical sciences as for the behavioral sciences.

There is a simple principle that evolves from these considerations. It is that replications yielding consistent results are maximally informative and maximally convincing if they are maximally separated from the first experiment and from each other along such dimensions as time, physical distance, personal attributes of the experimenters, experimenters' expectancies, and experimenters' degree of personal contact with one another. Keeping this principle in mind can go a long way in helping us to resolve the tensions of corroboration between "observation" and "hypothesis" as discussed earlier, particularly if we try to weigh replications in terms of the quality and uniqueness of the study. For example, in an area dominated by research on male subjects, the first study employing female subjects is worth more in terms of external validity than the tenth study employing only male subjects. In an area dominated by research on adults, the first study employing children as data collectors is worth more than the tenth study employing adult data collectors. And the first study employing performance measures of intellectual ability is worth more than the tenth study employing the more usual verbal measures of intellectual ability.

LIMITATIONS OF STRONG INFERENCE

There is another approach to replication, called *strong inference,* which ideally tries to deal with this tension between observation and hypothesis by letting one fact vie against another to form a higher synthesis (Platt, 1964). It is meant to be like climbing a tree, in that at each fork we choose to go to the right branch or to the left, until we have finally gotten to the top. The first step is to devise alternative predictions to represent rival causal hypotheses, on the basis of prior observation or the nature of the facts. The second step is to design a research study with alternative possible outcomes, each of which will (as nearly as possible) exclude one or more of the hypotheses. The third step is to carry out the research so as to get a clean result. The process is then repeated, making and testing new rival hypotheses to refine the possibilities that remain.

One problem with strong inference is that it is not always possible to get a clean result, given the complex nature of behavior. Further, when we do not get a clean result this simply may mean that there is more than one direction of causal pattern operating. To give an example, Dean Keith Simonton (1976*b*) had two rival hypotheses vying against one another in a cross-lag design replicated over many periods. One hypothesis was that the ascent and decline of civilizations is a result of changes in personal needs and values, an idea that he derived from research done by McClelland (1961). The rival hypothesis, which was derived from research by Sorokin (1964), was that personal beliefs are a response to prevailing political and cultural events. The design Simonton used resembled the one shown in Chapter 8 (see Figure 8.2), except that his sample consisted of 122 consecutive 20-year intervals from 540 B.C. to A.D. 1900 for which there were archival data available on measures of philosophical beliefs and political contexts. He reasoned that if variation in a political variable always preceded variation in a philosophical variable, then personal beliefs are probably the function of sociocultural context (Sorokin's hypothesis). On the other hand, if variation in a philosophical variable always preceded variation in a political variable, then personal beliefs may possess sociocultural consequences (McClelland's hypothesis). Depending upon the circumstances of the variables surveyed, Simonton found that both causal patterns have existed throughout history.

In other words, Simonton found that *a* may cause *b* but that *b* may also cause *a*. There are, to be sure, examples of similar outcomes at other levels of inquiry in behavioral research. For instance, there has recently been some debate in social psychology over the question of whether attitudes cause behaviors or whether behaviors cause attitudes. In spite of a lack of theoretical agreement, there now seems to be convincing evidence emerging that both hypotheses are correct. What seems to be true is that the specific causal sequence is intimately tied to the nature of the situation, and that attitudes cause behaviors in some situations while behaviors cause attitudes in other situations (Bentler & Speckart, 1981).

Thus it is possible that the hypothesis that is ruled out by strong inference may only be "incorrect" under the given set of conditions in which it was tested. To give a further example, there has been considerable research on the nature of the "clustering process" by which the mind consolidates related ideas and perceptions into distinct categories and stereotypes. Some researchers have argued that this clustering involves an averaging principle, while others have asserted that it involves an adding principle. What seems to be true, however, is that both hypotheses are correct (cf. Rosnow & Arms, 1968; Rosnow, Wainer, & Arms, 1970). Suppose that two persons, A and B, each have an income of $100 a day and that a third person, C, has an income of $40 a day. The total income of a group consisting of A, B, and C is higher than the total income of a group consisting only of A and B, but the average income of A and B is higher than the average income of A, B, and C. Were we to ask people which of these two groups enjoys a higher economic status, we would find that most people will perceive that the group with the higher *average* income is better off financially (the averaging principle). However, if we said that these were two families, we would then find that most people will perceive that the group with the higher *total* income is better off financially (the adding princi-ple). Because we do some of both, we would not want to rule out either principle by *blindly* following the logic of strong inference.

ASSESSING LIMITATIONS LOGICALLY

The tension between observation and hypothesis exists at all levels of behav-ioral research, where we deal with the meanings of social facts on the basis of data which always have an element of uncertainty. In any given situation, the best we can do is to try to deduce the limitations of the data on the basis of common sense and the evidence we have in hand.

Let us say we want to make a reasonable guess as to how subjects' volun-teer status interacts with the variables under investigation. To make a guess, we need to know a little about the characteristics that serve to differentiate volunteers for behavioral research from nonvolunteers. To give an example, in the 1940s and early 1950s Alfred C. Kinsey and his associates conducted land-mark studies which were also a source of great controversy. Kinsey and his associates conducted intensive interviews with about 8000 American men and 12,000 American women in order to uncover the predominant patterns of sex-ual behavior in the United States (Kinsey, Pomeroy, & Martin, 1948; Kinsey, Pomeroy, Martin, & Gebhard, 1953). Since the subjects were all volunteers, however, it was reasonable to question the generalizability of the findings. Some of the critics suggested that Kinsey's findings might have been biased in the direction of overreporting of sexual activity as a consequence of the sub-jects' volunteer status (Cochran, Mosteller, & Tukey, 1953; Dollard, 1953; Hyman & Sheatsley, 1954).

One critic, Abraham Maslow, based his belief on both observation and hypothesis. Maslow (1942) had observed that subjects who scored high on a self-esteem test tended to express unconventional sexual attitudes. He also observed that Brooklyn College students who volunteered for the Kinsey inter-view scored higher in self-esteem than did nonvolunteers (Maslow & Sakoda, 1952). On the basis of this evidence, Maslow logically hypothesized that Kin-sey's results might have overestimated the population values because his respondents, too, were volunteers who were presumably more self-disclosing about their unconventional attitudes.

In recent years, a great deal more has been learned about the characteristics of the volunteer subject. Table 15.1 lists those characteristics that deserve some degree of confidence in their stability, roughly in order of the degree of confidence we can have in each based on the empirical evidence (Rosenthal & Rosnow, 1975). There are five characteristics listed under maximum confidence: that volunteers tend to be better educated, to have higher social-class status, to be more intelligent, to be higher in the need for social approval, and to be more sociable than nonvolunteers. Under considerable confidence, we find that volunteers tend to be more motivated to seek arousal, to be more unconventional, to be females, to be less authoritarian, to be Jewish or Protestant, and to be less conforming than nonvolunteers. Under some confidence, we see that volunteers tend to be from small towns and to be more interested in religion than nonvolunteers (especially in questionnaire studies). We also find that volunteers tend to be more altruistic and self-disclosing than nonvolunteers. When recruitment of subjects is for research with drugs, hypnosis, high temperatures, or some vaguely described experiment, or when subject recruitment is for medical research, we find that volunteers are usually more malad-

Table 15.1 Volunteer characteristics grouped by degree of confidence of conclusion

I. *Maximum confidence*
  1. Educated
  2. Higher social class
  3. Intelligent
  4. Approval-motivated
  5. Sociable

II. *Considerable confidence*
  6. Arousal-seeking
  7. Unconventional
  8. Female
  9. Nonauthoritarian
  10. Jewish > Protestant > Catholic
  11. Nonconforming

III. *Some confidence*
  12. From smaller town
  13. Interested in religion
  14. Altruistic
  15. Self-disclosing
  16. Maladjusted
  17. Young

Source: R. Rosenthal and R. L. Rosnow, *The Volunteer Subject,* Wiley-Interscience, New York, 1975, by permission of the publisher.

justed than nonvolunteers. Volunteers are also usually younger than nonvolunteers (especially when volunteering is for laboratory research and when the subjects are women).

Given these seventeen characteristics, it is possible to make a good guess as to the direction of the volunteer bias in any particular investigation, either experimental or nonexperimental, using volunteer subjects. Suppose we had developed a new IQ test and wanted to standardize it by testing a large number of people in order to develop scoring norms. If we gave the test only to volunteer subjects, we may guess that the norms would be artificially inflated. That is because volunteers tend to be better educated (characteristic 1) and usually score higher on intelligence tests than nonvolunteers (characteristic 3). On the other hand, were we attempting to standardize a new test of authoritarianism on volunteers, that would probably produce underestimates of normative values (conclusion 9).

It also follows that if we know the interactions between these seventeen characteristics and the variables of interest, we should be able to hypothesize whether our research findings based on the behavior of volunteers err on the positive or negative side. Suppose we wanted to find out how persuasive a propaganda appeal was before using it in a field setting. One simple experimental procedure would be to expose a group of people to it and then to compare their reactions with others who were not exposed to it. If we used volunteer subjects, however, there would be an increased probability of a type I error. First of all, volunteers tend to be higher in the need for approval than nonvolunteers (characteristic 4). Second, there is evidence that those people who score high in need for approval tend to be more readily influenced than low-scorers (Buckhout, 1965; Crowne & Marlowe, 1964). Therefore, our volunteer subjects will probably be more influenced by the appeal than a sample of nonvolunteers. This would probably also lead to some distortion in the estimated magnitude of the difference between the experimental and the control group, and we would want to take this possibility into consideration when generalizing from the research findings. If we did not take this possibility into account, we might well be led to draw the false conclusion that the appeal was more persuasive than it actually would be in the population as a whole.

The opposite type of error can also be anticipated. Suppose an investigator were interested in the effects of some experimental manipulation on the dependent variable of gregariousness. If a sample of highly sociable volunteers were drawn, any manipulation designed to increase gregariousness might be too harshly judged as ineffective simply because the control group would already be unusually high on this variable (characteristic 5). The same manipulation might prove effective in increasing the gregariousness of the experimental group relative to the gregariousness of the control group if the total subject sample were characterized by a less restricted range of gregariousness. At least in principle, then, the use of volunteer subjects could also lead to a predictable increase in type II errors. Thus we see how it may be possible to deduce the limitations of our data in very specific ways based on common sense and the limited evidence at hand.

GATHERING EVIDENCE

Previously we said that, ideally, we search for some plausible combination of social facts which can be further corroborated by observation and hypothesis. The examples given above illustrate how we are able sometimes to assess the limits of data on the basis of logic and evidence. This evidence is usually the end product of a methodical and extensive literature review, as these examples clearly show. Because the inferences made in literature reviews are as central to the validity of scientific knowledge as those made in individual experimental and nonexperimental studies, they also require that we pay the same careful attention to details of rigorous methodology. Harris M. Cooper (1980) has analyzed the five stages in a literature review, which parallel the stages of individual studies, and his analysis helps us to focus on considerations which lead to the most objective reviews.

The first stage involves the *formulation of the research problem*, including the definition of variables and a rationale (usually a theory or specific hypothesis) for why they are related to one another. In this way, even if we start with a very broad conception, we can begin to think about how to narrow the vast body of literature into a more manageable entity. As we proceed, we may find that there are different operational definitions and levels of abstraction for the same or similar kinds of variables, but our theoretical definition will help us to distinguish relevant from irrelevant studies. Occam's razor is a good principle to keep in mind, for the more abstract our theoretical definition, the less able we are to discriminate among various studies. On the other hand, it is almost always better to be exhaustive in our coverage rather than to exclude a possibly relevant study because our conception of the problem was too narrow. Similarly, the more operational details examined, the more externally valid will our review conclusions be—since we present more information about situational and individual variations.

The second stage is the *collection of data*, and we begin by deciding what procedures should be used to find relevant evidence. This is not unlike defining the population of subjects that will be relevant in an experimental study, in that we must consider both those elements that we hope to represent in the study and those that are actually accessible to us. Some evidence is inaccessible to reviewers simply because it is not in print. It has been found that about half of researchers who produce a rejection of the null hypothesis will submit a report for publication, while only 6 percent who fail to reject the null hypothesis ever attempt to publish (Greenwald, 1975). This suggests a decided bias in favor of statistically significant research findings, although there are sometimes techniques for retrieving the unpublished reports as well.

For example, among the techniques for information retrieval mentioned by Cooper, one involves the "invisible college" of scientists working on similar problems who are usually aware of one another's interests and exchange published and unpublished reports of research findings. A second technique, called the "ancestry approach," involves tracking relations from one study to another on the basis of the list of references or notes in each report. A third technique, particularly useful in the case of published reports, is to use abstracting services, such as *Psychological Abstracts, Child Development Abstracts and Bibliography,* or the *Educational Resources Information Center Files.* Summaries of dissertations can be found in *Dissertation Abstracts International,* and there are other such archival references available in most research libraries. A speedy retrieval technique is the on-line computer search, where we supply a list of key words or phrases and the computer scans several abstracting services for us. No technique is perfect, however, and we will want to use more than one retrieval system to ensure that we have not omitted any relevant evidence.

The third step is the *evaluation of data* stage. Having amassed a body of data, we must now decide what evidence should be included in the review. Cooper suggests that, in research reviewing, there is only one criterion for discarding data: the internal validity of the study in question. Other workers in this field, however, feel that no data should be discarded; instead these workers feel that the quality of the research should be one of the factors examined to help us decide about the determinants of large versus small effects (e.g., Glass, McGaw, & Smith, 1981; Rosenthal, 1976; Rosenthal & Rosnow, 1975).

The fourth step involves the *analysis and interpretation* of the separate studies in order to lead to a set of unified statements about the research problem. An example would be the set of unified statements about volunteer bias which were developed on the basis of the separate data points in Table 15.1. Statistical aids have recently been developed for helping us quantitatively synthesize or integrate data in order to tease out systematic patterns, and we return to this subject in a later chapter when we discuss the meta-analysis of evidence. We must be very careful, whatever method we use, that we do not misinterpret evidence as supporting causality when it does not. As we shall see in the later chapters, we should also keep in mind that different statistical methods of analysis may tend to obscure some results or produce conflicting results. Therefore, we may need to reanalyze the previously published findings.

The final stage in the review process is the *public presentation* of the results to the scientific community. The traditional medium for communicating research results is scientific journals, and in Appendix A we discuss the preparation of a typical manuscript for journal publication. Most publication manuals discuss the nature of abbreviated research reviews that appear as introductions to new experimental or nonexperimental data, but ignore the more extensive research reviews of the type that we have been discussing. There are models available, nonetheless. Some excellent examples of review articles can be found in *Psychological Bulletin* and similar journals in other areas of behavioral science, although many of the more extensive reviews appear in book-length manuscripts (monographs). Whatever form it takes, a research review is never useful even at first if it does not address all of the significant variables and relations that are relevant to an area. To do the job carefully and thoroughly will involve many hours of hard work, paying particular attention to rigorous methodology in the same way we would if we were doing an experiment or a survey study.

STATISTICAL ANALYSIS OF DATA

So far we have concentrated on the nature and methods of data collection and on the logic of drawing conclusions on the basis of data which already have an element of error or uncertainty. In the chapters that follow we show various ways of analyzing quantitatively the data we have collected in our research.

The unifying theme of these chapters is that there will almost always be two kinds of information we want to have for each of our research questions: the size of the effect and its statistical significance. This theme is well expressed by a fundamental conceptual equation which we shall repeatedly refer to:

$$\text{Significance test} = \text{size of effect} \times \text{size of study}$$

This equation tells us that for any given size of effect (e.g., correlation coefficient) and for any given size of study (e.g., number of subjects) there will be a corresponding test of significance. Much of the data-analytic work of the behavioral sciences consists in deciding how we shall define these three elements of our equation in any particular study.

FUNDAMENTALS OF DATA ANALYSIS

Chapter **16.** **Describing Data**

Chapter **17.** **Correlations**

Chapter **18.** **Comparing Two Means: The *t* Test**

SIXTEEN

DESCRIBING DATA

DISPLAYS

Much of the fundamental work in behavioral science involves the description of a group of *sampling units,* that is, the people or things being studied. Sampling units are most often people or other animals, but they can be things like countries, states, cities, precincts, school districts, schools, classrooms, businesses, hospitals, wards, or clinics. Some type of number is assigned to each sampling unit on any particular variable, and the task of describing our data is that of summarizing the numbers representing the sampling units on that variable.

Suppose that we had measured nine people on a scale of anxiety and obtained the following numbers:

$$5, 8, 7, 6, 4, 6, 7, 5, 6$$

We might begin by ordering these numbers from lowest to highest to get a better view of their beginning and ending points and where they clump or bunch:

$$4, 5, 5, 6, 6, 6, 7, 7, 8$$

We can further clarify the nature of our observations by arranging them to reduce the number of categories to just the number of different score values:

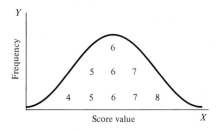

This kind of arrangement is called a *distribution* with score values increasing from left to right and the height of the curve reflecting the frequency of occurrence of the scores. Note that one axis is labeled X and the other Y; when describing research findings we *usually* plot the independent variable on the X-axis and the dependent variable on the Y-axis. Thus, distributions of research data show the rise and fall of frequencies as we move over varying values of our independent variable. Another name for the horizontal axis, or X-axis, is the *abscissa*; another name for the vertical axis, or Y-axis, is the *ordinate*.

There is, however, no hard-and-fast rule that displays must resemble the figure above. Data may also be plotted sideways, as in the following distribution:

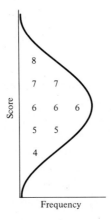

It is possible to combine the ordering of our data with the construction of a distribution. Imagine the following scores obtained from fifteen persons:

66, 87, 47, 74, 56, 51, 37, 70, 82, 66, 41, 52, 62, 79, 69

Since these are two-digit numbers we can save space by listing the leading digits only once and recording for each of these leading digits the second digits attached to them:

Leading digit	Second digits			
8	7	2		
7	4	0	9	
6	6	6	2	9
5	6	1	2	
4	7	1		
3	7			

The leading digits are referred to as "stems," and the second digits as "leaves," because that is how they looked to John Tukey, the statistician who designed and developed this *stem-and-leaf display* methodology (Tukey, 1977). The eye takes in the stem-and-leaf plot as it does any other frequency distribution, but the original data are preserved with greater precision in a stem-and-leaf plot than would be the case with ordinary frequency distributions. It is useful, too, after having recorded all the data in a stem-and-leaf display as above to rearrange the leaves from smallest to largest on each stem. Rearranging the display above yields:

Stem	Leaves			
8	2	7		
7	0	4	9	
6	2	6	6	9
5	1	2	6	
4	1	7		
3	7			

Quantitative summaries of the data displayed in stem-and-leaf plots often include (1) a listing of the scores falling at each of the following percentile locations: 100, 75, 50, 25, 0; (2) the range from the 75th to 25th percentile; (3) the standard deviation estimated; and (4) the mean, concepts now to be reviewed.

MEASURES OF LOCATION

One characteristic of distributions that we almost always want to describe is the location of their bulk or the central or typical values. Several measures are available for this purpose.

The *mode* is the score that occurs with the greatest frequency. In the series of scores 3, 4, 4, 4, 5, 5, 6, 6, 7, the modal score is 4. The series 3, 4, 4, 4, 5, 5, 6, 7, 7, 7 has two modes (at the values 4 and 7) and is called "bimodal."

The *median* is the midmost score in a series of n scores when n is an odd number. When n is an even number, the median is half the distance between the two midmost numbers. In the series 2, 3, 3, 4, 4, 5, 6, 7, 7, 8, 8, the median value is 5; in the series 2, 3, 3, 4, 4, 7, the median value is 3.5, halfway between the 3 and the 4 at the center of the set of scores. Ties create a problem. The series 3, 4, 4, 4, 5, 6, 7 has one score below 4 and three above, four scores below 5 and two above, four scores below 4.5 and three above. What shall we regard as our median? A useful procedure is to view our series as perfectly ranked, so that a series 1, 2, 3, 3, 3 is seen as made up of a 1, a 2, a small 3, a larger 3, and a still larger 3 on the assumption that more precise measurement procedures would have allowed us to break the ties. Thus, in the series 1, 2, 3, 3, 3 we would regard 3, the "smallest" 3, as our median. There are two scores below this particular 3 and two above it. In reporting this median we can simply specify the median's value as 3 or we could further specify that it was the "smallest" 3.

The *mean* is the arithmetic average of our scores written symbolically as

$$\frac{\Sigma X}{N}$$

and read as "the sum of the scores divided by the number of scores."

Trimmed means are sometimes useful. We trim by dropping a particular percentage of the scores from both ends of the distribution and computing the mean of the remaining scores. A mean trimming 10 percent of the scores from each end of the following series, -20, 2, 3, 6, 7, 9, 9, 10, 10, 10, is 7.0, the untrimmed mean is 4.6. The median is unaffected by trimming, so the median of the data just presented is 8 with or without trimming. The mode, which may be affected by trimming, is 10 before trimming but bimodal at 9 and 10 after trimming. In general, we prefer medians and trimmed means to ordinary means when the distribution of scores is strongly asymmetric. Their use protects us from possibly misleading interpretations based on very unusual scores. For example, if we listed the family income for ten families and found nine of them with zero income and one with a $10 million income, the mean income of $1 million would be highly unrepresentative compared to the trimmed mean, median, or (in this case) even the mode. Medians and trimmed means also protect us somewhat against the intrusion of "wild" scores. Suppose a series 4, 5, 5, 6, 6, 6, 7, 7, 8 of which the mean, median, mode, and trimmed mean are all 6. However, suppose the key-puncher erred and instead punched the values 4, 5, 5, 6, 6, 6, 7, 7, 80. Our new (erroneous) mean would now be 14, but our median or trimmed mean would remain unaffected.

MEASURES OF SPREAD

In addition to knowing the central tendency (or roughly the typical value of a set of scores), we almost always also want to know about the degree to which scores deviate from these measures of central tendency (or how spread out the scores are). Several measures of spread, dispersion, or variability are available.

The *range* is the distance between the highest and lowest scores. In the series 2, 3, 4, 4, 6, 7, 9, we can define the *crude range* as the highest score (9) minus the lowest score (2), i.e., $9 - 2 = 7$. A refinement is often introduced that takes into account the fact that a score of 9 might, under conditions of more accurate measurement, fall somewhere between 8.5 and 9.5, while a score of 2 might, under conditions of more accurate measurement, fall somewhere between 1.5 and 2.5. Therefore, we can view the *extended range*, or corrected range, as running from a high of 9.5 to a low of 1.5, i.e., $9.5 - 1.5 = 8$. The use of the extended, or corrected, range, therefore, adds a half unit at the top of the distribution and a half unit at the bottom of the distribution, or a total of one full unit. The extended range is, therefore, defined as the highest score (H) minus the lowest score (L) plus one unit, or ($H - L$) + 1 unit. If the units are integers we have ($H - L$) + 1 as the definition of the extended range. However, if the units are tenths of integers we have ($H - L$) + .1 as the definition of the extended range. Consider the series 8.4, 8.7, 8.8, 9.0, 9.1. The crude range is 9.1 − 8.4 = 0.7, the extended range runs from 9.15 to 8.35; and 9.15 − 8.35 = 0.8, or ($H - L$) + .1.

For most practical purposes we can use either the crude or the extended range. When measurement is not very accurate and when the crude range is small, however, we obtain a more accurate picture of the actual range when we employ the extended range. We illustrate with an extreme example. Suppose we have employed a 3-point rating scale in our research and all our judges made ratings at the midpoint value, say 2 on a scale of 1 to 3. Then our crude range would be zero (2 − 2), but our extended range would be 1 (2.5 − 1.5), since some of our judges might have rated nearly as high as 2.5 and some nearly as low as 1.5 had those ratings been possible. If a crude but quantitative index is desired to help us decide between the crude and extended range, we can divide the former by the latter. This index (CR/ER) yields zero in the extreme example just given and .90 if the crude range were 9 and the extended range were 10. With CR/ER as high as .90 it seems reasonable to report either of the ranges. With CR/ER much lower, it might be more informative to report the extended range.

The range is very convenient to compute and quite informative for describing the spread of certain well-behaved distributions. It suffers badly, however, from being very much affected by even a single very deviant score. (Such "wild" scores are sometimes due to recording errors, such as recording a 10 as 100.)

Trimmed ranges refer to a type of range designed to make the index of spread less affected by a small number of extreme scores. The general principle is to drop some proportion of the data from both ends of the distribution and then report the range, usually the crude range, for the data that remain. Suppose we decide to drop the extreme 10 percent of the data from each end; that would leave as the highest remaining score $X_{.90}$ (i.e., the score falling at the 90th percentile) and would leave $X_{.10}$ (i.e., the score falling at the 10th percentile) as the lowest remaining score. The trimmed range of the middle 80 percent of the scores then would be $X_{.90} - X_{.10}$. However, before we can compute this range we must find $X_{.90}$ and $X_{.10}$. We find $X_{.90}$ by computing the location of the $X_{.90}$th score as ($N + 1$).90 and the location of the $X_{.10}$th score as ($N + 1$).10. Given the scores 10, 11, 12, 13, 14, 15, 16, 17, 18, 28, we have $N = 10$, so ($N + 1$).90 = 11(.90) = 9.9 and ($N + 1$).10 = 1.1. We must keep in mind that 9.9 and 1.1 are *not* the scores we want but the *locations* of the scores we want. The 9.9th score is nine-tenths of the way between the 9th and 10th scores, which for our example is nine-tenths of the way between 18 and 28, or 27. The 1.1th score is one-tenth of the way between the first and second scores, which for our example, is one-tenth of the way between 10 and 11, or 10.1. Then the trimmed range $X_{.90} - X_{.10} = 27 - 10.1 = 16.9$.

A particular trimmed range that is frequently used is $X_{.75} - X_{.25}$, the *quartile range*. We find the required endpoints by $(N + 1).75$ and $(N + 1).25$, respectively. Thus for scores of 4, 6, 9, 11, 15, $N = 5$, $(N + 1).75 = 6(.75) = 4.5$, and $(N + 1).25 = 6(.25) = 1.5$. The locations we want, therefore, are the 4.5th score and 1.5th score, or 13 and 5 respectively. The quartile range $X_{.75} - X_{.25}$, then, is $13 - 5 = 8$. In the normal distribution (to be reviewed below) the quartile range is roughly equivalent to $1\frac{1}{3}$ standard deviations. There is one particular point in the distribution we have encountered earlier, $X_{.50}$, which is the median, and it is located by $(N + 1).50$.

The *average deviation* tells the average distance from the mean of all the scores in our series. To compute the average deviation $(\bar{D})$ we subtract the mean $(\bar{X})$ from each score (X) in turn, add these differences (D) disregarding signs, and divide by the number of scores (N) in the series:

$$\bar{D} = \frac{\Sigma|X - \bar{X}|}{N} = \frac{\Sigma|D|}{N}$$

Given a series of scores 4, 5, 5, 6, 10, we find the mean to be 30/5 = 6. The signed deviations, D, are found to be $-2, -1, -1, 0, +4$ for the values 4, 5, 5, 6, 10, respectively. The sum of the signed or *algebraic* deviations about the mean is always zero, but the sum of the unsigned or *absolute values* is not. For example, this sum is 8 for the present scores $(2 + 1 + 1 + 0 + 4)$ which, when divided by N, or 5 for this series, yields an average deviation of 8/5 = 1.6. The average deviation uses more of the information in a series of scores than does the range (which uses only the largest and smallest scores), but it is less convenient to compute or estimate than the range.

The *variance* of a set of scores is the mean of the squared deviations of the scores (X) from their mean $(\bar{X})$. Symbolically, the variance or σ^2 (read as sigma-squared) is written as:

$$\sigma^2 = \frac{\Sigma(X - \bar{X})^2}{N}$$

The square root of the variance, $\sqrt{\sigma^2} = \sigma$, is called the *standard deviation*, perhaps the most widely used of all measures of dispersion, spread, or variability. Both the variance, σ^2, and the standard deviation, σ, are often computed for our samples of scores. If our aim is to estimate the σ^2 of the population from which our sample has been randomly drawn, we can estimate it more accurately by a slightly different statistic, S^2, which is defined as

$$S^2 = \frac{\Sigma(X - \bar{X})^2}{N - 1}$$

and is the *unbiased estimator of the population value of* σ^2. Unbiased estimators of population values such as σ^2 are estimators that, in the long run, under repeated sampling, give the most accurate estimates. Interestingly, it turns out that S is not an unbiased estimator of the population value of σ, but that fact rarely works a hardship on us.

We illustrate the computation of σ^2, σ, S^2, and S for the following set of scores: 2, 4, 4, 5, 7, 8. The mean of these scores

$$\bar{X} = \frac{\Sigma X}{N} = \frac{2 + 4 + 4 + 5 + 7 + 8}{6} = \frac{30}{6} = 5$$

where X refers to each score and N refers to the number of scores. Therefore,

$$\sigma^2 = \frac{\Sigma(X - \bar{X})^2}{N} = \frac{(2 - 5)^2 + (4 - 5)^2 + (4 - 5)^2 + (5 - 5)^2 + (7 - 5)^2 + (8 - 5)^2}{6}$$

$$= \frac{24}{6} = 4$$

$$\text{and } \sigma = \sqrt{\sigma^2} = \sqrt{4} = 2$$

while

$$S^2 = \frac{\Sigma(X - \bar{X})^2}{N - 1} = \frac{(2 - 5)^2 + (4 - 5)^2 + (4 - 5)^2 + (5 - 5)^2 + (7 - 5)^2 + (8 - 5)^2}{(6 - 1)}$$

$$= \frac{24}{5} = 4.8$$

and $S = \sqrt{S^2} = \sqrt{4.8} = 2.19$

In most situations in which we want to *generalize* to some population we employ S^2 (or S); in most situations in which we want only to *describe* a particular set of scores (as in a classroom test) we employ σ^2 (or σ).

THE NORMAL DISTRIBUTION

The *normal distribution* is that special bell-shaped distribution that can be completely described from just our knowledge of the mean and the standard deviation. It is very useful in a wide variety of statistical procedures; descriptively it is especially useful (as we shall see shortly) because we can specify what proportion of the area is to be found in any region of the curve. In addition, many biological, psychological, and sociological attributes are actually distributed in a normal or nearly normal manner or can be transformed so that they will be distributed normally or nearly normally.

In a normal distribution as shown in Figure 16.1, about two-thirds of the scores fall between -1σ and $+1\sigma$, and about 95 percent of the scores fall between -2σ and $+2\sigma$. Over 99 percent of the scores fall between -3σ and $+3\sigma$, but the tails of the normal curve never do quite touch down.

A normal curve with mean set equal to zero and σ set equal to one is called a *standard normal curve*. Any score obtained on any normally distributed

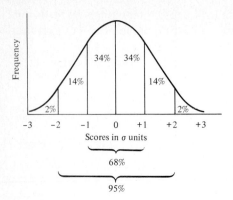

Figure 16-1 Areas in various segments of the normal distribution.

measure can be transformed into a score corresponding to a location on the abscissa of a standard normal curve by subtracting from the obtained score the mean obtained score and dividing this difference by the standard deviation of the original distribution. For example, assuming a mean ($\bar{X}$) and standard deviation (σ) of 500 and 100 for the SAT tests (a standard assumption), an obtained SAT score of 625 is equivalent to a standard deviation score (or *standard score*, or *Z score*) of 1.25. That is,

$$Z \text{ score} = \frac{X - \bar{X}}{\sigma} = \frac{625 - 500}{100} = 1.25$$

Employing a table of such Z values (see Appendix B, Table 1) shows that only about 10.6 percent of those tested score as high as 625 or higher, while about 89.4 percent score lower.

A positive Z score is above the mean, a negative Z score is below the mean. An important use of Z scores is to permit the comparison (and the averaging) of scores from distributions of widely differing means and standard deviations. For example, by computing Z scores for height and weight we can tell whether a person is taller than he or she is heavy, relative to others in the distribution of height and weight. Or suppose we had two measures of course grades, one based on a midterm multiple-choice exam of 100 points with $\bar{X} = 70$ and $\sigma = 12$, another on a final essay exam of 10 points with $\bar{X} = 6$ and $\sigma = 1$. It would make no sense to sum or average a person's scores on the two exams. For instance, consider three students earning a total of 76 points:

| | | Raw scores | | |
Student	Exam I	Exam II	Total	Average
1	70	6	76	38
2	73	3	76	38
3	67	9	76	38

However, if we convert each raw score to a standard score (Z score) we find:

Student	Exam I[a]	Standard scores Exam II[b]	Total	Average
1	0.00	0.00	0.00	0.00
2	0.25	-3.00	-2.75	-1.38
3	-0.25	3.00	2.75	1.38

[a] $\bar{X} = 70$, $\sigma = 12$ for the class as a whole
[b] $\bar{X} = 6$, $\sigma = 1$ for the class as a whole

Our first student scored at the mean both times. Our second student was slightly above average on the first test but far below average on the second. Our third student was slightly below average on the first test but far above average on the second test. The sums and averages of the Z scores take these facts into account, while the sums and averages of the raw scores are quite misleading as indices of students' course performance. Finally, Z scores can be weighted if we want them to be. In our example we weighted the Z scores for midterm and final equally (Z scores come equally weighted because their σ's are all alike, i.e., unity); if we want to weight the final exams double, we need only multiply the Exam II Z scores by 2 before adding. If we did that, our three students would now have sums of weighted Z scores equal to 0.00, -5.75, and $+5.75$ respectively. Note that the sums of Z scores are *not* themselves Z scores of the distribution of summed Z scores. If we want these sums Z scored, we must compute their mean and standard deviation and convert each sum of Z scores to a new Z by

$$Z = \frac{X - \bar{X}}{\sigma}$$

SEVENTEEN

CORRELATIONS

PEARSON *r*

One of the major purposes of all the sciences is to describe relationships, and there is no more widely employed index of relationship than the *Pearson r,* short for *Karl Pearson's product-moment correlation coefficient.* The Pearson *r* can take on values between -1.00 and $+1.00$. A value of .00 means that there is no linear relationship between the two variables we are examining. (A linear relationship is one in which a fixed change in one variable is always associated with a fixed change in the other variable.) A value of $+1.00$ means that there is a perfect positive linear relationship between the variables (X and Y) such that as scores on one variable (X) increase, there are perfectly predictable *increases* in the scores on the other variable (Y). A value of -1.00 means that there is a perfect negative linear relationship between the variables such that as scores on X increase there are perfectly predictable *decreases* in the scores on Y. Correlations (r's) of $+1.00$, .00, and -1.00 are illustrated in Table 17-1 for three sets of four subjects, each of whom has been measured on two tests of personality, X and Y. (Also see Figure 17-1.)

Illustration A in Table 17-1 shows that two variables may be perfectly correlated in the sense of Pearson's *r* even though the scores on X and Y never agree. Thus, if we are computing the degree of correlation between two judges of classroom behavior, such as degree of teacher warmth, we can achieve a high degree of correlation even though one judge rates systematically higher than the other. Inspection of Illustration A shows also that the values of Y were chosen to be exactly twice the values of X. If the values of Y had been identical to the corresponding values of X, the Pearson *r* would have been 1.00. Some-

Table 17-1 Illustrations of three correlation coefficients (*r*'s)

	A $r = 1.00$		B $r = .00$		C $r = -1.00$	
	X	Y	X	Y	X	Y
Subject 1	8	16	8	6	8	−4
Subject 2	6	12	6	4	6	−3
Subject 3	4	8	4	4	4	−2
Subject 4	2	4	2	6	2	−1
Σ	20	40	20	20	20	−10

what surprisingly to many students, doubling the values of one of the variables has no effect on the Pearson *r*. Thus, even when *Y* is chosen to be equal to 2*X*, the Pearson *r* is still 1.00. In general, it is the case that multiplying the values of either or both variables by any (nonzero) constant, or adding any constant to either or both variables, does not affect the value of the Pearson *r*. Such behavior is what we might expect if each set of scores (*X* and *Y*) were standard scored (*Z* scored) before we computed *r*. Indeed, that is exactly what is done since *r* can be defined as:

$$r_{xy} = \frac{\Sigma Z_x Z_y}{N}$$

That is, the correlation r_{xy} between *X* and *Y* is equal to the sum of the cross-products of the *Z* scores of *X* and *Y* divided by the number (*N*) of pairs of *X* and *Y* scores. Now we can see why *r* is called a "product-moment correlation." It is because the *Z*'s are distances from the mean (also called *moments*) that are multiplied by each other to form *products*.

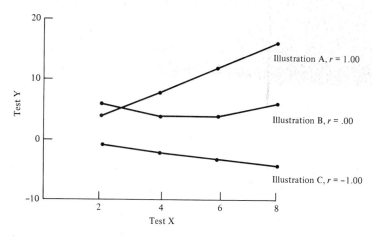

Figure 17-1 Plots of illustrations A, B, and C.

Table 17-2 Computation of r

	X	Z_x	Y	Z_y	Z_xZ_y
Subject 1	8	1.34	16	1.34	1.80
Subject 2	6	0.45	12	0.45	0.20
Subject 3	4	−0.45	8	−0.45	0.20
Subject 4	2	−1.34	4	−1.34	1.80
Σ	20	0	40	0	4.00
$\bar{X}$	5	0	10	0	1.00*
σ	2.24	1.00	4.47	1.00	—

* This is the value of r.

To employ the formula above for computation, we begin by transforming our X and Y scores to Z scores. Returning to Illustration A in Table 17-1, we find $(X - \bar{X})/\sigma_x = Z_x$ and $(Y - \bar{Y})/\sigma_y = Z_y$ for each person and then compute the products Z_xZ_y (often called the "cross products"), as shown in Table 17-2.

It should be noted that the Z scores for Y (Z_y) are identical to those for X although $Y = 2X$. That is because multiplying a set of scores by a constant also multiplies the standard deviation of that set of scores by the same constant, so that constancy of scale is preserved when Z scores are employed. The last column above shows the cross-products of the Z scores and their mean, $(\Sigma Z_xZ_y)/N$, equals r; in this case $4/4 = 1.00$.

Examining the formula for r shows that larger positive r's will be found when Z scores far above the mean of X are found alongside Z scores far above the mean of Y. Larger positive r's will also be found when Z scores far below the mean of X are found alongside Z scores far below the mean of Y (a large negative Z score multiplied by a large negative Z score yields an even larger *positive* Z score). The formula defining r is very clear conceptually but is not necessarily the most convenient formula for computing r. If a calculator is available that does not automatically compute r from the raw data of X and Y but does cumulate scores and squares of scores, the following formula is more convenient:

$$r_{xy} = \frac{N\Sigma XY - (\Sigma X)(\Sigma Y)}{\sqrt{[N\Sigma X^2 - (\Sigma X)^2][N\Sigma Y^2 - (\Sigma Y)^2]}}$$

Table 17-3 Alternative computation of r

	X	X^2	Y	Y^2	XY
Subject 1	8	64	16	256	128
Subject 2	6	36	12	144	72
Subject 3	4	16	8	64	32
Subject 4	2	4	4	16	8
Σ	20	120	40	480	240

Applied to the data of Illustration A we have the results shown in Table 17-3, and we find

$$r_{xy} = \frac{4(240) - (20)(40)}{\sqrt{[4(120) - (20)^2][4(480) - (40)^2]}} = \frac{160}{\sqrt{(80)(320)}} = \frac{160}{160} = 1.00$$

INTERPRETATIONS OF CORRELATIONS

Although it is very useful to think of r simply as an index number such that a larger positive r represents a higher degree of linear relationship than does a smaller positive r, a number of other useful interpretations are possible.

Proportion of Variance

Perhaps the most commonly employed interpretation involves r^2 rather than r; r^2 is interpreted as the proportion of the variance shared by X and Y; that is, the proportion of the variance among the Y scores that is attributable to variation in the X scores, and the proportion of the variance among the X scores that is attributable to variation in the Y scores. It is sometimes expressed as

$$r^2 + k^2 = 1.00$$

where r^2 is called the *coefficient of determination* (proportion of variance "accounted for") and k^2 is called the *coefficient of nondetermination* (the proportion of variance "not accounted for"). Although useful in some statistical applications (e.g., multiple regression and analysis of variance) the r^2 interpretation of correlation is only a poor reflection of the practical value of any given correlation coefficient (Rosenthal and Rubin, 1982). We shall return to that idea later in this chapter.

As an illustration of the r^2 interpretation of r, consider two predictor variables X_1 and X_2 that have been employed to predict or explain the dependent variable Y, as shown in Table 17-4.

Table 17-4 Two predictors of a dependent variable

	Predictor variables		Dependent variable
	X_1	X_2	Y
Subject 1	3	3	6
Subject 2	3	1	4
Subject 3	1	3	4
Subject 4	1	1	2
Σ	8	8	16
$\bar{X}$	2	2	4
σ	1	1	1.41
σ^2	1	1	2

Table 17-5 Predictor variables with unequal variances

	Predictor variables		Dependent variable
	X_1	X_2	$Y(X_1 + X_2)$
Subject 1	3	4	7
Subject 2	3	0	3
Subject 3	1	4	5
Subject 4	1	0	1
Σ	8	8	16
$\bar{X}$	2	2	4
σ	1	2	2.24
σ^2	1	4	5

The correlation between the two predictor variables is .00, and the correlation (r) between either X_1 or X_2 and Y is .707. Squaring r yields $r^2 = (.707)^2 = .500$, the proportion of variance among the Y scores predictable from *either* the X_1 *or* the X_2 scores. That this proportion of variance of .500 should be found seems appropriate; since we actually created variable Y by adding up variables X_1 and X_2 and seeing to it that they would be weighted equally by ensuring that they had equal variances or standard deviations. If they did not have equal variances, the predictor with larger variance would correlate more highly with their sum, as shown in Table 17-5.

For example, increasing the standard deviation of X_2 from 1 to 2 does not affect the correlation between X_1 and X_2 (still zero), but now the correlation between X_2 and Y has increased to .894 ($r^2 = .80$), and the correlation between X_1 and Y has decreased to .447 ($r^2 = .20$). This example shows that the ratio of the two r^2's .80/.20 is proportional to the ratio of the variances of the two predictor variables 4/1. For either example given (i.e., equal r^2's or unequal r^2's) it is useful to note that the proportions of variance in the dependent variable (Y) predictable from X_1 and X_2 are additive and, when added, yield what is called the multiple R^2. In this case $R^2 = 1.00$ because .50 + .50 = 1.00 and .80 + .20 = 1.00. Whenever we are given predictor variables that are uncorrelated ($r = .00$) with each other, the multiple R^2 (which can take any value between .00 and 1.00) between the entire battery of predictor variables and the dependent variable is simply the sum of the individual r^2's. It is not common in practice, however, for predictor variables to show a zero correlation with each other.

BINOMIAL EFFECT-SIZE DISPLAY

Another interpretation of r involves a method of displaying the practical importance of r. The procedure is called the *binomial effect-size display* (BESD) and has been described in detail elsewhere (Rosenthal and Rubin, 1979 b; 1982).

(The term *binomial* refers to the fact that in the BESD the research results are cast into dichotomous outcomes, such as success vs. failure, improved vs. not improved, or survived vs. died.) Rosenthal and Rubin found that neither experienced behavioral researchers nor experienced statisticians had a good intuitive sense of the practical meaning of such indices of *effect size* (see Chapter 2) as r^2 or such near relatives of r^2 as omega^2 (Hays, 1981) and epsilon^2 (Welkowitz, Ewen, & Cohen, 1976). The BESD was introduced because (a) its interpretation was quite transparent to researchers, students, and lay persons, (b) it was applicable whenever r was employed, and (c) it was very conveniently computed.

The specific question addressed by BESD is: What is the effect on the *success rate* (e.g., survival rate, cure rate, improvement rate, selection rate, etc.) of the institution of a new treatment procedure? It therefore displays the change in success rate attributable to the new treatment procedure. A meta-analytic example shows the appeal of the display.

In Chapter 4 we briefly alluded to a type of descriptive research known as *meta-analysis,* literally meaning the "analysis of analyses." One such study has been reported by Mary Lee Smith and Gene Glass (1977), who coded and systematically integrated the results of nearly 400 controlled evaluations of psychotherapy and counseling. On the average, they found, the typical psychotherapy client is better off than 75 percent of untreated "control" individuals, which would seem to provide evidence of the efficacy of psychotherapy. Smith and Glass reported their observations in terms of effect sizes, that is, the degree to which the null hypothesis is false—the overall effect was calculated to be equivalent to an r of .32. Instead of agreeing with Smith and Glass's conclusion, some critics argued that the results of this meta-analysis sounded the "death knell" for psychotherapy because of the "modest" size of the effect, which accounted for "only 10 percent of the variance." To resolve this inconsistency in interpretation, it might be well to examine the BESD corresponding to an r of .32. For our illustration we choose a dependent variable of extreme importance—life or death. While most dependent variables are less important than life or death, we want to emphasize that the interpretation of the BESD is not affected by the choice of dependent variable.

Table 17-6 is the BESD corresponding to an r of .32 or an r^2 of .10. For convenience and consistency we set the row and column totals of the display to 100; however, the data yielding the r's we want to display in the BESD do *not* require equal or fixed totals.

Clearly it is absurd to label as "modest" an effect size equivalent to increasing the survival rate from 34 percent to 66 percent. Even so small an r as .20, accounting for "only" 4 percent of the variance, is associated with a decrease in death rate from 60 percent to 40 percent, hardly a trivial decrease. The same statistical interpretation would apply no matter what the treatment outcome measure was, whether it was survival rate, cure rate, selection rate, and so on.

A great convenience of the BESD is how easily we can convert it to r (or r^2)

Table 17-6 The BESD for an example accounting for "only" 10 percent of the variance

| | Treatment outcome | | |
	Alive	Dead	Total
Treatment condition	66	34	100
Control condition	34	66	100
Total	100	100	200

and how easily we can go from r (or r^2) to the display. Table 17-7 shows systematically the increase in *success rates* associated with various values of r^2 and r. Thus an r of .30, accounting for 9 percent of the variance, is associated with an increase in success rate from 35 percent to 65 percent. The last column of the table shows that the difference in success rates is identical to r. Consequently the experimental-group success rate in the BESD is computed as .50 + $r/2$, whereas the control-group success rate is computed as .50 − $r/2$.

The use of the BESD to display the increase in success rate due to treatment or to selection more clearly communicates the real-world importance of

Table 17-7 Increases in success rate corresponding to various values of r^2 and r

r^2	r	Success rate increased From	To	Difference in success rates (r)
.00	.02	.49	.51	.02
.00	.04	.48	.52	.04
.00	.06	.47	.53	.06
.01	.08	.46	.54	.08
.01	.10	.45	.55	.10
.01	.12	.44	.56	.12
.03	.16	.42	.58	.16
.04	.20	.40	.60	.20
.06	.24	.38	.62	.24
.09	.30	.35	.65	.30
.16	.40	.30	.70	.40
.25	.50	.25	.75	.50
.36	.60	.20	.80	.60
.49	.70	.15	.85	.70
.64	.80	.10	.90	.80
.81	.90	.05	.95	.90
1.00	1.00	.00	1.00	1.00

treatment or selection effects than do the commonly used effect-size estimators based on the proportion of variance accounted for (Rosenthal & Rubin, 1982).

It might appear that the BESD can be employed only when the outcome variable is dichotomous, but that is not the case. It can be shown that for many distributions, there is quite good agreement between (a) the correlation r between the treatment variable and the continuously distributed outcome variable and (b) the correlation ϕ (phi) between the treatment variable and the dichotomized outcome variable (Rosenthal & Rubin, 1982).

One effect of the routine employment of a display procedure such as the 2×2 table of the BESD to index the *practical validity* of our research results would be to give us more useful and realistic assessments of how well we are doing in behavioral science.

Appropriate usage of the BESD requires that for any significance test computed, the effect-size estimate (r) associated with that test be reported as well. The interpretation of that r then is in terms of improvement in success rates as shown in Table 17-7. If we want to state this as a percentage, then we simply multiply $r \times 100$. Thus, $r = .40$ is equivalent to a 40 percent difference in success rates.

SPEARMAN RANK CORRELATION

Most of the useful correlation coefficients are product-moment correlations, and they are generally special cases of the Pearson r we have been discussing. When the data are in ranked form we apply the *Spearman rho*, but that is nothing more than a Pearson r computed on numbers that happen to be ranks. However, because ranked numbers are more predictable (in the sense that knowing only the number of pairs of scores [N] tells us both the mean and standard deviation of the scores obtained), we have a simpler computational formula for scores that have been ranked. The only new ingredient in the definitional formula is D, the difference between the ranks assigned to the two members of each pair of sampling units. The Spearman rho (ρ), then, is computed as:

$$\rho = 1 - \frac{6\Sigma D^2}{N^3 - N}$$

In the example shown in Table 17-8, four schools have been ranked by two observers on the warmth of the psychological climate created by the school's principal. The column headed D shows the difference between the ranks assigned by observers A and B. The column headed D^2 shows these differences squared, and the sum of these D^2's (ΣD^2) is required for the computation of ρ (rho). The columns headed Z_A and Z_B show the Z scores of the ranks assigned by observers A and B respectively. The last column $Z_A Z_B$ shows the cross-products of the Z-scored ranks assigned by observers A and B. Ordinarily we

Table 17-8 Two observers' rankings of four schools

| | Observers | | | | | | |
	A	B	D	D^2	Z_A	Z_B	$Z_A Z_B$
School 1	2	1	1	1	-0.45	-1.34	0.60
School 2	1	2	-1	1	-1.34	-0.45	0.60
School 3	3	3	0	0	0.45	0.45	0.20
School 4	4	4	0	0	1.34	1.34	1.80
Σ	10	10	0	2	0	0	3.20
$\bar{X}$	2.5	2.5	—	—	0	0	0.80
σ	1.12	1.12	—	—	1.00	1.00	—

$$\rho = 1 - \frac{6(2)}{4^3 - 4} = 1 - \frac{12}{60} = .80$$

$$r = \frac{\Sigma Z_A Z_B}{N} = \frac{3.20}{4} = .80$$

would need no Z scores to compute ρ, but here we wanted to illustrate the fact that ρ is equivalent to the Pearson r computed on the ranks.

The Spearman rank correlation coefficient is employed when the scores to be correlated are already in ranked form, as when raters have been asked to rank a set of sampling units. In addition, however, ρ is sometimes employed as a very quick index of correlation when ρ is easy and painless to compute and r is hard and slow. Consider computing r between the pairs of scores as shown in Table 17-9 when no calculator is available.

Computing r would be painful, but computing ρ was easy because ranks are so easy to work with. Had we computed r we would have obtained a value of .627. In this case, where $r = .627$ and $\rho = .800$, which is the better estimate of "true" correlation? That question cannot be answered readily. If, for some reason, we regarded the obtained scores as being on just the scale of measure-

Table 17-9 Computation of ρ

	X	Y	Rank X	Rank Y	D	D^2
Pair 1	6.8	79.713	2	1	1	1
Pair 2	12.2	47.691	1	2	-1	1
Pair 3	1.7	28.002	3	3	0	0
Pair 4	0.3	11.778	4	4	0	0

$$\rho = 1 - \frac{6(2)}{4^3 - 4} = 1 - \frac{12}{60} = .80$$

Table 17-10 Square root transformations

	X	Y	$\sqrt{X}$	$\sqrt{Y}$
Pair 1	6.8	79.713	2.61	8.93
Pair 2	12.2	47.691	3.49	6.91
Pair 3	1.7	28.002	1.30	5.29
Pair 4	0.3	11.778	0.55	3.43

$$r_{xy} = .627$$

$$r_{\sqrt{x}\sqrt{y}} = .799$$

$$\rho_{xy} = .800$$

$$\rho_{\sqrt{x}\sqrt{y}} = .800$$

ment required, we might prefer r to ρ. However, if there is nothing sacrosanct about the particular scale employed, and usually there is not, we might in any case choose to transform our scores to achieve greater symmetry (or lack of skewness) of distribution. Such transformations tend to increase the accuracy of statistical analyses, and ranking the scores is one form of transforming the data to reduce skewness. In this case we might have decided that the·data should have been transformed to improve the symmetry of our distributions since, in general, symmetrical distributions are preferable to skewed distributions for subsequent statistical analyses (Tukey, 1977). We might, for example, have decided to take the square roots of the data obtained. Had we done so, the illustration in Table 17-10 shows that the r between our square root transformed scores has become .799, in this case essentially the same value we obtained from the rank correlation, ρ.

In this example transforming the data to improve symmetry led to a higher r. Sometimes transforming the data leads to a lower r, however. Consider the data in Table 17-11 and their plots in Figure 17-2.

The correlation between X and Y is .9999, but the correlation between the more symmetrical transformed data (logs to the base 10 of X and Y) is only .80, precisely the value obtained by employing the rank correlation, ρ. In this case ranking the data was a better transformation than the original data; i.e., better

Table 17-11 Logarithmic transformations

	X	Y	$\log X$	$\log Y$
Pair 1	100	10	2	1
Pair 2	10	100	1	2
Pair 3	1000	1000	3	3
Pair 4	10000	10000	4	4

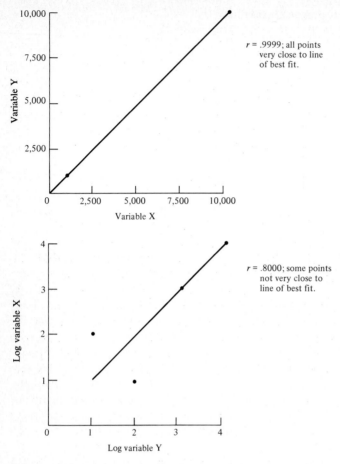

Figure 17-2 Plots of the relationship between variables X and Y and variables log X and log Y.

from the point of view of achieving symmetry; ranking the data had the same effect as taking the logs of the original data.

POINT BISERIAL CORRELATION

Another special case of the product-moment correlation r is the point biserial correlation, r_{pb}. In this case one of the variables is continuous (as are the variables employed for the usual case of r) while the other variable is dichotomous with arbitrarily applied numerical values, such as 0 and 1 or -1 and $+1$. (Such quantification of the two levels of a dichotomous variable is often called "dummy coding.") A typical illustration might have us compare females with males on some measure of verbal skill with results as follows:

Males	Females
2	4
3	5
3	5
4	6

Here we have two groups of scores. But the situation does not look like the typical situation for correlation coefficients where we would expect to see *pairs* of scores (i.e., X and Y) for each subject, not just one score (Y) as above. In this example, scores on Y (the verbal skill measure) are shown, but X is hidden. The reason, of course, is that the group identification, male vs. female, implies the X scores. Rewriting the data array into a form that "looks more correlational" yields Table 17-12.

The correlation between verbal skill and gender for these eight pairs of scores was .816. Although we shall be reviewing the t test in a subsequent chapter, we may note here, in anticipation, the special relationship between t and the point biserial correlation r_{pb}. The t statistic enables us to assess the probability that the means of two samples could differ by the obtained amount if in nature, i.e., the population, there were a zero difference between the means, or if the null hypothesis of no relationship between the independent variable and the dependent variable were true. The independent variable in the case of the t test is membership in one of the two groups being compared (usually scored as 0 and 1 or -1 and $+1$) while the dependent variable is the

Table 17-12 Correlation between gender and verbal skill

	Verbal skill	Gender (0 = male; 1 = female)	Z_x	Z_y	$Z_x Z_y$
Subject 1	2	0	-1.64	-1	1.64
Subject 2	3	0	-0.82	-1	0.82
Subject 3	3	0	-0.82	-1	0.82
Subject 4	4	0	0.00	-1	0.00
Subject 5	4	1	0.00	1	0.00
Subject 6	5	1	0.82	1	0.82
Subject 7	5	1	0.82	1	0.82
Subject 8	6	1	1.64	1	1.64
Σ	32	4	0	0	6.56
N	8	8	8	8	
$\bar{X}$	4.0	0.5	0	0	
σ	1.22	0.5	1	1	

score earned on the measures we want to compare for the two groups. As shown in Table 17-13, computing the t test for the sex-difference data yields $t = 3.46$.

Table 17-13 Illustration of a t test

	Males	Females
	2	4
	3	5
	3	5
	4	6
Σ	12	20
$\bar{X}$	3	5

$$t = \frac{\bar{X}_1 - \bar{X}_2}{\sqrt{\left(\dfrac{1}{n_1} + \dfrac{1}{n_2}\right)S^2 \text{ pooled}}} = \frac{5 - 3}{\sqrt{\left(\dfrac{1}{4} + \dfrac{1}{4}\right)0.6667}} = 3.46$$

which with 6 df is significant at $p < .01$, one-tailed test.* This result tells us that a t this large would be obtained less than 1 percent of the time if we were drawing random samples from the populations of females and males (from which our subjects were randomly sampled), if those parent populations of females and males showed zero difference between the means *or* a zero correlation between the obtained scores (Y) and the dichotomously scored (e.g., 0, 1 or -1, $+1$) variable (X) of group membership.

For the data above we now have both a correlation r_{pb} of .816 and a t value of 3.46. If it was so easy to obtain either r or t for the same data, it must be possible to obtain t directly from r or r directly from t; and so it is. Indeed, there is a very important general relationship between r's of any form (or any other measure of the size of an effect or a relationship) and a test of significance, which we introduced at the end of Chapter 15.

$$\text{Significance test} = \text{size of effect} \times \text{size of study}$$

Thus, for any given (nonzero) effect size (such as r) t, or any other test of significance, will increase as the size of the study (i.e., the number of sampling units) increases. The particular index of the size of the study, e.g., N, df, $\sqrt{N}$, $\sqrt{df}$, varies with the particular index of effect size employed, which might be r, r^2, or $r/\sqrt{1 - r^2}$ depending on the test of significance involved and the index of

---

* Degrees of freedom (df) refer to the number of observations diminished by the number of restrictions limiting the observations' freedom to vary. Thus the df for a single sample of size n is equal to $n - 1$ because once the mean of the sample has been determined, only $n - 1$ of the observations are still free to vary. Analogously, when two samples are involved, as in the case of the t test, one df is lost or "used up" for each of the two samples so $df = (n_1 - 1) + (n_2 - 1) = n_1 + n_2 - 2 = N - 2$.

the size of the study. In the case of t and r the appropriate equation is:

$$t = \frac{r}{\sqrt{1 - r^2}} \times \sqrt{df}$$

In this equation the size of the effect is defined as $r/\sqrt{1 - r^2}$ and the size of the study is defined as $\sqrt{df}$ (or, in this application, as $N - 2$). The quantity $r/\sqrt{1 - r^2}$ may be seen as the square root of $r^2/(1 - r^2)$, which is the ratio of the proportion of variance explained by r to the proportion of variance not explained by r, or a kind of signal-to-noise ratio. For our example, r was .816, so $r/\sqrt{1 - r^2} = 1.41$; the df (the number of pairs of scores minus 2) for r was $8 - 2 = 6$, so $t = 1.41 \times \sqrt{6} = 3.46$.

The general formula we gave for computing a significance test follows the scientific logic of first estimating the size of the relationship, and from that, by employing an index of the size of the study, computing the test of significance that provides information about the probability that the null hypothesis of no relationship between X and Y is true. In practice, however, researchers have traditionally computed the significance test before they have computed the size of the effect (e.g., the correlation coefficient) because of the primacy of significance testing (Chapter 2). In such cases it is easy to obtain the effect-size estimate r from the obtained t by means of the following relationship:

$$r = \sqrt{\frac{t^2}{t^2 + (n_1 + n_2 - 2)}}$$

where n_1 and n_2 represent the sizes of the samples on which each of the means being compared was based.

The t test for the significance of a correlation coefficient applies not only to the point biserial correlation r_{pb}, but to the Pearson r and to the rank-correlation coefficient ρ as well (although in the case of ρ we would want to have at least seven pairs of scores to obtain a good approximation; a rule of thumb suggested by a comparison of Tables A11[i] and A11[ii] in Snedecor & Cochran, 1980).

PHI COEFFICIENT

Another special case of the product-moment correlation r is the phi coefficient, ϕ. In this case both of the variables are dichotomous with arbitrarily applied numerical values such as 0 and 1 or -1 and $+1$. A typical illustration might have us compare Democrats with Republicans on their answer (yes or no) to a survey question with results as follows:

	Democrats	Republicans	Σ
Yes	1	4	5
No	4	1	5
Σ	5	5	10

The 2 × 2 table of counts, also called a *contingency table*, shows that one Democrat and four Republicans answered yes while four Democrats and one Republican answered no. At first glance this contingency table does not resemble the typical situation for correlation coefficients, where we would expect to see pairs of scores (i.e., X and Y for each subject. Closer evaluation shows, however, that the independent variable of party membership can be given numerical values, e.g., 0 and 1, and that the dependent variable of response to the question can be given similar numerical values. We noted earlier that this procedure of giving arbitrary numerical values to the two levels of a dichotomous variable is sometimes called "dummy coding" (especially when the numerical values assigned are 0 and 1) and was employed in our discussion of the point biserial correlation. Rewriting the data of our 2 × 2 table yields the arrangement shown in Table 17-14.

In our rewriting of the data of the 2 × 2 table, respondent 1 occupies the upper-left cell (the Democrat who said yes), respondents 2, 3, 4, and 5 occupy the upper-right cell (the Republicans who said yes), respondents 6, 7, 8, and 9 occupy the lower-left cell (the Democrats who said no), and respondent 10 occupies the lower-right cell (the Republican who said no).

The Pearson r ($\Sigma Z_x Z_y / N$) between party membership and response was .60 for these data, suggesting that Republicans were more likely to say yes to this particular question. In this example, because both variables were dichotomous, we call the obtained r a phi (ϕ) to remind us of the dichotomous nature of both variables. If our sample size (N) is not too small (that is, $N > 20$), and if both variables are not too far from a 50 : 50 split of zeros and ones (that is, no greater

Table 17-14 Correlation between response and party membership

	Party (X) (Rep. = 1; Dem. = 0)	Response (Y) (Yes = 1; No = 0)	Standard scores for variables X and Y		
			Z_x	Z_y	$Z_x Z_y$
Respondent 1	0	1	−1	1	−1
Respondent 2	1	1	1	1	1
Respondent 3	1	1	1	1	1
Respondent 4	1	1	1	1	1
Respondent 5	1	1	1	1	1
Respondent 6	0	0	−1	−1	1
Respondent 7	0	0	−1	−1	1
Respondent 8	0	0	−1	−1	1
Respondent 9	0	0	−1	−1	1
Respondent 10	1	0	1	−1	−1
Σ	5	5	0	0	6
N	10	10	10	10	
$\bar{X}$	.5	.5	0	0	
σ	.5	.5	1	1	

than 75–25), we can test the significance of phi coefficients by t tests. Since

$$t = \frac{r}{\sqrt{1 - r^2}} \times \sqrt{df}$$

For our data,

$$t = \frac{.60}{\sqrt{1 - (.60)^2}} \times \sqrt{8} = 2.12$$

which is significant at the .034 level, one-tailed (see expanded t table in Appendix B). This application of the t test for testing the significance of the phi coefficient is not well known but is well-documented (Cochran, 1950; Lunney, 1970; Snedecor & Cochran, 1967). The more common test of significance of the phi coefficient is the χ^2 test, which will be reviewed below. It comes as a surprise to many to learn that the χ^2 test does not necessarily yield more accurate tests of the significance of phi than does the t test under discussion (Cochran, 1950; Lunney, 1970).

So far in our discussion of phi we have treated it no differently from any other product-moment correlation. For two reasons, however, it will be useful to adopt an alternative approach to the phi coefficient. The first of these is computational convenience; the second is the availability of additional approaches to testing the significance of phi. Our alternative approach takes advantage of the fact that the data come to us in a 2×2 contingency table. In the table below we display again the data on the relationship between political-party affiliation and response to a survey question. This time, however, we add one of four labels to each of the four cells, A, B, C, D:

	Democrats	Republicans	Σ
Yes	A 1	4 B	(A + B) = 5
No	C 4	1 D	(C + D) = 5
Σ	(A + C) = 5	(B + D) = 5	(A + B + C + D) = 10

We can compute phi from

$$\phi = \frac{BC - AD}{\sqrt{(A + B)(C + D)(A + C)(B + D)}} = \frac{(4)(4) - (1)(1)}{\sqrt{(5)(5)(5)(5)}} = \frac{15}{25} = .60$$

Earlier we noted the general relationship between tests of significance and measures of effect size and size of experiment:

$$\frac{\text{Significance}}{\text{test}} = \frac{\text{size of}}{\text{effect}} \times \frac{\text{size of}}{\text{study}}$$

For the phi coefficient another test of significance is χ^2 with one *df* [written as $\chi^2(1)$], which can be employed whenever N is not too small (that is, $N > 20$) and the two variables are not too far from a 50:50 split of zeros and ones. It is computed as

$$\chi^2(1) = \phi^2 \times N$$

in which ϕ^2 represents the size of the effect and N represents the size of the study.

For the data we have been examining, then,

$$\chi^2(1) = (.60)^2 \times 10 = 3.60$$

which is significant at the .058 level from a table of critical values of χ^2 such as that shown in Appendix B. For χ^2 with one *df*, i.e., based on a 2×2 (or a 1×2) table, the tabled values of χ^2 are two-tailed with respect to the direction of the correlation (plus or minus), so that we divide the tabled p value by two if a one-tailed test is desired.

Sometimes χ^2 is computed before ϕ and then two formulas are available:

$$\chi^2(1) = \frac{N(BC - AD)^2}{(A + B)(C + D)(A + C)(B + D)}$$

which for the data above yields:

$$\chi^2(1) = \frac{10[(4)(4) - (1)(1)]^2}{(5)(5)(5)(5)} = \frac{2250}{625} = 3.60$$

Alternatively,

$$\chi^2(1) = \Sigma \frac{(O - E)^2}{E}$$

which is read as: the sum of the squared differences between the observed frequencies (O) and the expected frequencies (E) with each squared difference first divided by the expected frequency. The null hypothesis of no correlation (that is, that $\phi = 0$) leads to our computation of the expected frequencies. If the observed frequencies are nearly the same as those expected under the null hypothesis of no correlation, then $O - E$ will be small and $\chi^2(1)$ will be small, and it will not strongly suggest that the null hypothesis is false.

We compute the expected frequency (E) for any cell by multiplying the total of the row in which we find the cell by the total of the column in which we find the cell and dividing this product by the total number of observations (N). For the data we have been examining, the expected frequencies are all alike because $(5 \times 5)/10 = 2.5$ for all four cells. In the following display we show O and E for all four cells:

	Democrats	Republicans	Σ
Yes	$O = 1$ $E = 2.5$	$O = 4$ $E = 2.5$	$\Sigma O = 5$ $\Sigma E = 5$
No	$O = 4$ $E = 2.5$	$O = 1$ $E = 2.5$	$\Sigma O = 5$ $\Sigma E = 5$
	$\Sigma O = 5$ $\Sigma E = 5$	$\Sigma O = 5$ $\Sigma E = 5$	$\Sigma\Sigma O = 10$ $\Sigma\Sigma E = 10$

Then,

$$\chi^2(1) = \Sigma \frac{(O - E)^2}{E} = \frac{(1 - 2.5)^2}{2.5} + \frac{(4 - 2.5)^2}{2.5}$$

$$+ \frac{(4 - 2.5)^2}{2.5} + \frac{(1 - 2.5)^2}{2.5} = 3.60$$

If we compute $\chi^2(1)$ before computing phi we can obtain ϕ as follows:

$$\phi = \sqrt{\frac{\chi^2(1)}{N}}$$

The sign we give our phi depends on how we want to dummy code our variables. In the present example there is a positive correlation between being Republican and saying yes if we score being Republican as 1 and being a Democrat as 0, while scoring a yes response as 1 and a no response as 0. If the balance of the observed over the expected frequencies favors the cells agreeing in value of the dummy coding (1, 1 or 0, 0) we call phi "positive"; if the balance favors the cells disagreeing in value of the dummy coding (0, 1 or 1, 0) we call phi "negative."

Before leaving the topic of $\chi^2(1)$ as a test of significance for ϕ we should mention that *corrections for continuity* are suggested in many textbooks for χ^2 computed from 2×2 tables. The effect of these corrections is to reduce the size of the $\chi^2(1)$ obtained, by diminishing the absolute difference between O and E by .5 before squaring to adjust for the difference between discrete and continuous distributions. More recent work suggests, however, that this correction sometimes does more harm than good in terms of yielding accurate p values (Camilli & Hopkins, 1978; Conover, 1974). In any case the correction described should definitely *not* be employed if our object is to compute phi as in the equation just above. That computation of phi requires that $\chi^2(1)$ be defined in the standard (not "corrected") manner.

Related to the $\chi^2(1)$ approach to the testing of the significance of a phi coefficient is the approach via the standard normal deviate, Z. In this case the relationship between the test of significance and (1) the size of the effect and (2) the size of the study is given by:

$$Z = \phi \times \sqrt{N}$$

For the data we have been using for illustration $\phi = .60$ and $N = 10$, so

$$Z = .60 \times \sqrt{10} = 1.90$$

which is significant at the .029 level, one-tailed test, from a table of p values associated with standard normal deviates, Z's; such a table is found in Appendix B. That value agrees perfectly with the one-tailed p value based on the $\chi^2(1)$ approach to testing the significance of phi. It *should,* since $\sqrt{\chi^2(1)}$ is identical to Z.

It is also useful to keep in mind the relationship

$$\phi = \frac{Z}{\sqrt{N}}$$

because we sometimes want to compute someone else's phi from their reported p value. Suppose a research report gives a $p = .005$ but neglects to give us any effect-size estimate. As long as we can find N, the total size of the study, in the report, it is a simple matter to estimate phi. Employing a table of standard normal deviates, i.e., a table of areas in the tails of the normal curve, we can find the Z associated with a p level of .005, one-tailed, to be 2.58. If we found N to be 36 we would be able to compute phi as follows:

$$\phi = \frac{2.58}{\sqrt{36}} = .43$$

CURVILINEAR (QUADRATIC) CORRELATION

So far our discussion has been only of linear correlation in which the dependent variable (Y) can be seen to increase regularly as a function of regular increases (or decreases) in the independent variable (X). Sometimes, however, our predictions are not linear but *curvilinear*, as when we predict that performance (Y) will be better for medium levels of arousal (X) than for either high or low levels of arousal. The data below show the Pearson r between performance level (Y) and arousal level (X) for six subjects (see Table 17-15). The correlation is quite modest ($r = .13$), and the plot of the level of performance as a function of anxiety level shows why. The relationship between X and Y is not very linear; it seems instead to be substantially curvilinear; more specifically, it seems to be substantially *quadratic* (i.e., shaped like a U or an inverted U; see, for example, Figure 17-3). How can we compute a coefficient of curvilinear (quadratic) correlation between X and Y?

A number of procedures are available, and one of the simplest requires us only to redefine the variable X from amount of X (low to high) to extremeness

Table 17-15 Correlation between performance and arousal

	Arousal level (X)	Performance level (Y)	Z_x	Z_y	Z_xZ_y
Subject 1	4	1	−1.24	−1.58	+1.96
Subject 2	5	6	−1.04	0.00	0.00
Subject 3	8	9	−0.41	+0.95	−0.39
Subject 4	11	10	+0.21	+1.27	+0.27
Subject 5	15	7	+1.04	+0.32	+0.33
Subject 6	17	3	+1.45	−0.95	−1.38
Σ	60	36	0.00	0.00	+0.79
N	6	6			
$\bar{X}$	10	6			
σ	4.83	3.16			

$$r = \frac{\Sigma Z_xZ_y}{N} = \frac{+0.79}{6} = .13$$

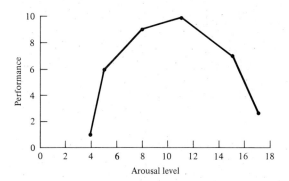

Figure 17-3 Curvilinear relationship between arousal level and performance.

Table 17-16 Correlation between performance and extremeness of arousal

	Extremeness of arousal level ($|X - \bar{X}|$)	Performance level (Y)	Z_x	Z_y	Z_xZ_y
Subject 1	6	1	+0.78	−1.58	−1.23
Subject 2	5	6	+0.31	0.00	0.00
Subject 3	2	9	−1.09	+0.95	−1.04
Subject 4	1	10	−1.56	+1.27	−1.98
Subject 5	5	7	+0.31	+0.32	+0.10
Subject 6	7	3	+1.25	−0.95	−1.19
Σ	26	36	0.00	0.00	−5.34
N	6	6			
$\bar{X}$	4.33	6			
σ	2.13	3.16			

$$r = \frac{\Sigma Z_xZ_y}{N} = \frac{-5.34}{6} = -.89$$

of X (distance from the mean of X). Table 17-16 shows this redefinition. Each value of X is replaced by the absolute (unsigned) value of that score's difference from the mean score. Therefore, a positive correlation between the extremeness of X and Y will mean that more extreme levels of arousal are associated with higher levels of performance, while a negative correlation will mean that more extreme levels of arousal are associated with lower levels of performance.

In their original form the scores on the X variable (arousal level) showed little correlation with the Y variable (performance level). In their redefined form ($|X - \bar{X}|$), however, the scores indicating absolute distance from the mean were very substantially correlated with performance level, $r = -.89$, showing that more extreme levels of arousal were associated with poorer performance (see Table 17-16). Later chapters will deal with the topic of curvilinear relationships in more detail.

In this chapter we have described five different product-moment correlations. Table 17-17 summarizes the chief characteristics of each.

Table 17-17 Product-moment correlations

Correlation	Characteristics of variables	Tests of significance*
Pearson r	both continuous	t
Spearman rho (ρ)	both ranked	t (or exact probability test if $N < 7$)
Point biserial (r_{pb})	one continuous, one dichotomous	t
Phi (ϕ)	both dichotomous	χ^2, Z, t
Curvilinear r	both continuous	t

* Appendix B has a table for critical values of p associated with correlations based on varying df where df = number of pairs of observations minus 2.

EIGHTEEN

COMPARING TWO MEANS: THE t TEST

t AND d

One of the most common situations in behavioral science is that in which we want to compare the means of two groups, e.g., an experimental vs. a control group, one diagnostic category vs. another, or one school system vs. another. Perhaps the most common method of "comparing two means" is to employ the t test of the hypothesis that there is in the populations from which we have drawn our samples either (a) no difference between the two means or, equivalently, (b) no relationship between the independent variable of membership in one of the groups and the dependent variable of score on the response variable. The t test is a test of significance and as such is made up of two components, the size of the effect and the size of the study:

$$\begin{matrix} \text{Significance} \\ \text{test} \end{matrix} = \begin{matrix} \text{size of} \\ \text{effect} \end{matrix} \times \begin{matrix} \text{size of} \\ \text{study} \end{matrix}$$

In the preceding chapter on correlations we saw that when the size of the effect of the independent variable is indexed by r the general relationship above can be rewritten more specifically as

$$t = \frac{r}{\sqrt{1 - r^2}} \times \sqrt{df}$$

Thus, we can compute the point biserial r between membership in one of the two groups (coded, for example, as 0, 1 or -1, $+1$) and the dependent variable and find t from this equation, which requires only that we also know the df for r. For this application $df =$ the number of pairs of scores less two ($N - 2$).

An alternative to indexing the size of the effect by means of r is to index it by the standardized difference between the group means, $(M_1 - M_2)/S$, in which the difference between the group means is divided by the square root of the unbiased estimate of the population variance (S^2) pooled from the two groups:

$$t = \frac{M_1 - M_2}{S} \times \frac{1}{\sqrt{\dfrac{1}{n_1} + \dfrac{1}{n_2}}}$$

or alternatively

$$t = \frac{M_1 - M_2}{S} \times \sqrt{\frac{n_1 n_2}{n_1 + n_2}}$$

It should be noted that in these alternative formulas we have changed not only the size-of-effect component but the size-of-study component as well. That is, just as $\dfrac{M_1 - M_2}{S}$ does not equal $\dfrac{r}{\sqrt{1 - r^2}}$, neither does $\sqrt{\dfrac{n_1 n_2}{n_1 + n_2}} = \sqrt{df}$. Ordinarily, whenever we change the size-of-effect index we also change the size-of-study index.

Sometimes we prefer to view the size of the effect as measured in standard score units (Z's) derived from the samples themselves. In these cases our interest is usually fixed on the effect size in the sample per se rather than on the effect size of the sample as an estimate of the effect size in the population. Therefore, our index of effect size changes from $\dfrac{M_1 - M_2}{S}$ to $\dfrac{M_1 - M_2}{\sigma}$ — sometimes called "Cohen's d" (after Cohen, 1977)—where S is based on pooling the quantities $\sqrt{\dfrac{\Sigma(X - \bar{X})^2}{N - 1}}$ and σ is based on pooling the quantities $\sqrt{\dfrac{\Sigma(X - \bar{X})^2}{N}}$. When we employ pooled σ rather than pooled S, the relationship between the test of significance, t, the effect size, $(M_1 - M_2)/\sigma = d$, and the size of the study becomes

$$t = \frac{M_1 - M_2}{\sigma} \times \left[\frac{\sqrt{n_1 n_2}}{(n_1 + n_2)} \times \sqrt{df} \right]$$

When $n_1 = n_2$ the first term in the brackets simplifies to $\frac{1}{2}$ and we can write

$$t = d \times \frac{\sqrt{df}}{2}$$

Sometimes, as part of a quantitative summary of a research domain, we would like to estimate d from other investigators' reports. We can do so readily if they have given us the results of their t test and their sample sizes n_1 and n_2

Table 18-1 Underestimation of *d* by "equal *n*" formula

Study	n_1	n_2	Accurate *d**	Estimated *d*†	Difference
1	50	50	.61	.61	.00
2	60	40	.62	.61	−.01
3	70	30	.66	.61	−.05
4	80	20	.76	.61	−.15
5	90	10	1.01	.61	−.40
6	95	5	1.39	.61	−.78
7	98	2	2.16	.61	−1.55
8	99	1	3.05	.61	−2.44

$$* \, d = \frac{t(n_1 + n_2)}{\sqrt{df}\,\sqrt{n_1 n_2}} = \text{general formula.}$$

$$\dagger \, d = \frac{2t}{\sqrt{df}} = \text{``equal } n \text{'' formula.}$$

since

$$d = \frac{t(n_1 + n_2)}{\sqrt{df}\,\sqrt{n_1 n_2}}$$

when $n_1 = n_2$ this simplifies to

$$d = \frac{2t}{\sqrt{df}}$$

If other investigators report their *t*'s and *df*'s but not their sample sizes, we can get a conservative estimate of *d* from using $d = 2t/\sqrt{df}$. When the investigator's sample sizes were equal, *d* will be accurate; but as n_1 and n_2 become more and more different, *d* will be progressively underestimated. Table 18-1 shows for eight studies, all with $t = 3.00$ and $df = n_1 + n_2 - 2 = 98$, the increasing underestimation of *d* when we employ the "equal *n*" formula. When the split is no more extreme than 70 : 30, however, the underestimation is still less than 10 percent.

MAXIMIZING *t*

Examination of the last four equations for computing *t* shows that *t* is maximized in three ways:

1. Driving the means further apart
2. Decreasing *S* or σ, the variability within groups
3. Increasing the effective size of the study.

In planning our research we can maximize t by doing what we can to achieve the three goals above. For example, strong treatment effects will drive the means further apart. If our hypothesis were that longer treatment sessions were more beneficial than shorter treatment sessions, we would be more apt to find a significant difference if we compared sessions lasting 15 minutes to sessions lasting 45 minutes than if we compared sessions lasting 30 minutes to sessions lasting 35 minutes.

S or σ, the variability of response within groups, is decreased by maximizing the standardization of our procedures and employing subject samples that are fairly homogeneous in those characteristics that are substantially correlated with the dependent variable.

Finally, when the sample sizes (n_1 and n_2) are increased, the size of t will be increased. And, for any given total N (i.e., $n_1 + n_2$), we can try to make n_1 and n_2 as nearly equal as possible since t tests thrive more when sample sizes are not too different for any fixed total N. Table 18-2 shows for various values of n_1 and n_2 (when $n_1 + n_2$ is fixed, e.g., $N = 100$) (1) the difference between n_1 and n_2 which serves as an index of sample-size inequality, (2) the arithmetic mean of the two sample sizes, (3) the harmonic mean of the two sample sizes, (4) an index of the effective size of the study, (5) the reduction in t as we have increasing inequality of n_1 and n_2, and (6) the effective loss of total sample size (N) as we have increasing inequality of n_1 and n_2. Compared to a study with $n_1 = n_2 = 50$, a study with $n_1 = 99$ and $n_2 = 1$ will show a decrease of t of 80 percent, the same effect we would have if we had lost 96 of our 100 subjects! Put another way, for any given effect size ($M_1 - M_2)/S$, t would be about the same size if we had 99 subjects in one group and 1 subject in the other group as if we had 2 subjects in each group.

Table 18-2 Effects on t of unequal sample sizes

n_1	n_2	$n_1 - n_2$	Arithmetic mean ($\bar{n}_A$)*	Harmonic mean ($\bar{n}_H$)†	$\sqrt{\dfrac{n_1 n_2}{n_1 + n_2}}$ ‡	Proportion reduction in t§	Loss of N¶
50	50	0	50	50	5.00	.00	0
60	40	20	50	48	4.90	.02	4
70	30	40	50	42	4.58	.08	16
80	20	60	50	32	4.00	.20	36
90	10	80	50	18	3.00	.40	64
95	5	90	50	9.50	2.18	.56	81
98	2	96	50	3.92	1.40	.72	92.16
99	1	98	50	1.98	0.99	.80	96.04

* $(n_1 + n_2)/2$.

† $1/\frac{1}{2}\left(\dfrac{1}{n_1} + \dfrac{1}{n_2}\right)$.

‡ Index of effective size of study (I).

§ $(5 - I)/5$ (for any nonzero t).

¶ $2(\bar{n}_A - \bar{n}_H)$.

INTERPRETING *t*

Behavioral and social researchers ordinarily like large *t* values from their investigations because larger *t* values are rarer events, i.e., events unlikely to occur if the null hypothesis were true. The two major ways of thinking about the null hypothesis for the *t* test situation are: (1) the means do not differ in the populations from which we have randomly sampled our subjects, and (2) there is no relationship between the independent variable of group membership (X) and the dependent or response variable (Y). We illustrate each of these two ways of thinking about the null hypothesis with the following example. Imagine two populations of patients requiring treatment for some problem. These populations are identical in all ways except that one population received treatment procedure A while the other population received treatment procedure B. The null hypothesis would be true in our first way of thinking if the mean benefit score of the population receiving treatment A was identical to that of the population receiving treatment B. The null hypothesis would be true in our second way of thinking if the correlation between treatment condition (coded, e.g., A = 1, B = 0) and benefit score were exactly zero for the members of populations A and B combined.

We think of the *t* test as a single test of statistical significance, and so it is in terms of the formulas we have seen above. In some ways, however, we might better think of the *t* test as a family of tests of significance, a family of infinite size. There is a different distribution of *t* values for every possible value of $n_1 + n_2 - 2$ or *df*. The two most extreme *t* distributions are those when *df* = 1 and *df* = ∞. When *df* = ∞ the *t* distribution is the normal distribution. When *df* = 1 the *t* distribution is lower in frequency in the center and higher in frequency in the tails, so that it takes a larger *t* value to reach the same level of significance than it does when *df* are larger. Figure 18-1 shows the two most extreme *t* distributions.

The vast majority of all *t* distributions look much more like the normal distribution than like the *t* distribution when *df* = 1, and it is only when *df* quite small that the divergence from normality is marked. All *t* distributions,

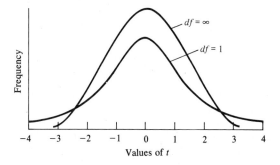

Figure 18-1 The two most extreme *t* distributions.

however, resemble the standard normal distribution in being symmetrical, in being centered at zero so that half the values are positive and half are negative, in having their greatest frequency near the center of the distribution, and in having tails that never do touch down, i.e., the upper and lower limits are $+ \infty$ and $- \infty$. Table 18-3 illustrates the differences in t distribution by giving the areas found in the right-hand tail of selected t distributions. A more complete table of t values is in Appendix B.

Studying Table 18-3 shows that for any level of significance p, the t value required to reach that level is smaller and smaller as df increases. In addition, of course, for any df a higher t value is required to reach more extreme (smaller) p levels. The most surprising fact about this table is the difference in t values required to reach the .001 level; when df is very large, a t of only about 3 is required, when $df = 1$, however, a t of about 318 is required!

One way to think about t is that if the null hypothesis were true—i.e., that the means in the population did not differ or that there were an r of zero between group membership (X) and scores on the dependent variable (Y)—the most likely value of t would be zero. However, even if the population mean difference were truly zero, we would often find nonzero t values by sheer chance alone. For example, with $df = 8$ we would obtain a t value of $+1.40$ or greater about 10 percent of the time, or of 1.86 or greater about 5 percent of the time, or of 4.50 or greater about one tenth of one percent of the time.

Table 18-3 t values required for significance at various p levels

One-tailed $p =$	.25	.10	.05	.025	.005	.001
df						
1	1.00	3.08	6.31	12.71	63.66	318.31
2	.82	1.89	2.92	4.30	9.92	22.33
3	.76	1.64	2.35	3.18	5.84	10.21
4	.74	1.53	2.13	2.78	4.60	7.17
5	.73	1.48	2.02	2.57	4.03	5.89
6	.72	1.44	1.94	2.45	3.71	5.21
8	.71	1.40	1.86	2.31	3.36	4.50
10	.70	1.37	1.81	2.23	3.17	4.14
15	.69	1.34	1.75	2.13	2.95	3.73
20	.69	1.32	1.72	2.09	2.84	3.55
25	.68	1.32	1.71	2.06	2.79	3.45
30	.68	1.31	1.70	2.04	2.75	3.38
40	.68	1.30	1.68	2.02	2.70	3.31
60	.68	1.30	1.67	2.00	2.66	3.23
80	.68	1.29	1.66	1.99	2.64	3.20
100	.68	1.29	1.66	1.98	2.63	3.17
1,000	.68	1.28	1.65	1.96	2.58	3.10
10,000	.68	1.28	1.64	1.96	2.58	3.09
∞	.67	1.28	1.64	1.96	2.58	3.09

We must decide for ourselves whether we will regard any given *t* as an event rare enough to make us doubt that the null hypothesis is true. The larger the *t* and the smaller the *p* (more significant *p*'s are *smaller*), the less likely it is that the null hypothesis is true. American behavioral researchers have an informal agreement to regard as "statistically significant" *t* values (and other tests of significance) with associated *p* levels of .05 or less, i.e., $p \leq .05$. There is evidence that decisions to believe or not believe (accept or reject) the null hypothesis are made in a binary manner based simply on whether *p* does or does not reach the .05 level (Rosenthal & Gaito, 1963, 1964).

The most experienced data-analytic statisticians do not share this view of a fixed critical level of significance and regard it as far wiser to report the actual *p* level obtained along with a statement of the size of the effect obtained (e.g., Snedecor & Cochran, 1967). There is something absurd in regarding as a "real" effect one that is supported by a $p = .05$ and as a zero effect one that is supported by a $p = .06$, yet this binary decision process does occur (Rosenthal & Gaito, 1964). It is helpful to keep in mind the general relationship

$$\frac{\text{Significance}}{\text{test}} = \frac{\text{size of}}{\text{effect}} \times \frac{\text{size of}}{\text{study}}$$

which shows that for any size of effect that is not precisely zero we can achieve any level of significance desired simply by adding to the size of the study (N).

COMPUTING *t*

We have already given several formulas for computing *t* as summarized below:

$$\frac{\text{Significance}}{\text{test}} = \frac{\text{size of}}{\text{effect}} \times \frac{\text{size of}}{\text{study}}$$

$$(1) \quad t = \frac{r}{\sqrt{1 - r^2}} \times \sqrt{df}$$

$$(2) \quad t = \frac{M_1 - M_2}{S} \times \frac{1}{\sqrt{\dfrac{1}{n_1} + \dfrac{1}{n_2}}}$$

$$(3) \quad t = \frac{M_1 - M_2}{S} \times \sqrt{\frac{n_1 n_2}{n_1 + n_2}}$$

$$(4) \quad t = \frac{M_1 - M_2}{\sigma} \times \left[\frac{\sqrt{n_1 n_2}}{(n_1 + n_2)} \times \sqrt{df} \right]$$

$$(5) \quad t = d \times \frac{\sqrt{df}}{2}$$

While all of these formulas are useful conceptually and often useful computationally, they are not as compact as we might like for a primary computational formula. Perhaps the most generally useful computational formula for a t test designed to compare the means of two independent groups is based on equation (2) above, which is rewritten more compactly as follows:

$$t = \frac{M_1 - M_2}{\sqrt{\left(\frac{1}{n_1} + \frac{1}{n_2}\right) S^2}}$$

where M_1 and M_2 (or $\bar{X}_1$ and $\bar{X}_2$) are the means of the two groups, n_1 and n_2 are the number of sampling units in each of the two groups, and S^2 is the pooled estimate of the population variance computed as

$$S^2 = \frac{\Sigma(X_1 - \bar{X}_1)^2 + \Sigma(X_2 - \bar{X}_2)^2}{n_1 + n_2 - 2}$$

Suppose we had obtained the following scores from two groups of subjects with $n_1 = n_2 = 4$

	Group 1	Group 2
	2	1
	3	2
	4	1
	5	2
Σ	14	6
n	4	4
$M = \bar{X}$	3.5	1.5

For each group we compute the sum of the squares of the deviations of the scores from their mean:

	Group 1			Group 2		
(X_1)	$(X_1 - \bar{X}_1)$	$(X_1 - \bar{X}_1)^2$	(X_2)	$(X_2 - \bar{X}_2)$	$(X_2 - \bar{X}_2)^2$
2	-1.5	2.25	1	-0.5	0.25
3	-0.5	0.25	2	0.5	0.25
4	0.5	0.25	1	-0.5	0.25
5	1.5	2.25	2	0.5	0.25
Σ 14	0	5.00	6	0	1.00
$\bar{X}$ 3.5	0		1.5	0	

Then $\quad S^2 = \dfrac{\Sigma(X_1 - \bar{X}_1)^2 + \Sigma(X_2 - \bar{X}_2)^2}{n_1 + n_2 - 2} = \dfrac{5 + 1}{4 + 4 - 2} = 1.00$

so
$$t = \frac{3.5 - 1.5}{\sqrt{(\frac{1}{4} + \frac{1}{4})\, 1.00}} = \frac{2}{\sqrt{.5}} = 2.83$$

with 6 df, a t of 2.83 is significant at about the .02 level, one-tailed test.

There is an alternative to the computation of S^2 that is more convenient when a hand-held calculator for obtaining sums of squared scores is available:

$$S^2 = \frac{\left(\Sigma X_1^2 - \dfrac{(\Sigma X_1)^2}{n_1}\right) + \left(\Sigma X_2^2 - \dfrac{(\Sigma X_2)^2}{n_2}\right)}{n_1 + n_2 - 2}$$

For the data given above

	Group 1		Group 2	
	(X_1)	$(X_1)^2$	(X_2)	$(X_2)^2$
	2	4	1	1
	3	9	2	4
	4	16	1	1
	5	25	2	4
Σ	14	54	6	10
$\bar{X}$	3.5	—	1.5	—

Then
$$S^2 = \frac{\left(54 - \dfrac{(14)^2}{4}\right) + \left(10 - \dfrac{(6)^2}{4}\right)}{4 + 4 - 2} = \frac{5 + 1}{6} = 1.00$$

Table 18-4 Alternative computations of t

Significance test	=	Size of effect	×	Size of study	=	For the data above	=	t
t	=	$\dfrac{r}{\sqrt{1 - r^2}}$	×	$\sqrt{df}$	=	$\dfrac{.756}{\sqrt{1 - (.756)^2}} \times \sqrt{6}$	=	2.83
t	=	$\dfrac{M_1 - M_2}{S}$	×	$\dfrac{1}{\sqrt{\dfrac{1}{n_1} + \dfrac{1}{n_2}}}$	=	$2.00 \times \dfrac{1}{\sqrt{\frac{1}{4} + \frac{1}{4}}}$	=	2.83
t	=	$\dfrac{M_1 - M_2}{S}$	×	$\sqrt{\dfrac{n_1 n_2}{n_1 + n_2}}$	=	$2.00 \times \sqrt{\dfrac{(4)(4)}{4 + 4}}$	=	2.83
t	=	$\dfrac{M_1 - M_2}{\sigma}$	×	$\left[\dfrac{\sqrt{n_1 n_2}}{n_1 + n_2} \times \sqrt{df}\right]$	=	$2.31 \times \left[\dfrac{\sqrt{(4)(4)}}{4 + 4} \times \sqrt{6}\right]$	=	2.83
t	=	d	×	$\dfrac{\sqrt{df}}{2}$	=	$2.31 \times \dfrac{\sqrt{6}}{2}$	=	2.83

Sometimes we want to compute t but do not have access to the original data. Instead, we may have access to certain summary statistics of the original data (our own or others') such as r, means, S, σ, d, n's, or df. Depending on which of these summary statistics we have available, different formulas for t will be useful. In Table 18-4 t is computed from the five formulas presented earlier. Had r and df been given, we would have employed the first-listed formula to obtain t. Had $(M_1 - M_2)/S$ been given, we would have employed the second- or third-listed formula. Finally, had $(M_1 - M_2)/\sigma$ (or d) been given, we would have employed the fourth- or fifth-listed formula; the fourth formula if n_1 and n_2 were different, the fifth formula if n_1 and n_2 were equal or nearly so.

t TESTS FOR NONINDEPENDENT SAMPLES

So far in our discussion of t tests employed to compare the means of two groups we have assumed the two groups of scores to be independent. That is, we thought of the scores in one group as having no relationship to the scores in the other group. Suppose, for example, that the two groups we have been comparing were two groups of children aged 10 to 11 who had been rated by judges on a 5-point scale of sociability. If group 1 had been the girls and group 2 had been the boys, might we not conclude that the children of groups 1 and 2 were independent of each other? Not necessarily. It might be the case, for example, that the four boys and four girls all came from just four families, as in Table 18-5.

When we examine the girls' and boys' scores over the four families we find that a family member's sociability score is to some degree predictable from a knowledge of family membership. For example, Table 18-5 shows that the Smith children are judged to be most sociable while the Brown children are judged to be least sociable. For these data, then, common family membership has introduced a degree of relatedness between the observations of group 1 and group 2. Other ways in which a degree of correlation might have been introduced include membership in the same dyad, as when female and male couple members are to be compared to each other. Perhaps the most common example is the so-called repeated-measures design in which the same subjects are each

Table 18-5 Sociability scores

Family	Girls: group 1	Boys: group 2	Mean
Brown	2	1	1.5
Clark	3	2	2.5
Jones	4	1	2.5
Smith	5	2	3.5
$\bar{X}$	3.5	1.5	2.5

Table 18-6 Sociability differences

Family	Girls	Boys	D
Brown	2	1	1
Clark	3	2	1
Jones	4	1	3
Smith	5	2	3
Σ	14	6	8
$\bar{X}$	3.5	1.5	2

measured twice—perhaps once after a treatment condition and once after a control condition, or once before and once after having been exposed to a learning experience.

Whenever pairs of observations *could* have been lined up next to each other because they were from the same family, the same dyad, or the same person, but were *not* lined up next to each other, we typically obtain *t* tests that are too small. That is because in these situations there is usually a positive correlation between scores earned by the two paired observations. In the example above, this correlation was .45. More rarely this type of correlation between pairmates is negative, and in those cases the resulting *t* will be too large if the *t* is computed ignoring this negative correlation.

In these *t* tests for correlated data (or repeated measurements, or matched pairs) we perform our calculations not on the original $n_1 + n_2$ scores but on the *differences* between the n_1 and n_2 scores. For example, given the family data above we compute the difference score $(X_1 - X_2 = D)$ for each pair of lined-up scores as shown in Table 18-6.

We then calculate *t* from*

$$t = \frac{\bar{D}}{\sqrt{\left(\frac{1}{n}\right) S_D^2}} = \frac{2}{\sqrt{(\frac{1}{4})1.333}} = 3.46$$

where

$$S_D^2 = \frac{\Sigma(D - \bar{D})^2}{n - 1} = \frac{4}{3} = 1.333$$

Earlier, when we computed *t* for the two groups of scores above, forgetting about the fact that they were not independent, we obtained a *t* of 2.83, which with 6 *df* was significant at about the .02 level, one-tailed test. In the case of the matched pair *t* of 3.46 for the same data, our *df* are not 6 (i.e., $n_1 + n_2 - 2$) but only 3, because we operated on only a single sample of four difference scores,

---

* The same formula can be employed when a single set of scores is to be compared to some specific theoretical value. Then we can form a *D* score for each person by subtracting the specific theoretical value from each person's obtained score. That is, *D* would equal *X* obtained minus *X* hypothesized-from-theory.

and so $df = n - 1 = 3$. For a t of 3.46 and $df = 3$ our p value is still about .02 because our larger t was offset by the loss of 3 df. Ordinarily sample sizes are larger than in this illustration, and when the data of the two groups are substantially correlated we find substantial increases in t accompanied by substantially lower (more significant) p levels.

For the matched pair t we can show the relationship to effect size and to size of the study as in Table 18-7.

The relationships of t for correlated observations to size of effect and size of study are analogous to the situation of the t for independent observations, keeping in mind that for matched pairs there are only n pairs to operate upon rather than $n_1 + n_2$ observations. In the third equation, d is defined as $\bar{D}/\sigma_D$, or the mean of the difference scores divided by the σ of the difference scores; df refers to $n - 1$ *pairs* of scores or $n - 1$ difference scores. In the second equation, S_D refers to S computed on the n difference scores, and n refers to the number of difference scores. In the first equation, r refers to the correlation between membership in group (girls vs. boys) and observed score *corrected for family membership*. It does *not* refer to the correlation between the first and second measurement made within families, dyads, or individuals. It also does not refer to the correlation of the eight scores uncorrected for family membership with membership in the groups (girls vs. boys). If we computed this r (scoring e.g., girls = 1, boys = 0) we would obtain the point biserial r corresponding to the t test for uncorrelated observations, with $r = .756$ rather than .894.

There are two ways to understand where we get the r for the size of the treatment or group effect for matched pair t tests. One way is via the analysis of variance, which will be reviewed and discussed beginning in the following chapter. In this approach we compute the "sums of squares" for the group or condition effect and for the "error term" for the group or condition effect, and then find r as

$$r = \sqrt{\frac{SS_{\text{groups}}}{SS_{\text{groups}} + SS_{\text{error}}}}$$

Table 18-7 Alternative computations of t (nonindependent)

Significance test	=	Size of effect	×	Size of study	=	For the data above	=	t
t	=	$\dfrac{r}{\sqrt{1 - r^2}}$	×	$\sqrt{df}$	=	$\dfrac{.894}{\sqrt{1 - (.894)^2}} \times \sqrt{3}$	=	3.46
t	=	$\dfrac{\bar{D}}{S_D}$	×	$\sqrt{n}$	=	$\dfrac{2}{1.155} \times \sqrt{4}$	=	3.46
t	=	d	×	$\sqrt{df}$	=	$\dfrac{2}{1.000} \times \sqrt{3}$	=	3.46

For the present data our table of variance is

Source	SS	df	MS	F	t	r
Pairs	4	3	1.333			
Gender groups	8	1	8.000	12.00	3.46	.894
Residual or error	2	3	0.667			

and, therefore

$$r = \sqrt{\frac{8}{8+2}} = \sqrt{.80} = .894$$

Another approach to understanding where we get the r for the size of the treatment or group effect for matched pairs is by "correcting" the original data for the systematic effects of membership in a particular pair (e.g., the family, dyad, or individual that generated the two scores). This is accomplished by subtracting for each member of a pair the mean of the two pair members. This procedure has the effect of eliminating differences between the means of fami-

Table 18-8 Correlation after correction for family membership

Family	Girls (X_1)	Boys (X_2)	Mean ($\bar{X}$)	Mean-corrected $X_1 - \bar{X}$	Mean-corrected $X_2 - \bar{X}$
Brown	2	1	1.5	+0.5	−0.5
Clark	3	2	2.5	+0.5	−0.5
Jones	4	1	2.5	+1.5	−1.5
Smith	5	2	3.5	+1.5	−1.5
Σ	14	6	10.00	4.0	−4.0
$\bar{X}$	3.5	1.5	2.5	1.0	−1.0

Children	Gender (1 = female, 0 = male)	Score (corrected)	Gender Z_x	Score Z_y	$Z_x Z_y$
1	1	0.5	1	0.45	0.45
2	1	0.5	1	0.45	0.45
3	1	1.5	1	1.34	1.34
4	1	1.5	1	1.34	1.34
5	0	−0.5	−1	−0.45	0.45
6	0	−0.5	−1	−0.45	0.45
7	0	−1.5	−1	−1.34	1.34
8	0	−1.5	−1	−1.34	1.34
Sum	4	0	0	0	7.16

$$r = \frac{\Sigma Z_x Z_y}{N} = \frac{7.16}{8} = .895$$

lies, dyads, or individuals. Having thus removed statistically the effect of belonging to a particular pair, we can then compute the point biserial correlation between group membership (coded as 0, 1 or as -1, 1, for example) and the corrected observed score. However, in the process of correcting for pair membership we lose all the df for pairs. Since in our example there were four pairs, we lose $4 - 1 = 3$ df in the process of computing r from our pair-corrected or residual scores, as shown in Table 18-8.

Therefore, our r based on computations from residuals (i.e., differences between scores and family means) agrees within rounding error with our r based on the analysis of variance. This process of correcting for pair membership will be described further in subsequent chapters dealing with two-way analysis of variance.

ASSUMPTIONS UNDERLYING THE USE OF t TESTS

Several assumptions are made in our use of t tests, and to the extent that these assumptions are not met, we may make incorrect inferences from our t tests. The basic assumptions are sometimes summarized by the statement that errors are IID Normal, where "errors" refers to the deviation of each score from the mean of its group or condition, and IID Normal is read as "independently and identically distributed in a normal distribution" (Box, Hunter, & Hunter, 1978, p. 78). The shorthand format of IID Normal translates into three assumptions about the distribution of observations within conditions ("errors").

1. The Errors Are Independent

If the errors are not independent of one another, the t we obtain may be very much in error. For example, if observations are strongly positively correlated, the obtained t may be several times larger than the accurate t (Snedecor & Cochran, 1980). Correlations among errors can be introduced in many ways. Suppose that we want to compare two types of group therapy. We assign thirty patients to each of the two types and within each type assign ten patients to each of three groups. It might turn out that being in the same therapy group has made the patients in each group "too much alike," so that they are no longer independent or uncorrelated. If that were so, thinking that we had thirty independent sampling units in each condition could be quite misleading. In such a situation we might have to regard *groups* rather than persons as our sampling units, and we would thereby suffer a loss of df from 58, or $(30 + 30 - 2)$, to 4, or $(3 + 3 - 2)$. In this example each person within a group would be seen as a "repeated measurement" of each group. The analysis of such data is considered in Chapter 22. A valuable discussion of problems of independence can be found in the recent volume by Charles Judd and David Kenny (1981).

2. The Errors Are Identically Distributed

For the *t* test situation in which two groups are being compared, the *t* obtained will be more accurate if the variances of the populations from which our data were drawn are more nearly equal. Only if the two population variances are very different *and* if the two sample sizes are very different is the violation of this assumption likely to lead to serious consequences. If just this situation has occurred, we can often transform the data to make the variances more nearly equal and then perform the *t* test on the transformed data. The most commonly used transformations involve taking the (a) square root, (b) logs, (c) reciprocal square root, or (d) reciprocals of the original data. George Box, William Hunter, and Stuart Hunter (1978), and John Tukey (1977) give more detailed guidance on when to use which transformation or reexpression of the data. The goal in this case, however, is clear. We want the one that makes our transformed data most nearly homogeneous in its variances.

3. The Errors Are Normally Distributed

If the errors are very nonnormally distributed, some inaccuracy may be introduced into the *t* test. However, if the distributions are not *too* skewed or not *too* bimodal, there seems to be little cause for concern unless sample sizes are tiny (Hays, 1981).

The assumptions we have discussed as underlying the use of the *t* test are also important to keep in mind during the reading of the following chapters that deal with the use of the *F* test. *The very same assumptions described above as underlying the appropriate use of* t *also underlie the appropriate use of* F.

SEVEN

FUNDAMENTALS OF ANALYSIS OF VARIANCE

Chapter **19.**   **Comparing Several Means: The Analysis of Variance**

Chapter **20.**   **Factorial Design of Experiments**

Chapter **21.**   **Interaction Effects**

COMPARING SEVERAL MEANS: THE ANALYSIS OF VARIANCE

THE F TEST

In the last chapter we discussed the comparison of two means by employing the *t* test. In the present chapter we discuss the comparison of two or more means by employing the *F* test. The *F* test can be used to test the hypothesis that there is in the population from which we have drawn our two or more samples (a) no difference between the two or more means, or equivalently (b) no relationship between membership in any particular group and score on the response variable. The *F* test, like the *t* test, is a test of significance and is, therefore, made up of two components, the size of the effect and the size of the study.

Significance test = size of effect × size of study

When there are only two means to be compared and when we index the size of the effect by r^2, the general relationship above can be rewritten more specifically as

$$F = \frac{r^2}{1 - r^2} \times df$$

We can, therefore, compute the point biserial *r* between membership in one of the two groups (coded, for example, as 0, 1 or -1, $+1$) and the dependent variable and find *F* from this equation, which requires only that we also know the *df* for *r*; for this application *df* = the number of pairs of scores less two or $N - 2$.

If we take the square root of both sides of the equation above we have:

$$\sqrt{F} = \frac{r}{\sqrt{1 - r^2}} \times \sqrt{df}$$

The right-hand side of this equation equals not only $\sqrt{F}$ but t as well, as we saw in the beginning of the chapter on the t test. For the special case of the comparison of two groups, then, $F = t^2$ or $\sqrt{F} = t$, and we could use either test to investigate the plausibility of the hypothesis that in the population from which we have drawn our samples there is no relationship between the independent and dependent variable, i.e., that $r = 0$. Just as is the case for t, the distribution of F is readily available in tables for the case of $r = 0$, so we can easily look up the probability that an F as large or larger than the one we obtained could have occurred if r were, in fact, zero. How, then, shall we decide whether to use t or F?

The advantage of t is that it is a signed statistic; i.e., it can be positive or negative in value, so that we can tell whether r is positive or negative or, put another way, whether the mean of the first group is greater than or less than the mean of the second group; F operates on r^2 or on the squared difference between the means, so F is the same whether the obtained r is positive or negative or whether group A is smaller or larger by the obtained amount than group B.

The limitation of t is that it can be employed only when there are just two means to be compared; the advantage of F is that it operates just as well for three groups, or four, or *any* number of groups as it does for just two groups. When more than two means are being compared, the relationship between F and the size of the effect and the size of the study is generalized to:

$$F = \frac{eta^2}{1 - eta^2} \times \frac{df\ error}{df\ means}$$

where eta^2 is a correlation index defined as the proportion of variance in the dependent variable attributable to group membership, $df\ error$ is analogous to the term df when we were discussing the t test, and $df\ means$ is the number (k) of means being compared less one, or $k - 1$. Later in this chapter we shall be more precise about the definition of eta and $df\ error$.

When we were discussing t in Chapter 18 we noted that the size of the effect could be indexed by r or by an index of standardized distance between the group means $(M_1 - M_2)/S$. In this latter index the difference between means is divided by the square root of the unbiased estimate of the population variance (S^2) pooled from the two groups. How might we incorporate the idea of standardized distances among means for the situation in which more than two means are to be compared? We might take all possible pairs of distances between means and take their average. This average distance between means, when divided by S computed from all the groups' data, would yield an *average*

$(M - M)/S$ with signs disregarded. Such an index *would* be fairly informative, but it turns out to be less useful for *subsequent* statistical procedures than an index that focused on squared differences among means, or S^2_{means} defined as

$$S^s_{means} = \frac{\Sigma(M_k - \bar{M})^2}{k - 1}$$

where M_k is any of the k means being compared, $\bar{M}$ is the mean of these k means, and k is the number of means being compared.

A large S^2_{means} indicates that the means are far apart in the sense of squared distances from the grand mean. However, the actual meaning of "far" depends on the particular metric employed in the particular research, and we shall want to standardize the distance index S^2_{means} by the particular unit of measurement employed. We can accomplish this by dividing S^2_{means} by S^2, the variance computed separately within each group and averaged for all groups. For the situation in which we want to compare the means of any number of independent groups we can also define F in terms of this new effect-size estimate and n, the number of sampling units in each of the groups when all groups have the same n:

$$F = \frac{S^2_{means}}{S^2} \times n$$

When the n's of the groups are not equal, n may be replaced (for a conservative estimate of F) by the harmonic mean of the sample sizes. The estimate of F based on the harmonic mean of the sample sizes is conservative in the sense that the harmonic mean of unequal sample sizes is always smaller than the arithmetic mean of these sample sizes. The harmonic mean of the sample sizes ($\bar{n}_h$) is found by:

$$\bar{n}_h = 1 \Big/ \frac{1}{k}\left(\frac{1}{n_1} + \frac{1}{n_2} \cdots \frac{1}{n_k}\right) = k \Big/ \left(\frac{1}{n_1} + \frac{1}{n_2} \cdots \frac{1}{n_k}\right)$$

where k is the number of means being compared and n_1 to n_k are the sizes of the samples upon which the various means are based.

AN ILLUSTRATION

Suppose we had twelve patients available for an experiment comparing four different treatment conditions or groups. We allocate three patients at random to each of the four conditions and obtain the improvement scores shown in Table 19-1.

Table 19-1 Improvement scores in four conditions

	Psychotherapy plus drug treatment	Psychotherapy plus no drug treatment	No psychotherapy plus drug treatment	No psychotherapy plus no drug treatment
	9	6	5	4
	8	4	4	2
	7	2	3	0
Σ	24	12	12	6
M_k or $\bar{X}$	8	4	4	2
S_k^2	1.0	4.0	1.0	4.0

Based on these scores,

$$\bar{M} = (8 + 4 + 4 + 2)/4 = 4.5$$

Since $F = \dfrac{S^2_{means}}{S^2} \times n$

we begin by computing S^2_{means}:

$$S^2_{means} = \frac{\Sigma(M_k - \bar{M})^2}{k - 1} = \frac{(8 - 4.5)^2 + (4 - 4.5)^2 + (4 - 4.5)^2 + (2 - 4.5)^2}{4 - 1}$$

$$= \frac{(3.5)^2 + (-0.5)^2 + (-0.5)^2 + (-2.5)^2}{3} = \frac{19}{3} = 6.33$$

Next we want S^2, the pooled within group variance collected over all groups:

$$S^2 = \frac{\Sigma(n_k - 1)S_k^2}{\Sigma(n_k - 1)} = \frac{(2)(1.0) + (2)(4.0) + (2)(1.0) + (2)(4.0)}{2 + 2 + 2 + 2} = \frac{20}{8} = 2.50$$

$$\text{So } F = \frac{S^2_{means}}{S^2} \times n = \frac{6.33}{2.50} \times 3 = \frac{19.00}{2.50} = 7.60$$

Once we have computed F we refer it to a table of the F distribution to learn the p level associated with an F value of that magnitude or greater. We shall return shortly to the use of F tables.

The formula we employed for computing F was useful for showing F to be a product of the size of the effect (S^2_{means}/S^2) and the size of the study (n), as is the case for all tests of significance. Although that formula is conceptually instructive, it is less computationally convenient for a variety of purposes.

The analysis of variance has the computation of F tests as only one of its purposes. The major general purpose of the analysis of variance is to divide up the total variance of all the observations into a number of separate sources of variance that can be compared to one another for purposes of both effect-size estimation and significance testing. In our present illustration of comparing the means of four groups, the total variation among the twelve scores is divided into two sources of variation: (a) variation between groups or conditions, and (b) variation within groups or conditions. It will be useful here to look again at the basic idea of variance

$$S^2 = \frac{\Sigma(X - \bar{X})^2}{N - 1}$$

where S^2 is the unbiased estimate of the population value σ^2, and σ^2 for a sample differs from S^2 only in that the denominator $N - 1$ is replaced by N. The quantity S^2 is sometimes referred to as a "mean square" because the sum of the squares of the deviations [i.e., the $\Sigma(X - \bar{X})^2$] is divided by $N - 1$ (or df) yielding the squared deviation per df, a kind of average.

In the analysis of variance we are especially interested in the numerators of our various S^2's, e.g., for between conditions and for within conditions. The reason for that is the additive property of the numerators or "sums of squares of deviations about the mean." That is, these sums of squares add up to the total sums of squares in the following fashion:

Total sum of squares = between conditions sum of squares
+ within conditions sum of squares

The standard abbreviation for sum of squares is SS, so we have:

Total SS = between conditions SS + within conditions SS

or   Total SS = between SS + within SS

The analysis of variance generally begins with the computation of these three sums of squares. Their definitions are as follows:

Total $SS = \Sigma(X - \bar{M})^2$

where X is each observation and $\bar{M}$ is the mean of the condition means. Here we add up as many squared deviations as there are scores altogether.

Between conditions $SS = \Sigma[n_k(M_k - \bar{M})^2]$

where n_k is the number of observations in the kth condition; M_k is the mean of the kth condition, and $\bar{M}$ is the mean of the condition means. Here we add up as many quantities as there are conditions.

Within conditions $SS = \Sigma(X - M_k)^2$

where X is each observation and M_k is the mean of the condition to which X belongs. Here we add up as many quantities as there are scores altogether.

Then, for the data of this illustration:

Total $SS = (9 - 4.5)^2 + (8 - 4.5)^2 + (7 - 4.5)^2 + (6 - 4.5)^2$
$+ (4 - 4.5)^2 + (2 - 4.5)^2 + (5 - 4.5)^2 + (4 - 4.5)^2$
$+ (3 - 4.5)^2 + (4 - 4.5)^2 + (2 - 4.5)^2 + (0 - 4.5)^2 = 77$

Between conditions $SS = 3(8 - 4.5)^2 + 3(4 - 4.5)^2 + 3(4 - 4.5)^2$
$+ 3(2 - 4.5)^2 = 57$

Within conditions $SS = (9 - 8)^2 + (8 - 8)^2 + (7 - 8)^2 + (6 - 4)^2$
$+ (4 - 4)^2 + (2 - 4)^2 + (5 - 4)^2 + (4 - 4)^2$
$+ (3 - 4)^2 + (4 - 2)^2 + (2 - 2)^2 + (0 - 2)^2 = 20$

As a check on our arithmetic we add the sum of squares between conditions to the sum of squares within conditions to see whether their sum equals the total sum of squares. In this case they do since

Total SS = between conditions SS + within conditions SS
$77 = 57 + 20$

A final comment about sums of squares: because they are sums of *squared* deviations they can take on only values of zero or above. Sums of squares are never negative. Therefore, F's also are never negative.

THE TABLE OF VARIANCE

The results of an analysis of variance are displayed in the form shown in Table 19-2. The first column labels the source of variance, in this case simply the between conditions and within conditions sources. The second column lists the SS, and the third column lists the degrees of freedom for each source of variance. Since there were four conditions being compared, or four means, three of those means were free to vary once the mean of the means was determined. Thus if there are k conditions, the degrees of freedom (df) for conditions are $k - 1$, or 3 in this case. The degrees of freedom within conditions are best obtained by determining the df within each condition and then adding. Within each condition we have $n - 1$ degrees of freedom, since within each condition of n scores only $n - 1$ of them are free to vary once we determine the mean of that condition. Thus the df within conditions are found by $\Sigma(n_k - 1)$, which in our present illustration is:

$$\Sigma(n_k - 1) = (3 - 1) + (3 - 1) + (3 - 1) + (3 - 1) = 8$$

When we compute the df for between and within conditions as shown, we can check our computations by adding these df to see whether they agree with the df for total computed directly as $N - 1$, the total number of observations less one. In the present case we have

$$df \text{ total} = df \text{ between} + df \text{ within}$$
$$11 = 3 + 8$$

Table 19-2 Table of variance

Source	SS	df	MS	F	eta	p
Between conditions	57	3	19.0	7.60	.86	.01
Within conditions	20	8	2.5			
Total	77	11	7.0			

The fourth column of the table of variance shows the mean squares obtained simply by dividing the sums of squares by the corresponding df. These quantities, the mean squares (or MS), can be viewed as the amounts of the total variation (measured in SS) attributable per df. The larger the MS for the between condition source of variance relative to the within condition source of variance, the less likely the null hypothesis of no difference between the condition means becomes. If the null hypothesis were true, then variation per df should be roughly the same for the df's between groups and the df's within groups.

The fifth column of our table of variance shows F, which is obtained by dividing the mean square between conditions by the mean square within conditions in applications of this type. F tests are also called "F ratios," since they are generally obtained by forming a ratio of two mean squares. The denominator mean square, often referred to as the *mean square for error*, serves as a kind of base rate for "noise level," or typical variation, while the numerator serves to inform us simultaneously about the size of the effect and the size of the study. Thus a numerator MS can be large relative to a denominator MS because the effect size (defined, for example, as eta^2 or as S^2_{means}/S^2) is large or the n per condition is large, or both are large. Large F's, therefore, should not be interpreted as reflecting large effects. Any conclusions about the size of the effect must be based on the direct calculation of an effect-size estimator. In the case of F perhaps the most generally useful such effect-size estimate is *eta,* defined as

$$eta = \sqrt{\frac{SS \text{ between}}{SS \text{ between} + SS \text{ within}}}$$

Eta, then, is the square root of the proportion of the sums of squares (between + within) associated with the between conditions source of variation. An equivalent computational formula that is convenient when we have access to an F but not to the original sums of squares is:

$$eta = \sqrt{\frac{F(df \text{ between})}{F(df \text{ between}) + df \text{ within}}}$$

For the present illustration the sixth column in Table 19.2 shows *eta* computed as

$$eta = \sqrt{\frac{57}{57 + 20}} = \sqrt{.7403} = .86 \text{ or, as}$$

$$eta = \sqrt{\frac{7.6(3)}{7.6(3) + 8}} = \sqrt{\frac{22.8}{22.8 + 8}} = .86$$

Eta^2 is interpreted as a proportion of variance accounted for, and the range, therefore, is like that for r^2, i.e., zero to one. However, r represents an index of linear relationship, and *eta* can serve as an index of any type of relationship. When there is only a single df between conditions, as, for example, when there are only two conditions being compared, *eta* and *r* are identical and may both be regarded as indices of linear relationships. As we shall see in our subsequent discussions of contrasts, we shall only rarely be interested in *eta*'s based on more than a single *df*. Such *eta*'s are difficult if not impossible to interpret in a substantively meaningful way. In addition, such *eta*'s tend to be overestimates of the population values of *eta*, sometimes very gross overestimates. This overestimation is most severe when the number of *df* of the numerator of *F* is large relative to the number of *df* of the denominator of *F* (Guilford & Fruchter, 1978).

The final column of our table of variance gives the probability, *p*, that an *F* of the size obtained or larger could have been obtained if the null hypothesis were true and there were really no differences in the population between the means of the conditions of our research investigation. An alternative interpretation is that the *p* expresses the probability that an *eta* of the size obtained or larger could have occurred if the relationship between the independent variable of condition membership and the dependent variable of score on the response variable were actually zero in the population.

DISTRIBUTIONS OF *F*

In our discussion of the interpretation of *t* we noted that there was a different distribution of *t* values for every possible value of $n_1 + n_2 - 2$ (i.e., *df*). The situation for *F* is similar but more complicated because for every *F* ratio there are *two* relevant *df* to take into account; the *df* between conditions and the *df* within conditions. For every combination of *df* between and *df* within there is a different *F* distribution. While *t* distributions are centered at zero, with negative values running to negative infinity and positive values running to positive infinity, *F* distributions all begin at zero and range upward to positive infinity. The expected value of *t* is zero when the null hypothesis is true; the expected value of *F*, however, is $df/(df - 2)$ where the *df* are for within conditions. For most values of *df*, then, the expected value of *F* is a little more than 1.0. Just as was the case for *t*, values of *F* closer to zero are likely when the null hypothesis of no difference between groups is true, but values further from zero are unlikely and are used as evidence to suggest that the null hypothesis is probably false.

Inspection of a large number of *F* distributions shows that critical values of *F* required to reach the .05, .01, and .001 levels decrease as *df* within increase for any given *df* between. Similarly, critical values of *F* decrease as *df* between increase for any given *df* within, except for the special cases of *df* within = 1 or 2. For *df* within = 1 there is a substantial increase in the *F*'s required to reach various critical levels as the *df* between increase from 1 to infinity. For *df* within = 2 there is only a very small increase in the *F*'s required to reach various critical levels as the *df* between increase from 1 to infinity. In practice, however, there are very few studies with large *df* between and only 1 or 2 *df* within. A sample *F* distribution is shown in Figure 19-1 with *df* between and within = 3 and 16, respectively.

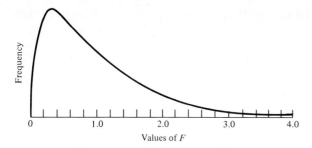

Figure 19-1 The F distribution for df of 3 and 16.

Table 19-3 illustrates the differences in various F distributions by giving the areas found in the right-hand tail of selected distributions. For each combination of df between and df within, two values are given, the F values required to reach the .05 and .01 levels respectively. A much more detailed table of F values is found in Appendix B.

In the example of an analysis of variance we have been discussing, we obtained an F of 7.60 with 3 df in the numerator (between) and 8 df in the denominator (within or error), a result we write as $F(3,8) = 7.60$. When we refer this value to Table 19-3 we find at the intersection of 3 df for between and 8 df for within the values 4.07 and 7.59. Our obtained F, therefore, is substantially larger than an F required to be significant at $p = .05$ and almost exactly the size required to be significant at $p = .01$. How shall we interpret this result? The p value of .01 means that we would obtain an F of this size or larger (for numerator $df = 3$, denominator $df = 8$) only once in 100 times if we repeatedly conducted a study of four groups of size 3 each if there were, in the population, no differences among the four means or if there were no relationship between group membership and the response variable.

Before leaving our discussion of the distributions of F we should note that the F's we compute in actual research situations will usually be distributed only approximately as F. The assumptions to be met before we can regard computed F's to be actually distributed as F were given at the end of the last chapter (IID Normal; that is, independently and identically distributed in a normal distribution). Of the three assumptions, the assumption of independence of errors (or sampling units) is most important, because if it is badly violated, our interpretation of F can go very wrong. Violations of the other two assumptions (homogeneity of variance and normality) are less serious in that F tends to be robust in the face of even some fairly serious violations of these assumptions.

AFTER THE F

Now we know that for the data of our example the group means are not likely to be so far apart if the null hypothesis were true. What does that tell us about the results of our experiment? By itself, not very much. After all, we conducted

Table 19-3 F values required for significance at the .05 (upper entry) and .01 levels

Degrees of freedom within conditions (denominator)	Degrees of freedom between conditions (numerator)						Expected value of F when H_0 true
	1	2	3	4	6	∞	
1	161	200	216	225	234	254	
	4052	4999	5403	5625	5859	6366	—
2	18.5	19.0	19.2	19.2	19.3	19.5	
	98.5	99.0	99.2	99.2	99.3	99.5	—
3	10.1	9.55	9.28	9.12	8.94	8.53	
	34.1	30.8	29.5	28.7	27.9	26.1	3.00
4	7.71	6.94	6.59	6.39	6.16	5.63	
	21.2	18.0	16.7	16.0	15.2	13.5	2.00
5	6.61	5.79	5.41	5.19	4.95	4.36	
	16.3	13.3	12.1	11.4	10.7	9.02	1.67
6	5.99	5.14	4.76	4.53	4.28	3.67	
	13.7	10.9	9.78	9.15	8.47	6.88	1.50
8	5.32	4.46	4.07	3.84	3.58	2.93	
	11.3	8.65	7.59	7.01	6.37	4.86	1.33
10	4.96	4.10	3.71	3.48	3.22	2.54	
	10.0	7.56	6.55	5.99	5.39	3.91	1.25
15	4.54	3.68	3.29	3.06	2.79	2.07	
	8.68	6.36	5.42	4.89	4.32	2.87	1.15
20	4.35	3.49	3.10	2.87	2.60	1.84	
	8.10	5.85	4.94	4.43	3.87	2.42	1.11
25	4.24	3.38	2.99	2.76	2.49	1.71	
	7.77	5.57	4.68	4.18	3.63	2.17	1.09
30	4.17	3.32	2.92	2.69	2.42	1.62	
	7.56	5.39	4.51	4.02	3.47	2.01	1.07
40	4.08	3.23	2.84	2.61	2.34	1.51	
	7.31	5.18	4.31	3.83	3.29	1.81	1.05
∞	3.84	2.99	2.60	2.37	2.09	1.00	
	6.63	4.60	3.78	3.32	2.80	1.00	1.00

our research to learn about the effects of psychotherapy and drug therapy separately and together. Knowing that the four groups of our study probably differ does not tell us whether psychotherapy helps, whether drugs help, whether both together help, whether one helps more than the other, etc. At the very least we need now to examine the means of the four groups:

Psychotherapy		No psychotherapy	
Drug	No drug	Drug	No drug
8	4	4	2

If the overall difference among the means is significant, then the greatest difference between the means is significant as well. In this case the greatest difference is that between the group receiving both psychotherapy and drug therapy and the group receiving neither psychotherapy nor drug therapy. To check the more exact significance of that difference we can compute t as described in the chapter on t:

$$t = \frac{M_1 - M_2}{\sqrt{\left(\frac{1}{n_1} + \frac{1}{n_2}\right) S^2}}$$

In this application of t, i.e., as a followup to an analysis of variance, we compute S^2 based on all the groups of the experiment, not just those directly involved in the t test. If we return to the definition of our mean square within (SS_{within}/df_{within})

$$MS_{within} = \frac{\Sigma(X - M_k)^2}{N - k}$$

where N is the total number of sampling units in the study and k is the number of conditions, we see that the MS within is actually the S^2 pooled over, or collected from, all the conditions of the analysis. Then for the means of interest

$$t = \frac{8 - 2}{\sqrt{\left(\frac{1}{3} + \frac{1}{3}\right) 2.5}} = \frac{6}{1.29} = 4.65$$

which is significant at $p < .001$, one-tailed, or .002, two-tailed, when referred to a table of the t distribution with $df = 8$. Because we have based our computation of S^2 (or MS within, or MS error) on all the data of the experiment, not just on the data of the two groups being compared, our t test is made on the t distribution with df equal to that of the S^2, *not*, in this case, on $n_1 + n_2 - 2$. For many applications of the analysis of variance we assume homogeneity or similarity of variance from condition to condition, so that an S^2 or MS within based on more groups is more likely to be a better estimate of the population value of σ^2. The number of df available to estimate σ^2, therefore, defines the t distribution to which we refer our obtained t. The n_1 and n_2 of the denominator of the t test still reflect the actual number of cases per group on which the t is based. Thus, it is not our sample sizes that are increased by our using a more stable estimate of σ^2, only the df used for referring to t tables.

We might also want to compare the benefits of receiving both psychotherapy *and* drug (mean $= 8$) with the benefits of receiving *either* psychotherapy (mean $= 4$) *or* drug (mean $= 4$). In both cases

$$t = \frac{8 - 4}{\sqrt{\left(\frac{1}{3} + \frac{1}{3}\right) 2.5}} = \frac{4}{1.29} = 3.10$$

which is significant at $p < .01$, one-tailed, when referred to the $t(8)$ distribution.

We might want to compare the benefits of receiving either psychotherapy or drug with the no-treatment control condition. Both comparisons yield

$$t = \frac{4 - 2}{\sqrt{\left(\frac{1}{3} + \frac{1}{3}\right) 2.5}} = \frac{2}{1.29} = 1.55$$

which is significant at about the .08 level, one-tailed. We have now compared each group with every other except for psychotherapy alone vs. drug alone, which by inspection yields a $t = 0$. Other comparisons are possible, taking more than one group at a time. Identifying the four groups as PD, P, D, and O we could also make the following comparisons:

$$
\begin{array}{rcl}
(PD + P) & vs. & (D + O) \\
(PD + D) & vs. & (P + O) \\
(PD + O) & vs. & (P + D) \\
(PD + P + D) & vs. & (O) \\
(PD + P + O) & vs. & (D) \\
(PD + D + O) & vs. & (P) \\
(P + D + O) & vs. & (PD)
\end{array}
$$

PROTECTING AGAINST "TOO MANY t TESTS"

So far, then, thirteen fairly obvious comparisons are possible. If we were to make them all, we might expect some of those thirteen t tests to yield significant results even if the null hypothesis were true. Generally, the more tests of significance computed on data for which the null hypothesis is true, the more significant results will be obtained, i.e., the more type I errors will be made. In Chapter 23, on contrasts, we shall deal with the issue in more detail. Here it is enough to offer only some brief and preliminary advice.

1. Plan the t tests of interest before the data are collected and conduct those t tests whether or not the overall F is significant. To perform these t tests only, no F need be computed; indeed our only reason for computing an analysis of variance is to reap the benefit of a more stable estimate of the σ^2 required for the denominator of our t tests. That is, each of our t tests is now based on the n_1 and n_2 of the two groups being compared, but the t distribution referred to in the tables is the one with the df of our error term (MS within), usually $N - k$.

2. If there are unexpected but interesting results for which t tests are computed, compute the overall F. If that F is significant, the t's computed are said to be "protected" against the problem of "capitalizing on chance," since some of the t's *must* be "legitimately" significant if the overall F is significant. For most practical purposes, the use of these protected t's is at least an adequate solution and, quite possibly, an optimal one (Balaam, 1963; Carmer & Swanson, 1973; Snedecor & Cochran, 1967, 1980).

3. Either for the case of planned t tests or for the case of unexpected results if many t tests are computed and (a) the overall F is not significant *and* (b) the investigators are worried lest they are capitalizing on chance, a simple and quite conservative procedure can be employed to adjust the interpretation of the p values obtained. The basic idea of this procedure, the Bonferroni procedure, is to divide the alpha level selected by the number of tests performed explicitly or implicitly (Harris, 1975; Morrison, 1976; Myers, 1979).

    Suppose, for example, that we plan to perform four t tests on our data but want to keep our overall alpha at the .05 level. If we divide .05 by 4, the number of tests planned, we find .0125 to be the adjusted level we would want to obtain to declare any of the four t's to be significant. If we have not planned our t tests and include only the largest obtained t's, we must divide the usual alpha level we prefer (most commonly, $p = .05$) by the number of *implicit* t tests. For example, if we have five groups to compare in our study and we test the three largest differences, we divide the .05 level not by 3 but by $(5 \times 4)/2 = 10$, the number of possible pairwise comparisons of five means; in this case we would require a p of $.05/10 = .005$ before we would declare a t test significant at an adjusted .05 level.

TWENTY

FACTORIAL DESIGN OF EXPERIMENTS

AN ECONOMY OF DESIGN

Suppose, that for the example we discussed in the last chapter, a major question was whether psychotherapy was effective. Given the means of our four conditions

$$\frac{PD}{8} \quad \frac{P}{4} \quad \frac{D}{4} \quad \frac{O}{2}$$

we could test the difference between the psychotherapy-only group (P) and the no-treatment control group (O). We have already made this test and found $t(8) = 1.55$, with $p = .08$, one-tailed. However, inspection of the four means shows another comparison that could be made to test the effect of psychotherapy; PD vs. D. This comparison [with $t(8) = 3.10$, $p < .01$ as reported earlier] is parallel to the earlier comparison of P vs. O, except that now both the psychotherapy and the no-psychotherapy conditions are receiving drug therapy.

   Rather than conduct two t tests, P vs. O and PD vs. D, we could conduct one simultaneous t test of (PD + P)/2 vs (D + O)/2 so that the conditions including psychotherapy could be compared to those not including psychotherapy. The advantage of thus combining our tests is that it increases the n_1 and n_2 of the denominator of the t test so that t will have greater power to "reject the null hypothesis" if the null hypothesis is false. An equally sensible and quite analogous test might ask whether drug therapy is beneficial, i.e., (PD + D)/2 vs.

(P + O)/2. The t test for psychotherapy would be computed as:

$$t = \frac{(8 + 4)/2 - (4 + 2)/2}{\sqrt{\left(\frac{1}{6} + \frac{1}{6}\right) 2.5}} = \frac{6 - 3}{0.913} = 3.29$$

which is significant at $p = .006$, one-tailed, when referred to the $t(8)$ distribution. The results for the drug effect turn out in this example to be identical.

Sir Ronald Fisher, for whom the F test was named, and who was responsible for so much of the development of the analysis of variance, noticed that in many cases a one-way analysis of variance could be rearrayed to form a two-dimensional (or higher-order) design of much greater power to reject the null hypothesis. Such experimental designs are called *factorial,* and they require that the two or more levels of each factor (variable) be administered in combination with the two or more levels of every other factor. For example, to rearrange the four means of the one-way analysis of variance that has served as our illustration into a factorial design we rearray from

PD	P	D	O
8[3ᵃ]	4[3]	4[3]	2[3]

[a] The number of units upon which each mean is based

to

		Psychotherapy		
		Present	Absent	Mean
Drug therapy	Present	8[3]	4[3]	6[6]
	Absent	4[3]	2[3]	3[6]
	Mean	6[6]	3[6]	4.5[12]

Now the comparison of the two column means is the test of the effect of psychotherapy, and the comparison of the two row means is the test of the effect of drug therapy. The number of observations upon which each mean is based has been doubled, from 3 to 6, as we moved from a comparison of one group with another group to a comparison of a column (or row) comprising two groups with another column (or row) also comprising two groups. Here then is the great economy of the factorial design; each condition or group contributes data to several comparisons. In the present example of a two-way analysis, the upper-left condition contributes its $n = 3$ to the comparison between columns and to the comparison between rows simultaneously.

EFFECTS AND THE STRUCTURE OF ANALYSIS OF VARIANCE

We can better understand our particular data, and we can better understand the nature of analysis of variance in general, by thinking of our obtained scores or means as being made up of two or more components that can be added to construct our obtained scores or means. Let us consider only the four means of our example:

		Psychotherapy	
		Present	Absent
Drug	Present	8	4
therapy	Absent	4	2

We can decompose these four means into two components, one due to the grand mean and one due to the *effect* of being in a particular group. If we compute the grand mean of our four condition means we find (8 + 4 + 4 + 2)/4 = 4.5. We subtract this value from each of our four means to obtain:

		Psychotherapy	
		Present	Absent
Drug	Present	3.5	−0.5
therapy	Absent	−0.5	−2.5

The differences between the cell means we started with and the grand mean are displayed above; they are called *residuals* (or leftovers) or *effects* of group or condition membership. We can write

Residual (condition) effects	=	group means	−	grand mean
3.5	=	(8)	−	(4.5)
−0.5	=	(4)	−	(4.5)
−0.5	=	(4)	−	(4.5)
−2.5	=	(2)	−	(4.5)
Σ 0.0	=	18	−	18.0

or

Group means	=	grand mean	+	residual (condition) effects
8	=	(4.5)	+	(3.5)
4	=	(4.5)	+	(−0.5)
4	=	(4.5)	+	(−0.5)
2	=	(4.5)	+	(−2.5)
Σ 18	=	18.0	+	0.0

The sum of the condition *effects* or *residuals* is always equal to zero, so that examining them highlights which groups score the most above average (i.e., the most positive signed mean) and which score the most below average (i.e., the most negative signed mean). The grand mean plus the condition *residual* or *effect* for each group mean is equal to the group mean.

When we move from a one-way analysis of variance to a two-way analysis of variance, such as in the case of a two-way factorial design, the condition *effects* or *residuals* are subdivided into *row effects, column effects,* and left-over, or *residual,* or *interaction effects.* So

$$\text{Group mean} = \text{grand mean} + \text{residual (condition) effect}$$

becomes

$$\text{Group mean} = \text{grand mean} + \text{row effect} + \text{column effect} + \text{interaction effect}$$

In order to decompose the group means into their four components we must compute the grand mean, the row effect, the column effect, and the interaction effect. The grand mean is the mean of all cell means. The row effect for each row is the mean of that row minus the grand mean; the column effect for each column is the mean of that column minus the grand mean. For our example:

		Psychotherapy Present	Psychotherapy Absent	Row means	Row effects
Drug therapy	Present	8	4	6	1.5
	Absent	4	2	3	−1.5
	Column means	6	3	4.5 (grand mean)	
	Column effects	1.5	−1.5		

The row effects are 6 − 4.5 and 3 − 4.5 for drug present and absent respectively; the column effects are 6 − 4.5 and 3 − 4.5 for psychotherapy present and absent respectively. The interaction effect is computed from:

$$\text{Interaction effect} = \text{group mean} - \text{grand mean} - \text{row effect} - \text{column effect}$$

so for our example, the four interaction effects are:

	Group mean	−	grand mean	−	row effect	−	column effect	=	interaction effect
PD	8	−	(4.5)	−	(1.5)	−	(1.5)	=	0.5
D	4	−	(4.5)	−	(1.5)	−	(−1.5)	=	−0.5
P	4	−	(4.5)	−	(−1.5)	−	(1.5)	=	−0.5
O	2	−	(4.5)	−	(−1.5)	−	(−1.5)	=	0.5
Σ	18	−	18.0	−	0	−	0	=	0

For the time being we think of interaction effects simply as the "leftover effects," but we shall have a great deal more to say about them in the next chapter. To show how the group means are composed of additive pieces we can rewrite the above as follows, noting that all effects (row, column, and interaction) add up to zero when added over all four conditions PD, D, P, and O, a characteristic of all residuals from a mean:

Group mean	=	grand mean	+	row effect	+	column effect	+	interaction effect
PD	8	=	4.5	+	(1.5)	+	(1.5)	+	(0.5)
D	4	=	4.5	+	(1.5)	+	(−1.5)	+	(−0.5)
P	4	=	4.5	+	(−1.5)	+	(1.5)	+	(−0.5)
O	2	=	4.5	+	(−1.5)	+	(−1.5)	+	(0.5)
Σ	18	=	18.0	+	0	+	0	+	0

What can be learned about the results of our experiment from studying the table of effects just above? The grand mean tells us the general "level" of our measurements and is usually not of great intrinsic interest. The row effect shows us that the groups receiving drugs do better than those not receiving drugs. The column effect shows us that the groups receiving psychotherapy do better than those not receiving psychotherapy. The interaction effect shows us that the group receiving *both* psychotherapy and drug and the group receiving *neither* psychotherapy nor drug both benefit more than do the groups receiving *either* psychotherapy or drug. That is not to say, of course, that for the present study it is better overall to receive neither psychotherapy nor drug than to receive either psychotherapy or drug. Although it is slightly better from the point of view of the *interaction effect alone* to receive neither treatment, this advantage in the interaction effect (i.e., 0.5) is more than offset by the disadvantage in the row effect (i.e., −1.5) and in the column effect (i.e., −1.5) to be receiving neither treatment.

INDIVIDUAL DIFFERENCES AS ERROR

We have seen how the mean of each group or condition can be decomposed into elements made up of the grand mean, the row effect, the column effect, and the interaction effect in the case of a two-dimensional design, such as a two-way factorial design. That does not quite tell the whole story, however, because it does not take into account that the various *scores* found in each condition show variability from the *mean* of that condition. That is, each score can be rewritten as a deviation or residual from the mean of that condition. The magnitude of these deviations reflects how poorly we have done in predicting individual scores from a knowledge of condition or group membership; these deviations or residuals are accordingly called *error*. A particular score shows a "large error" if it falls far from the mean of its condition but only a "small error" if it falls close to the mean of its condition. We can write error as

$$\text{Error} = \text{score} - \text{group mean}$$

so that

$$\text{Score} = \text{group mean} + \text{error}$$

but

$$\text{Group mean} = \text{grand mean} + \text{row effect}$$

$$+ \text{ column effect} + \text{interaction effect}$$

so

$$\text{Score} = \text{grand mean} + \text{row effect} + \text{column effect}$$

$$+ \text{ interaction effect} + \text{error}$$

From this we can show the makeup of each of the original twelve scores of the study we have been using as our illustration (see Table 20-1). We can employ the decomposition of the individual scores to understand better the computation of the various terms of the analysis of variance. Beneath each column of the display we show the sum of the twelve values (ΣX) and the sum of the squares of the twelve values (ΣX^2). Earlier, when we analyzed the results of the present study as a one-way analysis of variance we computed three sources of variance:

$$\text{Total } SS = \Sigma(X - \bar{M})^2 = 77$$
$$\text{Between-conditions } SS = \Sigma[n_k(M_k - \bar{M})^2] = 57$$
$$\text{Within-conditions } SS = \Sigma(X - M_k)^2 = 20$$

Table 20-1 Table of effects

Condition	Patient	Score	=	Grand mean	+	Row effect	+	Column effect	+	Interaction effect	+	Error
PD	1	9	=	4.5	+	(1.5)	+	(1.5)	+	(0.5)	+	(1)
PD	2	8	=	4.5	+	(1.5)	+	(1.5)	+	(0.5)	+	(0)
PD	3	7	=	4.5	+	(1.5)	+	(1.5)	+	(0.5)	+	(−1)
D	4	5	=	4.5	+	(1.5)	+	(−1.5)	+	(−0.5)	+	(1)
D	5	4	=	4.5	+	(1.5)	+	(−1.5)	+	(−0.5)	+	(0)
D	6	3	=	4.5	+	(1.5)	+	(−1.5)	+	(−0.5)	+	(−1)
P	7	6	=	4.5	+	(−1.5)	+	(1.5)	+	(−0.5)	+	(2)
P	8	4	=	4.5	+	(−1.5)	+	(1.5)	+	(−0.5)	+	(0)
P	9	2	=	4.5	+	(−1.5)	+	(1.5)	+	(−0.5)	+	(−2)
O	10	4	=	4.5	+	(−1.5)	+	(−1.5)	+	(0.5)	+	(2)
O	11	2	=	4.5	+	(−1.5)	+	(−1.5)	+	(0.5)	+	(0)
O	12	0	=	4.5	+	(−1.5)	+	(−1.5)	+	(0.5)	+	(−2)
	ΣX	54	=	54	+	0	+	0	+	0	+	0
	ΣX^2	320	=	243	+	27	+	27	+	3	+	20

The total SS is defined as the sum of the squared differences between every single score and the grand mean, i.e., $(9 - 4.5)^2 \ldots + \ldots (0 - 4.5)^2 = 77$. Alternatively, we can subtract the sum of the squared grand means shown in Table 20-1 as 243 (and expressed symbolically as $N\bar{M}^2$ or as $(\Sigma X)^2/N$) from the sum of the squared scores shown above as 320 (and expressed symbolically as ΣX^2) to obtain the same value, 77. In the one-way analysis of variance this total SS is allocated to two sources of variance, a between conditions and a within conditions source. In moving from a one-way to a two-way analysis of variance, the *within-conditions* source of variance, the source attributable to error, remains unchanged. Table 20-1, showing the contributions of various sources to each score, shows that the sum of the squared effects due to error is 20, as before. However, the *between-conditions* source of variance has now been further broken down into three components as follows:

$$\frac{\text{Between-}}{\text{conditions } SS} = \frac{\text{row-}}{\text{effect } SS} + \frac{\text{column-}}{\text{effect } SS} + \frac{\text{interaction-}}{\text{effect } SS}$$
$$57 \quad = \quad 27 \quad + \quad 27 \quad + \quad 3$$

where 57 is the between conditions SS computed earlier showing the overall variation among the four treatment conditions, and the row, column, and inter- action effects of 27, 27, and 3, respectively, are shown in the bottom row of the table of all twelve scores. The table of variance for the two-way analysis differs from the table of variance for the one-way analysis in reflecting the further subdivision of the between-conditions SS.

THE TABLE OF VARIANCE

Examination of this table of variance shows a large ($eta = .76$) and signifi- cant ($p = .012$) effect of drug and a large ($eta = .76$) and significant ($p = .012$) effect of psychotherapy. The table of effects (Table 20-1) indicates that it

Table 20-2 The table of variance for a two-way analysis

Source	SS	df	MS	F	eta[a]	p
(Between conditions	57	3	19.0	7.60	.86	.01)
Drug (row)	27	1	27.0	10.80	.76	.012
Psychotherapy (column)	27	1	27.0	10.80	.76	.012
Interaction	3	1	3.0	1.20	.36	.30
Within conditions	20	8	2.5			
Total	77	11	7.0			

$$^a eta = \sqrt{\frac{SS \text{ effect}}{SS \text{ effect} + SS \text{ within}}}$$

was more beneficial to have the drug than not to have it, and more beneficial to have the psychotherapy than not to have it. The interaction effect, the residual between conditions variation after the row and column effects were removed, was not close to statistical significance, though the size of the effect (*eta* = .36) was not trivial in magnitude. Because of the importance of interaction effects in two-way and higher-order analyses of variance, and because of the frequency with which they are misinterpreted by even very experienced investigators, we shall return later to discuss interaction effects in some detail.

The table of variance shown as Table 20-2 employs *eta* as its estimate of effect size. Earlier in our discussion of the one-way analysis of variance we defined *eta* as

$$eta = \sqrt{\frac{SS \text{ between}}{SS \text{ between} + SS \text{ within}}}$$

Eta, therefore, is similar to *r* in representing the square root of the proportion of variance accounted for. However, *eta* is a very nonspecific index of effect size when it is based on a source of variance with $df > 1$ and is, therefore, much less informative than *r*, which tells us about linear relationship. For example, in Table 20-2, the *eta* of .86 based on 3 *df* for the between conditions effect is large, but we cannot say much about what makes it large. The three *etas* listed below that *eta*, however, are each based on just a single *df*, and as noted earlier, when *eta* is of this special type ($df = 1$) *eta* is identical to *r* and may be interpreted as *r*. That helps quite a bit, as we can now say that the size of the effect of drug is $r = .76$ with all the different ways we have of interpreting that, including the BESD described in our discussion of correlations in Chapter 17. For the table of variance shown as Table 20-2, the size of the effect of psychotherapy is also $r = .76$, and the size of the effect of interaction is $r = .36$, which, while not significant with such a small-size study, is of at least promising magnitude. Our use of *eta* or *r* as an effect-size estimate in the context of the analysis of variance regards each effect of the analysis (e.g., row, column, and interaction effects) as though it were the only one investigated in that study. We mention this fact so that it will not seem strange that the sum of the r^2s or the eta^2s may exceed 1.00. Table 20-3 illustrates this.

Table 20-3 Summing *eta²*'s in a study

Source	SS	Proportion of total SS	r² or eta²
Drug	27	.35	.574
Psychotherapy	27	.35	.574
Interaction	3	.04	.130
Within conditions	20	.26	—
Total	77	1.00	1.278

In looking at the column for proportion of total SS, we see what proportion of all the SS of the study is associated with each source of variation including the error term. The definition, therefore, is

$$\text{Proportion of total } SS = \frac{SS \text{ effect of interest}}{\begin{array}{c}SS \text{ effect} \\ \text{of interest}\end{array} + \begin{array}{c}SS \text{ all other} \\ \text{between effects}\end{array} + SS \text{ within}}$$

In this definition, therefore, we keep increasing the size of the denominator as we keep increasing the number of variables investigated. Ordinarily, however, when we define proportion of variance as r^2 or eta^2, we disregard all between effects except for the one whose magnitude we are estimating. Therefore in our more usual usage we define r^2 or eta^2 as follows:

$$r^2 \text{ or } eta^2 = \frac{SS \text{ effect of interest}}{SS \text{ effect of interest} + SS \text{ within}}$$

TESTING THE GRAND MEAN

Earlier in our discussion of the grand mean we noted that we were ordinarily not interested in any intrinsic way in the magnitude of the grand mean. That is due in part to the arbitrary units of measurement often employed in behavioral research. Scores on ability tests, for example, might be equally well expressed as IQ scores with $M = 100$ and $\sigma = 20$, or as T scores with $M = 50$ and $\sigma = 10$, or as Z scores with $M = 0$ and $\sigma = 1$. The constant of measurement, then (e.g., 100, 50, 0), would be of little interest.

Sometimes, however, the constant of measurement may be of interest. For example, we may want to compare our sample of subjects with an earlier sample just to see whether the overall means are similar. That might be the case if we had failed to replicate a relationship obtained by an earlier investigator and wondered if our sample differed so much from the earlier one on the dependent variable that differences in sample characteristics might account for our failure to replicate the earlier result.

A second reason why we might be interested in our grand mean is that our dependent variable might estimate some skill that might or might not be better than chance. For example, in various measures of sensitivity to nonverbal communication, it would be of interest to know whether, on the average, a particular skill, such as understanding tone of voice, was better than a chance level of accuracy (Rosenthal, 1979; Rosenthal, Hall, DiMatteo, Rogers, & Archer, 1979).

A third reason why we might be interested in our grand mean is that our dependent variable might already be a difference score, such as the difference between a pre and a post measurement. In that case a test of the grand mean is equivalent to a *matched-pair t test* and tells us whether the two measurements, pre and post, differ systematically. Related closely to the assessment of change is the assessment of experimental difference, as when a sample of teachers or of experimenters is led to expect superior performance from some students or subjects. Then the dependent variable per teacher or experimenter sometimes is defined as the difference between (a) the performance obtained from the student or subject for whom the higher expectation had been created and (b) the performance obtained from the student or subject of the control condition. In that case a test of the grand mean tells us whether, overall, teachers or experimenters tended to obtain the results they had been led to expect (Rosenthal, 1966, 1976; Rosenthal & Jacobson, 1968; Rosenthal & Rubin, 1978).

The t Test

The general formula for the t test on the grand mean is

$$t = \frac{\bar{M} - C}{\sqrt{\left(\frac{1}{N}\right) MS \text{ error}}}$$

where $\bar{M}$ is the grand mean, C is the comparison score established on theoretical grounds, N is the total number of subjects or other sampling units, and MS error is the estimate of the variation of the scores of the sampling units within their experimental conditions, i.e., the MS within. For the illustration we have been considering, if we wanted to know whether the grand mean of 4.5 was significantly greater than zero, we would find

$$t = \frac{4.5 - 0}{\sqrt{\left(\frac{1}{12}\right) 2.5}} = 9.86$$

which, with 8 df (the df for the MS error or MS within), is significant at $p < .000005$, one-tailed.

Suppose that we were interested also in comparing our grand mean to the comparison score based on the grand mean of a large norm group of patients. In that case C would not be zero, but the grand mean of the norm group. Suppose that value were 5.0. Then,

$$t = \frac{4.5 - 5.0}{\sqrt{\left(\frac{1}{12}\right) 2.5}} = -1.10$$

which, with 8 df, has an associated p value of about .30, two-tailed. We might conclude that there is not a very significant difference between the average score of our twelve patients and the average score of the patients of the norm group. Of course, with a sample of only twelve patients our power to reject the null hypothesis is quite low unless the true effect size is quite large, and we are likely to make many type II errors (see Chapter 24).

In our examples employing the t test we have so far assumed that our comparison score was a theoretical score that was known exactly rather than a score that was itself only an estimate of a population value. Suppose, for example, that we wanted to compare our grand mean of 4.5 to the grand mean of 3.0 we obtained in an earlier study employing six patients. If we employed the same t test described so far, we would have obtained

$$t = \frac{4.5 - 3.0}{\sqrt{\left(\frac{1}{12}\right) 2.5}} = 3.29$$

which, with 8 df, is significant at about the .01 level, two-tailed. This p level is accurate if we assume the comparison score of 3.0 to be a theoretical value, but is not accurate if we want to take into account the fact that the comparison level is only an estimate based on six patients. Assuming the same MS error for both studies we compute this type of t by employing both sample sizes in the denominator:

$$t = \frac{\bar{M} - C}{\sqrt{\left(\frac{1}{N_{\bar{M}}} + \frac{1}{N_C}\right) MS \text{ error}}}$$

For our data,

$$t = \frac{4.5 - 3.0}{\sqrt{\left(\frac{1}{12} + \frac{1}{6}\right) 2.5}} = 1.90$$

which, with 8 df, is significant at about the .10 level, two-tailed. Employing the actual sample size upon which the comparison score is based will generally tend to decrease the obtained t from what it would have been had we employed a theoretical comparison score, and this decrease is greater when the actual sample size is smaller.

In this example we assumed that the MS error for the two studies was equivalent but that we did not actually know the MS error for the comparison score. Therefore, we employed as the MS error for our t test only the MS error for our new study. The df for our t test was, therefore, only 8, since that was the number of df upon which our MS error was based. If we had known the MS error for the earlier study we could have pooled the MS error for the two studies as follows:

$$MS \text{ error pooled} = \frac{df_1 \, MS \text{ error}_1 + df_2 \, MS \text{ error}_2}{df_1 + df_2}$$

then we could compute t from

$$t = \frac{\bar{M} - C}{\sqrt{\left(\frac{1}{N_{\bar{M}}} + \frac{1}{N_C}\right) MS \text{ error pooled}}}$$

The *df* for this *t* would be the sum of the *df* of the two pooled *MS* errors, i.e., $df_1 + df_2$.

The *F* Test

Early in our discussion of the analysis of variance we saw that $t^2 = F$ for the situation of only a single *df* for the numerator of *F*. *F* tests on the grand mean of any one study involve only a single *df* for the numerator of *F*, so that all of the *t* test procedures we have been discussing can be employed as *F* test procedures simply by squaring the computational formulas for *t*.

If we happen to be working with totals rather than means, the direct *F* test of the hypothesis that the grand mean differs from zero is obtained by

$$F = \frac{(\Sigma X)^2/N}{MS \ \text{error}}$$

where $(\Sigma X)^2$ is the square of the sum of all scores and N is the number of all such scores. For the example we have been using, the grand sum was 54 (i.e., the grand mean of 4.5 multiplied by the N of 12) so that

$$F = \frac{(54)^2/12}{2.5} = \frac{243}{2.5} = 97.20$$

which, with *df* of 1 for numerator and 8 for denominator, is significant at $p < .00001$. The square root of the obtained *F* is 9.86, precisely the value of *t* we obtained earlier when we tested the difference between the grand mean of 4.5 and zero.

We can relate the result of the preceding *F* test to our earlier discussion of individual differences as error (see Table 20-1). There we showed the decomposition of each of the twelve individual scores and the sum of the squared entries for each source of variance as follows:

		grand		row		column		interaction		
	Score =	mean	+	effect	+	effect	+	effect	+	error
ΣX^2	320 =	243	+	27	+	27	+	3	+	20

The entry for the grand mean, the sum of the twelve values of 4.5, each of which had been squared [i.e., $12(4.5)^2$], is identical to the numerator of the *F* test above, of the hypothesis that the grand mean differs from zero. If we subtract that value from the sum of the raw scores squared, we find $320 - 243 = 77$, the total sum of squares of deviations about the grand mean.

COMPUTATIONAL PROCEDURES: EQUAL AND UNEQUAL SAMPLE SIZES

In the case of a one-way analysis of variance it did not matter for the computational procedure whether we had the same number of units per condition or not. In a two-way or higher-order analysis, however, special care must be taken when the number of sampling units varies from condition to condition. Several procedures are available for dealing with this situation, of which the most wasteful is discarding a random subset of the units of each condition until the sample sizes of all conditions are equal. That procedure is almost never justified.

Several multiple-regression procedures are also available for handling the computations of a two-way analysis of variance with unequal sample sizes per condition (Overall & Spiegel, 1969; Overall, Spiegel, & Cohen, 1975). All of these procedures yield identical results when sample sizes are equal, but can differ fairly substantially as sample sizes become increasingly unequal. The procedure we present here can be employed when sample sizes are equal *or* unequal; it is intuitively appealing, and it is computationally convenient. Furthermore, it yields results closer to the "fully simultaneous multiple-regression method" (FSMR) recommended by Overall, Spiegel, and Cohen (1975) than do the competing methods described by Overall and Spiegel (1969). Indeed, for factorial designs of any size, having always two levels per factor, i.e., a 2^k factorial, it yields results that are identical to those obtained by the FSMR method (Horst & Edwards, 1982). In general, the multiple-regression approaches to the analysis of variance proceed by converting the independent variables of the analysis of variance to dummy variables all of which can then be used as predictors of the dependent variable.

Employing Unweighted Means

The procedure we present is called the *unweighted means analysis*. It can be used for situations of equal *or* unequal sample sizes and it requires only three simple steps (Walker & Lev, 1953).

1. Compute a *one-way* analysis of variance on the k groups or conditions.
2. Compute a two-way (or higher-way) analysis of variance on the *means* of all conditions just as though each condition had yielded only a single score (i.e., the mean).
3. Compute the error term required for the analysis in step 2 by multiplying the *MS* error from step 1 by $1/n_h$ where n_h is the harmonic mean of the various sample sizes of the different conditions. The quantity $1/n_h$, the factor by which we scale down the *MS* error from step 1 to make it the "right size" for the analysis of step 2, is computed by

$$\frac{1}{n_h} = \frac{1}{k}\left(\frac{1}{n_1} + \frac{1}{n_2} \cdots \frac{1}{n_k}\right)$$

where n_h is the harmonic mean of the sample sizes, k is the number of conditions, and the various n's (n_1 to n_k) are the number of sampling units per condition.

We now apply these steps to the set of data that has been serving as our illustration. As it happens, this set of data does have equal sample sizes, but the computational procedures are identical whether sample sizes are equal or unequal.

1. The one-way analysis of variance of our data

	PD	P	D	O
	9	6	5	4
	8	4	4	2
	7	2	3	0
Means	8	4	4	2

yields the following table of variance as reported earlier:

Source	Table of variance					
	SS	df	MS	F	eta	p
Between conditions	57	3	19.0	7.60	.86	.01
Within conditions	20	8	2.5			

Recall from Chapter 19 that equal sample sizes are *not* required for a one-way analysis of variance.

2. The two-way analysis of variance on the *means* of all conditions is computed as follows:

$$\text{Total } SS = \Sigma(M - \bar{M})^2$$

where M is the mean of each condition and $\bar{M}$ is the grand mean. Here we add up as many squared deviations as there are conditions altogether.

$$\text{Row } SS = \Sigma[c(M_R - \bar{M})^2]$$

where c is the number of columns contributing to the computation of M_R, the mean of each row, and $\bar{M}$ is the grand mean. Here we add up as many quantities as there are rows.

$$\text{Column } SS = \Sigma[r(M_C - \bar{M})^2]$$

where r is the number of rows contributing to the computation of M_C, the mean of each column, and $\bar{M}$ is the grand mean. Here we add up as many quantities as there are columns.

$$\text{Interaction } SS = \text{total } SS - \text{row } SS - \text{column } SS$$

For the data of our present illustration we have:

		Psychotherapy		
		Present	Absent	Mean
Drug	Present	8	4	6
therapy	Absent	4	2	3
	Mean	6	3	4.5

$$\text{Total } SS = (8 - 4.5)^2 + (4 - 4.5)^2 + (4 - 4.5)^2 + (2 - 4.5)^2 = 19$$
$$\text{Row } SS = 2(6 - 4.5)^2 + 2(3 - 4.5)^2 = 9$$
$$\text{Column } SS = 2(6 - 4.5)^2 + 2(3 - 4.5)^2 = 9$$
$$\text{Interaction } SS = 19 - 9 - 9 = 1$$

Note that in working only with condition means we have set all our "sample sizes" equal, i.e., they all equal 1, the one mean of the condition.

3. The error term (MS error) required for the sources of variance just computed from the means of conditions is obtained by multiplying the MS error from step 1 (found to be 2.5) by $1/n_h$, the reciprocal of the harmonic mean of the sample sizes, here found to be

$$\frac{1}{n_h} = \frac{1}{4}\left(\frac{1}{3} + \frac{1}{3} + \frac{1}{3} + \frac{1}{3}\right) = \frac{1}{3}$$

Therefore, our new error term, appropriately scaled down, is found to be $\frac{1}{3} \times 2.5 = 0.833$. Our table of variance, based on this set of computational procedures, is then displayed as shown in Table 20-4.

Earlier, we showed the table of variance for the same study but with computations based on the original twelve scores rather than on the means of the four different conditions. The results of F tests and the magnitudes of *eta* and of p are identical to those obtained by the method of unweighted means

Table 20-4 Unweighted means analysis

Source	SS	df	MS	F	eta[a]	p
Drug (row)	9	1	9	10.80	.76	.012
Psychotherapy (column)	9	1	9	10.80	.76	.012
Interaction	1	1	1	1.20	.36	.30
Error term ($MS_E \times 1/n_h$)	—	8	0.833			

$$^a eta = \sqrt{\frac{(F)(df \text{ numerator})}{(F)(df \text{ numerator}) + (df \text{ denominator})}}$$

shown in Table 20-4. However, the magnitudes of all SS and MS are smaller in the present table by a factor of $1/n_h$, the reciprocal of the harmonic mean sample size per condition. The effect of employing the unweighted means analysis, then, is to shrink the SS and MS in a uniform way that has no effect whatever on either significance tests or effect-size estimates. This example illustrates that when sample sizes are equal, the unweighted-means analysis yields results identical to those obtained from an ordinary analysis employing all of the original scores.

Effects on F of Unequal Sample Sizes

Earlier, in our discussion of increasing the size of t, we saw that for any given total N, and given that the true effect size was not zero, t would increase as the sizes of each sample became more nearly equal. The same situation holds for F, that for any given total N, F will increase as the sizes of the two or more samples or conditions become more nearly equal. We can demonstrate this for the data we have been employing for our illustration. The four groups were of equal size (3, 3, 3, 3) with a total N of twelve patients. Table 20-5 shows the effects on F, eta, and p when the sample sizes are made increasingly heterogeneous. For our example we show the F, eta, and p only for the drug (row) effect, but that is sufficient to illustrate the point.

Table 20-5 shows that as the sample sizes become more heterogeneous, where *heterogeneity* is defined by the relative magnitude of the σ of the sample sizes, F and eta both decrease and p becomes larger, i.e., less significant. F decreases by as much as 57 percent, eta decreases by as much as 20 percent, and the quite significant p of .012 goes to "nonsignificance" ($p = .064$), a result that would cause greatest pain to researchers endorsing dichotomous decisions about whether to believe or not believe the null hypothesis, a view we do not encourage.

The results shown in Table 20-5 are by no means extreme. When the total N increases, much more extreme effects are possible. For example, for the four conditions of the experiment that has been serving as our example, if the N had

Table 20-5 Effects on F, Eta, and p of heterogeneity of sample sizes

Sample sizes	σ^*	n_h	$1/n_h$	MS error $(2.5 \times 1/n_h)$	$F(1, 8)$	eta†	p
3, 3, 3, 3	0	3.00	.333	0.833	10.80	.76	.012
2, 2, 4, 4	1.00	2.67	.375	0.938	9.59	.74	.015
1, 1, 5, 5	2.00	1.67	.600	1.500	6.00	.65	.040
1, 1, 1, 9	3.46	1.29	.778	1.944	4.63	.61	.064

* Of the four sample sizes.

† $eta = \sqrt{\dfrac{(F)(df \text{ num.})}{(F)(df \text{ num.}) + (df \text{ denom.})}}$

been 100, equal-size samples of 25 each would have yielded an $F(1, 96)$ of 131.58 keeping the effect size of $eta = .76$ constant. However, if the N of 100 had been allocated as heterogeneously as possible (1, 1, 1, 97), $F(1, 96)$ would have been 7.00 and eta would have been .26, a reduction in F of 95 percent and a reduction in eta of 66 percent!

HIGHER-ORDER FACTORIAL DESIGNS

So far in our discussion of factorial designs we have dealt only with two-way, or two-dimensional, designs, but there are many occasions to employ higher-order designs. For example, suppose that the experiment we have been describing had been carried out twice, once for female patients and once for male patients. We could reap the general benefit of factorial designs of using subjects for more comparisons and building up the sample sizes per comparison by analyzing these two experiments as a single, higher-order factorial experiment with design and results as shown in Table 20-6. This design is referred to as a "2 × 2 × 2 factorial design" or as a "2^3 factorial," because there are three factors each with two levels: drug (present vs. absent), psychotherapy (present vs. absent), and sex of patient (female vs. male). Assume that there were three patients in each condition, so that $N = 2 \times 2 \times 2 \times 3 = 24$. Assume further that our preliminary one-way analysis of variance (step 1 of the unweighted means procedure) happened to yield an MS error of 2.5, exactly what we found in our earlier one-way analysis of the original twelve scores. Step 3 of the unweighted means procedure requires us to multiply this MS error of 2.5 by $1/n_h$ which for this study is

$$\frac{1}{n_h} = \frac{1}{8}\left(\frac{1}{3} + \frac{1}{3} + \frac{1}{3} + \frac{1}{3} + \frac{1}{3} + \frac{1}{3} + \frac{1}{3} + \frac{1}{3}\right) = \frac{1}{3}$$

so that our error term will be $2.5 \times \frac{1}{3} = 0.833$, exactly the same error term we found before. It only remains now to compute the three-way analysis of variance on the eight means shown in the table.

Computations via Subtables

In a three-way analysis of variance we will compute three main effects, one for each factor, three two-way interactions of all factors taken two at a time, and

Table 20-6 Improvement scores in eight conditions

	Female patients		Male patients	
	Psychotherapy	No psychotherapy	Psychotherapy	No psychotherapy
Drug	10	5	6	3
No drug	4	1	4	3

Table 20-7 Two-way tables of a three-way design

Subtable 1		Female	Male	Mean
Sex of patient × drug combination	Drug	7.5^{2} *	4.5^{2}	6.0^{4}
	No drug	2.5^{2}	3.5^{2}	3.0^{4}
	Mean	5.0^{4}	4.0^{4}	4.5^{8}

Subtable 2		Female	Male	Mean
Sex of patient × psycho-therapy combination	Psychotherapy	7.0^{2}	5.0^{2}	6.0^{4}
	No psychotherapy	3.0^{2}	3.0^{2}	3.0^{4}
	Mean	5.0^{4}	4.0^{4}	4.5^{8}

Subtable 3		Psychotherapy	No psychotherapy	Mean
Drug × psychotherapy combination	Drug	8^{2}	4^{2}	6^{4}
	No drug	4^{2}	2^{2}	3^{4}
	Mean	6^{4}	3^{4}	4.5^{8}

* The number of means upon which this mean is based.

one three-way interaction. Computations require us to construct the three two-way tables by averaging the two means (in this example) that contribute to the mean of each of the 2 × 2 tables (see Table 20-7).

The entries of our three 2 × 2 tables are found as follows: The mean for females given drugs, the top-left condition of subtable 1, is found by averaging the two conditions in which there are females given drugs; females given drugs who are also given psychotherapy ($M = 10$) and females given drugs who are not given psychotherapy ($M = 5$). The row and column means can be checked readily because each factor produces row or column means in two different 2 × 2 tables. Thus the female and male mean improvement scores can be compared in subtables 1 and 2, the drug and no-drug mean scores can be compared in subtables 1 and 3, and the psychotherapy and no-psychotherapy mean scores can be compared in subtables 2 and 3.

The general strategy is to compute the main effects first, then the two-way interactions which are residuals when the two contributing main effects are subtracted from the variation in the two-way tables, and the three-way interaction which is a residual when the three main effects and three two-way interactions are subtracted from the total variation among the eight condition means. The computational formulas follow:

$$\text{``Total''} \; SS = \Sigma(M - \bar{M})^2$$

where M is the mean of each condition and $\bar{M}$ is the grand mean of all conditions. Here we add up as many squared deviations as there are conditions altogether. (We have put quotation marks around "Total" as a reminder that this is a "total" SS only when we are considering the data of the analysis to consist only of the condition means.)

$$\text{Sex of patient } SS = \Sigma[dp(M_S - \bar{M})^2]$$

where d is the number of levels of the drug factor, p is the number of levels of the psychotherapy factor, M_S is the mean of all conditions of a given sex, and $\bar{M}$ is the grand mean. Here we add up as many quantities as there are levels of the factor sex of patient. Note that we have given up the row and column designations because with higher-order designs we run out of things to call factors, e.g., in a five-way design. Accordingly, in higher-order designs we simply employ the names of the factors as the names of the dimensions.

$$\text{Drug } SS = \Sigma[sp(M_D - \bar{M})^2]$$

where s is the number of levels of the sex of patient factor, p and $\bar{M}$ are as above, and M_D is the mean of all the conditions contributing observations to each level of the drug factor. Here we add up as many quantities as there are levels of the drug factor.

$$\text{Psychotherapy } SS = \Sigma[sd(M_P - \bar{M})^2]$$

where s, d, and $\bar{M}$ are defined as above and M_P is the mean of all the conditions contributing observations to each level of the psychotherapy factor. Here we add up as many quantities as there are levels of the psychotherapy factor.

$$\text{Sex} \times \text{drug interaction } SS = \Sigma[p(M_{SD} - \bar{M})^2] - \text{sex } SS - \text{drug } SS$$

where M_{SD} is the mean of all conditions contributing observations to each mean of subtable 1 of Table 20-7 and other terms are as defined above. Here we add up as many quantities as there are entries in that subtable.

$$\text{Sex} \times \text{psychotherapy interaction } SS = \Sigma[d(M_{SP} - \bar{M})^2]$$
$$- \text{sex } SS - \text{psychotherapy } SS$$

where M_{SP} is the mean of all conditions contributing observations to each mean of subtable 2 and other terms are as defined above. Here we add up as many quantities as there are entries in that subtable.

$$\text{Drug} \times \text{psychotherapy interaction } SS = \Sigma[s(M_{DP} - \bar{M})^2]$$
$$- \text{drug } SS - \text{psychotherapy } SS$$

where M_{DP} is the mean of all conditions contributing observations to each mean of subtable 3 and other terms are as defined above. Here we add up as many quantities as there are entries in that subtable.

Sex $\times$ drug $\times$ psychotherapy interaction SS = total SS
  $- $ sex $SS - $ drug $SS - $ psychotherapy $SS - $ sex $\times$ drug SS
  $- $ sex $\times$ psychotherapy $SS - $ drug $\times$ psychotherapy SS.

For the data of our $2 \times 2 \times 2$ factorial design we find

$$\text{Total } SS = (10 - 4.5)^2 + (5 - 4.5)^2 + (6 - 4.5)^2 + (3 - 4.5)^2 + (4 - 4.5)^2$$
$$+ (1 - 4.5)^2 + (4 - 4.5)^2 + (3 - 4.5)^2 = 50$$

Sex of patient $SS = 2 \times 2(5 - 4.5)^2 + 2 \times 2(4 - 4.5)^2 = 2$

Drug $SS = 2 \times 2(6 - 4.5)^2 + 2 \times 2(3 - 4.5)^2 = 18$

Psychotherapy $SS = 2 \times 2(6 - 4.5)^2 + 2 \times 2(3 - 4.5)^2 = 18$

Sex $\times$ drug $SS = 2(7.5 - 4.5)^2 + 2(4.5 - 4.5)^2 + 2(2.5 - 4.5)^2$
$+ 2(3.5 - 4.5)^2 - $ sex $SS - $ drug $SS = 8$

Sex $\times$ psychotherapy $SS = 2(7 - 4.5)^2 + 2(5 - 4.5)^2 + 2(3 - 4.5)^2$
$+ 2(3 - 4.5)^2 - $ sex $SS - $ psychotherapy
$SS = 2$

Drug $\times$ psychotherapy $SS = 2(8 - 4.5)^2 + 2(4 - 4.5)^2 + 2(4 - 4.5)^2$
$+ 2(2 - 4.5)^2 - $ drug $SS - $ psychotherapy
$SS = 2$

Sex $\times$ drug $\times$ psychotherapy $SS = $ total $SS - SS_S - SS_D - SS_P - SS_{SD}$
$- SS_{SP} - SS_{DP} = 0$

Table of Variance

These computations are summarized in the table of variance shown as Table 20-8. When we examine the effects of drug, psychotherapy, and the interaction of drug and psychotherapy, we find that the effect sizes (*eta*'s) of .76, .76, and .36, respectively, are identical to the effect sizes obtained in our earlier two-way analysis of variance. That is as it should be, of course, since the subtable of the drug $\times$ psychotherapy combination (Table 20-7, subtable 3) shows exactly the same four means as were shown by the two-way table of our earlier 2×2 factorial analysis of variance, and, in addition, our error term has remained the same. Although our *eta*'s have not changed, our F's have all increased, and our p levels are much smaller in the present analysis relative to our earlier two-way analysis. That too is what we would expect since the *size* of our study has

Table 20-8 Unweighted means analysis

Source	SS	df	MS	F(1, 16)	eta*	p
Sex of patient	2	1	2	2.40	.36	.14
Drug	18	1	18	21.61	.76	.0003
Psychotherapy	18	1	18	21.61	.76	.0003
Sex $\times$ drug	8	1	8	9.60	.61	.007
Sex $\times$ psychotherapy	2	1	2	2.40	.36	.14
Drug $\times$ psychotherapy	2	1	2	2.40	.36	.14
Sex $\times$ drug $\times$ psychotherapy	0	1	0	0.00	.00	1.00
Error term ($MS_E \times 1/n_h$)	—	16	0.833†			

* $eta = \sqrt{\dfrac{F(df \text{ num.})}{F(df \text{ num.}) + (df \text{ denom.})}}$

† Based on our finding that $MS_E = 2.5$.

increased. In fact, as discussed at the beginning of Chapter 19, our F tests have doubled because the size of our experiment (df for error) has doubled since

$$F = \frac{r^2}{1 - r^2} \times df$$

Inspection of the table of variance shown as Table 20-8 suggests a tendency ($eta = .36$) for the sex of the patient to make some difference, and subtables 1 and 2 of Table 20-7 show that females earned higher improvement scores than did males. We will postpone discussion of the remaining interaction effects of this table of variance until Chapter 21. The topic of interaction is so important and so widely misunderstood, not perhaps in theory but in practice, that we want to highlight the topic in a chapter of its own.

Generalizing Computational Procedures

It is not at all unusual for behavioral researchers to employ factorial designs of more than three dimensions. For example, it is easy to imagine repeating the three-way factorial just described for two or more levels of age, e.g., patients between 20 and 40 and patients between 40 and 60. The computations for this 2^4 factorial design (or $2 \times 2 \times 2 \times 2$) are quite analogous to those described for the 2^3 design. We proceed by constructing all possible two-way tables (AB, AC, AD, BC, BD, CD) and all possible three-way tables (ABC, ABD, ACD, BCD), and then compute the required four main effects, six two-way interactions, four three-way interactions, and one four-way interaction.

TWENTY-ONE

INTERACTION EFFECTS

SEPARATION OF INTERACTION FROM MAIN EFFECTS

In the last chapter we introduced the idea of interaction effects briefly but postponed detailed discussion to the present chapter. We did that to give the topic of interaction effects the status of an independent chapter, which it deserves for three reasons: (1) the *frequency* with which interactions occur and are discussed in the behavioral sciences, (2) the *importance* of interactions in so many substantive areas of the behavioral sciences, and (3) the widespread *misunderstanding* surrounding the concept of interaction.

Referees and advisory editors for various journals in the behavioral sciences, and consultants in research methods, find the misinterpretation of interaction effects to be one of the most common methodological errors made. The nature of the error is almost always the same: the effects of the interaction are not separated from the main effects.

An Illustration

Suppose we are comparing a new method of teaching reading to an old method and have employed both female and male pupils as our subjects. The tables of means and of variance are as shown, respectively, in Table 21-1 and Table 21-2. In the published report an investigator might accurately state that there was a significant effect of method such that pupils taught by the new method performed better than those taught by the old method. The investigator might also

Table 21-1 Table of means

	Females	Males	Means
Experimental (new method)	4	10	7
Control (old method)	4	2	3
Means	4	6	5

state correctly that there was no significant effect of sex of pupil on performance. Finally, the investigator might say, *but it would be wrong,* that the significant interaction effect shown in Figure 21-1 demonstrated that males but not females benefited from the new teaching method.

Table 21-2 Table of variance

Source	SS	df	MS	F	eta	p
Method	16	1	16	4.00	.25	.05
Sex of pupil	4	1	4	1.00	.13	—
Interaction	16	1	16	4.00	.25	.05
Error term (MS error $\times \frac{1}{16}$)	240	60	4			

In what way has the investigator erred in referring the reader to this figure? The figure is a perfectly accurate display of the *overall* results of the study including *both* main effects *plus* an interaction, but it is *not* an accurate display of the interaction the investigator believed was being displayed. An accurate display of the interaction might appear as shown in Figure 21-2.

Here we see that the *interaction* shows that males benefit from the new method precisely to the same degree that females are harmed by it. The diagram of the interaction is X-shaped; indeed, it is true *in general* that in any 2 × 2 analysis of variance the display of the interaction will be X-shaped. This will become clearer as we proceed.

DEFINING INTERACTION

Interaction effects are residual effects, or effects remaining in any analysis after lower-order effects have been removed, as explained in Chapter 20. In a two-way design (A × B), the interaction effects are the effects remaining after the row and column effects (the effects of A and B) have been removed. In a three-way design (A × B × C), and in higher-order designs, there are four or more different interactions. In an A × B × C design there are three two-way interactions (A × B, A × C, B × C), each of which is the residual set of effects remaining after the removal of the two main effects designated by the letters naming the interaction; there is also a three-way interaction (A × B × C) which is the residual set of effects remaining after the removal of the three main

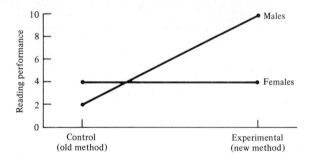

Figure 21-1 Figure showing two main effects as well as interaction.

effects and the three two-way interactions. In an A × B × C × D, or four-way design, there are six two-way interactions (A × B, A × C, A × D, B × C, B × D, C × D), four three-way interactions (A × B × C, A × B × D, A × C × D, B × C × D), and one four-way interaction. In general, a *higher-order interaction* is defined as the residual set of effects remaining after the main effects and all lower-order interactions relevant to the higher-order interaction have been removed. Thus the A × B × C × D interaction is defined as the set of effects remaining after the four main effects, the six two-way interactions, and the four three-way interactions have been subtracted from the total of all between-conditions effects.

DISPLAYING THE RESIDUALS

Before an interaction effect can be understood it must be identified and examined, i.e., the residuals defining the interaction must be displayed. The logic is straightforward, but in a very-high-order interaction the computation can become burdensome, and regrettably there are very few social science data-analytic packages (e.g., Data-text) that routinely provide the residuals. In a two-dimensional design, however, the computations are simple. Consider the

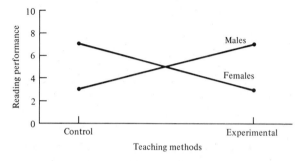

Figure 21-2 Figure showing interaction effect.

Table 21-3 Reading scores in four conditions

| | | Sex of pupils | | Means | Row effects |
		Females	Males		
Teaching method	New (experimental)	4	10	7	2
	Old (control)	4	2	3	−2
	Means	4	6	5	
	Column effects	−1	1		

(handwritten annotations: top row "3 4 -2 -1   7 10 -2 -1"; bottom row "7 4 - 2 -1   3 2 - 2 -1")

results of our experiment on the effects of a new method of teaching reading on reading performance scores, as shown in Table 21-3.

To find the interaction effects we must subtract the row and column effects from each condition of the experiment. *Row effects* are defined for each row as the mean of that row minus the grand mean. The row effects are $7 - 5 = 2$ for the new teaching method and $3 - 5 = -2$ for the old teaching method. To remove the row effect we subtract the row effect from every condition within that row. Subtracting 2 from the top row in Table 21-3 yields means of 2 and 8; subtracting −2 from the bottom row yields means of 6 and 4 (recall that subtracting a negative value is equivalent to adding a positive value). The table of means we started with, now with row effects removed (or "corrected for" row effects), has been amended as shown in Table 21-4.

We must still remove the effects of columns. *Column effects* are defined for each column as the mean of that column minus the grand mean. The column effects are $4 - 5 = -1$ for the females and $6 - 5 = 1$ for the males. To remove the column effect we subtract it from every condition within that column. Subtracting −1 from the first column of the row-corrected table shown as Table 21-4 yields means of 3 and 7; subtracting 1 from the second column yields means of 7 and 3. The table of means we started with, now with both row and column effects removed, has been amended as shown in Table 21-5. Once the row and column effects are all zero, we can be sure that what is left is only the set of residuals defining the interaction effect, sometimes with, and sometimes without, the grand mean added.

Table 21-4 Reading scores corrected for row effects

| | | Sex of pupils | | Means | Row effects |
		Females	Males		
Teaching method	New	2	8	5	0
	Old	6	4	5	0
	Means	4	6	5	
	Column effects	−1	1		

Table 21-5 Reading scores corrected for row and column effects

		Sex of pupils			Row effects
		Females	Males	Means	
Teaching method	New	3	7	5	0
	Old	7	3	5	0
	Means	5	5	5	
	Column effects	0	0		

It is these means that were shown in Figure 21-2 displaying the correct interaction effects. However, these interaction effects are inflated by the presence of the grand mean, an inflation useful for display purposes earlier when we wanted to compare the results of the experiment defined as the condition means, with the interaction effect alone. In most situations, however, we prefer to display the interaction effects freed of the effect of the grand mean. To remove the grand mean from Table 21-5 simply subtract it from every condition of the experiment. For our example that yields the results shown in Table 21-6.

It should be noted that all four conditions show the same absolute value of the interaction effects, only the signs differ. That is always the case in a 2 × 2 analysis, and the signs on one of the diagonals are always different from the signs on the other diagonal if the interaction is not precisely zero. It is thus convenient to think of an interaction in a 2 × 2 table as the difference between the means of the two diagonals, just as it is convenient to think of the row or column effects as the differences between the row means or the column means.

Returning now to Figure 21-1, we can see that it is an accurate display of the results of the experiment. It does show that females did not benefit from the new teaching method but that males did. That statement, however, is not a statement about the interaction effect per se but a statement made up in part of (1) a method effect (the new method is better), in part of (2) a sex effect (males score higher, though not significantly so), and in part of (3) an interaction effect

Table 21-6 Reading scores corrected for row and column effects and for the grand mean

		Sex of pupils			Row effects
		Females	Males	Means	
Teaching method	New	−2	2	0	0
	Old	2	−2	0	0
	Means	0	0	0	
	Column effects	0	0		

which we interpret as showing that females are hurt by the new method as much as males are helped by it.

Constructing Tables of Means

It is useful as a check on our students' understanding of interaction effects and the additive nature of the analysis of variance to ask them to construct tables of means to our specifications. We list a series of 2 × 2 tables with no entries in them and ask students to fill in the four means to match the following specifications, one for each 2 × 2 table; by "effects" we mean any nonzero effect.

1. Column effect only
2. Row effect only
3. Row effect and column effect only, with row effect larger
4. Interaction effect only
5. Interaction effect and row effect, with interaction effect larger
6. Interaction effect and column effect, with column effect larger
7. Row effect, column effect, and interaction effect, with row effect largest and column effect smallest

As an illustration of how to approach such practice problems begin with an empty A × B table:

	A_1	A_2	Means	Row effect
B_1				
B_2				
Means				
Column effect				

Beginning with the grand mean, choose any value—positive, zero, or negative—but keep to a single-digit integer for simplicity. If a grand mean of 2 were chosen, we would have:

	A_1	A_2	Means	Row effect
B_1	2	2	2	0
B_2	2	2	2	0
Means	2	2	2	
Column effect	0	0		

Since we want the column effect to be smallest, choose the smallest possible integers ($+1$ and -1) to add to each condition within each of the two columns yielding:

	A_1	A_2	Means	Row effect
B_1	3	1	2	0
B_2	3	1	2	0
Means	3	1	2	
Column effect	$+1$	-1		

In order that the interaction effect be larger than the column effect we might choose the values of $+2$ and -2, adding the former value to the conditions on one diagonal and the latter to the conditions on the other diagonal, yielding:

	A_1	A_2	Means	Row effect
B_1	5	-1	2	0
B_2	1	3	2	0
Means	3	1	2	
Column effect	$+1$	-1		

Finally, in order that the row effect be larger than the interaction, we might choose the values of $+3$ and -3, to add to each condition within each of the two rows, yielding:

	A_1	A_2	Means	Row effect
B_1	8	2	5	$+3$
B_2	-2	0	-1	-3
Means	3	1	2	
Column effect	$+1$	-1		

As a check on the construction of the 2×2 table we can decompose it, as in the last chapter, into its various additive components.

	Group mean	=	grand mean	+	row effect	+	column effect	+	interaction effect
A_1B_1	8	=	2	+	(3)	+	(1)	+	(2)
A_2B_1	2	=	2	+	(3)	+	(−1)	+	(−2)
A_1B_2	−2	=	2	+	(−3)	+	(1)	+	(−2)
A_2B_2	0	=	2	+	(−3)	+	(−1)	+	(2)
ΣX	8	=	8	+	0	+	0	+	0
ΣX^2	72	=	16	+	36	+	4	+	16

Examination of the four group means above and their additive components shows that row effects were larger than interaction effects, which in turn were larger than column effects, as required by our specifications. In a 2×2 table the absolute values of the two row effects are identical, with one of the signs positive and the other sign negative. Exactly the same situation holds for the column effects. For the interaction, all four effects are identical in absolute value, but the two effects on one diagonal are opposite in sign to the two effects on the other diagonal. In this case, therefore, we can rank-order the sizes of effects by rank-ordering the absolute values of the three effects contributing to any one of our four means.

MORE COMPLEX TWO-WAY DESIGNS

So far we have considered only the simple case of interaction in a 2×2 design. In such a design we have seen that the residuals defining the interaction are all identical in absolute value, with positive signs on one diagonal and negative signs on the other diagonal. In larger designs the situation is more complex. Because this is a chapter on interaction, our focus in the following example will be on the study of the interaction effects. This emphasis is not due to our regarding interaction effects as in any way more important than main effects. Rather, it is because interaction effects are so much more often misinterpreted than are main effects.

Table 21-7 Improvement scores in twelve conditions

		Treatment conditions				
Patient type		A_1 ECT(10)	A_2 ECT(3)	A_3 Supp. + drug	A_4 Supp. only	Mean
B_1	Psychotic depression	8	6	4	2	5
B_2	Neurotic depression	11	8	5	8	8
B_3	Paranoid reaction	2	4	6	8	5
Mean		7	6	5	6	6

For our example we consider an experiment in which four different treatment procedures are administered to three different types of patients, with results as shown in Table 21-7.

Patients of each of the three types were assigned at random to one of four treatment conditions: (1) a course of ten electroconvulsive treatments, (2) a course of three electroconvulsive treatments, (3) a combination of supportive psychotherapy and chemotherapy, and (4) supportive psychotherapy alone. In order to see the interaction of treatment × patient type, both the row and column effects must be subtracted off. Usually it is desirable also to subtract off the grand mean, and we begin by doing that. Since the grand mean is 6, simply subtract 6 from every one of the 3 × 4, or 12, condition means, yielding:

	A_1	A_2	A_3	A_4	Mean
B_1	2	0	-2	-4	-1
B_2	5	2	-1	2	2
B_3	-4	-2	0	2	-1
Mean	1	0	-1	0	0

Once the grand mean has been subtracted, the new row means are the row effects, and the new column means are the column effects. To remove the row effects, simply subtract the effect of each row (row mean minus grand mean) from every condition within that row. Doing that for the present data yields:

	A_1	A_2	A_3	A_4	Mean
B_1	3	1	-1	-3	0
B_2	3	0	-3	0	0
B_3	-3	-1	1	3	0
Mean	1	0	-1	0	0

Subtracting the column effect from every condition mean within that column then yields:

	A_1	A_2	A_3	A_4	Mean
B_1	2	1	0	-3	0
B_2	2	0	-2	0	0
B_3	-4	-1	2	3	0
Mean	0	0	0	0	0

Now that the grand mean, row effects, and column effects have been removed, we are left with the interaction effect shown just above. The effects contributing most to the interaction are the effects furthest from zero, and one way to approach the interpretation of the interaction is one residual at a time, starting with the largest absolute value. In this case the A_1B_3 condition shows the greatest residual (-4), suggesting that least improvement is shown by paranoid patients given a course of ten ECT treatments, disregarding row and column effects. The next two largest residuals are the A_4B_1 and A_4B_3 conditions. The former suggests that support alone offered to psychotic depressive patients is relatively damaging (-3), while the latter suggests that support alone offered to paranoid patients is *relatively* quite beneficial (3). The term "relatively" is used here to emphasize that the effects shown by certain combinations of treatments and patients are large or small only in relation to other effects shown here *after the removal of the main effects of treatments and patients*.

We can be more systematic in our examination of the residuals by listing them in order of magnitude as shown in Table 21-8. Examining first the positive residuals suggests that paranoid patients may do better given support, while depressive patients may do better given ECT. Examining the negative residuals suggests that paranoid patients may do worse given ECT, while depressive patients may do worse given support. It may be of value to simplify our design from four treatments to two by combining the two conditions receiving ECT and the two conditions receiving support. We can further simplify our design from three patient types to two by combining the two depressed groups. That

Table 21-8 Systematic ordering of residuals

Residual	Patient	Treatment
3	Paranoid	Support Only
2	Psychotic depression	ECT 10
2	Neurotic depression	ECT 10
2	Paranoid	Support + drug
1	Psychotic depression	ECT 3
0	Psychotic depression	Support + drug
0	Neurotic depression	ECT 3
0	Neurotic depression	Support Only
−1	Paranoid	ECT 3
−2	Neurotic depression	Support + drug
−3	Psychotic depression	Support Only
−4	Paranoid	ECT 10

yields a 2 × 2 table in each quarter of which we can record the sum of the residuals contributing to that quarter as shown below:

	ECT $(A_1 + A_2)$	Support $(A_3 + A_4)$	Mean
Depressives $(B_1 + B_2)$	5	−5	0
Paranoids (B_3)	−5	5	0
Mean	0	0	0

This simplification of the interaction to a 2 × 2 table represents one reasonable attempt to understand the patterning of the residuals defining the interaction. In subsequent chapters dealing with contrasts we shall give more details about the simplification of complex interaction effects.

The complexity of an interaction depends in part on the df associated with the interaction, with df computed as the product of the df associated with each of its constituent elements. In the study we have just now been discussing, there were four treatment conditions, so $df = 3$ for treatments, and three types of patients, so $df = 2$ for patient type; therefore df for the treatment × patient-type interaction = 3 × 2 = 6. Finding a pattern in these 6 df, such as the one shown just above as a 2 × 2 table, represents simplifying the 6 df interaction to a 1 df portion of that interaction. Elsewhere we provide procedures for assessing how well we have done in simplifying the interpretation of an interaction with multiple df in the numerator of its F test and, more generally, how well we have done in the interpretation of any effect, interaction or main effect, with multiple df in the numerator of the F test when we impose a simplifying structure.

An accurate description of the simplified structure of our interaction might be: depressed patients are benefited by ECT to the same degree that they are harmed by support, while paranoid patients benefit from support to the same degree that they are harmed by ECT. Note that we are describing the *interaction* effects or residuals and not necessarily the original condition means, which are a reflection *not* merely of the interaction but of the row and column effects as well.

An alternative simplification of the 6 df interaction might involve keeping in mind the amount of ECT administered as well as whether ECT was administered. Thus we might have three levels of ECT:

	(A_1) High (ECT 10)	(A_2) Low (ECT 3)	$(A_3 + A_4)$ No ECT	Mean
Depressives $(B_1 + B_2)$	4	1	−5	0
Paranoids (B_3)	−4	−1	5	0
Mean	0	0	0	0

Interpretation of this simplification might be that in going from none to some to more ECT, depressives are increasingly more benefited, while paranoids are increasingly less benefited.

Constructing Tables of Means

Earlier in this chapter we noted that it was useful to invite students to construct 2×2 tables of means to our specifications. We have also found it useful to do so with larger tables. For example, one can list a series of empty tables ranging in dimensions from 2×3 to 4×5 and, for each one, ask students to fill in means such that row effects would be largest, interaction effects intermediate, and column effects smallest, etc., with different specifications for each empty table.

THREE-WAY DESIGNS

Near the end of Chapter 20 we presented a table of variance for a $2 \times 2 \times 2$ design (see Table 20-8), but we postponed discussion of the interaction effects until the present chapter. In that study there were three two-way interactions, and for the purpose of computation of the three-way analysis of variance, we constructed three subtables of means, one for each two-way combination of the three factors of the study (see Table 20-7). The three factors were sex of patient, drug, and psychotherapy. Since we have already given several illustrations of how to go from a table of means to a table of effects, we will here simply show the table of effects corresponding to each table of means. In the tables of effects shown as Tables 21-9a to 21-9c the row and column "means" are the row and column effects, respectively, and the four entries in the 2×2 table are the residuals defining the interaction.

The interaction of sex of patient $\times$ drug was found to be significant ($p = .007$) and large ($eta = .61$). Now our examination of the residuals tells us that females did as much better with the drug as they did worse without it, while males did as much better without the drug as they did worse with it. Does this mean that males are better off without the drug? No, in this study there is a large main effect of drug, and it is better to have the drug than not have it for

Table 21-9a Sex of patient × drug combination

	Table of means			Table of effects		
	Female	Male	Mean	Female	Male	Mean
Drug	7.5	4.5	6.0	1.0	−1.0	1.5
No drug	2.5	3.5	3.0	−1.0	1.0	−1.5
Mean	5.0	4.0	4.5	0.5	−0.5	0

Table 21-9b Sex of patient × psychotherapy combination

	Table of means			Table of effects		
	Female	Male	Mean	Female	Male	Mean
Psychotherapy	7.0	5.0	6.0	0.5	−0.5	1.5
No psychotherapy	3.0	3.0	3.0	−0.5	0.5	−1.5
Mean	5.0	4.0	4.5	0.5	−0.5	0

males as well as females. The interaction tells us only that the benefits of the drug are less for males than they are for females, not that the drug is disadvantageous to males in any *absolute* sense.

The interaction of sex of patient × psychotherapy was found to be "significant" at only the .14 level, though the effect size was not trivial (*eta* = .36). Examination of the residuals shows that females did better with psychotherapy, while males did better without psychotherapy relative to females receiving no psychotherapy and males receiving psychotherapy. Phrased another way, we could say that psychotherapy benefited females [(0.5) − (−0.5) = 1.0] more than it benefited males [(−0.5) − (0.5) = −1.0].

The interaction of drug × psychotherapy also did not reach the conventional level of significance (*p* = .14), but its effect size was substantial (*eta* = .36). The residuals defining this interaction show that psychotherapy is more beneficial to those receiving the drug, and that the absence of psychotherapy is more beneficial to those not receiving the drug relative to the remaining two combinations (disregarding the main effects, as interactions always do). Phrased another way we could say that the interaction shows that receiving *both* drug and psychotherapy and receiving *neither* drug nor psychotherapy was more beneficial than receiving *either* one of the treatments alone. Once again we must emphasize that this does not mean that patients are better off receiving no treatment than receiving either treatment alone. On the contrary, the table of means in Table 21-9c shows that either drug or psychotherapy alone is more beneficial than neither treatment. However, considering *only* the inter-

Table 21-9c Drug × psychotherapy combination

	Table of means			Table of effects		
	Psychotherapy	No psychotherapy	Mean	Psychotherapy	No psychotherapy	Mean
Drug	8	4	6	0.5	−0.5	1.5
No drug	4	2	3	−0.5	0.5	−1.5
Mean	6	3	4.5	1.5	−1.5	0

action component of the variation among the means, it *is* true that neither treatment is better than either treatment.

Defining Three-Way Interactions

Interactions are defined by residuals, and we have now had some experience in computing these residuals for two-way interactions. In the case of three-way interactions we subtract off all three main effects and all three two-way interactions in order to find the residuals defining the three-way interaction. From the three subtables we have been examining we can find all the needed effects to be able to calculate the residuals for the three-way interactions. The original table of means was as shown in Table 21-10.

For illustration we focus on the top-left condition with a mean of 10. We begin by subtracting off the grand mean, which Tables 21-9a, 21-9b, and 21-9c all show to be 4.5, yielding the mean as a residual from the grand mean as 10 − 4.5 = 5.5. From this condition effect we will in turn subtract the three main effects and the three two-way interactions.

The mean of 10 is for the condition of female patients who do receive the drug and the psychotherapy. The table of effects of Table 21-9a shows at the bottom of column 1 the effect of being female at 0.5 and at the end of the top row the effect of receiving the drug at 1.5. The table of effects of Table 21-9b shows at the end of the top row the effect of receiving psychotherapy at 1.5. Each of these effects could also have been found in an alternative location: the effect of being female at the bottom of column 1 of the table of effects of Table 21-9b, the effect of receiving the drug at the end of the top row of the table of effects of Table 21-9c, and the effect of receiving psychotherapy at the bottom of column 1 of the table of effects of Table 21-9c. Now we subtract each of these three main effects from the residual defining the condition effect of 5.5 yielding:

$$\frac{\text{Condition}}{\text{effect}} - \frac{\text{sex}}{\text{effect}} - \frac{\text{drug}}{\text{effect}} - \frac{\text{psychotherapy}}{\text{effect}} = \frac{\text{combined}}{\text{interaction effect}}$$
$$5.5 \quad - \quad 0.5 \quad - \quad 1.5 \quad - \quad 1.5 \quad = \quad 2.0$$

The value of 2.0 is now made up of all the contributions to the condition effect made up of all three two-way interactions plus the three-way interaction. To find the three-way interaction residual, therefore, we will want only to subtract the three two-way interaction residuals from this value of 2.0. The

Table 21-10 Table of means

	Female patients		Male patients	
	Psychotherapy	No psychotherapy	Psychotherapy	No psychotherapy
Drug	10	5	6	3
No drug	4	1	4	3

three two-way interaction residuals are found in Tables 21-9a, 21-9b, and 21-9c. The upper-left condition of the table of effects of Table 21-9a shows the sex of patient × drug interaction effect to be 1.0 for females receiving drugs. The upper-left condition of the table of effects of Table 21-9b shows the sex of patient × psychotherapy interaction effect to be 0.5 for females receiving psychotherapy. The upper-left condition of the table of effects of Table 21-9c shows the drug × psychotherapy interaction effect to be 0.5 for those receiving both drug and psychotherapy.

In finding the interaction effect relevant to the condition mean or residual we are trying to decompose into its elements, great care must be taken to select the particular residual that applies to the mean we are working with. In a three-way design, when we are working with the mean of condition $A_1B_1C_1$ the AB residual we need is A_1B_1, the AC residual we need is A_1C_1, and the BC residual we need is B_1C_1. For the present case the combined interaction effect had a residual value of 2.0, from which we subtract the residuals of the three two-way interactions to find the residual defining the three-way interaction:

$$\frac{\text{Combined interaction effect}}{2.0} - \frac{\text{sex} \times \text{drug interaction}}{1.0} - \frac{\text{sex} \times \text{psycho-therapy interaction}}{0.5} - \frac{\text{drug} \times \text{psycho-therapy interaction}}{0.5} = \frac{\text{three-way interaction}}{0}$$

If we repeated this procedure for each of the eight condition means of the present experiment we would find that all the three-way interaction effects would be zero; i.e., there was no three-way interaction effect whatever in the present study. Table 21-11 summarizes the main effects and interactions that add up to yield each of the eight means of the present experiment. It is analogous to, and an extension of, an earlier example of how condition means may be viewed as made up of additive pieces (see page 260).

We can employ the decomposition of the condition means in Table 21-11 to understand better the computation of the various terms of the analysis of variance. Beneath each column of the display in the table we show the sum of the

Table 21-11 Table of effects

Mean	=	Grand mean	+ Sex	+ Drug	+ Psycho-therapy	+ S × D	+ S × P	+ D × P	+ S × D × P
10	=	4.5	+ (0.5)	+ (1.5)	+ (1.5)	+ (1.0)	+ (0.5)	+ (0.5)	+ 0
5	=	4.5	+ (0.5)	+ (1.5)	+ (−1.5)	+ (1.0)	+ (−0.5)	+ (−0.5)	+ 0
4	=	4.5	+ (0.5)	+ (−1.5)	+ (1.5)	+ (−1.0)	+ (0.5)	+ (−0.5)	+ 0
1	=	4.5	+ (0.5)	+ (−1.5)	+ (−1.5)	+ (−1.0)	+ (−0.5)	+ (0.5)	+ 0
6	=	4.5	+ (−0.5)	+ (1.5)	+ (1.5)	+ (−1.0)	+ (−0.5)	+ (0.5)	+ 0
3	=	4.5	+ (−0.5)	+ (1.5)	+ (−1.5)	+ (−1.0)	+ (0.5)	+ (−0.5)	+ 0
4	=	4.5	+ (−0.5)	+ (−1.5)	+ (1.5)	+ (1.0)	+ (−0.5)	+ (−0.5)	+ 0
3	=	4.5	+ (−0.5)	+ (−1.5)	+ (−1.5)	+ (1.0)	+ (0.5)	+ (0.5)	+ 0
ΣX 36	=	36	+ 0	+ 0	+ 0	+ 0	+ 0	+ 0	+ 0
ΣX^2 212	=	162	+ 2	+ 18	+ 18	+ 8	+ 2	+ 2	+ 0

eight values (ΣX) and the sum of the squares of the eight values (ΣX^2). For all three main effects, for all three two-way interactions, and for the three-way interaction, these sums of squared residuals are identical to the SS computed near the end of the last chapter from the seven computational formulas provided there (see Table 20-8).

Computing the residuals that define the three-way interaction was not especially difficult, but it did take some time. Defining a four-way, five-way, or higher-order interaction is also not especially difficult, but it takes more and more time to do the arithmetic required. As noted earlier, some behavioral science computer packages, such as Data-text, automatically provide the residuals defining all interactions tested. When they do not, and when investigators have not themselves computed the residuals, the probability of an error in the interpretation of a higher-order interaction is increased to an unacceptable level.

FURTHER NOTES ON INTERPRETATION

Organismic Interactions

Although interactions are defined by, and therefore completely described by, a table of residuals, such a table is not usually of interest to the investigator without some additional interpretation. In an abstract discussion of interaction we can view a 2×3 table of residuals without labeling the rows and columns and without thinking about the scientific meaning of the interaction. Investigators of a substantive problem, however, must go further. They must try to make sense of the phenomenon. Consider the simple interaction:

	Drug A	Drug B
Male	+1	−1
Female	−1	+1

If our entries are effectiveness scores we conclude that, at least for the interaction component of our results, drug A is relatively better for males while drug B is relatively better for females. The term "relatively" is used here to emphasize that the effects shown by certain combinations of drug and gender are large or small only in relation to other effects shown *after the removal of the main effects of drug and gender.*

It often happens in behavioral research that different treatment techniques are differentially effective for different subgroups. Such interactions, known as *organismic interactions,* reflect the fact that some types of interventions are especially effective for some but not other types of persons.

Synergistic Effects

Sometimes two or more treatments are applied simultaneously and synergistic effects occur such that receiving both treatments leads to better results than would have been predicted from a knowledge of the effects of each treatment taken alone. For example, in the following instance it appears that treatment A alone or treatment B alone has no beneficial value, but that the combination of treatments A and B is very beneficial:

		Treatment A	
		Present	Absent
Treatment B	Present	4	0
	Absent	0	0

Such a *positive synergistic* effect is probably best described in just that way, i.e., that both treatments are required for any benefits to result. Note, however, that such a description is of the four means and not of the residuals. If we subtract the grand mean, row effects, and column effects, we will find an interaction effect that tells quite a different story and that is identical in magnitude to the row effects and to the column effects. The interaction, taken by itself, will tell us that both treatments or neither treatment is superior to either one treatment or the other.

It is often the case, when row, column, and interaction effects are all of comparable magnitudes, that we would do well to interpret the results by examining the means apart from the row, column, and interaction effects preplanned by our design. In a later chapter on contrasts (Chapter 23), we shall see that if we had planned a study expecting the results shown just above, it would have been poor data-analytic procedure to cast the data into a 2 × 2 factorial design and analyze it without the use of a planned contrast.

Negative synergistic effects are also possible as shown here:

		Treatment A	
		Present	Absent
Treatment B	Present	0	4
	Absent	4	4

These results suggest that the treatments are harmful when taken together and not helpful when taken in isolation, since neither does better than the control group of no treatment. The results of this study, like those of the preceding one, are made up of row effects, column effects, and interaction effects that are all identical in size. The residual defining the interaction would suggest that receiving either treatment in isolation is better than receiving both treatments or neither treatment. As in the example of positive synergism, if we had anticipated results of this type, a 2×2 factorial design would not have been optimal; discussion of this is to be found in the later chapter on contrasts. Before leaving the topic of negative synergism we should note that a possible basis for negative synergism is a ceiling effect, as when the measuring instrument is simply unable to record benefits above a certain level. In that case the results might appear as follows:

		Treatment A	
		Present	Absent
Treatment B	Present	4	4
	Absent	4	0

Crossed-Line Interactions

Crossed-line interactions are interactions in which residuals for one group of subjects or sampling units show a relatively linear increase while residuals for another group of subjects show a relatively linear decrease. Actually, all 2×2 interactions are of this type since they are all characterized by an X shape, e.g., one group improves in going from control to experimental condition, and the other group gets worse in going from control to experimental condition. However, we usually consider interactions to be of the crossed-line type only when there are three or more levels for each of the groups being compared.

As an illustration, consider three measures of sensitivity to nonverbal communication that have been administered to female and male students. The three measures are designed to measure sensitivity to the face, to the body, and to tone of voice, respectively. Of these three channels, the face is thought to be most easily controlled, and tone is thought to be least easily controlled (Rosenthal & DePaulo, 1979a, 1979b). A fairly typical result in research of this type might yield the following accuracy scores:

	Channel			
	Face	Body	Tone	Mean
Female	6	4	2	4.0
Male	3	2	1	2.0
Mean	4.5	3.0	1.5	3.0

For which the table of effects would be as follows:

	Channel			
	Face	Body	Tone	Mean
Female	0.5	0.0	−0.5	1.0
Male	−0.5	0.0	0.5	−1.0
Mean	1.5	0.0	−1.5	0.0

The row effects show that females are better decoders of nonverbal cues than are males, a well-known result (Hall, 1979). The column effects show that face cues are easiest to decode and tone of voice cues are hardest to decode of these three types of cues, also a well-known result (Rosenthal et al., 1979). The interaction effects show that as the type of cue becomes more controllable by the encoder, the females' advantage over the males increases, a frequently obtained result (Rosenthal & DePaulo, 1979a, 1979b). A plot of these results would show an X-shaped figure (such as that shown in Figure 21-2 near the beginning of this chapter) with one group increasing as the other group is decreasing. A convenient way to display crossed-line interactions is to plot the *difference* between the residuals for the two groups. In this case such a plot would show a linear increase in the superiority of women over men as the channels became more controllable:

	Channel		
	Face	Body	Tone
Female	0.5	0.0	−0.5
Male	−0.5	0.0	0.5
Difference (female advantage)	1.0	0.0	−1.0

Crossed-Quadratic Interactions

Sometimes the residuals of one group are U-shaped while the residuals of the other group are shaped like an inverted U, or ∩. This type of nonlinear shape, where the line changes direction once (going up and then down, or vice versa) is called a *quadratic curve.* Curves changing direction twice (going up, down, and up again, or vice versa) are called *cubic curves.* With each additional change in direction cubic curves become *quartic curves, quartic* curves become *quintic curves*, and so on. (Chapter 23 provides illustrations of some of these curves.)

As an illustration of a crossed-quadratic interaction consider two groups of children tested under three conditions of arousal. The younger group of children seems less affected by arousal level than the older group, as shown in the following results:

		Low	Medium	High	Mean
			Arousal level		
Age	Younger	3	6	3	4
	Older	5	11	5	7
	Mean	4.0	8.5	4.0	5.5

For which the table of effects would be as follows:

		Low	Medium	High	Mean
			Arousal level		
Age	Younger	0.5	−1.0	0.5	−1.5
	Older	−0.5	1.0	−0.5	1.5
	Mean	−1.5	3.0	−1.5	0.0

The row effects show that the older children perform better than the younger children, and the column effects show that medium arousal level is associated with better performance than is either low or high arousal level. The residuals show crossed quadratic curves, with younger children showing a U-shaped performance curve relative to the older children, who show an inverted-U-shaped performance curve. Once again we must emphasize that these residuals refer exclusively to the interaction component of the results. Inspection of the condition means shows both groups of children producing an inverted-U-shaped function. The older children simply show more of one relative to the younger children.

Constructing Tables of Interaction Residuals

Earlier in this chapter we noted that it was useful for students to construct tables of means to our specifications. Here we add that we have also found it useful to ask our students to construct tables of interaction residuals to our specifications. We employ a range of table dimensions from 2 × 2 to 2 × 5 and ask students to place residual values into a series of empty tables to illustrate such types of interaction as organismic, positive and negative synergistic, crossed-line, and crossed-quadratic interactions. We also suggest having students label each level of each row and column in a plausible way. Students will know that their tables are exclusively made up of interaction effects when their row and column means are all equal to zero.

SIMPLIFYING COMPLEX TABLES OF RESIDUALS

A general principle for the simplification of tables of residuals is to subtract one level of a factor from the other level of that factor for any two-level factor for which the difference between levels can be regarded as substantively meaningful. Following this procedure, a two-way interaction may be viewed as a change in a main effect due to the introduction of a second independent variable; a three-way interaction may be viewed as a change in a main effect due to the introduction of a two-way interaction, or as a change in a two-way interaction due to the introduction of a third independent variable.

Another general principle for the simplification of tables of residuals involves a process of concept formation for the diagonals of a table of residuals, usually a 2 × 2 table. If a suitable concept can be found to describe each diagonal of a 2 × 2 table of residuals, the interpretation of the interaction will be simplified to the interpretation of a main effect of diagonals. We will illustrate each of these two methods.

The Method of Meaningful Differences

We have already had a brief exposure to this method in our discussion of crossed-line interactions. In that example we subtracted the residuals for males from the residuals for females to create difference scores that represented the advantage of being female over male in the decoding of nonverbal cues. We then compared these female advantage scores for three types of measures of sensitivity to nonverbal cues and were thus able to interpret an interaction of test × sex as simply the main effect of test on the differences between the sexes. An even simpler example might be:

		A	B	A − B
Subjects	Type X	+1	−1	2
	Type Y	−1	+1	−2

In this case two treatments, A and B, are each administered to two types of people, types X and Y. By taking the difference between treatments A and B we form a new measure, the advantage of treatment A over B. These advantage scores (A − B) can then be compared for persons of type X and Y. In this example the advantage of treatment A over B is greater for type X than for type Y people because 2 is greater than −2. By subtracting B from A we have reduced a two-dimensional display of residuals to a one-dimensional display.

The Method of Meaningful Diagonals

In this method we simplify the table of residuals by imposing substantive meaning on the residuals located on the diagonals, usually of a 2 × 2 table. For example we might be studying the outcome of psychotherapy as a function of the sex of the therapists and the sex of the patients with interaction effects as follows:

| | | Sex of therapist | |
		Female	Male
Sex of	Female	+1	−1
patient	Male	−1	+1

The diagonal going from upper left to lower right might be conceptualized as the *same-sex dyad* diagonal, while the diagonal going from lower left to upper right might be conceptualized as the *opposite-sex dyad* diagonal. We could then state that the mean residual for same sex dyads is greater (+1) than that for opposite sex dyads (−1). By employing a construct to describe the diagonals, we have reduced a two-dimensional display of residuals to a one-dimensional display as shown:

	Same-sex dyad	Opposite-sex dyad
	+1	−1
	+1	−1
Mean	+1	−1

Combined Methods

It is often possible to combine the two methods we have described to achieve a greater simplification of a fairly complex interaction. Consider the following three-way interaction in which male and female experimenters administered a task to male and female subjects, sometimes having been led to expect high achievement, sometimes having been led to expect low achievement from their subjects:

	Low expectations		High expectations	
	Female E	Male E	Female E	Male E
Female S	−1	+1	+1	−1
Male S	+1	−1	−1	+1

We begin the simplification process by applying the *method of meaningful differences*. In this case it makes the most substantive sense to subtract the residuals for low expectations from the residuals for high expectations. These differences then represent expectancy effects, positive in sign when they are in the predicted direction (high > low) and negative in sign when they are in the opposite direction (high < low). The results of this first step are as shown:

Table of differences (High − Low)		
	Female E	Male E
Female S	+2	−2
Male S	−2	+2

Now the three-way interaction of sex of experimenter, sex of subject, and expectancy has been simplified to a two-way interaction of sex of experimenter and sex of subject with the dependent variable of difference scores or expectancy effect scores. We can now apply the *method of meaningful diagonals* to this two-way table and interpret the originally complex three-way interaction as showing that same-sex dyads show greater expectancy effects than do opposite-sex dyads.

A Five-Way Interaction

The same general procedures can often be applied to an even more complicated situation, a five-way interaction, as shown in the following case. This time we have female and male experimenters who are either black or white, administering a task to male and female subjects who are either black or white, sometimes having been led to expect high, and sometimes low, performance. The design, then, is a race of E × sex of E × race of S × sex of S × expectancy of E factorial, each with two levels of each factor, a $2 \times 2 \times 2 \times 2 \times 2$, or 2^5,

Table 21-12 Residuals defining a five-way interaction

| | Black E | | | | White E | | | |
| | Male E | | Female E | | Male E | | Female E | |
(Expectancy)	High	Low	High	Low	High	Low	High	Low
Black S								
Male S	+1	−1	−1	+1	−1	+1	+1	−1
Female S	−1	+1	+1	−1	+1	−1	−1	+1
White S								
Male S	−1	+1	+1	−1	+1	−1	−1	+1
Female S	+1	−1	−1	+1	−1	+1	+1	−1

factorial design. The effects for the five-way interaction are as shown in Table 21-12.

Our first step again is to eliminate one dimension of the design by subtracting the low expectancy residuals from the high expectancy residuals, yielding the results shown in Table 21-13.

The entries of this table of difference scores can be viewed as a 2 × 2 interaction (race of E × race of S) of 2 × 2 interactions (sex of E × sex of S). The upper-left and lower-right 2 × 2 tables are identical to each other and opposite in signs to the 2 × 2 tables of the upper right and lower left. The first-named diagonal describes the same-race dyads, the second-named diagonal describes the opposite-race dyads. Within each of the four quadrants of the larger 2 × 2 table there are smaller 2 × 2 tables in which one diagonal describes same-sex dyads and in which the other diagonal describes opposite-sex dyads. Keeping that in mind leads us to our interpretation of the five-way interaction. Expectancy effects are greater for same-sex dyads that are also same-race dyads or different-sex dyads that are also different-race dyads than for dyads differing only on sex or only on race. We can redisplay this five-way interaction

Table 21-13 Table of expectancy effects (high-low)

| | Black E | | White E | |
	Male E	Female E	Male E	Female E
Black S				
Male S	+2	−2	−2	+2
Female S	−2	+2	+2	−2
White S				
Male S	−2	+2	+2	−2
Female S	+2	−2	−2	+2

Table 21-14 Table of mean expectancy effects

		Race of dyad	
		Same	Different
Sex of dyad	Same	+2	−2
	Different	−2	+2

(or four-way interaction of difference scores) as a two-way interaction of two-way interactions of difference scores (see Table 21-14).

Employing the principle illustrated in our earlier example, we made a single factor (same vs. different) of the race of E × race of S interaction, and a single factor (same vs. different) of the sex of E × sex of S interaction.

Such simplification of complex interactions is not always possible, though it is more likely when there is conceptual meaning to the diagonal cells of any 2×2 contained within a 2^n factorial design. In general, too, such simplification is more likely when there are fewer levels to the factors of the experiment and thus fewer *df* associated with the higher-order interaction that we are trying to understand. Some higher-order interactions will prove more intractable than others, but by careful examination of the residuals, by employing the methods of meaningful differences and meaningful diagonals, and by employing the contrast procedures discussed in detail in later chapters, we can often make some progress.

A Note on Complexity

Sometimes our research questions are complex, and complex designs and analyses may be required. However, just because we know how to deal with complexity is no reason to value it for its own sake. If our questions are simple, simpler designs and simpler analyses are possible. Especially for the beginning researcher, there is considerable practical benefit to be derived from keeping the designs and analyses as simple as possible, in the same way that we use Occam's razor for developing parsimonious hypotheses.

EIGHT

INTERMEDIATE TOPICS IN DATA ANALYSIS

Chapter **22.** **Repeated-Measures Designs**

Chapter **23.** **Contrasts: An Introduction**

Chapter **24.** **Considerations of Power**

REPEATED-MEASURES DESIGNS

USE OF REPEATED MEASURES

So far in our discussion of analysis of variance, each of our sampling units was observed only once. Thus, for example, each subject, patient, school, city, or other sampling unit contributed only one observation to the total number of observations. Such designs are called *between subjects* designs because all of the variation among the obtained scores is based on individual differences between subjects. In these designs subjects are said to be *nested* within their treatment conditions. By "nested" we mean that subjects are observed under only a single condition of the study. Often, however, it is very efficient to administer two or more treatment conditions to the same sampling units, thereby permitting sampling units to "serve as their own control." In these designs subjects are said to be *crossed* by treatment conditions rather than nested within them. By "crossed" we mean that subjects are observed under two or more conditions of the study. The more the scores of the sampling units under one condition of the experiment are correlated with the scores of the sampling units under another condition of the experiment, the more advantageous it is to employ the sampling units under more than one condition, i.e., to employ them for *repeated measures*.

Sometimes, too, the very nature of the research question seems to call for a repeated-measures-type design. For example, if we are interested in examining the effects of practice on the performance of a learning task, or the effects of age in a longitudinal study of development, it seems natural to employ the same sampling units repeatedly over time. Another very common research situation in which it is natural and advantageous to employ a repeated-measures design is that in which a series of tests or subtests is to be administered to a group of subjects. For example, we might want to administer the eleven subtests of a standardized test of intelligence, or the fifteen subtests of a standardized test of personality, or the four subtests of a measure of sensitivity to nonverbal cues. The main effect of subtests in these cases tells only whether subtest means differ, a result in which there may be no great interest. However, interaction of type of subject with subtest would tell which type of person is relatively better and worse at which type of subtest, a result that is frequently of great interest. Similarly, of course, we might want to administer two or more different types of tests, such as a test of intelligence and a test of personality.

COMPUTATIONS

Suppose we want to examine the effects on performance scores of repeated practice sessions. Four subjects are administered the same task on three occasions with results as shown in Table 22-1.

The layout is called a 4 × 3 arrangement, since there are four levels of the between-subjects factor and three levels of the within-subjects factor (i.e., each subject is measured on three occasions). The analysis begins just like that of any two-way analysis of variance, yielding a row effect (subjects in this case), a column effect (sessions in this case), and a row × column interaction effect (subjects × sessions in this case). The analysis differs from other two-way designs we have seen earlier in that there is only a single observation in each combination of row and column. The required sums of squares are obtained as follows:

$$\text{Total } SS = \Sigma(X - \bar{M})^2$$

where X is each individual score and $\bar{M}$ is the grand mean. Here we add up as many squared deviations as there are scores altogether.

$$\text{Row } SS = \Sigma[c(M_R - \bar{M})^2]$$

where c is the number of columns contributing to the computation of M_R, the mean of each row, and $\bar{M}$ is the grand mean. Here we add up as many quantities

Table 22-1 Performance scores on three occasions

	Session 1	Session 2	Session 3	Mean
Subject 1	0	7	3	3.33
Subject 2	1	7	4	4.00
Subject 3	3	8	5	5.33
Subject 4	4	8	6	6.00
Mean	2.0	7.5	4.5	4.67

as there are rows.

$$\text{Column } SS = \Sigma[r(M_C - \bar{M})^2]$$

where r is the number of rows contributing to the computation of M_C, the mean of each column, and $\bar{M}$ is the grand mean. Here we add up as many quantities as there are columns. Finally,

$$\text{Interaction } SS = \text{total } SS - \text{row } SS - \text{column } SS$$

For the data of our illustration we have

$$\begin{aligned}
\text{Total } SS = {} & (0 - 4.67)^2 + (7 - 4.67)^2 + (3 - 4.67)^2 + (1 - 4.67)^2 \\
& + (7 - 4.67)^2 + (4 - 4.67)^2 + (3 - 4.67)^2 + (8 - 4.67)^2 \\
& + (5 - 4.67)^2 + (4 - 4.67)^2 + (8 - 4.67)^2 + (6 - 4.67)^2 = 76.67
\end{aligned}$$

$$\begin{aligned}
\text{Row } SS = {} & 3(3.33 - 4.67)^2 + 3(4.00 - 4.67)^2 + 3(5.33 - 4.67)^2 + \\
& 3(6.00 - 4.67)^2 = 13.35
\end{aligned}$$

$$\text{Column } SS = 4(2.0 - 4.67)^2 + 4(7.5 - 4.67)^2 + 4(4.5 - 4.67)^2 = 60.67$$

$$\text{Interaction } SS = 76.67 - 13.35 - 60.67 = 2.65$$

The table of variance is best set up so that the distinction between the within-subjects and the between-subjects sources of variance is highlighted. Earlier we saw that between-subjects sources of variance were those associated with individual differences between subjects. Within-subjects sources of variance are those associated with differences in individual subjects' scores from condition to condition.

In the table of variance shown as Table 22-2 we have distinguished sharply between the sources of variance that are due to within- vs. between-subject variation. Such sharp distinctions are useful when there are several sources of variation due to between-subject sources and several due to within-subject sources of variation. The distinctions simplify our bookkeeping and, as we shall see, help us employ the appropriate error term for tests of significance.

Table 22-2 Table of variance: Repeated measures

Source	SS	df	MS	F	eta	p
*Between subjects**	13.35	3	4.45			
Within subjects†						
Sessions	60.67	2	30.33	68.93	98	<.001
Sessions × subjects‡	2.65	6	0.44			

* This term, the Subjects effect, would not normally be tested for significance.

  † Note that in earlier chapters when we referred to *within* sources of variance we were referring to variation that was within *conditions* but *between* subjects.

   ‡ Error term for Sessions effect.

FIXED AND RANDOM EFFECTS

There is another distinction that will help us employ the appropriate error term, that is the distinction between fixed and random factors. *Fixed* factors are those in which we have selected particular levels of the factor in question not by random sampling but because we are interested in those particular effects. We are not entitled to view these levels as representative of any other levels of the factor in question, i.e., we cannot generalize to other levels of the fixed factor. Most factors involving experimental manipulations, or such organismic variables as gender, race, and social class, and such repeated measures factors as time, sessions, subtests, etc., are fixed factors.

Random factors are those in which we view the levels of the factor as having been randomly sampled from a larger population of such levels. The most common random factor in behavioral research is that of sampling units, especially persons or other organisms. In Table 22-2, if we regard the subjects factor as a random factor we can test its significance only very conservatively. If we regard it as a fixed factor, so that we restrict any inferences only to these four subjects, we can test the significance of the subjects factor against the sessions × subjects interaction, though the test will be conservative when sessions are also regarded as fixed effects. To clarify these issues we will consider all combinations of fixed and random effects for between- and within-subject factors.

Imagine that we want to study four countries as our between sampling units factor. If we are interested only in these four countries and do not choose to view them as a sample from a larger population of countries, we regard them as fixed. Alternatively, we can view them as a sample from which we want to generalize, and we must then regard them as random.

Imagine further a diachronic (longitudinal) design in which we have a summary score for each country for each of three decades. These three scores are our repeated measures, or within sampling units factor. We regard these scores as fixed if we have chosen them specifically as critical decades of the century in question. We regard the scores as random, however, if we view them as a sample of the decades to which we want to generalize. Thus we can have four combinations of between (e.g., countries) and within (e.g., decades) sampling units factors and fixed and random effects. The four combinations are shown in Table 22-3, and each combination is then discussed in turn. Our discussion is intended as a kind of reference manual rather than as an exposition of the underlying mathematical models which would be required for a more theoretically based discussion. See, for example, Green and Tukey (1960), Snedecor and Cochran (1967, 1980), and Winer (1971).

Type A (between Fixed, within Fixed)

The interaction *MS* can be employed as the error term for the *MS* between and the *MS* within subjects, but it is likely to lead to *F*'s that are too conservative. Only if there is *in nature* a zero interaction effect will the *F* tests be accurate.

Table 22-3 Four types of design

		Within sampling units	
		Fixed	Random
Between *sampling* *units*	Fixed	Type A	Type B
	Random	Type C	Type D

The only way to test whether the interaction effect really is likely to be zero is to make multiple observations for each combination of row and column effects. Such multiple observations might be made by randomly sampling several years from each decade in our example of four countries studied for three decades. This within combination *MS*, computed as any other within condition source of variance, is the appropriate error term for the between effect, the repeated-measures effect, and the interaction effect. When the interaction *MS* is used as the error term for the row or column effect, a large *F* can be trusted to be at least that large, but a small *F* may or may not reflect the absence of a row or column effect. The table of variance shown as Table 22-4 illustrates the Type A situation. The abbreviations employed in Table 22-4 and in the following three tables are as follows:

B = Between subjects *MS*
W = Within subjects *MS*
BW = Between × within subjects interaction *MS*
0 = Ordinary error; i.e., *MS* for replications within combinations of B × W

Table 22-4 Illustration of Type A design
(Both factors fixed)

Source	Abbreviations	Error term "proper"	Error term "conservative"*
Between countries†	B	0	BW
Within countries			
Decades‡	W	0	BW
Decades × countries§	BW	0	—
Years within decade × country combinations¶	0	—	—

* Used when 0 is not available, as when only a single observation has been made for every B × W combination.
† Computed as is the row effect of any two-way factorial design.
‡ Computed as is the column effect of any two-way factorial design.
§ Computed as is the interaction effect of any two-way factorial design.
¶ Computed as is the within-cell error of any two-way factorial design.

Table 22-5 Illustration of Type B design
(Between factor fixed, within factor random)

Source	Abbreviations	Error term "proper"	Error term "conservative"*
Between countries	B	BW†	—
Within countries			
Decades	W	0	BW
Decades × countries	BW	0	—
Years within BW	0	—	—

* Used when 0 is not available.
† Use of 0 as error term can lead to F's that are seriously inflated.

Type B (between Fixed, within Random)

The interaction *MS* is the appropriate error term for the between sampling units effect, but is the appropriate error term for the within or repeated measures effect only if the interaction effect is really zero. The appropriate error term for the within subjects effect (and for the interaction) is the variation of the multiple observations made for each combination of row and column, as shown in Table 22-5.

Type C (between Random, within Fixed)

The interaction *MS* is the appropriate error term for the within sampling units effect, but is the appropriate error term for the between sampling units effect only if the interaction effect is really zero. The appropriate error term for the between subjects effect (and for the interaction) is the variation of the multiple observations made for each combination of row and column, as shown in Table 22-6.

Table 22-6 Illustration of Type C design
(Between factor random, within factor fixed)

Source	Abbreviations	Error term "proper"	Error term "conservative"*
Between countries	B	0	BW
Within countries			
Decades	W	BW†	—
Decades × countries	BW	0	—
Years within BW	0	—	—

* Used when 0 is not available.
† Use of 0 as error term can lead to F's that are seriously inflated.

Table 22-7 Illustration of Type D design
(Both factors random)

Source	Abbreviations	Error term "proper"	Error term "conservative"*
Between countries	B	BW†	—
Within countries			
Decades	W	BW†	—
Decades × countries	BW	0	—
Years within BW	0	—	—

* Not applicable to this design.
† Use of 0 as error term can lead to F's that are seriously inflated.

Type D (between Random, within Random)

The interaction MS is the appropriate error term for both the between- and within-subject effects. The interaction effect could be tested against the variation of the multiple observations made for each combination of row and column as shown in Table 22-7. More detailed information about the consequences for significance testing of various combinations of fixed and random factors can be found in Green and Tukey (1960), Snedecor and Cochran (1967, 1980), and Winer (1971).

LATIN SQUARES

In the example we gave of four subjects, each measured three times, there was no alternative to administering the three sessions of testing in the sequence 1, 2, 3. However, suppose that we were administering three drugs, A, B, and C, to four patients. If we employed the design:

	Drug A	Drug B	Drug C
Subject 1			
Subject 2			
Subject 3			
Subject 4			

such that each subject were given the three drugs in the same sequence A, then B, then C, (or ABC), we would have entangled, or *confounded,* two different variables. The variable of drug (A vs. B vs. C) and the variable of order or position in the sequence (first drug vs. second drug vs. third drug) would be confounded.

Suppose our hypothesis had been that drug A would be best and we found from our study that drug A was indeed best. It would not be appropriate to conclude that drug A actually was better than drugs B and C. A plausible rival hypothesis is that the first-administered drug is best. To avoid this type of confounding we employ a technique called *counterbalancing* (a counterbalance is a weight balancing another weight). To counterbalance, the sequence of administration of treatments is balanced (or varied systematically) so that, on the average, there is no longer a relationship between, or confounding of, the variables that had been entangled, such as order (first-presented) and drug type (drug A) in the present example.

Counterbalancing is essential when we are interested in studying matters of organization and sequencing in the presentation of stimuli. For example, an important research question for social psychologists is to determine the circumstances under which it is advantageous to present a message before the opposition has a chance to reach the audience or afterward, in order to have the last word. Those researchers who investigate this question use the term *primacy* to refer to the case where opinions or actions are influenced more by the arguments presented first, and *recency* where they are influenced more by the arguments presented last. To test for primacy and recency, it is necessary to use a counterbalanced design. Half of the subjects, at random, receive a pro and then a con argument; the remaining subjects receive a con and then a pro argument. In this way, it is possible to avoid the problem of confounding primacy vs. recency effects with the specific effects of the pro vs. con arguments (Rosnow, 1968).

A commonly employed design that has counterbalancing built in is called the *latin square*, a design in which the number of rows equals the number of columns. A latin square requires a square array of letters (or numbers) in which each letter (or number) appears once and only once in each row and in each column. Frequently the rows represent sequences of administration of the treatments, the columns represent the order of administration of the treatments, and the letters represent specific treatments administered in particular orders as part of particular sequences.

	Order of administration		
	1	2	3
Sequence 1 (ABC)	A	B	C
Sequence 2 (BCA)	B	C	A
Sequence 3 (CAB)	C	A	B

In sequence 1 treatments are administered in the sequence first A, then B, then C. In sequences 2 and 3 the treatments are administered in different

Table 22-8 Some latin squares and their sources of variance

3 × 3 latin square				Sources of variance	
Order				Source	df
1	*2*	*3*		Sequences	2
				Orders	2
Sequence 1	A	B	C	(Sequences × orders	4)
Sequence 2	B	C	A	Treatments	2
Sequence 3	C	A	B	Residual sequences × orders	2

4 × 4 latin square					Sources of variance	
Order					Source	df
1	*2*	*3*	*4*		Sequences	3
					Orders	3
Sequence 1	A	B	C	D	(Sequences × orders	9)
Sequence 2	B	C	D	A	Treatments	3
Sequence 3	C	D	A	B	Residual sequences × orders	6
Sequence 4	D	A	B	C		

5 × 5 latin square						Sources of variance*	
Order						Source	df
1	*2*	*3*	*4*	*5*		Sequences	4
						Orders	4
Sequence 1	A	B	C	D	E	(Sequences × orders	16)
Sequence 2	B	C	D	E	A	Treatments	4
Sequence 3	C	D	E	A	B	Residual sequences × orders	12
Sequence 4	D	E	A	B	C		
Sequence 5	E	A	B	C	D		

* In any of these latin squares we could also think of the sequences effect as part of the treatment × order interaction effect and the orders effect as part of the treatment × sequences interaction effect. These are only conceptual alternatives that do not yield different statistical results.

For an example of the computations, assume that four patients have been administered four treatments in counterbalanced order with results shown in Table 22-9; note that sequences are completely confounded with patients, i.e., we could label sequences as subjects if we preferred.

$$
\begin{aligned}
\text{Total } SS = {}& (4 - 6)^2 + (3 - 6)^2 + (8 - 6)^2 + (5 - 6)^2 + (0 - 6)^2 + (6 - 6)^2 \\
& + (7 - 6)^2 + (7 - 6)^2 + (2 - 6)^2 + (2 - 6)^2 + (10 - 6)^2 + (10 - 6)^2 \\
& + (6 - 6)^2 + (5 - 6)^2 + (7 - 6)^2 + (14 - 6)^2 = 186
\end{aligned}
$$

Table 22-9 Effects of four treatments

		Order				
		1	*2*	*3*	*4*	Mean
Sequence 1	(ABCD)	4	3	8	5	5
Sequence 2	(BCDA)	0	6	7	7	5
Sequence 3	(CDAB)	2	2	10	10	6
Sequence 4	(DABC)	6	5	7	14	8
Mean		3	4	8	9	6

Sequences $SS = 4(5 - 6)^2 + 4(5 - 6)^2 + 4(6 - 6)^2 + 4(8 - 6)^2 = 24$

Orders $SS = 4(3 - 6)^2 + 4(4 - 6)^2 + 4(8 - 6)^2 + 4(9 - 6)^2 = 104$

Sequences $\times$ orders $SS = 186 - 24 - 104 = 58$

To compute the treatment SS we will have to collect the scores associated with each of the four treatments, A, B, C, and D. To minimize clerical errors we can rearrange the data obtained from a sequence $\times$ order to a sequence $\times$ treatments data display as follows:

	Treatments				
	A	B	C	D	Mean
Sequence 1	4	3	8	5	5
Sequence 2	7	0	6	7	5
Sequence 3	10	10	2	2	6
Sequence 4	5	7	14	6	8
Mean	6.5	5.0	7.5	5.0	6

Then,

Treatment $SS = 4(6.5 - 6)^2 + 4(5.0 - 6)^2 + 4(7.5 - 6)^2 + 4(5.0 - 6)^2 = 18$

and Residual $SS = 58 - 18 = 40$

The resulting table of variance then is:

Source	SS	df	MS	F	eta	p
Sequences	24	3	8.00	1.20	.61	.39
Orders	104	3	34.67	5.20	.85	.042
(Sequences $\times$ orders)	(58)	(9)				
Treatments	18	3	6.00	0.90	.56	.49
Residual sequences $\times$ orders	40	6	6.67			

OTHER COUNTERBALANCING DESIGNS

Latin squares are employed when the number of subjects or other sampling units equals the number of treatments we wish to administer to each subject. But suppose that we have more sampling units than we have treatments, what is to be done? Two general strategies are useful, *multiple squares* and *rectangular arrays*.

Rectangular Arrays

If we had three treatments to administer to six subjects we could randomly assign half the subjects to each of two squares of size 3×3 and treat each square as a different experiment or as a replication of the same experiment. Alternatively, however, we could assign each of the six subjects a unique sequence of the three treatments. Since the number of unique sequences of treatments is $t!$ (where t is the number of treatments) and $3! = 6$, we have just the right number of subjects for this study.* If we had four treatments to administer to each subject and we wanted each subject to have a unique sequence, we would need $4! = 24$ subjects, etc. Such designs may be called $t \times t!$ designs, and their analysis is analogous to that of the latin square. Examples of $t \times t!$ designs are given in Table 22-10 for $t = 3$ and $t = 4$. When $t = 2$ we have our familiar 2×2 latin square once again.

If we have fewer sampling units available than the $t!$ required by our design, we can form a series of latin squares instead, or sample randomly from the $t!$ sequences, but with the constraint that each treatment occur in each order as nearly equally often as possible. The employment of this constraint tends to maximize the degree of counterbalancing that *is* possible even though complete counterbalancing may *not* be possible.

If we have more sampling units available than the $t!$ required by our design, two general strategies are useful: *multiple rectangular arrays* and *subjects within sequences designs*.

Subjects within Sequences Designs

If we had $2 \times t!$ subjects available, we could randomly assign half the subjects to each of two rectangular arrays of size $t \times t!$ We then treat each array as a different experiment or as a replication of the same experiment. The same type of procedure can be employed for any multiple of $t!$ subjects, of course. Alternatively, we could assign several subjects at random to each of the $t!$ sequences in such a way as to keep the number of subjects per sequence as nearly equal as possible.

As an example, suppose we had eighteen subjects available for a study of three treatment procedures. The six possible sequences of three treatments ($3! = 6$) are as displayed in the following $t \times t!$ ($t = 3$) design (Table 22-10), and we

---

* Recall that $N! = N$ factorial $= N(N - 1)(N - 2) \ldots (2)(1)$ so that $3! = (3)(2)(1) = 6$.

Table 22-10 Examples of $t \times t!$ designs

$t \times t!$ design: $t = 3$				Sources of variance	
Order				Source	df
	1	*2*	*3*	Sequences	5
				Orders	2
Sequence 1	A	B	C	(Sequences × orders)	(10)
Sequence 2	A	C	B	Treatments	2
Sequence 3	B	A	C	Residual sequences × orders	8
Sequence 4	B	C	A		
Sequence 5	C	A	B		
Sequence 6	C	B	A		

$t \times t!$ design: $t = 4$					Sources of variance	
Order					Source	df
	1	*2*	*3*	*4*	Sequences	23
					Orders	3
Sequence 1	A	B	C	D	(Sequences × orders)	(69)
Sequence 2	A	B	D	C	Treatments	3
Sequence 3	A	C	B	D	Residual sequences × orders	66
Sequence 4	A	C	D	B		
Sequence 5	A	D	B	C		
Sequence 6	A	D	C	B		
Sequence 7	B	A	C	D		
Sequence 8	B	A	D	C		
Sequence 9	B	C	A	D		
Sequence 10	B	C	D	A		
Sequence 11	B	D	A	C		
Sequence 12	B	D	C	A		
Sequence 13	C	A	B	D		
Sequence 14	C	A	D	B		
Sequence 15	C	B	A	D		
Sequence 16	C	B	D	A		
Sequence 17	C	D	A	B		
Sequence 18	C	D	B	A		
Sequence 19	D	A	B	C		
Sequence 20	D	A	C	B		
Sequence 21	D	B	A	C		
Sequence 22	D	B	C	A		
Sequence 23	D	C	A	B		
Sequence 24	D	C	B	A		

Table 22-11 Sources of variance: Subjects within sequences

Source	df	Comments
Between subjects	(17)	
(Seq.) Sequences	5	tested against Ss
(Ss) Subjects within sequences	12	
Within subjects	(36)*	
(Ord.) Orders	2	tested against Ord. $\times$ Ss
(Ord. $\times$ seq.) Orders $\times$ sequences†	10	usually not tested
(Treat.) Treatments	2	tested against Ord. $\times$ Ss
(Resid.) Residual ord. $\times$ seq.	8	tested against Ord. $\times$ Ss
(Ord. $\times$ Ss) Orders $\times$ subjects within seq.	24	

* Computed as (N of subjects) $\times$ (df for levels of repeated measures).
† This term is subdivided into the following two terms.

assign three subjects at random to each of these six sequences. In this design subjects are *not* confounded with sequences as they are in latin squares or rectangular arrays lacking replications for each sequence. Instead, subjects are *nested* within sequences so that the differences between sequences can be tested. The sources of variance for this example are as shown in Table 22-11.

There are a number of noteworthy features of this design and analysis. First, there is more than a single error term in the design. In the earlier chapters on analysis of variance, there had always been only a single error term; and it had always been associated with the individual differences among subjects (or other sampling units) collected from within each of the conditions of the study. In the present design there is also such an error term (subjects within sequences), and it is used to test whether the sequences of the experiment differ from one another. We want to note especially that this error term is within *conditions* but *between* subjects. The other error term in this design is the orders $\times$ subjects within sequences interaction. This error term is used to test all the within-subjects sources of variation, and it is itself a *within-subjects* source of variation. It is typical for error terms employed to test within-subjects sources of variation that they are formed by crossing the repeated-measures factors by the random factor of sampling units, usually subjects or subjects within conditions.

There is another feature of this design which is common to latin square and rectangular array repeated measures designs. It is the fact that to test for treatments we must reach into the order $\times$ sequence interaction and pull out the variation of the treatment means around the grand mean. That represents only a minor complication for the analysis.

The computation of this analysis is a simple extension of the computational procedures we have seen so far in this chapter. It is easiest to begin with a 3 $\times$ 18 design in mind, three levels of order and eighteen levels of subjects. The between-subjects SS is then broken down into a sequences SS and a subjects-within-sequences *SS*. The latter can be obtained as the difference between the between-subjects *SS* and the sequences *SS*. The order *SS* is computed in the usual manner, and the order × subjects interaction is broken down into an order × sequences *SS* and an order × subjects-within-sequences *SS*. The latter can be obtained as the difference between the order × subjects *SS* and the order × sequences *SS*.

THREE OR MORE FACTORS

So far in our discussion of repeated-measures designs we have examined only two-factor designs, one factor as a between-subjects factor and one factor as a within-subjects or repeated-measures factor. Repeated-measures designs, however, are frequently more complex in having two or more between-subjects factors, two or more within-subjects factors, or both.

Two or More Between-Subjects Factors

Increasing the number of between-subjects factors does not increase the complexity of the design as much as increasing the number of within-subjects factors. Suppose, for example, that we wanted to examine the effects on four subtests of a personality test of three age levels and two genders. Our design might appear as in Table 22-12.

If we assume two subjects for each of the 3 × 2 = 6 between-subjects conditions, the sources of variance and *df* would be as follows:

Source	df	
Between subjects	(11)	
Age	2	
Sex	1	
Age × sex	2	
Subjects (within conditions)	6	
Within subjects	(36)*	
Subtests	3	
Subtests × age	6	⎫
Subtests × sex	3	⎬ Subtests × between subjects
Subtests × age × sex	6	⎪
Subtests × subjects (within conditions)	18	⎭

* Computed as (*N* of subjects) × (*df* for levels of repeated measures).

The computation of the *SS* involves nothing new. It is easiest to think of the design, for computational purposes, as a twelve-subject × four-measurements array. We compute first all the between-subjects *SS*'s, beginning with the total

Table 22-12 Design comprised of two between factors and one within factor

(Between subjects)		Subtests (Repeated measures)			
		1	2	3	4
Age	*Sex*				
12	Female				
	Male				
14	Female				
	Male				
16	Female				
	Male				

between subjects SS. We then compute the age SS, the sex SS, the age × sex SS, and subtract these three SS's from the total between-subjects SS. This gives us the subjects-within-conditions SS. As designs become more complicated, computing the df for each source of variance becomes increasingly useful as a check on whether we have left out any sources of variance. For example, since there are twelve subjects in this design we know there are $12 - 1 = 11$ df available between subjects. We also know the df for age ($3 - 1 = 2$), sex ($2 - 1 = 1$), age × sex ($[3 - 1 = 2] \times [2 - 1 = 1] = 2$), and subjects-within conditions ($[2 - 1] \times 6 = 6$). These four sources of variance are a decomposition of the total between subjects source of variance, and the sum of their df should equal the df for the total between-subjects variance. In this case we find this requirement to be satisfied.

The within-subjects sources of variation are made up of the main effect of subtests ($df = 3$) and the subtests × between-subjects interaction ($df = 3 \times 11 = 33$). This latter interaction is further decomposed into a series of interactions: subtests × age, subtests × sex, subtests × age × sex, and subtests × subjects (within conditions). The df of these four interactions add up ($6 + 3 + 6 + 18$) to 33, the total df for the subtests × between subjects interaction.

A Computational Example

We illustrate the required computations with the data given in Table 22-13. We begin by regarding the design as a simple twelve-subject × four-subtests array for which we will compute first the row (subjects) and column (subtests) sums of squares as shown at the beginning of this chapter.

$$\text{Total } SS = \Sigma(X - \bar{M})^2 = (2 - 5)^2 + (3 - 5)^2 + (7 - 5)^2 + \cdots +$$
$$(5 - 5)^2 + (7 - 5)^2 + (8 - 5)^2 = 340$$

Table 22-13 Results of a repeated-measures study with two between-subjects factors and one within-subjects factor

Age	Sex	Subject	Subtests (Repeated measures)				Mean
			1	2	3	4	
12	Female	1	2	3	7	8	5.0
12	Female	2	1	2	3	6	3.0
12	Male	3	1	1	3	3	2.0
12	Male	4	1	2	1	4	2.0
14	Female	5	5	4	7	8	6.0
14	Female	6	4	5	8	7	6.0
14	Male	7	1	2	4	5	3.0
14	Male	8	1	4	6	9	5.0
16	Female	9	5	9	9	9	8.0
16	Female	10	6	5	8	9	7.0
16	Male	11	5	6	9	8	7.0
16	Male	12	4	5	7	8	6.0
	Mean		3.0	4.0	6.0	7.0	5.0

Row (subject) $SS = \Sigma[c(M_R - \bar{M})^2] = 4(5.0 - 5)^2 + 4(3.0 - 5)^2$

$\qquad + 4(2.0 - 5)^2 + \cdots + 4(7.0 - 5)^2 + 4(7.0 - 5)^2 + 4(6.0 - 5)^2 = 184$

Column (repeated-measures) $SS = \Sigma[r(M_c - \bar{M})^2] = 12(3.0 - 5)^2$

$\qquad + 12(4.0 - 5)^2 + 12(6.0 - 5)^2 + 12(7.0 - 5)^2 = 120$

Row $\times$ column interaction SS = total SS − row SS − column SS
$\qquad = 340 - 184 - 120 = 36$

Of the sums of squares computed above only the column SS (or subtest SS) is one we will use directly in our final table of variance. The remaining sums of squares above will be used in the computation of other sums of squares required for our final table of variance.

Our next step is to decompose the row (or subject) SS into its components of subject age SS, subject sex SS, subject age $\times$ sex SS, and subjects-within-conditions SS, by means of the following formulas:

$$\text{Subject age } SS = \Sigma[nst(M_A - \bar{M})^2]$$

where n is the number of subjects in each of the conditions formed by the crossing of the two between-subjects factors, s is the number of levels of the sex factor, t is the number of levels of the subtests (column) factor, M_A is the mean of all conditions of a given age, and $\bar{M}$ is the grand mean, i.e., the mean of all condition means.

$$\text{Subject sex } SS = \Sigma[nat(M_S - \bar{M})^2]$$

where a is the number of levels of the age factor, n, t, and $\bar{M}$ are as above, and M_S is the mean of all conditions of a given sex.

$$\text{Subject age} \times \text{sex } SS = \Sigma[nt(M_{AS} - \bar{M})^2]$$
$$- \text{subject age } SS - \text{subject sex } SS$$

where M_{AS} is the mean of all observations contributing to each of the combinations of the two between-subjects facors, and n, t, and $\bar{M}$ are as above.

Subjects within conditions SS = row (subject) SS
$$- \text{subject age } SS - \text{subject sex } SS - \text{subject age} \times \text{sex } SS$$

where the row (subject) SS was computed from our initial twelve-subject × four-subtest array.

Our arithmetic is simplified if we construct the table of means formed by the crossing of the two between-subjects factors as shown in Table 22-14.

For the data of the present study we find:

Age $SS = 2 \times 2 \times 4(3.0 - 5)^2 + 2 \times 2 \times 4(5.0 - 5)^2 + 2 \times 2 \times 4(7.0 - 5)^2$
$= 128$

Sex $SS = 2 \times 3 \times 4(5.83 - 5)^2 + 2 \times 3 \times 4(4.17 - 5)^2 = 33$

Age × sex $SS = 2 \times 4(4.0 - 5)^2 + 2 \times 4(2.0 - 5)^2 + 2 \times 4(6.0 - 5)^2$
$$+ 2 \times 4(4.0 - 5)^2 + 2 \times 4(7.5 - 5)^2 + 2 \times 4(6.5 - 5)^2$$
$$- \text{age } SS - \text{sex } SS$$
$$= 164 - 128 - 33 = 3$$

Subjects within conditions $SS = 184 - 128 - 33 - 3 = 20$

Table 22-14 Table of means: Age × sex of subject

Age	Sex of subject		Mean
	Female	Male	
12	4.0[8]*	2.0[8]	3.0[16]
14	6.0[8]	4.0[8]	5.0[16]
16	7.5[8]	6.5[8]	7.0[16]
Mean	5.83[24]	4.17[24]	5.0[48]

* The number of observations upon which each type of mean is based.

Now that we have computed all the needed between-subject sources of variance we turn our attention to the within-subjects sources of variance that are made up of the main effect of subtests (the already-computed column effect) and the crossing of this main effect with age, sex, age $\times$ sex, and subjects (within conditions) to form four interactions. The interaction sums of squares are computed as follows:

$$\text{Subtests} \times \text{age } SS = \Sigma[ns(M_{TA} - \bar{M})^2] - \text{subtests } SS - \text{age } SS$$

where M_{TA} is the mean of all observations contributing to each combination of subtest (T) and age (A), and all other terms are as above.

$$\text{Subtests} \times \text{sex } SS = \Sigma[na(M_{TS} - \bar{M})^2] - \text{subtests } SS - \text{sex } SS$$

where M_{TS} is the mean of all observations contributing to each combination of subtest and sex, and all other terms are as above.

$$\text{Subtests} \times \text{age} \times \text{sex } SS = \Sigma[n(M_{TAS} - \bar{M})^2] - \text{subtests } SS$$
$$- \text{age } SS - \text{sex } SS - \text{subtests} \times \text{age } SS$$
$$- \text{subtests} \times \text{sex } SS - \text{age} \times \text{sex } SS$$

where M_{TAS} is the mean of all observations contributing to each combination of subtest, age, and sex, and all other terms are as above.

$$\text{Subtests} \times \text{subjects within conditions } SS = \text{row} \times \text{column interaction } SS$$
$$- \text{subtests} \times \text{age } SS - \text{subtests} \times \text{sex } SS - \text{subtests} \times \text{age} \times \text{sex } SS$$

where the row $\times$ column interaction SS was computed earlier from our initial 12-subject $\times$ 4-subtest array.

Again, our arithmetic will be simplified if, for each of the next three interactions to be computed, we construct the appropriate table of means (see Tables

Table 22-15 Table of means: Subtests $\times$ age

Age	Subtests				
	1	2	3	4	Mean
12	1.25[4]*	2.00	3.50	5.25	3.00[16]
14	2.75	3.75	6.25	7.25	5.00
16	5.00	6.25	8.25	8.50	7.00
Mean	3.00[12]	4.00	6.00	7.00	5.00[48]

* The number of observations upon which each type of mean is based.

Table 22-16 Table of means: Subtests × sex

Sex	Subtests				Mean
	1	2	3	4	
Female	3.83[6]*	4.67	7.00	7.83	5.83[24]
Male	2.17	3.33	5.00	6.17	4.17
Mean	3.00[12]	4.00	6.00	7.00	5.00[48]

* The number of observations upon which each type of mean is based.

22-15 to 22-17). Then, from Table 22-15 we find:

$$\text{Subtests} \times \text{age } SS = 2 \times 2(1.25 - 5)^2 + 2 \times 2(2.00 - 5)^2 + 2 \times 2(3.50 - 5)^2$$
$$+ \cdots + 2 \times 2(6.25 - 5)^2 + 2 \times 2(8.25 - 5)^2$$
$$+ 2 \times 2(8.50 - 5)^2 - \text{subtests } SS -$$
$$\text{age } SS = 252 - 120 - 128 = 4$$

From Table 22-16 we find:

$$\text{Subtests} \times \text{sex } SS = 2 \times 3(3.83 - 5)^2 + 2 \times 3(4.67 - 5)^2 + \cdots$$
$$+ 2 \times 3(5.00 - 5)^2 + 2 \times 3(6.17 - 5)^2 - \text{subtests } SS$$
$$- \text{sex } SS = 154 - 120 - 33 = 1$$

From Table 22-17 we find:

$$\text{Subtests} \times \text{age} \times \text{sex } SS = 2(1.5 - 5)^2 + 2(2.5 - 5)^2 + \cdots + 2(8.0 - 5)^2$$
$$+ 2(8.0 - 5)^2 - \text{subtests } SS - \text{age } SS$$
$$- \text{sex } SS - \text{subtests} \times \text{age } SS$$
$$- \text{subtests} \times \text{sex } SS - \text{age} \times \text{sex } SS$$
$$= 300 - 120 - 128 - 33 - 4 - 1 - 3 = 11$$

$$\text{Subtests} \times \text{subjects within conditions } SS = 36 - 4 - 1 - 11 = 20$$

Table 22-17 Table of means: Subtests × age × sex

Age	Sex	Subtests				Mean
		1	2	3	4	
12	Female	1.5[2]*	2.5	5.0	7.0	4.0[8]
12	Male	1.0	1.5	2.0	3.5	2.0
14	Female	4.5	4.5	7.5	7.5	6.0
14	Male	1.0	3.0	5.0	7.0	4.0
16	Female	5.5	7.0	8.5	9.0	7.5
16	Male	4.5	5.5	8.0	8.0	6.5
	Mean	3.0[12]	4.0	6.0	7.0	5.0[48]

* The number of observations upon which each type of mean is based.

Table 22-18 Table of variance: Two between-subjects factors and one within-subjects factor

Source	SS	df	MS	F	eta*	p
Between subjects	*(184)*	*(11)*				
Age	128	2	64.00	19.22	.93	.003
Sex	33	1	33.00	9.91	.79	.02
Age × Sex	3	2	1.50	0.45	.36	.66
Subjects						
(within conditions)	20	6	3.33			
Within subjects	*(156)*	*(36)*				
Subtests	120	3	40.00	36.04	.93	.0001
Subtests × age	4	6	.67	0.60	.41	.73
Subtests × sex	1	3	.33	0.30	.22	.82
Subtests × age × sex	11	6	1.83	1.65	.60	.19
Subtests × subjects						
(within conditions)	20	18	1.11			

$$* \ eta = \sqrt{\frac{F \ (df \ \text{num.})}{F \ (df \ \text{num.}) + (df \ \text{denom.})}}$$

We have now computed all the ingredients required to complete our table of variance (see Table 22-18). The analysis of variance of these data shows that all three main effects were significant. Although none of the interactions were significant we note that the effect sizes (*eta*'s) were quite substantial for several of these interactions, suggesting that replications with larger sample sizes might reach statistical significance.

The example we have been following employed an equal number of subjects ($n = 2$) within each combination of the between-subjects factor. Had these numbers not been equal we could still have employed the same computational procedures with only one small modification. We would simply have replaced n, wherever it occurred, by n_h, the harmonic mean of the sample sizes. We recall from the discussion of the factorial design of experiments in Chapter 20 that n_h is defined as

$$\frac{1}{\frac{1}{k} \left(\frac{1}{n_1} + \frac{1}{n_2} + \cdots + \frac{1}{n_k} \right)}$$

Returning to the table of variance shown as Table 22-18 we can see that the four interactions involving subtests are formed readily by crossing the subtests factor with each of the between-subjects effects in turn. We can illustrate this by adding an additional between-subjects factor to the present design, say diagnosis. We assume that half the children in each of the six conditions are hyperactive and half are not, so that our design becomes:

(Between subjects)			Subtests			
			(Repeated measures)			
			1	2	3	4
Age	*Sex*	*Diagnosis*				
	Female	Hyperactive				
12		Normal				
	Male	Hyperactive				
		Normal				
	Female	Hyperactive				
14		Normal				
	Male	Hyperactive				
		Normal				
	Female	Hyperactive				
16		Normal				
	Male	Hyperactive				
		Normal				

Assuming for the present example that we had five subjects in each of our twelve between-subjects conditions, our new listing of sources of variance is:

Source	df
Between subjects	(59)
Age	2
Sex	1
Diagnosis	1
Age × sex	2
Age × diagnosis	2
Sex × diagnosis	1
Age × sex × diagnosis	2
Subjects (within conditions)	48
Within subjects	(180)*
Subtests	3
Subtests × age	6
Subtests × sex	3
Subtests × diagnosis	3
Subtests × age × sex	6
Subtests × age × diagnosis	6
Subtests × sex × diagnosis	3
Subtests × age × sex × diagnosis	6
Subtests × subjects	144

* Computed as (*N* of subjects) × (*df* for levels of repeated measures).

Once again, all interactions involving the within-subjects factor, subtests in this case, are formed simply by prefixing the within-subjects factor to each of the between-subjects factors in turn. Even with this four-factor design (three between and one within) computations are not difficult. They may be tedious, however, if the number of subjects per condition is large and a calculator rather than a computer is to be employed. Again it is easiest to think of the design as a subjects × subtests design, with all between-subjects main effect and interaction SS's subtracted from the total between-subjects SS to yield the subjects-within-conditions SS.

No matter how many between-subjects sources of variance there are, all of them are tested against the MS for subjects within conditions.* It is essential to keep in mind, however, that the various between-subjects sources of variance have meaning only if the *sum* of the repeated-measures scores is meaningful. For example, if the four subtests of the personality test we have been using as our illustration were all scored such that a high number were reflective of "good adjustment" (or "poor adjustment"), then the sum of these scores would be meaningful, and all the between-subjects effects would be interpretable. However, if some of the subtests reflected good adjustment and some reflected poor adjustment, the sum (and the mean) of the four scores would be meaningless, and all between-subjects effects would be essentially meaningless.

It should also be noted that when we decide that the sum of the repeated-measures scores is meaningful, the components of this sum have not necessarily contributed equally to the sum. Those components that are more variable (in the sense of S^2) contribute more heavily to the variation in the sum of the components. Thus, if the S^2's differ appreciably from each other, and if we want all components to contribute equally to the variation in the sum, we first transform each component to its standard score with mean $= 0$ and $\sigma^2 = 1$.

Even if the between-subjects sources of variance were meaningless because the sum of the repeated measures was not a meaningful variable, the within-subjects sources of variance may be quite informative. The interactions of the within-subjects factor and the between-subjects factors indicate the extent to which the main effect of the repeated measure (subtest in our present example) is affected by the various between-subjects sources of variance.

When there is only a single within-subjects factor, as in the present illustrations, there is only a single error term for all the within-subjects sources of variation, the repeated-measures factor × subjects-within-conditions interaction, or the subtests × subjects-within-conditions interaction in our present example. However, as we add within-subjects factors, the number of error terms grows very quickly, such that every main effect within subjects and every interaction between two or more within-subjects factors has its own error term. These error terms are generally formed by the crossing of each source of

---

* Assuming that all between-subjects sources of variance are regarded as fixed effects, the most frequent situation. A little later we discuss the situation in which these effects are not all regarded as fixed.

Table 22-19 Number of within-subjects error terms required as a function of number of within-subjects factors

Number of factors	Number of error terms
1	1
2	3
3	7
4	15
5	31
6	63
7	127
8	255
9	511
10	1023

variance by the subjects-within-conditions source of variance. Table 22-19 shows how quickly the number of error terms for the within-subjects sources of variance grows as the number of within-subjects factors grows. Table 22-19 shows that for each additional within-subjects factor, the number of error terms more than doubles. We shall illustrate only for three and for seven error terms.

TWO WITHIN-SUBJECTS FACTORS

Suppose our subjects were five female and five male teachers, each of whom was assigned a different set of four pupils to teach in a brief teaching situation. Of each of these ten sets of four pupils, two were female and two were male. Furthermore, one of the female and one of the male pupils was designated (at random) to her or his teacher as showing special intellectual promise (high expectancy) while nothing was said of the remaining pupils (low expectancy). The main conditions of our design might be displayed as follows:

(Between subjects)		(Repeated measures)			
		Female		Male	
		Low	High	Low	High
Sex of teacher	Female				
	Male				

Special note should be taken of the fact that the four *different* pupils can still be regarded as providing repeated measures. That is because we decided

Table 22-20 Error terms for two within-subjects factors

Source	df	Error terms
Between subjects	9	
Sex of teacher	1	
Teachers (within sex)	8	Error term for preceding line
Within subjects	30*	
Expectancy	1	
Expectancy × sex of teacher	1	
Expectancy × teachers (within sex)	8	Error term for preceding two lines
Pupil sex	1	
Pupil sex × sex of teacher	1	
Pupil sex × teachers (within sex)	8	Error term for preceding two lines
Expectancy × pupil sex	1	
Expect. × pupil sex × sex of teacher	1	
Expect. × pupil sex × teachers (within sex)	8	Error term for preceding two lines

* Computed as (N of subjects) × (df for levels of repeated measures); this design has four levels of repeated measures, two levels of expectancy for each of two genders.

that we would employ teachers as our sampling units (a random factor) and each child's score would be viewed as a repeated measurement of the teacher who taught that child. Further note should be taken of the fact that the four repeated measurements can, in this study, be viewed as a 2×2 design: two levels of expectancy × two levels of pupil sex. The sources of variance, *df*, and error terms would be as shown in Table 22-20.

It should be noted that each of the three repeated-measures error terms was formed by crossing the relevant repeated-measures factor by the random factor of sampling units—in this case, teachers (within sex).

A Computational Example

We illustrate the required computations with the data of Table 22-21. We begin by regarding the design as a simple ten-teacher × four-levels of repeated measurement array for which we will compute first the row (teachers) and column (repeated measures) sums of squares as shown in the preceding section on computing a two between-factors and one within-factor study.

$$\text{Total } SS = \Sigma(X - \bar{M})^2 = (3 - 5)^2 + (7 - 5)^2 + (2 - 5)^2 + \cdots$$

$$+ (8 - 5)^2 + (4 - 5)^2 + (3 - 5)^2 = 260$$

$$\text{Row (teacher) } SS = \Sigma[c(M_R - \bar{M})^2] = 4(5.0 - 5)^2 + 4(5.0 - 5)^2$$

$$+ 4(6.0 - 5)^2 + \cdots + 4(4.0 - 5)^2 + 4(5.0 - 5)^2 + 4(5.0 - 5)^2 = 72$$

$$\text{Column (repeated-measures) } SS = \Sigma[r(M_c - \bar{M})^2] = 10(4.0 - 5)^2$$

$$+ 10(8.0 - 5)^2 + 10(3.0 - 5)^2 + 10(5.0 - 5)^2 = 140$$

Row × column-interaction SS = total SS − row SS − column SS
$$= 260 - 72 - 140 = 48$$

Our next step is to decompose the row (or teacher) SS into its components of sex-of-teacher SS and teachers-within-sex SS by means of the following formulas:

$$\text{Sex of teacher } SS = \Sigma[npe(M_S - \bar{M})^2]$$

where n is the number of teachers within each sex of teacher (or n_h if these n's are not equal), p is the number of levels of the pupil sex factor, e is the number of levels of the expectancy factor, M_S is the mean of all conditions of a given teacher sex, and $\bar{M}$ is the grand mean, i.e., the mean of all condition means.

$$\text{Teachers within sex } SS = \text{row (teacher) } SS - \text{sex of teacher } SS$$

For the present study the mean scores obtained by female teachers and male teachers were 6.0 and 4.0, respectively. Therefore,

$$\text{Sex of teacher } SS = 5 \times 2 \times 2 \,(6.0 - 5)^2 + 5 \times 2 \times 2 \,(4.0 - 5)^2 = 40$$

and,

$$\text{Teachers within sex } SS = 72 - 40 = 32$$

We now turn our attention to the various within-teachers sources of variance. We consider first the SS for expectancy, expectancy × sex of teacher, and expectancy × teachers (within sex):

$$\text{Expectancy } SS = \Sigma[nsp(M_E - \bar{M})^2]$$

Table 22-21 Results of a repeated-measures study with one between-subjects factor and two within-subjects factors

	Teacher	Repeated measures				Mean
		Female pupil		Male pupil		
		Low	High	Low	High	
Female teachers	1	3	7	2	8	5.0
	2	3	9	3	5	5.0
	3	5	8	5	6	6.0
	4	7	10	4	7	7.0
	5	7	11	6	4	7.0
Male teachers	6	2	6	0	4	3.0
	7	1	5	1	5	3.0
	8	3	7	3	3	4.0
	9	4	9	2	5	5.0
	10	5	8	4	3	5.0
	Mean	4.0	8.0	3.0	5.0	5.0

where s is the number of levels of the sex-of-teacher factor, M_E is the mean of all conditions of a given level of expectancy, and the other terms are as above.

Expectancy × sex of teacher $SS = \Sigma[np(M_{ES} - \bar{M})^2]$

$$- \text{expectancy } SS - \text{sex of teacher } SS$$

where M_{ES} is the mean of all observations contributing to each combination of expectancy and teacher sex, and the other terms are as above.

Expectancy × teachers within sex $SS = \Sigma[p(M_{ET} - \bar{M})^2]$

$$- \text{expectancy } SS - \text{row (teacher) } SS* - \text{expectancy × sex of teacher } SS$$

where M_{ET} is the mean of all observations contributing to each combination of expectancy and individual teacher, and the other terms are as above.

To help our arithmetic we construct a table of the appropriate means (see Table 22-22). From this table we find:

Expectancy $SS = 5 \times 2 \times 2\,(3.5 - 5)^2 + 5 \times 2 \times 2\,(6.5 - 5)^2 = 90$

Condensing the table to obtain the means of the expectancy × sex-of-teacher combinations (M_{ES}) gives:

	Expectancy	
Teacher sex	Low	High
Female	4.5$\underline{|10}$*	7.5
Male	2.5	5.5

* The number of observations per condition.

Expectancy × sex of teacher $SS = 5 \times 2(4.5 - 5)^2 + 5 \times 2(7.5 - 5)^2$

$$+ 5 \times 2(2.5 - 5)^2 + 5 \times 2(5.5 - 5)^2$$

$$- \text{expectancy } SS - \text{sex of teacher } SS$$

$$= 130 - 90 - 40 = 0$$

Expectancy × teachers within sex $SS = 2(2.5 - 5)^2 + 2(7.5 - 5)^2 + \cdots$

$$+ 2(4.5 - 5)^2 + 2(5.5 - 5)^2$$

$$- \text{expectancy } SS - \text{row (teacher) } SS*$$

$$- \text{expectancy × sex of teacher } SS$$

$$= 180 - 90 - 72 - 0 = 18$$

* Note that this is identical to sex of teacher SS + teachers within sex SS.

Table 22-22 Table of means: Expectancy × teachers

	Teachers	Expectancy		
		Low	High	Mean
Female teachers	1	2.5[2]*	7.5	5.0[4]
	2	3.0	7.0	5.0
	3	5.0	7.0	6.0
	4	5.5	8.5	7.0
	5	6.5	7.5	7.0
Male teachers	6	1.0	5.0	3.0
	7	1.0	5.0	3.0
	8	3.0	5.0	4.0
	9	3.0	7.0	5.0
	10	4.5	5.5	5.0
	Mean	3.5[20]	6.5	5.0[40]

* The number of observations upon which each type of mean is based.

We consider next the SS for pupil sex, pupil sex × sex of teacher, and pupil sex × teachers (within sex).

$$\text{Pupil-sex } SS = \Sigma[nse(M_P - \bar{M})^2]$$

where M_P is the mean of all conditions of a given level of pupil sex, and the other terms are as above.

$$\text{Pupil-sex × sex of teacher } SS = \Sigma[ne(M_{PS} - \bar{M})^2] - \text{pupil sex } SS$$
$$- \text{ sex of teacher } SS$$

where M_{PS} is the mean of all observations contributing to each combination of pupil sex and teacher sex, and the other terms are as above.

$$\text{Pupil sex × teachers within sex } SS = \Sigma[e(M_{PT} - \bar{M})^2] - \text{pupil sex } SS$$
$$- \text{ row (teacher) } SS^* - \text{ pupil sex × sex of teacher } SS$$

where M_{PT} is the mean of all observations contributing to each combination of pupil sex and individual teacher, and the other terms are as above.

Again we construct a table of the appropriate means (see Table 22-23). From this table we find:

$$\text{Pupil sex } SS = 5 \times 2 \times 2(6.0 - 5)^2 + 5 \times 2 \times 2(4.0 - 5)^2 = 40$$

* Note that this is identical to sex of teacher SS + teachers within sex SS.

Table 22-23 Table of means: Pupil sex × teachers

		Pupil sex		
	Teachers	Female	Male	Mean
Female teachers	1	$5.0^{[2]}$*	5.0	$5.0^{[4]}$
	2	6.0	4.0	5.0
	3	6.5	5.5	6.0
	4	8.5	5.5	7.0
	5	9.0	5.0	7.0
Male teachers	6	4.0	2.0	3.0
	7	3.0	3.0	3.0
	8	5.0	3.0	4.0
	9	6.5	3.5	5.0
	10	6.5	3.5	5.0
	Mean	$6.0^{[20]}$	4.0	$5.0^{[40]}$

* The number of observations upon which each type of mean is based.

Condensing the table to obtain the means of the pupil-sex × sex-of-teacher combinations (M_{PS}) gives:

	Pupil sex	
Teacher sex	Female	Male
Female	$7.0^{[10]}$*	5.0
Male	5.0	3.0

* The number of observations per condition.

Pupil sex × sex of teacher $SS = 5 \times 2(7.0 - 5)^2 + 5 \times 2(5.0 - 5)^2$

$$+ 5 \times 2(5.0 - 5)^2 + 5 \times 2(3.0 - 5)^2$$

$$- \text{pupil sex } SS - \text{sex of teacher } SS$$

$$= 80 - 40 - 40 = 0$$

Pupil sex × teachers-within-sex $SS = 2(5.0 - 5)^2 + 2(5.0 - 5)^2 + \cdots \cdots$

$$+ 2(6.5 - 5)^2 + 2(3.5 - 5)^2$$

$$- \text{pupil sex } SS - \text{row (teacher) } SS*$$

$$- \text{pupil sex } \times \text{ sex of teacher } SS$$

$$= 128 - 40 - 72 - 0 = 16$$

* Note that this is identical to sex of teacher SS + teachers within sex SS.

Finally, we consider the SS for expectancy $\times$ pupil sex, expectancy $\times$ pupil sex $\times$ sex of teacher, and expectancy $\times$ pupil sex $\times$ teachers (within sex).

Expectancy $\times$ pupil sex SS

$$= \Sigma[ns(M_{EP} - \bar{M})^2] - \text{expectancy } SS - \text{pupil sex } SS$$

where M_{EP} is the mean of all observations contributing to each combination of expectancy and pupil sex, and the other terms are as above.

Expectancy $\times$ pupil sex $\times$ sex of teacher $SS = \Sigma[n(M_{EPS} - \bar{M})^2]$

- expectancy SS - pupil sex SS - sex of teacher SS

- expectancy $\times$ pupil sex SS - expectancy $\times$ sex of teacher SS

- pupil sex $\times$ sex of teacher SS

where M_{EPS} is the mean of all observations contributing to each combination of expectancy, pupil sex, and sex of teacher, and where the other terms are as above.

Expectancy $\times$ pupil sex $\times$ teachers within sex $SS = \Sigma[(M_{EPT} - \bar{M})^2]$*

- expectancy SS - pupil sex SS - row (teacher) SS

- expectancy $\times$ pupil sex SS - expectancy $\times$ sex of teacher SS

- pupil sex $\times$ sex of teacher SS - expectancy $\times$ pupil sex

$\times$ sex of teacher SS - expectancy $\times$ teachers within sex SS

- pupil sex $\times$ teachers within sex SS (or, more compactly, total SS

- all other sums of squares)

where M_{EPT} is the mean of all observations contributing to each combination of expectancy, pupil sex, and individual teacher. In this example, there is only one such observation for each combination of these three factors, and the original 10 teachers $\times$ 4 repeated measures table shows these observations.

We begin with a condensed version of the original table of the results of the present study to show the means of the expectancy $\times$ pupil-sex combinations (M_{EP}):

	Pupil sex	
Expectancy	Female	Male
Low	4.0[10]*	3.0
High	8.0	5.0

* The number of observations per condition.

* Identical in this case to $\Sigma(X - \bar{M})^2 = $ total SS.

Expectancy $\times$ pupil sex $SS = 5 \times 2(4.0 - 5)^2 + 5 \times 2(3.0 - 5)^2$

$$+ 5 \times 2(8.0 - 5)^2 + 5 \times 2(5.0 - 5)^2$$

$$- \text{expectancy } SS - \text{pupil sex } SS$$

$$= 140 - 90 - 40 = 10$$

Next we show the table of eight means (M_{EPS}) required for the three-way interaction of expectancy $\times$ pupil sex $\times$ sex of teacher:

Teacher sex	Female		Male	
	Low	High	Low	High
Female	5.0⌊5*	9.0	4.0	6.0
Male	3.0	7.0	2.0	4.0

* The number of observations per condition.

Expectancy $\times$ pupil sex $\times$ sex of teacher SS

$$= 5(5.0 - 5)^2 + 5(9.0 - 5)^2 + \cdots \cdot + 5(2.0 - 5)^2 + 5(4.0 - 5)^2$$

$$- 90 - 40 - 40 - 10 - 0 - 0 = 180 - 180 = 0$$

Expectancy $\times$ pupil sex $\times$ teachers within sex SS

$$= 260(\text{total } SS) - 90 - 40 - 72 - 10 - 0 - 0 - 0 - 18 - 16 = 14$$

We have now computed all the SS required to complete our table of variance (see Table 22-24). The analysis of variance of these data shows all three main effects and one two-way interaction to be significant.

The present example employed an equal number of teachers ($n = 5$) in each condition of teacher sex. Had these numbers not been equal, we could still have employed the same computational procedures with just one modification. We could simply have replaced the quantity n by n_h wherever n was called for. We recall that n_h is the harmonic mean of the sample sizes found in each between-subjects condition of the study, i.e.,

$$n_h = \cfrac{1}{\dfrac{1}{k}\left(\dfrac{1}{n_1} + \dfrac{1}{n_2} + \cdots \cdot + \dfrac{1}{n_k}\right)}$$

Aggregating Error Terms

When the number of df per error term is small, as it is in this example, we want to consider aggregating the three within-subjects error terms in order to obtain

Table 22-24 Table of variance: One between-subjects factor and two within-subjects factors

Source	SS	df	MS	F	eta*	p
Between subjects	(72)	(9)				
Sex of teacher	40	1	40.00	10.00	.75	.013
Teachers (within sex)	32	8	4.00			
Within subjects	(188)	(30)				
Expectancy	90	1	90.00	40.00	.91	.0002
Expectancy × sex of teacher	0	1	0.00	0.00	.00	1.00
Expectancy × teachers (within sex)	18	8	2.25			
Pupil sex	40	1	40.00	20.00	.85	.002
Pupil sex × sex of teacher	0	1	0.00	0.00	.00	1.00
Pupil sex × teachers (within sex)	16	8	2.00			
Expectancy × pupil sex	10	1	10.00	5.71	.65	.043
Expectancy × pupil sex × sex of teacher	0	1	0.00	0.00	.00	1.00
Expectancy × pupil sex × teachers (within sex)	14	8	1.75			

$$* \ eta = \sqrt{\frac{F(df \text{ num.})}{F(df \text{ num.}) + (df \text{ denom.})}}$$

a more stable single estimate; in this example based on 24 *df*. This averaging together of error terms (each weighted by its *df*) is usually recommended only if the ratio of the largest to the smallest error term is about 2.0 or less (Green & Tukey, 1960).

In the analysis of variance we have just completed, the three within-subjects error terms range from 1.75 to 2.25, with the ratio of the largest mean square to the smallest mean square only $2.25/1.75 = 1.29$. Therefore, these three error terms are good candidates for aggregation. The general formula for the aggregation of *k* error terms is:

$$MS \text{ aggregated} = \frac{MS_1(df_1) + MS_2(df_2) + \cdots + MS_k(df_k)}{df_1 + df_2 + \cdots + df_k}$$

where MS_1 to MS_k are the *k* error terms to be aggregated, and df_1 to df_k are the *k* *df* associated with the *k* *MS*'s for error. For the data of Table 22-24 we have:

$$MS \text{ aggregated} = \frac{2.25(8) + 2.00(8) + 1.75(8)}{8 + 8 + 8} = 2.00$$

When it is more convenient to work with sums of squares, the general formula is written as:

$$MS \text{ aggregated} = \frac{SS_1 + SS_2 + \cdots + SS_k}{df_1 + df_2 + \cdots + df_k}$$

where SS_1 to SS_k are the k sums of squares of the k error sources of variance, and df_1 to df_k are their associated df. For the data of Table 22-24 we have

$$MS \text{ aggregated} = \frac{18 + 16 + 14}{8 + 8 + 8} = 2.00$$

Once we have computed an aggregated error term it replaces all the individual error terms that contributed to its computation. Some of the F's computed using the new error term will be larger (those in which the original MS error was larger) and some will be smaller (those in which the original MS error was smaller).

THREE WITHIN-SUBJECTS FACTORS

In our example of three within-subjects factors, we retain the basic plan of the preceding example but assume that each teacher teaches eight pupils instead of four. In addition, we assume that for each combination of expectancy and pupil sex, there is one hyperactive child and one normal child:

	(Repeated measures)							
	Female				Male			
	Hyperactive		Normal		Hyperactive		Normal	
(Between subjects)	Low	High	Low	High	Low	High	Low	High
Sex of Female								
teacher Male								

The sources of variance, df, and error terms of this design would be as shown in Table 22-25. Note how easily we could generate all new sources of variance simply by adding the new within-subjects factor of diagnosis and then crossing that term systematically with all preceding sources of variance. Just as in the previous example, we want to consider aggregating the various error terms to form a more stable overall error term. In this example we have one error term that is a four-way interaction, three error terms that are three-way interactions, and three error terms that are two-way interactions. In this situation it is useful to begin with the higher-order interactions and aggregate them first. For example, we might begin by aggregating (if $F < 2$) the three-way interactions (along with the four-way since there is just one) to form the new error term for all terms tested by any of these error terms. We might then aggregate the two-way interaction error terms (if $F < 2$) to form the new error term for all terms tested by any of these error terms. Finally, if the two new error terms are themselves aggregable ($F < 2$) we can use this new supererror

Table 22-25 Error terms for three within-subjects factors

Source	df	Error terms
Between subjects	9	
Sex of teacher	1	
Teachers (within sex)	8	Error term for preceding line
Within subjects	70*	
Expectancy	1	
Expectancy × sex of teacher	1	
Expectancy × teachers (within sex)	8	Error term for preceding two lines
Pupil sex	1	
Pupil sex × sex of teacher	1	
Pupil sex × teachers (within sex)	8	Error term for preceding two lines
Expectancy × pupil sex	1	
Expectancy × pupil sex × sex of teacher	1	
Expectancy × pupil sex × teachers (within sex)	8	Error term for preceding two lines
Diagnosis	1	
Diagnosis × sex of teacher	1	
Diagnosis × teachers (within sex)	8	Error term for preceding two lines
Diagnosis × expectancy	1	
Diagnosis × expectancy × sex of teacher	1	
Diagnosis × expectancy × teachers (within sex)	8	Error term for preceding two lines
Diagnosis × pupil sex	1	
Diagnosis × pupil sex × sex of teacher	1	
Diagnosis × pupil sex × teachers (within sex)	8	Error term for preceding two lines
Diagnosis × expectancy × pupil sex	1	
Diagnosis × expectancy × sex (P) × sex (T)	1	
Diagnosis × expectancy × sex (P) × teachers (within sex)	8	Error term for preceding two lines

* Computed as (N of subjects) × (df for levels of repeated measures); this design has eight levels arranged as a 2 × 2 × 2 format.

term to test all within-subjects sources of variation. In any of the aggregations described, the error terms should be weighted by their df.

FIXED OR RANDOM FACTORS

So far in our discussion of three or more factors in designs employing repeated measures, we have assumed that all factors other than subjects-within conditions have been fixed factors rather than random factors. That is, in fact, the most common situation. We should, however, note the consequences for significance testing of having other factors in the design that are random rather than fixed. For our illustration assume we have chosen five female and five male teachers from each of four schools to teach a brief lesson to two pupils, one of whom has been designated at random as a pupil of high intellectual potential. Our design can be displayed as follows:

(Between subjects)		(Repeated measures)	
School	Sex	Control	High expectancy
1	Female		
	Male		
2	Female		
	Male		
3	Female		
	Male		
4	Female		
	Male		

The sources of variance, *df*, and error terms are:

Source	*df*	Error terms*
Between subjects	*39*	
Sex of teacher	1	
School	3	
Sex of teacher × school	3	Error term for sex of teacher
Teachers (within conditions)	32	Error term for preceding two lines
Within subjects	*40†*	
Expectancy	1	
Expectancy × sex of teacher	1	
Expectancy × school	3	Error term for expectancy
Expectancy × sex of teacher × school	3	Error term for expectancy × sex of teacher
Expectancy × teachers	32	Error term for preceding two lines

* Assuming school to be a random rather than a fixed factor.
† Computed as (*N* of subjects) × (*df* for levels of repeated measures).

If all of our factors, including school, had been fixed, there would have been only two error terms. Teachers (within conditions) would have served as the error term for all three between-subjects effects, and expectancy × teachers would have served as the error term for all four within-subjects effects. However, with schools considered a random factor, we find there to be five error terms rather than two. Now the sex-of-teacher effect is tested against the sex of teacher × school interaction, an error term that has only three *df*. This is in contrast to the 32 *df* associated with the error term we would employ if schools were a fixed rather than random factor. The advantage of considering schools as a random factor is that we can then generalize to the population of schools represented by these four schools. The disadvantage of considering schools as a random factor is the low power to reject the null hypothesis associated with our having only four schools in our study.

In practice, it sometimes happens that we can have the best of both worlds. This happens when the mean square error considering the effect random is about the same size as the mean square error considering the effect fixed. In our example that would occur if the mean square for sex of teacher × school were about the same size as the mean square for teachers within conditions. If that *were* the case we could aggregate the two error terms. We would weight each by its *df,* and use the new pooled error term instead of either of the two components.

Let us turn now to the within-subjects factors. We find that expectancy is tested against the expectancy × school interaction, and the expectancy × sex of teacher interaction is tested against the expectancy × sex of teacher × school interaction. The comments made above in the discussion of the sex-of-teacher effect apply here also. Note that both of the fixed effects (sex of teacher, expectancy) and their interaction (sex of teacher × expectancy) are tested against error terms formed by crossing the effect to be tested by the random effect (schools in this example). More detailed discussions of forming error terms in repeated measures designs are available in Winer (1971).

DID REPEATED MEASURES HELP?

Our basic reason for employing repeated-measures designs is "to use subjects as their own control" in hopes of increasing the precision of our experiment. As we said at the beginning of this chapter, the more the scores of the subjects (or other sampling units) under one condition of the experiment are correlated with the scores of the subjects under another condition of the experiment, the more advantage accrues to us when we employ repeated-measures designs. Very low correlations between scores earned under one condition and scores earned under other conditions of the experiment suggest that there was little statistical advantage to our having employed a repeated-measures design.* Consider a very simple repeated-measures design in which five subjects are each tested on three subtests:

	Subtests		
	1	2	3
Subject 1	5	6	7
Subject 2	3	6	4
Subject 3	3	4	6
Subject 4	2	2	3
Subject 5	1	4	4

* There may still be a logistical advantage, however, since it is usually more efficient to measure *n* subjects *k* times each than to measure *n* × *k* subjects once each.

For these five subjects we can compute the correlation (r) between their performance on subtests 1 and 2, 1 and 3, and 2 and 3. These three r's were .64, .80, and .58 respectively, with a mean $\bar{r}$ of .67. This very substantial average correlation suggests that a repeated-measures design would be very efficient compared to a between-subjects design. Computing the mean of three r's was not arduous. Suppose, however, that there were ten subtests instead of three. Then there would be (10×9)/2 = 45 correlations to compute and to average. A much easier approach is available via the analysis of variance, and it involves computation of the *intraclass r*.

The Intraclass *r*

The intraclass r is an index of the degree of similarity of observations made on a given sampling unit, such as a subject. If there is a high correlation between pairs of observations made on subjects (e.g., subtest 1 and subtest 2), then the intraclass r will tend to be high. In fact, the intraclass r tends to be a good estimate of the mean correlation obtained by correlating all possible pairs of observations made on subjects (e.g., subtest 1 with 2, 1 with 3, 2 with 3, etc.). To compute the intraclass r we begin with the mean squares of the analysis of variance. For our example we have:

Source	SS	df	MS
Between subjects	24.0	4	6.00
Within subjects			
Subtests	11.2	2	5.60
Subtests × subjects	6.8	8	0.85

The intraclass r is computed by

$$r_I = \frac{MS_S - MS_{S \times K}}{MS_S + (k - 1)MS_{S \times K}}$$

where MS_S = mean square for subjects, $MS_{S \times K}$ = mean square for subjects × repeated measures factor, and k = number of levels of the repeated measures factor. For our example,

$$r_I = \frac{6.00 - 0.85}{6.00 + (3 - 1)0.85} = .67$$

a value which agrees with the mean r of .67 reported earlier. In more complicated designs involving additional between-subjects and/or additional within-subjects factors, the intraclass r can be computed by defining MS_S as the between-subjects error term and $MS_{S \times K}$ as the within-subjects error term. If the various within-subjects error terms are approximately equal in size, and if the *df* for these error terms are few, it may be helpful to aggregate these error terms weighting each error term by its *df*. This new error term is then used to test all effects tested by any of the original error terms, and is used to compute the intraclass *r*.

A NOTE ON ASSUMPTIONS

Before leaving our discussion of repeated-measures analyses of variance, we should note that the *F*'s we compute in actual research situations will usually be distributed only approximately as *F*. Three of the assumptions to be met before we can regard computed *F*'s to be actually distributed as *F* were given at the end of the chapter on *t* tests (Chapter 18) and again in Chapter 19 in our discussion of the distributions of *F*. These assumptions were (1) independence of errors (or sampling units), (2) homogeneity of variance, and (3) normality (with all three summarized as IID Normal).

In the case of repeated-measures analyses, there is an *additional* assumption having to do with the relative magnitudes of the intercorrelations among the various levels of the repeated-measures factors. For practical purposes, we regard this assumption as met to the degree that we have homogeneity of correlation coefficients among the various levels of the repeated-measures factors (Hays, 1981; Winer, 1971). This assumption only applies to *F* tests on repeated measures with more than a single *df* in the numerator. Therefore, any *F* test in which there are only two levels of the repeated-measures factor does not need to meet this assumption. Indeed, when there are only two levels, only one correlation is possible! Even when there are more than two levels of the repeated-measures factor, however, this assumption is not needed when we have tested some focused hypothesis about the results by means of a contrast, since contrasts also have only a single *df* for the numerator of the *F* used to test them. We now turn to the topic of contrasts.

TWENTY-THREE

CONTRASTS: AN INTRODUCTION

BACKGROUND

We introduce the topic of *contrasts* (or comparisons) with a hypothetical example of a one-way analysis of variance. A developmental psychologist administered a cognitive task to a total of fifty children in a cross-sectional study. There were ten children at each of the following age levels: 8, 9, 10, 11, 12. Tables 23-1 and 23-2 show the mean obtained at each age level and the analysis of variance of these data.

The tables show us that F for age levels = 1.03, $p = .40$, i.e., that the differences among the five means are far from significant. Shall we conclude that for this study age was not an effective variable? If we did so we would be making a very grave error, though unfortunately a fairly common one.

Figure 23-1 shows the performance means of the five age levels; we see clearly that the resulting plot does not appear consistent with the conclusion that age and performance are not related. Indeed, the correlation of the levels of age and levels of performance yield $r(3) = .992$, $p < .001$ (two-tailed).

How can we reconcile such clear and obvious results (the plot, the r, the p) with the results of the analysis of variance telling us that age did not matter? The answer is that the F above addresses a question that may be of relatively little interest to us. The question is diffuse and unfocused, i.e., are there *any* differences among the five groups, disregarding entirely the arrangement of the ages that constitute the levels of the independent variable. Thus arranging the ages 8, 9, 10, 11, 12, would yield the same F as arranging them 12, 11, 10, 9, 8, or 10, 9, 11, 12, 8. This diffuse question is unlikely to have been the one our

Table 23-1 Mean performance score at five age levels*

	Age levels			
8	9	10	11	12
2.0	3.0	5.0	7.0	8.0

* n = 10 at each age level

Table 23-2 Analysis of variance of performance scores

Source	SS	df	MS	F	p
Age levels	260	4	65	1.03	.40
Within	2835	45	63		

developmental researcher wanted to address. Far more likely he or she wanted to know whether performance increased with age or whether there was a *quadratic* (upright or inverted U; U or ∩) trend.

The correlation we computed addressed the more focused question of whether performance increased linearly with age. In this example the *r* worked well, but note that we had only 3 *df* for testing the significance of that *r*. We shall want a more general, flexible, and powerful way of asking focused questions of our data. Once we learn how to do this there will be relatively few circumstances under which we will want to use unfocused, diffuse, or omnibus *F* tests. That, then, is the purpose of contrasts—to permit us to ask more focused questions of our data. What we get in return for the small amount of computation required to employ contrasts is very much greater statistical power and very much greater clarity of substantive interpretation of research results.

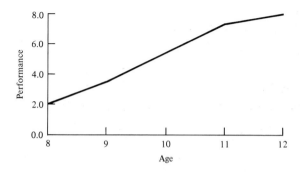

Figure 23-1 Mean performance score at five age levels.

DEFINITIONS AND AN EXAMPLE

Contrasts are comparisons, employing two or more groups, set up in such a way that the results obtained from the several conditions involved in the research are compared (or "contrasted") to the predictions based on theory, hypothesis, or hunch. These predictions are expressed as weights (called λ and pronounced "lambda"), and they can take on any convenient numerical value so long as the sum of the weights (Σλ) is zero for any given contrast. Contrasts are quite easy to compute within the context of the analysis of variance. The following formula (Snedecor & Cochran, 1967, p. 308) shows the computation of a contrast in terms of a sum of squares for the single *df* test being made. Because contrasts are based on only one *df,* the sum of squares is identical to the mean square and needs only to be divided by the appropriate mean square for error to yield an *F* test for the contrast:

$$MS \text{ contrast} = SS \text{ contrast} = \frac{L^2}{n\Sigma\lambda^2}$$

where *L* = sum of all condition totals (*T*) each of which has been multiplied by the weight (λ) called for by the hypothesis, or:

$$L = \Sigma[T\lambda] = T_1\lambda_1 + T_2\lambda_2 + T_3\lambda_3 + \cdots + T_k\lambda_k$$

k = number of conditions
n = number of observations in each condition, given equal *n* per condition*
λ = weights required by the hypothesis such that the sum of the weights equals zero.

We can apply this formula directly to the data of our example. The means were given as 2.0, 3.0, 5.0, 7.0, and 8.0, each mean based on an *n* of 10. To obtain the required values of *T* we multiply these means by *n* and get 20, 30, 50, 70, and 80. For each *T* we also need a λ based on our theory. If our prediction were that there would be a linear trend, i.e., that there would be a regular increment of performance for every regular increment of age, we might first think of using age levels as our λ's, and they would be 8, 9, 10, 11, 12. However, the sum of these λ's is not zero, as required, but 50. Fortunately, that is easy to correct. We simply subtract the mean age level of 10 (i.e., 50/5) from each of our λ's and thus obtain (8 − 10), (9 − 10), (10 − 10), (11 − 10), (12 − 10), or −2, −1, 0, +1, +2, a set of weights that does sum to zero. To save ourselves the effort of having to calculate these weights, Table 23-3 on page 352 provides them for linear, quadratic, and cubic orthogonal (i.e., independent) trends, curves, or polynomials (algebraic expressions of two or more terms) (after Snedecor & Cochran, 1967, p. 572). Later in this chapter these orthogonal polynomials will be described in more detail.

---

* Later in this chapter we discuss the situation of unequal *n* per condition.

For our present example we have:

Age level	8	9	10	11	12	Σ
T	20	30	50	70	80	250
λ	-2	-1	0	$+1$	$+2$	0
$T\lambda$	-40	-30	0	70	160	160

For our formula for SS contrast we need L^2, n, and $\Sigma\lambda^2$. $L = \Sigma[T\lambda] = 160$, so $L^2 = (160)^2$; $n = 10$ as given earlier, and $\Sigma\lambda^2 = (-2)^2 + (-1)^2 + (0)^2 + (+1)^2 + (+2)^2 = 10$. So,

$$\frac{L^2}{n\Sigma\lambda^2} = \frac{(160)^2}{10(10)} = 256 = SS \text{ contrast} = MS \text{ contrast}$$

To compute the F test for this contrast we need only divide it by the mean square for error of our analysis of variance to find $F(1,45) = \frac{256}{63} = 4.06$, $p = .05$. Since all F's employed to test contrasts have only one df in the numerator, we can always take the square root of these F's to obtain the t test for the contrast, in case we want to make a one-tailed t test. In this example a one-tailed t test would be quite sensible, and $t(45) = 2.02$, $p = .025$, one-tailed.

It is characteristic of contrast sums of squares that they are identical whether we employ a given set of weights or their opposite, i.e., the weights multiplied by -1. Thus, had we used the weights $+2$, $+1$, 0, -1, -2 instead of the weights -2, -1, 0, $+1$, $+2$ in the preceding example we would have obtained identical results, namely SS contrast $= 256$, and $F(1,45) = 4.06$, $p = .05$. This p value, though one-tailed in the F distribution (in that it refers only to the right-hand portion of the F distribution) is two-tailed with respect to the hypothesis that performance increases with age. If we take $\sqrt{F} = t$ we must be very careful in making one-tailed t tests to be sure that the results do in fact bear out our prediction and not its opposite. A convenient device is to give t a positive sign when the result is in the predicted direction (e.g., performance improves with age) and a negative sign when the result is in the opposite direction (e.g., performance worsens with age).

To estimate the size of the effect of the linear relationship between performance and age we can employ the information that

$$r = \sqrt{\frac{(df \text{ numerator}) F}{(df \text{ numerator}) F + df \text{ denominator}}} = \sqrt{\frac{t^2}{t^2 + df}}$$

$$= \sqrt{\frac{4.06}{4.06 + 45}} = .29$$

Thus, the correlation (r) between age level and average performance level is of moderate size. An alternative computational formula for the effect size r is

$$r = \sqrt{\frac{SS \text{ contrast}}{SS \text{ contrast} + SS \text{ error}}} = \sqrt{\frac{256}{256 + 2835}} = .29$$

What if we had divided the SS contrast by the total SS between age groups and taken the square root? We would have found $\sqrt{\frac{256}{260}} = .992$, exactly the r we obtained earlier by direct computation of the correlation between age level and mean performance level. This r, based on only 3 df, was valuable to us as an alerting device that we were about to make an error by forgetting to take account of the increasing nature of age. However, the r of .992 is a poor estimate of the relationship between individual children's age and performance, though it does a better job of estimating the correlation of age and performance for the mean age and mean performance of groups of children, with $n = 10$ per group. (Not only in this example but generally as well, it is often the case that correlations based on groups or other aggregated data are higher than those based on the original nonaggregated data.)

ADDITIONAL EXAMPLES

Testing for linear trend in age is a natural procedure for developmental researchers, but other contrasts may be preferred under some conditions. Suppose our investigator were confident only that 12-year-olds would be superior to 8-year-olds. The investigator could have chosen weights (λ's) as follows:

Age level	8	9	10	11	12	Σ
T	20	30	50	70	80	250
λ	-1	0	0	0	$+1$	0
$T\lambda$	-20	0	0	0	$+80$	60

The SS contrast then would have been $\dfrac{L^2}{n\Sigma\lambda^2} = \dfrac{(60)^2}{10(2)} = 180 = MS$ contrast, which, when divided by the mean square for error of our earlier analysis of variance, yields $F(1,45) = \dfrac{180}{63} = 2.86$, $t(45) = 1.69$, $p = .05$, one-tailed.

Comparing the 12-year-olds to the 8-year-olds is something we knew how to do even before we knew about contrasts (see Chapter 18). We could simply compute the t test to compare those groups. Had we done so we would have found

$$t = \frac{M_1 - M_2}{\sqrt{\left(\dfrac{1}{n_1} + \dfrac{1}{n_2}\right) MS \text{ error}}} = \frac{8.0 - 2.0}{\sqrt{\left(\dfrac{1}{10} + \dfrac{1}{10}\right) 63}} = 1.69, \, df = 45$$

(the df associated with the mean square error), $p = .05$, one-tailed. Comparing the ordinary t test with the contrast t test shows them to be identical, as indeed they should be.

Suppose now that our hypothesis had been that both the 8- and 9-year-olds would score significantly lower than the 12-year-olds. We could then have chosen weights (λ's) as follows:

Age level	8	9	10	11	12	Σ
T	20	30	50	70	80	250
λ	-1	-1	0	0	$+2$	0
$T\lambda$	-20	-30	0	0	160	110

(Recall that our λ's must add to zero, so that the $\lambda = +2$ of the 12-year-olds is needed to balance the -1 and -1 of the 8- and 9-year-olds.)

The SS contrast would have been $\dfrac{L^2}{n\Sigma\lambda^2} = \dfrac{(110)^2}{10(6)} = 201.67 = MS$ contrast, which, when divided by the mean square for error of our earlier analysis of variance, yields $F(1,45) = \dfrac{201.67}{63} = 3.20$, $t(45) = 1.79$, $p = .04$, one-tailed.

Had we decided to compute a simple t test between the mean of the 8- and 9-year-olds and the mean of the 12-year-olds we could have done so as follows:

$$t = \frac{M_1 - M_2}{\sqrt{\left(\dfrac{1}{n_1} + \dfrac{1}{n_2}\right) MS \text{ error}}} = \frac{8.0 - 2.5^*}{\sqrt{\left(\dfrac{1}{10} + \dfrac{1}{20\dagger}\right) 63}} = 1.79,$$

$$df = 45, \, p = .04, \text{ one-tailed.}$$

Once again the two methods of computing t yield identical results.

UNEQUAL n PER CONDITION

So far in our discussion of contrasts we have assumed equal n per condition. When n's are not equal we employ an unweighted means approach (see Chap-

---

* $(2.0 + 3.0)/2 = 2.5$
† n (8-year-olds) + n (9-year-olds) = 20

ter 20). Our basic formula for computing SS contrast is

$$\frac{L^2}{n\Sigma\lambda^2} \text{ which can be rewritten as } \frac{(\Sigma T\lambda)^2}{n\Sigma\lambda^2}$$

To employ the unweighted means procedure we redefine the T and the n of the just preceding formula, so that n becomes the harmonic mean of the n's, and T becomes the mean of the condition multiplied by the harmonic mean of the n's thus:

$$\text{Redefined } n = \frac{k}{\Sigma\frac{1}{n}} = n_h \text{ (harmonic mean } n)$$

where k is the number of conditions and $\Sigma\frac{1}{n}$ is the sum of the reciprocals of the n's, and redefined $T = Mn_h$ where M is the mean of a condition and n_h is n as redefined above.

If we had a study of five conditions in which the n's were 10, 10, 10, 10, and 10, the arithmetic mean n and the harmonic mean n would both $= 10$. If the same fifty observations were allocated to conditions as 4, 6, 10, 14, 16, the arithmetic mean n would still be 10 but the harmonic mean n would only be 7.69, since

$$\frac{k}{\Sigma\frac{1}{n}} = \frac{5}{\left(\frac{1}{4} + \frac{1}{6} + \frac{1}{10} + \frac{1}{14} + \frac{1}{16}\right)} = 7.69$$

It would always be appropriate to employ the redefined n and redefined T, since they are required when n's are unequal and are identical to the original definitions of n and T when n's are equal, because

$$n_h = \frac{k}{\Sigma\frac{1}{n}} = \frac{k}{k\left(\frac{1}{n}\right)} = n \text{ when } n\text{'s are equal.}$$

ORTHOGONAL CONTRASTS

When we consider a set of research results based on k conditions it is possible to compute up to $k - 1$ contrasts, each of which is uncorrelated with, or *orthogonal* to, every other contrast. Contrasts are orthogonal to each other when the correlation between them is zero, and the correlation between them will be zero when the sum of the products of the corresponding weights or λ's is zero. Thus the following two sets of contrast weights are orthogonal:

Contrast	Condition				
	A	B	C	D	Σ
λ_1 set	−3	−1	+1	+3	0
λ_2 set	+1	−1	−1	+1	0
Product $\lambda_1\lambda_2$	−3	+1	−1	+3	0

The set of contrast weights λ_1 can be seen to represent four points on a straight line, while the set λ_2 can be seen to represent four points on a U-shaped function. The third row, labeled $\lambda_1\lambda_2$ shows the products of these linear and quadratic weights, which add up to zero (−3, +1, −1, +3, when added yield zero) and are thus orthogonal.

A particularly useful set of orthogonal contrasts based on the coefficients of orthogonal polynomials (curves or trends) should be considered whenever the k conditions of the study can be arranged from the smallest to the largest levels of the independent variable, as is the case when age levels, dosage levels, learning trials, or other ordered levels comprise the independent variable. Table 23-3 shows us that when there are three levels or conditions (represented as $k = 3$), the weights defining a linear trend are −1, 0, +1, while the orthogonal weights defining the quadratic trend are +1, −2, +1. No matter how many levels of k there may be, the linear trend λ's always show a consistent gain (or loss), while the quadratic trend λ's always show a change in direction from down to up in a U curve (or up to down in a ∩ curve). Cubic trends, which can be assessed when there are four or more conditions, show two changes of direction from up to down to up (or down to up to down).

Figure 23-2 shows the results of three hypothetical studies that were (a) perfectly linear, (b) perfectly quadratic, and (c) perfectly cubic. The three figures show idealized results. In most real-life applications we find combinations of linear and nonlinear results. For example, the results in Figure 23-3 show a curve that has both strong linear and strong quadratic components.

We have noted that it is possible to compute up to $k − 1$ orthogonal contrasts among a set of k means or totals. Thus if we had four conditions we could compute three orthogonal contrasts, each based on a different polynomial or trend, the linear, quadratic, and cubic. The sums of squares of these three contrasts would add up to the total sum of squares among the four conditions. However, although there are only $k − 1$ orthogonal contrasts in a given set, such as those based on orthogonal polynomials, there is an infinite number of *sets* of contrasts that could be computed, each of which is made up of $k − 1$ orthogonal contrasts. The *sets* of contrasts, however, would not be

Table 23-3 Weights for orthogonal polynomial-based contrasts

		Ordered conditions									
k*	Polynomial†	1	2	3	4	5	6	7	8	9	10
2	Linear	−1	+1								
3	Linear	−1	0	+1							
	Quadratic	+1	−2	+1							
4	Linear	−3	−1	+1	+3						
	Quadratic	+1	−1	−1	+1						
	Cubic	−1	+3	−3	+1						
5	Linear	−2	−1	0	+1	+2					
	Quadratic	+2	−1	−2	−1	+2					
	Cubic	−1	+2	0	−2	+1					
6	Linear	−5	−3	−1	+1	+3	+5				
	Quadratic	+5	−1	−4	−4	−1	+5				
	Cubic	−5	+7	+4	−4	−7	+5				
7	Linear	−3	−2	−1	0	+1	+2	+3			
	Quadratic	+5	0	−3	−4	−3	0	+5			
	Cubic	−1	+1	+1	0	−1	−1	+1			
8	Linear	−7	−5	−3	−1	+1	+3	+5	+7		
	Quadratic	+7	+1	−3	−5	−5	−3	+1	+7		
	Cubic	−7	+5	+7	+3	−3	−7	−5	+7		
9	Linear	−4	−3	−2	−1	0	+1	+2	+3	+4	
	Quadratic	+28	+7	−8	−17	−20	−17	−8	+7	+28	
	Cubic	−14	+7	+13	+9	0	−9	−13	−7	+14	
10	Linear	−9	−7	−5	−3	−1	+1	+3	+5	+7	+9
	Quadratic	+6	+2	−1	−3	−4	−4	−3	−1	+2	+6
	Cubic	−42	+14	+35	+31	+12	−12	−31	−35	−14	+42

* Number of conditions.
† Shape of trend.

orthogonal to one another. For example, in the following contrasts, Set I is comprised of mutually orthogonal contrasts, as is Set II, but none of the three contrasts in Set I is orthogonal to any of the contrasts of Set II:

	Contrast Set I				Contrast Set II			
	A	B	C	D	A	B	C	D
λ_1	−3	−1	+1	+3	−1	−1	−1	+3
λ_2	+1	−1	−1	+1	−1	−1	+2	0
λ_3	−1	+3	−3	+1	−1	+1	0	0

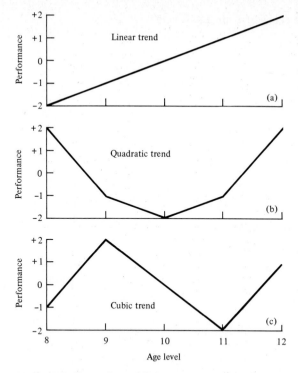

Figure 23-2 Illustrations of linear, quadratic, and cubic trends.

NONORTHOGONAL CONTRASTS

Although there is some advantage to employing orthogonal contrasts, in that each contrast addresses a fresh and nonoverlapping question, there is no a priori reason not to employ correlated (or nonorthogonal) contrasts. An especially valuable use of these contrasts is in the comparison of certain plausible

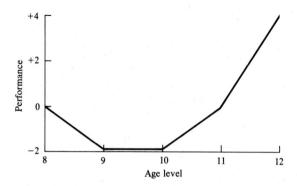

Figure 23-3 Curve showing linear and quadratic components.

Table 23-4 Mean performance score at four age levels*

		Age levels			
	6	8	10	12	Σ
Means	4.0	4.0	5.0	7.0	20
Hypothesis I λ's	−3	−1	+1	+3	0
Hypothesis II λ's	−1	−1	−1	+3	0

* $n = 10$ at each age level.

$$SS_I = \frac{L^2}{n\Sigma\lambda^2} = \frac{(\Sigma T\lambda)^2}{n\Sigma\lambda^2} = \frac{[40(-3) + 40(-1) + 50(+1) + 70(+3)]^2}{10[(+3)^2 + (+1)^2 + (-1)^2 + (-3)^2]} = 50$$

$$SS_{II} = \frac{L^2}{n\Sigma\lambda^2} = \frac{(\Sigma T\lambda)^2}{n\Sigma\lambda^2} = \frac{[40(-1) + 40(-1) + 50(-1) + 70(+3)]^2}{10[(-1)^2 + (-1)^2 + (-1)^2 + (+3)^2]} = 53.3$$

$$SS \text{ between conditions} = \frac{(40)^2}{10} + \frac{(40)^2}{10} + \frac{(50)^2}{10} + \frac{(70)^2}{10} - \frac{(200)^2}{40} = 60$$

rival hypotheses. Suppose we tested children at age levels 6, 8, 10, and 12. One plausible developmental prediction (which we call hypothesis I) is for a constant rate of improvement with age, while a rival hypothesis (II) predicts only that 12-year-olds will differ from all younger children. Table 23-4 shows the results of this research, the contrast weights used to test each hypothesis, the sums of squares associated with each contrast, and the sums of squares between all conditions ($df = 3$).

Both the contrasts do a good job of fitting the data, with SS_I taking up 50/60 (or 83 percent) of the between-conditions SS, and SS_{II} taking up 53.3/60 (or 89 percent) of the between-conditions SS. Hypothesis II did a bit better than hypothesis I but probably not enough better to make us give up hypothesis I. That both hypotheses did well should not surprise us too much, since the correlation between the weights representing the two hypotheses was quite substantial ($r = .77$). There might even have been a third hypothesis that predicted that 6- and 12-year-olds would differ most but that 8- and 10-year-olds would not differ from one another. Such a prediction would have been expressed by hypothesis III λ's of −1, 0, 0, +1. Hypothesis III would have been correlated .95 with hypothesis I and .82 with hypothesis II. The SS contrast for this set of weights would be 45, accounting for 75 percent of the total variance among conditions.

TWENTY-FOUR

CONSIDERATIONS OF POWER

POWER ANALYSIS

It is often the case that we can improve the design of our research studies by giving careful consideration to an analysis of the *power* of the research. To introduce the procedures of power analysis we will want to review the basic types of errors referred to in Chapter 2. The type I error (or "error of the first kind") involves rejecting the null hypothesis when it is in fact true. In its usual application in the behavioral sciences the type I error represents an error of gullibility or of overeagerness. It claims an effect or a relationship where none exists. The type II error (or "error of the second kind") involves failing to reject the null hypothesis when it is in fact false. In its usual application in the behavioral sciences the type II error represents an error of conservatism or blindness to a relationship. It denies the existence of an effect or a relationship that does exist. By convention, the probability of a type I error is called alpha (α), and the probability of a type II error is called beta (β).

Power is defined as the probability of rejecting the null hypothesis when the null hypothesis is false and, therefore, in need of rejecting. Power increases as the probability of a type II error (β) decreases or, more specifically:

$$\text{Power} = 1 - \beta$$

Put another way, power is the probability of *not* making a type II error, i.e., of not overlooking an effect or a relationship that is really there.

Two major purposes of power analysis include (1) the planning of research and (2) the evaluation of research already completed. In the planning of research a power analysis is conducted to determine the size of the sample needed to reach a given alpha (α) level for any particular size of effect that might be expected. In the evaluation of completed research and its accompanying inferences, we employ a power analysis to help us decide whether a given failure to detect an effect at a given alpha (α) was likely to have been due primarily to the employment of too small a sample. Let us consider an example.

Smith conducts an experiment on the effects of her new treatment of learning disabilities by randomly assigning forty children to the experimental condition and forty children to the control condition. Smith reports that the treatment-condition children improved significantly more than the control-condition children at $t(78) = 2.21$, $p < .05$. Jones is skeptical and decides to check on Smith's results by assigning children at random to the same two conditions. Jones has twenty children available for the research, and he assigns ten to each condition. His results show $t(18) = 1.06$, p not even close to .05 (actually greater than .30). Jones publishes his findings, claiming Smith's results were unreplicable, or the results of an artifact, or otherwise not to be believed.

Readers relying on p levels to tell them whether the research had been replicated or not might be seriously misled by Jones's conclusions of nonreplication. A closer look at Jones's data showed not only that Jones's results were in the same direction as Smith's but, more importantly, that Jones's effect size of $\frac{1}{2}\sigma$ (computed as $2t/\sqrt{df}$) was exactly the same as Smith's effect size of $\frac{1}{2}\sigma$ (computed as $2t/\sqrt{df}$). In short, the two studies showed the same result, but Smith's sample size was large enough to show an effect at $p < .05$ (actual power for her t test was about .6), while Jones's sample size was not large enough to show the effect at $p < .05$ (actual power for his t test was only about .2, or one-third as great as Smith's).

In a given study the determination of the level of power at which we would be operating depends on (1) the particular statistic we employ to determine the level of significance, (2) the level of alpha (α) we select, (3) the size of the sample we employ, and (4) the size of the effect we are studying.

EFFECT SIZE

There are a great many different ways in which to represent the size of the effects under investigation. We shall consider a number of these in due course, but for now we focus our attention on two of the most common, most serviceable, and most easily understood, *eta* and *d*.

Eta, which was described earlier in Chapter 19, can be defined as the square root of the proportion of variance accounted for. It can also be defined as the square root of the ratio of the sum of squares of the effect to the sum of squares of the effect plus the sum of squares of the error, or

$$eta = \sqrt{\frac{SS \text{ effect}}{SS \text{ effect} + SS \text{ error}}} \tag{1}$$

If the sums of squares are not available, only a little rearrangement of terms is required to show that we can give *eta* in terms of *F* instead:

$$eta = \sqrt{\frac{(F)(df \text{ effect})}{(F)(df \text{ effect}) + (df \text{ error})}} \quad (2)$$

The interpretation of *eta* is analogous to the interpretation of the Pearson product-moment correlation coefficient (*r*), but with the understanding that *eta* may refer to nonlinear as well as to linear relationships. *Eta* may be seen as the general case of which *r* is a special instance.

Particularly when the research involves the comparison of two groups, it is common to index the size of the effect by examining the difference between the means. Such differences, however, have little meaning apart from the (often arbitrary) scale of measurement employed. It is useful, therefore, to divide the difference between the means by the common within-group σ so that the effect size will be represented in σ units. Jacob Cohen (1969, 1977), in his extensive treatment of this topic, refers to such standardized differences as units of *d*— units that were decribed earlier in our chapter on the *t* test (Chapter 18).

$$d = \frac{\text{Mean 1} - \text{Mean 2}}{\sigma} \quad (3)$$

In experimental research we often try to maximize *d*. We do this by increasing the numerator and by decreasing the denominator of the expression above. We try to increase the mean difference (the numerator) by selecting treatment conditions we believe to be as powerful as possible; and we try to decrease the within-groups σ (the denominator) by increasing the standardization of our procedures, by increasing the reliability of our measurements, by selecting more homogeneous sampling units for our study, and by related methods for increasing precision, i.e., decreasing uncontrolled variation.

Often when we would like to determine *d* or σ for a published study, we find that they have not been reported. In addition, it may happen that the *MS* for error has not been reported, so that we cannot calculate σ ourselves ($\sigma \cong \sqrt{MS}$ error). In those cases we can get a good approximation to *d* by doubling the associated *t* value and dividing by the $\sqrt{df}$ (or $N - 2$) on which the *t* test was based (Friedman, 1968; a procedure we discussed in Chapter 18):

$$d = \frac{2t}{\sqrt{df}} \quad (4)$$

Table 24-1 helps us review the use of the indices of effect size discussed so far. The results of the study shown are in the form of dichotomous (0, 1) scores for both conditions of the study. Dichotomous data work well and are easy to work with computationally.

First we compute *eta* according to formula (1), which gives:

$$eta = \sqrt{\frac{1.80}{1.80 + 3.20}} = .60$$

Table 24-1 Experimental results and the table of variance

Experimental results		Table of variance					
Control	Experimental	Source	SS	df	MS	F	t*
1	1	Between conditions	1.80	1	1.800	10.11	3.18
1	1	Within conditions	3.20	18	0.178		
0	1						
0	1						
0	1						
0	1						
0	1						
0	1						
0	0						
0	0						
Σ 2	8						
$\bar{X}$ 0.2	0.8						
σ 0.4	0.4						

* $t = \sqrt{F}$ when F is based on only a single df in the numerator.

Then we compute *eta* according to formula (2), which gives:

$$eta = \sqrt{\frac{(10.11)(1)}{(10.11)(1) + 18}} = .60$$

Next we compute d according to formula (3), which gives:

$$d = \frac{0.8 - 0.2}{.4} = 1.50$$

Finally, we compute d according to formula (4), which gives:

$$d = \frac{2(3.18)}{\sqrt{18}} = 1.50$$

For the situation in which F has only a single df in the numerator, *eta* can be seen as simply r. We can show the relationship between r and d so that given one we can easily find the other. Given r we can find d by

$$d = \frac{2r}{\sqrt{1 - r^2}}$$

and, given d we can find r by

$$r = \frac{d}{\sqrt{d^2 + 4}}$$

The experimental results we reported above were chosen not only to be very easy to work with computationally, but also to show a simple generalization of our procedures to the case of a 2×2 contingency table. We can redisplay the data above as follows:

Score	Control	Experimental	Σ
1	2	8	10
0	8	2	10
Σ	10	10	20

Recalling from our chapter on correlations that

$$\chi^2(1) = \sum \frac{(O - E)^2}{E}$$

we find for these data that $\chi^2(1) = 7.2$. This value, when divided by our total N of 20, equals .36, of which the square root is .60. That turns out to be both the phi (ϕ) coefficient summarizing the data of the contingency table and also the *eta* we computed earlier on the same data. In general, for a 2×2 contingency table, we compute phi (ϕ), a product-moment correlation, as follows:

$$\phi = \sqrt{\frac{\chi^2}{N}}$$

By convention, whether our effect size is indexed by d or r or ϕ, we employ a positive sign when the effect is in the predicted direction and a negative sign when the effect is in the unpredicted direction.

POWER TABLES

The most comprehensive, elegant, and useful discussion of power analysis in behavioral research is that by Cohen (1969, 1977). He has provided a large number of tables that are indispensable to behavioral researchers, and Table 24-2 is a composite based on many of those tables. For each of seven statistics ranging from t to F the effect-size index suggested by Cohen is given, along with his definitions of "small," "medium," and "large" effect sizes. The rest of the table allows us to read the sample sizes required to operate at each power level from .15 to .90 or to read the power at which we were operating for any given sample size. In section A the power and sample size equivalences are given for an alpha level of .05, two-tail, and for medium-effect sizes as defined by Cohen. Section B gives the equivalences for medium effects tested at .01, two-tail. Section C gives the equivalences for small effects at .05, two-tail.

Whenever the table involves the comparison of two or more samples (e.g., t, F, $r_1 - r_2$, $P_1 - P_2$) the sample sizes are assumed equal. When sample sizes

Table 24-2 Multipurpose power tables

				Statistics and effect sizes			
Statistic	t	r	$r_1 - r_2$	$P - .50$	$P_1 - P_2$	χ^2	F
Effect size	d	r	q	g	h	w	f
a. small	.20	.10	.10	.05	.20	.10	.10
b. medium	.50	.30	.30	.15	.50	.30	.25
c. large	.80	.50	.50	.25	.80	.50	.40

A   Sample size (rounded) required to detect "medium" effect at .05, two-tail

Power	t	r	$r_1 - r_2$	$P - .50$	$P_1 - P_2$	χ^2 $(df = 1)$	F $(df = 1$ for numerator)
.15	10	10	20	<10	<10	<25	10
.20	10	15	30	10	10	<25	10
.30	20	25	50	20	20	25	20
.40	25	35	70	35	25	30	25
.50	30	40	90	45	30	45	30
.60	40	55	115	55	40	55	40
.70	50	65	140	70	50	70	50
.80	65	85	175	90	65	90	65
.90	85	115	235	110	85	120	85
definition of n:	a	b	c	d	c	d	a

B   Sample size (rounded) required to detect "medium" effect at .01, two-tail

Power	t	r	$r_1 - r_2$	$P - .50$	$P_1 - P_2$	χ^2 $(df = 1)$	F $(df = 1)$
.15	20	30	55	30	20	25	20
.20	25	35	70	40	25	35	25
.30	35	45	95	50	35	45	35
.40	45	60	125	60	45	60	45
.50	55	70	150	70	55	75	55
.60	65	85	180	85	65	90	65
.70	80	100	220	100	75	110	80
.80	95	125	260	130	95	130	95
.90	120	160	330	160	120	160	120

C   Sample size (rounded) required to detect "small" effect at .05, two-tail

Power	t	r	$r_1 - r_2$	$P - .50$	$P_1 - P_2$	χ^2 $(df = 1)$	F $(df = 1)$
.15	45	85	170	90	40	80	45
.20	65	125	250	120	65	125	65
.30	105	200	400	200	105	200	105
.40	150	300	600	300	140	300	150
.50	200	400	800	400	200	400	200
.60	250	500	1000	500	250	500	250
.70	300	600	1250	650	300	600	300
.80	400	800	1600	800	400	800	400
.90	550	1000	2100	1000	500	1000	550

a. each group or condition   b. n of score pairs   c. n of *each* sample   d. total N

Source: Based on J. Cohen, *Statistical Power Analysis for the Behavioral Sciences,* Academic Press, New York, 1977.

are not equal, we employ the harmonic mean (n_h) of the sample sizes as our approximation.

INDICES OF EFFECT SIZE

We turn now to a consideration of each of the seven statistics of Table 24.2 and the index of effect size associated with each.

t The effect size associated with *t* is called *d*, and we have already defined *d* as:

$$\frac{(M_1 - M_2)}{\sigma}$$

We note in our inspection of the entries under *t* in sections A, B, and C in Table 24-2 that to achieve even the modest power level of .50 we will require sample sizes of 30, 55, and 200, *in each group* for the three combinations of expected effect size and alpha respectively.

r The effect size associated with *r* is, of course, *r* itself. The definitions of small, medium, and large effects are not quite consistent between *r* and *t*. The table below shows in the third column the levels of *r* that are equivalent to each level of *d*. Thus Cohen requires a somewhat larger effect when examining *r* than when examining *t* when medium and especially, large effects are under discussion:

	d	Cohen's *r*	*r* equivalent to *d**
Small	.20	.10	.10
Medium	.50	.30	.24
Large	.80	.50	.37

* Where *r* is obtained from *d* by: $r = \dfrac{d}{\sqrt{d^2 + 4}}$

To achieve the moderate power level of .50 we will require sample sizes of 40, 70, and 400 sampling units for the three combinations of expected effect size and alpha shown in sections A, B, and C of Table 24-2. Comparison of sample sizes listed for *t* and for *r* show the sample sizes required for *r* to be uniformly higher. It should be noted, however, that the entries under *t* are the *n*'s for each of two groups, while the entries for *r* are the total sample size. In fact, for most power levels and for most effect sizes and alpha levels, the total sample sizes required by *r* are smaller than those required by *t*. That appears to be due partly to the fact that "medium" and "large" effects are actually larger for *r* than for *d*, and partly to the fact that *t* cannot take advantage of both between-group and within-group linearity of regression. The table below shows t for the comparison between two sets of two scores each:

		t					r	
Subject	Treatment condition	Within condition specific prediction	Score	$\bar{X}$	Subject	Treatment condition	Within condition specific prediction	Score
1	Control	None	2	3.0	1	Control	-3	2
2	Control	None	4		2	Control	-1	4
3	Experimental	None	6	7.0	3	Experimental	1	6
4	Experimental	None	8		4	Experimental	3	8
$t(2) = 2.83, p < .11, r = .89$					$r(2) = 1.00, t \to \infty, p \to 0$			

There is no effect on t if the scores within each group are rearranged. There is an effect on r, however, of having accurately predicted on the basis of some theory which of the scores in each group should be higher; the correlation over all four scores is perfect. If even one of the pairs of numbers of the experimental or control group had been interchanged in the right-hand section of the table above, however, r would have dropped from 1.00 to .80 ($t = 1.89$, $df = 2$, $p <$ .20). In short, where there really is a more nearly perfect linear regression between the predicted and obtained results, r is likely to be more powerful than t. That is because t has lost some of the information in the independent variable (or predictor variable) by dichotomizing the four discriminable predictor values (-3, -1, $+1$, $+3$) to just two levels of -1 and $+1$.

$r_1 - r_2$ The difference between correlation coefficients is indexed by q, the difference between the Fisher z transformations associated with each r. Fisher's z is defined as: $\frac{1}{2} \log_e \frac{1 + r}{1 - r}$. To achieve a power level of .50, we need 90, 150, and 800 sampling units for *each* r for the three combinations of expected effect size and alpha shown in sections A, B, and C of Table 24-2.

It is worth noting that the testing of differences between correlation coefficients is a more "difficult" enterprise than is usually realized, often requiring enormous sample sizes to detect differences. Why should it be so difficult to detect the differences between the value of one r and another r when it is so much easier to detect the difference between the value of one r and zero? The answer lies in the difference between the confidence interval around a second observed r and that around a theoretical value of zero. The latter, of course, has no confidence interval, while the former has a real confidence interval "to be overcome." Consider an r of .30 based on an N of 45. The t associated with this r is 2.01 and $p = .05$. The 95 percent confidence interval around the obtained r is between .01 and .54. There is no overlap with zero. Now imagine that we wanted to compare this obtained r with another obtained r of 0.0 based on the same sample size of 45. The confidence interval of this latter r runs from $-.29$ to $+.29$ and overlaps very considerably with the confidence interval of our r of .30 as shown in Figure 24-1. It is this overlap that keeps the r's from being found to differ significantly. In short, it is easier to be found to be bigger than a point than to be found bigger than the mean of a distribution.

$P - .50$ The difference between an obtained proportion (P) and .50 is referred to as g. To achieve a power level of .50, we need 45, 70, and 400 sampling units for the three combinations of expected effect size and alpha shown in sections A, B, and C of Table 24-2.

$P_1 - P_2$ The difference between two obtained proportions is indexed by the difference, h, between the arcsin transformations of the two proportions. This transformation, like that employed for r, makes equal differences in the transformed scale equally detectable (Cohen, 1977). To achieve a power level of .50 requires 30, 55, and 200 sampling units *for each sample* for the three combinations of expected effect size and alpha shown in sections A, B, and C of Table 24-2.

χ^2 The effect size associated with χ^2 is called w. It is defined as the square root of the sum over all cells (of any size table of frequencies) of the square of the difference between the proportion expected and the proportion obtained in each cell divided by the proportion expected in that cell, or

$$w = \sqrt{\Sigma \frac{(P \text{ expected} - P \text{ obtained})^2}{P \text{ expected}}}$$

The definition of w, then, looks like the square root of the definition of χ^2 except that the raw frequencies employed in the computation of χ^2 have been

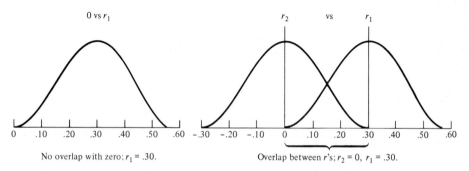

Figure 24-1 Comparison of a correlation coefficient with (a) a theoretical value of zero and with (b) a correlation coefficient of zero.

replaced by the proportions of total N found in each cell or expected in each cell. For a 2×2 table w is equivalent to phi (ϕ), so $\phi = w = \sqrt{\chi^2/N}$. In terms of the contingency coefficient C (where $C = \sqrt{\chi^2/(\chi^2 + N)}$), $w = \sqrt{C^2/(1 - C^2)}$. To achieve a power level of .50, we will require 45, 75, and 400 sampling units for the three combinations of expected effect size and alpha shown in sections A, B, and C of Table 24-2.

F The effect size associated with F is called f and is defined as the σ of the means divided by the σ within conditions. In the case of just two groups, f is related to d by $f = d/2$. More generally f is related to the correlation ratio, *eta*, by

$$f = \sqrt{\frac{eta^2}{1 - eta^2}}$$

To achieve a power level of .50 (or any other given power level), when only two groups are involved, the sample sizes required are identical to those required for t. When F is based on more than two groups, we should note that power decreases in tests of main effects as the number of df of the between-group factors increases for a given fixed total N. In addition, power for an interaction decreases as the number of df of the interaction increases for a given fixed total N.

In using Cohen's (1977) power tables we redefine n to n^1 before entering the tables, where

$$n^1 = \frac{df \text{ error} + df \text{ effect} + 1}{df \text{ effect} + 1}$$

Thus, given the sample sizes shown below:

	A_1	A_2	A_3	Σ
B_1	10	10	10	30
B_2	10	10	10	30
B_3	10	10	10	30
B_4	10	10	10	30
Σ	40	40	40	120

we would find df to be as follows:

$$df \text{ error} = 120 - 12 = 12(10 - 1) = 108$$

$$df \text{ effect A} = 3 - 1 = 2$$

$$df \text{ effect B} = 4 - 1 = 3$$

$$df \text{ effect AB} = (3 - 1) \times (4 - 1) = 6$$

Therefore, n^1 for the A effect $= \dfrac{108 + 2 + 1}{2 + 1} = 37$

and n^1 for the B effect $= \dfrac{108 + 3 + 1}{3 + 1} = 28$

and n^1 for the AB effect $= \dfrac{108 + 6 + 1}{6 + 1} = 16.4$

Using the required power tables provided by Cohen (1977) we would find the power levels for alpha $= .05$ and a medium effect size of $f = .25$ to be .65, .58, and .46 for the A, B, and AB effects, respectively. These results illustrate the loss of power involved when, for a fixed total N, the df for various effects show an increase. Here, then, is a major reason to organize our scientific questions into focused questions such as are addressed by t tests, F tests with a single df in the numerator, χ^2's with 1 df, and more generally, by contrasts of any type.

NINE

ADDITIONAL TOPICS IN DATA ANALYSIS

Chapter **25. Comparing and Combining Independent Research Results**

Chapter **26. Chi-Square and the Analysis of Tables**

Chapter **27. Multivariate Procedures**

TWENTY-FIVE

COMPARING AND COMBINING INDEPENDENT RESEARCH RESULTS

BACKGROUND

It has become almost obligatory to end research reports with the clarion call for further research. Yet it seems fair to say that we have been better at issuing such calls than at knowing what to do with the answers. There are many areas of behavioral science for which we do in fact have available the results of numerous studies all addressing essentially the same question. The summaries of the results of these sets of studies, however, have not been nearly as informative as they might have been, either with respect to summarized significance levels or with respect to summarized effect sizes. Even the best reviews of research by the most sophisticated workers have rarely told us more about each study of a set of studies than that it did or did not reach a given p level and the direction of the relationship between the variables investigated. This state of affairs is beginning to change, however. More and more reviews of the literature are moving from the traditional, literary format to the quantitative format (e.g., Cooper & Rosenthal, 1980; Glass, McGaw, & Smith, 1981; Rosenthal, 1980, with the latter two providing useful overviews; and our discussion of meta-analysis in Chapter 4).

If one were to trace historically (and ever so briefly) the development of the movement to quantify runs of studies, we might begin with Sir Ronald Fisher (1938), for his thinking about the combination of the significance levels of independent studies; move through Frederick Mosteller and Robert Bush (1954) for their broadening of the Fisher perspective both in (a) introducing several new methods of combining independent probability levels to social and behavioral scientists and (b) showing that effect sizes as well as significance levels could be usefully combined; and end in the present day with an expanding number of investigators such as Gene V Glass (1976, 1980) and others (including Hall, 1980; Light & Smith, 1971; Pillemer & Light, 1980; Rosenthal, 1969, 1978, 1980; Rosenthal & Rubin, 1978, 1980; Smith, 1980; Smith & Glass, 1977; Smith, Glass, & Miller, 1980) as well as still others cited in the references of each of these workers.

COMPARING TWO STUDIES

Even when we have been quite rigorous and sophisticated in the interpretation of the results of a single study, we are often prone to err in the interpretation of two or more studies. Earlier we reported an example of such error involving a report by an investigator (say Smith) of a significant relationship between X and Y followed by a rebuttal by another investigator (say Jones) that there was no such relationship. A closer look at their data showed that Smith's results— $t(78) = 2.21$, $p < .05$, $d = .50$, $r = .24$—were more significant than Jones's results—$t(18) = 1.06$, $p > .30$, $d = .50$, $r = .24$—but that the studies were in perfect agreement as to their estimated sizes of effect defined by either d or r. A comparison of their respective significance levels by procedures to be described below reveals, furthermore, that these p's are not significantly different ($p = .42$). Clearly Jones was wrong in claiming that he had failed to replicate Smith's results. We shall begin this section by considering some procedures for comparing quantitatively the results of two independent studies, e.g., studies conducted with different research participants or other sampling units.

Significance Testing

Ordinarily when we compare the results of two studies we are more interested in comparing their effect sizes than their p values. However, sometimes we cannot do any better than comparing their p values, and here is how we do it (Rosenthal & Rubin, 1979a): For each of the two test statistics we obtain an accurate p level, accurate say to two digits (not counting zeros before the first nonzero value), such as $p = .43$ or .024, or .0012. That is, if $t(30) = 3.03$ we give p as .0025, not as "$< .05$." Extended tables of the t distribution are helpful here (e.g., Federighi, 1959, which is reproduced in Appendix B). For each p we find Z, the standard normal deviate corresponding to the p value. The last row of the table just cited and the table of Z's of Appendix B will both be useful in finding the accurate Z. Both p's should be one-tailed, and the corresponding Z's will have the same sign if both studies show effects in the same direction, but different signs if the results are in the opposite direction. The difference between the two Z's when divided by $\sqrt{2}$ yields a new Z that corresponds to the p value that the difference between the Z's could be so large, or larger, if the two Z's did not really differ. Recapping,

$$\frac{Z_1 - Z_2}{\sqrt{2}} \quad \text{is distributed as } Z,$$

so we can enter this newly calculated Z in a table of Z's (Appendix B) to find the p value associated with finding a Z of the size obtained or larger.

Example 1 Studies A and B yield results in opposite directions, and neither is "significant." One p is .06, one-tailed, the other is .12, one-tailed but in the opposite tail. The Z's corresponding to these p's are found in a table of the normal curve to be $+1.56$ and -1.18 (note the opposite signs to indicate results in opposite directions). Then, from the preceding equation we have

$$\frac{Z_1 - Z_2}{\sqrt{2}} = \frac{(1.56) - (-1.18)}{1.41} = 1.94$$

as the Z of the difference between the two p values or their corresponding Z's. The p value associated with a Z of 1.94 is .026 one-tailed or .052 two-tailed. The two p values thus may be seen to differ significantly, or nearly so, suggesting that the results of the two studies are not consistent even allowing for normal sampling fluctuation.

Example 2 Studies A and B yield results in the same direction, and both are significant. One p is .04, the other is .000025. The Z's corresponding to these p's are 1.75 and 4.06 (since both Z's are in the same tail they have the same sign). From the preceding equation we have

$$\frac{Z_1 - Z_2}{\sqrt{2}} = \frac{(4.06) - (1.75)}{1.41} = 1.64$$

as our obtained Z of the difference. The p associated with that Z is .050 one-tailed or .100 two-tailed, so we may want to conclude that the two p values differ significantly, or nearly so. It should be emphasized, however, that finding one Z greater than another does not tell us whether that Z was greater because the size of the effect was greater, the size of the study was greater, or both.

Example 3 Studies A and B yield results in the same direction, but one is "significant" ($p = .05$) and the other is not ($p = .06$). This illustrates the worst-case scenario for inferential errors where investigators might conclude that the two results are "inconsistent" because one is significant and the other is not. Regrettably, this example is not merely theoretical. Just such errors have been made and documented (Rosenthal & Gaito, 1963, 1964). The Z's corresponding to these p's are 1.64 and 1.55. From the preceding equation we have

$$\frac{Z_1 - Z_2}{\sqrt{2}} = \frac{(1.64) - (1.55)}{1.41} = .06$$

as our obtained Z of the difference between a p value of .05 and .06. The p value associated with this difference is .476 one-tailed or .952 two-tailed. This example shows clearly just how nonsignificant the difference between significant and nonsignificant results can be.

Effect-Size Estimation

When we ask whether two studies are telling the same story, what we usually mean is whether the results (in terms of the estimated effect size) are reasonably consistent with each other or whether they are significantly heterogeneous. For the purpose of the present chapter the discussion will be restricted to r as the effect-size indicator, but analogous procedures are available for comparing such other effect-size indicators as Cohen's (1977) d or differences between proportions (Hsu, 1980; Rosenthal & Rubin, 1982).

For each of the two studies to be compared we compute the effect-size r and find for each of these r's the associated Fisher z^* defined as $\frac{1}{2}\log_e [(1 + r)/ (1 - r)]$. A table to convert our obtained r's to Fisher z's is available in Appendix B. Then, when N_1 and N_2 represent the number of sampling units (e.g., subjects) in each of our two studies, the quantity

$$\frac{z_1 - z_2}{\sqrt{\dfrac{1}{N_1 - 3} + \dfrac{1}{N_2 - 3}}}$$

is distributed as Z (Snedecor & Cochran, 1967, 1980).

Example 4 Studies A and B yield results in opposite directions with effect sizes of $r = .60$ ($N = 15$) and $r = -.20$ ($N = 100$), respectively. The Fisher z's corresponding to these r's are .69 and $-.20$, respectively (note the opposite signs of the z's to correspond to the opposite signs of the r's). Then, from the preceding equation we have

$$\frac{(.69) - (-.20)}{\sqrt{\dfrac{1}{12} + \dfrac{1}{97}}} = 2.91$$

as the Z of the difference between the two effect sizes. The p value associated with a Z of 2.91 is .002 one-tailed or .004 two-tailed. These two effect sizes, then, differ significantly.

Example 5 Studies A and B yield results in the same direction with effect sizes of $r = .70$ ($N = 20$) and $r = .25$ ($N = 95$), respectively. The Fisher z's corresponding to these r's are .87 and .26, respectively. From the preceding

---

* In this chapter we employ the lower-case z for the Fisher transformation and the capital Z for the standard normal deviate.

equation we have

$$\frac{(.87) - (.26)}{\sqrt{\dfrac{1}{17} + \dfrac{1}{92}}} = 2.31$$

as our obtained Z of the difference. The p associated with that Z is .01 one-tailed or .02 two-tailed. Here is an example of two studies that agree there is a significant positive relationship between variables X and Y, but disagree significantly in their estimates of the size of the relationship.

Example 6 Studies A and B yield effect-size estimates of $r = .00$ ($N = 17$) and $r = .30$ ($N = 45$), respectively. The Fisher z's corresponding to these r's are .00 and .31, respectively. From the preceding equation we have

$$\frac{(.00) - (.31)}{\sqrt{\dfrac{1}{14} + \dfrac{1}{42}}} = -1.00$$

as our obtained Z of the difference between our two effect-size estimates. The p associated with that Z is .16 one-tailed or .32 two-tailed. Here we have an example of two effect sizes, one zero ($r = .00$) the other ($r = .30$) significantly different from zero [$t(43) = 2.06$, $p < .025$ one-tailed], which do not differ significantly from one another.* This illustrates well how careful we must be in concluding that results of two studies are heterogeneous just because one is significant and the other is not or because one has a zero estimated effect size and the other does not.

COMBINING TWO STUDIES

Significance Testing

After comparing the results of any two independent studies it is an easy matter also to combine the p levels of the two studies. In this way we get an overall estimate of the probability that the two p levels might have been obtained if the null hypothesis of no relationship between X and Y were true. Many methods for combining the results of two or more studies are available and have been described elsewhere (Rosenthal, 1978, 1983). Here it is necessary to give only the simplest and most versatile of the procedures, the method of adding Z's called the *Stouffer method* by Mosteller and Bush (1954).

This method, just like the method of comparing p values, asks us first to obtain accurate p levels for each of our two studies and then to find the Z corresponding to each of these p levels. Both p's must be given in one-tailed

* This somewhat counterintuitive result is explained in detail in Chapter 24.

form, and the corresponding Z's will have the same sign if both studies show effects in the same direction. They will have different signs if the results are in the opposite direction. The sum of the two Z's when divided by $\sqrt{2}$ yields a new Z. This new Z corresponds to the p value that the results of the two studies combined, or results even further out in the same tail could have occurred if the null hypothesis of no relationship between X and Y were true. Recapping,

$$\frac{Z_1 + Z_2}{\sqrt{2}}$$

is distributed as Z.

Example 7 Studies A and B yield results in opposite directions, and both are significant. One p is .05, one-tailed; the other is .0000001, one-tailed but in the opposite tail. The Z's corresponding to these p's are found in a table of normal deviates (see Appendix B) to be -1.64 and 5.20, respectively (note the opposite signs to indicate results in opposite directions). Then from the preceding equation we have

$$\frac{Z_1 + Z_2}{\sqrt{2}} = \frac{(-1.64) + (5.20)}{1.41} = 2.52$$

as the Z of the combined results of studies A and B. The p value associated with a Z of 2.52 is .006 one-tailed or .012 two-tailed. Thus, the combined p supports the result of the more significant of the two results. If these were actual results we would want to be very cautious in interpreting our combined p. That is because the two p's we combined were so very significantly different from each other. We would try to discover what differences between studies A and B might have led to results so significantly different.

Example 8 Studies A and B yield results in the same direction, but neither is significant. One p is .11, the other is .09, and their associated Z's are 1.23 and 1.34, respectively. From the preceding equation we have

$$\frac{(1.23) + (1.34)}{1.41} = 1.82$$

as our combined Z. The p associated with that Z is .034 one-tailed or .068 two-tailed.

Effect-Size Estimation

When we want to combine the results of two studies, we are as interested in the combined estimate of the effect size as we are in the combined probability. Just as was the case when we compared two effect-size estimates, we shall consider r as our effect-size estimate in the combining of effect sizes. However, we note that many other estimates are possible (e.g., Cohen's d or differences between proportions).

For each of the two studies to be combined, we compute r and the associated Fisher z and have

$$\frac{z_1 + z_2}{2} = \bar{z}$$

as the Fisher z corresponding to our mean r. We use an r to z or z to r table (see Appendix B) to look up the r associated with our mean $\bar{z}$. Tables are preferable to finding r from z from the following: $r = (e^{2z} - 1)/(e^{2z} + 1)$. Should we want to do so we could weight each z by its df, i.e., $N - 3$ (Snedecor & Cochran, 1967, 1980).

The weighted mean z is obtained as follows:

$$\text{Weighted } \bar{z} = \frac{z_1(N_1 - 3) + z_2(N_2 - 3)}{(N_1 + N_2 - 6)}$$

where N_1 is the number of sampling units upon which z_1 is based, and N_2 is the number of sampling units upon which z_2 is based.

We illustrate with the data of Example 6, where we had r's of .00 and .30 based on N's of 17 and 45, respectively. The Fisher z's corresponding to our two r's are .00 and .31. Therefore our

$$\text{Weighted } \bar{z} = \frac{.00(17 - 3) + .31(45 - 3)}{(17 + 45 - 6)} = .232$$

which corresponds to an r of .23.

Example 9 Studies A and B yield results in opposite directions, one $r = .80$, the other $r = -.30$. The Fisher z's corresponding to these r's are 1.10 and -0.31, respectively. From the preceding equation we have

$$\frac{z_1 + z_2}{2} = \frac{(1.10) + (-0.31)}{2} = .395$$

as the mean Fisher z. From our z to r table we find a z of .395 associated with an r of .38.

Example 10 Studies A and B yield results in the same direction, one $r = .95$, the other $r = .25$. The Fisher z's corresponding to these r's are 1.83 and .26, respectively. From the preceding equation we have

$$\frac{1.83 + .26}{2} = 1.045$$

as the mean Fisher z. From our z to r table we find a z of 1.045 to be associated with an r of .78. Note that if we had averaged the two r's without first transforming them to Fisher z's we would have found the mean r to be $(.95 + .25)/2 = .60$, substantially smaller than .78. This illustrates that the use of Fisher's z gives heavier weight to r's that are further from zero in either direction.

Finally, it should be noted that before combining tests of significance, or effect-size estimates, it is very useful first to test the significance of the difference between the two p values or the two effect sizes. If the results of the studies *do* differ we should be most cautious about combining their p values or effect sizes—especially when their results were in opposite directions.

COMPARING THREE OR MORE STUDIES

Although we can do quite a lot in the way of comparing and combining the results of sets of studies with just the procedures given so far, it does happen often that we have three or more studies of the same relationship that we want to compare and/or combine. The purpose of this section is to present generalizations of the procedure given in the last section so that we can compare and combine the results of any number of studies.

Significance Testing

Given three or more p levels to compare, we first find the standard normal deviate, Z, corresponding to each p level. All p levels must be one-tailed, and the corresponding Z's will have the same sign if all studies show effects in the same direction. They will have different signs if the results are not in the same direction. The statistical significance of the heterogeneity of the Z's can be obtained from a χ^2 computed as follows (Rosenthal & Rubin, 1979a):

$$\Sigma(Z_j - \bar{Z})^2 \quad \text{is distributed as } \chi^2 \text{ with } K - 1 \, df$$

In this equation Z_j is the Z for any one study, and $\bar{Z}$ is the mean of all the Z's obtained. A significant $\chi^2(K - 1)$ tells us that the Z's we have tested for heterogeneity (or the p's associated with those Z's) differ significantly among themselves.

Example 11 Studies A, B, C, and D yield one-tailed p values of .15, .05, .01, and .001, respectively. Study C, however, shows results opposite in direction from those of studies A, B, and D. From our normal table we find the Z's corresponding to the four p levels to be 1.04, 1.64, -2.33, and 3.09. (Note the negative sign for the Z associated with the result in the opposite direction.) Then, from the preceding equation we have

$$\Sigma(Z_j - \bar{Z})^2 = [(1.04 - (0.86)]^2 + [(1.64) - (0.86)]^2$$
$$+ [(-2.33) - (0.86)]^2 + [(3.09) - (0.86)]^2 = 15.79$$

as our χ^2 value which for $K - 1 = 4 - 1 = 3 \, df$ is significant at $p = .0013$. The four p values we compared, then, are clearly significantly heterogeneous. Beyond the question of whether a set of p levels differ significantly among themselves, we sometimes want to test specific hypotheses about which studies will show the more significant p levels. This can be done by computing contrasts among the obtained p levels (Rosenthal & Rubin, 1979 a).

Effect-Size Estimation

Here we want to assess the statistical heterogeneity of three or more effect-size estimates. We again restrict our discussion to r as the effect-size estimator, though analogous procedures are available for comparing such other effect-size estimators as d or differences between proportions (Rosenthal & Rubin, 1982).

For each of the three or more studies to be compared we compute the effect-size r, its associated Fisher z, and $N - 3$, where N is the number of sampling units on which each r is based. Then the statistical significance of the heterogeneity of the r's can be obtained from a χ^2 computed as follows (Snedecor & Cochran, 1967, 1980):

$$\Sigma[(N_j - 3)(z_j - \bar{z})^2] \quad \text{is distributed as } \chi^2 \text{ with } K - 1 \text{ } df$$

In this equation z_j is the Fisher z corresponding to any r, and $\bar{z}$ is the weighted mean z, i.e.,

$$\frac{\Sigma[(N_j - 3)z_j]}{\Sigma(N_j - 3)}$$

Example 12 Studies A, B, C, and D yield effect sizes of $r = .70$ ($N = 30$), $r = .45$ ($N = 45$), $r = .10$ ($N = 20$), and $r = -.15$ ($N = 25$), respectively. The Fisher z's corresponding to these r's are found from our table of Fisher z to be .87, .48, .10, and $-.15$, respectively. The weighted mean z is found from the equation just above to be

$$\frac{[27(.87) + 42(.48) + 17(.10) + 22(-.15)]}{[27 + 42 + 17 + 22]} = \frac{42.05}{108} = .39$$

Then, from the equation for χ^2 above, we have

$$\Sigma[(N_j - 3)(z_j - \bar{z})^2] = 27(.87 - .39)^2 + 42(.48 - .39)^2 + 17(.10 - .39)^2 + 22(-.15 - .39)^2 = 14.41$$

as our χ^2 value which for $K - 1 = 3$ df is significant at $p = .0024$. The four effect sizes we compared are clearly significantly heterogeneous. Just as was the case for a set of p values, procedures are also available for computing contrasts among the obtained effect-size estimates (Rosenthal & Rubin, 1982).

COMBINING THREE OR MORE STUDIES

Significance Testing

After comparing the results of any set of three or more studies it is an easy matter also to combine the p levels of the set of studies to get an overall estimate of the probability that the set of p levels might have been obtained if the null hypothesis of no relationship between X and Y were true. Of the various methods available, we present here only the generalized version of the method presented earlier in our discussion of combining the results of two groups.

This method requires only that we obtain Z for each of our p levels, all of which should be given as one-tailed. Z's disagreeing in direction from the bulk of the findings are given negative signs. Then, the sum of the Z's divided by the square root of the number (K) of studies yields a new statistic distributed as Z. Recapping,

$$\frac{\Sigma Z_j}{\sqrt{K}} \quad \text{is distributed as } Z$$

Example 13 Studies A, B, C, and D yield one-tailed p values of .15, .05, .01, and .001, respectively. Study C, however, shows results opposite in direction from the results of the remaining studies. The four Z's associated with these four p's, then, are 1.04, 1.64, −2.33, and 3.09. From the preceding equation we have

$$\frac{\Sigma Z_j}{\sqrt{K}} = \frac{(1.04) + (1.64) + (-2.33) + (3.09)}{\sqrt{4}} = 1.72$$

as our new Z value, which has an associated p value of .043 one-tailed, or .086 two-tailed. We would normally employ the one-tailed p value if we had correctly predicted the bulk of the findings but the two-tailed p value if we had not. The combined p that we obtained in this example supports the results of the majority of the individual studies. However, even if these p values (.043 and .086) were more significant, we would want to be very cautious about drawing any simple overall conclusion because of the very great heterogeneity of the four p values we were combining. Example 11, which employed the same p values, showed that this heterogeneity was significant at $p = .0013$. It should be emphasized again, however, that this great heterogeneity of p values could be due to heterogeneity of effect sizes, heterogeneity of sample sizes, or both. To find out about the sources of heterogeneity we would have to look carefully at the effect sizes and sample sizes of each of the studies involved.

Effect-Size Estimation

When we combine the results of three or more studies we are as interested in the combined estimate of the effect size as we are in the combined probability. We follow here our earlier procedure of considering r as our effect-size estimator while recognizing that many other estimates are possible. For each of the three or more studies to be combined, we compute r and the associated Fisher z and have

$$\frac{\Sigma z}{K} = \bar{z}$$

as the Fisher $\bar{z}$ corresponding to our mean r. We use a table of Fisher z to find the r associated with our mean z. Should we want to do so, we could weight each z by its *df* (Snedecor & Cochran, 1967, 1980).

Example 14 Studies A, B, C, and D yield effect sizes of r = .70, .45, .10, and −.15, respectively. The Fisher z values corresponding to these r's are .87, .48, .10, and −.15, respectively. Then, from the preceding equation we have

$$\frac{\Sigma z}{K} = \frac{(.87) + (.48) + (.10) + (-.15)}{4} = .32$$

as our mean Fisher z. From our table of Fisher z values we find a z of .32 to correspond to an r of .31. Just as in the previous example of combined p levels, however, we would want to be very cautious in our interpretation of this combined effect size. If the r's we have just averaged were based on substantial sample sizes, as was the case in Example 12, they would be significantly heterogeneous. Therefore, averaging without special thought and comment would be inappropriate.

THE FILE DRAWER PROBLEM

Both behavioral researchers and statisticians have long suspected that the studies published in the behavioral and social sciences are a biased sample of the studies that are actually carried out (Bakan, 1967; McNemar, 1960; Smart, 1964; Sterling, 1959). The extreme view of this problem, the *file drawer problem*, is that the journals are filled with the 5 percent of the studies that show type I errors, while the file drawers back at the lab are filled with the 95 percent of the studies that show nonsignificant (e.g., p > .05) results.

In the past there was very little we could do to assess the net effect of studies tucked away in file drawers that did not make the magic .05 level (Rosenthal & Gaito, 1963, 1964). Now, however, although no definitive solution to the problem is available, we can establish reasonable boundaries on the problem and estimate the degree of damage to any research conclusion that could be done by the file drawer problem. The fundamental idea in coping with the file drawer problem is simply to calculate the number of studies averaging null results that must be in the file drawers before the overall probability of a type I error can be just brought to any desired level of significance, say p = .05. This number of filed studies, or the tolerance for future null results, is then evaluated for whether such a tolerance level is small enough to threaten the overall conclusion drawn by the reviewer. If the overall level of significance of the research review will be brought down to the level of *just significant* by the addition of just a few more null results, the finding is not resistant to the file drawer threat.

Computation

To find the number (X) of new, filed, or unretrieved studies averaging null results required to bring the new overall p to any desired level, say, just significant at $p = .05$ ($Z = 1.645$), one simply writes:

$$1.645 = k\bar{Z}_k/\sqrt{k + X}$$

where k is the number of studies combined, and $\bar{Z}_k$ is the mean Z obtained for the k studies.

Rearrangement shows that

$$X = (k/2.706)[k(\bar{Z}_k)^2 - 2.706]$$

An alternative formula that may be more convenient when the sum of the Z's (ΣZ) is given rather than the mean Z, is as follows:

$$X = [\Sigma Z)^2/2.706] - k$$

One method based on counting rather than adding Z's may be easier to compute and can be employed when exact p levels are not available; but it is probably less powerful. If X is the number of new studies required to bring the overall p to .50 (not to .05), s is the number of summarized studies significant at $p < .05$, and n is the number of summarized studies not significant at .05, then

$$X = 19s - n$$

Another conservative alternative (to be used when exact p levels are not available) is to set $Z = .00$ for any nonsignificant result and to set $Z = 1.645$ for any result significant at $p < .05$.

The equations above all assume that each of the k studies is independent of all other $k - 1$ studies, at least in the sense of employing different sampling units. There are other senses of independence, however. For example, we can think of two or more studies conducted in a given laboratory as less independent than two or more studies conducted in different laboratories. Such nonindependence can be assessed by such procedures as intraclass correlations. Whether nonindependence of this type serves to increase type I or type II errors appears to depend in part on the relative magnitude of the Z's obtained from the studies that are "correlated" or "too similar." If the correlated Z's are, on the average, as high (or higher) as the grand mean Z corrected for nonindependence, the combined Z we compute treating all studies as independent will be too large. If the correlated Z's are, on the average, clearly low relative to the grand mean Z corrected for nonindependence, the combined Z we compute treating all studies as independent will tend to be too small.

Illustration In 1969, ninety-four experiments examining the effects of interpersonal self-fulfilling prophecies, such as those discussed in Chapter 9, were summarized (Rosenthal, 1969). The mean Z of these studies was 1.014, k was 94, and Z for the studies combined was $9.83 = 94(1.014)/(94)^{1/2}$.

How many new, filed, or unretrieved studies (X) would be required to bring this very large Z down to a barely significant level ($Z = 1.645$)? From the second equation of the preceding section,

$$X = (94/2.706)[94(1.014)^2 - 2.706] = 3263$$

One finds that 3263 studies averaging null results ($\bar{Z} = .00$) must be crammed into file drawers before one would conclude that the overall results were due to sampling bias in the studies summarized by the reviewer. In a more recent summary of the same area of research (Rosenthal & Rubin, 1978) the mean Z of 345 studies was estimated to be 1.22, k was 345, and X was 65,123. Thus, over 65,000 unreported studies averaging a null result would have to exist somewhere before the overall results could reasonably be ascribed to sampling bias.

The Tolerance Table

Table 25-1 is a table of tolerance values with five convenient mean Z values heading the columns and various numbers of available studies (k) indexing the rows. The intersection of any row and column yields the number of new studies (X) required to bring the combined p for all studies, old and new together, down to the level of being just significant at $p = .05$ ($Z = 1.645$).

There is both a sobering and a cheering lesson to be learned from this table and from the equations given above. The sobering lesson is that small numbers of studies, even when their combined p is significant, if they are not *very* significant, may well be misleading. That is because only a few studies filed away could change the combined significant results to a nonsignificant one. Thus, fifteen studies averaging a Z of $+0.50$ have a combined p of .026. But if there were only six studies tucked away showing a mean Z of 0.00, the tolerance level for null results (five in this case) would be exceeded, and the significant result would become nonsignificant. Or, if there were two studies averaging a Z of $+2.00$, the combined p would be about .002. But uncovering four new studies averaging a Z of 0.00 would bring p into the "not significant" region, because four exceeded the tabled tolerance level of three shown in the tolerance table.

The cheering lesson is that when the number of studies available grows large and/or the mean directional Z grows large, the file drawer as a plausible rival hypothesis can be safely ruled out. If 300 studies are found averaging a Z of $+1.00$, it would take 32,959 + 1 studies to bring the new combined p to a nonsignificant level. That many file drawers full are simply too improbable.

At the present time no firm guidelines can be given as to what constitutes an unlikely number of unretrieved or unpublished studies. For some areas of research 100 or even 500 unpublished and unretrieved studies may be a plausible state of affairs, while for others even 10 or 20 seems unlikely. Probably any rough-and-ready guide should be based partly on k, so that as more studies are known it becomes more plausible that other studies in that area may be in those file drawers. Perhaps we could regard as robust to the file drawer

Table 25-1 Tolerances for future null results as a function of mean Z ($\bar{Z}$) and number of studies summarized (k)

k	$\bar{Z}$ +0.50	+1.00	+1.50	+2.00	+2.50
1	—	—	—	—	1
2	—	—	1	3	7
3	—	—	4	10	17
4	—	1	9	19	32
5	—	4	15	31	52
6	—	7	23	47	77
7	—	11	33	65	106
8	—	15	45	86	139
9	—	20	58	110	178
10	—	26	73	137	220
15	5	68	172	317	504
20	16	127	312	571	903
25	32	205	494	898	1,418
30	53	302	718	1,300	2,048
40	107	551	1,290	2,325	3,655
50	180	873	2,028	3,645	5,724
60	272	1,270	2,933	5,261	8,254
80	511	2,285	5,241	9,380	14,701
100	823	3,595	8,214	14,681	22,996
150	1,928	8,164	18,558	33,109	51,817
200	3,495	14,581	33,059	58,927	92,187
300	8,014	32,959	74,533	132,737	207,571
500	22,596	91,887	207,371	369,049	576,920

Note: The p values corresponding to the mean $Z(\bar{Z})$ values are .308, .159, .067, .023, and .006, respectively. Dashes in the table indicate that $X < 1$ (X is the number of new studies required to bring the combined p for all studies to the level of being just significant at $p = .05$).

problem any combined results for which the tolerance level (X) reaches $5 k + 10$. That seems a conservative but reasonable tolerance level; the $5 k$ portion suggests that it is unlikely that the file drawers have more than five times as many studies as the reviewer, and the $+10$ sets the minimum number of studies that could be filed away at 15 (when $k = 1$).

It appears that more and more reviewers of research literature will be estimating average effect sizes and combined p's of the studies they summarize. It would be very helpful to readers if for each combined p they presented, reviewers also gave the tolerance for future null results associated with their overall significance level.

TWENTY-SIX

CHI-SQUARE AND THE ANALYSIS OF TABLES

TABLE ANALYSIS AND CHI-SQUARE

There are so many data-analytic procedures useful to the student and practitioner of behavioral research that no one book can present them all in sufficient detail to be useful. In this chapter we present some material on the analysis of frequency counts cast into tabular form that we feel will be useful even though we can only be introductory in our exposition.

In previous chapters we repeatedly referred to the relationship between tests of significance and measures of effect size and size of study:

$$\frac{\text{Significance}}{\text{test}} = \frac{\text{size of}}{\text{effect}} \times \frac{\text{size of}}{\text{study}}$$

For 2×2 tables of counts, one specific form of this general relationship is:

$$\chi^2(1) = \phi^2 \times N$$

where $\chi^2(1)$ is the test statistic on $df = 1$. We determine df in any two-dimensional table of counts as (number of rows $-$ 1) $\times$ (number of columns $-$ 1). Thus, for a 2×2 table we have $(2 - 1) \times (2 - 1) = 1$ df. The term ϕ^2 (phi^2) is the squared product-moment correlation between the variable defined by the two rows and the variable defined by the two columns. As usual, N is the total number of sampling units in our study. A χ^2, therefore, is a test of significance of the effect-size estimate ϕ^2. To be consistent with our preference for product-moment correlation coefficients, rather than their squares, as effect-size estimates, we might prefer to say that Z, the standard normal deviate and the square root of $\chi^2(1)$, is a test of significance of ϕ because

$$Z = \phi \times \sqrt{N}$$

In our computation of χ^2's from 2×2 tables of counts we must keep in mind that there must be N independent sampling units, each having contributed to only one of the four cells of the 2×2 table. It would not do, for example, to have $N/2$ sampling units, each having contributed two observations to the total number of observations (N).

We also would like the frequencies expected in each cell, if the null hypothesis of no relationship were true, not to be too small. At one time it was thought that the expected frequency should not fall below 5 for any cell. Evidence now indicates, however, that very usable χ^2 values can be obtained even with expected frequencies as low as 1, as long as the total number of independent observations (N) is not too small. We know from the work of Gregory Camilli and Kenneth Hopkins (1978) that an N of 20 is large enough, but small expected frequencies may work quite well in even smaller studies. The same workers have also shown that corrections for continuity may do more harm than good. One correction for continuity, the *Yates correction*, involves reducing each occurrence of the term $O - E$ by 0.5 before employing the computational formula for $\chi^2(1)$:

$$\chi^2(1) = \sum \frac{(O - E)^2}{E}$$

where O is the observed frequency in each cell, and E is the expected frequency in that cell (see the discussion of the phi coefficient in Chapter 17).

LARGER TABLES OF COUNTS

There is a large and growing literature on the analysis of tables of counts of any size, much of it emphasizing the "log-linear model." A definitive text is that by Yvonne Bishop, Stephen Fienberg, and Paul Holland (1975), an excellent brief introduction is provided by Hays (1981), and discussions of intermediate length are available in texts by Everitt (1977), Fienberg (1977), and Upton (1978). The *log-linear model* approaches tables of counts in a manner analogous to the analysis of variance. Although we do not describe the log-linear model in this chapter, our approach to larger tables of counts is consistent with the use of log-linear contrasts and our own general preference for testing specific rather than omnibus, unfocused hypotheses. Just as in our approach to the F statistic we want the numerator df to be no greater than unity, we will want the df for our χ^2 tests to be no greater than unity. (The denominator df for F is roughly analogous to N in the case of tables of counts, and given a choice, we like *those* quantities to be large rather than small.)

Quantifying Qualitative Data

In Chapter 17 we saw how we could quantify qualitative data in the case of a 2 × 2 table.

	Democrats	Republicans	Σ
Yes	1	4	5
No	4	1	5
Σ	5	5	10

The qualitative difference Republican vs. Democrat can be quantified by assigning a 0 to one of these and a 1 to the other. If we give being a Republican a 1 and being a Democrat a 0, we have a scale of "Republicanness"; if we assign the 1 to the Democrats we have a scale of "Democraticness." Similarly, we assign a 0 or a 1 to the dependent variable of item response. If we assign a 1 to yes and a 0 to no, we have a scale of agreement with the item or "yesness"; if we reverse the numbers assigned, we have a scale of disagreement or "noness." In this example, we find a phi coefficient of .60 when Republican was coded 1 and yes was coded 1 while Democrats and no were coded 0. Suppose, however, that instead of a 2 × 2 table we had a 2 × 3 table:

		Independent variable			
		Democrats	Republicans	Others	Σ
Dependent variable	Yes	1	4	2	7
	No	4	1	2	7
	Σ	5	5	4	14

We could still "dummy code" the dependent variable of yes vs. no as before, but what shall we do with the three levels of the independent variable? Assuming that we know very little about "Others," it would make no sense to call Others .5. If we did, that would mean we had created a scale in which Others fall halfway between the anchoring ends of our scale Democrat–Republican. That might be a reasonable numerical assignment for some political group, but not for one about which we knew nothing. Instead, we would create a series of dummy variables as follows:

"Democraticness":	Democrats = 1;	Republicans = 0;	Others = 0
"Republicanness":	Republicans = 1;	Democrats = 0;	Others = 0
"Otherness":	Others = 1;	Democrats = 0;	Republicans = 0

Given the three dummy-coded independent variables, and the single dummy-coded dependent variable of "Yesness" (or agreement with the item presented), we can rewrite the data of the preceding table as shown in Table 26-1. The table of intercorrelations (phi coefficients) among the four variables in the table is:

	Agreement	"Democraticness"	"Republicanness"	"Otherness"
Agreement	—	−.45	+.45	.00
"Democraticness"		—	−.56	−.47
"Republicanness"			—	−.47
"Otherness"				—

Inspecting the correlation matrix above shows that Republicans, compared to non-Republicans (Democrats plus Others), are more likely to agree with the item (answer it *yes*). Democrats, compared to non-Democrats (Republicans plus Others), are less likely to agree; and being in the category "Other" rather

Table 26-1 Variables × respondent data matrix

	Variables			
	Dependent	Independent		
	Agreement	"Democraticness"	"Republicanness"	"Otherness"
Respondent 1	1	1	0	0
Respondent 2	1	0	1	0
Respondent 3	1	0	1	0
Respondent 4	1	0	1	0
Respondent 5	1	0	1	0
Respondent 6	1	0	0	1
Respondent 7	1	0	0	1
Respondent 8	0	1	0	0
Respondent 9	0	1	0	0
Respondent 10	0	1	0	0
Respondent 11	0	1	0	0
Respondent 12	0	0	1	0
Respondent 13	0	0	0	1
Respondent 14	0	0	0	1

than non-Other (Democrats plus Republicans) is unrelated to agreement. The three correlations among the independent variables are all fairly strongly negative, as we would expect, since the more one belongs to group A the "less" one can belong to group B or group C. In the extreme case of just two variables (e.g., Democratic vs. Republican) the intercorrelation would be -1.00, so no information would be added by using both variables.

Sometimes we can do better than dummy coding the variables. Instead, if we can order the levels of a dimension on some underlying conceptual continuum, we can create a score based on each row's or column's position on that continuum. Suppose that we had obtained the following data:

| | Improvement scores | | | |
	None	Slight	Moderate	Σ
Mildly depressed	1	2	5	8
Moderately depressed	2	5	1	8
Severely depressed	5	2	1	8
Σ	8	9	7	24

Rather than forming a series of dummy variables we could create a scaled independent variable of severity of depression such that

$$
\begin{array}{lll}
\text{Mildly depressed} & = 1 & \left(\text{or } 0\right. \quad \left(\text{or } -1\right. \\
\text{Moderately depressed} & = 2 & \left.\text{or } 1\right) \quad \left.\text{or } 0\right) \\
\text{Severely depressed} & = 3 & \left.\text{or } 2\right/ \quad \left.\text{or } +1\right/
\end{array}
$$

Similarly, we could create a scaled dependent variable of degree of improvement after therapy such that

$$
\begin{array}{lll}
\text{No improvement} & = 1 & \left(\text{or } 0\right. \quad \left(\text{or } -1\right. \\
\text{Slight improvement} & = 2 & \left.\text{or } 1\right) \quad \left.\text{or } 0\right) \\
\text{Moderate improvement} & = 3 & \left.\text{or } 2\right/ \quad \left.\text{or } +1\right/
\end{array}
$$

We could then simply compute the correlation r between degree of depression and degree of improvement. We would have one pair of scores 1, 1; two pairs of scores 1, 2; five pairs of scores 1, 3 for the first row, etc., and $r = -.52$, suggesting that more severe levels of depression are associated with lower levels of improvement. We could test the significance of that r by means of t. It would *not* do to test significance by means of the $\chi^2(4)$ test of the 3×3 table. The reason is not simply because the expected frequencies might be somewhat low for our taste. Rather it is because that overall χ^2 with $(3 - 1) \times (3 - 1) = 4$ *df* tests a different and more diffuse hypothesis, namely, that there is some type of relationship between the rows and columns, instead of the more focused hypothesis of a linear relationship tested by the *t* test for *r*.

Distributions of Chi-Square

The computation of χ^2 for a table of any size is most easily accomplished by

$$\chi^2 = \sum \frac{(O - E)^2}{E}$$

This quantity, when based on independent observations and expected frequencies not too small, tends to be distributed as chi-square on *df* = (number of rows − 1) × (number of columns − 1).

   Just as was the case for *F* (see Chapter 19), there is a different chi-square distribution for every value of *df*. Also as for *F*, all chi-square distributions begin at zero and range upward to infinity. We recall that the expected value of *t* was zero when the null hypothesis was true, and that the expected value of *F* was $df/(df - 2)$ where *df* are for the denominator mean square. For chi-square distributions the expected value, when the null hypothesis of no relationship is true, is equal to the *df* defining that chi-square distribution. Thus for χ^2 based on

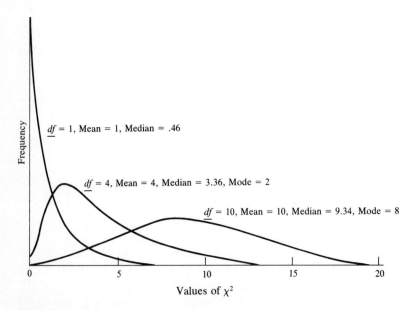

Figure 26-1 Three chi-square distributions: $df = 1$, 4, and 10.

Table 26-2 χ^2 **values required for significance at various p levels**

df	.80	.50	.30	.20	.10	.05	.02	.01	.001
					p levels				
1	.06	.46	1.07	1.64	2.71	3.84	5.41	6.64	10.83
2	.45	1.39	2.41	3.22	4.60	5.99	7.82	9.21	13.82
3	1.00	2.37	3.66	4.64	6.25	7.82	9.84	11.34	16.27
4	1.65	3.36	4.88	5.99	7.78	9.49	11.67	13.28	18.46
5	2.34	4.35	6.06	7.29	9.24	11.07	13.39	15.09	20.52
6	3.07	5.35	7.23	8.56	10.64	12.59	15.03	16.81	22.46
8	4.59	7.34	9.52	11.03	13.36	15.51	18.17	20.09	26.12
10	6.18	9.34	11.78	13.44	15.99	18.31	21.16	23.21	29.59
15	10.31	14.34	17.32	19.31	22.31	25.00	28.26	30.58	37.70
20	14.58	19.34	22.78	25.04	28.41	31.41	35.02	37.57	45.32
25	18.94	24.34	28.17	30.68	34.38	37.65	41.57	44.31	52.62
30	23.36	29.34	33.53	36.25	40.26	43.77	47.96	50.89	59.70

Note: For $df > 30$ the p value for any χ^2 can be estimated by first finding the standard normal deviate, Z, associated with that p, e.g., a Z of 1.96 is associated with a p of .05 (two-tailed). We find Z from:

$$Z = \sqrt{2\chi^2} - \sqrt{2df - 1}$$

1, 4, or 10 df, the average value of the χ^2 obtained if the null hypothesis were true would be 1, 4, and 10, respectively. The median of a given distribution tends to be just less than the mean (df), and the mode for chi-square distributions of $df = 2$ or more is $df - 2$.

Just as was the case for F, values of χ^2 further and further into the right-hand tail are less and less likely if the null hypothesis were true and are used as evidence to suggest that the null hypothesis is probably false. Although in data-analytic work we use tables of χ^2 rather than pictured distributions, it is instructive to see some examples of χ^2 distributions, as in Figure 26-1 (after Lindquist, 1953).

Comparison of the three distributions in the figure shows that they move to the right with increases in df, and they tend to greater symmetry as well. Table 26-2 illustrates the differences in various chi-square distributions by giving the areas found to the right of the tabled values. Thus for 1 df the table shows that a χ^2 value of 3.84 or greater is found only .05 of the time if the null hypothesis of no relationship is true. A value of 10.83 or greater is found only .001 of the time.

AN ILLUSTRATION

For our illustration of the analysis of a table larger than 2 × 2, we present the results of a 3 × 3 study (Gilbert, McPeek, & Mosteller, 1977). In this study a set of fifty-three investigations was categorized into three levels of experimental control achieved by the investigators while simultaneously being categorized into three levels of enthusiasm shown by the investigators for their newly tested medical treatments. The results were as follows:

| | Degree of enthusiasm | | | |
Degree of control	High	Medium	Low	Σ
High	0	3	3	6
Medium	10	3	2	15
Low	24	7	1	32
Σ	34	13	6	53

As a preliminary step, and to illustrate the computation, we begin by applying the general formula for χ^2

$$\chi^2 = \sum \frac{(O - E)^2}{E}$$

The table above gives us our O's (observed values) and the table below our E's (expected values). If the null hypothesis of no relationship between the rows and columns were true, we would expect the O's and E's to be equal. That is, we would find the observed entry for each cell to be the product of the row total of the row to which the cell belongs and the column total of the column to which the cell belongs divided by the total number of observations, N. This, of course, is the formula for computing the expected frequencies, that is,

$$E = \frac{\text{row total} \times \text{column total}}{N}$$

In this case, the expected frequencies are as follows:

| | Degree of enthusiasm | | | |
Degree of control	High	Medium	Low	Σ
High	3.85	1.47	0.68	6.00
Medium	9.62	3.68	1.70	15.00
Low	20.53	7.85	3.62	32.00
Σ	34.00	13.00	6.00	53.00

Note that the row and column totals are identical in the two tables. To compute χ^2 we use only the cell data as follows:

$$\chi^2(4) = \sum \frac{(O - E)^2}{E} = \frac{(0 - 3.85)^2}{3.85} + \frac{(3 - 1.47)^2}{1.47} + \frac{(3 - 0.68)^2}{0.68}$$

$$+ \frac{(10 - 9.62)^2}{9.62} + \frac{(3 - 3.68)^2}{3.68} + \frac{(2 - 1.70)^2}{1.70}$$

$$+ \frac{(24 - 20.53)^2}{20.53} + \frac{(7 - 7.85)^2}{7.85} + \frac{(1 - 3.62)^2}{3.62} = 16.13,$$

$$p = .0028.$$

A result this large or larger (occurring only .0028 of the time in repeated samplings if the null hypothesis of no relationship between the variables of experimental control and enthusiasm of the investigator were true) unfortunately tells us only that there is likely to be some sort of relationship, but it says nothing about what type of relationship there might be. This is analogous to the situation of an overall diffuse F test with more than one df in the numerator in which we must look at the condition means to see what the results actually show. More satisfactory approaches to the analysis of larger tables of counts are available than settling for unfocused, omnibus χ^2 tests of $df > 1$.

THE ANALYSIS OF VARIANCE OF QUALITATIVE DATA

Our alternative to the χ^2 test of qualitative data involves the application of the analysis of variance. In this approach, suggested by William Cochran (1950), we begin by quantifying the qualitative data as shown earlier in this chapter. If the various rows or columns representing the dependent variable can be scaled or ordered, as in our earlier example of three levels of improvement (scored 1, 2, or 3), then each subject or other sampling unit can be assigned one of several numbers to serve as the dependent variable scores. Even if such scaling is not possible, we can still create a number of dependent variables, each one dummy coded (0 or 1). Once we have scaled or dummy-coded (a special case of scaling) a score for each subject, we compute the analysis of variance in the usual way. However, now the subjects' scores will be only 0 or 1; 1, 2, or 3; or some other (usually small) set of possible values.

Except for very small studies (say $df < 20$), and for very extreme splits of 0 vs. 1 data,* the F tests obtained from the analysis of variance give quite accurate results (Edward, 1972; Hsu & Feldt, 1969; Lunney, 1970; Snedecor & Cochran, 1967, 1980; Winer, 1971). Indeed, Cochran (1950) has suggested that such results based on F might, under some conditions, be more accurate than

---

* We might regard as an extreme split one in which 90 percent of the observations were of one type (0 or 1) and 10 percent were of the other type.

those based on χ^2. Ralph D'Agostino (1971; following Snedecor & Cochran, 1967) has shown that for even fairly extreme splits, transformations (e.g., arcsin, logit) can be employed to make the analysis of variance still work well.

An Illustration

We illustrate the use of the analysis of variance employing the same data we employed in the preceding example of χ^2 (Gilbert, McPeek, & Mosteller, 1977). In this example we can do better than dichotomize the dependent variable of degree of enthusiasm. We can assign the scores 1, 2, and 3 to the categories low, medium, and high levels of enthusiasm, respectively. We can now write the scores for each of the three levels of the independent variable of degree of experimental control as follows:

Degree of control	Listing of scores
(6 observations) high	2 2 2 1 1 1
(15 observations) medium	3 3 3 3 3 3 3 3 3 3 2 2 2 1 1
(32 observations) low	3 3 3 3 3 3 3 3 3 3 3 3 3 3 3 3 3 3 3 3 3 3 3 3 2 2 2 2 2 2 2 1

The analysis of variance of these data is summarized as follows:

Source	SS	df	MS	F	eta	p
			Table of variance			
Between conditions	7.505	2	3.753	10.60	.55	.00015
Within conditions	17.702	50	0.354			

We note that the omnibus F is more significant than the omnibus χ^2 (.00015 vs. .0028). We might have expected this if we felt that degree of enthusiasm would be affected by degree of control, since the scores employed in the analysis of variance were able to use the information that $3 > 2 > 1$. The χ^2 result would not have been any different even if our levels of enthusiasm (columns) had been interchanged. Although our F has used more information than our χ^2 it is still somewhat diffuse or omnibus ($df = 2$ for numerator rather than 1), though less diffuse or unfocused than the χ^2 ($df = 4$). What does the analysis of variance show us? The means of the three conditions were as follows.

Degree of control	Condition means
High	1.50
Medium	2.53
Low	2.72

These means indicate that studies showing a higher degree of control elicited less enthusiasm from their investigators than did studies showing a lower degree of control. The p value for that statement, however, has not been determined. Our omnibus F test tells only that the means differ somehow. Had we planned the appropriate comparison we might simply have computed the t test between the high and low degree of control conditions but employing the MS error from the overall analysis of variance as shown:

$$t(50) = \frac{M_1 - M_2}{\sqrt{\left(\frac{1}{n_1} + \frac{1}{n_2}\right) MS \text{ error}}} = \frac{2.72 - 1.50}{\sqrt{\left(\frac{1}{32} + \frac{1}{6}\right)} 0.354} = 4.61,$$

$$p = .000028, \text{ two-tailed}, r = .61.$$

A conceptually similar test could be made employing a linear contrast on the means of the three groups (Chapter 23 gives computational details). For these data the contrast $F(1,50) = 23.84$, $t = \sqrt{F} = 4.88$, $p = .000011$, two-tailed, $r = .57$. This contrast, based on an unweighted means analysis of variance, agrees well with the results of the ordinary (weighted means) t test with r's of .57 and .61, respectively. (Actually, both these r's are more accurately given as negative, since higher scores on the independent variable are associated with lower scores on the dependent variable.)

A third and quite direct estimate of the size of the relationship between degree of experimental control and degree of investigator enthusiasm is available. Since we can scale the independent variable of degree of experimental control (high = 3, medium = 2, low = 1), we can simply correlate for the fifty-three investigators their degree of enthusiasm scored 1, 2, or 3 with the degree of experimental control scored 1, 2, or 3. This correlation was $r(51) = -.49$, $t(51) = 3.97$, $p = .00023$, two-tailed, a result in fairly good agreement with those obtained by our two alternative methods, the t on the extreme groups omitting the intermediate condition and the linear contrast following the unweighted means analysis of variance.

TESTING SPECIFIC HYPOTHESES BY SUBDIVIDING LARGER TABLES

By employing the analysis of variance approach to tables of counts, we were able to apply familiar methods (t tests, contrasts, and correlations) to the investigation of specific hypotheses rather than having to settle for an overall unfocused, diffuse χ^2. Methods are available for computing contrasts in the log-linear models, but we will not discuss those here. For a detailed discussion see *Discrete Multivariate Analysis* (Bishop, Fienberg, & Holland, 1975). Here we shall describe only some simple, useful methods for subdividing tables of counts into one or more 2 × 2 tables each of which is based on only a single *df*. That is, each table addresses only a single question. Although these are not contrasts in the technical sense, they are very much in the spirit of contrasts.

The Chi-Square Corner Cells Test

When the data in both the rows and columns can be arranged in some meaningful order from more to less of that variable, a very simple $\chi^2(1)$ test can be performed on the four corner cells of the contingency table. Because this test does not use as much of the information as does the analysis of variance with contrasts, we recommend it only as a quick preliminary test. A good example is our illustration of degree of experimental control and degree of enthusiasm. The table of counts was:

	Degree of enthusiasm		
Degree of control	High	Medium	Low
High	0	3	3
Medium	10	3	2
Low	24	7	1

Because both the rows and columns are arranged in order of magnitude, (high, medium, low), our corner cells test is applicable. The corners are:

	High	Low	Σ
High	0	3	3
Low	24	1	25
Σ	24	4	28

The expected frequencies computed from the marginals of the 2×2 table above are:

	High	Low	Σ
High	2.57	0.43	3.00
Low	21.43	3.57	25.00
Σ	24.00	4.00	28.00

The resulting $\chi^2(1)$ is 20.16, $p = .000007$, phi $= .85$. The size of the effect is, of course, "inflated" by our having compared extreme groups rather than having used all, or nearly all, of the scores. There is nothing wrong with this, since good research design often involves choosing extreme groups. However, it is important to keep in mind that the large χ^2 and phi are due in part to our having chosen extreme groups on both the independent and dependent variable. There is another issue to be addressed for this χ^2; the expected frequency of 0.43 is probably too small for comfort. One way to get an "independent opinion" about the correct significance level is to compute the *Fisher exact probability test* (Siegel, 1956).

The Fisher Exact Probability Test

A detailed discussion is available in Siegel (1956) and a briefer one in Hays (1981). Still more briefly, we find Fisher's exact test useful when we have a 2 × 2 table of independent observations, as in a 2 × 2 χ^2 type situation but when expected frequencies are very low. The test gives the one-tailed p that a particular table of counts or one reflecting a still stronger relationship between the two variables could have occurred if the null hypothesis of no relationship between the two variables were true and if the row and column totals were viewed as fixed. With cells labeled as:

		Score		
		High	Low	
Group	High	A	B	(A + B)
	Low	C	D	(C + D)
		(A + C)	(B + D)	N

we find p for any one outcome (i.e., our obtained outcome, or one more extremely disconfirming of the null hypothesis of no relationship between the two variables) from the following relationship:

$$p = \frac{(A + B)!(C + D)!(A + C)!(B + D)!}{N!A!B!C!D!}$$

In using the Fisher exact test we compute p for our obtained table *and for each possible table showing a more extreme outcome than the one we obtained*. The p we want as a test of our hypothesis of no relationship is the sum of these p's.

The data for which we were seeking a second opinion were:

		Enthusiasm		
		High	Low	Σ
Degree	High	0	3	3
of control	Low	24	1	25
	Σ	24	4	28

In this case our result is the most extreme one (the most inconsistent with the null hypothesis of no relationship between the variables) we could obtain given our row and column totals. Therefore, we will need to obtain only a single p for our test. (When one of the cell entries is zero we cannot have a more extreme result given fixed marginal totals.) For the table above we find

$$p = \frac{3!25!24!4!}{28!0!3!24!1!} = .0012$$

We interpret this to mean that there was only a 12 in 10,000 chance of obtaining cell entries as extreme as this if there were no relationship between the independent and dependent variables and given the row and column totals for our data. (Computing p was burdensome before the advent of inexpensive hand-held calculators, because factorials are unpleasant to compute by hand; e.g., $10! = 1 \times 2 \times 3 \times 4 \times 5 \times 6 \times 7 \times 8 \times 9 \times 10 = 3,628,800$; recall too that $0! = 1$. Siegel [1956] provides useful tables for the Fisher exact test, but it is preferable to compute the actual p rather than to use only critical values of p.)

Our Fisher exact probability result of .0012, while quite significant, is not nearly so significant as the p based on our chi-square corner cells test. That difference appears to be primarily due to the unusually small expected frequency (0.43) in cell B of our χ^2 test.

What about an effect-size estimate? A serviceable approximation is obtained by finding the standard normal deviate Z that corresponds to our obtained p. Squaring Z and dividing by N gives us an estimate of the effect size analogous to that obtained by $\chi^2(1)/N = \phi^2$. Because we prefer the unsquared effect-size estimate, we employ

$$\phi \text{ estimated} = \sqrt{\frac{Z^2}{N}}$$

$$\text{since } \phi = \sqrt{\frac{\chi^2(1)}{N}}$$

$$\text{and } \chi^2(1) = Z^2$$

For our data, p was .0012; so Z was 3.04 and

$$\phi \text{ estimated} = \sqrt{\frac{(3.04)^2}{28}} = .57$$

an effect-size estimate which, though quite substantial, is much smaller than the ϕ of .85 obtained from our $\chi^2(1)$ test. That effect size [as well as the $\chi^2(1)$] was inflated primarily by the small expected frequency in cell B. The ϕ estimated at .57 agrees very well with the r's obtained earlier when we compared the high and low degree of control conditions following the analysis of variance. The r based on the unweighted means contrast was .57, that for the t test (weighted means) was .61.

In our example, the four cell entries were the most extreme that could have occurred as evidence against the hypothesis of no relationship between the variables given the four marginal totals. Earlier we noted that if the outcome obtained is not the most extreme possible we must compute p for our result *and for every outcome more extreme*. The p we employ then is the sum of the p's obtained from all of our tables, i.e., our own data-outcome p plus the p's of all outcomes more extreme. For example, suppose we had obtained these results:

	High	Low	Σ
High	1	2	3
Low	23	2	25
Σ	24	4	28

then $p = \dfrac{3!25!24!4!}{28!1!2!23!2!} = .044.$

The p of .044 is the p of this particular result, but the p we want is the p of our result and any more extreme. Therefore, we must also compute p for the more extreme result. In this case the only more extreme result possible is the one we really did obtain with $p = .0012.$* Now we add our p to those more extreme to get the value we need.

$$p = .044 + .0012 = .045$$

Note that the margins remain the same for the computation of each p. Only the cell counts change.

Before leaving this section of the Fisher exact test as a procedure for getting a second opinion on a χ^2 test, it will be useful to comment briefly on both these tests as examples of *nonparametric* statistical procedures. Nonparametric procedures are those in which it is less important to know the shape of the population distribution from which the research samples were drawn (Snedecor & Cochran, 1980). We know that t tests and F tests depend on the assumption of normal distributions, though both are fairly effective even when that assumption is not met. It is widely believed that χ^2 tests are nonparametric in the sense that no assumption about the population distribution is made. Cochran (1950), however, has pointed out that χ^2 tests may depend as much as do F tests on the assumption of normality, so χ^2 tests may not be so nonparametric after all. The Fisher exact test is far more truly nonparametric.

In this book generally we have not tried to cover nonparametric procedures, because data transformations often make the more flexible and powerful

---

* One approach to finding all outcomes more extreme than a given outcome is to reduce by one the smallest cell frequency, a procedure which increases by one the two adjacent frequencies and decreases by one the diagonally opposite frequency. We continue this procedure until one of our cell frequencies is zero.

"parametric" procedures work about as well as do the nonparametric procedures.

Combined Category Chi-Square Test

We employed the Fisher exact test to get a second opinion when our expected frequencies became very small, as they sometimes do in the corner cells test. Another way to get a second opinion is to combine adjacent rows or columns that have been meaningfully arranged from higher to lower levels of the variables that are defined by the rows and columns. Our corner cells test involved the four corners of the original data table:

	Degree of enthusiasm			
Degree of control	High	Medium	Low	Σ
High	0	3	3	6
Medium	10	3	2	15
Low	24	7	1	32
Σ	34	13	6	53

The expected frequencies for the four corner cells were

	High	Low
High	2.57	0.43
Low	21.43	3.57

where the upper-right corner, cell B, showed the very low expected frequency. Therefore, cell B is most in need of having its expected frequency increased. There are two ways to increase that expected frequency by combining categories: we can recruit (1) the row or (2) the column adjacent to cell B (or any other cell in need of augmented expected frequency). Recruiting the adjacent row yields the following tables of obtained and expected frequencies:

	Obtained frequencies				Expected frequencies		
	High	Low	Σ		High	Low	Σ
High	10	5	15	High	12.75	2.25	15.00
Low	24	1	25	Low	21.25	3.75	25.00
Σ	34	6	40	Σ	34.00	6.00	40.00

Recruiting the adjacent column yields the following tables of obtained and expected frequencies:

	Obtained frequencies				Expected frequencies		
	High	Low	Σ		High	Low	Σ
High	0	6	6	High	3.79	2.21	6.00
Low	24	8	32	Low	20.21	11.79	32.00
Σ	24	14	38	Σ	24.00	14.00	38.00

For the present example, recruiting the adjacent row yielded $\chi^2(1) = 6.32$, $p = .012$, phi $= .40$. Recruiting the adjacent column yielded $\chi^2(1) = 12.21$, $p = .0005$, phi $= .57$. It goes without saying that one does not compute both $\chi^2(1)$'s and present only the results of the more "favorable" $\chi^2(1)$. We either present both $\chi^2(1)$'s, p's, and phi's or we adopt a set of rules beforehand telling us which $\chi^2(1)$ to compute. For example, rule 1 might be: we choose the table of which the smallest expected frequency is 5 or greater. If both tables (or neither table) give an expected frequency of 5 or greater, we go to rule 2, which might be that we choose the table with the more nearly equal (in percentage of total N) column totals on the grounds that binomial data are better behaved when the splits are closer to 50–50.

Another rule, rule 3, if it were needed, might be that we choose the table with the more nearly equal (in percentage of total N) row totals, on the grounds that more nearly equal-sized groups generally yield more powerful tests of significance. Note that in our terminology we have used columns to refer to the dependent variable and rows to refer to the independent variable. If we choose to set up our table differently, the rows and columns of rules 2 and 3 above become the columns and rows, respectively.

If we had applied our rules to the present situation, rule 1 would not have helped, since neither the recruitment of rows nor the recruitment of columns led to the smallest expected frequency reaching or exceeding 5. Rule 2, however, would have led us to choose the column recruitment method, since it yielded a column split of $.63 - .37$, whereas the row recruitment method yielded a column split of $.85 - .15$. In this example the column recruitment method yielded a phi of $.57$, a value that agreed well with the correlations obtained by the various other procedures described earlier.

Sometimes it happens that neither the recruitment of rows nor the recruitment of columns helps much to increase the expected frequency of the cell with the smallest expected frequency. In that case we simply continue to recruit columns or rows until we have achieved a satisfactory expected frequency.

COMPLETE PARTITIONING OF LARGER TABLES

The chapter on contrasts (Chapter 23) shows that for any diffuse, overall F test with k df in the numerator we can compute a set of k orthogonal contrasts each of which addresses a focused, precise question. In an analogous way we can take a table of counts larger than 2×2 with $df =$ (number of rows $-$ 1) $\times$ (number of columns $-$ 1) $= k$ and subdivide or partition it into a set of k 2×2 tables that address focused, precise questions. A summary of procedures for partitioning, and a general method for computing $\chi^2(1)$ for any of the resulting 2×2 tables, is presented by Jean Bresnahan and Martin Shapiro (1966).

One procedure for the complete partitioning of a table is to begin in, e.g., the upper-left corner cell, so that for the top row the two new cells will contain the frequency of the upper-left cell and the remainder of the frequencies in that row, respectively. For the bottom row the two new cells will contain the frequency of the first column minus the frequency of the top-left cell and the balance of all frequencies not in either the top row or the leftmost column, respectively. We illustrate with the data of our example of degree of enthusiasm as a function of degree of experimental control:

	Enthusiasm			
Control	High	Medium	Low	Σ
High	0	3	3	6
Medium	10	3	2	15
Low	24	7	1	32
Σ	34	13	6	53

The midmost vertical and horizontal lines show where we made the partitions of the overall table to yield *subtable 1*.

	High	Lower	Σ
High	0	6	6
Lower	34	13	47
Σ	34	19	53

We obtain *subtable 2* by omitting the first column completely and repeating the procedure shown for the remainder of the table.

	Medium	Low	Σ
High	3	3	6
Medium	3	2	5
Low	7	1	8
Σ	13	6	19

The midmost vertical and horizontal lines show where we made the partitions of the remainder table to yield *subtable 2*.

	Medium	Low	Σ
High	3	3	6
Lower	10	3	13
Σ	13	6	19

We have now run out of columns to drop, so we begin to drop rows. We return to our original table and drop the top row, leaving as our remainder table:

	High	Medium	Low	Σ
Medium	10	3	2	15
Low	24	7	1	32
Σ	34	10	3	47

The midmost vertical and horizontal lines show where we made the partitions of the remainder table to yield *subtable 3*.

	High	Lower	Σ
Medium	10	5	15
Lower	24	8	32
Σ	34	13	47

We have now run out of rows to drop, but we can return to dropping columns, i.e., the first column of the remainder table just above, leaving us the remainder table below, which turns out also to be the final subtable, *subtable 4*.

	Medium	Low	Σ
Medium	3	2	5
Low	7	1	8
Σ	10	3	13

Computing $\chi^2(1)$'s for Partitioned Tables

The general formula for computing $\chi^2(1)$'s for each table is

$$\chi^2(1) \text{ partitioned} = \text{``}\chi^2\text{'' cells} - \text{``}\chi^2\text{'' rows} - \text{``}\chi^2\text{'' columns} + \text{``}\chi^2\text{'' total}$$

$$\text{where ``}\chi^2\text{'' cells} = \sum^4 \frac{(O_c - E_c)^2}{E_c}$$

the sum (over the 4 cells of the subtable) of the standard χ^2 quantity $(O - E)^2/E$ but where the expected frequencies have been computed not from the subtable but from the *full table;*

$$\text{where ``}\chi^2\text{'' rows} = \sum^2 \frac{(O_r - E_r)^2}{E_r}$$

the sum (over the two row totals of the subtable) of the standard χ^2 quantity $(O - E)^2/E$. Here, the observed row total is based on the subtable, but the expected row total is obtained from the full table-derived expected frequencies found in the subtable;

$$\text{where ``}\chi^2\text{'' columns} = \sum^2 \frac{(O_k - E_k)^2}{E_k}$$

defined as for rows above, and

$$\text{where ``}\chi^2\text{'' total} = \frac{(O_t - E_t)^2}{E_t}$$

the squared difference between the observed and expected total (N) for the subtable.

To illustrate the computations we begin with the expected frequencies of the original table:

	Enthusiasm			
Control	High	Medium	Low	Σ
High	3.85	1.47	0.68	6.00
Medium	9.62	3.68	1.70	15.00
Low	20.53	7.85	3.62	32.00
Σ	34.00	13.00	6.00	53.00

Table 26-3 Subtables of observed (and expected) frequencies

	Observed frequencies			Expected frequencies		
Subtable 1						
	0	6	6	3.85	2.15	6.00
	34	13	47	30.15	16.85	47.00
	34	19	53	34.00	19.00	53.00
Subtable 2						
	3	3	6	1.47	0.68	2.15
	10	3	13	11.53	5.32	16.85
	13	6	19	13.00	6.00	19.00
Subtable 3						
	10	5	15	9.62	5.38	15.00
	24	8	32	20.53	11.47	32.00
	34	13	47	30.15	16.85	47.00
Subtable 4						
	3	2	5	3.68	1.70	5.38
	7	1	8	7.85	3.62	11.47
	10	3	13	11.53	5.32	16.85

Next we display our four subtables each with its corresponding table of expected frequencies. These are based *not* on the subtable, but on the full table.

Finally we display the results of each step of our computation in a table designed to provide computational checks (see Table 26-4).

Table 26-4 Results of computations of partitioned $\chi^2(1)$'s

	Partitioned $\chi^2(1)$ =	"χ^2" cells −	"χ^2" rows −	"χ^2" columns +	"χ^2" total
Subtable 1	12.12	= 12.12	− 0	− 0	+ 0
Subtable 2	2.95	= 10.72	− 7.77	− 0	+ 0
Subtable 3	0.31	= 1.68	− 0	− 1.37	+ 0
Subtable 4	0.76	= 2.17	− 1.08	− 1.21	+ 0.88
Σ	16.14	= 26.69	− 8.85	− 2.58	+ 0.88

We illustrate the computational details only for subtable 4 of Table 26-3.

$$\text{``}\chi^2\text{'' cells} = \frac{(3 - 3.68)^2}{3.68} + \frac{(2 - 1.70)^2}{1.70} + \frac{(7 - 7.85)^2}{7.85} + \frac{(1 - 3.62)^2}{3.62} = 2.17$$

$$\text{``}\chi^2\text{'' rows} = \frac{(5 - 5.38)^2}{5.38} + \frac{(8 - 11.47)^2}{11.47} = 1.08$$

$$\text{``}\chi^2\text{'' columns} = \frac{(10 - 11.53)^2}{11.53} + \frac{(3 - 5.32)^2}{5.32} = 1.21$$

$$\text{``}\chi^2\text{'' total} = \frac{(13 - 16.85)^2}{16.85} = 0.88$$

The sum of the four partitioned $\chi^2(1)$'s is identical (within rounding error) to the overall $\chi^2(4)$ based on the original 3×3 table of frequencies. Now we can see which of the components of the overall χ^2 made the greatest contribution to the overall χ^2. This contribution is based in part on the strength of the correlation ϕ found in each table and partly on the N for each table. Therefore, as usual, we want to compare phi's as much as we want to compare $\chi^2(1)$'s, as in the summary table below:

Subtable	$\chi^2(1)$	p	phi
1	12.12	.0005	.48
2	2.95	.09	.39
3	0.31	.58	.08
4	0.76	.38	.24

Subtable 1 showed both the largest and the most significant result. That subtable presented data showing higher levels of enthusiasm to be associated with lower levels of experimental control.

Subtable 2, while not significant at .05, showed nearly as large an effect as subtable 1; but the interpretation of the result should be cautious. Examining the expected frequencies for subtable 2 shows that most of the "χ^2" cells is due to the upper-right cell with expected frequency of only 0.68. Consequently, we may not want to put too much confidence in the result of subtable 2. Subtables 3 and 4 appear to require little comment.

A further word of caution is required. When interpreting the individual 2×2 $\chi^2(1)$ results, there is a tendency to look only at the observed frequencies. Accurate interpretation of the computed χ^2's, however, requires that we examine the observed frequencies *in relation to the expected frequencies*.

The particular partitioning of the overall 3×3 table is not unique. Just as there are many sets of k orthogonal contrasts that can be computed for an F of k df in the numerator, so there are many alternative sets of k 2×2 tables that can be computed for a χ^2 with k df. For example, instead of beginning with the upper-left cell of the full table we could have followed the exactly analogous procedure beginning with some other corner. When we begin with the lower-left cell we obtain the four sets of observed and expected frequencies, $\chi^2(1)$'s, p's, and phi's, shown in Table 26-5.

Each of the four subtables in Table 26-5 supports the same hypothesis that greater levels of enthusiasm are associated with lower levels of experimental control; but the size of the effect and its level of significance vary.

Just because it is possible completely to partition a table of frequencies is no reason to do so. It is a useful exploratory data-analytic procedure and is quite valuable as a source of hypotheses for further investigation. Typically, however, we would approach the 2×2 $\chi^2(1)$ tests in the same spirit as we approach contrasts following an analysis of variance. We compute the $df = 1$ tests that we planned to make—those that address the questions of interest to us.

The Corner Cells Test Subtable

When the data are ordered from more to less in both the rows and columns (as was the case for the example we have been using), it is natural to employ the

Table 26-5 Analyses of four subtables

	Observed frequencies		Expected frequencies		χ^2	p	ϕ
Subtable 1							
	10	11	13.47	7.53	4.13	.042	.28
	24	8	20.53	11.47			
Subtable 2							
	6	5	5.15	2.38	2.36	.12	.35
	7	1	7.85	3.62			
Subtable 3							
	0	6	3.85	2.15	8.29	.004	.63
	10	5	9.62	5.38			
Subtable 4							
	3	3	1.47	0.68	1.34	.25	.35
	3	2	3.68	1.70			

corner cells test we described earlier. The modification we make here is based on the idea of partitioning a table completely. It involves our using the expected frequencies computed from the full table, not just from the corner cells alone. Our computations are just as for any of the subtables of a partitioned table where

Partitioned $\chi^2(1)$ = "χ^2" cells − "χ^2" rows − "χ^2" columns + "χ^2" total

For the corner cells test of our example

	Obtained frequency				Expected frequency		
	High	Low	Σ		High	Low	Σ
High	0	3	3	High	3.85	0.68	4.53
Low	24	1	25	Low	20.53	3.62	24.15
Σ	24	4	28	Σ	24.38	4.30	28.68

$$\chi^2(1) = 14.25 - 0.55 - 0.03 + 0.02 = 13.69,$$
$$p = .00011, \phi = .70$$

This corner cells test with expected frequencies based on the entire table yielded a somewhat more conservative value of χ^2 and of ϕ compared to the original corner cells test with expected frequencies based only on the data from the four corner cells. That $\chi^2(1)$ had been 20.16, $\phi = .85$, probably inflated by an unusually low expected frequency of 0.43 in one of the cells.

Contrasts in Proportions

Throughout our discussion of the subdividing of larger tables we have emphasized the conceptual relationship between the study of contrasts following the analysis of variance and the study of 2×2 tables following the analysis of larger tables. It sometimes happens for larger tables that one dimension can be ordered from more to less, and that information from the other dimension can be expressed as a proportion of the total frequency found in each level of the ordered dimension. In situations of that sort, contrasts can be computed directly, and we illustrate this method for the example we have been following.

		Enthusiasm			
Control		High	Medium	Low	Σ
A {	High	0	3	3	6
	Medium	10	3	2	15
B	Low	24	7	1	32
$N = (A + B) \Sigma$		34	13	6	53

Because it leads to a more nearly 50 : 50 split we designate the bottom row rather than the top row as B; the two top rows together are designated A. For each of our three columns, we will also want the quantities $P = B/N$; $S_p^2 = P(1 - P)/N$, the squared standard error of the proportion; and λ, the contrast weights. From these ingredients we can compute a Z test of significance of the contrast by means of a formula suggested by Donald B. Rubin (1981).

	High	Medium	Low
$P = B/N$	.71	.54	.17
$S_p^2 = \dfrac{P(1 - P)}{N}$	.0061	.0191	.0232
λ	+1	0	−1

Since $Z = \dfrac{\Sigma P\lambda}{\sqrt{\Sigma S_p^2 \lambda^2}}$

$$Z = \frac{.71(+1) + .54(0) + 17(-1)}{\sqrt{.0061(1) + .0191(0) + .0232(1)}} = \frac{.54}{\sqrt{.0293}} = 3.15$$

$p = .0016$, two-tailed, $Z^2 = \chi^2(1) = 9.92$, $\phi = .43$.

This result is somewhat more conservative than those of the various alternative analyses, e.g., the contrasts following the analysis of variance. The reason appears to be the loss of information involved in treating the top two rows of our data table as though they were homogeneous. Actually, those two rows provide additional evidence in support of the relationship between degree of experimental control and level of enthusiasm. We can demonstrate this by repeating our contrast in the proportions of just the top two rows.

		High	Medium	Low	Σ
A	High	0	3	3	6
B	Medium	10	3	2	15
N	Σ	10	6	5	21
P		1.0000	0.5000	0.4000	
S_p^2		0	.0417	.0480	
λ		+1	0	−1	

$$Z = \frac{1.0(+1) + .5(0) + .4(-1)}{\sqrt{0(1) + .0417(0) + .0480(1)}} = \frac{.60}{\sqrt{.0480}} = 2.74$$

$p = .0062$, two-tailed, $Z^2 = \chi^2(1) = 7.51$, $\phi = .60$.

Therefore, the data in the top two rows alone provide additional strong support for the relationship between degree of control and level of enthusiasm.

An alternative procedure we might have employed would have performed the contrast in the proportions omitting the medium level of degree of experimental control. That would have yielded a Z of 3.46, $p = .00054$, $\phi = .56$, a value in good agreement with those obtained following the analysis of variance. The r based on the unweighted means contrast had been .57, that for the t test (weighted means) had been .61.

STANDARDIZING ROW AND COLUMN TOTALS

As tables of counts grow very large it becomes almost impossible to determine by inspection just what is going on in the data. A major problem is that our eye is likely to be attracted to very large values. For example, in the following table, what stands out?

24	10	6
36	15	9
48	20	12
132	55	33

We are most likely to see the 132 as a standout cell. Actually, however, that value is just what we would expect if the null hypothesis of no relationship between the variables were true. It is a large value only because it falls in a large row and a large column. We could do better than inspecting the raw counts by making a table of partial χ^2 values, i.e., computing $(O - E)^2/E$ for each cell. At least that would tell us where the bulk of the χ^2 value is coming from. However, what shall we do about very small expected frequencies that yield perhaps exaggeratedly large values of partial χ^2?

Computing $(O - E)^2/E$ for each cell is one way of taking the size of the row and column into account. A very valuable alternative has been described by Frederick Mosteller (1968), who shows us how to take the size of the row and column totals into account. The method has been called *standardizing the margins,* and it proceeds by setting all row totals equal to each other and all column totals equal to each other. We illustrate the method with our continuing example.

		Enthusiasm		
Control	High	Medium	Low	Σ
High	0	3	3	6
Medium	10	3	2	15
Low	24	7	1	32
Σ	34	13	6	53

An example We begin by dividing each cell count by the sum of the column in which we find the count.

	High	Medium	Low	Σ
High	.00	.23	.50	.73
Medium	.29	.23	.33	.85
Low	.71	.54	.17	1.42
Σ	1.00	1.00	1.00	3.00

This first step has equalized (standardized to 1.00 in this case) the column totals, but the row totals are far from equal. To set them equal we now divide each entry of this new table by its row total, yielding:

	High	Medium	Low	Σ
High	.00	.32	.68	1.00
Medium	.34	.27	.39	1.00
Low	.50	.38	.12	1.00
Σ	.84	.97	1.19	3.00

For simplicity we are presenting only two decimal places, but it is usually wise to employ three or four decimal places while calculating. We now continue the process of dividing the counts of each new table by the column totals, which unequalizes the row totals. We then divide the counts of the following table by the row totals, and so on until the row totals are all equal and the column totals are all equal. The individual row totals will not equal the individual column totals except in cases where the number of rows and columns are equal. We continue the process of dividing by column totals, then by row totals. The tables on the right always follow the table immediately to their left.

	Dividing by column totals				Dividing by row totals			
	High	Medium	Low	Σ	High	Medium	Low	Σ
High	.00	.33	.58	0.91	.00	.36	.64	1.00
Medium	.41	.28	.32	1.01	.40	.28	.32	1.00
Low	.59	.39	.10	1.08	.55	.36	.09	1.00
Σ	1.00	1.00	1.00	3.00	.95	1.00	1.05	3.00
High	.00	.36	.61	0.97	.00	.37	.63	1.00
Medium	.42	.28	.30	1.00	.42	.27	.31	1.00
Low	.58	.36	.09	1.03	.56	.35	.09	1.00
Σ	1.00	1.00	1.00	3.00	.98	.99	1.03	3.00
High	.00	.37	.62	0.99	.00	.38	.62	1.00
Medium	.43	.27	.30	1.00	.43	.27	.30	1.00
Low	.57	.36	.08	1.01	.57	.35	.08	1.00
Σ	1.00	1.00	1.00	3.00	1.00	1.00	1.00	3.00

The row and column totals have now all converged to unity; we have finished standardizing the margins. There is one more step, however, that will throw our results into bolder relief, and that is to subtract from each entry of the final table the grand mean of all cells. In this case that value is $3.00/9 = .33$, yielding as our table of residuals the following:

	Enthusiasm		
Control	High	Medium	Low
High	−.33	.05	.29
Medium	.10	−.06	−.03
Low	.24	.02	−.25

The interpretation of this display is quite direct and, of course, quite consistent with the results we have been examining in our continuing analyses of these data. The greatest overrepresentation is in the upper-right and lower-left corners, while the greatest underrepresentation is in the upper-left and lower-right corners. Clearly, the higher the degree of control, the lower the level of enthusiasm. The entries from the middle row and middle column are all fairly small. It is the corners where the action is. The crossed linear contrast weights shown below fit these results very well.

	High	Medium	Low
High	−1	0	+1
Medium	0	0	0
Low	+1	0	−1

In fact, the correlation (r) (over the nine cells) of the relative frequencies and the contrast weights is .966, showing how good the fit of the data is to the crossed linear contrast weights.

A more complex example In this more complex illustration, 1264 college students were cross-classified by (a) the field of study (humanities, social, biological, or physical science) in which they intended to concentrate (the rows) and (b) the field of study in which they actually took their degree (the columns).

Intended field of study	Field in which degree was awarded				
	Humanities	Social science	Biological science	Physical science	Σ
Humanities	133	158	14	4	309
Social science	57	312	17	5	391
Biological science	16	72	94	10	192
Physical science	34	102	56	180	372
Σ	240	644	181	199	1264

After the first step in standardizing the margin we obtain the following table:

	Humanities	Social science	Biological science	Physical science	Σ
Humanities	.55	.25	.08	.02	.90
Social science	.24	.48	.09	.03	.84
Biological science	.07	.11	.52	.05	.75
Physical science	.14	.16	.31	.90	1.51
Σ	1.00	1.00	1.00	1.00	4.00

We omit the next ten such tables and report the final table in which the margins have been successfully standardized.

	Humanities	Social science	Biological science	Physical science	Σ
Humanities	.60	.26	.09	.05	1.00
Social science	.27	.55	.12	.06	1.00
Biological science	.08	.13	.66	.13	1.00
Physical science	.05	.06	.13	.76	1.00
Σ	1.00	1.00	1.00	1.00	4.00

For our final table of residuals from the mean (4.00/16 = .25) we then have:

	Humanities	Social science	Biological science	Physical science
Humanities	.35	.01	−.16	−.20
Social science	.02	.30	−.13	−.19
Biological science	−.17	−.12	.41	−.12
Physical science	−.20	−.19	−.12	.51

The overwhelming result, of course, is that students are much more likely to graduate in their intended field than in any other. We could provide contrast weights to help us assess the extent to which that is the case. Our weights are given below:

	H	SS	BS	PS
H	3	−1	−1	−1
SS	−1	3	−1	−1
BS	−1	−1	3	−1
PS	−1	−1	−1	3

The correlation (r) (over the sixteen cells) of the relative frequencies and the contrast weights is .951, showing a very good fit between the data and the contrast weights.

We can go a little further in understanding the data if we note that the four fields of study can be arrayed on a dimension of "soft" to "hard." That is, humanities are "softer" than the social sciences, which in turn are softer than the biological sciences, and these in turn are softer than the physical sciences. If that is a reasonable ordering, theoretically speaking, then we might suggest that when people do not graduate in their intended field they are more likely to graduate in a field more adjacent (rather than not adjacent) on the scale of soft-hard. The weights below are appropriate to this hypothesis and are orthogonal to the weights shown in the preceding table.

	H	SS	BS	PS
H	0	2	−1	−1
SS	1	0	1	−2
BS	−2	1	0	1
PS	−1	−1	2	0

The correlation (r) (over the sixteen cells) of the relative frequencies and these contrast weights was .193, suggesting at least a moderate relationship between second choices of field for graduation and adjacency to original choice.

TWENTY-SEVEN
MULTIVARIATE PROCEDURES

BACKGROUND

In the following pages we provide an overview of the statistical procedures generally called *multivariate*. However, as we shall see, some of the procedures described in detail in earlier sections of this book were in some senses also multivariate. Our intent here is to provide acquaintanceship with the major multivariate procedures within the framework of a system of classification that will make it easier to think about the many different techniques.

Whereas in earlier sections we provided computational procedures for all the methods presented, we shall not do so here. First, there is not space enough left. Second, the computations are generally complex and unpleasant even with the help of an excellent hand-held calculator. Finally, the computations are almost always done by computer; happily, however, there are many packaged programs available to get the computations done.

Because we are only illustrative in this section, details must be found elsewhere. Of the many excellent sources on multivariate methods of analysis we have found especially useful the books by Jacob Cohen and Patricia Cohen (1975), William Cooley and Paul Lohnes (1971), Richard Harris (1975), Donald Morrison (1976), and Norman Nie, C. Hadlai Hull, Jean Jenkins, Karin Steinbrenner, and Dale Bent (1975). Although we cannot describe even briefly all the various multivariate procedures, the classification and overview we provide should be sufficient that most omitted procedures may be viewed as (a) close relatives of those described, (b) special cases of those described, or (c) combinations of those described.

It simplifies our thinking about multivariate procedures if we conceive of one or more sets of independent or predictor variables and one or more sets of dependent or criterion variables. Then our first classificatory principle is simply whether the procedure is concerned with *either* the independent (predictor) or the dependent (criterion) variables or whether it is concerned with *both* the independent (predictor) *and* the dependent (criterion) variables. We begin our discussion with the former.

RELATIONSHIPS WITHIN SETS OF VARIABLES: REDESCRIPTORS

The first class of procedures has in common that a set of variables—either independent (predictor) variables or dependent (criterion) variables—is to be redescribed in such a way as to meet one or more of the following goals:

1. *Reduce the number of variables* required to describe, predict, or explain the phenomena of interest.
2. *Assess the psychometric properties* of standardized measures or measures under construction.
3. *Improve the psychometric properties* of measures under construction by suggesting (a) how test and subtest reliability might be improved by adding relatively homogeneous items or variables, (b) how subtests are related to each other, and (c) what new subtests might be usefully constructed.
4. *Test hypotheses* derived from theories implying certain types or patterns of descriptors emerging from the analyses.
5. *Generate hypotheses* in the spirit of exploratory data analysis on the basis of unexpected descriptors emerging from the analyses.

   Of the many specific procedures falling into this class we focus on one to give a flavor of the usage of that procedure. We also describe some others falling into this class, but only very briefly.

Principal Components Analysis

Suppose that a number of variables, say eleven, have been administered to a large group of people and we want to know whether we could do an adequate job of describing the total variation in the data on all eleven variables with a much smaller number of "supervariables" or components. *Principal components analysis* rewrites the original set of eleven variables into a new set of eleven components (usually) that have the following properties. The first principal component rewrites the original variables into the linear combination that does the best job of discriminating among the subjects of our sample. It is the single supervariable that accounts for the maximum possible variance in all of the original variables.

The second principal component is essentially the same *type* of supervariable, except that it operates on the variation in the data remaining after removal of the variation attributable to the first principal component. Thus they are orthogonal, since there is no overlap between the first and second principal components. That is, the second operates only on the leftovers of the first. After the second principal component has been extracted, the third is computed, and so on until as many components have been computed as there are variables. (If one or more of the original variables is completely predictable from the other original variables, the total number of components computed is reduced accordingly.)

How does it help us in our search for "supervariables" to rewrite eleven variables as eleven components? The logic of the method is such that the first few components computed tend to account for much more of the total variation among subjects on the full set of variables than would be the case for an equal number of the original variables, chosen at random. Thus, the first principal component alone might account for 30, 40, or 50 percent of the total variation among the subjects on ten or twenty variables. In contrast, only 10 percent or 5 percent would be expected if the early components were no more "supervariables" than any variable chosen randomly from the original set.

We can illustrate with the small example below how just a few components can reexpress most of the information in several variables. As in principal components (and related) procedures we begin with the matrix of intercorrelations. Here we show only five variables intercorrelated:

			Variables		
Variables	A	B	C	D	E
A	1.00	.80	.70	.10	.00
B	.80	1.00	.90	.20	.10
C	.70	.90	1.00	.10	.00
D	.10	.20	.10	1.00	.80
E	.00	.10	.00	.80	1.00

Since the lower-left and upper-right large triangles of this correlation matrix are mirror images we can concentrate on just one of these, say the lower-left. To call attention to the major features we decompose the large triangle into three smaller geometric shapes, a triangle, a rectangle, and a square:

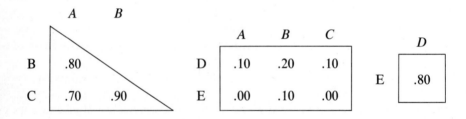

The triangle of three correlations represents all the intercorrelations of variables A, B, and C, which a more formal analysis would show to be important contributors to the first principal component. The median intercorrelation is .80. The square represents the correlation (.80) of variables D and E, which a more formal analysis would show to be important contributors to the second principal component. The rectangle shows the correlations between the variables A, B, and C and the variables D and E. The median correlation is .10. The diagram below gives the average intercorrelation *within* a group of variables comprising a supervariable and the average intercorrelation *between* the variables comprising a supervariable:

I   II

.80 ——————————— .10 ——————————— .80

The difference between the median of all within and the median of all between correlations, .80 vs. .10 in this case, provides information on the strength and "purity" of the supervariable. In this example the two supervariables are nearly independent of each other and highly consistent internally.

This example is not technically an example of principal components analysis, but it serves to convey the spirit of the enterprise. Actually the example is an illustration of one of the related procedures called *cluster analysis*.

The process of principal components analysis also begins with the intercorrelation of all the variables. Then the components are computed, and the *loading* (or component loading or factor loading) of each variable on each component is computed. These loadings are the correlations between each variable (usually the rows) and the newly computed components (usually the columns). Each component is understood or interpreted in terms of the pattern of loadings. We illustrate this presently.

Typically, however, the components as first extracted from the correlations among the variables are not very interpretable (except perhaps the first component). They are typically made more interpretable by a process called *rotation*. We illustrate this process by showing a plot of the data of the following matrix of correlations of variables with components; just the first two components are shown (see Figure 27-1).

	Loadings before rotation	
	Component I	Component II
Variable 1	.60	.55
Variable 2	.50	.50
Variable 3	.70	.60
Variable 4	.50	−.50
Variable 5	.60	−.55
Variable 6	.70	−.60

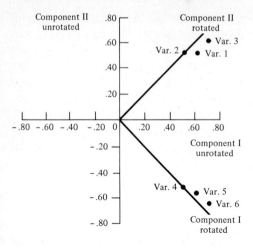

Figure 27-1 Loadings of six variables on two rotated and unrotated components (or factors).

With respect to the original unrotated components, I and II, all the variables loaded highly on component I, while half the variables showed a strong positive and half showed a strong negative loading on component II. When we rotate the axes, in this particular case 45 degrees clockwise, we find that three of the variables load highly only on one rotated component, while the other three load highly only on the other rotated component. The new *rotated component loadings* have now become:

	Loadings after rotation	
	Component I	Component II
Variable 1	.04	.82
Variable 2	.00	.70
Variable 3	.06	.92
Variable 4	.70	.00
Variable 5	.82	.04
Variable 6	.92	.06

If we were now told that variables 1, 2, and 3 were alternative measures of sociability, and variables 4, 5, and 6 were alternative measures of intellectual ability, the rotated components would be far more useful than the unrotated. The latter would be very difficult to interpret; the former would suggest that our six variables could be reduced to two supervariables (sociability and intellectual ability) that were independent of each other (orthogonal). That is, when we rotated the axes of components I and II, we kept them orthogonal (at right angles to one another). Sometimes it is useful to allow the rotations to be nonorthogonal, as when the hypothesized underlying supervariables are thought to be somewhat correlated in the real world. Such nonorthogonal rotations are called *oblique*.

The most commonly used method of orthogonal rotation is called *varimax*; it tries to maximize the variation of the squared loadings for each component by making the loadings go to zero or to 1.00 to the extent possible. This method of rotation helps make components easier to interpret.

Applications: Construct Validity

As part of the construct validation of a new measure of sensitivity to nonverbal cues, the PONS test, it was important to assess the independence of this measure from measures of intellectual functioning (Rosenthal, Hall, Di Matteo, Rogers, & Archer, 1979). For a sample of 110 high school students we had available their PONS subtest scores to items reflecting sensitivity to nonverbal cues that were positive and submissive in content, positive and dominant, negative and submissive, and negative and dominant.

In addition, we had available scores on the verbal SAT, the math SAT, and the Otis IQ test. If the PONS were really independent of intellectual ability, as hoped and hypothesized, we should obtain two principal components which, after varimax rotation, should yield an "intelligence component" and an orthogonal "nonverbal sensitivity component." Here is what was found:

| | Loadings after rotation | |
Variable	Component 1	Component 2
Otis IQ	.19	.64
Verbal SAT	−.02	.89
Math SAT	−.07	.84
PONS: Pos.-Sub.	.66	.02
PONS: Pos.-Dom.	.82	−.00
PONS: Neg.-Sub.	.77	.06
PONS: Neg.-Dom.	.78	.06

These results, then, were in good agreement with the predictions and the hopes. The first rotated component was essentially a PONS component; the second was an intellectual component. Just as had been the case for our simpler hypothetical example above, before rotation the first principal component had shown positive loadings by all the variables; the second principal component had shown positive loadings by some of the variables (the three intellectual variables) and negative loadings by some of the variables (the four sensitivity-to-nonverbal-cues variables).

Applications: Subtest Construction

The preceding application of principal components analysis was to construct validation. The next application is to *subtest formation*. The PONS test of sensitivity to nonverbal cues was made up of 220 items, 20 in each of 11 channels. The channels were in either the visual or the auditory domain as follows:

	Visual channels			
Auditory channels	None	Face	Body	Face + body
None		1	2	3
Content-filtered	4	5	6	7
Random-spliced	8	9	10	11

Face-channel items showed only facial cues, body-channel items showed only body cues, while face + body–channel items showed both. Content-filtered items preserved tone but not content, by removing high frequencies. Random-spliced items preserved different aspects of tone but not content by random scrambling of speech.

After intercorrelating the eleven channels and channel combinations shown above, extracting four principal components and rotating orthogonally (varimax), we obtained the loadings shown in Table 27-1.

The first component was characterized by face presence, reflecting ability to decode nonverbal cues from any combination of channels as long as the face was included as a source of information. The second and third principal components each reflected a specific skill: decoding random-spliced and content-filtered cues respectively, in the absence of any visual cues. The fourth principal component reflected ability to decode body cues in the absence of facial cues.

The first row at the bottom of the matrix of loadings shows the sum of the squared loadings, the amount of variance accounted for by that factor. (Alter-

Table 27-1 Eleven PONS subtests' loadings on four components

Variables	Loadings on components			
	1	2	3	4
Face	.62	.12	.10	.15
Face + body	.68	.07	.11	.24
Face + random-spliced	.70	.02	.06	.22
Face + content-filtered	.65	−.03	.09	.20
Face + body + random-spliced	.67	.30	.09	.05
Face + body + content-filtered	.70	.06	.10	.32
Random-spliced	.14	.95	.03	.12
Content-filtered	.20	.04	.96	.14
Body	.47	−.04	.02	.59
Body + random-spliced	.33	.07	.12	.57
Body + content-filtered	.11	.13	.08	.82
Sum of squared loadings	3.11	1.04	1.01	1.66
Percentage of variance	28%	9%	9%	15%
Number of variables defining components	6	1	1	3
Number of items defining components	120	20	20	60

native terms for this quantity are "eigenvalue," "latent root," "characteristic root," or just "root;" Armor, 1974.) The second row at the bottom of Table 27-1 shows the percentage of variance accounted for by each component. It is computed by dividing the sum of the squared loadings for that component by the total number of variables, eleven in this illustration. For the present analysis these first two rows show that the first and fourth components are more important in the sense of accounting for more variance than are the second and third components. Note that this can occur only after rotation. Before rotation no succeeding component can be larger than a preceding component, because each succeeding component is extracted only from the residuals of the preceding component.

The third row at the bottom of Table 27-1 lists the number of variables serving to define each component. The last row lists the number of raw test items contributing to the variables defining each component.

A variety of procedures are available for forming scales from principal components analyses. Many of these generate scores for each subject for each component in such a way as to keep scores on the various components uncorrelated with each other. In our own work, however, we have used a simple procedure that often leads to psychologically more interpretable scales, subtests, or supervariables, although our supervariables may no longer be entirely uncorrelated with each other. We simply combine all the variables serving to define each component. How we combine variables depends on their form. If they are all measured on similar scales and have similar standard deviations we simply add or average the variables.* That was the situation for the analysis above. Since scores of each variable could range from 0 to 20 and standard deviations were similar, we simply added subjects' scores on the variables serving to define each component.

Thus, each subject could earn a score of 0 to 120 on the supervariable based on the first rotated component, scores of 0 to 20 on the second and third rotated components, and scores of 0 to 60 on the fourth rotated component.

When the variables are not all on the same scale or metric we would transform all variables to standard scores before adding or averaging. When there are no missing data it may not matter whether we add or average the scores on the variables defining each component. However, when there may be missing data it is safer to use the mean of the variables rather than their sum as the new or super variable.

One rarely is very interested in seeing the loadings of as many principal components (either unrotated or rotated) as there are variables. A number of quantitative criteria are available to help decide how many to examine. For subtest or supervariable construction we recommend a step-up approach in which we examine in turn the rotated first two components, then the first three, then the first four, and so on. The solution we choose should be the one that makes the most substantive sense. Experience suggests that looking only at the rotated end result (i.e., the loadings of all variables on all the components extracted based on any of several quantitative rules for stopping the extraction process) typically yields more components than are needed to construct useful, meaningful subtests or supervariables and fewer components that are interpretable. It should be noted that at each step up, the definition of each component changes. Thus the first component after rotating two components will not be the same component as the first component after rotating three or four or more components.

Applications: Reliability Analysis

Since the first unrotated principal component is the best single summarizer of the linear relationships among all the variables, it can be employed as the basis for an estimate of the internal-consistency reliability of a test. We would probably employ such an estimate only where it made substantive sense to think of an overall construct tapped by all the variables to some degree. Such might be the case for many measures of ability, adjustment, achievement, and the like.

It would make sense, for example, to think of an ability to decode nonverbal cues. We might, therefore, estimate the internal consistency of the PONS test from the first principal component *before rotation*. After rotation it would

---

* This assumes that all variables have loadings of the same sign or are positively correlated with each other. A variable negatively correlated with the others can be employed only after changing its scale into the proper direction, e.g., by multiplying each observation by -1.

no longer be the best single summarizer, though it would probably give a far better structure to the data working in concert with other rotated components.

David Armor (1974) provides the computational formula for his index of reliability, theta, an index that gives a maximum possible reliability:

$$\text{theta} = \frac{V}{V-1}\left(\frac{L-1}{L}\right)$$

where V is the number of variables and L is the latent root (eigenvalue or sum of squared loadings). For the 220 items of the PONS test with each item regarded as a variable, we found

$$\text{theta} = \frac{220}{219}\left(\frac{13.217-1}{13.217}\right) = .929$$

The analogous reliability based on the eleven channels rather than the 220 items was

$$\text{theta} = \frac{11}{10}\left(\frac{4.266-1}{4.266}\right) = .842$$

It should be noted that the latent root of 4.266 for the eleven-variable analysis is substantially (37 percent) larger than the latent root of 3.113 obtained for the first principal component after rotation.

Before leaving this brief discussion of reliability it may be useful to ask how it is possible that a test (e.g., the PONS) could be made up of several orthogonal principal components and still have high internal-consistency reliability. By definition, we know that the orthogonal components cannot be making any contribution of correlation to each other. However, the way internal-consistency reliability for a total test score is defined, this reliability increases as the mean of the intercorrelations increases and as the number of items increases. Therefore, a mean intercorrelation lowered by the presence of orthogonal components can be compensated for by an increase in the number of items that correlate positively with some other items. Longer tests, therefore, can have high internal-consistency reliability even when they are comprised of orthogonal components or factors.

Other Redescriptors

The most commonly used alternative to the principal components method for the redescription of variables is actually an entire family of alternatives called *factor analysis*. Sometimes principal components analysis is viewed as a special type of factor analysis, but there are subtle differences between principal components and other forms of factor analysis. For example some forms of factor analysis make more assumptions than are required for principal components analysis and introduce a greater series of options for viewing the data. As a result, different investigators exercising different options will obtain different factor structures from the same data. Beginners would do well to employ principal components with varimax rotation as their standard procedure. Stanley Mulaik (1972) and R. J. Rummel (1967) provide detailed comparisons of various types of factor analysis, and Jae-On Kim (1975) provides a briefer overview.

Cluster analysis represents a family of methods for grouping variables ranging from some very simple to some very complicated procedures. A very simple form of cluster analysis was illustrated when we first introduced principal components analysis; there we used as a criterion of cluster tightness the difference between the average within-cluster intercorrelations and the average between-cluster correlations. Kenneth Bailey (1974) gives a detailed summary of the methods, and Ki Hang Kim and Fred Roush (1980) give a brief but quite mathematical discussion.

In clustering, it is not necessary that it be variables that are grouped together. We could instead cluster the subjects or other sampling units for whom measurements had been obtained. Then, instead of grouping variables together that correlated highly over a list of persons, we could group persons together that correlated highly over a list of variables. A typology of persons or other sampling units could thereby be constructed, as, for example, was alluded to at the very end of our discussion of definitions in Chapter 3.

It should be noted, however, that factor analysis and principal components analysis can also be employed to the same end. We illustrate what is involved with a small example; these procedures involve what amounts to an exchange of rows with columns, assuming that we always intercorrelate columns with an eye to their redescription.

Data matrices											
IA Redescribing variables*						IIA Redescribing persons†					
	Var. 1	Var. 2	Var. 3	Var. 4	Var. 5		Persons 1	2	3	4	5 6
Person 1						Variable 1					
Person 2						Variable 2					
Person 3						Variable 3					
Person 4						Variable 4					
Person 5						Variable 5					
Person 6											

* To redescribe the variables as clusters, factors, or types.

† To redescribe the persons as clusters, factors, or types.

We call the two tables above *data matrices*; the one on the left has each person's scores on all variables in one row, while the one on the right has each variable's scores for each person in one row. From these data matrices we compute the correlation matrices shown below by correlating each column's scores with every other column's scores:

Correlation matrices												
IB						**IIB**						
Var. 1	Var. 2	Var. 3	Var. 4	Var. 5		Persons 1	2	3	4	5	6	
Variable 1						Person 1						
Variable 2						Person 2						
Variable 3						Person 3						
Variable 4						Person 4						
Variable 5						Person 5						
						Person 6						

Note: The matrix above has each correlation based on six observations, i.e., the six persons.

Note: The matrix above has each correlation based on five observations, i.e., the five variables.

Clustering or factoring the correlation matrices above would lead to a redescription of the five variables in terms of some (usually smaller) number of groupings of variables in the case of the matrix on the left (IB), and to a redescription of the six persons in terms of some (usually smaller) number of groupings of persons in the case of the matrix on the right (IIB). Our example of six persons measured on five variables was convenient as an illustration, but we should note that, in general, factors will be more reliable when the N on which each correlation is based is much larger than the number of variables or persons being intercorrelated and factor analyzed.

Many other procedures have been developed to serve as redescriptors. They have in common that they examine the relationships among objects or stimuli in terms of some measure of similarity or dissimilarity, and then try to infer some number of dimensions that would meaningfully account for the obtained pattern of similarities or dissimilarities among the objects or stimuli. The methods have been called *dimensional analysis,* a term referring to distance analysis, multidimensional scaling, multidimensional unfolding, proximity analysis, similarity analysis, smallest-space analysis, and other procedures summarized by various authors (see Coombs, Dawes, & Tversky, 1970; Rummel, 1967; and the more detailed discussions by Guttman, 1966; Lazarsfeld & Henry, 1968; Torgerson, 1958; and especially by Shepard, Romney, & Nerlove, 1972).

RELATIONSHIPS AMONG SETS OF VARIABLES

The remaining multivariate procedures that will be summarized only briefly are those in which we are interested in the relationship among two or more sets of

Table 27-2 Multivariate procedures for examining relationships among sets of variables

Traditionally labeled		Dependent-variable status	
		Single	Multiple*
Correlational	Method pair 1	Multiple correlation	Canonical correlation
	Method pair 2	Discriminant function	Multiple discriminant function
	Method pair 3	Path analysis	Multiple path analysis
	Method pair 4	Multiple partial correlation	Complex multiple partial correlation
Analysis of variance	Method pair 5	Multilevel analysis of variance	Multivariate multilevel analysis of variance
	Method pair 6	Analysis of covariance	Multivariate analysis of covariance

* Interpretation of the results of these procedures is almost always ambiguous, and special caution should be exercised before any of these are employed in any but the most exploratory spirit.

variables heuristically classified as independent (predictor) and dependent (criterion) variables. Table 27-2 provides a structure for the survey of these procedures.

The left half of the table lists the procedures in which a set of independent or predictor variables is assessed for its relationship to a single dependent or criterion variable. The right half of the table lists the analogous procedure but where there is more than one dependent or criterion value. Thus each of the six method pairs of the table has one member of the pair based on a single dependent variable and one based on multiple dependent variables.

The first four method pairs are labeled "correlational," and the last two method pairs are labeled "analysis of variance." While this traditional distinction is useful in helping us find our way to the various packaged computer programs, it is also useful for conceptual purposes to view the analysis-of-variance procedures as special cases of the correlational procedures both subsumed under the same fundamental model for the analysis of data, the general linear model (Cohen & Cohen, 1975). In what follows we describe briefly each of the method pairs in turn.

Method pair 1: Multiple (canonical) correlation *Multiple correlation* (also briefly discussed in Chapter 17) is the correlation between two or more predictor variables and a single dependent variable. The multiple correlation coefficient R is a Pearson product-moment correlation between the dependent variable and a composite independent variable. This composite variable is made up, to varying degrees, of the individual independent variables in proportion to their importance in helping to maximize the value of R. Thus we can learn from the procedures of multiple correlation and regression both the absolute value as a predictor of the entire set of predictors and the relative value as a predictor of each independent variable compared to the others. By dummy coding the various factors of an analysis of variance and employing these as independent variables, many, but not all (i.e., fixed but not random factor designs), models of the analysis of variance can be approached readily by way of multiple correlation or regression. (It should be noted that we are using the terms "correlation" and "regression" interchangeably in this context. A more technical usage would have us refer to *regression* in contexts where we want to relate changes in level of x to changes in level of y, whereas we would refer to *correlation* as a more global index of closeness of relationship.)

Canonical correlation is the correlation between two or more predictor variables and two or more dependent variables. The canonical correlation coefficient CR is a Pearson product-moment correlation between a composite independent and a composite dependent variable. These composite variables are constructed by weighting each constituent variable in proportion to the importance of its contribution to maximizing the value of CR. Multiple R can be seen as a special case of CR when there is only one dependent variable. When there are more dependent variables we can compute more CR's, in fact as many CR's as there are dependent variables (or independent variables if there are fewer of them than of dependent variables). Each successively computed CR is again a correlation between a composite independent and a composite dependent variable, but with each computed so as to be independent of the preceding composites computed. Since each CR is operating on the residuals from the preceding CR, successive CR's grow smaller and smaller just as successive principal components do.

From a practical point of view, we would not often recommend the use of canonical correlation, since the results obtained are only rarely interpretable. For the situation for which canonical correlations apply, we have found it more useful to generate several reasonably uncorrelated independent supervariables (with the help of principal components or cluster analysis) and several reasonably uncorrelated dependent supervariables (with the help of principal components or cluster analysis). We would then employ ordinary correlation and multiple correlation separately for each of the relatively orthogonal dependent variables.

Method pair 2: (Multiple) discriminant function The *discriminant function* is the set of optimal weights (given the predictor variables) that does the best job of discriminating whether subjects or other sampling units are members of one or another group. Since we can dummy code group membership as 0 and 1, we can regard discriminant function analysis as a special case of multiple correlation or regression where we have a dichotomous (0,1) dependent variable.

The *multiple discriminant function* is the set of optimal weights given each predictor variable that does the best job of discriminating among subjects' memberships in three or more groups. Since multiple groups can be turned into multiple dependent variables by dummy coding (so that we have one less variable than we had groups), we can regard multiple discriminant function analysis as a special case of canonical correlation where the dependent variables are dichotomous. (It should be noted that we get the same result whether we regard the dummy-coded group membership variables as the dependent variables or as the independent variables.)

The same note of caution on practical usage we offered in the case of canonical correlation applies to this special case.

Method pair 3: (Multiple) path analysis *Path analysis* is a special case of multiple regression in which the goal is usually the drawing of causal inference, and in which we have a strong basis for ordering causal priorities. For example, if our predictor variables included gender, social class, and education, we could order these three variables on a dimension of time with gender being determined first, then social class (defined, say, as parental income and occupation when the subject began formal education), and finally education of subject (defined as number of years). We would then employ multiple regression in a repeated way with each variable contributing to the prediction of every other variable coming later in time. If the dependent variable were income, all three predictors would be relevant to income, with gender contributing directly to income but also by way of influencing social class and education, which in turn also affect the dependent variable. Social class, having been partially affected by gender, then can affect income directly but also by way of education. Education, having been affected by gender and social class, can then also affect income directly. The diagram in Figure 27-2 summarizes the lines of influence.

Multiple path analysis is a logically implied special case of canonical correlation again involving the repeated application of multiple correlational methods to time-ordered variables, but with two or more ultimate dependent vari-

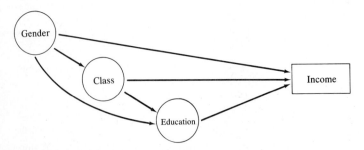

Figure 27-2 Path analysis showing the prediction of income from three time-ordered variables.

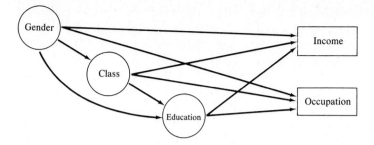

Figure 27-3 Multiple path analysis showing the prediction of income and occupation from three time-ordered variables.

ables. A composite dependent variable is constructed with weights maximizing the predictive relationships between the time-ordered predictor variables and the composite dependent variable. As many sets of predictive relationships can be computed as there are dependent variables. This procedure has been little employed to date but may prove useful in the future. The diagram in Figure 27-3 summarizes the procedure.

Method pair 4: (Complex) multiple partial correlation *Multiple partial correlation* is ordinary multiple correlation or regression performed on a set of variables from which the effects of one or more other variables have been removed. The effects of these "third party" variables (also called *covariates* or *control variables*) can be removed from either the independent or dependent variable set (*multiple part correlations*) or from both (*multiple partial correlations*); for details see Cooley and Lohnes (1971).

Complex multiple partial correlation is ordinary canonical correlation performed on a set of variables from which the effects of one or more other variables have been removed. The effects of the "third-party" variables can be removed from either the independent or dependent variable set (complex multiple part correlation) or from both (complex multiple partial correlation). For details see Jacob Cohen's paper on *set correlation* (1982).

Method pair 5: (Multivariate) multilevel analysis of variance *Multilevel analysis of variance* has been discussed in detail in many of the earlier chapters of this book. We list it here only to be consistent, since the procedure does involve more than one independent variable. Even a one-way analysis of variance, if there are more than two levels, can be viewed as made up of a series of (dummy-coded) independent variables. Given a series of independent variables and a single dependent variable, we could approach many types of analysis very readily by means of multiple correlation or regression. Fixed-effects analyses could be handled very easily, for example, but random-effects analyses could be handled only with considerably greater difficulty.

Multivariate multilevel analysis of variance is the generalization of the analysis of variance to more than a single dependent variable. As such, it can be seen as closely akin to canonical correlation, especially the type of canonical correlation in which one set of variables is dichotomous (multiple discriminant function). Many types of multivariate analysis-of-variance problems can be approached readily through canonical correlation if the independent variables are fixed rather than random.

Method pair 6: (Multivariate) analysis of covariance *Analysis of covariance* is essentially an analysis of variance performed on a dependent variable that has been corrected or adjusted for a subject's score on some other variable (a covariate) that correlates (usually substantially) with the dependent variable. Analysis-of-covariance procedures are used successfully to increase the precision of the analysis, and with more dubious success to reduce bias in nonexperimental studies (Judd & Kenny, 1981). These procedures are closely related to those of the multiple partial correlation and other multiple regression procedures.

Multivariate analysis of covariance is analysis of covariance for the situation of multiple dependent variables. It is closely related to complex multiple partial correlation.

As a practical matter we would only rarely recommend the use of either the multivariate analysis of variance or covariance. With correlated dependent variables we have found it more useful to generate several fairly orthogonal supervariables (usually by means of principal component or clustering methods described earlier) to serve as our dependent variables; following this by analysis of variance or covariance separately for each dependent variable.

A final word about multivariate procedures. It is just about as easy to have the computer produce a multiple discriminant function analysis as a *t* test, and we have seen eager researchers call for them by the dozen. But as we have argued against the diffuse, unfocused *F* test (or effect-size estimators) based on more than a single *df* in the numerator, we want to argue against the diffuse, unfocused tests of significance and effect-size estimates that typically emerge from many of the multivariate procedures. We encourage their use, however, in exploratory contexts and as preliminary tests analogous to the omnibus *F* of the analysis of variance when they are to be followed up by focused and precise tests of significance and effect-size estimates.

WRITING THE RESEARCH REPORT

COMMUNICATING IDEAS

A researcher's work is not finished when the study is completed. The ability to communicate the results is at least as significant as the skills and expertise required to arrive at them. Science is a process in which there is a gradual evolution of ideas that challenge, support, and build on one another. The report of each individual research project is a link in this evolutionary chain. One scientist has described the role the written word plays as follows:

> The literature of science, a permanent record of the communication between scientists, is also the history of science: a record of the search for truth, of observations and opinions, of hypotheses that have been ignored or have been found wanting or have withstood the test of further observation and experiment. Science is a continuing endeavor in which the end of one investigation may be the starting point for another. *Scientists must write*, therefore, so that their discoveries may be known to others (Barrass, 1978, p. 25).

For behavioral scientists, whatever area they specialize in, there are stylistic techniques and tried-and-true writing formulas that constitute almost recipes for terse, readable reports. In this appendix we discuss the two aspects of the task at hand: the paper's form and content. Those two aspects are detailed in this appendix separately, although in the finished paper they should ideally blend to form a cohesive presentation.

By the paper's *form* we mean a group of stylistic elements that, taken together, constitute the way in which the paper is presented. The kinds of things to be considered when we talk about form include the process of gathering information, formulating an outline, and techniques for beginning, writing, and revising the paper. Within this category fall specific elements of style, such as spelling, punctuation, and the proper formats for presenting footnotes, charts, figures, and references.

The second aspect to be considered is the paper's *content*, which refers to the formula for the presentation of the substantive work. Here we first consider the formulation of an introduction, then the specification of methods and procedures. Next we consider the analysis of the results, the discussion of findings, the conclusion, and finally how to write a summary (or abstract).

FORM

It is assumed that the processes of formulating and researching a specific hypothesis have, as one of their outcomes, sufficiently narrowed the topic so that this need not be a consideration as we begin to plan the paper. At this point, while the research findings are fresh in mind, it is well to arrive at a working title. It should be succinct while at the same time adequately descriptive of the paper's objective. The title can be changed, but a good working title gives a direction and keeps the writer's thoughts on course. It should contain key words that pinpoint what the research is about, so that a reader leafing through the table of contents of a journal will be able to determine readily whether or not it pertains to his or her field of interest.

The next concern is gathering further information to ensure that we have covered our topic thoroughly. A good deal of work will have been done already, during the course of data collection and analysis and even before the research was undertaken. But there may be fresh insights and ideas which should send us back to the literature. There is no adequate substitute for a thorough literature review (discussed in Chapter 15), whenever possible in the primary materials rather than in secondary sources.* In searching for primary materials we can make use of the library and its resources (including especially the reference librarian), of any bibliographies that may be available, and of the suggestions of other researchers whose work is related to our own. Other primary sources of information not to be overlooked are personal correspondence and observations, and students may also get good clues about where to look from class lecture notes.

No matter what sources we use, it cannot be stressed too strongly that it is of prime importance to take accurate notes and to document them fully. Many

---

* There is a classic example to illustrate how an interpretation or hypothesis, no matter how elegant and persuasive it is, is simply wrong if the information or observation on which it is based is mistaken. Sigmund Freud rested an important interpretation in his psychoanalytical study of Leonardo da Vinci on the erroneous understanding that a bird in one of Leonardo's early memories was a vulture. But it turned out that Freud was relying on an inaccurate translation of the Italian word, which actually means another kind of bird, a kite (Anderson, 1981).

experienced researchers have found that a convenient way to take notes is to use index cards and to alphabetize them by author. Begin by writing the author, title, publisher, and year of the work, using a separate card for each source. In making use of these sources we can either paraphrase or quote directly. In either case we must note down the page numbers, and in the case of a direct quote we must be sure to copy it exactly and enclose it within quotation marks.

We are now ready to make an outline which we can use as a guide to map out and structure our ideas as well as to bring order to notes we have taken and raw data we have collected. If the outline is done properly, the paper will practically write itself. The outline can take the form of sentence, topic, or paragraph, but in any case should proceed from the most general to the most specific. Think of the first outline as making a list—that is to say, a rough grouping—of the points we wish to include in the paper. The process of taking notes and ordering them will help us to reorganize the sections of the outline into a cohesive unit that will direct the writing of the paper. The important point is that the final outline will reflect each of the main ideas we have chosen to consider, and they will be fleshed out with specifics that illustrate or amplify those ideas.

Using the outline as a starting point we are ready to begin to write. It is important to keep in mind the level of sophistication of the audience for whom the paper is intended and to fit the style to those expectations. Another stylistic element to keep in mind is to avoid the use of sexist language. Among other things this means that we must be specific in the use of personal pronouns, such as "he" and "she," so as not to incorrectly imply similarities or generalizations where there are or could be sex differences. (A good reference source on this subject is "Guidelines for Nonsexist Language in APA Journals," which is available from the American Psychological Association, by sending a stamped self-addressed envelope to: Publication Manual, Change Sheet 2, APA, 1200 Seventeenth Street, N.W., Washington, D.C. 20036.) It is also well to define any terms that will be used in the paper. Some writers find it helpful to include a glossary at the back of the paper, if it is a technical report, especially if the writing involves technical or specific language that calls for the use of different or unusual words and expressions. Structure the paper around a topic sentence that states what is to be investigated. We use additional sentences to modify, specify, and build on those foundations. There are some words and phrases that can help the reader to follow the thread of the writing more easily, for example, "first," "in addition," "finally," "another important," "even more important." A phrase like "not only but also" can give direction to a sentence or a paragraph.

There are several accepted style manuals, and if we are writing for a journal there is always a specific prescribed style that the journal will explicitly recommend. Submitting a paper written in an inappropriate style conveys the idea that the writer is lazy and has not bothered with form or content. Along with a reliable style manual, a good dictionary is invaluable not only as a spelling and definition reference but as a guide to the singulars and plurals, usages, and abbreviations of Latin words that commonly appear in scientific reports. Some of the more common abbreviations used in footnotes and bibliographies are:

op. cit., from *opere citato* ("in the work cited")
ibid., from *ibidem* ("in the same place")
et al., from *et alii* ("and others")
i.e., from *id est* ("that is")
cf., from *confer* ("compare")
e.g., from *exempli gratia* ("for example")

Without going into details of content, which will be considered in the next section, we proceed with the writing of the paper. When the paper has been completed it is well, if there is time, to put it aside for a day or two. It is then possible to begin the process of revision, which is the next step, from a fresh point of view. To revise, it is necessary to read the paper carefully with a critical eye. Be on guard against lapses in logic, awkward or trite phrasing, run-on sentences, incomplete sentences, as well as faulty punctuation and spelling. We are now ready to rewrite the paper, section by section, cutting whatever is superfluous and rewording transitions between paragraphs so that the flow of the writing is smooth and tight.

Once we are completely satisfied that we have done the best job we can, a clean typewritten copy of the manuscript should be made. Choose one or two readers whose judgment is sound and who will give the work an objective critical analysis. We must be open-minded to all kinds of feedback, including suggestions for substantive as well as grammatical and stylistic changes. In this way the paper will be improved and our writing skills sharpened.

CONTENT

It is customary to begin the research report with an introduction. This section should contain a clear statement of the problem to be considered and a discussion of the way in which the paper builds on what others have said so that there is a logical thread throughout. It is often helpful to include a literature review in order to show the development of the hypotheses and the reason the research was done as well as the particular methods chosen to accomplish the research. One way of knowing that a poor transition has been made between the introductory section of a research paper and the methods section is to be surprised by the methods described. One purpose of the introduction is to prepare the reader for the particular methods employed. The strongest introductions describe the questions posed in such a way as to make the methods section appear to be an inexorable consequence of those questions. Reader's reactions should be, "Well, of course, that's what the authors had to do to get decent answers to their questions."

The second section of the report is usually a specification of methods and procedures, in which we spell out what method of inquiry we have chosen. It is also important to give detailed information as to our choice of subjects: who they are, how they were recruited (did they volunteer?), their age and sex, the number of subjects who dropped out or were dropped by the researcher, and any other information that we think may be pertinent to the study's generalizability. We must also detail the particular instruments and measurements used. If they are standardized tests, it is sufficient simply to name them. But if not, they should be treated at greater length, particularly with regard to their validity and reliability.

The analysis of the results follows this section. To present the results in a manner that can be easily understood, it is often helpful to use tables, graphs, or charts. When these are used, be sure to label, title, and caption them completely. Indicate where they belong in the body of the text ("Insert Figure 1 about here" or "See appendix for pertinent tables and graphs"). Follow standard practices as to format, and here it is helpful if we refer to style manuals. It is important to reiterate findings shown in figures within the body of the text so that the information is presented in verbal as well as in pictorial form. In discussing the analysis we want to be specific and detailed, but not redundant. Raw data should be saved. If a reader wants to analyze our principal findings, he or she then has the necessary data to do so by writing to us. At the same time it is necessary to be selective about what is included in this section. We should strive to avoid "telling all we know" so as not to make the paper too discursive. We should also avoid false or needless precision (as discussed in Chapter 7).

The next major section of the paper is that in which we discuss the findings. To begin to pull the paper together, it is well at this point to refer to the introductory section. If there was more than one hypothesis, discuss each of these in turn to show their relationships to the findings. There may be serendipitous findings, and these too should be treated in depth. Consider specifically how various types of validity might be affected by the conditions of the investigation. It is always a good idea to try to anticipate criticisms and to deal with the imagined objections before they arise.

The final section deals with the conclusions we have reached, although it is also stylistically correct to include this section as the final part of the discussion. The conclusions should be given as specifically and succinctly as we can. We should try to derive implications based on the results and, if possible, to suggest further study or areas of future research.

The summary (or abstract) is written once the main body of the paper has been completed, although in typing the paper it may appear at the beginning. The summary should highlight and tie together the objectives, findings, and conclusions as succinctly as possible. It tells the reader briefly what the paper is about and provides key information that can help the reader determine whether the paper is pertinent to the work he (or she) wishes to pursue.

TYPING THE PAPER

The following pages show a typewritten manuscript by Thomas et al. (1979)*
that was prepared according to one preferred format. A similar format is that
recommended by the American Psychological Association, which is spelled out
in detail in its *Publication Manual*. The APA style manual has been adopted by
many American and international journals. It is not the only style manual used
by journals, and the writer should check a recent issue of the journal to which
the paper is to be submitted.

* *Source:* C. B. Thomas et al., "Evaluation Apprehension, Social Desirability, and the Interpretation of Test Correlations," *Social Behavior and Personality,* 1979, *7*, 193–197. Reprinted by permission of the first author and the journal.

Standard footnote of acknowledgement, although in some style manuals (such as the *APA Manual*) footnotes of acknowledgement are not numbered while text footnotes should be numbered. Type all footnotes double-spaced on a separate sheet (see page 12).

The title summarizes the main idea or the major variables or theoretical issues of the paper simply.

For multiple authors from separate institutions, the names are typed on separate lines. Where there are multiple authors indicated, it is assumed that all made substantial scientific contributions to the study.

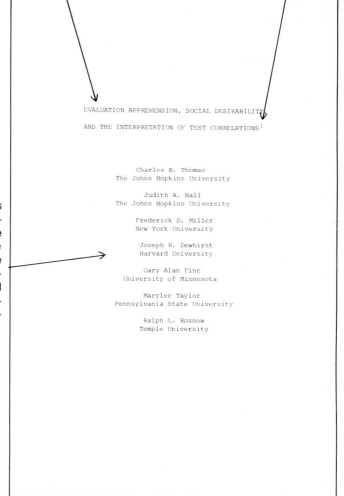

EVALUATION APPREHENSION, SOCIAL DESIRABILITY,

AND THE INTERPRETATION OF TEST CORRELATIONS[1]

Charles B. Thomas
The Johns Hopkins University

Judith A. Hall
The Johns Hopkins University

Frederick D. Miller
New York University

Joseph R. Dewhirst
Harvard University

Gary Alan Fine
University of Minnesota

Marylee Taylor
Pennsylvania State University

Ralph L. Rosnow
Temple University

Objective or purpose of the research study.

Abstract of a research paper should contain specific statements of the methods and results, saving more detailed general statements for the body of the paper or text.

The abstract briefly summarizes the content and purpose of the paper. In some journals it takes the place of a concluding summary, and thus allows readers to anticipate the content of the paper.

Abstract

This paper investigates the relationship between the concepts of social desirability and evaluation apprehension. The Marlowe-Crowne Social Desirability Scale and the Taylor Manifest Anxiety Scale were administered to 63 Harvard and Radcliffe students. As predicted, there was a moderate negative correlation between social desirability and manifest anxiety in the (nonanonymous) high evaluation apprehension condition ($r = -.35$, $p = .05$); and a substantially reduced correlation in the (anonymous) low evaluation apprehension conditions ($r = -.04$). Nonanonymous subjects also had a lower mean score on the Taylor Manifest Anxiety Scale than did anonymous subjects. The results demonstrate a link between evaluation apprehension and social desirability, and indicate the importance of the nature of the testing situation in clinical or applied settings.

Conclusion and implication of the results.

Title is repeated, so that if editor removes title page for blind reviewing the referees will still be apprised of the title.

Double quotation marks to introduce a work or phrase used in a special way.

Because the function of the introduction is obvious, it is not labeled with a heading.

Always check the typed copy of quoted material against the original.

EVALUATION APPREHENSION, SOCIAL DESIRABILITY,

AND THE INTERPRETATION OF TEST CORRELATIONS

Weber and Cook (1972, p. 287) have noted the connection between the concept of "evaluation apprehension" in psychological experiments (Rosenberg, 1965, 1969) and the concept of "social desirability" in personality testing: "The apprehensive subject role, "they wrote," is obviously related to the literature on social desirability ... though explicit links still need to be made." (See also Rosenberg, 1969, p. 280, footnote). The present study demonstrates just such an empirical link.

Rosenberg (1965, 1969) introduced the notion that evaluation apprehension can affect subjects' behavior in psychological experiments, and can lead to invalid causal inference. Rosenberg (1969, p. 281) defined evaluation apprehension as "an active, anxiety-toned concern that he (the subject) win a positive evaluation from the experimenter, or a least that he provide no grounds for a negative one." As a result of evaluation apprehension, subjects have conformed less in conformity studies and exhibited quicker conditioning in conditioning studies as part of a positive self-presentation (Weber and Cook, 1972). Other research on evaluation apprehension has shown that when they must make a choice, subjects are more concerned with presenting themselves in favorable light (this has been called the "apprehensive subject role") than with "helping the experimenter" to validate the experi-

If a work has more than two authors, include first author followed by "et al."

Some manuals prefer that these abbreviations not be italicized (that is, not be underlined) — check the journal.

Acronyms on their first appearance should be explained.

mental hypothesis (the "good subject role") (Rosnow et al., 1973).

Concern with giving a positive self-presentation is also implicit in the "social desirability" concept. This concept refers to a tendency to give the "socially desired response" — e.g., a response that would typically be considered "well-adjusted" -- in answering items on personality measures. This response set is important for personality researchers because it threatens valid interpretation of test results. Crowne and Marlow (1964), for example, found a moderate negative correlation (-.25) between scores on the Taylor Manifest Anxiety Scale (TMAS) and the Marlowe-Crowne Social Desirability Scale (MCSDS): Subjects with a high need to manifest socially desirable traits and behaviors reported themselves to be less anxious (the socially desirable response) than subjects with lower MCSDS scores.

Rosenberg (1969) demonstrated an empirical link between evaluation apprehension and social desirability. In his studies (Rosenberg, 1969, pp. 295, 306), subjects with high versus low desirability scores on tne Marlowe-Crowne Social Desirability Scale were found to be differentially responsive to the experimental manipulation of evaluation apprehension. In a related way, we hoped to demonstrate in this study that the impact of social desirability as a response set affecting personality test scores is mediated by evalu-

Some journals, however, prefer that you not use the first person.

ation apprehension. We hypothesized that in a high evaluation apprehension condition there would be a moderately
negative correlation (approximating the -.25 found by
Marlowe and Crowne, 1964) between scores on the MCSDS and
scores on another personality measure, namely, the Taylor
Manifest Anxiety Scale; and this correlation between TMAS
and MCSDS would be substantially reduced in the low evaluation apprehension condition. High evaluation apprehension

Operational definitions in terms of manipulations that were used.

was operationalized as informing subjects that they were to
be tested nonanonymously; low evaluation apprehension subjects were tested anonymously. This was done on the assumption that subjects who believe they can be identified should
be more concerned with making a positive self-presentation
than subjects who believe they are anonymous. Research by
Silverman (1968) and by Rosnow et al. (1973) indicates that

Empirical support or operational definition.

anonymity-nonanonymity effectively manipulates evaluation
apprehension.

It is important to note two points about the nature of
the hypothesis. The prediction is made for the correlational
results in the two conditions (high vs. low evaluation apprehension). No prediction is made regarding possible mean
differences. The predicted correlational result can be ob-

Italics for emphasis.

tained for any of seven patterns of mean differences: The
experimental group (nonanonymous condition) mean may exceed
the control group (anonymous condition) mean for (1) both
MCSDS and TMAS, (2) neither MCSDS nor TMAS, (3) TMAS alone,

(4) MCSDS alone. The control group mean may exceed the experimental group mean for (5) both MCSDS and TMAS, (6) TMAS
alone, (7) MCSDS alone. The second important feature of
the hypothesis to note is that the maximum difference between
the correlation (between MCSDS and TMAS) in the experimental
condition and the correlation in the control condition is expected to be about .25-.00 = .25. (Crowne and Marlow [1964,
Chapter 2] give theoretical reasons why correlations found
in this type of research would not be expected to be much
more strongly negative than $r = -.25$).

Method

All 33 items of the MCSDS (Crowne and Marlow, 1964) and
all 50 items of the TMAS (Taylor, 1953) were administered to
63 men and women who were students at Harvard and Radcliffe
Colleges, enrolled in an intermediate-level undergraduate
course. The experimental manipulation consisted of varying
instructions concerning anonymity. Half of the subjects
received booklets in which they were instructed to write
their name, sex, and graduating class. Booklets for the
other half of the subjects contained instructions to write
sex and graduating class only. The cover pages of the
booklets were identical in both manipulations. To ran-
domize the sample, test booklets were initially stacked so
that nonanonymous and anonymous test booklets alternated,
booklets were then distributed in this order so that every
other student was in the nonanonymous condition. Items
from the two scales were randomly interspersed in the booklet.
The experiment was carried out during the lecture hour,

The Method Section tells how the study was conducted.

Sex of subjects, and whether they were volunteers or "captive subjects".

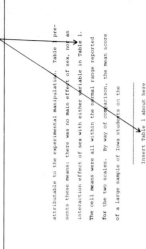

attributable to the experimental manipulation. Table 1 presents these means; there was no main effect of sex, nor an interaction effect of sex with either variable in Table 1. The cell means were all within the normal range reported for the two scales. By way of comparison, the mean score of a large sample of Iowa students on the

Insert Table 1 about here

TMAS was 14.56 (Taylor, 1953), with regard to the MCSDS, Crowne and Marlowe (1964) reported the range for college students to be 10.06 (Dartmouth men) to 16.04 (University of North Dakota women). Examining the cell means separately for each test revealed no differences on the MCSDS ($t < 1$), but there were fewer anxious symptoms reported by nonanonymous than by anonymous subjects on the TMAS ($t = 1.69$, $p <$ .10, two-tailed test). This noteworthy finding suggests that evaluation apprehension can affect the rate at which anxiety symptoms are self-reported.

Although prediction in this experiment was limited to the correlational result, the pattern of mean differences

Although the printed article will not appear this way, it is necessary for handling by the copy editor and the printer to type tables on a separate page.

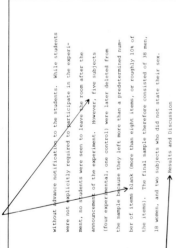

without advance notification to the students. While students were not explicitly required to participate in the experiment, no students were seen to leave the room after the announcement of the experiment. However, five subjects (four experimental, one control) were later deleted from the sample because they left more than a predetermined number of items blank (more than eight items, or roughly 10% of the items). The final sample therefore consisted of 38 men, 18 women, and two subjects who did not state their sex.

Results and Discussion

The hypothesis entertained in this study dealt with the relationship between the dependent variables. For the group as a whole the Pearson product-moment correlation between TMAS scores and MCSDS scores was -.19. For the nonanonymous group ($n = 27$) this correlation was significant ($r = -.35$, $p = .054$, one-tailed), while for the anonymous group ($n = 31$) the correlation was negligible ($r = -.04$). Thus, as hypothesized, subjects in the high evaluation apprehension condition replicated the relationship originally reported in Crowne and Marlowe (1964), whereas the correlation vanished in the low evaluation apprehension condition.[2,3] We also explored for possible effects on the scale means

Why, and how many, subjects were dropped.

The Results and Discussion Sections may be combined in a short paper.

Two footnotes here, since one of these is later refered to specifically.

443

tion found by Marlowe-Crowne. Further, there is a sizable difference in variance explained by the correlation in the experimental condition compared to that explained by the correlation in the control condition.

There is also a matter of interpretation to be considered. Perhaps the results of this experiment are due to a "carelessness factor" rather than to the experimental manipulation. That is, perhaps the MCSDS or TMAS was less valid or internally consistent when taken anonymously than when taken nonanonymously. Perhaps subjects in the anonymous condition took the test less seriously and responded in a more slipshod fashion. The fact that there were no differences in reliability between experimental and control subjects on MCSDS (.76 vs. .76 reliability) or on TMAS (.90 vs. .86 [see footnote 2] counts as evidence against this rival interpretation. Furthermore, the research of Silverman (1968) and Rosnow et al. (1973) and the fact that more experimental than control subjects had their data deleted for incomplete responding (see Method section above) support an evaluation apprehension rather than "carelessness factor" explanation.

Conclusion

This study demonstrated one empirical link between evaluation apprehension and social desirability. It is hoped that the work reported here will serve as a useful

---

Again an attempt to anticipate the reader's questions.

Reference to earlier footnote.

Emphasizes the relatively exploratory nature of the study and the need for an independent replication.

---

found is understandable. The correlational results indicate that social desirability operated in the experimental condition (where a moderate negative correlation between MCSDS and TMAS was found) but not the control condition (where a zero correlation was found). Thus, it is not surprising that subjects in the experimental condition reported fewer symptoms of anxiety (the socially desired response) than did subjects in the control condition. The finding of no mean difference between experimental and control subjects on MCSDS is also what might be expected, since randomization procedures would be expected to produce roughly equal distributions of MCSDS scores (a trait, as opposed to state, variable) for subjects in each condition of the experiment.

Some additional issues merit consideration. First, it should be noted that, with a relatively small sample such as used in this research, it is more difficult to obtain a statistically significant result than with a larger sample size (Cohen, 1969). A further question involves the appropriate statistical test to employ. It is inappropriate to use a test for the significance of the difference between two correlation coefficients because of the constraints on the correlations. The correlation between the tests for the anonymous condition (r = -.04) is as small as it can be; and the correlation for the nonanonymous condition is about as high as it can reasonably be expected to be in this area of research (Crowne and Marlowe, 1964). Our correlation of r = -.15 is actually stronger than the -.25 correla-

---

The authors attempt to anticipate the reader's questions.

Choose references judiciously and cite them accurately.

Book with one author.

Book with two authors.

Journal article with one author.

Year, journal volume, and pages.

Article is an edited book.

Journal article with more than two authors.

Here all authors are listed, instead of the "first author et al."

Several references by the same author are arranged by year of publication.

REFERENCES

Cohen, J. Statistical power analysis for the behavioral sciences. New York: Academic Press, 1969.

Crowne, D. P. and Marlowe, D. The approval motive: Studies in evaluative dependence. New York: Wiley, 1964.

Rosenberg, M. J. When dissonance fails: On eliminating evaluation apprehension from attitude measurement. Journal of Personality and Social Psychology, 1965, 1, 28-42.

Rosenberg, M. J. The conditions and consequences of evaluation apprehension. In R. Rosenthal and R. L. Rosnow (Eds.), Artifact in behavioral research. New York: Academic Press, 1969.

Rosnow, R. L., Goodstadt, B. E., Suls, J. M. and Gitter, A. G. More on the social psychology of the experiment: When compliance turns to self-defense. Journal of Personality and Social Psychology, 1973, 27, 337-343.

Silverman, I. Role-related behavior of subjects in laboratory studies of attitude change. Journal of Personality and Social Psychology, 1968, 8, 343-348.

Taylor, J. A. A personality scale of manifest anxiety. Journal of Abnormal and Social Psychology, 1953, 48, 285-290.

Weber, S. J. and Cook, T. D. Subject effects in laboratory research: An examination of subject roles, demand characteristics, and valid inference. Psychological Bulletin, 1972, 77, 273-295.

Attempts to evaluate and further specify the implications of this research.

point of departure for future work of both an empirical and a theoretical nature.

The result reported here also has implications for personality researchers and for those working in clinical or applied settings. This experiment demonstrates that an observed relationship between scores on a specimen personality test and scores on a test of social desirability may be moderated in an important way by the nature of the testing situation (specifically, whether the testing situation was anonymous or nonanonymous). It was also found (at $p <$ .10) that evaluation apprehension can affect the rate at which anxiety symptoms are self-reported. The nature of the testing situation should be carefully considered when: (1) interpreting the correlation between a personality test and a measure of social desirability; and (2) interpreting the actual scores on personality measures (such as the TMAS) which seem strongly susceptible to the influence of social desirability.

Attempts to present the data in a more easily comprehensible form to supplement the text.

Acronyms were defined in the text.

Brief but clearly explanatory title.

Standard abbreviations.

Left-hand column usually lists major independent variable.

Table 1

Means and Standard Deviations on the TMAS and MCSDS

for Subjects Tested Anonymously and Nonanonymously

Experimental Conditions	TMAS		MCSDS	
	M	SD	M	SD
Anonymity ($\underline{n}$ = 31)	17.19	7.89	9.55	4.79
Nonanonymity ($\underline{n}$ = 27)	13.63	8.22	10.18	4.66

Type all footnotes double-spaced on a separate sheet.

If the paper is to be blind reviewed, type the authors's acknowledgement footnote on a separate sheet.

FOOTNOTES

1. This study was supported by an allocation from the Department of Psychology and Social Relations at Harvard University, where the last author was a visiting professor. The first author expresses his gratitude to four of his colleagues at The Johns Hopkins University for valuable comments on an earlier draft of this paper: Linda Gottfriedson, John Hollifield, James McPartland, and especially Robert Slavin.

2. The correlation for anonymity accounts for 12.1% less variance than the correlation for nonanonymity. The difference between the two correlations (after transformation of each by Fisher's z), or q = .125, corresponds to what Cohen (1969) has called a "medium" effect size.

3. Reliabilities for the four conditions of the experiment were computed using Cronbach's alpha. For anonymity, MCSDS reliability = .76; and for nonanonymity, MCSDS reliability = .76. For anonymity, TMAS reliability = .86; and for nonanonymity, TMAS reliability = .90.

STATISTICAL TABLES

Table 1. Table of standard normal deviates (Z) 448
Table 2. Summary table of t 449
Table 3. Extended table of t 450
Table 4. Table of F 453
Table 5. Table of χ^2 457
Table 6. Significance levels of r 458
Table 7. Table of Fisher's z transformation of r 459
Table 8. Table of r equivalents of Fisher's z 460
Table 9. Table of random digits 461

Table 1 Table of standard normal deviates (Z)

Second digit of Z

Z	.00	.01	.02	.03	.04	.05	.06	.07	.08	.09
.0	.5000	.4960	.4920	.4880	.4840	.4801	.4761	.4721	.4681	.4641
.1	.4602	.4562	.4522	.4483	.4443	.4404	.4364	.4325	.4286	.4247
.2	.4207	.4168	.4129	.4090	.4052	.4013	.3974	.3936	.3897	.3859
.3	.3821	.3783	.3745	.3707	.3669	.3632	.3594	.3557	.3520	.3483
.4	.3446	.3409	.3372	.3336	.3300	.3264	.3228	.3192	.3156	.3121
.5	.3085	.3050	.3015	.2981	.2946	.2912	.2877	.2843	.2810	.2776
.6	.2743	.2709	.2676	.2643	.2611	.2578	.2546	.2514	.2483	.2451
.7	.2420	.2389	.2358	.2327	.2296	.2266	.2236	.2206	.2177	.2148
.8	.2119	.2090	.2061	.2033	.2005	.1977	.1949	.1922	.1894	.1867
.9	.1841	.1814	.1788	.1762	.1736	.1711	.1685	.1660	.1635	.1611
1.0	.1587	.1562	.1539	.1515	.1492	.1469	.1446	.1423	.1401	.1379
1.1	.1357	.1335	.1314	.1292	.1271	.1251	.1230	.1210	.1190	.1170
1.2	.1151	.1131	.1112	.1093	.1075	.1056	.1038	.1020	.1003	.0985
1.3	.0968	.0951	.0934	.0918	.0901	.0885	.0869	.0853	.0838	.0823
1.4	.0808	.0793	.0778	.0764	.0749	.0735	.0721	.0708	.0694	.0681
1.5	.0668	.0655	.0643	.0630	.0618	.0606	.0594	.0582	.0571	.0559
1.6	.0548	.0537	.0526	.0516	.0505	.0495	.0485	.0475	.0465	.0455
1.7	.0446	.0436	.0427	.0418	.0409	.0401	.0392	.0384	.0375	.0367
1.8	.0359	.0351	.0344	.0336	.0329	.0322	.0314	.0307	.0301	.0294
1.9	.0287	.0281	.0274	.0268	.0262	.0256	.0250	.0244	.0239	.0233
2.0	.0228	.0222	.0217	.0212	.0207	.0202	.0197	.0192	.0188	.0183
2.1	.0179	.0174	.0170	.0166	.0162	.0158	.0154	.0150	.0146	.0143
2.2	.0139	.0136	.0132	.0129	.0125	.0122	.0119	.0116	.0113	.0110
2.3	.0107	.0104	.0102	.0099	.0096	.0094	.0091	.0089	.0087	.0084
2.4	.0082	.0080	.0078	.0075	.0073	.0071	.0069	.0068	.0066	.0064
2.5	.0062	.0060	.0059	.0057	.0055	.0054	.0052	.0051	.0049	.0048
2.6	.0047	.0045	.0044	.0043	.0041	.0040	.0039	.0038	.0037	.0036
2.7	.0035	.0034	.0033	.0032	.0031	.0030	.0029	.0028	.0027	.0026
2.8	.0026	.0025	.0024	.0023	.0023	.0022	.0021	.0021	.0020	.0019
2.9	.0019	.0018	.0018	.0017	.0016	.0016	.0015	.0015	.0014	.0014
3.0	.0013	.0013	.0013	.0012	.0012	.0011	.0011	.0011	.0010	.0010
3.1	.0010	.0009	.0009	.0009	.0008	.0008	.0008	.0008	.0007	.0007
3.2	.0007									
3.3	.0005									
3.4	.0003									
3.5	.00023									
3.6	.00016									
3.7	.00011									
3.8	.00007									
3.9	.00005									
4.0*	.00003									

Note: All p values are one-tailed in this table.

* Additional values of Z are found in the bottom row of Table 3 since t values for $df = \infty$ are also Z values.

Source: Reproduced from S. Siegel, *Nonparametric Statistics,* McGraw-Hill, New York, 1956, p. 247, with the permission of the publisher.

Table 2 Summary table of _t_

df	p = .9	.8	.7	.6	.5	.4	.3	.2	.1	.05	.02	.01
1	.158	.325	.510	.727	1.000	1.376	1.963	3.078	6.314	12.706	31.821	63.657
2	.142	.289	.445	.617	.816	1.061	1.386	1.886	2.920	4.303	6.965	9.925
3	.137	.277	.424	.584	.765	.978	1.250	1.638	2.353	3.182	4.541	5.841
4	.134	.271	.414	.569	.741	.941	1.190	1.533	2.132	2.776	3.747	4.604
5	.132	.267	.408	.559	.727	.920	1.156	1.476	2.015	2.571	3.365	4.032
6	.131	.265	.404	.553	.718	.906	1.134	1.440	1.943	2.447	3.143	3.707
7	.130	.263	.402	.549	.711	.896	1.119	1.415	1.895	2.365	2.998	3.499
8	.130	.262	.399	.546	.706	.889	1.108	1.397	1.860	2.306	2.896	3.355
9	.129	.261	.398	.543	.703	.883	1.100	1.383	1.833	2.262	2.821	3.250
10	.129	.260	.397	.542	.700	.879	1.093	1.372	1.812	2.228	2.764	3.169
11	.129	.260	.396	.540	.697	.876	1.088	1.363	1.796	2.201	2.718	3.106
12	.128	.259	.395	.539	.695	.873	1.083	1.356	1.782	2.179	2.681	3.055
13	.128	.259	.394	.538	.694	.870	1.079	1.350	1.771	2.160	2.650	3.012
14	.128	.258	.393	.537	.692	.868	1.076	1.345	1.761	2.145	2.624	2.977
15	.128	.258	.393	.536	.691	.866	1.074	1.341	1.753	2.131	2.602	2.947
16	.128	.258	.392	.535	.690	.865	1.071	1.337	1.746	2.120	2.583	2.921
17	.128	.257	.392	.534	.689	.863	1.069	1.333	1.740	2.110	2.567	2.898
18	.127	.257	.392	.534	.688	.862	1.067	1.330	1.734	2.101	2.552	2.878
19	.127	.257	.391	.533	.688	.861	1.066	1.328	1.729	2.093	2.539	2.861
20	.127	.257	.391	.533	.687	.860	1.064	1.325	1.725	2.086	2.528	2.845
21	.127	.257	.391	.532	.686	.859	1.063	1.323	1.721	2.080	2.518	2.831
22	.127	.256	.390	.532	.686	.858	1.061	1.321	1.717	2.074	2.508	2.819
23	.127	.256	.390	.532	.685	.858	1.060	1.319	1.714	2.069	2.500	2.807
24	.127	.256	.390	.531	.685	.857	1.059	1.318	1.711	2.064	2.492	2.797
25	.127	.256	.390	.531	.684	.856	1.058	1.316	1.708	2.060	2.485	2.787
26	.127	.256	.390	.531	.684	.856	1.058	1.315	1.706	2.056	2.479	2.779
27	.127	.256	.389	.531	.684	.855	1.057	1.314	1.703	2.052	2.473	2.771
28	.127	.256	.389	.530	.683	.855	1.056	1.313	1.701	2.048	2.467	2.763
29	.127	.256	.389	.530	.683	.854	1.055	1.311	1.699	2.045	2.462	2.756
30	.127	.256	.389	.530	.683	.854	1.055	1.310	1.697	2.042	2.457	2.750
∞	.12566	.25335	.38532	.52440	.67449	.84162	1.03643	1.28155	1.64485	1.95996	2.32634	2.57582

Note: All _p_ values are _two-tailed_ in this table. Table 3 presents a more detailed table of _t_ values for _one-tailed p_ ≤ .25.
Source: Reproduced from E. F. Lindquist, _Design and Analysis of Experiments in Psychology and Education_, Houghton Mifflin, Boston, 1953, p. 38, with the permission of the publisher.

Table 3 Extended table of *t*

df \ p	.25	.10	.05	.025	.01	.005	.0025	.001
1	1.000	3.078	6.314	12.706	31.821	63.657	127.321	318.309
2	.816	1.886	2.920	4.303	6.965	9.925	14.089	22.327
3	.765	1.638	2.353	3.182	4.541	5.841	7.453	10.214
4	.741	1.533	2.132	2.776	3.747	4.604	5.598	7.173
5	.727	1.476	2.015	2.571	3.365	4.032	4.773	5.893
6	.718	1.440	1.943	2.447	3.143	3.707	4.317	5.208
7	.711	1.415	1.895	2.365	2.998	3.499	4.029	4.785
8	.706	1.397	1.860	2.306	2.896	3.355	3.833	4.501
9	.703	1.383	1.833	2.262	2.821	3.250	3.690	4.297
10	.700	1.372	1.812	2.228	2.764	3.169	3.581	4.144
11	.697	1.363	1.796	2.201	2.718	3.106	3.497	4.025
12	.695	1.356	1.782	2.179	2.681	3.055	3.428	3.930
13	.694	1.350	1.771	2.160	2.650	3.012	3.372	3.852
14	.692	1.345	1.761	2.145	2.624	2.977	3.326	3.787
15	.691	1.341	1.753	2.131	2.602	2.947	3.286	3.733
16	.690	1.337	1.746	2.120	2.583	2.921	3.252	3.686
17	.689	1.333	1.740	2.110	2.567	2.898	3.223	3.646
18	.688	1.330	1.734	2.101	2.552	2.878	3.197	3.610
19	.688	1.328	1.729	2.093	2.539	2.861	3.174	3.579
20	.687	1.325	1.725	2.086	2.528	2.845	3.153	3.552
21	.686	1.323	1.721	2.080	2.518	2.831	3.135	3.527
22	.686	1.321	1.717	2.074	2.508	2.819	3.119	3.505
23	.685	1.319	1.714	2.069	2.500	2.807	3.104	3.485
24	.685	1.318	1.711	2.064	2.492	2.797	3.090	3.467
25	.684	1.316	1.708	2.060	2.485	2.787	3.078	3.450
26	.684	1.315	1.706	2.056	2.479	2.779	3.067	3.435
27	.684	1.314	1.703	2.052	2.473	2.771	3.057	3.421
28	.683	1.313	1.701	2.048	2.467	2.763	3.047	3.408
29	.683	1.311	1.699	2.045	2.462	2.756	3.038	3.396
30	.683	1.310	1.697	2.042	2.457	2.750	3.030	3.385
35	.682	1.306	1.690	2.030	2.438	2.724	2.996	3.340
40	.681	1.303	1.684	2.021	2.423	2.704	2.971	3.307
45	.680	1.301	1.679	2.014	2.412	2.690	2.952	3.281
50	.679	1.299	1.676	2.009	2.403	2.678	2.937	3.261
55	.679	1.297	1.673	2.004	2.396	2.668	2.925	3.245
60	.679	1.296	1.671	2.000	2.390	2.660	2.915	3.232
70	.678	1.294	1.667	1.994	2.381	2.648	2.899	3.211
80	.678	1.292	1.664	1.990	2.374	2.639	2.887	3.195
90	.677	1.291	1.662	1.987	2.368	2.632	2.878	3.183
100	.677	1.290	1.660	1.984	2.364	2.626	2.871	3.174
200	.676	1.286	1.652	1.972	2.345	2.601	2.838	3.131
500	.675	1.283	1.648	1.965	2.334	2.586	2.820	3.107
1,000	.675	1.282	1.646	1.962	2.330	2.581	2.813	3.098
2,000	.675	1.282	1.645	1.961	2.328	2.578	2.810	3.094
10,000	.675	1.282	1.645	1.960	2.327	2.576	2.808	3.091
∞	.674	1.282	1.645	1.960	2.326	2.576	2.807	3.090

Note: All *p* values are one-tailed in this table. For *p* values > .25 see Table 2.

Table 3 (*Continued*)

df \ p	.0005	.00025	.0001	.00005	.000025	.00001
1	636.619	1,273.239	3,183.099	6,366.198	12,732.395	31,830.989
2	31.598	44.705	70.700	99.992	141.416	223.603
3	12.924	16.326	22.204	28.000	35.298	47.928
4	8.610	10.306	13.034	15.544	18.522	23.332
5	6.869	7.976	9.678	11.178	12.893	15.547
6	5.959	6.788	8.025	9.082	10.261	12.032
7	5.408	6.082	7.063	7.885	8.782	10.103
8	5.041	5.618	6.442	7.120	7.851	8.907
9	4.781	5.291	6.010	6.594	7.215	8.102
10	4.587	5.049	5.694	6.211	6.757	7.527
11	4.437	4.863	5.453	5.921	6.412	7.098
12	4.318	4.716	5.263	5.694	6.143	6.756
13	4.221	4.597	5.111	5.513	5.928	6.501
14	4.140	4.499	4.985	5.363	5.753	6.287
15	4.073	4.417	4.880	5.239	5.607	6.109
16	4.015	4.346	4.791	5.134	5.484	5.960
17	3.965	4.286	4.714	5.044	5.379	5.832
18	3.922	4.233	4.648	4.966	5.288	5.722
19	3.883	4.187	4.590	4.897	5.209	5.627
20	3.850	4.146	4.539	4.837	5.139	5.543
21	3.819	4.110	4.493	4.784	5.077	5.469
22	3.792	4.077	4.452	4.736	5.022	5.402
23	3.768	4.048	4.415	4.693	4.972	5.343
24	3.745	4.021	4.382	4.654	4.927	5.290
25	3.725	3.997	4.352	4.619	4.887	5.241
26	3.707	3.974	4.324	4.587	4.850	5.197
27	3.690	3.954	4.299	4.558	4.816	5.157
28	3.674	3.935	4.275	4.530	4.784	5.120
29	3.659	3.918	4.254	4.506	4.756	5.086
30	3.646	3.902	4.234	4.482	4.729	5.054
35	3.591	3.836	4.153	4.389	4.622	4.927
40	3.551	3.788	4.094	4.321	4.544	4.835
45	3.520	3.752	4.049	4.269	4.485	4.766
50	3.496	3.723	4.014	4.228	4.438	4.711
55	3.476	3.700	3.986	4.196	4.401	4.667
60	3.460	3.681	3.962	4.169	4.370	4.631
70	3.435	3.651	3.926	4.127	4.323	4.576
80	3.416	3.629	3.899	4.096	4.288	4.535
90	3.402	3.612	3.878	4.072	4.261	4.503
100	3.390	3.598	3.862	4.053	4.240	4.478
200	3.340	3.539	3.789	3.970	4.146	4.369
500	3.310	3.504	3.747	3.922	4.091	4.306
1,000	3.300	3.492	3.733	3.906	4.073	4.285
2,000	3.295	3.486	3.726	3.898	4.064	4.275
10,000	3.292	3.482	3.720	3.892	4.058	4.267
∞	3.291	3.481	3.719	3.891	4.056	4.265

Note: All *p* values are one-tailed in this table.

Table 3 (*Continued*)

df	.000005	.0000025	.000001	.0000005	.00000025	.0000001
1	63,661.977	127,323.954	318,309.886	636,619.772	1,273,239.545	3,183,098.862
2	316.225	447.212	707.106	999.999	1,414.213	2,236.068
3	60.397	76.104	103.299	130.155	163.989	222.572
4	27.771	33.047	41.578	49.459	58.829	73.986
5	17.807	20.591	24.771	28.477	32.734	39.340
6	13.555	15.260	17.830	20.047	22.532	26.286
7	11.215	12.437	14.241	15.764	17.447	19.932
8	9.782	10.731	12.110	13.257	14.504	16.320
9	8.827	9.605	10.720	11.637	12.623	14.041
10	8.150	8.812	9.752	10.516	11.328	12.492
11	7.648	8.227	9.043	9.702	10.397	11.381
12	7.261	7.780	8.504	9.085	9.695	10.551
13	6.955	7.427	8.082	8.604	9.149	9.909
14	6.706	7.142	7.743	8.218	8.713	9.400
15	6.502	6.907	7.465	7.903	8.358	8.986
16	6.330	6.711	7.233	7.642	8.064	8.645
17	6.184	6.545	7.037	7.421	7.817	8.358
18	6.059	6.402	6.869	7.232	7.605	8.115
19	5.949	6.278	6.723	7.069	7.423	7.905
20	5.854	6.170	6.597	6.927	7.265	7.723
21	5.769	6.074	6.485	6.802	7.126	7.564
22	5.694	5.989	6.386	6.692	7.003	7.423
23	5.627	5.913	6.297	6.593	6.893	7.298
24	5.566	5.845	6.218	6.504	6.795	7.185
25	5.511	5.783	6.146	6.424	6.706	7.085
26	5.461	5.726	6.081	6.352	6.626	6.993
27	5.415	5.675	6.021	6.286	6.553	6.910
28	5.373	5.628	5.967	6.225	6.486	6.835
29	5.335	5.585	5.917	6.170	6.426	6.765
30	5.299	5.545	5.871	6.119	6.369	6.701
35	5.156	5.385	5.687	5.915	6.143	6.447
40	5.053	5.269	5.554	5.768	5.983	6.266
45	4.975	5.182	5.454	5.659	5.862	6.130
50	4.914	5.115	5.377	5.573	5.769	6.025
55	4.865	5.060	5.315	5.505	5.694	5.942
60	4.825	5.015	5.264	5.449	5.633	5.873
70	4.763	4.946	5.185	5.363	5.539	5.768
80	4.717	4.896	5.128	5.300	5.470	5.691
90	4.682	4.857	5.084	5.252	5.417	5.633
100	4.654	4.826	5.049	5.214	5.376	5.587
200	4.533	4.692	4.897	5.048	5.196	5.387
500	4.463	4.615	4.810	4.953	5.094	5.273
1,000	4.440	4.590	4.781	4.922	5.060	5.236
2,000	4.428	4.578	4.767	4.907	5.043	5.218
10,000	4.419	4.567	4.756	4.895	5.029	5.203
∞	4.417	4.565	4.753	4.892	5.026	5.199

Note: All p values are one-tailed in this table.
Standard normal deviates (Z) corresponding to t can be estimated quite accurately from:

$$Z = \left[df \log_e \left(1 + \frac{t^2}{df} \right) \right]^{1/2} \left[1 - \frac{1}{2df} \right]^{1/2}$$

Source: Reproduced from E. T. Federighi, Extended tables of the percentage points of Student's t-distribution, *Journal of the American Statistical Association*, 1959, *54*, 683–688, with the permission of the publisher.

Table 4 Table of F

df_2	p	1	2	3	4	5	6	8	12	24	∞
1	.001	405284	500000	540379	562500	576405	585937	598144	610667	623497	636619
	.005	16211	20000	21615	22500	23056	23437	23925	24426	24940	25465
	.01	4052	4999	5403	5625	5764	5859	5981	6106	6234	6366
	.025	647.79	799.50	864.16	899.58	921.85	937.11	956.66	976.71	997.25	1018.30
	.05	161.45	199.50	215.71	224.58	230.16	233.99	238.88	243.91	249.05	254.32
	.10	39.86	49.50	53.59	55.83	57.24	58.20	59.44	60.70	62.00	63.33
	.20	9.47	12.00	13.06	13.73	14.01	14.26	14.59	14.90	15.24	15.58
2	.001	998.5	999.0	999.2	999.2	999.3	999.3	999.4	999.4	999.5	999.5
	.005	198.50	199.00	199.17	199.25	199.30	199.33	199.37	199.42	199.46	199.51
	.01	98.49	99.00	99.17	99.25	99.30	99.33	99.36	99.42	99.46	99.50
	.025	38.51	39.00	39.17	39.25	39.30	39.33	39.37	39.42	39.46	39.50
	.05	18.51	19.00	19.16	19.25	19.30	19.33	19.37	19.41	19.45	19.50
	.10	8.53	9.00	9.16	9.24	9.29	9.33	9.37	9.41	9.45	9.49
	.20	3.56	4.00	4.16	4.24	4.28	4.32	4.36	4.40	4.44	4.48
3	.001	167.5	148.5	141.1	137.1	134.6	132.8	130.6	128.3	125.9	123.5
	.005	55.55	49.80	47.47	46.20	45.39	44.84	44.13	43.39	42.62	41.83
	.01	34.12	30.81	29.46	28.71	28.24	27.91	27.49	27.05	26.60	26.12
	.025	17.44	16.04	15.44	15.10	14.89	14.74	14.54	14.34	14.12	13.90
	.05	10.13	9.55	9.28	9.12	9.01	8.94	8.84	8.74	8.64	8.53
	.10	5.54	5.46	5.39	5.34	5.31	5.28	5.25	5.22	5.18	5.13
	.20	2.68	2.89	2.94	2.96	2.97	2.97	2.98	2.98	2.98	2.98
4	.001	74.14	61.25	56.18	53.44	51.71	50.53	49.00	47.41	45.77	44.05
	.005	31.33	26.28	24.26	23.16	22.46	21.98	21.35	20.71	20.03	19.33
	.01	21.20	18.00	16.69	15.98	15.52	15.21	14.80	14.37	13.93	13.46
	.025	12.22	10.65	9.98	9.60	9.36	9.20	8.98	8.75	8.51	8.26
	.05	7.71	6.94	6.59	6.39	6.26	6.16	6.04	5.91	5.77	5.63
	.10	4.54	4.32	4.19	4.11	4.05	4.01	3.95	3.90	3.83	3.76
	.20	2.35	2.47	2.48	2.48	2.48	2.47	2.47	2.46	2.44	2.43
5	.001	47.04	36.61	33.20	31.09	29.75	28.84	27.64	26.42	25.14	23.78
	.005	22.79	18.31	16.53	15.56	14.94	14.51	13.96	13.38	12.78	12.14
	.01	16.26	13.27	12.06	11.39	10.97	10.67	10.29	9.89	9.47	9.02
	.025	10.01	8.43	7.76	7.39	7.15	6.98	6.76	6.52	6.28	6.02
	.05	6.61	5.79	5.41	5.19	5.05	4.95	4.82	4.68	4.53	4.36
	.10	4.06	3.78	3.62	3.52	3.45	3.40	3.34	3.27	3.19	3.10
	.20	2.18	2.26	2.25	2.24	2.23	2.22	2.20	2.18	2.16	2.13
6	.001	35.51	27.00	23.70	21.90	20.81	20.03	19.03	17.99	16.89	15.75
	.005	18.64	14.54	12.92	12.03	11.46	11.07	10.57	10.03	9.47	8.88
	.01	13.74	10.92	9.78	9.15	8.75	8.47	8.10	7.72	7.31	6.88
	.025	8.81	7.26	6.60	6.23	5.99	5.82	5.60	5.37	5.12	4.85
	.05	5.99	5.14	4.76	4.53	4.39	4.28	4.15	4.00	3.84	3.67
	.10	3.78	3.46	3.29	3.18	3.11	3.05	2.98	2.90	2.82	2.72
	.20	2.07	2.13	2.11	2.09	2.08	2.06	2.04	2.02	1.99	1.95
7	.001	29.22	21.69	18.77	17.19	16.21	15.52	14.63	13.71	12.73	11.69
	.005	16.24	12.40	10.88	10.05	9.52	9.16	8.68	8.18	7.65	7.08
	.01	12.25	9.55	8.45	7.85	7.46	7.19	6.84	6.47	6.07	5.65
	.025	8.07	6.54	5.89	5.52	5.29	5.12	4.90	4.67	4.42	4.14
	.05	5.59	4.74	4.35	4.12	3.97	3.87	3.73	3.57	3.41	3.23
	.10	3.59	3.26	3.07	2.96	2.88	2.83	2.75	2.67	2.58	2.47
	.20	2.00	2.04	2.02	1.99	1.97	1.96	1.93	1.91	1.87	1.83
8	.001	25.42	18.49	15.83	14.39	13.49	12.86	12.04	11.19	10.30	9.34
	.005	14.69	11.04	9.60	8.81	8.30	7.95	7.50	7.01	6.50	5.95
	.01	11.26	8.65	7.59	7.01	6.63	6.37	6.03	5.67	5.28	4.86
	.025	7.57	6.06	5.42	5.05	4.82	4.65	4.43	4.20	3.95	3.67
	.05	5.32	4.46	4.07	3.84	3.69	3.58	3.44	3.28	3.12	2.93
	.10	3.46	3.11	2.92	2.81	2.73	2.67	2.59	2.50	2.40	2.29
	.20	1.95	1.98	1.95	1.92	1.90	1.88	1.86	1.83	1.79	1.74
9	.001	22.86	16.39	13.90	12.56	11.71	11.13	10.37	9.57	8.72	7.81
	.005	13.61	10.11	8.72	7.96	7.47	7.13	6.69	6.23	5.73	5.19
	.01	10.56	8.02	6.99	6.42	6.06	5.80	5.47	5.11	4.73	4.31
	.025	7.21	5.71	5.08	4.72	4.48	4.32	4.10	3.87	3.61	3.33
	.05	5.12	4.26	3.86	3.63	3.48	3.37	3.23	3.07	2.90	2.71
	.10	3.36	3.01	2.81	2.69	2.61	2.55	2.47	2.38	2.28	2.16
	.20	1.91	1.94	1.90	1.87	1.85	1.83	1.80	1.76	1.72	1.67

Table 4 (*Continued*)

df_2	p	df_1 1	2	3	4	5	6	8	12	24	∞
10	.001	21.04	14.91	12.55	11.28	10.48	9.92	9.20	8.45	7.64	6.76
	.005	12.83	9.43	8.08	7.34	6.87	6.54	6.12	5.66	5.17	4.64
	.01	10.04	7.56	6.55	5.99	5.64	5.39	5.06	4.71	4.33	3.91
	.025	6.94	5.46	4.83	4.47	4.24	4.07	3.85	3.62	3.37	3.08
	.05	4.96	4.10	3.71	3.48	3.33	3.22	3.07	2.91	2.74	2.54
	.10	3.28	2.92	2.73	2.61	2.52	2.46	2.38	2.28	2.18	2.06
	.20	1.88	1.90	1.86	1.83	1.80	1.78	1.75	1.72	1.67	1.62
11	.001	19.69	13.81	11.56	10.35	9.58	9.05	8.35	7.63	6.85	6.00
	.005	12.23	8.91	7.60	6.88	6.42	6.10	5.68	5.24	4.76	4.23
	.01	9.65	7.20	6.22	5.67	5.32	5.07	4.74	4.40	4.02	3.60
	.025	6.72	5.26	4.63	4.28	4.04	3.88	3.66	3.43	3.17	2.88
	.05	4.84	3.98	3.59	3.36	3.20	3.09	2.95	2.79	2.61	2.40
	.10	3.23	2.86	2.66	2.54	2.45	2.39	2.30	2.21	2.10	1.97
	.20	1.86	1.87	1.83	1.80	1.77	1.75	1.72	1.68	1.63	1.57
12	.001	18.64	12.97	10.80	9.63	8.89	8.38	7.71	7.00	6.25	5.42
	.005	11.75	8.51	7.23	6.52	6.07	5.76	5.35	4.91	4.43	3.90
	.01	9.33	6.93	5.95	5.41	5.06	4.82	4.50	4.16	3.78	3.36
	.025	6.55	5.10	4.47	4.12	3.89	3.73	3.51	3.28	3.02	2.72
	.05	4.75	3.88	3.49	3.26	3.11	3.00	2.85	2.69	2.50	2.30
	.10	3.18	2.81	2.61	2.48	2.39	2.33	2.24	2.15	2.04	1.90
	.20	1.84	1.85	1.80	1.77	1.74	1.72	1.69	1.65	1.60	1.54
13	.001	17.81	12.31	10.21	9.07	8.35	7.86	7.21	6.52	5.78	4.97
	.005	11.37	8.19	6.93	6.23	5.79	5.48	5.08	4.64	4.17	3.65
	.01	9.07	6.70	5.74	5.20	4.86	4.62	4.30	3.96	3.59	3.16
	.025	6.41	4.97	4.35	4.00	3.77	3.60	3.39	3.15	2.89	2.60
	.05	4.67	3.80	3.41	3.18	3.02	2.92	2.77	2.60	2.42	2.21
	.10	3.14	2.76	2.56	2.43	2.35	2.28	2.20	2.10	1.98	1.85
	.20	1.82	1.83	1.78	1.75	1.72	1.69	1.66	1.62	1.57	1.51
14	.001	17.14	11.78	9.73	8.62	7.92	7.43	6.80	6.13	5.41	4.60
	.005	11.06	7.92	6.68	6.00	5.56	5.26	4.86	4.43	3.96	3.44
	.01	8.86	6.51	5.56	5.03	4.69	4.46	4.14	3.80	3.43	3.00
	.025	6.30	4.86	4.24	3.89	3.66	3.50	3.29	3.05	2.79	2.49
	.05	4.60	3.74	3.34	3.11	2.96	2.85	2.70	2.53	2.35	2.13
	.10	3.10	2.73	2.52	2.39	2.31	2.24	2.15	2.05	1.94	1.80
	.20	1.81	1.81	1.76	1.73	1.70	1.67	1.64	1.60	1.55	1.48
15	.001	16.59	11.34	9.34	8.25	7.57	7.09	6.47	5.81	5.10	4.31
	.005	10.80	7.70	6.48	5.80	5.37	5.07	4.67	4.25	3.79	3.26
	.01	8.68	6.36	5.42	4.89	4.56	4.32	4.00	3.67	3.29	2.87
	.025	6.20	4.77	4.15	3.80	3.58	3.41	3.20	2.96	2.70	2.40
	.05	4.54	3.68	3.29	3.06	2.90	2.79	2.64	2.48	2.29	2.07
	.10	3.07	2.70	2.49	2.36	2.27	2.21	2.12	2.02	1.90	1.76
	.20	1.80	1.79	1.75	1.71	1.68	1.66	1.62	1.58	1.53	1.46
16	.001	16.12	10.97	9.00	7.94	7.27	6.81	6.19	5.55	4.85	4.06
	.005	10.58	7.51	6.30	5.64	5.21	4.91	4.52	4.10	3.64	3.11
	.01	8.53	6.23	5.29	4.77	4.44	4.20	3.89	3.55	3.18	2.75
	.025	6.12	4.69	4.08	3.73	3.50	3.34	3.12	2.89	2.63	2.32
	.05	4.49	3.63	3.24	3.01	2.85	2.74	2.59	2.42	2.24	2.01
	.10	3.05	2.67	2.46	2.33	2.24	2.18	2.09	1.99	1.87	1.72
	.20	1.79	1.78	1.74	1.70	1.67	1.64	1.61	1.56	1.51	1.43
17	.001	15.72	10.66	8.73	7.68	7.02	6.56	5.96	5.32	4.63	3.85
	.005	10.38	7.35	6.16	5.50	5.07	4.78	4.39	3.97	3.51	2.98
	.01	8.40	6.11	5.18	4.67	4.34	4.10	3.79	3.45	3.08	2.65
	.025	6.04	4.62	4.01	3.66	3.44	3.28	3.06	2.82	2.56	2.25
	.05	4.45	3.59	3.20	2.96	2.81	2.70	2.55	2.38	2.19	1.96
	.10	3.03	2.64	2.44	2.31	2.22	2.15	2.06	1.96	1.84	1.69
	.20	1.78	1.77	1.72	1.68	1.65	1.63	1.59	1.55	1.49	1.42
18	.001	15.38	10.39	8.49	7.46	6.81	6.35	5.76	5.13	4.45	3.67
	.005	10.22	7.21	6.03	5.37	4.96	4.66	4.28	3.86	3.40	2.87
	.01	8.28	6.01	5.09	4.58	4.25	4.01	3.71	3.37	3.00	2.57
	.025	5.98	4.56	3.95	3.61	3.38	3.22	3.01	2.77	2.50	2.19
	.05	4.41	3.55	3.16	2.93	2.77	2.66	2.51	2.34	2.15	1.92
	.10	3.01	2.62	2.42	2.29	2.20	2.13	2.04	1.93	1.81	1.66
	.20	1.77	1.76	1.71	1.67	1.64	1.62	1.58	1.53	1.48	1.40

Table 4 (*Continued*)

	p	1	2	3	4	5	6	8	12	24	∞
df_2 / df_1											
19	.001	15.08	10.16	8.28	7.26	6.61	6.18	5.59	4.97	4.29	3.52
	.005	10.07	7.09	5.92	5.27	4.85	4.56	4.18	3.76	3.31	2.78
	.01	8.18	5.93	5.01	4.50	4.17	3.94	3.63	3.30	2.92	2.49
	.025	5.92	4.51	3.90	3.56	3.33	3.17	2.96	2.72	2.45	2.13
	.05	4.38	3.52	3.13	2.90	2.74	2.63	2.48	2.31	2.11	1.88
	.10	2.99	2.61	2.40	2.27	2.18	2.11	2.02	1.91	1.79	1.63
	.20	1.76	1.75	1.70	1.66	1.63	1.61	1.57	1.52	1.46	1.39
20	.001	14.82	9.95	8.10	7.10	6.46	6.02	5.44	4.82	4.15	3.38
	.005	9.94	6.99	5.82	5.17	4.76	4.47	4.09	3.68	3.22	2.69
	.01	8.10	5.85	4.94	4.43	4.10	3.87	3.56	3.23	2.86	2.42
	.025	5.87	4.46	3.86	3.51	3.29	3.13	2.91	2.68	2.41	2.09
	.05	4.35	3.49	3.10	2.87	2.71	2.60	2.45	2.28	2.08	1.84
	.10	2.97	2.59	2.38	2.25	2.16	2.09	2.00	1.89	1.77	1.61
	.20	1.76	1.75	1.70	1.65	1.62	1.60	1.56	1.51	1.45	1.37
21	.001	14.59	9.77	7.94	6.95	6.32	5.88	5.31	4.70	4.03	3.26
	.005	9.83	6.89	5.73	5.09	4.68	4.39	4.01	3.60	3.15	2.61
	.01	8.02	5.78	4.87	4.37	4.04	3.81	3.51	3.17	2.80	2.36
	.025	5.83	4.42	3.82	3.48	3.25	3.09	2.87	2.64	2.37	2.04
	.05	4.32	3.47	3.07	2.84	2.68	2.57	2.42	2.25	2.05	1.81
	.10	2.96	2.57	2.36	2.23	2.14	2.08	1.98	1.88	1.75	1.59
	.20	1.75	1.74	1.69	1.65	1.61	1.59	1.55	1.50	1.44	1.36
22	.001	14.38	9.61	7.80	6.81	6.19	5.76	5.19	4.58	3.92	3.15
	.005	9.73	6.81	5.65	5.02	4.61	4.32	3.94	3.54	3.08	2.55
	.01	7.94	5.72	4.82	4.31	3.99	3.76	3.45	3.12	2.75	2.31
	.025	5.79	4.38	3.78	3.44	3.22	3.05	2.84	2.60	2.33	2.00
	.05	4.30	3.44	3.05	2.82	2.66	2.55	2.40	2.23	2.03	1.78
	.10	2.95	2.56	2.35	2.22	2.13	2.06	1.97	1.86	1.73	1.57
	.20	1.75	1.73	1.68	1.64	1.61	1.58	1.54	1.49	1.43	1.35
23	.001	14.19	9.47	7.67	6.69	6.08	5.65	5.09	4.48	3.82	3.05
	.005	9.63	6.73	5.58	4.95	4.54	4.26	3.88	3.47	3.02	2.48
	.01	7.88	5.66	4.76	4.26	3.94	3.71	3.41	3.07	2.70	2.26
	.025	5.75	4.35	3.75	3.41	3.18	3.02	2.81	2.57	2.30	1.97
	.05	4.28	3.42	3.03	2.80	2.64	2.53	2.38	2.20	2.00	1.76
	.10	2.94	2.55	2.34	2.21	2.11	2.05	1.95	1.84	1.72	1.55
	.20	1.74	1.73	1.68	1.63	1.60	1.57	1.53	1.49	1.42	1.34
24	.001	14.03	9.34	7.55	6.59	5.98	5.55	4.99	4.39	3.74	2.97
	.005	9.55	6.66	5.52	4.89	4.49	4.20	3.83	3.42	2.97	2.43
	.01	7.82	5.61	4.72	4.22	3.90	3.67	3.36	3.03	2.66	2.21
	.025	5.72	4.32	3.72	3.38	3.15	2.99	2.78	2.54	2.27	1.94
	.05	4.26	3.40	3.01	2.78	2.62	2.51	2.36	2.18	1.98	1.73
	.10	2.93	2.54	2.33	2.19	2.10	2.04	1.94	1.83	1.70	1.53
	.20	1.74	1.72	1.67	1.63	1.59	1.57	1.53	1.48	1.42	1.33
25	.001	13.88	9.22	7.45	6.49	5.88	5.46	4.91	4.31	3.66	2.89
	.005	9.48	6.60	5.46	4.84	4.43	4.15	3.78	3.37	2.92	2.38
	.01	7.77	5.57	4.68	4.18	3.86	3.63	3.32	2.99	2.62	2.17
	.025	5.69	4.29	3.69	3.35	3.13	2.97	2.75	2.51	2.24	1.91
	.05	4.24	3.38	2.99	2.76	2.60	2.49	2.34	2.16	1.96	1.71
	.10	2.92	2.53	2.32	2.18	2.09	2.02	1.93	1.82	1.69	1.52
	.20	1.73	1.72	1.66	1.62	1.59	1.56	1.52	1.47	1.41	1.32
26	.001	13.74	9.12	7.36	6.41	5.80	5.38	4.83	4.24	3.59	2.82
	.005	9.41	6.54	5.41	4.79	4.38	4.10	3.73	3.33	2.87	2.33
	.01	7.72	5.53	4.64	4.14	3.82	3.59	3.29	2.96	2.58	2.13
	.025	5.66	4.27	3.67	3.33	3.10	2.94	2.73	2.49	2.22	1.88
	.05	4.22	3.37	2.98	2.74	2.59	2.47	2.32	2.15	1.95	1.69
	.10	2.91	2.52	2.31	2.17	2.08	2.01	1.92	1.81	1.68	1.50
	.20	1.73	1.71	1.66	1.62	1.58	1.56	1.52	1.47	1.40	1.31
27	.001	13.61	9.02	7.27	6.33	5.73	5.31	4.76	4.17	3.52	2.75
	.005	9.34	6.49	5.36	4.74	4.34	4.06	3.69	3.28	2.83	2.29
	.01	7.68	5.49	4.60	4.11	3.78	3.56	3.26	2.93	2.55	2.10
	.025	5.63	4.24	3.65	3.31	3.08	2.92	2.71	2.47	2.19	1.85
	.05	4.21	3.35	2.96	2.73	2.57	2.46	2.30	2.13	1.93	1.67
	.10	2.90	2.51	2.30	2.17	2.07	2.00	1.91	1.80	1.67	1.49
	.20	1.73	1.71	1.66	1.61	1.58	1.55	1.51	1.46	1.40	1.30

Table 4 (*Continued*)

df_2 \ df_1	p	1	2	3	4	5	6	8	12	24	∞
28	.001	13.50	8.93	7.19	6.25	5.66	5.24	4.69	4.11	3.46	2.70
	.005	9.28	6.44	5.32	4.70	4.30	4.02	3.65	3.25	2.79	2.25
	.01	7.64	5.45	4.57	4.07	3.75	3.53	3.23	2.90	2.52	2.06
	.025	5.61	4.22	3.63	3.29	3.06	2.90	2.69	2.45	2.17	1.83
	.05	4.20	3.34	2.95	2.71	2.56	2.44	2.29	2.12	1.91	1.65
	.10	2.89	2.50	2.29	2.16	2.06	2.00	1.90	1.79	1.66	1.48
	.20	1.72	1.71	1.65	1.61	1.57	1.55	1.51	1.46	1.39	1.30
29	.001	13.39	8.85	7.12	6.19	5.59	5.18	4.64	4.05	3.41	2.64
	.005	9.23	6.40	5.28	4.66	4.26	3.98	3.61	3.21	2.76	2.21
	.01	7.60	5.42	4.54	4.04	3.73	3.50	3.20	2.87	2.49	2.03
	.025	5.59	4.20	3.61	3.27	3.04	2.88	2.67	2.43	2.15	1.81
	.05	4.18	3.33	2.93	2.70	2.54	2.43	2.28	2.10	1.90	1.64
	.10	2.89	2.50	2.28	2.15	2.06	1.99	1.89	1.78	1.65	1.47
	.20	1.72	1.70	1.65	1.60	1.57	1.54	1.50	1.45	1.39	1.29
30	.001	13.29	8.77	7.05	6.12	5.53	5.12	4.58	4.00	3.36	2.59
	.005	9.18	6.35	5.24	4.62	4.23	3.95	3.58	3.18	2.73	2.18
	.01	7.56	5.39	4.51	4.02	3.70	3.47	3.17	2.84	2.47	2.01
	.025	5.57	4.18	3.59	3.25	3.03	2.87	2.65	2.41	2.14	1.79
	.05	4.17	3.32	2.92	2.69	2.53	2.42	2.27	2.09	1.89	1.62
	.10	2.88	2.49	2.28	2.14	2.05	1.98	1.88	1.77	1.64	1.46
	.20	1.72	1.70	1.64	1.60	1.57	1.54	1.50	1.45	1.38	1.28
40	.001	12.61	8.25	6.60	5.70	5.13	4.73	4.21	3.64	3.01	2.23
	.005	8.83	6.07	4.98	4.37	3.99	3.71	3.35	2.95	2.50	1.93
	.01	7.31	5.18	4.31	3.83	3.51	3.29	2.99	2.66	2.29	1.80
	.025	5.42	4.05	3.46	3.13	2.90	2.74	2.53	2.29	2.01	1.64
	.05	4.08	3.23	2.84	2.61	2.45	2.34	2.18	2.00	1.79	1.51
	.10	2.84	2.44	2.23	2.09	2.00	1.93	1.83	1.71	1.57	1.38
	.20	1.70	1.68	1.62	1.57	1.54	1.51	1.47	1.41	1.34	1.24
60	.001	11.97	7.76	6.17	5.31	4.76	4.37	3.87	3.31	2.69	1.90
	.005	8.49	5.80	4.73	4.14	3.76	3.49	3.13	2.74	2.29	1.69
	.01	7.08	4.98	4.13	3.65	3.34	3.12	2.82	2.50	2.12	1.60
	.025	5.29	3.93	3.34	3.01	2.79	2.63	2.41	2.17	1.88	1.48
	.05	4.00	3.15	2.76	2.52	2.37	2.25	2.10	1.92	1.70	1.39
	.10	2.79	2.39	2.18	2.04	1.95	1.87	1.77	1.66	1.51	1.29
	.20	1.68	1.65	1.59	1.55	1.51	1.48	1.44	1.38	1.31	1.18
120	.001	11.38	7.31	5.79	4.95	4.42	4.04	3.55	3.02	2.40	1.56
	.005	8.18	5.54	4.50	3.92	3.55	3.28	2.93	2.54	2.09	1.43
	.01	6.85	4.79	3.95	3.48	3.17	2.96	2.66	2.34	1.95	1.38
	.025	5.15	3.80	3.23	2.89	2.67	2.52	2.30	2.05	1.76	1.31
	.05	3.92	3.07	2.68	2.45	2.29	2.17	2.02	1.83	1.61	1.25
	.10	2.75	2.35	2.13	1.99	1.90	1.82	1.72	1.60	1.45	1.19
	.20	1.66	1.63	1.57	1.52	1.48	1.45	1.41	1.35	1.27	1.12
∞	.001	10.83	6.91	5.42	4.62	4.10	3.74	3.27	2.74	2.13	1.00
	.005	7.88	5.30	4.28	3.72	3.35	3.09	2.74	2.36	1.90	1.00
	.01	6.64	4.60	3.78	3.32	3.02	2.80	2.51	2.18	1.79	1.00
	.025	5.02	3.69	3.12	2.79	2.57	2.41	2.19	1.94	1.64	1.00
	.05	3.84	2.99	2.60	2.37	2.21	2.09	1.94	1.75	1.52	1.00
	.10	2.71	2.30	2.08	1.94	1.85	1.77	1.67	1.55	1.38	1.00
	.20	1.64	1.61	1.55	1.50	1.46	1.43	1.38	1.32	1.23	1.00

Source: Reproduced from E. F. Lindquist, *Design and Analysis of Experiments in Psychology and Education,* Houghton Mifflin, Boston, 1953, pp. 41–44, with the permission of the publisher.

Table 5 Table of χ²

df	Probability													
	.99	.98	.95	.90	.80	.70	.50	.30	.20	.10	.05	.02	.01	.001
1	.0³157	.0²628	.00393	.0158	.0642	.148	.455	1.074	1.642	2.706	3.841	5.412	6.635	10.827
2	.0201	.0404	.103	.211	.446	.713	1.386	2.408	3.219	4.605	5.991	7.824	9.210	13.815
3	.115	.185	.352	.584	1.005	1.424	2.366	3.665	4.642	6.251	7.815	9.837	11.345	16.268
4	.297	.429	.711	1.064	1.649	2.195	3.357	4.878	5.989	7.779	9.488	11.668	13.277	18.465
5	.554	.752	1.145	1.610	2.343	3.000	4.351	6.064	7.289	9.236	11.070	13.388	15.086	20.517
6	.872	1.134	1.635	2.204	3.070	3.828	5.348	7.231	8.558	10.645	12.592	15.033	16.812	22.457
7	1.239	1.564	2.167	2.833	3.822	4.671	6.346	8.383	9.803	12.017	14.067	16.622	18.475	24.322
8	1.646	2.032	2.733	3.490	4.594	5.527	7.344	9.524	11.030	13.362	15.507	18.168	20.090	26.125
9	2.088	2.532	3.325	4.168	5.380	6.393	8.343	10.656	12.242	14.684	16.919	19.679	21.666	27.877
10	2.558	3.059	3.940	4.865	6.179	7.267	9.342	11.781	13.442	15.987	18.307	21.161	23.209	29.588
11	3.053	3.609	4.575	5.578	6.989	8.148	10.341	12.899	14.631	17.275	19.675	22.618	24.725	31.264
12	3.571	4.178	5.226	6.304	7.807	9.034	11.340	14.011	15.812	18.549	21.026	24.054	26.217	32.909
13	4.107	4.765	5.892	7.042	8.634	9.926	12.340	15.119	16.985	19.812	22.362	25.472	27.688	34.528
14	4.660	5.368	6.571	7.790	9.467	10.821	13.339	16.222	18.151	21.064	23.685	26.873	29.141	36.123
15	5.229	5.985	7.261	8.547	10.307	11.721	14.339	17.322	19.311	22.307	24.996	28.259	30.578	37.697
16	5.812	6.614	7.962	9.312	11.152	12.624	15.338	18.418	20.465	23.542	26.296	29.633	32.000	39.252
17	6.408	7.255	8.672	10.085	12.002	13.531	16.338	19.511	21.615	24.769	27.587	30.995	33.409	40.790
18	7.015	7.906	9.390	10.865	12.857	14.440	17.338	20.601	22.760	25.989	28.869	32.346	34.805	42.312
19	7.633	8.567	10.117	11.651	13.716	15.352	18.338	21.689	23.900	27.204	30.144	33.687	36.191	43.820
20	8.260	9.237	10.851	12.443	14.578	16.266	19.337	22.775	25.038	28.412	31.410	35.020	37.566	45.315
21	8.897	9.915	11.591	13.240	15.445	17.182	20.337	23.858	26.171	29.615	32.671	36.343	38.932	46.797
22	9.542	10.600	12.338	14.041	16.314	18.101	21.337	24.939	27.301	30.813	33.924	37.659	40.289	48.268
23	10.196	11.293	13.091	14.848	17.187	19.021	22.337	26.018	28.429	32.007	35.172	38.968	41.638	49.728
24	10.856	11.992	13.848	15.659	18.062	19.943	23.337	27.096	29.553	33.196	36.415	40.270	42.980	51.179
25	11.524	12.697	14.611	16.473	18.940	20.867	24.337	28.172	30.675	34.382	37.652	41.566	44.314	52.620
26	12.198	13.409	15.379	17.292	19.820	21.792	25.336	29.246	31.795	35.563	38.885	42.856	45.642	54.052
27	12.879	14.125	16.151	18.114	20.703	22.719	26.336	30.319	32.912	36.741	40.113	44.140	46.963	55.476
28	13.565	14.847	16.928	18.939	21.588	23.647	27.336	31.391	34.027	37.916	41.337	45.419	48.278	56.893
29	14.256	15.574	17.708	19.768	22.475	24.577	28.336	32.461	35.139	39.087	42.557	46.693	49.588	58.302
30	14.953	16.306	18.493	20.599	23.364	25.508	29.336	33.530	36.250	40.256	43.773	47.962	50.892	59.703

Note: For larger values of *df*, the expression $\sqrt{2\chi^2} - \sqrt{2df - 1}$ may be used as a normal deviate with unit variance, remembering that the probability for χ^2 corresponds with that of a single tail of the normal curve.

Source: Reproduced from E. F. Lindquist, *Design and Analysis of Experiments in Psychology and Education,* Houghton Mifflin, Boston, 1953, p. 29, with the permission of the publisher.

Table 6 Significance levels of r

(N-2)	Probability level				
	.10	.05	.02	.01	.001
1	.988	.997	.9995	.9999	1.000
2	.900	.950	.980	.990	.999
3	.805	.878	.934	.959	.991
4	.729	.811	.882	.917	.974
5	.669	.754	.833	.874	.951
6	.622	.707	.789	.834	.925
7	.582	.666	.750	.798	.898
8	.550	.632	.716	.765	.872
9	.521	.602	.685	.735	.847
10	.497	.576	.658	.708	.823
11	.476	.553	.634	.684	.801
12	.458	.532	.612	.661	.780
13	.441	.514	.592	.641	.760
14	.426	.497	.574	.623	.742
15	.412	.482	.558	.606	.725
16	.400	.468	.542	.590	.708
17	.389	.456	.528	.575	.693
18	.378	.444	.516	.561	.679
19	.369	.433	.503	.549	.665
20	.360	.423	.492	.537	.652
22	.344	.404	.472	.515	.629
24	.330	.388	.453	.496	.607
25	.323	.381	.445	.487	.597
30	.296	.349	.409	.449	.554
35	.275	.325	.381	.418	.519
40	.257	.304	.358	.393	.490
45	.243	.288	.338	.372	.465
50	.231	.273	.322	.354	.443
55	.220	.261	.307	.338	.424
60	.211	.250	.295	.325	.408
65	.203	.240	.284	.312	.393
70	.195	.232	.274	.302	.380
75	.189	.224	.264	.292	.368
80	.183	.217	.256	.283	.357
85	.178	.211	.249	.275	.347
90	.173	.205	.242	.267	.338
95	.168	.200	.236	.260	.329
100	.164	.195	.230	.254	.321
125	.147	.174	.206	.228	.288
150	.134	.159	.189	.208	.264
175	.124	.148	.174	.194	.248
200	.116	.138	.164	.181	.235
300	.095	.113	.134	.148	.188
500	.074	.088	.104	.115	.148
1000	.052	.062	.073	.081	.104
2000	.037	.044	.052	.058	.074

Note: All p values are two-tailed in this table.

Source: Reproduced from H. M. Walker and J. Lev, *Statistical Inference,* Holt, New York, 1953, p. 470, with the permission of the author and publisher.

Table 7 Table of Fisher's z transformation of r

Second digit of r

r	.00	.01	.02	.03	.04	.05	.06	.07	.08	.09
.0	.000	.010	.020	.030	.040	.050	.060	.070	.080	.090
.1	.100	.110	.121	.131	.141	.151	.161	.172	.182	.192
.2	.203	.213	.224	.234	.245	.255	.266	.277	.288	.299
.3	.310	.321	.332	.343	.354	.365	.377	.388	.400	.412
.4	.424	.436	.448	.460	.472	.485	.497	.510	.523	.536
.5	.549	.563	.576	.590	.604	.618	.633	.648	.662	.678
.6	.693	.709	.725	.741	.758	.775	.793	.811	.829	.848
.7	.867	.887	.908	.929	.950	.973	.996	1.020	1.045	1.071
.8	1.099	1.127	1.157	1.188	1.221	1.256	1.293	1.333	1.376	1.422

Third digit of r

r	.000	.001	.002	.003	.004	.005	.006	.007	.008	.009
.90	1.472	1.478	1.483	1.488	1.494	1.499	1.505	1.510	1.516	1.522
.91	1.528	1.533	1.539	1.545	1.551	1.557	1.564	1.570	1.576	1.583
.92	1.589	1.596	1.602	1.609	1.616	1.623	1.630	1.637	1.644	1.651
.93	1.658	1.666	1.673	1.681	1.689	1.697	1.705	1.713	1.721	1.730
.94	1.738	1.747	1.756	1.764	1.774	1.783	1.792	1.802	1.812	1.822
.95	1.832	1.842	1.853	1.863	1.874	1.886	1.897	1.909	1.921	1.933
.96	1.946	1.959	1.972	1.986	2.000	2.014	2.029	2.044	2.060	2.076
.97	2.092	2.109	2.127	2.146	2.165	2.185	2.205	2.227	2.249	2.273
.98	2.298	2.323	2.351	2.380	2.410	2.443	2.477	2.515	2.555	2.599
.99	2.646	2.700	2.759	2.826	2.903	2.994	3.106	3.250	3.453	3.800

Note: z is obtained as $\frac{1}{2}\log_e \frac{(1 + r)}{(1 - r)}$.

Source: Reprinted by permission from *Statistical Methods* by George W. Snedecor and William G. Cochran, 7th ed. (c) 1980 by the Iowa State University Press, Ames, Iowa 50010.

Table 8 Table of *r* equivalents of Fisher's *z*

z	.00	.01	.02	.03	.04	.05	.06	.07	.08	.09
.0	.000	.010	.020	.030	.040	.050	.060	.070	.080	.090
.1	.100	.110	.119	.129	.139	.149	.159	.168	.178	.187
.2	.197	.207	.216	.226	.236	.245	.254	.264	.273	.282
.3	.291	.300	.310	.319	.327	.336	.345	.354	.363	.371
.4	.380	.389	.397	.405	.414	.422	.430	.438	.446	.454
.5	.462	.470	.478	.485	.493	.500	.508	.515	.523	.530
.6	.537	.544	.551	.558	.565	.572	.578	.585	.592	.598
.7	.604	.611	.617	.623	.629	.635	.641	.647	.653	.658
.8	.664	.670	.675	.680	.686	.691	.696	.701	.706	.711
.9	.716	.721	.726	.731	.735	.740	.744	.749	.753	.757
1.0	.762	.766	.770	.774	.778	.782	.786	.790	.793	.797
1.1	.800	.804	.808	.811	.814	.818	.821	.824	.828	.831
1.2	.834	.837	.840	.843	.846	.848	.851	.854	.856	.859
1.3	.862	.864	.867	.869	.872	.874	.876	.879	.881	.883
1.4	.885	.888	.890	.892	.894	.896	.898	.900	.902	.903
1.5	.905	.907	.909	.910	.912	.914	.915	.917	.919	.920
1.6	.922	.923	.925	.926	.928	.929	.930	.932	.933	.934
1.7	.935	.937	.938	.939	.940	.941	.942	.944	.945	.946
1.8	.947	.948	.949	.950	.951	.952	.953	.954	.954	.955
1.9	.956	.957	.958	.959	.960	.960	.961	.962	.963	.963
2.0	.964	.965	.965	.966	.967	.967	.968	.969	.969	.970
2.1	.970	.971	.972	.972	.973	.973	.974	.974	.975	.975
2.2	.976	.976	.977	.977	.978	.978	.978	.979	.979	.980
2.3	.980	.980	.981	.981	.982	.982	.982	.983	.983	.983
2.4	.984	.984	.984	.985	.985	.985	.986	.986	.986	.986
2.5	.987	.987	.987	.987	.988	.988	.988	.988	.989	.989
2.6	.989	.989	.989	.990	.990	.990	.990	.990	.991	.991
2.7	.991	.991	.991	.992	.992	.992	.992	.992	.992	.992
2.8	.993	.993	.993	.993	.993	.993	.993	.994	.994	.994
2.9	.994	.994	.994	.994	.994	.995	.995	.995	.995	.995

Note: r is obtained as $\dfrac{e^{2z} - 1}{e^{2z} + 1}$.

Source: Reprinted by permission from *Statistical Methods* by George W. Snedecor and William G. Cochran, 7th ed. (c) 1980 by the Iowa State University Press, Ames, Iowa 50010.

Table 9 Table of random digits

00000	10097	32533	76520	13586	34673	54876	80959	09117	39292	74945
00001	37542	04805	64894	74296	24805	24037	20636	10402	00822	91665
00002	08422	68953	19645	09303	23209	02560	15953	34764	35080	33605
00003	99019	02529	09376	70715	38311	31165	88676	74397	04436	27659
00004	12807	99970	80157	36147	64032	36653	98951	16877	12171	76833
00005	66065	74717	34072	76850	36697	36170	65813	39885	11199	29170
00006	31060	10805	45571	82406	35303	42614	86799	07439	23403	09732
00007	85269	77602	02051	65692	68665	74818	73053	85247	18623	88579
00008	63573	32135	05325	47048	90553	57548	28468	28709	83491	25624
00009	73796	45753	03529	64778	35808	34282	60935	20344	35273	88435
00010	98520	17767	14905	68607	22109	40558	60970	93433	50500	73998
00011	11805	05431	39808	27732	50725	68248	29405	24201	52775	67851
00012	83452	99634	06288	98083	13746	70078	18475	40610	68711	77817
00013	88685	40200	86507	58401	36766	67951	90364	76493	29609	11062
00014	99594	67348	87517	64969	91826	08928	93785	61368	23478	34113
00015	65481	17674	17468	50950	58047	76974	73039	57186	40218	16544
00016	80124	35635	17727	08015	45318	22374	21115	78253	14385	53763
00017	74350	99817	77402	77214	43236	00210	45521	64237	96286	02655
00018	69916	26803	66252	29148	36936	87203	76621	13990	94400	56418
00019	09893	20505	14225	68514	46427	56788	96297	78822	54382	14598
00020	91499	14523	68479	27686	46162	83554	94750	89923	37089	20048
00021	80336	94598	26940	36858	70297	34135	53140	33340	42050	82341
00022	44104	81949	85157	47954	32979	26575	57600	40881	22222	06413
00023	12550	73742	11100	02040	12860	74697	96644	89439	28707	25815
00024	63606	49329	16505	34484	40219	52563	43651	77082	07207	31790
00025	61196	90446	26457	47774	51924	33729	65394	59593	42582	60527
00026	15474	45266	95270	79953	59367	83848	82396	10118	33211	59466
00027	94557	28573	67897	54387	54622	44431	91190	42592	92927	45973
00028	42481	16213	97344	08721	16868	48767	03071	12059	25701	46670
00029	23523	78317	73208	89837	68935	91416	26252	29663	05522	82562
00030	04493	52494	75246	33824	45862	51025	61962	79335	65337	12472
00031	00549	97654	64051	88159	96119	63896	54692	82391	23287	29529
00032	35963	15307	26898	09354	33351	35462	77974	50024	90103	39333
00033	59808	08391	45427	26842	83609	49700	13021	24892	78565	20106
00034	46058	85236	01390	92286	77281	44077	93910	83647	70617	42941
00035	32179	00597	87379	25241	05567	07007	86743	17157	85394	11838
00036	69234	61406	20117	45204	15956	60000	18743	92423	97118	96338
00037	19565	41430	01758	75379	40419	21585	66674	36806	84962	85207
00038	45155	14938	19476	07246	43667	94543	59047	90033	20826	69541
00039	94864	31994	36168	10851	34888	81553	01540	35456	05014	51176
00040	98086	24826	45240	28404	44999	08896	39094	73407	35441	31880
00041	33185	16232	41941	50949	89435	48581	88695	41994	37548	73043
00042	80951	00406	96382	70774	20151	23387	25016	25298	94624	61171
00043	79752	49140	71961	28296	69861	02591	74852	20539	00387	59579
00044	18633	32537	98145	06571	31010	24674	05455	61427	77938	91936

Table 9 (*Continued*)

00045	74029	43902	77557	32270	97790	17119	52527	58021	80814	51748
00046	54178	45611	80993	37143	05335	12969	56127	19255	36040	90324
00047	11664	49883	52079	84827	59381	71539	09973	33440	88461	23356
00048	48324	77928	31249	64710	02295	36870	32307	57546	15020	09994
00049	69074	94138	87637	91976	35584	04401	10518	21615	01848	76938
00050	09188	20097	32825	39527	04220	86304	83389	87374	64278	58044
00051	90045	85497	51981	50654	94938	81997	91870	76150	68476	64659
00052	73189	50207	47677	26269	62290	64464	27124	67018	41361	82760
00053	75768	76490	20971	87749	90429	12272	95375	05871	93823	43178
00054	54016	44056	66281	31003	00682	27398	20714	53295	07706	17813
00055	08358	69910	78542	42785	13661	58873	04618	97553	31223	08420
00056	28306	03264	81333	10591	40510	07893	32604	60475	94119	01840
00057	53840	86233	81594	13628	51215	90290	28466	68795	77762	20791
00058	91757	53741	61613	62269	50263	90212	55781	76514	83483	47055
00059	89415	92684	00397	58391	12607	17646	48949	72306	94541	37408
00060	77513	03820	86864	29901	68414	82774	51908	13980	72893	55507
00061	19502	37174	69979	20288	55210	29773	74287	75251	65344	67415
00062	21818	59313	93278	81757	05686	73156	07082	85046	31853	38452
00063	51474	66499	68107	23621	94049	91345	42836	09191	08007	45449
00064	99559	68331	62535	24170	69777	12830	74819	78142	43860	72834
00065	33713	48007	93584	72869	51926	64721	58303	29822	93174	93972
00066	85274	86893	11303	22970	28834	34137	73515	90400	71148	43643
00067	84133	89640	44035	52166	73852	70091	61222	60561	62327	18423
00068	56732	16234	17395	96131	10123	91622	85496	57560	81604	18880
00069	65138	56806	87648	85261	34313	65861	45875	21069	85644	47277
00070	38001	02176	81719	11711	71602	92937	74219	64049	65584	49698
00071	37402	96397	01304	77586	56271	10086	47324	62605	40030	37438
00072	97125	40348	87083	31417	21815	39250	75237	62047	15501	29578
00073	21826	41134	47143	34072	64638	85902	49139	06441	03856	54552
00074	73135	42742	95719	09035	85794	74296	08789	88156	64691	19202
00075	07638	77929	03061	18072	96207	44156	23821	99538	04713	66994
00076	60528	83441	07954	19814	59175	20695	05533	52139	61212	06455
00077	83596	35655	06958	92983	05128	09719	77433	53783	92301	50498
00078	10850	62746	99599	10507	13499	06319	53075	71839	06410	19362
00079	39820	98952	43622	63147	64421	80814	43800	09351	31024	73167
00080	59580	06478	75569	78800	88835	54486	23768	06156	04111	08408
00081	38508	07341	23793	48763	90822	97022	17719	04207	95954	49953
00082	30692	70668	94688	16127	56196	80091	82067	63400	05462	69200
00083	65443	95659	18288	27437	49632	24041	08337	65676	96299	90836
00084	27267	50264	13192	72294	07477	44606	17985	48911	97341	30358
00085	91307	06991	19072	24210	36699	53728	28825	35793	28976	66252
00086	68434	94688	84473	13622	62126	98408	12843	82590	09815	93146
00087	48908	15877	54745	24591	35700	04754	83824	52692	54130	55160
00088	06913	45197	42672	78601	11883	09528	63011	98901	14974	40344
00089	10455	16019	14210	33712	91342	37821	88325	80851	43667	70883

Table 9 (*Continued*)

00090	12883	97343	65027	61184	04285	01392	17974	15077	90712	26769
00091	21778	30976	38807	36961	31649	42096	63281	02023	08816	47449
00092	19523	59515	65122	59659	86283	68258	69572	13798	16435	91529
00093	67245	52670	35583	16563	79246	86686	76463	34222	26655	90802
00094	60584	47377	07500	37992	45134	26529	26760	83637	41326	44344
00095	53853	41377	36066	94850	58838	73859	49364	73331	96240	43642
00096	24637	38736	74384	89342	52623	07992	12369	18601	03742	83873
00097	83080	12451	38992	22815	07759	51777	97377	27585	51972	37867
00098	16444	24334	36151	99073	27493	70939	85130	32552	54846	54759
00099	60790	18157	57178	65762	11161	78576	45819	52979	65130	04860
00100	03991	10461	93716	16894	66083	24653	84609	58232	88618	19161
00101	38555	95554	32886	59780	08355	60860	29735	47762	71299	23853
00102	17546	73704	92052	46215	55121	29281	59076	07936	27954	58909
00103	32643	52861	95819	06831	00911	98936	76355	93779	80863	00514
00104	69572	68777	39510	35905	14060	40619	29549	69616	33564	60780
00105	24122	66591	27699	06494	14845	46672	61958	77100	90899	75754
00106	61196	30231	92962	61773	41839	55382	17267	70943	78038	70267
00107	30532	21704	10274	12202	39685	23309	10061	68829	55986	66485
00108	03788	97599	75867	20717	74416	53166	35208	33374	87539	08823
00109	48228	63379	85783	47619	53152	67433	35663	52972	16818	60311
00110	60365	94653	35075	33949	42614	29297	01918	28316	98953	73231
00111	83799	42402	56623	34442	34994	41374	70071	14736	09958	18065
00112	32960	07405	36409	83232	99385	41600	11133	07586	15917	06253
00113	19322	53845	57620	52606	66497	68646	78138	66559	19640	99413
00114	11220	94747	07399	37408	48509	23929	27482	45476	85244	35159
00115	31751	57260	68980	05339	15470	48355	88651	22596	03152	19121
00116	88492	99382	14454	04504	20094	98977	74843	93413	22109	78508
00117	30934	47744	07481	83828	73788	06533	28597	20405	94205	20380
00118	22888	48893	27499	98748	60530	45128	74022	84617	82037	10268
00119	78212	16993	35902	91386	44372	15486	65741	14014	87481	37220
00120	41849	84547	46850	52326	34677	58300	74910	64345	19325	81549
00121	46352	33049	69248	93460	45305	07521	61318	31855	14413	70951
00122	11087	96294	14013	31792	59747	67277	76503	34513	39663	77544
00123	52701	08337	56303	87315	16520	69676	11654	99893	02181	68161
00124	57275	36898	81304	48585	68652	27376	92852	55866	88448	03584
00125	20857	73156	70284	24326	79375	95220	01159	63267	10622	48391
00126	15633	84924	90415	93614	33521	26665	55823	47641	86225	31704
00127	92694	48297	39904	02115	59589	49067	66821	41575	49767	04037
00128	77613	19019	88152	00080	20554	91409	96277	48257	50816	97616
00129	38688	32486	45134	63545	59404	72059	43947	51680	43852	59693
00130	25163	01889	70014	15021	41290	67312	71857	15957	68971	11403
00131	65251	07629	37239	33295	05870	01119	92784	26340	18477	65622
00132	36815	43625	18637	37509	82444	99005	04921	73701	14707	93997
00133	64397	11692	05327	82162	20247	81759	45197	25332	83745	22567
00134	04515	25624	95096	67946	48460	85558	15191	18782	16930	33361

Table 9 (*Continued*)

00135	83761	60873	43253	84145	60833	25983	01291	41349	20368	07126
00136	14387	06345	80854	09279	43529	06318	38384	74761	41196	37480
00137	51321	92246	80088	77074	88722	56736	66164	49431	66919	31678
00138	72472	00008	80890	18002	94813	31900	54155	83436	35352	54131
00139	05466	55306	93128	18464	74457	90561	72848	11834	79982	68416
00140	39528	72484	82474	25593	48545	35247	18619	13674	18611	19241
00141	81616	18711	53342	44276	75122	11724	74627	73707	58319	15997
00142	07586	16120	82641	22820	92904	13141	32392	19763	61199	67940
00143	90767	04235	13574	17200	69902	63742	78464	22501	18627	90872
00144	40188	28193	29593	88627	94972	11598	62095	36787	00441	58997
00145	34414	82157	86887	55087	19152	00023	12302	80783	32624	68691
00146	63439	75363	44989	16822	36024	00867	76378	41605	65961	73488
00147	67049	09070	93399	45547	94458	74284	05041	49807	20288	34060
00148	79495	04146	52162	90286	54158	34243	46978	35482	59362	95938
00149	91704	30552	04737	21031	75051	93029	47665	64382	99782	93478
00150	94015	46874	32444	48277	59820	96163	64654	25843	41145	42820
00151	74108	88222	88570	74015	25704	91035	01755	14750	48968	38603
00152	62880	87873	95160	59221	22304	90314	72877	17334	39283	04149
00153	11748	12102	80580	41867	17710	59621	06554	07850	73950	79552
00154	17944	05600	60478	03343	25852	58905	57216	39618	49856	99326
00155	66067	42792	95043	52680	46780	56487	09971	59481	37006	22186
00156	54244	91030	45547	70818	59849	96169	61459	21647	87417	17198
00157	30945	57589	31732	57260	47670	07654	46376	25366	94746	49580
00158	69170	37403	86995	90307	94304	71803	26825	05511	12459	91314
00159	08345	88975	35841	85771	08105	59987	87112	21476	14713	71181
00160	27767	43584	85301	88977	29490	69714	73035	41207	74699	09310
00161	13025	14338	54066	15243	47724	66733	47431	43905	31048	56699
00162	80217	36292	98525	24335	24432	24896	43277	58874	11466	16082
00163	10875	62004	90391	61105	57411	06368	53856	30743	08670	84741
00164	54127	57326	26629	19087	24472	88779	30540	27886	61732	75454
00165	60311	42824	37301	42678	45990	43242	17374	52003	70707	70214
00166	49739	71484	92003	98086	76668	73209	59202	11973	02902	33250
00167	78626	51594	16453	94614	39014	97066	83012	09832	25571	77628
00168	66692	13986	99837	00582	81232	44987	09504	96412	90193	79568
00169	44071	28091	07362	97703	76447	42537	98524	97831	65704	09514
00170	41468	85149	49554	17994	14924	39650	95294	00566	70481	06905
00171	94559	37559	49678	53119	70312	05682	66986	34099	74474	20740
00172	41615	70360	64114	58660	90850	64618	80620	51790	11436	38072
00173	50273	93113	41794	86861	24781	89683	55411	85667	77535	99892
00174	41396	80504	90670	08289	40902	05069	95083	06783	28102	57816
00175	25807	24260	71529	78920	72682	07385	90726	57166	98884	08583
00176	06170	97965	88302	98041	21443	41808	68984	83620	89747	98882
00177	60808	54444	74412	81105	01176	28838	36421	16489	18059	51061
00178	80940	44893	10408	36222	80582	71944	92638	40333	67054	16067
00179	19516	90120	46759	71643	13177	55292	21036	82808	77501	97427

Table 9 (*Continued*)

00180	49386	54480	23604	23554	21785	41101	91178	10174	29420	90438
00181	06312	88940	15995	69321	47458	64809	98189	81851	29651	84215
00182	60942	00307	11897	92674	40405	68032	96717	54244	10701	41393
00183	92329	98932	78284	46347	71209	92061	39448	93136	25722	08564
00184	77936	63574	31384	51924	85561	29671	58137	17820	22751	36518
00185	38101	77756	11657	13897	95889	57067	47648	13885	70669	93406
00186	39641	69457	91339	22502	92613	89719	11947	56203	19324	20504
00187	84054	40455	99396	63680	67667	60631	69181	96845	38525	11600
00188	47468	03577	57649	63266	24700	71594	14004	23153	69249	05747
00189	43321	31370	28977	23896	76479	68562	62342	07589	08899	05985
00190	64281	61826	18555	64937	13173	33365	78851	16499	87064	13075
00191	66847	70495	32350	02985	86716	38746	26313	77463	55387	72681
00192	72461	33230	21529	53424	92581	02262	78438	66276	18396	73538
00193	21032	91050	13058	16218	12470	56500	15292	76139	59526	52113
00194	95362	67011	06651	16136	01016	00857	55018	56374	35824	71708
00195	49712	97380	10404	55452	34030	60726	75211	10271	36633	68424
00196	58275	61764	97586	54716	50259	46345	87195	46092	26787	60939
00197	89514	11788	68224	23417	73959	76145	30342	42077	11049	72049
00198	15472	50669	48139	36732	46874	37088	73465	09819	58869	35220
00199	12120	86124	51247	44302	60883	52109	21437	36786	49226	77837
00200	19612	78430	11661	94770	77603	65669	86868	12665	30012	75989
00201	39141	77400	28000	64238	73258	71794	31340	26256	66453	37016
00202	64756	80457	08747	12836	03469	50678	03274	43423	66677	82556
00203	92901	51878	56441	22998	29718	38447	06453	25311	07565	53771
00204	03551	90070	09483	94050	45938	18135	36908	43321	11073	51803
00205	98884	66209	06830	53656	14663	56346	71430	04909	19818	05707
00206	27369	86882	53473	07541	53633	70863	03748	12822	19360	49088
00207	59066	75974	63335	20483	43514	37481	58278	26967	49325	43951
00208	91647	93783	64169	49022	98588	09495	49829	59068	38831	04838
00209	83605	92419	39542	07772	71568	75673	35185	89759	44901	74291
00210	24895	88530	70774	35439	46758	70472	70207	92675	91623	61275
00211	35720	26556	95596	20094	73750	85788	34264	01703	46833	65248
00212	14141	53410	38649	06343	57256	61342	72709	75318	90379	37562
00213	27416	75670	92176	72535	93119	56077	06886	18244	92344	31374
00214	82071	07429	81007	47749	40744	56974	23336	88821	53841	10536
00215	21445	82793	24831	93241	14199	76268	70883	68002	03829	17443
00216	72513	76400	52225	92348	62308	98481	29744	33165	33141	61020
00217	71479	45027	76160	57411	13780	13632	52308	77762	88874	33697
00218	83210	51466	09088	50395	26743	05306	21706	70001	99439	80767
00219	68749	95148	94897	78636	96750	09024	94538	91143	96693	61886
00220	05184	75763	47075	88158	05313	53439	14908	08830	60096	21551
00221	13651	62546	96892	25240	47511	58483	87342	78818	07855	39269
00222	00566	21220	00292	24069	25072	29519	52548	54091	21282	21296
00223	50958	17695	58072	68990	60329	95955	71586	63417	35947	67807
00224	57621	64547	46850	37981	38527	09037	64756	03324	04986	83666

Table 9 (*Continued*)

00225	09282	25844	79139	78435	35428	43561	69799	63314	12991	93516
00226	23394	94206	93432	37836	94919	26846	02555	74410	94915	48199
00227	05280	37470	93622	04345	15092	19510	18094	16613	78234	50001
00228	95491	97976	38306	32192	82639	54624	72434	92606	23191	74693
00229	78521	00104	18248	75583	90326	50785	54034	66251	35774	14692
00230	96345	44579	85932	44053	75704	20840	86583	83944	52456	73766
00231	77963	31151	32364	91691	47357	40338	23435	24065	08458	95366
00232	07520	11294	23238	01748	41690	67328	54814	37777	10057	42332
00233	38423	02309	70703	85736	46148	14258	29236	12152	05088	65825
00234	02463	65533	21199	60555	33928	01817	07396	89215	30722	22102
00235	15880	92261	17292	88190	61781	48898	92525	21283	88581	60098
00236	71926	00819	59144	00224	30570	90194	18329	06999	26857	19238
00237	64425	28108	16554	16016	00042	83229	10333	36168	65617	94834
00238	79782	23924	49440	30432	81077	31543	95216	64865	13658	51081
00239	35337	74538	44553	64672	90960	41849	93865	44608	93176	34851
00240	05249	29329	19715	94082	14738	86667	43708	66354	93692	25527
00241	56463	99380	38793	85774	19056	13939	46062	27647	66146	63210
00242	96296	33121	54196	34108	75814	85986	71171	15102	28992	63165
00243	98380	36269	60014	07201	62448	46385	42175	88350	46182	49126
00244	52567	64350	16315	53969	80395	81114	54358	64578	47269	15747
00245	78498	90830	25955	99236	43286	91064	99969	95144	64424	77377
00246	49553	24241	08150	89535	08703	91041	77323	81079	45127	93686
00247	32151	07075	83155	10252	73100	88618	23891	87418	45417	20268
00248	11314	50363	26860	27799	49416	83534	19187	08059	76677	02110
00249	12364	71210	87052	50241	90785	97889	81399	58130	64439	05614
00250	59467	58309	87834	57213	37510	33689	01259	62486	56320	46265
00251	73452	17619	56421	40725	23439	41701	93223	41682	45026	47505
00252	27635	56293	91700	04391	67317	89604	73020	69853	61517	51207
00253	86040	02596	01655	09918	45161	00222	54577	74821	47335	08582
00254	52403	94255	26351	46527	68224	91083	85057	72310	34963	83462
00255	49465	46581	61499	04844	94626	02963	41482	83879	44942	61915
00256	94365	92560	12363	30246	02086	75036	88620	91088	67691	67762
00257	34261	08769	91830	23313	18256	28850	37639	92748	57791	71328
00258	37110	66538	39318	15626	44324	82827	08782	65960	58167	01305
00259	83950	45424	72453	19444	68219	64733	94088	62006	89985	36936
00260	61630	97966	76537	46467	30942	07479	67971	14558	22458	35148
00261	01929	17165	12037	74558	16250	71750	55546	29693	94984	37782
00262	41659	39098	23982	29899	71594	77979	54477	13764	17315	72893
00263	32031	39608	75992	73445	01317	50525	87313	45191	30214	19769
00264	90043	93478	58044	06949	31176	88370	50274	83987	45316	38551

Table 9 (*Continued*)

00265	79418	14322	91065	07841	36130	86602	10659	40859	00964	71577
00266	85447	61079	96910	72906	07361	84338	34114	52096	66715	51091
00267	86219	81115	49625	48799	89485	24855	13684	68433	70595	70102
00268	71712	88559	92476	32903	68009	58417	87962	11787	16644	72964
00269	29776	63075	13270	84758	49560	10317	28778	23006	31036	84906
00270	81488	17340	74154	42801	27917	89792	62604	62234	13124	76471
00271	51667	37589	87147	24743	48023	06325	79794	35889	13255	04925
00272	99004	70322	60832	76636	56907	56534	72615	46288	36788	93196
00273	68656	66492	35933	52293	47953	95495	95304	50009	83464	28608
00274	38074	74083	09337	07965	65047	36871	59015	21769	30398	44855
00275	01020	80680	59328	08712	48190	45332	27284	31287	66011	09376
00276	86379	74508	33579	77114	92955	23085	92824	03054	25242	16322
00277	48498	09938	44420	13484	52319	58875	02012	88591	52500	95795
00278	41800	95363	54142	17482	32705	60564	12505	40954	46174	64130
00279	63026	96712	79883	39225	52653	69549	36693	59822	22684	31661
00280	88298	15489	16030	42480	15372	38781	71995	77438	91161	10192
00281	07839	62735	99218	25624	02547	27445	69187	55749	32322	15504
00282	73298	51108	48717	92926	75705	89787	96114	99902	37749	96305
00283	12829	70474	00838	50385	91711	80370	56504	56857	80906	09018
00284	76569	61072	48568	36491	22587	44363	39592	61546	90181	37348
00285	41665	41339	62106	44203	06732	76111	79840	67999	32231	76869
00286	58652	49983	01669	27464	79553	52855	25988	18087	38052	17529
00287	13607	00657	76173	43357	77334	24140	53860	02906	89863	44651
00288	55715	26203	65933	51087	98234	40625	45545	63563	89148	82581
00289	04110	66683	99001	09796	47349	65003	66524	81970	71262	14479
00290	31300	08681	58068	44115	40064	77879	23965	69019	73985	19453
00291	26225	97543	37044	07494	85778	35345	61115	92498	49737	64599
00292	07158	82763	25072	38478	57782	75291	62155	52056	04786	11585
00293	71251	25572	79771	93328	66927	54069	58752	26624	50463	77361
00294	29991	96526	02820	91659	12818	96356	49499	01507	40223	09171
00295	83642	21057	02677	09367	38097	16100	19355	06120	15378	56559
00296	69167	30235	06767	66323	78294	14916	19124	88044	16673	66102
00297	86018	29406	75415	22038	27056	26906	25867	14751	92380	30434
00298	44114	06026	97553	55091	95385	41212	37882	46864	54717	97038
00299	53805	64150	70915	63127	63695	41288	38192	72437	75075	18570

Source: Reprinted from the Rand Corporation, *A Million Random Digits with 100,000 Normal Deviates,* Free Press, New York, 1955, with the permission of the Rand Corporation and the publisher.

GLOSSARY OF TERMS

Abscissa The horizontal axis of a distribution.

Acceptability stage The third (final) stage in the development of a scientific hypothesis, where the scientist accepts the plausibility of the research idea and molds it into a specific proposition or premise.

Activity Any intentional act or behavior or incident that is aimed at affecting the status of events—a natural unit of ethnographic field work.

Affective component An attitudinal dimension referring to a person's emotional evaluations or feelings about things.

After-only design A standard experimental design in which subjects' reactions are measured after the treatment has been administered.

Aggregating sources of variance Combining terms that are sufficiently similar, say $F < 2$.

Alias A source of variation completely confounded with another.

Alpha (α) Probability of a type I error.

Analogous Having a similar structure or logic.

Analysis of covariance Analysis of variance with dependent variable adjusted for one or more covariates or predictor variables.

Analysis of variance Subdivision of the total variance of a set of scores into its components.

Analytic survey A sample survey the purpose of which is to explore the relationships between variables.

Anova Analysis of variance.

a priori method Reasoning from cause to effect, or from a general to a particular instance, independently of any scientific observation.

Arcsin transformation Transformation for proportions making equal differences equally detectable.

Area probability sampling A type of probability sampling where the subclasses are geographical areas.

Arithmetic mean Arithmetic average.

Armor's theta An index of test reliability based on the eigenvalue of the first (unrotated) principal component.

Artifacts Specific threats to validity, or confounded aspects of the scientist's observations.

Assumed probability A probability that is taken for granted, where there is scientific evidence for belief that a particular relationship or phenomenon is likely to occur or prove true.

Average deviation The average distance from the mean of all scores.

Average error An index of the variability of a set of data around the most typical value.

468

Before-after design A standard research design in which subjects' reactions are measured both before and after they have undergone the experimental manipulation or a control substitute.

Behaviorism A point of view that the behavioral sciences should restrict themselves to a study of the relationships between observable stimuli and responses.

BESD Binomial effect-size display.

Beta (β) Probability of a type II error.

Bias Net systematic error.

Bimodal A distribution showing two modes.

Binomial effect-size display (BESD) Procedure for the display of the practical importance of a correlation (r) of any particular magnitude.

Biological variables That class of independent variables which consists of biological determinants of behavior.

Biosocial experimenter effects Those interactional effects which are a function of biosocial attributes of the experimenter.

Blind controls Research participants who are unaware of their experimental status.

Blocking Subdividing sampling units to increase precision and/or to detect interactions between independent and blocking variables.

Bonferroni procedure Redefining alpha level of significance to protect against post hoc selection of largest effects.

Boundary experiments A series of experiments designed to fix the range of application of relationships.

Built-in contrasts Contrasts that are obtained as a natural consequence of an experimental design, such as any source of variance in a 2^k factorial design (not including error terms).

Canonical correlation Correlation between two or more predictor variables and two or more dependent variables.

Category scale A recording scale, usually in the form of a checklist or tally sheet.

Causal inference The act or process of inferring that X causes Y.

Ceiling effect A certain level above which observations cannot be made (as when a test is too easy).

Central tendency Location of the bulk of a distribution measured by means, medians, modes, trimmed means, etc.

Central tendency error A type of response set where the observer hesitates to give extreme ratings and instead tends to rate in the direction of the mean of the total group.

Characteristic root Sum of squared factor loadings.

Chi-square (χ^2) A statistic employed to test the degree of agreement between the data actually obtained and those expected under a particular hypothesis (e.g., the null hypothesis).

Chi-square corner cells test Chi-square test performed on the four corners of a table of counts.

Chi-square (χ^2) distributions Family of distributions centered at the df for each χ^2 and ranging from zero to positive infinity.

Chi-square (χ^2) test A test of significance employed to judge the tenability of the null hypothesis of no relationship between two or more variables.

Cluster analysis Formal procedures for grouping variables or sampling units together.

Coefficient of correlation Index of correlation, typically Pearson r or related product-moment correlation.

Coefficient of determination Proportion of variance "accounted for" (r^2).

Coefficient of nondetermination Proportion of variance "not accounted for" (k^2).

Cognitive component An attitudinal dimension referring to a person's beliefs and how he or she tends to perceive things.

Cohen's d A measure of effect size in σ units.

Cohen's f Effect-size estimate employed with F tests of significance.

Cohen's g The difference between any proportion and .50.

Cohen's h The difference between two proportions after each has been transformed via arcsin.

Cohen's q The difference between two Pearson r's after they have been transformed to Fisher's z.

Cohen's w Effect-size estimate employed with χ^2 tests of significance.

Cohort   The term for a collection of people who were born in the same period.

Cohort-sequential design   A type of research design in which several cohorts are studied, with the initial measurements taken in successive years.

Column effects   Column means minus grand mean.

Combined category chi-square test   Chi-square test performed on redefined tables of counts in which adjacent rows and/or columns have been meaningfully combined.

Complex multiple partial correlation   Canonical correlation performed on variables from which the effects of third-party variables have been removed.

Component loading   See *Factor loading*.

Conative component   An attitudinal dimension referring to a person's disposition to overt behavior.

Concept   Thought, idea, cognition.

Concurrent validity   A type of test validity that asks the extent to which the test results are correlated with some criterion in the present.

Confidence interval   Region in which a population parameter is likely to be found.

Confounded variables   Variables that are correlated with one another.

Consensus tests   Checking for consensus among F tests formed from largest and smallest relevant error terms.

Construct   An abstract variable that is constructed from ideas or images in order to serve as an explanatory term.

Construct validation   The process by which a means for the measurement of a construct is devised and then related to subjects' performance in a variety of other spheres as the construct would predict. *Construct validity* is concerned with the psychological qualities contributing to the relationship between X and Y.

Content analysis   A multipurpose research method which permits quantification of subjective data based on exact counts of frequency.

Content validity   A type of test validity that asks whether the test adequately samples all of the relevant material.

Contingency table   A table in which the data are displayed as counts.

Contrasts   Tests of focused questions in which specific predictions can be tested by comparing or contrasting them to the obtained data.

Control group   A condition against which we compare the effects of the treatment (or experimental) condition. Also, a procedure to serve as a check on validity.

Convergent validity   The extent to which measures of different aspects of the same behavior yield some equivalent results.

Corner cells test   See *Chi-square corner cells test*.

Corrected range   Crude range plus one unit.

Correction for continuity   A procedure for decreasing the absolute difference between obtained and expected frequencies to adjust for the difference between discrete and continuous distributions.

Correlate   A quantifiable process that varies similarly to another quantifiable process.

Correlated data   Observations that are not independent of one another.

Correlation   Degree of relationship between variables.

Counterbalancing   Presenting treatment conditions in a sequence that eliminates confounding.

Covariance   Sum of products of deviations from the mean, i.e., $\Sigma(x - \bar{x})(y - \bar{y})$, divided by df.

Covary   Variations in one variable correlate with variations in another.

Criterion variable   An outcome variable, a variable that was predicted.

Cross-lag design   A diachronic research design where one variable is allowed to lag behind the other, thus using relational data to test a causal hypothesis.

Cross-sectional design   Any research design that takes a slice of time and compares subjects on one or more variables simultaneously.

Cross-sequential design   A research design in which different cohorts are observed over several periods, with the initial measurement(s) taken in the same period.

Crossed contrasts   Contrasts formed from the crossing of contrasts in two or more main effects.

Crossed sampling units   Sampling units observed under two or more conditions of a study.

Crossed-line interaction   Interaction residuals showing an ascending linear trend for one subgroup and a descending linear trend for another subgroup.

Crossed-quadratic interaction   Interaction residuals showing a U-shaped trend for one subgroup and an inverted U-shaped trend for another subgroup.

Crude range   Highest score minus lowest score.

Cubic trend   Curvilinear relationship between two variables in which the line changes direction twice.

Curvilinear (quadratic) correlation   The correlation between scores on one variable and extremeness of scores on the other variable.

D   The difference between scores or ranks.

D̄   The mean of a set of *D*'s.

d   See *Cohen's* d.

Degrees of freedom   The number of observations minus the number of restrictions limiting the observations' freedom to vary.

Demand characteristics   The mixture of various hints and cues that govern the subject's perception of his or her role and of the experimenter's hypothesis.

Dependent variable   A variable whose changes are viewed as being dependent or consequent on changes in one or more independent variables.

Descriptive inquiry   Any method of research that seeks to map out what happens behaviorally, to tell "how things are."

Determinative relationship   The assumption that changes in one variable probably serve to determine changes in another variable.

df   Degrees of freedom.

df **between conditions**   Degrees of freedom for means of conditions.

df **error**   Degrees of freedom for denominator of *F* ratio.

df **means**   Degrees of freedom for numerator of *F* ratio.

df **within conditions**   Degrees of freedom for observations within conditions.

Diachronic research   Referring to a temporal research approach in which a phenomenon or variable is observed in such a way as to uncover changes that occur during successive periods of time.

Dialectical pattern   A pattern of change based on the progressive balancing of opposing forces. In philosophy, the *dialectic method* refers to a series of questions and answers, often in contradiction to one another, used to arrive at the truth or falsity of a proposition.

Difference in success rates   See *Binomial effect-size display*.

Diffuse tests of significance   Significance tests addressing unfocused questions, as in χ^2 with $df > 1$ or F with numerator $df > 1$.

Diffusion   Having reference to the effects of changes in a response on other responses that are close in time to the primary one. Also termed *irradiation* or the *spread of effect*.

Dimensional analysis   Set of redescriptors of relationships among objects in terms of measures of similarity or dissimilarity.

Discovery   A term used by philosophers of science to refer to the origin, creation, and invention of hypotheses.

Discriminant function   Special case of multiple correlation with a dichotomous dependent variable.

Discriminant validity   The extent to which measures of different aspects of the same behavior yield some nonequivalent results.

Disguised measures   Those measuring instruments that are used to study behavior indirectly or unobtrusively.

Dispersion   Spread or variability.

Distance analysis   Set of redescriptors of relationships among objects in terms of measures of similarity or dissimilarity.

Distribution   The relative frequencies as we move over varying values of our independent variable.

Drunkard's search The principle that much effort is lost or vitiated when we look in a convenient place but not in the most likely one.

Dummy-coding Giving arbitrary numerical values to the two levels of a dichotomous variable.

Edgington method of adding probabilities Procedure for combining *p* values of a set of studies.

Effect size The magnitude of an experimental effect.

Effective reliability The reliability of the mean of two or more judges' ratings.

Effects See *Residuals*.

Efficient cause The propelling factor that produces something, sets it into motion, or changes it.

Eigenvalue Sum of squared factor loadings.

Empirical method Any effective manner or mode of procedure using experience, observation, or experiment to map out the nature of reality.

Enumerative survey A sample survey the purpose of which is to count (enumerate) a representative group and then make inferences about the population on the basis of the sample values.

Equal-appearing-intervals method A procedure in attitude-scale construction where values are obtained for statements or items on the basis of how they were sorted as interval data.

Equivalent-forms method A means of evaluating reliability in test construction based on data from comparable forms of the same test.

Error term The denominator of an *F* ratio in the analysis of variance.

Errors Deviations of scores from the mean of the group or condition.

Eta Index of correlation not limited to linear relationships.

Eta² Proportion of variance accounted for.

Ethics The system of moral values by which behavior is judged.

Ethnography That type of field observation in which a society's culture is studied.

Evaluation apprehension Subjects' fears that an experimenter intends to evaluate some aspect of their competence.

Expectancy control design A research design in which the expectancy variable is permitted to operate separately from the primary independent variable.

Expected frequencies Counts expected under various conditions if certain hypotheses (e.g., the null hypothesis) were true.

Experimental group A group in which there is controlled manipulation of some independent variable.

Experimenter One who tests or tries some observational method, using human or animal subjects, in order to gather scientific data about behavior.

Experimental inquiry Any method of research which seeks to describe what happens behaviorally when something of interest to the experimenter is introduced into the situation, to tell "how things are and how they got to be that way."

Experimental realism Referring to the psychological impact of an experimental manipulation on the participants.

Experimenter expectancy effect That which results when the hypothesis held by the investigator leads unintentionally to behavior toward the subjects which increases the likelihood that their behavior, in turn, will confirm the hypothesis.

Extended range Crude range plus one unit.

External validity The approximate validity with which conclusions are drawn about the generalizability of a causal relationship.

External variables Independent variables that can "pull" a human being in a particular direction or toward a specific goal or object.

f See *Cohen's* f.

F **distributions** Family of distributions centered at $(df)/(df - 2)$ (when *df* are for the denominator of the *F* ratio) and ranging from zero to positive infinity.

F **ratios** Ratios of mean squares that are distributed as *F* when the null hypothesis is true.

F **test** A test of significance employed to judge the tenability of the null hypothesis of no relationship between two or more variables.

Fact-finding experiment   Any experiment aimed at determining some magnitude or property of the dependent variable.

Factor analysis   The rewriting of a set of variables into a new set of orthogonal factors.

Factor loading   Correlations between variables and factors serving as their redescriptors.

Factorial designs   Experimental designs in which each level of one dimension or factor is administered in combination with each level of another dimension or factor.

False precision   When something relatively vague is reported as if the measuring instrument were sensitive to very slight differences.

Falsifiability   The principle that a theoretical system is "scientific" only if it is stated in such a way that it can, if incorrect, be falsified by empirical tests.

File drawer problem   Completed but unreported studies serving to complicate the quantitative summary of research domains.

Final cause   The end reason for which a person or thing tends naturally to strive; also called the *teleologic factor*.

Fisher exact probability test   Test of significance for a 2×2 table of counts based on exact probability rather than reference to a distribution.

Fisher method of adding logs   Procedure for combining p values of a set of studies.

Fisher's z transformation   Transformation for Pearson r's making equal differences equally detectable.

Fixed effects   Levels of a factor chosen because of our specific interest rather than as representatives of a population of levels of a factor.

Focused tests of significance   Tests of significance addressing precise questions, as in any 1 *df* contrast.

Forced-choice   Where the respondent is "forced" to accept some statements that are clearly unfavorable or to reject some statements that are clearly favorable.

Formal cause   The implicit form or meaning of something.

Fractional factorials   Design in which higher-order interactions are intentionally confounded with lower-order effects.

Frequency distribution   A set of data scores arranged according to incidence of occurrence.

g   See *Cohen's* g.

Good subject   The research participant who "puts his best foot forward" by eagerly cooperating with the experimenter—a characterisic which is more common among volunteer than nonvolunteer subjects.

Grand mean   Mean of means.

Graphic scale   A type of rating scale in the form of a straight or segmented line with cue words attached.

h   See *Cohen's* h.

H$_0$ Null hypothesis.

Halo effect   A type of response set where the bias results from the judge's forming a favorable impression of someone with regard to some central trait and then tending to paint a rosier picture of the person on other characteristics.

Harmonic mean   The reciprocal of the arithmetic mean of values that have been transformed to their reciprocals.

Hawthorne effect   The mere fact of being observed that has somehow influenced the behavior under investigation.

Hereditary variables   That class of independent variables which consists of genetic determinants of behavior.

Heterogeneous   That certain elements are essentially different from one another.

Heuristic experiment   Designed to generate ideas, provide leads for further inquiry, and open up new lines of investigation.

Hierarchical structure   A system in which one thing is ranked above another.

High antecedent probability   That a research idea is believed, even before being empirically tested, to be sound and likely to prove relevant to the problem under investigation.

Higher-order interaction   Residuals remaining after all main effects and all lower-order interactions relevant to the higher-order interaction have been subtracted.

History   A plausible threat to internal validity when an event or incident that takes place between the premeasurement and the postmeasurement contaminates the results of an experiment.

Homogeneity of covariances   Degree of similarity of covariances found between any two levels of a repeated measures factor.

Homogeneous   That certain elements are essentially alike.

Hypothesis   A research idea which serves as a premise or proposition to organize certain facts.

IID Normal   Assumptions underlying use of t and F tests, that errors be independently and identically distributed in a normal distribution.

Incomplete factorial design   Design in which higher-order interactions are intentionally confounded with lower-order effects.

Independent variable   A variable on which the dependent variable depends. Also, an observable or measurable event manipulated by an experimenter to determine whether there is any effect upon another event (the dependent variable).

Indirect measures   Those instruments used to study behavior when the subject is aware of being observed but not of the consequences of his or her behavior, for example, the Rorschach test.

Inferential validity   A summary term referring to the fact that a laboratory relationship between two variables has a high degree of internal and external validity.

Initial thinking   The first stage in the development of a scientific hypothesis, characterized by the relative vagueness of ideas or first impressions.

Instrumentation   A plausible threat to internal validity when changes in the measuring instrument bias the results of an experiment, for example, if the measuring instrument has deteriorated over time.

Intensive case study   The gathering and organization of information about a particular set of circumstances in great depth.

Intentional effect   That type of noninteractional experimenter effect which results in error due to the researcher's dishonesty in reporting data.

Interaction effects   Condition means minus grand mean, row effects, and column effects.

Interaction process analysis   A particular example of a category scale and observational procedure developed by R. F. Bales to study small-group interactions.

Interactional experimenter effects   Effects of the experimenter that operate by affecting the actual response of the participant.

Interpreter effect   That type of noninteractional experimenter effect which results in error during the interpretation-of-data phase of the research process.

Internal validity   The degree of validity of statements made about whether X causes Y.

Interdisciplinary research   Where a scientist draws heavily on the theoretical orientations and methods of more than one field.

Internal variables   Independent variables that can "push" a human being in a particular direction or toward a specific goal or object.

Interval data   Stimuli or values whose quantitative distances from one another on some attribute can be measured.

Intraclass correlation   Procedure for estimating the average intercorrelation among the repeated observations obtained from a set of sampling units.

Item analysis   A procedure for selecting items for a Likert scale. Consists of calculating the extent to which each item is correlated with the total score and then choosing those items that correlate well for the final scale.

Joint method   J. S. Mill's joint method of agreement and difference, which tells us that X is both necessary and sufficient for the occurrence of Y.

Justification   A term used by philosophers of science to refer to the evaluation, defense, truth, and confirmation of hypotheses.

k   Coefficient of alienation or "noncorrelation."

k^2   Coefficient of nondetermination.

L   Sum of the products of condition totals and contrast weights (λ).

Lambda (λ) Weights derived from theory serving to define a contrast.

Latent root Sum of squared factor loadings.

Latin square A square of letters or numbers in which each letter or number appears once and only once in each row and in each column.

Learning A relatively stable or permanent change in behavior potential which occurs as a result of practice.

Leaves The trailing digits of a stem-and-leaf display.

Leniency error A type of response set where the judge tends to rate someone who is very familiar, or someone with whom the judge is ego-involved, more positively than the person deserves.

Likert scale See *Summated ratings*.

Linear trend Straight-line relationship between two variables.

Loading See *Factor loading*.

Location measures Measures of central tendency.

Log-linear model An approach to the analysis of tables analogous to the analysis of variance.

Logical error in rating A type of response set where the judge gives similar ratings for variables or traits that seem logically related.

Longitudinal design Any research design in which the subjects are studied over a period of time.

M The mean of a set of scores.

$\bar{M}$ Grand mean.

Matched pairs Pairs of observations made on the same sampling units.

Material cause The material out of which something is made or comes about.

Maturation A plausible threat to internal validity when the results of an experiment are contaminated by the participants' having grown older or wiser or stronger or more experienced between the pretest and the posttest.

Maximum possible benefit of a contrast Upper limit of gain due to employing contrast; $(df - 1)/df$.

MPBS Maximum possible benefit score.

MPC$-F$ Maximum possible contrast F.

Maximum possible contrast F The F from which the contrast is to be carved, multiplied by its numerator df.

Mean The arithmetic average of a set of scores.

Mean polish Removing grand mean, row, and column effects to expose residuals defining the interaction.

MS Mean square.

MS between Mean square between conditions.

MS error Mean square used as denominator of F ratio.

MS within Mean square within conditions.

Mechanistic model The metatheory which compares social causation to a complex machine and assumes human nature to be a matter of social engineering.

Median The midmost score of a distribution.

Meta-analysis The analysis of the results of sets of studies of a particular research question.

Metaphor A word or phrase applied to a concept or phenomenon that it does not literally denote.

Metatheory A conceptual scheme.

Method of adding logs Procedure for combining independent probabilities.

Method of adding probabilities Procedure for combining independent probabilities.

Method of adding t's Procedure for combining independent probabilities.

Method of adding Z's Procedure for combining independent probabilities.

Method of adding weighted Z's Procedure for combining independent probabilities.

Method of agreement If X, then Y—which means that X is a sufficient condition of Y.

Method of authority When an idea is held to be true merely because it is approved by some authority.

Method of difference If not-X, then not-Y—which means that X is a necessary condition of Y.

Method of meaningful diagonals Forming a concept to summarize the data found on the diagonals of a two-way table of means or of residuals.

Method of meaningful differences Reducing a two-dimensional display of residuals to a one-dimensional display.

Method of tenacity Clinging tenaciously to an idea because it brings peace of mind.

Method of testing mean p Procedure for combining independent probabilities.

Method of testing mean z Procedure for combining independent probabilities.

Methodological experiment Serves to develop or to improve some particular technique of inquiry.

Mode The score occurring with greatest frequency.

Modeling effects Those interactional effects which are a function of the example set by the experimenter.

Multidimensional scaling (unfolding) Set of redescriptors of relationships among objects in terms of measures of similarity or dissimilarity.

Multilevel analysis of variance Analysis of variance with two or more independent variables and one dependent variable.

Multiple confirmation The use of two or more independent measures of the same behavior and the comparison of the results.

Multiple correlation Correlation between two or more predictor variables and a single dependent variable.

Multiple discriminant function Special case of canonical correlation with dichotomous dependent variables.

Multiple partial correlation Multiple correlation performed on variables from which the effects of third-party variables have been removed.

Multiple path analysis Canonical correlation with time-ordered predictor variables.

Multivariate analysis of covariance Analysis of covariance for the case of multiple dependent variables.

Multivariate multilevel analysis of variance Analysis of variance with two or more independent and two or more dependent variables.

Multivariate procedures Statistical procedures involving two or more independent (predictor) variables and/or two or more dependent (criterion) variables.

Mundane realism Referring to the extent to which laboratory events are likely to occur in a naturalistic setting.

N The number of scores in a study.

n The number of scores in a sample.

N_h The harmonic mean n.

Naturalistic observation Any research that looks at behavior in its usual natural environment.

Necessary condition A requisite or essential condition.

Negative synergistic effects Synergistic effects serving to lower scores.

Negativistic subject The type of research participant who approaches the investigation with an uncooperative attitude.

Nested sampling units Sampling units observed under only one condition of a study.

Net contrast benefit measure Improvement of our contrast over a randomly chosen contrast.

NCBM Net contrast benefit measure.

Net information per contrast df Improvement of our contrast over a randomly chosen contrast.

Noninteractional experimenter effects Those effects that occur without affecting the actual response of the human or animal subject.

Nonorthogonal contrasts Correlated contrasts.

Nonparametric statistical procedures Procedures that are less dependent on the shape of the population distribution from which our observations were drawn.

Nonreactive observation Any observation that does not affect the thing being observed.

Nonresponse bias Error that is due to nonresponse or nonparticipation.

Normal distribution Bell-shape curve that is completely described by mean and standard deviation.

No-show A person who volunteers to serve as a research subject, but then fails to show up; also called a *pseudovolunteer*.

Null hypothesis   The hypothesis that there is no relationship between two or more variables.

Numerical scale   A rating scale where the judges work with a sequence of defined numbers.

Oblique rotations   Rotations that are nonorthogonal.

Observed frequencies   Counts obtained under various conditions.

Observer effect   That type of noninteractional experimenter effect which results in overstatements or understatements of some criterion value during the observation and recording phase of the research process.

Occam's razor   The principle that hypotheses introduced to explain relationships should be as parsimonious as possible. Also known as the *principle of parsimony*.

Omnibus tests of significance   Significance tests addressing unfocused questions, as in χ^2 with $df > 1$ or F with numerator $df > 1$.

One-group pre-post design   A pre-experimental design in which the reactions of only one group of subjects are measured before and after exposure to the treatment.

One-shot case study   A pre-experimental design in which the reactions of only one group of subjects are measured once an event has occurred.

One-tailed test   Test of significance in which the null hypothesis is rejected only if the results are significant in one of the two possible directions.

Open-ended item   See *Unstructured items*.

Operational definition   The meaning of a variable in terms of the operations necessary to measure it in any concrete situation, or in terms of the experimental methods involved in its determination.

Ordinal data   Objects or events that can be ranked from high to low on some characteristic.

Ordinate   The vertical axis of a distribution.

Organismic interactions   Treatments showing different effects for different subgroups.

Organismic model   The metatheory which emphasizes the progressive changes in behavior patterns.

Orthogonal contrasts   Uncorrelated contrasts.

Orthogonal polynomial contrasts   Sets of orthogonal contrasts in which linear, quadratic, and higher-order trends can be evaluated.

Orthogonal relationship   Correlation equals zero.

Orthogonal rotations   Rotations in which axes are kept at right angles to one another.

Overall F test   An F test with $df > 1$ in the numerator which serves as appropriate protection for subsequent contrasts.

p value   Probability value or level obtained in a test of significance.

Paradigm case   A clear and unequivocal example or pattern of something.

Paradoxical incident   An occurrence characterized by seemingly self-contradictory aspects.

Paradox of sampling   That the appropriateness of a sample is validated by the method used to arrive at its appropriateness.

Paradox of usage   That the usage of words is validated by a method based on how the words are actually used.

Parsimony principle   See *Occam's razor*.

Partial aggregation   Aggregation of only a subset of all relevant sources of variance.

Participant observation   A method of observation in which a group or a community is studied from within by a researcher who makes careful records of the behavior as it proceeds.

Partitioning tables   Subdividing tables of counts into a set of 2×2 tables each of which addresses a precise question.

Path analysis   Multiple regression with time-ordered predictor variables.

Pearson r   Standard index of linear relationship.

Percentile   Location of a score in a distribution defining the point below which a given percentage of the cases fall. A score at the 90th percentile falls at a point such that 90 percent of the scores fall at or below that score.

Period centrism fallacy   The mistake of assuming that the results of an analysis of one particular moment are generalizable to apply to other periods.

Phi coefficient (ϕ)   Pearson r where both variables are dichotomous.

Placebo-control group   A control group in which a substance without any pharmacological effect is given as a "drug."

Planned contrasts   Contrasts intended before the data were examined.

Plausible rival hypothesis   A proposition, or set of propositions, that provides a reasonable alternative which rivals the working hypothesis as an explanation for the occurrence of some specified phenomenon.

Plausibility stage   The second stage in the development of a scientific hypothesis, in which the scientist evaluates the worthiness of ideas or first impressions.

Point-biserial correlation (r_{pb})   Pearson r where one of the variables is continuous and the other is dichotomous.

Pointer reading   any empirical reference point or value that serves to pin down or pinpoint a theoretical relationship at a moment in time.

Pointless precision   When a measure is more exact than can be taken advantage of in the situation.

PONS   Profile of Nonverbal Sensitivity; a test for measuring sensitivity to nonverbal cues.

Pooling sources of variance   Combining terms that are not too significantly different.

POPBS   Proportion of Possible Benefit Score (NCBM/MPBS).

Population   The organisms or other units from which we have drawn our samples and to which we want to generalize.

Positive synergistic effects   Synergistic effects serving to raise scores.

Postdictive validity   A type of test validity based on the extent to which the test results correlate with some criterion in the past.

Post hoc contrasts   Contrasts computed only after the data were examined.

Power   Probability of not making a type II error, or $1 - \beta$.

Practical validity   Social utility of established relationships.

Pre-analysis of an experiment   The statistical analysis of the data predicted by our theory to clarify how our predictions will be tested in our data-analytic model.

Precision   Sharpness or exactness of observations.

Predictive validity   A type of test validity based on the extent to which the test can "predict" the future.

Pre-experimental design   Any research design in which there is such a total absence of control that it is of minimal value in establishing causality.

Pre-post control group design   A before-after experimental design (e.g., the *Solomon design*).

Principal-components analysis   The rewriting of a set of variables into a new set of orthogonal components.

Probability   The mathematical chance of an event occurring.

Probability sampling   A sampling plan which specifies that the population will be divided into subclasses and then sampled in such a way as to ensure that each subclass is represented in proportion to its contribution to the population.

Product-moment correlation   Standard index of linear relationship.

Projective tests   Indirect disguised measures which operate on the principle that the subject will project some unconscious aspect of his or her life experience and emotions onto ambiguous stimuli in the spontaneous responses that come to mind, for example, the Rorschach test.

Protected t test t test computed under the umbrella of an overall F to minimize capitalizing on post hoc selection of largest effects.

Proximity analysis   Set of redescriptors of relationships among objects in terms of measures of similarity or dissimilarity.

Pseudovolunteer   See *No-show*.

Psychosocial experimenter effects   Those interactional effects which are a function of psychosocial attributes of the experimenter, for example, the experimenter's personality.

q   See *Cohen's q*.

Q-sort   A rating procedure where the judge sorts stimuli into piles to resemble a normal distribution.

Quadratic trend   Curvilinear relationship between two variables in which the line changes direction once (as in a U or ∩ curve).

Quartile range The range of scores found between the 75th and 25th percentiles.

Quasi-control subjects Participants who reflect on the context in which an experiment is conducted and speculate on ways in which the context might influence their own and research subjects' behavior.

Quasi-experiment Any design that resembles an experimental design (in that there are treatments, outcome measures, and experimental units) but where there is no random assignment to create the comparisons from which treatment-caused changes are inferred.

r Pearson's product-moment correlation.

r^2 Pearson's correlation squared; proportion of variance "accounted for."

r_{pb} See point biserial correlation.

Random effects Levels of a factor chosen as representative of a population of levels of a factor.

Random errors The effects of uncontrolled variables that cannot be specifically identified. Such effects theoretically are self-canceling, in that the average of these errors would probably equal zero.

Random sample A sample chosen by chance procedures and with known probabilities of selection, so that every individual in the population will have the same likelihood of being selected.

Range Distance between the highest and lowest score.

Rating scale The common name for a variety of measuring instruments where the observer gives a numerical value to certain judgments or assessments.

Raw contrast score Sum of the products of condition scores or residuals and contrast weights (λ) for each sampling unit.

Reactive observation An observation that affects the thing being observed.

Rectangular arrays Generalizations of latin squares to $t \times t!$ dimensions where t = number of treatments.

Redescriptors Multivariate procedures serving to redescribe a set of variables, often in a smaller set of variables.

Regression analysis Loosely equivalent to correlational analysis; more technically refers to relations of changes in level of Y to changes in levels of X.

Relational inquiry Any method of research that seeks to tell "how things are in relation to other things."

Reliability The degree to which observations are consistent or stable.

Repeated measurements Measurements made on the same sampling units.

Replicability The ability to repeat or duplicate a scientific observation, usually an experimental observation.

Representative research design Any design that involves sampling from both subjects and stimuli.

Residuals Effects left over when appropriate components are subtracted from scores or means.

Response The consequence of, or reaction to, a stimulus.

Response set That type of response bias in which a person's answers to questions or responses to a set of items are determined by a consistent mental set.

Response variable Dependent variable.

Rho (ρ) Spearman rank correlation.

Role-play A type of simulation where subjects act out a given scenario; known as *emotional role-play* when a high degree of experimental realism is achieved by increasing the subjects' emotional involvement.

Rotation of factors or components Rotation of axes on which variables have been located with the aim of making the factors or components more interpretable.

Row effects Row means minus grand mean.

Rule of thumb Where the researcher starts with some everyday occurrence or practitioner's rule based on experience and, seeing that it works, then tries to repeat the experience and explain it scientifically.

S Square root of the unbiased estimator of the population value of σ^2.

S^2 Unbiased estimator of the population value of σ^2.

S^2 **means** The variance of means around the grand mean.

S^2 **pooled** Variance collected from two or more samples.

Sample The subset of the population for whom we have obtained observations.

Sampling plan A design, scheme of action, or procedure that specifies how the participants are to be selected.

Sampling stability The assumption that all samples produced by the same sampling plan will yield essentially the same results.

Sampling units The organisms or objects being studied, e.g., people, schools, or countries.

Sampling with replacement A type of simple random selection in which the selected names are placed in the selection pool again and may be reselected on subsequent draws. This is contrasted with *sampling without replacement*, in which a previously selected name cannot be reselected and must be disregarded on any later draw.

Scheffé test Significance test appropriate for use when we have formulated our contrast after examining the data.

Scientific method A methodical system of scientific procedures and techniques that is believed to "work" or "produce" or "pay off."

Secondary analysis The reanalysis of existing data.

Selection A plausible threat to internal validity when different kinds of research subjects have been selected to take part in one experimental group than have been selected for another group.

Self-fulfilling prophecy The idea that someone who predicts an event may behave in ways that are likely to increase the probability that the event will occur—the prophet thus acts to fulfill his or her own prophecy.

Semantic differential A major type of rating scale which is used to measure subjective (or connotative) meaning.

Sentence-completion test A type of projective test in which the subject responds to an incomplete sentence with whatever comes to mind.

Sequence The pattern of presentation of two or more treatment conditions.

Serendipity The occurrence of discoveries in the course of investigations designed for another purpose.

Σ Instruction telling us to sum or add over a set of numbers.

σ The standard deviation of a set of scores.

σ^2 The variance of a set of scores.

Sign test Test of significance of the preponderance of positive vs. negative difference scores for matched-pair data.

Significance level The level of alpha.

Significance test Statistical test giving information on the tenability of the null hypothesis of no relationship between two or more variables.

Significance testing The use of statistical probability when a decision is made about a hypothesis.

Simple random selection A type of sampling plan in which the participants are selected individually on the basis of a table of random digits.

Simulation experiment An experiment which is based on a model in order to learn what will happen under conditions that are designed to mimic the environment in a definite way.

Situational experimenter effects Those interactional effects which are a function of situationally determined experimenter attributes.

Skewness A characteristic of distributions in which extreme scores are concentrated on one side of the mean.

Smallest-space analysis Set of redescriptors of relationships among objects in terms of measures of similarity or dissimilarity.

Social environmental variables That class of independent variables which consists of environmental determinants of behavior.

Social experimentation The application of experimental methods to the analysis of social problems and to the development, testing, and assessment of workable intervention procedures to reduce the problems.

Solomon design A four-group experimental design that was developed by R. L. Solomon. It is a means of assessing initial performance without having contaminated it by pretesting; it also allows us to determine the interaction of pretesting and the treatment.

Spearman rank correlation   Pearson r computed on scores in ranked form.

Split-half method   A means of evaluating reliability in test construction, in which the responses to a test that is split in half are correlated.

Spread   Dispersion or variability.

Standard deviation   An index of the variability of a set of data around the most typical value in a normal distribution.

Standard normal curve   Normal curve with mean $= 0$ and $\sigma = 1$.

Standard normal deviate Z score location on a normal distribution of zero mean and unit variance.

Standard score   Score converted to standard deviation unit.

Standardized contrast score   The contrast SS for each sampling unit.

Standardized measure   Referring to the fact that there are standards for administering, scoring, and interpreting a particular measure or instrument.

Standardizing the margins   Procedure for more clearly showing relationships in a table of counts by setting row totals equal to each other and by setting column totals equal to each other.

Statistical conclusion validity   The degree to which the presumed independent variable, X, and the presumed dependent variable, Y, are indeed related.

Statistical significance   The p value arbitrarily selected to define the test statistic (e.g., t, F, χ^2) as too large to make the null hypothesis tenable.

Stem   The leading digits of a stem-and-leaf display.

Stem-and-leaf display   The plot of a distribution in which the original data are preserved with any desired precision.

Stimulus   Any sensory contact which evokes a response.

Stouffer method of adding z's   Procedure for combining p values of a set of studies.

Strong inference   A type of research approach where one hypothesis or fact vies against another.

Structured items   Those items with clearcut response options.

Subjects-within-sequences designs   Designs in which more than one subject is assigned to some or all sequences of a repeated-measures design.

Sufficient condition   An adequate condition.

SS   Sum of squares.

SS between   Sum of squares between conditions.

SS total   Total sum of squares.

SS within   Sum of squares within conditions.

Summated ratings   A method of attitude-scale construction, developed by R. Likert, which uses *item analysis* to select the best items.

Symmetry   A characteristic of distributions in which the portions to the right and left of the mean are mirror images of each other.

Symptomatic volunteers   Research volunteers who most closely resemble those persons to whom we wish our generalizations to apply.

Synchronic research   Referring to a temporal approach in which a variable is observed as it exists at one brief period in time, not using information about its development.

Synergistic effects   Nonadditive effects of several treatments.

Systematic errors   The effects of uncontrolled variables that often can be specifically identified. Such effects are theoretically seen as *not* self-canceling, in contrast to the self-canceling effects of random errors.

t distributions   Family of distributions, centered at zero and ranging from negative to positive infinity.

t test   A test of significance employed to judge the tenability of the null hypothesis of no relationship between two variables.

Table analysis   Statistical analysis of frequency counts cast into tabular form.

Tacit knowledge   Facts or truths that we know but cannot easily communicate verbally.

Teleologic factor   See *Final cause*.

Test of significance   Statistical test giving information on the tenability of the null hypothesis of no relationship between two or more variables.

Testing error   Where familiarity with a test or scale artificially enhances performance.

Testing the grand mean Testing whether the grand mean differs from zero or some other value of theoretical interest.

Test-retest method A means of evaluating reliability in test construction, where the correlation coefficient is calculated on data obtained from the same test but from results gotten at different times.

Theoretical definition The meaning of a variable in relatively abstract terms. Also called the *conceptual definition* of a variable.

Thurstone scale See *Equal-appearing-intervals method.*

Time-sequential design A research design where subjects of different ages are observed at several different times.

Tolerance for future null results Number of filed (unavailable) studies with mean effect size of zero required to bring the combined probability to a nonsignificant level.

Total aggregation Aggregation of all relevant sources of variance.

Trimmed mean The mean of a distribution from which the highest and lowest X percent have been dropped.

Trimmed range Range remaining after highest and lowest X percent of the scores have been dropped.

Two-tailed test Test of significance in which the null hypothesis is rejected if the results are significant in either of the two possible directions.

Type I error The error in rejecting the null hypothesis when it is true.

Type II error The error in failing to reject the null hypothesis when it is false.

Typology A systematic classification of types.

Unbiased sample Based on a sampling plan which specifies that the sample values do not differ in the long run from the corresponding values in the population being studied.

Uncertainty principle W. Heisenberg's assertion that the accurate measurement of one of two related quantities (in quantum mechanics) produces uncertainties in the measurement of the other. Also, in behavioral science, predicting behavior is limited by reactive observations that impose uncertainties on the behavior.

Units of analysis The organisms or objects being studied, e.g., people, schools, or countries.

Unobtrusive measures Those instruments that are used to study behavior when the subject is unaware of being observed.

Unplanned contrasts Contrasts computed only after the data were examined.

Unstructured items Those items that offer the respondent an opportunity to express feelings, motives, or behavior quite spontaneously—also called *open-ended items.*

Unweighted-means analysis Analysis weighting all means equally even if sample sizes differ.

Validity The degree to which we observe what we purport to observe.

Values The standards or principles by which the worth of something is judged.

Variables Any observable or measurable events or things.

Variance The mean of the squared deviations of scores from their mean.

Varimax rotation Common method of orthogonal rotation that tries to make loadings as close to zero or to 1.00 as possible.

Volunteer bias That error which results when participants who volunteer respond differently than nonvolunteers.

w See *Cohen's* w.

Winer method of adding *t*'s Procedure for combining p values of a set of studies.

Word association test A type of projective test in which the subject is read a list of words and then responds with the first thing that comes to mind.

Working hypothesis A proposition, or set of propositions, that serves to guide and organize an empirical investigation.

X Any score.

$\bar{X}$ The mean of a set of scores.

$\bar{\bar{X}}$ Grand mean.

X-axis The horizontal axis of a distribution.

Y-axis The vertical axis of a distribution.

Yates correction for continuity Specific correction for continuity in which the absolute difference between obtained and expected frequencies is decreased by .5.

Yea-saying A type of response set in which the person tends to answer consistently in the affirmative.

Z Standard normal deviate.

Z score Score converted to standard deviation unit.

Zeitgeist The general "temper" or "feeling" characteristic of a particular period of time.

REFERENCES

Adair, J. G.: *The Human Subject: The Social Psychology of the Psychological Experiment,* Little, Brown, Boston, 1973.

Adcock, C. J.: A note on combining probabilities. *Psychometrika,* 1960, *25,* 303–305.

Adorno, T. W., E. Frenkel-Brunswik, D. J. Levinson, and R. N. Sanford: *The Authoritarian Personality,* Harper and Row, New York, 1950.

Allport, F. H., and M. Lepkin: Wartime rumors of waste and special privilege: Why some people believe them, *Journal of Abnormal and Social Psychology,* 1945, *40,* 3–36.

Allport, G. W., J. S. Bruner, and E. M. Jandorf: Personality under social catastrophe: Ninety life histories of the Nazi revolution, in C. Kluckhohn and H. A. Murray (eds.), *Personality: In Nature, Society, and Culture,* 2d ed, Knopf, New York, 1953, pp. 436–455.

—— and L. J. Postman: *The Psychology of Rumor,* Holt, Rinehart & Winston, New York, 1947.

Altmann, J.: Observational study of behavior: Sampling methods, *Behaviour,* 1974, *49,* 227–267.

American Psychological Association: *Publication Manual of the American Psychological Association,* 2d ed., American Psychological Association, Washington, D.C., 1974.

Anderson, J. W.: The methodology of psychological biography, *Journal of Interdisciplinary History,* 1981, *11,* 455–475.

Appelbaum, R.: *Theories of Social Change,* Markham, Chicago, 1970.

Armor, D. J.: Theta reliability and factor scaling, in H. L. Costner (ed.), *Sociological Methodology 1973–1974,* Jossey-Bass, San Francisco, 1974.

—— and A. S. Couch: *Data-Text Primer: An Introduction to Computerized Social Data Analysis,* Free Press, New York, 1972.

Arms, R. L., G. W. Russell, and M. L. Sandilands: Effects on the hostility of spectators of viewing aggressive sports, *Social Psychology Quarterly,* 1979, *42,* 275–279.

Aronson, E., and J. M. Carlsmith: Experimentation in social psychology, in G. Lindzey and E. Aronson (eds.), *The Handbook of Social Psychology,* 2d ed., Addison-Wesley, Reading, Mass., 1968, vol. 2, pp. 1–79.

Asch, S.: *Social Psychology,* Prentice-Hall, Englewood Cliffs, N.J., 1952.

Atwell, J. E.: Human rights in human subjects research, in A. J. Kimmel (ed.), *New Directions for Methodology of Social and Behavioral Science: Ethics of Human Subject Research,* no. 10, Jossey-Bass, San Francisco, 1981, pp. 81–90.

Axinn, S.: Fallacy of the single risk, *Philosophy of Science,* 1966, *33,* 154–162.

Babbie, E. R.: *The Practice of Social Research,* Wadsworth, Belmont, Calif., 1975.

Baenninger, R.: Some consequences of aggressive behavior: A selective review of the literature on other animals, *Aggressive Behavior,* 1974, *1,* 17–37.

————, R. D. Estes, and S. Baldwin: Anti-predator behavior of baboons and impalas toward a cheetah, *Journal of East African Wildlife,* 1977, *15,* 327–329.

Bailey, K. D.: Cluster analysis, in D. R. Heise (ed.), *Sociological Methodology 1975,* Jossey-Bass, San Francisco, 1974, pp. 59–128.

Bakan, D.: *On Method: Toward a Reconstruction of Psychological Investigation,* Jossey-Bass, San Francisco, 1967.

Balaam, L. N.: Multiple comparisons—A sampling experiment, *Australian Journal of Statistics,* 1963, *5,* 62–84.

Bales, R. F.: A set of categories for analysis of small group interaction, *American Sociological Review,* 1950, *15,* 257–263. (*a*)

————: *Interaction Process Analysis: A Method for the Study of Small Groups,* Addison-Wesley, Cambridge, Mass., 1950. (*b*)

Barber, B.: Resistance by scientists to scientific discovery, *Science,* 1961, *134,* 596–602.

———— and A. Inkeles (eds.): *Stability and Social Change,* Little, Brown, Boston, 1971.

Barber, T. X.: *Pitfalls in Human Research: Ten Pivotal Points,* Pergamon, New York, 1976.

Barrass, R.: *Scientists Must Write,* Chapman & Hall, London, 1978.

Baughman, E. E., and W. G. Dahlstrom: *Negro and White Children: A Psychological Study in the Rural South,* Academic Press, New York, 1968.

Bavelas, A.: Communication patterns in task-oriented groups, *Journal of the Acoustical Society of America,* 1950, *22,* 725–730.

Becker, H. S., and B. Geer: Participant observation: The analysis of qualitative field data, in R. N. Adams and J. J. Preiss (eds.), *Human Organization Research,* Dorsey, Homewood, Ill., 1960.

Beez, W. V.: Influence of biased psychological reports on teacher behavior and pupil performance, *Proceedings of the 76th Annual Convention of the American Psychological Association,* 1968, 605–606.

Benedict, R. F.: *Patterns of Culture,* Houghton, New York, 1934.

Bentler, P. M., and G. Speckart: Attitudes "cause" behaviors: A structural equation analysis, *Journal of Personality and Social Psychology,* 1981, *40,* 226–238.

Berelson, B.: *Content Analysis in Communication Research,* Free Press, Glencoe, Ill., 1952.

————: Content analysis, in G. Lindzey (ed), *Handbook of Social Psychology,* Addison-Wesley, Reading, Mass., 1954, vol. 1, pp. 488–522.

Billow, R. M.: Metaphor: A review of the psychological literature, *Psychological Bulletin,* 1977, *84,* 81–92.

Birnbaum, A.: Combining independent tests of significance, *Journal of the American Statistical Association,* 1954, *49,* 559–574.

Bishop, Y. M. M., S. E. Fienberg, and P. W. Holland: *Discrete Multivariate Analysis: Theory and Practice,* MIT Press, Cambridge, Mass., 1975.

Boder, D. P.: *I Did Not Interview the Dead,* University of Illinois Press, Urbana, 1949.

Bok, S.: *Lying: Moral Choice in Public and Private Life,* Pantheon, New York, 1978.

Boring, E. G.: *A History of Experimental Psychology,* 2d ed., Appleton-Century-Crofts, New York, 1950.

————: Perspective: Artifact and control, in R. Rosenthal and R. L. Rosnow (eds.), *Artifact in Behavioral Research,* Academic Press, New York, 1969, pp. 1–11.

Box, G. E. P.: Non-normality and tests on variances, *Biometrika,* 1953, *40,* 318–335.

————, W. G. Hunter, and J. S. Hunter: *Statistics for Experimenters,* Wiley, New York, 1978.

Bradburn, N. M.: Question-wording effects in surveys, in R. Hogarth (ed.), *New Directions for Methodology of Social and Behavioral Science: Question Framing and Response Consistency,* no. 11, Jossey-Bass, San Francisco, 1982, pp. 65–76.

Brady, J. V.: Ulcers in "executive" monkeys, *Scientific American,* 1958, *199,* 95–100.

————, G. Bigelow, H. Emurian, and D. M. Williams: Design of a programmed environment for experimental analysis of social behavior, in D. H. Carson (ed.), *Man-Environment Interactions: Evaluations and Applications. 7: Social Ecology,* Environmental Design Research Associates, Milwaukee, 1974, pp. 187–208.

———— and H. H. Emurian: Behavior analysis of motivational and emotional interactions in a programmed environment, in H. E. Howe, Jr., and R. A. Dienstbier (eds.), *Nebraska Symposium on Motivation 1978: Human Emotion,* vol. 26, University of Nebraska Press, Lincoln, 1979.

——, R. W. Porter, D. G. Conrad, and J. W. Mason: Avoidance behavior and the development of gastroduodenal ulcers, *Journal for the Experimental Analysis of Behavior,* 1958, *1,* 69–72.

Bresnahan, J. L., and M. M. Shapiro: A general equation and technique for the exact partitioning of chi-square contingency tables, *Psychological Bulletin,* 1966, *66,* 252–262.

Bridgman, P. W.: *The Logic of Modern Physics,* Macmillan, New York, 1937.

Brinton, J. E.: Deriving an attitude scale from semantic differential data, *Public Opinion Quarterly,* 1961, *25,* 289–295.

Brislin, R. W.: Comparative research methodology: Cross-cultural studies, *International Journal of Psychology,* 1976, *11,* 215–229.

Broad, W. J.: Paul Feyerabend: Science and the anarchist, *Science,* 1979, *206,* 534–537.

Brogden, W. J. Animal studies of learning, in S. S. Stevens (ed.), *Handbook of Experimental Psychology,* Wiley, New York, 1951, pp. 568–612.

Brozek, J., and K. Tiede: Reliable and questionable significance in a series of statistical tests, *Psychological Bulletin,* 1952, *49,* 339–341.

Brunswik, E.: *Systematic and Representative Design of Psychological Experiments,* University of California Press, Berkeley, 1947.

Buckhout, R.: Need for approval and attitude change, *Journal of Psychology,* 1965, *60,* 123–128.

Burnham, J. R.: Experimenter bias and lesion labeling, unpublished manuscript, Purdue University, 1966.

Buss, A. H.: Aggression pays, in J. L. Singer (ed.), *The Control of Aggression and Violence,* Academic Press, New York, 1971.

Buss, A. R.: Causes and reasons in attribution theory: A conceptual critique, *Journal of Personality and Social Psychology,* 1978, *36,* 1311–1321.

Camilli, G., and K. D. Hopkins: Applicability of chi-square to 2×2 contingency tables with small expected cell frequencies, *Psychological Bulletin,* 1978, *85,* 163–167.

Campbell, D. T.: The indirect assessment of attitudes, *Psychological Bulletin,* 1950, *47,* 15–38.

——: Prospective: Artifact and control, in R. Rosenthal and R. L. Rosnow (eds.), *Artifact in Behavioral Research,* Academic Press, New York, 1969, pp. 351–382.

——: Evolutionary epistemology, in P. A. Schilpp (ed.), *The Philosophy of Karl R. Popper,* Vol. 14, I & II, Library of Living Philosophers, Open Court, LaSalle, Ill., 1974, pp. 413–463, vol. 14-I.

——: A tribal model of the social system vehicle carrying scientific knowledge, *Knowledge: Creation, Diffusion, Utilization,* 1979, *1,* no. 2, 181–200.

—— and D. W. Fiske: Convergent and discriminant validation by the multitrait-multimethod matrix, *Psychological Bulletin,* 1959, *56,* 81–105.

—— and J. C. Stanley: *Experimental and Quasi-Experimental Designs for Research,* Rand McNally, Chicago, 1966.

Cannon, W. B.: *The Way of an Investigator,* Norton, New York, 1945.

Carmer, S. G., and M. R. Swanson: An evaluation of ten pairwise multiple comparison procedures by Monte Carlo methods, *Journal of the American Statistical Association,* 1973, *68,* 66–74.

Caws, P.: *The Philosophy of Science: A Systematic Account,* Van Nostrand, Princeton, N.J., 1965.

——: The structure of discovery, *Science,* 1969, *166,* 1375–1380.

Chamberlin, T. C.: The method of multiple working hypotheses, *Journal of Geology,* 1897, *5,* 838–848.

Cochran, W. G.: The comparison of percentages in matched samples, *Biometrika,* 1950, *37,* 256–266.

——: Some methods for strengthening the common χ^2 tests, *Biometrics,* 1954, *10,* 417–451.

—— and G. M. Cox: *Experimental Designs,* 2d ed., Wiley, New York, 1957. (First corrected printing, 1968.)

——, F. Mosteller, and J. W. Tukey: Statistical problems of the Kinsey report, *Journal of the American Statistical Association,* 1953, *48,* 673–716.

Cohen, J.: *Statistical Power Analysis for the Behavioral Sciences,* Academic Press, New York, 1969, rev. ed., 1977.

———: Set correlation as a general multivariate data-analytic method. *Multivariate Behavioral Research,* 1982, *17,* 301–341.

——— and P. Cohen: *Applied Multiple Regression/Correlation Analysis for the Behavioral Sciences,* Erlbaum, Hillsdale, N.J., 1975.

Cohen, M. R.: *Reason and Nature: An Essay on the Meaning of Scientific Method,* Dover, New York, 1959. (First published 1931, Harcourt Brace.)

Collins, B. E., and B. H. Raven: Group structure: Attraction, coalition, communication, and power, in G. Lindzey and E. Aronson (eds.), *The Handbook of Social Psychology,* rev. ed., Addison-Wesley, Reading, Mass., 1969, vol. 4, pp. 102–204.

Collins, H. M.: Science and the rule of replicability: A sociological study of scientific method, Paper presented at annual meeting of the American Association for the Advancement of Science in symposium on "Replication and Experimenter Effect," Washington, D.C., 1978.

Conover, W. J.: Some reasons for not using the Yates continuity correction on 2 × 2 contingency tables, *Journal of the American Statistical Association,* 1974, *69,* 374–376.

Cook, T. D., and D. T. Campbell: *Quasi-Experimentation: Design and Analysis Issues for Field Settings,* Rand McNally, Chicago, 1979.

Cooley, W. W., and P. R. Lohnes: *Multivariate Data Analysis,* Wiley, New York, 1971.

Coombs, C. H., R. M. Dawes, and A. Tversky: *Mathematical Psychology: An Elementary Introduction,* Prentice-Hall, Englewood Cliffs, N.J., 1970.

Cooper, H. M.: The literature review: Elevating its status to scientific inquiry, Technical report 238, Center for Research in Social Behavior, University of Missouri at Columbia, December 1980.

——— and R. Rosenthal: Statistical versus traditional procedures for summarizing research findings, *Psychological Bulletin,* 1980, *87,* 442–449.

Cooper, W. H.: Ubiquitous halo, *Psychological Bulletin,* 1981, *90,* 218–244.

Coren, S., and C. Porac: Fifty centuries of right-handedness: The historical record, *Science,* 1977, *198,* 631–632.

Cornell, F. G., and E. P. McLoone: Design of sample surveys in education, *Review of Educational Research,* 1963, *33,* 523–532.

Corrozi, J. F., and R. L. Rosnow: Consonant and dissonant communications as positive and negative reinforcements in opinion change, *Journal of Personality and Social Psychology,* 1968, *8,* 27–30.

Cox, D. R.: The use of a concomitant variable in selecting an experimental design, *Biometrika,* 1957, *44,* 150–158.

———: *Planning of Experiments,* Wiley, New York, 1958.

Crandall, V. C.: Personality characteristics and social and achievement behaviors associated with children's social desirability response tendencies, *Journal of Personality and Social Psychology,* 1966, *4,* 477–486.

Cronbach, L. J.: Response sets and test validity, *Educational and Psychological Measurement,* 1946, *6,* 475–494.

———: Further evidence on response sets and test design, *Educational and Psychological Measurement,* 1950, *10,* 3–31.

———: *Essentials of Psychological Testing,* 2d ed., Harper, New York, 1960.

——— and P. E. Meehl: Construct validity in psychological tests, *Psychological Bulletin,* 1955, *52,* 281–302.

Crowne, D. P., and D. Marlowe: *The Approval Motive: Studies in Evaluative Dependence,* Wiley, New York, 1964.

Dabbs, J. M., and I. L. Janis: Why does eating while reading facilitate opinion change?—An experimental inquiry, *Journal of Experimental Social Psychology,* 1965, *1,* 133–144.

D'Agostino, R. B.: A second look at analysis of variance on dichotomous data, *Journal of Educational Measurement,* 1971, *8,* 327–333.

Darroch, R. K., and I. D. Steiner: Role playing: An alternative to laboratory research? *Journal of Personality,* 1970, *38,* 302–311.

DeVore, I., and K. R. L. Hall: Baboon ecology, in I. DeVore (ed.), *Primate Behavior,* Holt, Rinehart & Winston, New York, 1965, pp. 20–52.

——— and S. L. Washburn: Baboon ecology and human evolution, in F. C. Howell and F. Bourlière (eds.), *African Ecology and Human Evolution,* Viking Fund, New York, 1963, pp. 335–367.

Dewey, E. R.: *Cycles: Selected Writings,* Foundation for the Study of Cycles, Pittsburgh, 1970.

Dohrenwend, B. S.: Interviewer biasing effects: Toward a reconciliation of findings, *Public Opinion Quarterly,* 1969, *33,* 121–125.

———, J. Colombotos, and B. P. Dohrenwend: Social distance and interviewer effects, *Public Opinion Quarterly,* 1968, *32,* 410–422.

Dollard, J.: The Kinsey report on women: A strangely flawed masterpiece, *New York Herald Tribune,* September 13, 1953, sec. 6, p. 3.

———, L. W. Doob, N. E. Miller, O. H. Mowrer, R. R. Sears, (C. S. Ford, C. I. Hovland, and R. T. Sollenberger): *Frustration and Aggression,* Yale University Press, New Haven, 1939.

Duhem, P.: *The Aim and Structure of Physical Theory,* Princeton University Press, Princeton, 1954.

Eagly, A. H.: Sex differences in influenceability, *Psychological Bulletin,* 1978, *85,* 86–116.

Easley, J. A. Scientific method as an educational objective, in L. C. Deighton (ed.), *The Encyclopedia of Education,* Free Press and Macmillan, New York, 1971, vol. 8, pp. 150–157.

——— and M. M. Tatsuoka: *Scientific Thought: Cases from Classical Physics,* Allyn & Bacon, Boston, 1968.

Edgington, E. S.: An additive model for combining probability values from independent experiments, *Journal of Psychology,* 1972, *80,* 351–363. (a)

———: A normal curve method for combining probability values from independent experiments, *Journal of Psychology,* 1972, *82,* 85–89. (b)

Edwards, A. L.: *Techniques of Attitude Scale Construction,* Appleton-Century-Crofts, New York, 1957.

———: *Experimental Design in Psychological Research,* 4th ed., Holt, Rinehart & Winston, New York, 1972.

Eron, L. D., and L. R. Huesmann: Sohn should let sleeping dogs lie, *American Psychologist,* 1980, *36,* 231–233.

———, L. R. Huesmann, M. M. Lefkowitz, and L. O. Walder: Does television violence cause aggression? *American Psychologist,* 1972, *27,* 253–263.

Everitt, B. S.: *The Analysis of Contingency Tables,* Wiley, New York, 1977.

Fear, D. E.: *Technical Writing,* 2d ed., Random House, New York, 1978.

Federighi, E. T.: Extended tables of the percentage points of Student's *t*-distribution, *Journal of the American Statistical Association,* 1959, *54,* 683–688.

Feldman, R. E.: Response to compatriot and foreigner who seek assistance, *Journal of Personality and Social Psychology,* 1968, *10,* 202–214.

Festinger, L.: *A Theory of Cognitive Dissonance,* Row, Peterson, Evanston, Ill., 1957.

Feyerabend, P.: *Against Method: Outline of an Anarchistic Theory of Knowledge,* New Left Books, London, 1975.

Fienberg, S. E.: *The Analysis of Cross-Classified Categorical Data,* MIT Press, Cambridge, Mass., 1977.

Filion, F. L.: Estimating bias due to nonresponse in mail surveys, *Public Opinion Quarterly,* 1975–76, *39,* 482–492.

Findley, J. D.: Programmed environments for the experimental analysis of human behavior, in W. K. Honig (ed.), *Operant Behavior: Areas of Research and Application,* Appleton-Century-Crofts, New York, 1966, pp. 827–848.

Firth, R.: Rumor in a primitive society, *Journal of Abnormal and Social Psychology,* 1956, *53,* 122–132.

Fishbein, M. (ed.): *Readings in Attitude Theory and Measurement,* Wiley, New York, 1967.

—— and I. Ajzen: *Belief, Attitude, Intention and Behavior: An Introduction to Theory and Research,* Addison-Wesley, Reading, Mass., 1975.

Fisher, R. A.: *The Design of Experiments,* Oliver & Boyd, London, 1935.

——: *Statistical Methods for Research Workers,* 7th ed., Oliver & Boyd, London, 1938.

Flacks, R.: The liberated generation: An exploration of the roots of social protest, *Journal of Social Issues,* 1967, *23,* 52–75.

Foa, U. G.: Three kinds of behavioral change, *Psychological Bulletin,* 1968, *70,* 460–473.

—— and Foa, E. B.: *Societal Structures of the Mind,* Charles C. Thomas, Springfield, Ill., 1974.

Friedman, C. J., and J. W. Gladden: Objective measurement of social role concept via the semantic differential, *Psychological Reports,* 1964, *14,* 239–247.

Friedman, H.: Magnitude of experimental effect and a table for its rapid estimation, *Psychological Bulletin,* 1968, *70,* 245–251.

Fruchter, B.: *Introduction to Factor Analysis,* Van Nostrand, Princeton, 1954.

Furno, O. F.: Sample survey designs in education—Focus on administrative utilization, *Review of Educational Research,* 1966, *37,* 552–565.

Gergen, K. J.: Social psychology as history, *Journal of Personality and Social Psychology,* 1973, *26,* 309–320.

——: Experimentation in social psychology: A reappraisal, *European Journal of Social Psychology,* 1978, *8,* 507–527.

Gilbert, J. P., B. McPeek, and F. Mosteller: Statistics and ethics in surgery and anesthesia, *Science,* 1977, *198,* 684–689.

Glass, G. V.: Primary, secondary, and meta-analysis of research, Paper presented at the meeting of the American Educational Research Association, San Francisco, April 1976.

——: Summarizing effect sizes, in R. Rosenthal (ed.), *New Directions for Methodology of Social and Behavioral Science: Quantitative Assessment of Research Domains,* no. 5, Jossey-Bass, San Francisco, 1980.

——, B. McGaw, and M. L. Smith: *Meta-Analysis in Social Research,* Sage, Beverly Hills, Calif., 1981.

Goffman, E.: On face-work: An analysis of ritual elements in social interaction, *Psychiatry: Journal for the Study of Interpersonal Processes,* 1955, *18,* 213–231.

——: Embarrassment and social organization, *American Journal of Sociology,* 1956, *62,* 264–274. (a)

——: The nature of deference and demeanor, *American Anthropologist,* 1956, *58,* 473–502. (b)

——: Alienation from interaction, *Human Relations,* 1957, *10,* 47–59.

Goldstein, J. H.: *Aggression and Crimes of Violence,* Oxford University Press, New York, 1975.

—— and R. L. Arms: Effects of observing athletic contests on hostility, *Sociometry,* 1971, *34,* 83–90.

Goode, W. J., and P. K. Hatt: *Methods in Social Research,* McGraw-Hill, New York, 1952.

Goodenough, W. H.: Ethnographic field techniques, in H. C. Triandis and J. W. Berry (eds.), *Handbook of Cross-Cultural Psychology: Methodology,* vol. 2, Allyn & Bacon, Boston, 1980, pp. 29–55.

Goodstadt, B., and D. Kipnis: Situational influences on the use of power, *Journal of Applied Psychology,* 1970, *54,* 201–207.

Gorden, R. L.: *Interviewing: Strategy, Techniques, and Tactics,* Dorsey, Homewood, Ill., 1969.

Gottman, J. M.: *Time-Series Analysis: A Comprehensive Introduction for Social Scientists,* Cambridge University Press, Cambridge, 1981.

Green, B. F., Jr., and J. W. Tukey: Complex analysis of variance: General problems, *Psychometrika,* 1960, *25,* 127–152.

Greenberg, M. S.: Role playing: An alternative to deception? *Journal of Personality and Social Psychology,* 1967, *7,* 152–157.

Greenwald, A.: Consequences of prejudices against the null hypothesis, *Psychological Bulletin,* 1975, *82,* 1–20.

Greenwald, A. G., and D. L. Ronis: Twenty years of cognitive dissonance: Case study of the evolution of a theory, *Psychological Review,* 1978, *85,* 53–57.

Grey, R. J., and D. Kipnis: Untangling the performance appraisal dilemma: The influence of perceived organizational context on evaluative processes, *Journal of Applied Psychology,* 1976, *61,* 329–335.

Grünbaum, A.: Causality and the science of human behavior, *American Scientist,* 1952, *40,* 665–676.

Guilford, J. P.: *Psychometric Methods,* 2d ed., McGraw-Hill, New York, 1954.

—— and B. Fruchter: *Fundamental Statistics in Psychology and Education,* 6th ed., McGraw-Hill, New York, 1978.

Guttman, L.: Order analysis of correlation matrices, in R. B. Cattell (ed.), *Handbook of Multivariate Experimental Psychology,* Rand McNally, Chicago, 1966, pp. 438–458.

Hackmann, W. D.: The relationship between concept and instrument design in eighteenth-century experimental science, *Annals of Science,* 1979, *36,* 205–224.

Hagenaars, J. A., and N. P. Cobben: Age, cohort and period: A general model for the analysis of social change, *Netherlands Journal of Sociology,* 1978, *14,* 58–91.

Hall, J. A.: Gender, gender roles, and nonverbal communication skills, in R. Rosenthal (ed.), *Skill in Nonverbal Communication: Individual Differences,* Oelgeschlager, Gunn & Hain, Cambridge, Mass., 1979, pp. 32–67.

——: Gender differences in nonverbal communication skills, in R. Rosenthal (ed.), *New Directions for Methodology of Social and Behavioral Science: Quantitative Assessment of Research Domains,* no. 5, Jossey-Bass, San Francisco, 1980.

Hanson, N. R.: *Patterns of Discovery,* Cambridge University Press, Cambridge, 1958.

——: The idea of a logic of discovery, in S. Toulmin and H. Woolf (eds.), *What I Do Not Believe and Other Essays,* D. Reidel, Dordrecht, Holland, 1971.

Harlow, H. F.: Love in infant monkeys, in S. Coopersmith (ed.), *Frontiers of Psychological Research,* W. H. Freeman, San Francisco, 1959, 1966, pp. 92–98.

—— and M. K. Harlow: The affectional systems, in A. M. Schrier, H. F. Harlow, and F. Stollnitz (eds.), *Behavior of Nonhuman Primates: Modern Research Trends,* vol. 2, Academic Press, New York, 1965, pp. 287–334.

—— and M. Harlow: Learning to love. *American Scientist,* 1966, *54,* 244–272.

—— and ——: The young monkeys, in P. Cramer (ed.), *Readings in Developmental Psychology Today,* CRM Books, Del Mar, Calif., 1970, pp. 93–97.

Harner, M. J.: Population pressures and the social evolution of agriculturists, *Southwestern Journal of Anthropology,* 1970, *26,* 67–86.

Harris, R. J.: *A Primer of Multivariate Statistics,* Academic Press, New York, 1975.

Hartmann, G. W.: A field experiment on the comparative effectiveness of "emotional" and "rational" political leaflets in determining election results, *Journal of Abnormal and Social Psychology,* 1936, *31,* 99–114.

Hasher, L., D. Goldstein, and T. Toppino: Frequency and the conference of referential validity, *Journal of Verbal Learning and Verbal Behavior,* 1977, *16,* 107–112.

Haviland, J. B.: Gossip as competition in Zinacantan, *Journal of Communication,* 1977, *27,* No. 1, 186–191.

Hays, W. L.: *Statistics,* 3d ed., Holt, Rinehart & Winston, New York, 1981.

Heberlein, T. A., and R. Baumgartner: Factors affecting response rates to mailed questionnaires: A quantitative analysis of the published literature, *American Sociological Review,* 1978, *43,* 447–462.

Heisenberg, W.: *Across the Frontiers,* Harper & Row, New York, 1974.

Hendrick, C. (ed.): Role-playing as a methodology for social research: A symposium, *Personality and Social Psychology Bulletin,* 1977, *3,* 454–522.

Henshel, R. L.: Seeking inoperative laws: Toward the deliberate use of unnatural experimentation, in L. Freese (ed.), *Theoretical Methods in Sociology, Seven Essays,* University of Pittsburgh Press, Pittsburgh, 1980. (a)

——: The purposes of laboratory experimentation and the virtues of deliberate artificiality, *Journal of Experimental Social Psychology,* 1980, *16,* 466–478. (b)

Hodgkinson, H.: Student protest—An institutional and national profile, *The Record* (*Columbia University Teachers' College*), 1970, *71*, 537–555.

Holden, C.: Ethics in social science research, *Science,* 1979, *206,* 537–540.

Holsti, O. R. (with the collaboration of J. K. Loomba and R. C. North): Content analysis, in G. Lindzey and E. Aronson (eds.), *The Handbook of Social Psychology,* 2d ed., Addison-Wesley, Reading, Mass., 1968, vol. 2, pp. 596–692.

Holton, G.: On the role of themata in scientific thought, *Science,* 1975, *188,* 328–334.

—— and R. S. Morison (eds.): *Limits of Scientific Inquiry,* Norton, New York, 1979.

Horowitz, I. A.: Effects of volunteering, fear, arousal, and number of communications on attitude change, *Journal of Personality and Social Psychology,* 1969, *11,* 34–37.

—— and B. H. Rothschild: Conformity as a function of deception and role playing, *Journal of Personality and Social Psychology,* 1970, *14,* 224–226.

Horowitz, I. L.: Methods and strategies in evaluating equity research. *Social Indicators Research,* 1979, *6,* 1–22.

Horst, P., and A. L. Edwards: Analysis of nonorthogonal designs: The 2^k factorial experiment, *Psychological Bulletin,* 1982, *91,* 190–192.

Hsu, L. M.: Tests of differences in p levels as tests of differences in effect sizes, *Psychological Bulletin,* 1980, *88,* 705–708.

Hsu, T. C., and L. S. Feldt: The effect of limitations on the number of criterion score values on the significance level of the F-test, *American Educational Research Journal,* 1969, *6,* 515–527.

Huck, S. W., and H. M. Sandler: *Rival Hypotheses,* Harper & Row, New York, 1979.

Hume, D.: *A Treatise of Human Nature,* Clarendon, Oxford, 1978. (Originally published 1739–40.)

Humphreys, L.: *Tearoom Trade: Impersonal Sex in Public Places,* 2d ed., Aldine, Chicago, 1975.

Hurvich, L. M.: Hering and the scientific establishment, *American Psychologist,* 1969, *24,* 497–514.

Hyman, H., and P. B. Sheatsley: The scientific method, in D. P. Geddes (ed.), *An Analysis of the Kinsey Reports,* New American Library, New York, 1954.

Janis, I. L., D. Kaye, and P. Kirschner: Facilitating effects of "eating-while-reading" on responsiveness to persuasive communications, *Journal of Personality and Social Psychology,* 1965, *1,* 181–186.

—— and L. Mann: Effectiveness of emotional role-playing in modifying smoking habits and attitudes, *Journal of Experimental Research in Personality,* 1965, *1,* 84–90.

Jones, F. P.: Experimental method in antiquity, *American Psychologist,* 1964, *19,* 419.

Jones, L. V., and D. W. Fiske: Models for testing the significance of combined results, *Psychological Bulletin,* 1953, *50,* 375–382.

Judd, C. M., and D. A. Kenny: *Estimating the Effects of Social Interventions,* Cambridge University Press, New York, 1981.

Kahn, R. L., and C. F. Cannell: *The Dynamics of Interviewing,* Wiley, New York, 1965.

Kamin, L.: *The Science and Politics of IQ,* Erlbaum, Potomac, Md., 1974.

Kaplan, A.: *The Conduct of Inquiry: Methodology for Behavioral Science,* Chandler, Scranton, Pa., 1964.

Katona, G.: *Psychological Economics,* Elsevier, New York, 1975.

——: Toward a macropsychology, *American Psychologist,* 1979, *34,* 118–126.

Kazdin, A. E., and A. H. Tuma (eds.): *New directions for methodology of social and behavioral science: Single-case research designs,* no. 13, Jossey-Bass, San Francisco, 1982.

Kelman, H. C.: *A Time to Speak: On Human Values and Social Research,* Jossey-Bass, San Francisco, 1968.

Keniston, K.: The sources of student dissent, *Journal of Social Issues,* 1967, *23,* 108–137.

——: You have to grow up in Scarsdale to know how bad things really are, *New York Times Magazine,* April 27, 1969.

Kenny, D. A.: *Correlation and Causality,* Wiley, New York, 1979.

Kidder, L. H.: On becoming hypnotized: How skeptics become convinced: A case of attitude change? *Journal of Abnormal Psychology,* 1972, *80,* 317–322.

Kim, J.-O.: Factor analysis, in N. H. Nie, C. H. Hull, J. G. Jenkins, K. Steinbrenner, and D. H. Bent, *SPSS: Statistical Package for the Social Sciences*, 2d ed., McGraw-Hill, New York, 1975, pp. 468–514.

Kim, K. H., and F. W. Roush: *Mathematics for Social Scientists*, Elsevier, New York, 1980.

Kinsey, A. C., W. B. Pomeroy, and C. E. Martin: *Sexual Behavior in the Human Male*, Saunders, Philadelphia, 1948.

———, ———, ———, and P. H. Gebhard: *Sexual Behavior in the Human Female*, Saunders, Philadelphia, 1953.

Kipnis, D.: *The Powerholders*, University of Chicago Press, Chicago, 1976.

——— and J. Cosentino: Use of leadership powers in industry, *Journal of Applied Psychology*, 1969, *53*, 460–466.

Kish, L.: *Survey Sampling*, Wiley, New York, 1965.

Kleinmuntz, B., and R. S. McLean: Computers in behavioral science: Diagnostic interviewing by digital computer, *Behavioral Science*, 1968, *13*, 75–80.

Klineberg, O.: *Social Psychology*, Henry Holt, New York, 1940.

Koch, H. L., M. Dentler, B. Dysart, and H. Streit: A scale for measuring attitudes toward the question of children's freedom, *Child Development*, 1934, *5*, 253–266.

Koertge, N.: The problem of appraising scientific theories, in P. D. Asquith and H. E. Hyburg, Jr. (eds.), *Current Research in Philosophy of Science*, Philosophy of Science Association, East Lansing, Mich., 1979, pp. 228–251.

Kolata, G. B.: NIH shaken by death of research volunteer, *Science*, 1980, *209*, 475–479.

Kordig, C. R.: Discovery and justification, *Philosophy of Science*, 1978, *45*, 110–117.

Kothandapani, V.: Validation of feeling, belief, and intention to act as three components of attitude and their contribution to prediction of contraceptive behavior, *Journal of Personality and Social Psychology*, 1971, *19*, 321–333.

Lana, R. E.: *Assumptions of Social Psychology*, Appleton-Century-Crofts, New York, 1969.

Lancaster, H. O.: The combination of probabilities: An application of orthonormal functions, *Australian Journal of Statistics*, 1961, *3*, 20–33.

Lanz, L.: The uncertainty principle, *Scientia*, 1976, *111*, 325–332.

Larsen, K. S., H. J. Martin, R. H. Ettinger, and J. Nelson: Approval seeking, social cost, and aggression: A scale and some dynamics, *Journal of Psychology*, 1976, *94*, 3–11.

Laslett, B.: Beyond methodology: The place of theory in quantitative historical research, *American Sociological Review*, 1980, *45*, 214–228.

Latané, B., and J. M. Darley: *The Unresponsive Bystander: Why Doesn't He Help?*, Appleton-Century-Crofts, New York, 1970.

Lazarsfeld, P. F., and N. W. Henry: *Latent Structure Analysis*, Houghton Mifflin, Boston, 1968.

Leavitt, H. J.: Some effects of certain communication patterns on group performance, *Journal of Abnormal and Social Psychology*, 1951, *46*, 38–50.

Lessac, M. S., and Solomon, R. L.: Effects of early isolation on the later adaptive behavior of beagles, *Developmental Psychology*, 1969, *1*, 14–25.

Levin, J., and A. J. Kimmel: Gossip columns: Media small talk, *Journal of Communication*, 1977, *27*, No. 1, 169–175.

Levin, S.: Behind every great man is a woman, behind every great woman there is none: A look at *Who's Who in America*, Unpublished data, Harvard University, 1974.

Light, R. J., and P. V. Smith: Accumulating evidence: Procedures for resolving contradictions among different research studies, *Harvard Educational Review*, 1971, *41*, 429–471.

Likert, R. A.: A technique for the measurement of attitudes, *Archives of Psychology*, 1932, *140*, 1–55.

Lindquist, E. F.: *Design and Analysis of Experiments in Psychology and Education*, Houghton-Mifflin, Boston, 1953.

Lindzey, G., and E. Aronson (eds.): *The Handbook of Social Psychology*, 2d ed., Addison-Wesley, Reading, Mass., 1968–69.

Linsky, A. S.: Stimulating responses to mailed questionnaires: A review, *Public Opinion Quarterly*, 1975, *39*, 83–101.

Linton, R.: *The Study of Man,* Appleton-Century-Crofts, New York, 1936.

London, P.: The rescuers: Motivational hypotheses about Christians who saved Jews from the Nazis, in J. Macaulay and L. Berkowitz (eds.), *Altruism and Helping Behavior: Social Psychological Studies of Some Antecedents and Consequences,* Academic Press, New York, 1970, pp. 241–250.

Lonner, W. J.: The search for psychological universals, in H. C. Triandis and R. W. Brislin (eds.), *Handbook of Cross-Cultural Psychology: Social Psychology,* Addison-Wesley, Boston, 1980, vol. 5.

Lorenz, K.: *On Aggression,* Harcourt, Brace & World, New York, 1966.

——: *Behind the Mirror,* Harcourt Brace Jovanovich, New York, 1977.

——: *The Year of the Greylag Goose,* Harcourt Brace Jovanovich, New York, 1979.

Lotz, J.: Social science research and northern development, *Arctic,* 1968, *21,* 291–294.

Lunney, G. H.: Using analysis of variance with a dichotomous dependent variable: An empirical study, *Journal of Educational Measurement,* 1970, *7,* 263–269.

McClelland, D.: *The Achieving Society,* Van Nostrand, Princeton, 1961.

McGinniss, J.: *The Selling of the President 1968,* Trident, New York, 1969.

McGrew, W. C., C. E. G. Tutin, and P. J. Baldwin: Chimpanzees, tools, and termites: Cross-cultural comparisons of Senegal, Tanzania, and Rio Muni, *Man,* 1979, *14,* 185–214.

McGuigan, F. J.: The experimenter: A neglected stimulus object, *Psychological Bulletin,* 1963, *60,* 421–428.

McGuire, W. J.: Inducing resistance to persuasion: Some contemporary approaches, in L. Berkowitz (ed.), *Advances in Experimental Social Psychology,* Academic Press, New York, 1964, vol. 1, pp. 191–229.

——: The yin and yang of progress in social psychology: Seven koan, *Journal of Personality and Social Psychology,* 1973, *26,* 446–456.

——: Historical comparisons: Testing psychological hypotheses with cross-era data, *International Journal of Psychology,* 1976, *11,* 161–183.

McNemar, Q.: Opinion-attitude methodology, *Psychological Bulletin,* 1946, *43,* 289–374.

——: At random: Sense and nonsense, *American Psychologist,* 1960, *15,* 295–300.

Maher, B. A.: Stimulus sampling in clinical research: Representative design reviewed, *Journal of Consulting and Clinical Psychology,* 1978, *46,* 643–647.

Mahler, I.: Attitudes toward socialized medicine, *Journal of Social Psychology,* 1953, *38,* 273–282.

Mahoney, M. J.: *Scientist as Subject: The Psychological Imperative,* Ballinger, Cambridge, Mass., 1976.

——: Experimental methods and outcome evaluation, *Journal of Consulting and Clinical Psychology,* 1978, *46,* 660–672.

Mann, L.: The effects of emotional role playing on smoking attitudes and behavior, *Journal of Experimental Social Psychology,* 1967, *3,* 334–348.

—— and I. L. Janis: A follow-up study on the long-term effects of emotional role playing, *Journal of Personality and Social Psychology,* 1968, *8,* 339–342.

Margolis, J.: *Knowledge and Existence: An Introduction to Philosophical Problems,* Oxford University Press, New York, 1973.

Martindale, C.: *Romantic Progression: The Psychology of Literary History,* Hemisphere, Washington, D.C., 1975.

——: The evolution of English poetry, *Poetics,* 1978, *7,* 231–248.

Maslow, A. H.: Self-esteem (dominance feelings) and sexuality, *Journal of Social Psychology,* 1942, *16,* 259–293.

——: *Toward a Psychology of Being,* Van Nostrand, New York, 1962.

—— and J. M. Sakoda: Volunteer-error in the Kinsey study, *Journal of Abnormal and Social Psychology,* 1952, *47,* 259–262.

Matarazzo, J. D., A. N. Wiens, and G. Saslow: Studies in interview speech behavior, in L. Krasner and L. P. Ullman (eds.), *Research in Behavior Modification,* Holt, Rinehart & Winston, New York, 1965, pp. 179–210.

Medawar, P. B.: *Advice to a Young Scientist,* Harper & Row, New York, 1979.

Merton, R. K.: *Social Theory and Social Structure,* enlarged ed., Free Press, New York, 1968.

———: Thematic analysis in science: Notes on Holton's concept, *Science,* 1975, *188,* 335–338.

Milgram, S.: Behavioral study of obedience, *Journal of Abnormal and Social Psychology,* 1963, *67,* 371–378.

———: Some conditions of obedience and disobedience to authority, *Human Relations,* 1965, *18,* 57–76.

———: *Obedience to Authority,* Harper & Row, New York, 1974.

———: *The Individual in a Social World: Essays and Experiments,* Addison-Wesley, Reading, Mass., 1977.

Miller, A. G.: Role playing: An alternative to deception? *American Psychologist,* 1972, *27,* 623–636.

Miller, G. A.: The magical number seven, plus or minus two: Some limits on our capacity for processing information, *Psychological Review,* 1956, *63,* 81–97.

———, A. S. Bregman, and D. A. Norman: The computer as a general purpose device for the control of psychological experiments, in R. W. Stacy and B. D. Waxman (eds.), *Computers in Biomedical Research,* Academic Press, New York, 1965, vol. 1, pp. 467–490.

Mischel, W.: *Personality and Assessment,* Wiley, New York, 1968.

Morrison, D. F.: *Multivariate Statistical Methods,* 2d ed., McGraw-Hill, New York, 1976.

Mosteller, F.: Association and estimation in contingency tables, *Journal of the American Statistical Association,* 1968, *63,* 1–28.

Mosteller, F. M. and R. R. Bush: Selected quantitative techniques, in G. Lindzey (ed.): *Handbook of Social Psychology,* vol. 1: *Theory and Method,* Addison-Wesley, Cambridge, Mass., 1954, pp. 328–331.

Mulaik, S. A.: *The Foundations of Factor Analysis,* McGraw-Hill, New York, 1972.

Murdock, G. P., et al. (eds.): Ethnographic atlas, *Ethnology,* 1962–67, vols. 1–6.

Myers, J. L.: *Fundamentals of Experimental Design,* 3d ed., Allyn & Bacon, Boston, 1979.

Nie, N. H., C. H. Hull, J. G. Jenkins, K. Steinbrenner, and D. H. Bent: *SPSS: Statistical Package for the Social Sciences,* 2d ed., McGraw-Hill, New York, 1975.

Oppenheim, A. N.: *Questionnaire Design and Attitude Measurement,* Basic Books, New York, 1966.

Oppenheimer, R.: *The Open Mind,* Simon & Schuster, New York, 1955.

Orne, M. T.: On the social psychology of the psychological experiment: With particular reference to demand characteristics and their implications, *American Psychologist,* 1962, *17,* 776–783.

———: Demand characteristics and the concept of quasi-controls, in R. Rosenthal and R. L. Rosnow (eds.), *Artifact in Behavioral Research,* Academic Press, New York, 1969, pp. 143–179.

———, P. W. Sheehan, and F. J. Evans: Occurrence of posthypnotic behavior outside the experimental setting, *Journal of Personality and Social Psychology,* 1968, *9,* 189–196.

Osgood, C. E., G. J. Suci, and P. H. Tannenbaum: *The Measurement of Meaning,* University of Illinois Press, Urbana, 1957.

Oskamp, S.: *Attitudes and Opinions,* Prentice-Hall, Englewood Cliffs, N.J., 1977.

OSS Assessment Staff: *Assessment of Men: Selection of Personnel for the Office of Strategic Services,* Rinehart, New York, 1948.

Overall, J. E., B. J. Goldstein, and B. Brauzer: Symptomatic volunteers in psychiatric research, *Journal of Psychiatric Research,* 1971, *9,* 31–43.

——— and D. K. Spiegel: Concerning least squares analysis of experimental data, *Psychological Bulletin,* 1969, *72,* 311–322.

———, ———, and J. Cohen: Equivalence of orthogonal and nonorthogonal analysis of variance, *Psychological Bulletin,* 1975, *82,* 182–186.

Overton, W. F.: The active organism in structuralism, *Human Development,* 1976, *19,* 71–86.

Page, M. M.: Effects of evaluation apprehension on cooperation in verbal conditioning, *Journal of Experimental Research in Personality,* 1971, *5,* 85–91.

Paine, R.: Lappish decisions, partnerships, information management, and sanctions—A nomadic pastoral adaptation, *Ethnology,* 1970, *9,* 52–67.

Pareek, U., and T. V. Rao: Cross-cultural surveys and interviewing, in H. C. Triandis and J. W.

Berry (eds.), *Handbook of Cross-Cultural Psychology: Methodology,* Allyn & Bacon, Boston, 1980, vol. 2, pp. 127–179.

Parten, M.: *Surveys, Polls, and Samples,* Harper, New York, 1950.

Pearson, K.: On the mathematical theory of errors of judgment with special reference to the personal equation, *Philosophical Transactions of the Royal Society of London,* 1902, *198,* 235–299.

Pepitone, A.: Toward a normative and comparative biocultural social psychology, *Journal of Personality and Social Psychology,* 1976, *4,* 641–653.

Pepper, S. C.: *World Hypotheses: A Study in Evidence,* University of California Press, Berkeley, 1942.

Peterson, R. E.: *The Scope of Organized Student Protest in 1967–68,* Princeton University Press, Princeton, 1968. (a)

——: The student left in American higher education, *Daedalus,* 1968, *97,* 293–317. (b)

Pillemer, D. B., and R. J. Light: Benefiting from variation in study outcomes, in R. Rosenthal (ed.), *New Directions for Methodology of Social and Behavioral Science: Quantitative Assessment of Research Domains,* no. 5, Jossey-Bass, San Francisco, 1980.

Platnick, N.: The evolution of courtship behaviour in spiders, *Bulletin of the British Arachnoid Society,* 1971, *2,* 40–47.

Platt, J.: Evidence and proof in documentary research: 1. Some specific problems of documentary research, *Sociological Review,* 1981, *29,* 31–52. (a)

——: Evidence and proof in documentary research: 2. Some shared problems in documentary research, *Sociological Review,* 1981, *29,* 53–66. (b)

Platt, J. R.: Strong inference. *Science,* 1964, *146,* 347–353.

Polanyi, M.: The potential theory of adsorption, *Science,* 1963, *141,* 1010–1013.

——: *The Tacit Dimension,* Doubleday Anchor, New York, 1966.

Popper, K. R.: *The Logic of Scientific Discovery,* Basic Books, New York, 1961.

Rabin, A. I. (ed.): *Projective Techniques in Personality Assessment,* Springer, New York, 1968.

RAND Corporation: *A Million Random Digits with 100,000 Normal Deviates,* Free Press, New York, 1955.

Reichenbach, H.: *Experience and Prediction,* University of Chicago Press, Chicago, 1938.

Reilly, F. E.: *Charles Peirce's Theory of Scientific Method,* Fordham University Press, New York, 1970.

Reynolds, P. D.: Value dilemmas in the professional conduct of social science, *International Social Science Journal,* 1975, *27,* 563–611.

Riecken, H. W.: Social experimentation, *Society,* July–August 1975, 34–41.

Riley, M. W.: Aging and cohort succession: Interpretation and misinterpretation, *Public Opinion Quarterly,* 1973, *37,* 35–49.

Rosenberg, M. J.: The conditions and consequences of evaluation apprehension, in R. Rosenthal and R. L. Rosnow (eds.), *Artifact in Behavioral Research,* Academic Press, New York, 1969, pp. 279–349.

Rosenthal, R.: *Experimenter Effects in Behavioral Research,* Appleton-Century-Crofts, New York, 1966; enlarged ed., Irvington, 1976.

——: Covert communication in the psychological experiment, *Psychological Bulletin,* 1967, *67,* 356–367.

——: Interpersonal expectation, in R. Rosenthal and R. L. Rosnow (eds.), *Artifact in Behavioral Research,* Academic Press, New York, 1969, pp. 181–277.

——: Estimating effective reliability in studies that employ judges' ratings, *Journal of Clinical Psychology,* 1973, *29,* 342–345. (a)

——: On the social psychology of the self-fulfilling prophecy: Further evidence for Pygmalion effects and their mediating mechanisms, MSS Modular Publication, New York, 1973, Module 53. (b)

——: The Pygmalion effect, *Psychology Today,* 1973, *7,* 56–63. (c)

——: Biasing effects of experimenters, *Et Cetera: A Review of General Semantics,* 1977, *34,* 253–264.

——: How often are our numbers wrong? *American Psychologist,* 1978, *33,* 1005–1008.

——: Combining results of independent studies, *Psychological Bulletin*, 1978, *85*, 185–193.

——: The "file drawer problem" and tolerance for null results, *Psychological Bulletin*, 1979, *86*, 638–641. (a)

—— (ed.): *Skill in Nonverbal Communication: Individual Differences*, Oelgeschlager, Gunn & Hain, Cambridge, Mass., 1979. (b)

—— (ed.): *New Directions for Methodology of Social and Behavioral Science: Quantitative Assessment of Research Domains*, no. 5, Jossey-Bass, San Francisco, 1980. (a)

——: Summarizing significance levels, in R. Rosenthal (ed.), *New Directions for Methodology of Social and Behavioral Science: Quantitative Assessment of Research Domains*, no. 5, Jossey-Bass, San Francisco, 1980. (b)

——: Conducting judgment studies. In K. R. Scherer and P. Ekman (eds.), *Handbook of Methods in Nonverbal Behavior Research*, Cambridge University Press, New York, 1982.

——: Toward a more cumulative social science, in L. Bickman (ed.), *Applied Social Psychology Annual*, vol. 4, Sage Publications, Beverly Hills, Calif., 1983.

—— and B. M. Depaulo: Sex differences in accommodation in nonverbal communication, in R. Rosenthal (ed.), *Skill in Nonverbal Communication: Individual Differences*, Oelgeschlager, Gunn & Hain, Cambridge, Mass., 1979, pp. 68–103. (a)

—— and ——: Sex differences in eavesdropping on nonverbal cues, *Journal of Personality and Social Psychology*, 1979, *37*, 273–285. (b)

—— and K. L. Fode: The effect of experimenter bias on the performance of the albino rat, *Behavioral Science*, 1963, *8*, 183–189.

—— and J. Gaito: The interpretation of levels of significance by psychological researchers, *Journal of Psychology*, 1963, *55*, 33–38.

—— and ——: Further evidence for the cliff effect in the interpretation of levels of significance, *Psychological Reports*, 1964, *15*, 570.

—— and J. A. Hall: Critical values of $\bar{z}$ for combining independent probabilities, *Replications in Social Psychology*, 1981, *1*(2), 1–6.

——, ——, M. R. DiMatteo, P. L. Rogers, and D. Archer: *Sensitivity to Nonverbal Communication: The PONS Test*, Johns Hopkins University Press, Baltimore, 1979.

—— and L. Jacobson: *Pygmalion in the Classroom*, Holt, Rinehart & Winston, New York, 1968.

—— and R. Lawson: A longitudinal study of the effects of experimenter bias on the operant learning of laboratory rats, *Journal of Psychiatric Research*, 1964, *2*, 61–72.

—— and R. L. Rosnow (eds.): *Artifact in Behavioral Research*, Academic Press, New York, 1969.

—— and ——: *The Volunteer Subject*, Wiley-Interscience, New York, 1975.

—— and D. B. Rubin: Interpersonal expectancy effects: The first 345 studies, *Behavioral and Brain Sciences*, 1978, *3*, 377–386.

—— and ——: Comparing significance levels of independent studies, *Psychological Bulletin*, 1979, *86*, 1165–1168. (a)

—— and ——: A note on percent variance explained as a measure of the importance of effects, *Journal of Applied Social Psychology*, 1979, *9*, 395–396. (b)

—— and ——: Comparing within- and between-subjects studies, *Sociological Methods and Research*, 1980, *9*, 127–136. (a)

—— and ——: Summarizing 345 studies of interpersonal expectancy effects, in R. Rosenthal (ed.), *New Directions for Methodology of Social and Behavioral Science: Quantitative Assessment of Research Domains*, no. 5, Jossey-Bass, San Francisco, 1980. (b)

—— and ——: A simple general purpose display of magnitude of experimental effect, *Journal of Educational Psychology*, 1982, *74*, 166–169. (a)

—— and ——: Comparing effect sizes of independent studies, *Psychological Bulletin*, 1982, *92*, 500–504.

Rosnow, R. L.: A "spread of effect" in attitude formation, in A. G. Greenwald, T. C. Brock, and T. M. Ostrom (eds.), *Psychological Foundations of Attitudes*, Academic Press, New York, 1968, pp. 89–107.

——: Gossip and marketplace psychology, *Journal of Communication*, 1977, *27*, No. 1, 158–163.

————: The prophetic vision of Giambattista Vico: Implications for the state of social psychological theory, *Journal of Personality and Social Psychology,* 1978, *36,* 1322–1331.

————: Psychology of rumor reconsidered, *Psychological Bulletin,* 1980, *87,* 578–591.

————: *Paradigms in Transition: The Methodology of Social Inquiry,* Oxford University Press, New York, 1981.

———— and L. S. Aiken: Mediation of artifacts in behavioral research, *Journal of Experimental Social Psychology,* 1973, *9,* 181–201.

———— and R. L. Arms: Adding versus averaging as a stimulus-combination rule in forming impressions of groups, *Journal of Personality and Social Psychology,* 1968, *10,* 363–369.

———— and D. J. Davis: Demand characteristics and the psychological experiment, *Et Cetera: A Review of General Semantics,* 1977, *34,* 301–313.

———— and G. A. Fine: *Rumor and Gossip: The Social Psychology of Hearsay,* Elsevier, New York, 1976.

————, B. E. Goodstadt, J. M. Suls, and A. G. Gitter: More on the social psychology of the experiment: When compliance turns to self-defense, *Journal of Personality and Social Psychology,* 1973, *27,* 337–343.

———— and E. J. Robinson: *Experiments in Persuasion,* Academic Press, New York, 1967.

———— and R. Rosenthal: Volunteer effects in behavioral research, in K. H. Craik et al., *New Directions in Psychology 4,* Holt, Rinehart & Winston, New York, 1970, pp. 211–277.

———— and ————: The volunteer subject revisited, *Australian Journal of Psychology,* 1976, *28,* 97–108.

———— and J. M. Suls: Reactive effects of pretesting in attitude research, *Journal of Personality and Social Psychology,* 1970, *15,* 338–343.

————, H. Wainer, and R. L. Arms: Personality and group impression formation as a function of the amount of overlap in evaluative meaning of the stimulus elements, *Sociometry,* 1970, *33,* 472–484.

Rothwell, N. J., and M. J. Stock: A role for brown adipose tissue in diet-induced thermogenesis, *Nature,* 1979, *281,* 31–35.

Rozin, P.: Specific aversions as a component of specific hungers, *Journal of Comparative and Physiological Psychology,* 1967, *64,* 237–242.

————: Adaptive food sampling patterns in vitamin deficient rats, *Journal of Comparative and Physiological Psychology,* 1969, *69,* 126–132.

Rozynko, V. V.: Social desirability in the sentence completion test, *Journal of Consulting Psychology,* 1959, *23,* 280.

Rubin, D. B.: Personal communication to R. Rosenthal, January 4, 1981.

Ruch, F. L.: A technique for detecting attempts to fake performance on a self-inventory type of personality test, in Q. McNemar and M. A. Merrill (eds.), *Studies in Personality,* McGraw-Hill, New York, 1942.

Ruehlmann, W.: *Stalking the Feature Story,* Writer's Digest, Cincinnati, 1977.

Rummel, R. J.: *Applied Factor Analysis,* Northwestern University Press, Evanston, Ill., 1970.

Ryder, N. B.: The cohort as a concept in the study of social change, *American Sociological Review,* 1965, *30,* 843–861.

Rysman, A.: How the "gossip" became a woman, *Journal of Communication,* 1977, *27,* No. 1, 176–180.

Schachter, S.: *The Psychology of Affiliation: Experimental Studies of the Sources of Gregariousness,* Stanford University Press, Stanford, 1959.

Schaie, K. W.: A general model for the study of developmental problems, *Psychological Bulletin,* 1965, *64,* 92–107.

Schuessler, K., D. Hittle, and J. Cardascia: Measuring responding desirability with attitude-opinion items, *Social Psychology Quarterly,* 1978, *41,* 224–235.

Scott, W. A., and M. Wertheimer: *Introduction to Psychological Research,* Wiley, New York, 1962.

Shaw, M. E., and J. M. Wright: *Scales for the Measurement of Attitudes,* McGraw-Hill, New York, 1967.

Shepard, R. N., A. K. Romney, and S. B. Nerlove (eds.): *Multidimensional Scaling*, 2 vols., Seminar Press, New York, 1972.

Sidman, M.: *Tactics of Scientific Research: Evaluating Experimental Data in Psychology*, Basic Books, New York, 1960.

Siegel, S.: *Nonparametric Statistics*, McGraw-Hill, New York, 1956.

Sigall, H., E. Aronson, and T. Van Hoose: The cooperative subject: Myth or reality? *Journal of Experimental Social Psychology*, 1970, *6*, 1–10.

Silverman, I.: *The Human Subject in the Psychological Laboratory*, Pergamon, New York, 1977.

Simonton, D. K.: Interdisciplinary creativity over historical time: A correlational analysis of generational fluctuations, *Social Behavior and Personality*, 1975, *3*, 181–188. (a)

———: Sociocultural context of individual creativity: A transhistorical time-series analysis, *Journal of Personality and Social Psychology*, 1975, *32*, 1119–1133. (b)

———: Ideological diversity and creativity: A re-evaluation of a hypothesis, *Social Behavior and Personality*, 1976, *4*, 203–207. (a)

———: The sociopolitical context of philosophical beliefs: A transhistorical causal analysis, *Social Forces*, 1976, *54*, 513–523. (b)

Skinner, B. F.: *Cumulative Record*, 3d ed., Appleton-Century-Crofts, New York, 1972.

———: *Notebooks* (edited by R. Epstein), Prentice-Hall, Englewood Cliffs, N.J., 1980.

Smart, R. G.: The importance of negative results in psychological research, *Canadian Psychologist*, 1964, *5a*, 225–232.

Smith, C.: Selecting a source of local television news in the Salt Lake City SMSA: A multivariate analysis of cognitive and affective factors for 384 randomly-selected news viewers, unpublished doctoral dissertation, Temple University School of Communication, November 1980.

Smith, M. B.: *Social Psychology and Human Values*, Aldine, Chicago, 1969.

Smith, M. L.: Integrating studies of psychotherapy outcomes, in R. Rosenthal (ed.), *New Directions for Methodology of Social and Behavioral Science: Quantitative Assessment of Research Domains*, No. 5, Jossey-Bass, San Francisco, 1980.

——— and G. V Glass: Meta-analysis of psychotherapy outcome studies, *American Psychologist*, 1977, *32*, 752–760.

———, G. V Glass, and T. I. Miller: *Benefits of Psychotherapy*, Johns Hopkins University Press, Baltimore, 1980.

Smith, T. W.: Happiness: Time trends, seasonal variations, intersurvey differences, and other mysteries, *Social Psychology Quarterly*, 1979, *42*, 18–30.

Snedecor, G. W., and W. G. Cochran: *Statistical Methods*, 6th ed., 7th ed., Iowa State University Press, Ames, 1967, 1980.

Snider, J. G.: Profiles of some stereotypes held by ninth-grade pupils, *Alberta Journal of Educational Research*, 1962, *8*, 147–156.

——— and C. E. Osgood (eds.): *Semantic Differential Technique: A Sourcebook*, Aldine, Chicago, 1969.

Solomon, R. L.: An extension of control group design, *Psychological Bulletin*, 1949, *46*, 137–150.

——— and M. S. Lessac: A control group design for experimental studies of developmental processes, *Psychological Bulletin*, 1968, *70*, 145–150.

Sorokin, P. A.: A survey of the cyclical conceptions of social and historical process, *Social Forces*, 1927, *6*, 28–40.

———: *Social and Cultural Mobility*, Free Press, New York, 1964.

Stanley, J. C.: Test reliability, in L. Deighton (ed.), *Encyclopedia of Education*, vol. 9, Macmillan and Free Press, New York, 1971.

Stephenson, W.: *The Study of Behavior: Q-Technique and Its Methodology*, University of Chicago Press, Chicago, 1953.

———: Independency and operationism in Q-sorting, *Psychological Record*, 1963, *13*, 269–272.

———: Newton's fifth rule and Q methodology: Application to educational psychology, *American Psychologist*, 1980, *35*, 882–889.

Sterling, T. D.: Publication decisions and their possible effects on inferences drawn from tests of significance—or vice versa, *Journal of the American Statistical Association*, 1959, *54*, 30–34.

Stouffer, S. A., E. A. Suchman, L. C. DeVinney, S. A. Star, and R. M. Williams, Jr.: *The American Soldier: Adjustment During Army Life,* vol. 1, Princeton University Press, Princeton, 1949.

Strong, D. R., Jr.: Null hypotheses in ecology, *Synthese,* 1981, *43,* 271–285.

Suls, J. M., and R. L. Rosnow: The delicate balance between ethics and artifacts in behavioral research, in A. J. Kimmel (ed.), *New Directions for Methodology of Social and Behavioral Science: Ethics of Human Subject Research,* no. 10, Jossey-Bass, San Francisco, 1981, pp. 55–67.

Sundland, D. M.: The construction of *Q* sorts: A criticism, *Psychological Review,* 1962, *69,* 62–64.

Symonds, P. M.: Notes on rating, *Journal of Applied Psychology,* 1925, *9,* 188–195.

Thomas, C. B., J. A. Hall, F. D. Miller, J. R. Dewhirst, G. A. Fine, M. Taylor, and R. L. Rosnow: Evaluation apprehension, social desirability, and the interpretation of test correlations, *Social Behavior and Personality,* 1979, *7,* 193–197.

Thurstone, L. L.: Theory of attitude measurement, *Psychological Bulletin,* 1929, *36,* 222–241.

——: *The Measurement of Social Attitudes,* University of Chicago Press, Chicago, 1929–34.

Torgerson, W. S.: *Theory and Methods of Scaling,* Wiley, New York, 1958.

Triandis, H. C.: Exploratory factor analyses of the behavioral component of social attitudes, *Journal of Abnormal and Social Psychology,* 1964, *68,* 420–430.

——: *Attitude and Attitude Change,* Wiley, New York, 1971.

—— et al. (eds.): *Handbook of Cross-Cultural Psychology,* 6 vols., Addison-Wesley, Boston, 1980.

Tukey, J. W.: *Exploratory Data Analysis,* Addison-Wesley, Reading, Mass., 1977.

Upton, G. J. G.: *The Analysis of Cross-Tabulated Data,* Wiley, New York, 1978.

Van de Geer, J. P.: *Introduction to Multivariate Analysis for the Social Sciences,* Freeman, San Francisco, 1971.

Walker, H. M., and J. Lev: *Statistical Inference,* Holt, New York, 1953.

Wallace, D. L.: Bounds on normal approximations to Student's and the chi-square distributions, *Annals of Mathematical Statistics,* 1959, *30,* 1121–1130.

Warner, S. B., Jr., and S. Fleisch: *Measurements for Social History,* Sage, Beverly Hills, Calif.: 1977.

Warwick, D. P., and C. A. Lininger: *The Sample Survey: Theory and Practice,* McGraw-Hill, New York, 1975.

Webb, E. J., D. T. Campbell, R. F. Schwartz, and L. Sechrest: *Unobtrusive Measures: Nonreactive Research in the Social Sciences,* Rand McNally, Chicago, 1966.

——, D. T. Campbell, R. D. Schwartz, L. Sechrest, and J. B. Grove: *Nonreactive Measures in the Social Sciences,* 2d ed., Houghton Mifflin, Boston, 1981.

Weick, K. E.: Systematic observational methods, in G. Lindzey and E. Aronson (eds.), *The Handbook of Social Psychology,* 2d ed., vol. 2, Addison-Wesley, Reading, Mass., 1968, pp. 357–451.

Weimer, W. B.: *Notes on the Methodology of Scientific Research,* Erlbaum, Hillsdale, N.J., 1979.

Weinstein, D.: Fraud in science, *Social Science Quarterly,* 1979, *59,* 639–652.

Weiss, C. H.: Interaction in the research interview: The effects of rapport on response, *Proceedings of the American Statistical Association: Social Statistics Section,* 1970, 17–20.

Welkowitz, J., R. B. Ewen, and J. Cohen: *Introductory Statistics for the Behavioral Sciences,* 2d ed., 3rd ed., Academic Press, New York, 1976, 1982.

Wheelwright, P. (ed.): *Aristotle,* Odyssey Press, New York, 1951.

Whiteley, J. M., M. Q. Burkhart, M. Harway-Herman, and R. M. Whiteley: Counseling and student development, *Annual Review of Psychology,* 1975, *26,* 337–366.

Wicker, A. W., and G. Bushweiler: Perceived fairness and pleasantness of social exchange situations: Two factorial studies of inequity, *Journal of Personality and Social Psychology,* 1970, *15,* 63–75.

Wilkins, L., and C. P. Richter: A great craving for salt by a child with corticoadrenal insufficiency, *Journal of the American Medical Association,* 1940, *114,* 866–868.

Wilkinson, B.: A statistical consideration in psychological research, *Psychological Bulletin,* 1951, *48,* 156–158.

Willis, R. H., and Y. A. Willis: Role playing versus deception: An experimental comparison, *Journal of Personality and Social Psychology,* 1970, *16,* 472–477.

Wilson, E. O.: *Sociobiology: The New Synthesis,* Belknap/Harvard University Press, Cambridge, Mass., 1975.

———: Competitive and aggressive behavior, in J. F. Eisenberg and W. S. Dillon (eds.), *Man and Beast: Comparative Social Behavior,* Smithsonian Institution Press, Washington, D.C., 1971, pp. 183–217.

Winer, B. J.: *Statistical Principles in Experimental Design,* 2d ed., McGraw-Hill, New York, 1971.

Wohlwill, J. F.: Methodology and research strategy in the study of developmental change, in L. Goulet and P. Baltes (eds.), *Life-Span Developmental Psychology,* Academic Press, New York, 1970, pp. 92–191.

Wrightsman, L. S.: Wallace supporters and adherence to "law and order," *Journal of Personality and Social Psychology,* 1969, *13,* 17–22.

Zajonc, R. F.: Social facilitation, *Science,* 1965, *149,* 269–274.

Zelen, M., and L. S. Joel: The weighted compounding of two independent significance tests, *Annals of Mathematical Statistics,* 1959, *30,* 885–895.

Zimbardo, P. G., G. Marshall, G. White, and C. Maslach, *Science,* 1973, *181,* 282–284.

NAME INDEX

Adair, John G., 106, 484
Adcock, C. J., 484
Adorno, T. W., 138, 484
Agnew, Spiro, 126
Aiken, Leona S., 80, 107, 497
Ajzen, Icek, 151, 489
Allport, Floyd H., 484
Allport, Gordon W., 6, 44–46, 67, 484
Altmann, J. 117–118, 484
Anderson, J. W., 432, 484
Appelbaum, Richard P., 4, 484
Archer, Dane, 114, 163, 264, 419, 496
Aristotle, 28
Armor, David J., 421, 484
Arms, Robert L., 186, 484, 489, 497
Aronson, Elliot, 67, 105, 124, 177, 484, 492, 498
Asch, Solomon E., 54–55, 484
Atwell, J. E., 174, 179, 484
Axinn, S., 22, 484

Babbie, Earl R., 158, 484
Bacon, Francis, 16
Baenninger, R., 38, 118, 484–485
Bailey, Kenneth D., 424, 485
Bakan, David, 21, 379, 485
Balaam, L. N., 253, 485
Baldwin, P. J., 493
Baldwin, S., 118, 485
Bales, Robert Freed, xvii, 122–123, 485
Barber, Bernard, 16, 58, 485
Barber, Theodore X., 106, 485
Barker, Pierce, xvi

Barrass, Robert, 431, 485
Baughman, Earl, xvii
Baughman, Emmett E., 130–132, 141, 485
Baumgartner, Robert, 160, 490
Bavelas, Alex, 35, 485
Becker, Howard S., 56, 485
Beez, W. Victor, 24, 485
Benedict, Ruth F., 56–57, 485
Bent, Dale H., 414, 494
Bentler, Peter M., 185, 485
Berelson, Bernard R., 124–125, 485
Bessel, F. W., 108
Bigelow, G., 66, 485
Billow, Richard M., 18, 485
Birnbaum, Allan, 485
Bishop, Yvonne M. M., 384, 393, 485
Boder, David P., 45–46, 485
Bok, Sissela, 175, 485
Boring, Edwin G., 87, 108, 485
Boudreau, Blair, xvii
Box, George E. P., 238–239, 485
Bradburn, N. M., 133–134, 141, 485
Brady, Joseph V., 8, 66–67, 70, 118, 485–486
Brauzer, B., 162, 494
Bregman, Albert S., 114, 494
Bresnahan, Jean L., 400, 486
Bridgman, Percy W., 37, 486
Brinton, James E., 144, 486
Brislin, Richard W., 486
Broad, William J., 7, 486
Brogden, W. J., 182, 486
Brown, William, 163
Brozek, Josef, 486
Bruner, Jerome S., 44–46, 484

Brunswik, Egon, 112, 486
Buckhout, Robert, 188, 486
Burkhart, Mary Q., 101, 167, 499
Burnham, J. Randolph, 112–113, 486
Burt, Cyril, 108
Bush, Robert R., 369, 373, 494
Bushweiler, Gary, 69, 499
Buss, Allan R., 34, 486
Buss, Arnold H., xvii, 37, 486
Butler, Robert A., 64

Camilli, Gregory, 221, 384, 486
Campbell, Donald T., 7, 10, 12, 71, 76, 79,
    90–91, 94–95, 101, 103, 105, 127, 130,
    486, 499
Cannell, Charles F., 128, 133, 491
Cannon, Walter B., 8, 486
Cardascia, J., 135, 497
Carlsmith, J. Merrill, 67, 177, 484
Carmer, G., 255, 486
Caws, Peter, 19, 78, 486
Chamberlin, T. C., 12, 486
Cobben, Niki P., 99–100, 167–168, 491
Cochran, William G., xvii, 159, 180–181, 186,
    217, 219, 231, 238, 255, 308, 346, 372, 375,
    377, 379, 391–392, 397, 486, 498
Cohen, Jacob, xvii, 22, 209, 226, 268, 357, 359,
    361, 363–365, 372, 414, 426, 429, 487, 494,
    499
Cohen, Morris R., 11, 27–28, 60, 180–181, 487
Cohen, Patricia, 414, 426, 487
Collins, Barry E., 35, 487
Collins, Harry M., 9–10, 487
Colombotos, John, 139, 488
Conover, W. J., 221, 487
Conrad, D. G., 8, 486
Cook, Thomas D., 76, 79, 90, 94, 101, 103,
    105, 487
Cooley, William W., 414, 429, 487
Coombs, Clyde H., 425, 487
Cooper, Harris M., 189–190, 369, 487
Cooper, W. H., 142, 144, 487
Coren, Stanley, 58, 487
Cornell, F. G., 158, 487
Corrozi, John F., 35, 487
Cosentino, Joseph, 123–124, 492
Couch, Arthur S., 139, 484
Cox, D. R., 487
Cox, Gertrude M., 486
Crandall, Virginia C., 135, 487
Cronbach, Lee, J., 78, 135, 142, 487
Crowne, Douglas P., 52–53, 55, 61–62, 78,
    135, 188, 487

Dabbs, James, 19, 487
D'Agostino, Ralph B., 392, 487
Dahlstrom, William G., xvii, 130–132, 141,
    485
Darley, John, 17–18, 492
Darroch, Russell K., 69, 488
Darwin, Charles, 5
da Vinci, Leonardo, 432n.
Davis, D. J., 105–106, 497
Dawes, Robyn M., 425, 487
Dentler, Mame, 492
DePaulo, Bella M., xvi, 294–295, 496
DeVinney, L. C., 499
DeVore, Irven, 25, 118, 488
Dewey, Edward R., 488
Dewhirst, Joseph R., 138, 499
DiMatteo, M. Robin, xvi, 114, 163, 264, 419,
    496
Dohrenwend, Barbara S., 139, 488
Dohrenwend, Bruce P., 139, 488
Dollard, John, 36–37, 45, 186, 488
Doob, Leonard W., 37, 45, 488
Duhem, Pierre M. M., 20, 488
Dysart, Bonnie, 492

Eagly, Alice H., 181–182, 488
Easley, John A., 36–37, 488
Edgington, Eugene S., 488
Edwards, Allen L., 268, 391, 488, 491
Einstein, Albert, 3, 16
Eisenhower, Dwight D., 45
Emurian, H., 66, 485
Eron, Leonard D., 488
Estes, R. D., 118, 485
Ettinger, Richard H., 135, 492
Evans, Frederick J., 107, 494
Everitt, B. S., 384, 488
Ewen, Robert B., xv, 209, 499

Fear, David E., 133, 488
Federighi, Enrico T., 488
Feldman, Roy E., 71, 488
Feldt, Leonard S., 391, 491
Festinger, Leon, 11–12, 17, 20–21, 488
Feyerabend, Paul, 7, 12, 486, 488
Fienberg, Stephen E., 384, 393, 485, 488
Filion, F. L., 159, 488
Findley, J. D., 488
Fine, Gary A., 138, 497, 499
Firth Raymond, 17, 56–57, 488
Fishbein, Martin, 151, 488
Fisher, Ronald A., 22, 257, 369, 489

Fiske, Donald W., 486
Fiske, Susan, xvi
Flachs, Richard, 47, 489
Fleisch, Sylvia, 48, 499
Foa, Edna, 19, 489
Foa, Uriel G., 19, 34, 489
Fode, Kermit L., 111, 496
Ford, C. S., 37, 45, 488
Frenkel-Brunswik, Else, 139, 484
Freud, Sigmund, 432*n*.
Friedman, C. Jack, xvii, 146, 489
Friedman, Herbert, 357, 489
Friedman, Howard S., xvi
Fruchter, Benjamin, 250, 489, 490
Furno, O. F., 158, 489

Gaito, John, 231, 371, 379, 496
Galileo, 27
Gebhard, Paul H., 186, 492
Geer, B., 56, 485
Genovese, Kitty, 17
Gergen, Kenneth J., 181, 489
Gilbert, John P., 389, 392, 489
Gitter, A. George, xvi, 105, 497
Gladden, John W., 146, 489
Glass, Gene V, 209, 369−370, 489, 498
Goffman, Erving, 489
Goldstein, B. J., 162, 494
Goldstein, David, xvi, 6, 490
Goldstein, Jeffrey H., 38, 489
Goode, William J., 57, 489
Goodenough, Ward H., 120, 489
Goodstadt, Barry E., 105, 124, 489, 497
Gordon, Raymond L., 128−130, 132, 489
Gottman, J. M., 60, 489
Green, Bert F., Jr., 308, 489
Greenberg, Martin S., 68−69, 489
Greenwald, Anthony G., 21, 189, 489
Grey, Ronald, J., 123−124, 490
Grove, Janet B., 10, 127, 499
Grünbaum, Adolph, 27, 490
Guilford, J. P., 141−144, 250, 490
Guttman, Louis, 425, 490

Hackmann, W. D., 84, 490
Hagenaars, Jacques A., 99−100, 167−168, 491
Hall, Judith A., xvi, 114, 138, 163, 264, 295, 370, 419, 490, 496, 499
Hall, K. R. L., 25, 488
Hanson, Norwood R., 490

Harlow, Harry F., 25, 62−66, 70, 72, 490
Harlow, Margaret K., 62, 64−65, 490
Harner, Michael J., 33, 59−60, 490
Harris, Richard J., 255, 414, 490
Hartmann, George W., 70, 490
Harway-Herman, Michelle, 101, 167, 499
Hasher, Lynn A., 6, 490
Hatt, P. K., 57, 489
Haviland, John B., xvii, 120−122, 490
Hays, William L., 209, 239, 343, 384, 395, 490
Heberlein, Thomas A., 160, 490
Heisenberg, Werner, 10, 490
Hendrick, Clyde, 69, 490
Henry, Neil W., 425, 492
Henshel, Richard L., 72, 84, 490
Hittle, D., 135, 497
Hodgkinson, H., 47, 491
Holden, Constance, 171−172, 491
Holland, Paul W., xvii, 384, 393, 485
Holsti, Ole R., 124, 491
Holton, Gerald, 170, 491
Hopkins, Kenneth D., 221, 384, 486
Horowitz, I. L., 491
Horowitz, Irwin A., 69, 80, 94, 491
Horst, Paul, 268, 491
Hovland, Carl I., 37, 45, 488
Hsu, Louis M., 372, 491
Hsu, Tse-Chi, 391, 491
Huck, Schuyler W., 13, 491
Huesmann, L. Rowell, 488
Hull, C. Hadlai, 414, 494
Hume, David, 29, 76, 491
Humphrey, Hubert, 126, 145
Humphreys, Laud, 171−172, 491
Hunter, J. Stuart, 238−239, 485
Hunter, William G., 238−239, 485
Hurvich, Leo M., 16, 491
Hyman, Herbert H., 186, 491

Inkeles, Alex, 58, 485
Isenberg, Dan, xvi

Jacobson, Lenore, 24, 496
Jandorf, E. M. 44−46, 484
Janis, Irving L., 18−19, 69−70, 72, 487, 493
Jenkins, Jean G., 414, 494
Joel, L. S., 500
Jones, Frank P., 88, 491
Jones, Lyle V., 491
Judd, Charles M., xvi, 238, 430, 491

Kahn, Robert L., 128, 133, 491
Kamin, Leon J., 109, 491
Kaplan, Abraham, 7, 9–11, 15–16, 22, 51–52, 62, 66, 75, 85, 155, 491
Katona, George, 4, 491
Kaye, Donald, 19, 491
Kazdin, A. E., 169, 491
Kelman, Herbert C., 175, 491
Keniston, Kenneth, 47, 139, 491
Kenny, David A., xvi, 96, 238, 430, 491
Kidder, Louise, H., xvii, 117–119, 491
Kim, Jae-On, 424, 492
Kim, Ki Hang, 424, 492
Kimmel, Allan J., 124, 492
Kinnebrook, D., 108
Kinsey, Alfred C., 186, 492
Kipnis, David, 123–124, 489, 490, 492
Kirschner, Paul, 19, 491
Kish, Leslie, 157–158, 492
Kleinmuntz, Benjamin, 114, 492
Klineberg, Otto, 57, 492
Koch, Helen L., 492
Koertge, N., 21, 492
Kolata, Gina B., 490
Kordig, C.R., 15, 492
Kothandapani, Virupaksha, 79, 151, 492
Krippendorff, Klaus, 124

Lana, Robert E., 28, 492
Lancaster, H.O., 492
Lanz, L., 10, 492
Larsen, Knud S., 135, 492
Laslett, Barbara, 60, 492
Latané, Bibb, 17–18, 492
Lavoisier, Antoine L., 16
Lawson, Reed, 111, 496
Lazarsfeld, Paul F., 425, 492
Leavitt, Harold J., 35, 492
Lefkowitz, Monroe M., 488
Lepkin, Milton, 6, 484
Lessac, Michael S., 92–94, 492, 498
Lev, Joseph, xvii, 163, 268, 499
Levin, Jack, 124, 492
Levin, Smadar, 492
Levinson, Daniel J., 139, 484
Light, Richard J., 370, 492, 495
Likert, Rensis A., 148, 151, 492
Lindquist, E.F., 492
Lindzey, Gardner, 124, 492
Lininger, Charles A., 56, 158, 499
Linsky, Arnold S., 160, 492
Linton, Ralph, 57, 493

Lohnes, Paul R., 414, 429, 487
London, Perry, 128, 493
Lonner, Walter J., 493
Loomba, Joanne K., 124, 491
Lorenz, Konrad, 5, 493
Lotz, J., 130, 493
Lunney, Gerald H., 219, 391, 493

McClelland, David C., 52, 185, 493
McGaw, Barry, 369, 489
McGinniss, Joe, 145, 493
McGrew, W.C., 493
McGuigan, Frank J., 114, 493
McGuire, William J., 17–19, 59, 493
McLean, Robert S., 114, 492
McLoone, E.P., 158, 487
McNemar, Quinn, 379, 493
McPeek, Bucknam, 389, 392, 489
Maher, Brendan, A., 112, 493
Mahler, Irwin, xvii, 148–149, 493
Mahoney, Michael J., 16, 101, 493
Malinowski, Bronislaw, 56–57
Mann, Leon, 69–70, 72, 493
Margolis, Joseph Z., 7, 493
Marlowe, David, 52–53, 55, 61–62, 78, 135, 188, 487
Martin, Clyde E., 186, 492
Martin, Harry J., 135, 492
Martindale, Colin E., 493
Maskelyne, N., 108
Maslow, Abraham, H., 36, 186, 493
Mason, J.W., 8, 486
Matarazzo, Joseph D., 25, 493
Mead, Margaret, 56–57, 122
Medawar, Peter B., 8, 15, 493
Meehl, Paul E., 78, 487
Merton, Robert K., 8, 494
Milgram, Stanley, 25, 68, 171–173, 176–177, 494
Mill, John Stuart, 29–30, 61, 76, 88–89
Miller, Arthur G., 68, 494
Miller, Frederick D., 138, 499
Miller, George A., 114, 494
Miller, Neal E., 37, 45, 488
Miller, Thomas I., 370, 498
Mischel, Walter, 85, 494
Morison, Robert S., 170, 491
Morrison, Donald F., 255, 414, 494
Mosteller, Frederick, xvii, 186, 369, 373, 389, 392, 408, 486, 489, 494
Mowrer, O. Hobart, 37, 45, 488
Mulaik, Stanley A., 424, 494
Murdock, George P., 494

Muskie, Edmund S., 126
Myers, Jerome L., 255, 494

Nelson, Joan, 135, 492
Nerlove, S.B., 425, 498
Newton, Isaac, 3, 180
Nie, Norman, 414, 494
Nietzsche, Friedrich W., 57
Nixon, Richard M., 126, 145
Norman, Donald A., 114, 494
North, Robert C., 124, 491

Oppenheim, Abraham N., 46, 55–56, 133–134, 494
Oppenheimer, J. Robert, 7, 494
Orne, Martin T., 104, 106–107, 494
Osgood, Charles E., 144–145, 494, 498
Oskamp, Stuart, 144, 494
OSS Assessment Staff, 41, 494
Overall, John E., 162, 268, 494
Overton, Willis F., 32, 494

Page, Monte M., 105, 494
Paine, R., 17, 494
Pareek, U., 132, 494
Parten, Mildred B., 159, 495
Pavelchak, Mark, xvi
Pearson, Karl, 184, 204, 495
Peirce, Charles Sanders, 6–7
Pepitone, Albert, 495
Pepper, Stephan C., 181, 495
Peterson, Richard E., 46–48, 50, 55, 495
Pfungst, Oskar, 110–111
Picasso, Pablo, 35
Pillemer, David B., 370, 495
Platnick, N., 59, 495
Platt, Jennifer, 49, 495
Platt, John R., 184, 495
Polanyi, Michael, 9, 16, 495
Pomeroy, Wardell B., 186, 492
Popper, Karl R., 20, 495
Porac, Clare, 58, 487
Porter, R.W., 8, 486
Postman, Leo J., 66, 484

Rabin, Albert I., 495
RAND Corporation, 495
Rao, T.V., 132, 494
Raven, Bertram H., 35, 487
Reichenbach, Hans, 495

Reilly, Francis E., 6, 495
Reynolds, Paul D., 170, 178, 495
Richter, C.P., 33, 499
Riecken, Henry W., 71, 495
Riley, Matilda W., 495
Robinson, Edward J., 497
Rogers, Peter L., 114, 163, 264, 419, 496
Romney, A.K., 425, 498
Ronis, David L., 21, 489
Rosenberg, Milton J., 105, 495
Rosengren, Karl, 124
Rosenthal, Mary Lu, xvii
Rosenthal, Robert, 11, 24, 49, 80, 82–83, 106, 109–112, 114, 160–161, 163–164, 187, 207–209, 211, 231, 264, 294–295, 369–373, 376–377, 379, 419, 487, 495–497
Rosnow, Mimi, xvii
Rosnow, Ralph L., xvi, 13, 28, 31, 35, 58, 60, 68, 80, 105–107, 138, 143, 160–161, 170, 186–187, 312, 487, 496–497, 499
Rothschild, Bertram H., 69, 491
Rothwell, Nancy J., 32, 497
Roush, F.W., 424, 492
Rozin, Paul, 33, 497
Rozynko, Vitali V., 135, 497
Rubin, Donald B., xvii, 24, 207–209, 211, 370, 372, 376–377, 407, 496–497
Ruch, Floyd L., 138, 497
Ruelmann, William, 128, 497
Rummel, Rudolph J., 424–425, 497
Russell, Gordon W., xvi, 484
Ryder, Norman B., 99, 497
Rysman, Alexander, 36, 497

Sakoda, James M., 186, 493
Sandilands, Mark L., 484
Sandler, Howard M., 13, 491
Sanford, R. Nevitt, 139, 484
Saslow, George, 25, 493
Schachter, Stanley, 52, 68–69, 497
Schaie, K. Warner, 99, 167, 497
Schuessler, K., 135, 497
Schwartz, Richard D., 10, 127, 499
Scott, William A., 48, 497
Sears, Robert R., 37, 45, 488
Sechrest, Lee, 10, 127, 499
Shapiro, Martin M., 400, 486
Shaw, Marvin E., 151, 497
Sheatsley, Paul B., 186, 491
Sheehan, Peter W., 107, 494
Shepard, Roger N., 425, 498
Sidman, Murray, 8, 169, 498

Siegel, Sidney, 395, 498
Sigall, Harold E., 105, 498
Silverman, Irwin, 105–l06, 498
Simonton, Dean K., 59, 185, 498
Skinner, B.F., 88, 498
Smart, R.G., 379, 498
Smith, Conrad, xvii, 129, 135, 137, 158, 498
Smith, Mahlon B., 176, 498
Smith, Mary Lee, 209, 369 489, 498
Smith, Paul V., 370, 492
Smith, T.W., 498
Snedecor, George W., 217, 219, 231, 238, 255, 308, 346, 372, 375, 377, 379, 391–392, 397, 498
Snider, James G., 145, 498
Sollenberger, R.T., 37, 45, 488
Solomon, Richard L., 92–94, 492, 498
Sorokin, Pitirim A., 60, 185, 498
Spearman, Charles, 163
Speckart, George, 185, 485
Spiegel, Douglas K., 268, 494
Stanley, Julian C., 10, 12, 71, 81, 90–91, 94–95, 486, 498
Star, S.A., 499
Steinbrenner, Karin, 414, 494
Steiner, Ivan D., 69, 488
Stephenson, William, 147–148, 498
Sterling, Theodore D., 379, 498
Stock, Michael, 32, 497
Stouffer, Samuel A., 499
Streit, Helen, 492
Strong, D.R., Jr., 22, 499
Suchman, E.A., 499
Suci, George J., 144, 494
Suls, Jerry M., 105–l06, 170, 497, 499
Sundland, D.M., 148, 499
Swanson, M.R., 255, 486
Symonds, P.M., 142, 499

Tannenbaum, Percy H., 144, 494
Tatsuoka, Maurice M., 36, 488
Taylor, Marylee, 138, 499
Thomas, Charles B., xvi, 138, 436, 499
Thurstone, L.L., 150–151, 499
Tiede, Kenneth, 486
Tolman, Edward, xvii
Toppino, Thomas C., 6, 490
Torgerson, Warren S., 425, 499
Triandis, Harry C., 144, 151, 499
Tufte, Ed, xvi
Tukey, John W., 186, 197, 213, 239, 308, 486, 489, 499

Tuma, A.H., 169, 491
Tutin, C.E.G., 493
Tversky, Amos, 425, 487

Upton, Graham J.G., 384, 499

Van de Geer, John P., 499
Van Hoose, Thomas A., 105, 498
van Wagenen, Gertrude, 63
von Osten, 110

Wainer, Howard, 186, 497
Walder, Leopold O., 488
Walker, Helen M., 163, 268, 499
Wallace, D.L., 499
Wallace, George, 126–127, 145
Walpole, Horace, 7
Warner, Sam B., Jr., 48, 499
Warwick, Donald P., 56, 158, 499
Washburn, Sherwood L., 118, 488
Webb, Eugene J., 10, 127, 499
Weick, Karl E., 499
Weimer, W. B., 499
Weinstein, D., 108, 499
Weiss, C.H., 139, 499
Welkowitz, Joan, xv, 209, 499
Wertheimer, Michael, 48, 497
Wheelwright, Philip, 28, 499
Whitely, John M., 101, 167, 499
Whitely, Rita M., 101, 167, 499
Wicker, Allan W., 69, 499
Wiens, Arthur N., 25, 493
Wilkins, L., 33, 499
Wilkinson, Bryan, 500
William of Occam, 11
Williams, D.M., 66, 485
Williams, R.M., Jr., 499
Willis, Richard H., 69, 500
Willis, Yolanda A., 69, 500
Wilson, Edward O., 5, 59, 500
Winer, B.J., 308, 343, 391, 500
Wohlwill, Joachim F., 99, 167, 500
Wright, J.M., 151, 497
Wrightsman, Lawrence S., Jr., 126, 151, 500

Zajonc, Robert F., 19, 500
Zelen, M., 500

A priori method, 6–7, 468
Abscissa, 196, 468
Abstracta, 52
Academic Press, xvii, 131, 360
Acceptability stage, 15, 468
Achievement motive, 52
Activity, 468
Adaptation, 5
Affective component, 468
Affiliation motive, 52
After-only design, 468
Age, controlling for, 98–99, 101
Aggregating sources of variance, 468
Aggression studies, 5, 37–38, 45
Agreement, method of, 89, 475
Alberta Journal of Educational Research, xvii, 145
Alias, 468
Allentown, Pennsylvania, 70
Alpha, 21–22, 355–356, 468
American Educational Research Association, xvii, 91, 95
American Psychological Association, xvii, 119, 175, 433, 436, 484
American Sociological Association, xvii, 123
Analogous, 468
Analysis:
  cluster, 417, 424–425
  content, 124–125, 470
  dimensional, 425, 471
  distance, 471
  principal components (*see* Principal components analysis)
  proximity, 478

Analysis(*Cont.*):
  regression, 479
  reliability, 422–423
  secondary, 49, 480
  time-series, 60
  unit of, 482
Analysis of covariance, 468
  multivariate, 430, 476
  (*See also* Analysis of variance)
Analysis of data, statistical, 190–191
Analysis of variance, 468
  computation of, 267–268, 272–276
  effects and structure of, 258–260
  multilevel, 429–430, 476
  of qualitative data, 391–393
Analytic survey, 55–56, 468
Anchor words, 142
Anova, 468
Anxiety studies, 68–69
Apollonian construct, 57
Approval, need for, studies of, 52–55
Arcsin transformation, 468
Area probability sampling, 158
Arithmetic mean, 468
Armor's theta, 422–433, 468
Artifacts, 468
Assessment, OSS, 41–44, 46, 51, 58, 62
Assumed probabilities, 3–4, 468
Assumptions, 343
Athens, 71
Attitudes, social, 79
Austria, 44
Authoritarian personality research, 138–139
Authority, method of, 6, 475

Auxiliary symbols, 52
Average deviation, 200, 468
Average error, 468

Baboon studies, 118
Before-after design, 469
Behavior studies, 25, 32
Behavioral control, 88
Behavioral genetics, 4
Behavioral medicine, 4
Behaviorism, 5, 469
Berkeley, University of California at, 138
BESD (binomial effect-size display), 208–211, 469
Beta, 21–22, 355–356, 469
Between-conditions, 261–262
Bias, 10–11, 49, 156, 469
    expectancy, 10, 110–111
    nonresponse, 159–160
    volunteer, 160–161, 482
Bimodal, 469
Bimodal score, 197
Binomial effect-size display (BESD), 208–211, 469
Biological variables, 32-33, 469
Biosocial experimenter effects, 109, 469
Blind controls, 107, 469
Blocking, 469
Bonferroni procedure, 255, 469
Boston, Massachusetts, 71
Boundary experiments, 66, 469
Brain-lesioned rats, 112–114
Brain-stimulation, 8
Brooklyn College students, 186
Built-in contrasts, 469
"Buster," 43
Butler box, 64, 66

Cambridge University, 8
Canadians, 145–146
Canonical correlation, 426–427, 469
Category scale, 122–124, 469
Causal description, 27
Causal inference, 26–27, 469
Causal patterns, 72
Causality, 26–30
Ceiling effect, 469
Central tendency, 469
Central tendency error, 143, 469
Characteristic root, 469
Chicago, University of, 48
Chicago, University of, Press, xvii, 150

Child Development Abstracts and Bibliography, 190
Chi-square, 469
    combined category test, 398–399, 470
    corner cells test, 394–395, 405–406, 469
    distributions of, 388–391, 469
    table of, 457
Civil rights protests, 47
Clear inference, 29–31
Clever Hans case, 110–111
Cluster analysis, 417, 424–425, 469
Cluster sampling, 158
Clustering process, 185–186
Coefficient of correlations, 469–470
    canonical, 426–427, 469
    cross-lag, 97–98
    interpretations of, 207–211, 223
    intraclass, 342–343, 474
    product moment, 204–224, 478
Coefficient of determination, 207, 469
Coefficient of nondetermination, 207, 469
Cognitive closure, 6
Cognitive component, 469
Cognitive dissonance, 12, 20–21
Cohen's d, 226, 469
Cohen's f, 469
Cohen's g, 469
Cohen's h, 469
Cohen's q, 469
Cohen's w, 469
Cohort, 470
    controlling for, 98–101
Cohort analyses, 100–101
Cohort-sequential design, 470
Cohort tables, 99, 168
Coinvestigators, 107
Collection of data, 189
Collier brothers, 88
Column effects, 259–260, 280–284, 470
Column totals, standardizing, 408–413
Combined category chi-square test, 398–399, 470
Combining studies, 369–370
    effect-size estimation in , 374–376, 378–379
    significance testing in, 373–374, 377–378
    Stouffer method of, 373–374
    three or more, 377–379
    two, 373–376
Communication patterns, effects of, 35
Comparing studies, 369–370
    effect-size estimation in, 372–373, 377
    significance testing in, 370–372, 376–377
    three or more, 376–377
    two, 370–373

Comparisons, historical, 59–60
Complex multiple partial correlation, 429, 470
Component loading, 470
Conative component, 470
Concentration-camp survivors, 45
Concept, 470
Concurrent validity, 82–83, 470
Conditions, constancy of, 87
Confidence interval, 470
Confirmation, multiple, 127, 476
Conflicting results, accounting for, 19
Confounded variables, 77, 470
Confounding, 105
Connecticut, University of, 48
Consensus tests, 470
Constancy of conditions, 87
Construct, 470
Construct validation, 470
Construct validity, 76, 78–79, 419–420
Constructing hypotheses, 11–13
Constructs, personality, 51–55
Content, 21
Content analysis, 124–125, 470
Content validity, 83–84, 470
Contingency table, 217–218, 470
Contrasts:
　background of, 344–345
　definitions of, 346–348
　examples of, 347–349
　nonorthogonal, 353–354, 476
　orthogonal, 350–353, 477
　unequal n per condition, 349–350
Control group, 88–90, 470
Control series, 87–88
Controls, 87–90, 103
　for age, 98–99
　behavioral, 88
　for cohort, 98–101
　constancy, 87
　for demand characteristics, 105–107
　for expectancy effects, 112–114
　in experimental design, 88
　placebo, 90
Convergent validity, 78–79, 470
Corner cells test, chi-square, 394–395, 405–406, 469
Corrected range, 470
Correction for continuity, 221, 470
Correlate, 470
Correlated data, 470
Correlated replicators, 183–184
Correlations (see Coefficient of correlations)
Corroboration, tensions of, 180–181, 184

Cost of doing, 170–173
Counterbalancing, 312–313, 470
Counterbalancing designs, 317–320
Counter-roll, 87
Covariance(s), 470
　homogeneity of, 474
　of variables, 76–77, 97–98
Covary, 470
Criterion variable, 43, 470
Critical period hypothesis, 92
Cross-lag design, 95–97, 470
　correlations, 97–98
Cross-products, 205–206
Cross-sectional analysis, 100–101
Cross-sectional design, 98–100, 470
Cross-sequential design, 470
Crossed contrasts, 470
Crossed-line interaction, 294–295, 471
Crossed-quadratic interaction, 295–297, 471
Crossed sampling units, 471
Crude range, 198–199, 471
Cubic curve, 295–296
Cubic trend, 471
Curvilinear (quadratic) correlation, 222–224, 471
Cyclic patterns, 59–60

$\underline{D}$, 471
$\overline{D}$, 471
d, 225–227, 471
Data:
　collection of, 117–118, 189
　interpretation of, 190
　statistical analysis of, 190–191
Data analysis, teaching of, xvi
Data matrices, 424–425
Data-text, 279, 292
Davidson County, Tennessee, 126
Debriefing, 176–178
Deception in research, 173–174
Definitions:
　operational, 36, 477
　theoretical, 36–38, 482
Degrees of freedom (df), 216, 471
Degrees of relationships, 35
Deliberate observation, 9–10
Demand characteristics, 104–106, 471
Dependent variables, 26–29, 34–35, 76–77, 471 (*See also* Variables)
Descriptive inquiry, 471
Descriptive research, 22–23, 25–26, 41–47, 49–51, 55, 471

Design(s):
  experimental (*see* Experimental designs)
  sampling: cohort-sequential, 167-168
    cross-sectional, 167–168
    simple cross-sectional, 167–168
    simple longitudinal, 167–168, 475
Determinative relationship, 26–27, 471
df, 216, 471
df between conditions, 471
df error, 471
df means, 471
df within conditions, 471
Diachronic research, 57–59, 471
Diagonal of indecision, 171
Dialectical patterns, 60, 471
Difference:
  method of, 89, 475
  in success rates, 471
Diffuse tests of significance, 471
Diffusion, 471
  of changes, 34–35
  of responsibility, 17–18
Dimensional analysis, 425, 471
Dionysian construct, 57
Discovery, 20, 471
Discriminant function, multiple, 428, 476
Discriminant validity, 78–79, 84, 471
Discriminating power of statistical procedure,
  85
Discrimination learning study, 112–114
Disguised measures, 125–127, 471
  indirect, 126, 474
  unobtrusive, 126–127, 482
Dispersion, 471
Displays, 195–197
Dissertation Abstracts International, 190
Distance analysis, 471
Distributions, 196, 471
  chi-square, 388–391, 469
  of *F*, 250–251, 472
  frequency, 195–197, 473
  normal, 201–203, 476
  t, 229–230, 481
Documentary research, 48–49
Drug-hazard study, 80–81
Drug symptoms, 30–31
Drunkard's search, principle of, 472
Dummy coding, 214–215, 218, 385–387, 472

Eating behavior, effects of biological variables
  on, 32
Economy of design, 256–257
Edgington method of adding probabilities, 472

*Educational Resources Information Center
  Files*, 190
Effect size, 22, 191, 356–365, 472
  estimation of, 372–379
  indices of, 361–365
  power tables, 359–361
Effective reliability, 163–166, 472
Effects, 259–260, 263, 472
  on *F*, 271–272
  fixed, 308–316, 473
  interaction (*see* Interaction effects)
  random, 308–316, 479
  residual, 259–260
  row, 259–260, 280–284, 279
  synergistic, 293–294, 481
  table of, 261
  (*See also* Residuals)
Efficient cause, 28, 472
Eigenvalue, 472
Elsevier Scientific Publishing Company, xvii,
  99
Empirical method, 472
Enumerative survey, 46–47, 472
Equal-appearing-intervals method, 150–151,
  472
Equal sample sizes, 267–271
Equivalent-forms method, 81, 472
Error term, 472
  aggregating, 336–338
Errors, 7, 75–76, 81, 260–261, 472
  average, 468
  of central tendency, 143, 469
  identically distributed, 239
  IID normal, 238, 474
  independent, 238
  insufficient precision, 84
  insufficient reliability, 81
  insufficient validity, 76
  internal validity, 91
  of leniency, 143,
  logical, in rating, 144, 475
  MS, 265–267, 475
  normally distributed, 239
  observer, 49
  random, 102–103, 479
  recording, 49
  systematic, 102–103, 481
  Type I, 21–22, 31, 355–356, 482
  Type II, 21–22, 31, 355–356, 482
Eta, 249–250, 262–264, 356–359, 472
Eta^2, 472
Ethical guidelines, 174–175
Ethics, 472
Ethnographic Atlas, 60

Ethnography, 120–122, 472
Etymology, 36
Evaluation apprehension, 105, 472
Evaluation of data, 190
Evidence, gathering of, 189–191
Expectancy bias, 10, 110–111
Expectancy control design, 11, 112–114, 472
Expected frequencies, 390–391, 472
Experimental designs, 29
  after-only, 468
  before-after, 469
  cross-lag, 95–98, 470
  cross-sectional, 98–100, 470
  economy of, 256–257
  four-group, 91–95
  longitudinal, 98–100, 475
  Solomon, 92–93, 480
  three-way, 288–292
  true, 90–91
  two-way, 284–288
Experimental group, 88–90, 472
Experimental inquiry, 22, 24–26, 472
Experimental method of reasoning, 29
Experimental realism, 67, 472
Experimental research, 50–63, 70–72
  (*See also* Research)
Experimenter, 472
Experimenter effects:
  interactional, 109–110, 474
    biosocial, 109, 469
    psychosocial, 109–110, 478
    situational, 110, 480
  noninteractional, 107–108, 476
    intentional, 108–109, 474
    interpreter, 108–109, 474
    observer, 107–109, 477
Experimenter expectancy effects, 110–114, 472
Experimenter expectation, 10–11
Experimenters' personalities, 109–110
Experiments:
  boundary, 66, 469
  fact-finding, 66, 473
  field, 70–71
  heuristic, 66, 473
  methodological, 66, 476
  simulation, 66–67, 480
Explanations, 28
Extended range, 198–199, 472
Extended table of *t*, 450–452
External invalidity, sources of, 94–95
  interaction of pretesting and X, 95
  interaction of selection and X, 95
External validity, 76, 79–81, 472
External variables, 34, 472

f, 472
F, table of, 252, 453–456
F distributions, 250–251, 472
F ratios, 472
F Scale, 138–139
F test, 243–248, 267, 427
  on the grand mean, 265–267
Fact-finding experiments, 66, 473
Factor analysis, 423–425, 473
Factor loading, 473
Factorial designs, 272–275, 473
  incomplete, 474
Factors:
  designs for three or more, 320–329
  fixed, 308–311, 339–341
  random, 308–311, 339–341
  three within-subjects, 338–341
  two within-subjects, 329–338
False conceptions, 16
False precision, 85, 473
Falsifiability, 20–22, 473
Fascism scale (F Scale), 138–139
Field experiments, 70–71
Field observations, 117–122
File drawer problem, 379–382, 473
  computation, 380–381
  tolerance table, 381–382
Final cause, 28, 473
Fisher exact probability test, 395–398, 473
Fisher method of adding logs, 473
Fisher's *z* transformation of *r*, 459, 473
Fixed effects, 308–316, 473
Fixed factors, 308–311, 339–341
Focused tests of significance, 473
Forced-choice rating scale, 142, 147, 473
Formal cause, 28, 473
Four-group design, Solomon, 91–95, 480
Fractional factorials, 473
Frankfurt, University of, 138
Free Press, 467
Frequency distribution, 195–197, 202, 473
Frustration-aggression hypothesis, 36–37, 45
FSMR (fully simultaneous multiple-regression
    method), 268

g, 473
Germany, 44–46
Good subject, 104, 473
Gossip, 13, 36
  studies of, 120–122, 124–125
Grand mean, 264–267, 473
  and *F* test, 267
  and *t* test, 265–267

Graphic scale, 142–143, 473
Greenwich Observatory, England, 107–108
Group profiles, 145–146
Guidelines, ethical, 174–175

h, 473
H_0 (null hypothesis), 229–231, 473
Halo effect, 141–142, 473
Harmonic mean, 245, 473
Harvard University, xv, 172
Hawthorne effect, 473
Helping behavior, studies of, 71
Hereditary variables, 473
Heroic behavior, interviews of, 128–129
Heterogeneous, 473
Heterogeneous sample sizes, 271
Heuristic experiments, use of, 66, 473
Heuristic hypotheses, 13
Heuristic models, 59–60
Hierarchical structure, 36, 473
High antecedent probability, 15, 473
Higher-order interaction, 43–46, 474
Historical comparisons, 59–60
History, 474
Holt (publisher), 458
Homogeneity of covariances, 474
Homogeneous, 474
Homosexuals, research on, 172–173
Houghton Mifflin Company, xvii, 91, 95, 453, 456–457
Human Relations Area Files, 48
Hypnosis studies, 107, 117–119
Hypothesis, 11–16, 19–24, 28, 92, 181, 184, 474

Ideal presidential curve, 145
IID normal, 238, 474
Incomplete factorial design, 474
Independent variables, 26–29, 31–34, 56, 76–77
  (*See also* Variables)
Indirect measures, 126, 474
Individual differences as error, 260
Inferential validity, 80, 474
Informed consent, 175
Initial thinking, 15, 474
Instrumentation, 84, 474
  self-report methods, 84–85
  simulation methods, 84
Insufficient precision, 84
Insufficient reliability, 81
Insufficient validity, 76

Intensive case study, 17, 474
Intentional effect, 108–109, 474
Interaction effects, 259–260, 474
  crossed-line, 294–295
  crossed-quadratic 295–297
  definition of, 278–279
  five-way, 299–301
  and main effects, 277–279
  organismic, 292
  three-way, 290–292
  two-way, 284–288
Interaction process analysis, 474
Interactional experimenter effects (*see*
  Experimenter effects, inter-
  actional)
Interdisciplinary research, 474
Internal consistency, 82, 423
Internal invalidity, 91–95
Internal validity, 76–78, 90–92, 474
  threats to, 77–78, 90–92
Internal variables, 33, 474
Interpretation(s):
  of correlations, 207–211, 223
  of data, 190
Interpreter effects, 108–109, 474
Interval data, 474
Intervening variables, 52
Interviews, 56, 128–133
  advantages of, 128
  disadvantages of, 130
  items for, 130–132
  schedule for, 131–133
Intraclass correlation, 342–343, 474
Invisible college, 190
Iowa State University Press, 459–460
IQ:
  age-curve, 98–99
  studies of, 108–109
Irradiation of changes, 34–35
Item analysis, 148, 474

Johns Hopkins University School of Medicine, 66
Joint method, 89, 474
Journal of the American Statistical Association, 452
Journal of Communication, xvii, 121
Journal Press, xvii, 149
Judges:
  and reliability of ratings, 163–166
  selection of, 162–163
Judgment studies, 54–55
Justification, 20, 474

k, 474
k^2, 474
"Kippy," 43
Königsberg, 108

L, 474
Lamda (λ), 475
Lapland, gossip in, 17
Laser study, 9
Latent root, 475
Latin squares, 311–316, 475
Lawful causality, 26–28
Learning, 475
    discrimination, study of, 112–114
Leaves, 196–197, 475
Levels of inquiry, 22–23
Likert scale, 148–149, 475
Limitations:
    assessing, 186–187
    of strong inference, 184–186
Linear patterns, 59–60
Linear trend, 475
Loading, 475
    rotated component, 417–422
        oblique, 419
        varimax, 419
Location, measures of, 197–198
Logarithmic transformations, 213–214
Logical error in rating, 144, 475
Log-linear model, 384, 475
Longitudinal design, 98–99, 475

M, 475
$\overline{M}$, 475
McGraw-Hill, xvii, 448
Main effects, 277–284
Manipulation check, 80
Manuscript format, 437–446
Marlowe-Crowne Social Desirability Scale,
    52–55, 62
Matched-pair t test, 264–265
Matched pairs, 475
Material cause, 28, 475
Maturation, 475
Maximum possible benefit of a contrast, 475
Maximum possible contrast F, 475
Mean, 198, 475
    arithmetic, 468
    harmonic, 245, 473
    trimmed, 198
Mean polish, 475
Mean square for error, 249

Meaningful diagonals, method of, 298–301, 475
Meaningful differences, method of, 299, 476
Measures, disguised (*see* Disguised measures)
Mechanistic model, 31–33, 475
Median, 197–198, 475
Meta-analysis, 49, 209, 475
Metaphor, 17–18, 475
Metatheory, 31, 475
Method of adding logs, 475
Method of adding probabilities, 475
Method of adding t's, 475
Method of adding Z's, 475
Method of adding weighted Z's, 475
Method of agreement, 89, 475
Method of authority, 6, 475
Method of difference, 89, 475
Method of equal-appearing intervals, 150–151,
    472
Method of meaningful diagonals, 298–301,
    475
Method of meaningful differences, 299, 476
Method of observation, 181, 184
Method of tenacity, 6, 476
Method of testing mean p, 476
Method of testing mean z, 476
Methodological experiments, use of, 66, 476
Michigan, University of, 48
Mode, 197, 476
Modeling effects, 476
Moments, 205
Monkey research, 8, 63–66
Mood of compliance, 18
Mood questionnaire, 143
Motive hierarchy, 36
MPBS, 475
MPC$-F$, 475
MS, 265–267, 475
MS between, 475
MS error, 265–267, 475
MS within, 475
Multidimensional scaling (unfolding), 476
Multilevel analysis of variance, 429–430, 476
Multiple confirmation, 127, 476
Multiple correlation, 426–427, 476
Multiple discriminant function, 428, 476
Multiple partial correlation, 476
Multiple path analysis, 428–429, 476
Multiple-regression method, 268
Multiple squares, 317
Multivariate analysis of covariance, 430, 476
Multivariate multilevel analysis of variance,
    429, 476
Multivariate procedures, 414–415, 476
Mundane, realism, 67, 476

N, 476
n, 476
N_h, 476
N-of-one research, 168–169
National Institutes of Health (NIH), 175–176
National Opinion Research Center (NORC), 48, 166–167
National Science Foundation, xvii
Natural selection, 5
Naturalistic experimentation, 70–72, 476
NCBM (net contrast benefit measure), 476
Necessary condition, 89, 476
Need for approval, studies of, 52–55
Negative synergistic effects, 293–294, 476
Negativistic subject, 105, 476
Nested sampling units, 476
Net contrast benefit measure (NCBM), 476
Net information per contrast df, 476
Netherlands, subjects from, 99–100
New York City, 17
Noninteractional experimenter effects (*see* Experimenter effects, noninteractional)
Nonorthogonal contrasts, 353–354, 476
Nonparametric statistical procedures, 397–398, 476
Nonrandomized selection, 166–169
  in cohort design, 166–167
  in quasi-experiments, 167
Nonreactive observation, 10, 476
Nonresponse bias, 159–160
Normal distribution, 201–203, 476
North Carolina, 79
No-show, 476
Null hypothesis, 22, 229–231, 477
Numerical scale, 140–142, 477

Obedience studies, 25, 68, 172–173
  and debriefing, 176–177
Oblique rotations, 419, 477
Observation:
  deliberate, 9–10
  field, 117–122
  method of, 181, 184
  nonreactive, 10, 476
  participant, 56–57, 477
Observed frequencies, 477
Observer effect, 107–109, 477
Observers, 122–125
Occam's razor, 11, 16, 477
OED (Oxford English Dictionary), 36
Office of Strategic Services (OSS), 41–44, 46, 49–51, 58, 62
Ohio State University, 52

Omnibus tests of significnce, 477
One-group pre-post design, 91, 477
One-shot case study, 90–91, 100, 477
One-tailed test, 477
Open-ended items, 130–132, 134, 477
Operational definition, 36, 477
Ordinal data, 477
Ordinal definitions, 36–37, 477
Ordinate, 196
Organismic interactions, 292, 477
Organismic model, 32–33, 477
Orthogonal contrasts, 350–353, 477
Orthogonal polynomial contrasts, 477
Orthogonal relationship, 477
Orthogonal rotations, 477
OSS (Office of Strategic Services) assessment study, 41–44, 46, 49–51, 58, 62
Overall F test, 477
Oxford English Dictionary (OED), 36

p value, 477
Paradigm cases, 41–43, 51–55, 62–65, 477
Paradox of sampling, 155, 477
Paradox of usage, 155, 477
Paradoxical incidents, 17, 477
Paris, 71
Parsimony principle, 11, 477
Partial aggregation, 477
Participant observation, 56–57, 477
Partitioning tables, 477
Path analysis, multiple, 428–429, 477
Pearson r, 204–207, 211–213, 477
Pearson r correlation, 224
Percentile, 477
Period centrism fallacy, 477
Personality constructs, 51–55
Personality of experimenter, 109–110
Phantoms, 16
Phi coefficient, 217–222, 224, 477
Placebo control group, 90, 478
Planned contrasts, 478
Plausibility stage, 15, 478
Plausible rival hypotheses, 12, 478
Point-biserial correlation, 214–217, 224, 478
Pointer reading, 72, 478
Pointless precision, 85, 156, 478
Political propaganda studies, 70–71
PONS (Profile of Nonverbal Sensitivity) test, 478
  and construct validity, 419–420
  and reliability analysis, 422–423
  and subtest construction, 420–422
Pooling sources of variance, 478

Population, 478
Population of Possible Benefit Score (POPBS), 478
Positive synergistic effects, 294, 478
Post hoc contrasts, 478
Postdictive validity, 82–83, 478
Power, 478
Power analysis, 355–356
Power tables, 359–361
Practical validity, 211, 478
Pre-analysis of an experiment, 478
Precise instrumentation, 84
Precision, 76, 84–86, 478
 false, 85, 473
 pointless, 85, 156, 478
Predictive validity, 82–83, 478
Predictor variables, 43, 207–208
Pre-experimental design, 478
 one-group pre-post, 91
 one-shot case study, 90–91
Preinquiry, 107
Pre-post control group design, 478
Primacy, 312
Primate behavior, 25
Principal components analysis, 415–419
 and construct validity, 419–422
 and reliability analysis, 422–423
 and subtest construction, 420–423
Principle of parsimony, 11, 477
Principle of uncertainty, 10, 482
Probabilities:
 assumed, 3–4, 468
 Edgington method of adding, 472
Probability, 478
Probability sampling, 156–158, 478
Procedures, data collection, 189
 field observations, 117–118
 laboratory experiments, 118
Product-moment correlation, 204–224, 478
Product-moment correlation coefficient, 204–207
Products, 205
Profile of Nonverbal Sensitivity (*see* PONS test)
Projective tests, 478
Propaganda studies, 70–71
Protected t test, 478
Protests, studies on:
 civil rights, 47
 student, 46–47
Proximity analysis, 478
Pseudovolunteer, 478
Psychological Abstracts, 190
Psychological consistency, 12

Psychological consonance, 12
Psychological economics, 4–5
Psychological Reports, xvii, 146
Psychologists, 4–5
Psychosocial experimenter effects, 109–110, 478
Public presentation of research results, 190–191
Pulsars, research on, 8
Pupils' learning study, 23–24

q, 478
Q-sort scale, 147–148, 478
Quadratic correlations, 222–224
Quadratic curves, 295–296
Quadratic trend, 478
Quartile range, 200, 479
Quasi-control subjects, 106–107, 479
Quasi-experiment, 479
Queens (New York City), 17
Questionnaires, 56, 128–137, 160

r, 479
 computation of, 212–213
 significance levels of, 458
r^2, 479
r_{pb}, 479
r equivalents of Fisher's z, table of, 460
Rand Corporation, xvii, 467
Random digits, table of, 156–157, 461–467
Random effects, 308–316, 479
Random errors, 102–103, 479
Random factors, 308–311, 339–341
Random method, 24
Random sample, 156–157, 479
Random sampling, 56, 111–112, 156–157
 area probability, 157–159
 cluster, 158
 stratified, 157–158
Range, 479
 crude, 198–199, 471
 extended, 198–199, 472
 quartile, 200, 479
 trimmed, 199–200, 482
Rat studies, 111–114
Rating scales (*see* Scales, rating)
Raw contrast score, 479
Reactive observation, 10, 479
Reactive organism, 32
Reasoning, experimental method of, 29
Recency, 312
Records, secondary, 48–49

Rectangular arrays, 317, 479
Redescriptors, 415, 479
Regression analysis, 479
Relational inquiry, 22–23, 25–26, 479
Relational research, 43–44, 46–48, 50–55, 60–61
Relationships:
  among sets of variables, 425–430
    and discriminant function, 427–428
    and multiple correlation, 426–427
    and path analysis, 428–429
  within sets of variables: construct validity, 419–420
    principal components analysis, 415–419
    redescriptors, 415
    reliability analysis, 422–423
    subtest construction, 420
Reliability, 76, 81–82, 86, 479
  evaluation of, 81–82
    equivalent forms method, 81, 472
    internal consistency method, 82
      split-half method, 82, 481
    test-retest method, 81, 482
  insufficient, 81
  in test construction, 81–82
Reliability analysis, 422–423
Reliability coefficient, 163–166
Repeated measures, 479
  computations of, 306–308
  use of, 305–306
Replicability, 9–10, 479
Replication, 111
  relative utility of, 182–183
Replicators, correlated, 183–184
Representative research design, 111–112, 479
Research:
  deception in, 173–174
  descriptive, 22–23, 25–26, 41–47, 49–51, 55, 471
  diachronic, 57–59, 471
  experimental, 50–63, 70–72
  interdisciplinary, 474
  monkey, 8, 63–66
  relational, 43–44, 46–48, 50–55, 60–61
  synchronic, 57–58, 481
Research design, representative, 111–112, 479
Research problem, formulation of, 189
Research reports:
  communicating idea in, 431–432
  content of, 434–435
  form of, 432–434
  typing of, 436
Research subjects (*see* Subjects, research)
Research team, 183–184
Residual effects, 259–260

Residuals, 278–301, 479
  and Data-text, 279
  displaying, 279–284
  and method of meaningful diagonals, 299–300
  and method of meaningful differences, 299
  tables of, 282–284, 296–301
Resource theory, 19
Response, 479
Response set, 479
Response variable, 26, 479
Responsibility, diffusion of, 17–18
rho (Spearman rank correlation), 211–214, 224, 479, 481
Righthandedness study, 58–59
Rival hypotheses, 12–13
Role motivations, 104–105
  and evaluation apprehension, 105
  in good subject, 104
  in negativistic subject, 105
Role-play, 479
Role-play experiments, 68–70
Role theory, 104–105
Roper Center, 48
Rotation, 417–422
  of factors or components, 479
Row effects, 259–260, 280–284, 479
Row totals, standardizing, 408–413
Rule of thumb, 17–18, 479
Rumor, 6, 12, 28
Rumor study, 67–68
Russians, 145–146

S, 479
S^2, 479
S^2 means, 479
S^2 pooled, 479
Sage Publishers, 124
St. Louis, 172
Sample, 48, 480
  unbiased, 482
Sample sizes:
  equal, 267–271
  heterogeneous, 271
  unequal, 267–272, 349–350
Sampling, 56, 111–112, 117
  area probability, 158
  cluster, 158
  paradox of, 155, 477
  probability, 156–158, 478
  random (*see* Random sampling)
  with replacement, 480
  requirements of: bias-free, 156
    stability, 156, 480

Sampling (*Cont.*):
  stratified random, 157–158
  survey, 156
Sampling design (*see* Design, sampling)
Sampling plan, 155, 480
Sampling stability, 156, 480
Sampling units, 195, 480
Scales:
  category, 122–124, 469
  F Scale, 138–139
  rating, 479
    forced-choice, 142, 147, 473
    graphic, 142–143, 473
    Likert, 148–149
    numerical, 140–142
    Q-sort, 147–148, 478
    semantic differential, 144–147, 480
    Thurstone, 150–151
Scheffé test, 480
Scientific imperatives, 178–179
Scientific method, 6–7, 480
Score value, 195–196
Secondary analysis, 49, 480
Secondary records, 48–49
Selection, 480
  nonrandomized, 166–169
  (*See also* Sampling)
Self-fulfilling prophecy, 11, 24, 110–111, 480
Semantic differential scale, 144–147, 480
  and group profiles, 145–146
  and three-dimensional representation, 146–147
Sentence completion test, 480
Sequence, 480
Serendip, 7
Serendipity, 7–8, 16, 480
Sign test, 480
Significance level(s), 480
  of *r*, 458
Significance test (*see* Test of significance)
Significance testing, 21, 370–374. 376–378, 480
Simple random selection, 480
  (*See also* Random sampling)
Simulation experiment, 66–67, 480
Simulation methods, 84
Single-case research, 168–169
Situational experimenter effects, 110, 480
Size:
  of effect, 191, 216, 219–222, 225–226, 231, 233, 236, 243–246
  of study, 191, 216, 219–222, 225–226, 231, 233, 236, 243–246
Skewness, 480
Skinner box study, 111

Sleep experiment, 175–176
Small-group studies, 122–123
Small-*N* research, 168–169
Smallest-space analysis, 480
Smoking, attitudes toward, study of, 69–70
Social attitudes, 79
Social Behavior and Personality, xvii, 436
Social causality, 28, 31
Social desirability, 52–55, 62
  coping with, 135, 138–139
Social environmental variables, 33, 480
Social experimentation, 71–72, 480
Social facilitation hypothesis, 19
Societal imperatives, 178–179
Solomon design, 91–95, 480
Spearman-Brown formula, 163–166
Spearman rank correlation (rho), 211–214, 224, 479, 481
Speech behavior, 25
Split-half method, 82, 481
Spread, measures of, 198–199, 480
Square root transformations, 213
SS, 247–249, 481
SS between, 481
SS total, 481
SS within, 481
Stability in sampling, 156
Standard deviation, 200–203, 481
Standard normal curve, 201–203, 481
Standard normal deviate(s) (*Z*), 221, 481
  table of, 448
Standard score, 202–203, 481
Standardized contrast score, 481
Standardized measure, 481
Standardized questions, 133
Standardizing the margins, 408–413, 481
Stanford University, 149
Station S, 42
Statistical conclusion validity, 76–77, 481
Statistical examples, xvi
Statistical probability, 21
Statistical procedures:
  discriminating power of, 85
  nonparametric, 397–398, 476
Statistical significance, 481
Stem, 196–197, 481
Stem-and-leaf display, 196–197, 481
Stimulus, 481
Stouffer method of adding *z*'s, 373–374, 481
Stratified random sampling, 157–158
Stress tolerance test, 42
Strong inference, limitations of, 184–186, 481
Structure of hierarchies, 36
Structured items, 130–134, 481
Student protests, 46–47

Subdividing larger tables of counts, 393–399
  chi-square corner cells test, 394–395
  combined category chi-square test, 398–399
  complete partitioning of, 400–408
    computing $\chi^2(1)$'s for partitioned tables, 402–405
    contrasts in proportions, 406–408
    corner cells test subtable, 405–406
  Fisher exact probability test, 395–398, 473
Subjects, research, 104–107
  good, 104
  negativistic, 105
  quasi-control, 106–107
  in surveys, 160–162
  volunteer status of, 186–189
Subjects-within-sequences designs, 317–320, 481
Success rates, 210–211
Sufficient condition, 89, 481
Sum of squares, 247–249
Summary table of t, 449
Summated ratings, 481
Survey data, 48
Survey Research Center, 48
Survey sampling, 156
Symmetry, 481
Symptomatic volunteers, 162, 481
Synchronic research, 57–58, 481
Synergistic effects, 293–294, 481
Systematic errors, 102–103, 481

t:
  computing, 231–234, 236
  and d, 225–227
  extended table of, 450–452
  interpreting, 229–231
  summary table of, 449
t distributions, 229–230, 481
t tests, 256–257, 481
  after the F, 251–255
  on the grand mean, formula for, 265–267
  matched-pair, 264–265
  for nonindependent samples, 234–236
  protected, 478
  and unequal sample sizes, 238
Table analysis, 481
Table of chi-square, 457
Table of effects, 261
Table of F, 252, 453–456
Table of Fisher's z transformation of r, 459
Table of r equivalents of Fisher's z, 460
Table of random digits, 156–157, 461–467
Table of standard normal deviates (Z), 448

Table of variance, 248–250, 262–263, 275–276
Tables of counts:
  larger, 384–391
  log-linear model, 384
  (*See also* Subdividing larger tables of counts)
Tables of residuals, 282–284, 296–301
Tacit knowledge, 9–10, 481
Tax-sticker study, 126–127
Teachers' behavior, 23–24
Teleologic factor, 28, 481
Temple University, xv, xvii
Tenacity, method of, 6, 476
Tensions of corroboration, 180–181, 184
Territorial behavior, 5
Test construction, reliability in, 81–82
Test record, 21
Test of significance, 191, 216, 219–222, 224–225, 231, 233, 243, 246, 481
  focused, 473
  omnibus, 477
Test validity, 82–83
  concurrent, 83
  content, 83
  postdictive, 82–83
  predictive, 82–83
Testing error, 481
Testing the grand mean, 265–267, 482
  (*See also* F test)
Test-retest method, 81, 482
Thaddeus Bolton Professorship, xvii
Theoretical definition, 36–38, 482
Theory, 20–21
Three-way designs, 288–292
Thurstone scale, 150–151, 482
Time sequential design, 482
Time-series analysis, 60
Tinker Toy, 42, 44
Tolerance for future null results, 482
Total aggregation, 482
Transformations:
  arcsin, 468
  logarithmic, 213–214
  r to z, 460
  square root, 213
  z to r, 459
Traumatic Index, 46
Trimmed means, 198, 482
Trimmed range, 199–200, 482
Two-tailed test, 482
Two-way designs, 284–288
Type I error, 21–22, 31, 355–356, 482
Type II error, 21–22, 31, 355–356, 482
Typology, 37–38, 482

Ulcer project, 8
Unbiased estimator of the population values, 200–201
Unbiased sample, 482
  (*See also* Sampling)
Uncertainty principle, 10, 482
Unequal sample sizes, 267–272, 349–350
  effects on *F*, 271–272
Unequal variances, 208
United Nations, 38
Units of analysis, 482
Unobtrusive disguised measures, 126–127, 482
Unplanned contrasts, 482
Unstructured items, 130–132, 134, 482
Unweighted means analysis, 268–271, 275–276, 482
Utility:
  of doing, 170–173
  variables affecting, 182–183

Validity, 76–81, 86, 482
  concurrent, 82–83, 470
  construct, 76, 78–79, 470
  content, 83–84, 470
  convergent, 78–79, 470
  discriminant, 78–79, 84, 471
  external, 76, 79–81, 472
  inferential, 80, 474
  insufficient, 76
  internal, 76–78, 90–92, 474
  practical, 211, 478
  predictive, 82–83, 478
  postdictive, 82–83, 478
  statistical conclusion, 76–77, 481
  test, 82–83
Values, 482
Variables, 26–28, 32, 36–37, 96–98, 469, 482
  affecting utility, 182–183
  covariance of, 76–77, 97–98
  external, 34, 472
  hereditary, 473
  independent, 26–29, 31–34, 56, 76–77
  internal, 33, 474
  intervening, 52
  predictor, 43, 207–208
  relationships among sets of, 429–430
  response, 26, 479

Variables (*Cont.*):
  social environmental, 33, 480
Variance(s), 200, 482
  proportion of, 207
  table of, 248–250, 262–263, 275–276
  unequal, 208
Varimax rotation, 419, 482
Verbal conditioning studies, 53–54
Vietnam, 47
Volunteer bias, 160–161, 482
  reduction methods, 161
Volunteer characteristics, 187–189
Volunteer status, 186–189
Volunteer subjects study, 80
Volunteers, 160–162
  symptomatic, 162

w, 482
Walter Reed Army Hospital, 8
Washington, D.C., 42
John Wiley & Sons Publishers, xvi, xvii
Winer method of adding *t*'s, 482
Wisconsin, University of, 63
Within conditions, 261–262
Within-subjects factors, 329–341
Word association test, 482
Working hypothesis, 11, 482
World War I, 99
World War II, 41, 45, 51, 99

X, 482
$\bar{X}$, 482
$\bar{\bar{X}}$, 482
X-axis, 196, 482

Y-axis, 196, 482
Yale University, 18, 48
Yates correction for continuity, 384, 483
Yea-saying, 138, 483

Z, 222, 370–371, 376, 378, 380–382, 384, 407–408, 483
Z score, 202–203, 205–206, 483
Zeitgeist, 28, 59, 483

SIGNIFICANCE TEST	=	SIZE OF EFFECT	×	SIZE OF STUDY
$\chi^2(1)$	=	ϕ^2	×	N
Z	=	ϕ	×	$\sqrt{N}$
t	=	$\dfrac{r}{\sqrt{1-r^2}}$	×	$\sqrt{df}$
t	=	$\dfrac{M_1 - M_2}{S}$	×	$\dfrac{1}{\sqrt{\dfrac{1}{n_1} + \dfrac{1}{n_2}}}$
t	=	$\dfrac{M_1 - M_2}{S}$	×	$\sqrt{\dfrac{n_1 n_2}{n_1 + n_2}}$
t	=	$\dfrac{M_1 - M_2}{\sigma}$	×	$\left[\dfrac{\sqrt{n_1 n_2}}{(n_1 + n_2)} \times \sqrt{df}\right]$